The Complete Guide to the
Theory and Practice of Materials
Development for Language Learning

The Complete Guide to the Theory and Practice of Materials Development for Language Learning

Brian Tomlinson
University of Liverpool
UK

Hitomi Masuhara
University of Liverpool
UK

WILEY Blackwell

Registered Office
John Wiley & Sons, Inc., 111 River Street, Hoboken, NJ 07030, USA

Editorial Office
9600 Garsington Road, Oxford, OX4 2DQ, UK

For details of our global editorial offices, customer services, and more information about Wiley products visit us at www.wiley.com.

Wiley also publishes its books in a variety of electronic formats and by print-on-demand. Some content that appears in standard print versions of this book may not be available in other formats.

Library of Congress Cataloging-in-Publication Data

Names: Tomlinson, Brian, 1943-, author. | Masuhara, Hitomi, author.
Title: The complete guide to the theory and practice of materials development
    for language learning / Brian Tomlinson, Hitomi Masuhara.
Description: Hoboken, NJ : John Wiley & Sons, Inc., [2017] | Includes index. |
Identifiers: LCCN 2016058002 (print) | LCCN 2017017087 (ebook) |
ISBN 9781119054788 (Adobe PDF) | ISBN 9781119054986 (ePub) | ISBN 9781119054764
    (cloth) | ISBN 9781119054771 (pbk.)
Subjects: LCSH: Language and languages–Study and teaching. | Teaching–Aids
    and devices.
Classification: LCC P53.15 (ebook) | LCC P53.15 .T76 2017 (print) |
    DDC 418.0071–dc23
LC record available at https://lccn.loc.gov/2016058002

Cover design by: Wiley

Set in 10/12pt WarnockPro by Aptara Inc., New Delhi, India
Printed and bound in Malaysia by Vivar Printing Sdn Bhd

1   2018

Contents

Preface

This book is a celebration of a journey that began officially in 1993 with our foundation of MATSDA (the Materials Development Association). Brian became the first Chair and Hitomi the first Secretary. Together we developed an association dedicated to bringing together researchers, writers, publishers and teachers to work towards the development of effective materials for L2 learners. At the same time Brian designed and delivered a dedicated MA in materials development at the University of Luton, and Hitomi (who was doing her PhD at the University of Luton at the time) started to contribute to it as a tutor. This MA was taken in reduced form to the National University of Singapore and then in its original full form to Leeds Metropolitan University when we moved there and started to deliver it together in 2000. It was also cloned (with permission) at IGSE (the International Graduate School of English) in Seoul. This MA, the MATSDA journal *Folio*, and the annual MATSDA workshops and conferences, as well as publications on materials development by us and by many others, have helped to create a situation in which students and teachers in training all over the world are now taking courses on materials development and many of them are devoting their postgraduate research to issues of relevance to it.

Since 1993 we have continued our research and have published, separately and together, on issues relevant to the principles and procedures of materials development for language learning. In 2004 we published a brief guide to materials development for teachers in Southeast Asia to use when writing or adapting materials (Tomlinson & Masuhara, 2004) and in 2010 we edited and published a collection of chapters reporting research on materials development from all over the world. Our 2004 book has been republished in Brazil, China, and South Korea and copied all over Southeast Asia. We are told that it has helped thousands of new or unqualified teachers to gain the awareness and confidence needed to make materials their own. Our 2010 book is now being supplemented by other edited collections of research reports from all over the world (e.g. Masuhara, Mishan, & Tomlinson, 2017; Maley & Tomlinson, in press), and McGrath (2013), Garton & Graves (2014) and Harwood (2014) have recently published books containing reports of worldwide research on materials development.

In 1998 Brian stated that there was a growing interest in exploring issues related to "the writing and exploitation of materials' and yet 'very few books have been published which investigate these issues" (Tomlinson, 1998: vii). Since then there has been an explosion of interest in materials development both as a field of academic study and as a practical undertaking, and fortunately there have been many resources developed to cater for this interest. In Tomlinson (1998) there is reference to the founding in 1993 of MATSDA as an association dedicated to the bringing together of researchers, writers, publishers, and teachers in a concerted effort to facilitate the development of effective materials (www.matsda.org). MATSDA is still going strong, Brian is now the President, and Hitomi is still the Secretary, and we have just organized with the University of Liverpool our thirtieth MATSDA conference. Other associations are also offering great support to students and practitioners of materials development (e.g. MAWSIG, the materials writing special interest group of IATEFL, as well as special interest groups of the American association TESOL and the Japanese association, JALT). There are now a number of journals dedicated to or focusing special issues on materials development (e.g. the MATSDA journal *Folio*, a new MAWSIG journal *ELT Materials Review*, the JALT newsletter *Between the Keys*, *The European Journal of Applied Linguistics and TEFL*, *Innovation in Language Learning and Teaching*). And there are many books focusing on both practical and theoretical issues in materials development (see Chapter 1).

At least four things have changed since Tomlinson (1998). One is the shift of emphasis from a focus on materials development for language teaching to a focus on materials development for language learning (e.g. Tomlinson & Masuhara, 2010). The second is an increased interest in research for materials development, with the emphasis not on achieving academic respectability but on evaluating the effectiveness of innovative interventions. The third is the massive increase in digital delivery of materials for language learning bringing with it numerous new affordances for language learning, but more a change so far we would argue in mode of delivery than in pedagogical approach (see Chapter 8). And the fourth is the coming together of materials development for the learning of English with materials development for the learning of other second or foreign languages. For example, we have had contributions to MATSDA conferences and to the MATSDA journal *Folio* relating to materials for the learning of Arabic, Chinese, French, German, Japanese, Portuguese, Russian, and Spanish, and we have both run materials development workshops for teachers of all those languages in countries around the world. In this book most of our references and examples relate directly to materials for the learning of English but all the principles and procedures we recommend are equally relevant to materials development for the learning of any second or foreign language. Also our references and examples in most chapters relate specifically to print materials, although we would argue that the principles that inform them apply equally to digital materials too. We have done this deliberately so as not to exclude those many teachers who as yet do not have easy and reliable access to the Internet (or even to conventional electronic materials) in their teaching environment, and we have devoted a sizeable chapter (Chapter 8) to the development and exploitation of digital materials.

What we have done in the *Complete guide to the theory and practice of materials development for language learning* is to combine the practicality and accessibility of our 2004 guide with the academic rigor of the 2010 reports on materials development in action. It has been our ambition for a long time to produce a book, which will be of value to all types of participants in what we find to be the exciting field of materials development. We want it to help teachers, researchers, students, publishers and writers to know, understand and be constructively critical of what has been achieved to date. We want it to help them to develop, adapt, use, publish, review and research materials for themselves. And we want the strong opinions and approaches we put forward in this book to inspire readers to think for themselves and to develop and apply strong opinions and approaches of their own.

References

Garton, S., & Graves, K. (Eds.). (2014). *International perspectives on materials in ELT*. Basingstoke: Palgrave Macmillan.

Harwood, N. (Ed.). (2014). *English language teaching textbooks: Content, consumption, production.* Basingstoke: Palgrave Macmillan.

Maley, A., & Tomlinson, B. (Eds.). (in press). *Authenticity in materials development for language learning.* Newcastle upon Tyne: Cambridge Scholars.

Masuhara, H., Mishan, F., & Tomlinson, B. (Eds.). (2017). *Practice and theory for materials development in L2 learning.* Newcastle upon Tyne: Cambridge Scholars.

McGrath, I. (2013). *Teaching materials and the roles of EFL/ESL teachers: Practice and theory.* London: Bloomsbury.

Tomlinson, B. (Ed.). (1998). *Materials development in language teaching.* Cambridge: Cambridge University Press

Tomlinson, B., & Masuhara, H. (2004). *Developing language course materials.* Singapore: RELC Portfolio Series.

Tomlinson, B., & Masuhara, H. (Eds.). (2010). *Research for materials development in language learning: evidence for best practice.* London: Continuum.

1

Materials Development So Far

Introduction

Materials Development

The term "materials development" is used in this book to refer to all the different processes in the development and use of materials for language learning and teaching. "Such
processes include materials evaluation, materials adaptation, materials design, materials production, materials exploitation and materials research." All of these processes are
important and should ideally "interact in the making of any materials designed to help
learners to acquire a language" (Tomlinson, 2012, pp. 143–144).

As well as being the practical undertaking described above, materials development
has also become, since the mid-1990s, a popular field of academic study that investigates the principles and procedures of the design, writing, implementation, and evaluation of materials. "Ideally these two aspects of materials development are interactive in
that the theoretical studies inform, and are informed by, the actual development and use
of learning materials" (Tomlinson, 2001, p. 66). This is true of many recent publications
about materials development, for example Tomlinson (2008, 2010a, 2011, 2013a, 2013c,
2015, 2016a), Mukundan (2009), Harwood (2010a, 2014), Tomlinson and Masuhara
(2010), McDonough, Shaw, and Masuhara (2013), McGrath (2013, 2016), Garton and
Graves (2014), Mishan and Timmis (2015), Masuhara, Mishan, and Tomlinson (2017),
and Maley and Tomlinson (in press). Nearly all the writers in these books are both practitioners and researchers and their focus is on the theoretical principles and the practical
realizations of materials development. The interaction between theory and practice and
between practice and theory is also a deliberately distinctive feature of *The complete
guide to the theory and practice of materials development for language learning*. Like
the other writers referred to above, we have both worked on many coursebooks, supplementary books and web materials (for example, for Bulgaria, China, Ethiopia, Japan,
Morocco, Namibia, Nigeria, Singapore, Zambia and the global market), we have worked
on many research projects, and we have published many articles and books on theoretical and practical aspects of materials development.

Materials

There are many different definitions of what language-learning materials are. For example, "any systematic description of the techniques and exercises to be used in classroom

The Complete Guide to the Theory and Practice of Materials Development for Language Learning,
First Edition. Brian Tomlinson and Hitomi Masuhara.
© 2018 John Wiley & Sons, Inc. Published 2018 by John Wiley & Sons, Inc.

teaching" (Brown, 1995, p. 139). Many of these definitions focus on exercises for teaching (as Brown's definition does). We prefer to focus on materials for learning and the definition we are using for this book is that materials are anything that can be used by language learners to facilitate their learning of the target language. So materials could be a coursebook, a CD ROM, a story, a song, a video, a cartoon, a dictionary, a mobile phone interaction, a lecture, or even a photograph used to stimulate a discussion. They could also be an exercise, an activity, a task, a presentation, or even a project.

> Materials can be informative (in that they inform the learner about the target language), instructional (in that they guide the learner to practice the language), experiential (in that they provide the learner with experience of the language in use), eliciting (in that they encourage the learner to use the language) or exploratory (in that they help the learner to make discoveries about the language). (Tomlinson, 2012, p. 143)

Since L2 language teaching began, the vast majority of institutions that have provided language learning classes have either bought materials for their learners or have required their learners to buy materials for themselves. Some experts question whether commercial materials are actually necessary (e.g. Thornbury & Meddings, 2001) and some institutions even forbid their use at certain levels. For example, the Berlitz schools actually forbid the use of reading and writing at the lower levels. Their classes do not have a coursebook and their classrooms do not have whiteboards. Instead, the learners have to rely on the teacher as the source of oral input and the model of the target language. Interestingly, a Berlitz teacher at a school in Germany tried to teach Brian beginner's German in this way. Brian just could not segment the flow of language he was being exposed to by the teacher and, in desperation, the teacher took out a cigarette packet and wrote his sentences on it—thus creating useful materials and facilitating learning of the German being taught.

Materials can also be in design, as designed, in action, or in reflection. Materials in design are those that are in the process of being developed; materials as designed are those that have been finalized and are in a form ready for use; materials in action are those that are actually in the process of being used, and materials in reflection are those that are represented when users of the materials recollect their use. In theory the more thorough and principled the design process is the more effective the materials as designed are likely to be both when in action and when in reflection. However, in reality, user factors such as teacher / student rapport, teacher impact, teacher beliefs and learner motivation can mean that principled design becomes ineffective use and vice versa. This means that, ideally, materials need to be evaluated in all four states. The first three states receive a lot of attention in this book but the concept of materials in reflection has only just occurred to us. This could be a fruitful area of enquiry as knowing how users represent the materials in their minds, which they have used, could be very informative. The four states mentioned above are not necessarily just progressive; they can be recursive and interactive too. For example, the perception of materials in reflection can influence the subsequent use of the materials and / or the redesign of the materials. See Chapters 3, 4, and 15 for discussion of pre-use, whilst-use and post-use evaluation, of adaptation and of use of materials, and Ellis (2016) for a distinction between materials as work plans and materials as work plans in implementation.

In our travels around the classrooms of the world we have seen many examples of resourceful teachers creating useful homemade materials when effective commercial materials were not available. For example, a teacher in a Vanuatu primary school presented an English version of a local folk story by unrolling it across the cut-out "screen" of a make-believe cardboard television for the students to read, as well as getting puppets made by the pupils to act out dialogues. A different teacher in another Vanuatu primary school passed round a single photo of a Vietnamese girl running screaming down a road to stimulate groups to discuss the effects of war. There was a remarkably rich resource room full of wonderful homemade materials, which embarrassed the teachers in an Ethiopian primary school. And we both talked to three 7 year olds in a Guangzhou primary school who were the only pupils who could not only chant out rehearsed responses to the textbook drills but could hold a conversation with us in English. All three were dissatisfied with the teachers' limited use of the coursebook and looked out for materials of their own. One surfed the web in English every night; one subscribed to a soccer magazine written for native-speaker adults, and one went to Foreigners' Corner every weekend to talk to foreigners in English. Our point is that language learning materials can be produced commercially by professionals, they can be created by teachers, they can be found by learners, and they can even be created by learners (as when a class at one level writes stories for a class at a lower level). All four types of materials can facilitate language learning. And all four types can fail to facilitate language learning too. It all depends on the match between the materials and the needs, wants, and engagement of the learners using them (see Chapter 3).

For a discussion of whether or not commercial materials are typically necessary and useful, see Chapter 2 in this book. For suggestions about how the teacher can help learners to look for English outside the classroom see Barker (2010), Tomlinson (2014a) and Pinnard (2016).

Commercial Publications

Coursebooks

Although often under attack for inflexibility, shallowness, and lack of local relevance, the coursebook has been (and arguably still is) the main aid to learning a second or foreign language since language classes began. For example, when the learning of English first became popular in China in the early part of the nineteenth century many coursebooks were written by eminent Chinese scholars for teachers to use in their classrooms. In Daoyi and Zhaoyi (2015) there are accounts of the coursebooks used in 1920 and a reference to a general review of textbooks that listed over 200 English coursebooks published in China in the period 1912–1949.

A coursebook is usually written to contain the information, instruction, exposure, and activities that learners at a particular level need in order to increase their communicative competence in the target language. Of course, this is never enough and ideally even the best coursebook ever written needs supplementation. However, the reality for many learners and teachers is that the coursebook is all they have, and they just have to make do with it. This has been true for hundreds of years and is still true today in, for example, the schools and colleges in West Kalimantan that we visited recently and where we talked to Indonesian students who are learning English in state institutions with government-approved, locally published coursebooks or in private institutions using global coursebooks published in the United Kingdom for worldwide consumption.

The early twentieth-century coursebooks referred to in Daoyi and Zhaoyi (2015) "normally used a form of the grammar-translation method (GTM) with a focus on reading skills rather than spoken English" (p. 29). However, in the late 1920s a version of Harold Edward Palmer's direct method started to influence some of the coursebooks being published and similar oral methods were soon driving many of the coursebooks. The teacher and her learners were dominated by the one coursebook they used, which was obeyed as an edict rather than used as a resource. This excessive reverence for the coursebook continued (according to Daoyi & Zhaoyi, 2015) until the 1990s when the shift began from "teaching the textbook" to "teaching with the textbook" (p. 122) and supplementary materials became available too. By now there were many foreign publishing firms located in China and their global coursebooks exerted an influence. Teachers complained that coursebooks were either too conventional and restricting or "they adopted new approaches unsuitable for the pedagogical situation of the local areas where the textbooks" were being used. Every teacher, it seems, used a coursebook, but no teacher was happy with the book they were using. It seemed to have been accepted that this situation was inevitable and teachers were encouraged (but not helped very much) to adapt their coursebook to make it more suitable for the learners they were using it with (see Chapter 4 for discussion of ways of doing this).

It seems that what was true for China was largely true throughout the world (certainly in our experience in Austria, Indonesia, Japan, Malaysia, Oman, Singapore, the United States, the United Kingdom, and Vietnam). And it seems that it is still true to some extent today with, according to research done by the British Council (2008) and by Tomlinson (2010b), most teachers in many different countries saying that they use a textbook, that their textbook is chosen for them, and that they are not satisfied that it really helps their learners to acquire the target language.

Daoyi and Zhaoyi (2015, pp. 124–126) show how the early GTM and direct method were gradually supplemented in China (but not entirely replaced) by the structural approach, then the audio-lingual method, then functional / notional approaches, then communicative language teaching, then the eclectic method, and now by task-based language teaching. This "progress" can be observed by putting a line of textbooks in chronological order from the 1920s to today (as they do in the Textbook Museum in Beijing) not just in China but in most other countries around the world. What can be observed by visiting classrooms to see lessons in action (as we have done fairly recently in China, Ethiopia, Singapore, Spain and Turkey) is that the coursebook might have new buzzwords on the blurb but the way that the teacher uses it does not differ much from the way they used their previous textbook and all the ones before that too. The explicit teaching and testing of grammar still seems to dominate most classrooms (and many coursebooks too—e.g the very popular *Headway* series) and very little seems to have changed in the way that languages are typically taught and learned. There are exceptions of course (see Darici and Tomlinson, 2016, for an example of a text-driven classroom in Turkey) but most classrooms reflect what is reported in Thomas and Reinders (2015). This book reports on the introduction of task-based materials in countries and institutions in Asia and almost without exception the chapters report how the task-based approach was weakened in order to allow teachers to continue to pre-teach declarative knowledge of the grammar point to be "practiced" in the task. In other words, the much-discredited Presentation-Practice-Production procedure still prevails regardless of the pedagogical label on the coursebook, as we have demonstrated in our coursebook evaluations in Tomlinson, Dat, Masuhara, & Rubdy (2001), Masuhara, Haan, Yi, & Tomlinson (2008), and Tomlinson and Masuhara (2013).

For a critical evaluation of the evolution of coursebook pedagogies see Mishan (2016); for a discussion about the value of coursebooks see Chapter 2 in this book, and for a summary of research reports of how teachers and learners actually use coursebooks see Chapters 5 and 15 in this book.

Digital Materials

In our experience, paper materials are still the main means in most countries of helping learners to acquire a language in the classroom. But there is no denying that digital materials are increasing almost every day in number, technological sophistication and quality of presentation. First, there came the desktop computer in the 1980s with forward-thinking language schools in the United Kingdom and the United States installing computer laboratories to impress, and hopefully help, their fee-paying students. Brian remembers how, as Director of Studies at a privileged language school in the United Kingdom, he spent a week in the shiny new lab with a group of teachers wondering what use they could put it to. Instead of asking the technician what the computers could do, they decided what they wanted the computers to do and then asked the technician to make sure that they could. As a result, the classes that were timetabled in the lab were actually popular and useful. A few years later Brian was a frequent visitor to schools in Indonesia where his meetings with principals were invariably held in unused computer labs because they were the only rooms with air conditioning and because the World Bank had provided the labs but not the training or spare parts that could make them effective. A few years after that, Hitomi was teaching in Singapore and was compelled to deliver 30% of her lessons through the computer regardless of its suitability for what she was helping students to learn. And today we received an e-mail referring us to a web article about the Tanzanian government's plan to link 2,000 primary schools to ICT facilities so that math and reading programs in particular can be delivered.

One big question about digital materials is whether or not they have provided the field with radical new modes of delivery of the same old pedagogy or whether they have stimulated new pedagogies too. Just as we were thinking about this question we received delivery of a new book published by the British Council (Kukulska-Hulme, Norris, and Donohue, 2015). Its title, *Mobile pedagogy for English language teaching: A guide for teachers,* suggests that its authors think that their pedagogy is as innovative as its delivery. A quick glance at a random pair of pages (pp. 20–21) reveals the following benefits of mobile pedagogy:

- recording and documenting learning practices;
- recording problems when they occur;
- providing learner choice of task, text, medium, intended outcome, etc.;
- recording critical reflection;
- providing an audience;
- producing multimedia texts;
- finding and recording the target language outside the classroom;
- sharing outputs with peers and other communities;
- compiling a portfolio for continuous assessment.

All these benefits are valuable and are probably best provided by student use of their mobiles. However, none of these activities, or the many more described and exemplified throughout the book, actually represent a new pedagogy. What they do is to make use of the affordances of mobile technology to achieve creative exploitation of existing pedagogies. Unlike the activities in some digital materials that we have experienced, they are informed by language-learning principles and they provide a rich variety of new opportunities. We once worked as advisors and writers on a major online English-through-football course. We were initially excited by the creative potential of multimedia delivery but were eventually dismayed by being restricted by the software being used and by "learner expectations" to such stock activities as multiple choice, filling in the blanks, and sentence completion. And today one of our postgraduate students informed us of the apparent success of the online Middlebury Interactive Language program in increasing attendance and performance in schools in Hartford, United States. The innovative pedagogy seems to consist of so-called scaffolding interventions, which aid learner comprehension (e.g. difficult words in the reading texts have pop-up boxes with visual, audio and written definitions).

Brian was once invited by Microsoft to review the pedagogies of all the major existing computer-assisted language courses and to make use of this review to recommend the optimum pedagogy for such courses. Predictably most of the courses just reproduced, in more "glamorous" form, the stock activity types to be found in most paper-based courses. However, in his recommendations Brian was able to combine some of the more creative uses of pedagogy in the courses with principles and procedures he had already developed himself. We have no idea what happened to his recommendations as, like most research undertaken for publishers, his report was totally confidential and was never actually responded to. This issue of confidential research undertaken for publishers is taken up and developed in Chapter 15.

Although there have been radical developments in the use of new technologies to deliver language learning materials (both in stand-alone courses and as supplementary materials for print delivered coursebooks) there are very few books (or even articles) that focus on the pedagogical principles and development of these materials. Most of the publications on using new technologies to deliver language courses have focused, until very recently, on the technological innovations of the delivery (for a useful article on the technologies available to teachers see Levy, 2012) and on ways of exploiting the new affordances offered by these innovations. For example, the award-winning *CALICO Journal* (accessed September 30, 2016) lists only one article amongst its list of seminal articles that appears to relate computer-assisted language learning (CALL) to materials development. However, this article (Salaberry, 1996), although suggesting in its title a focus on pedagogical tasks, is actually an excellent article about the pedagogical affordances of computer-assisted language learning. This is true also of many other articles in this and other highly respected CALL journals (e.g. *Language Learning and Technology, CALL* and *ReCALL*). They provide very useful overviews of how technology can help teachers to apply the principles of second-language acquisition (SLA) theory to classroom practice in new and effective ways but have often little to offer on materials development (though see Chapter 8 for examples of publications, mainly chapters in books, which do suggest and report effective ways of developing principled digital materials).

Although aware of the obvious benefits brought to the field by digital delivery of language learning materials, some materials developers have warned against the control of language teachers and learners by technology. For example, Mukundan (2008b, p. 109) points out the danger of educationalists thinking that "multimedia can drive pedagogically sound methodology" and gives the example of Malaysia where he thinks teaching courseware "directs teaching in a prescriptive manner." Maley (2011, p. 390) is positive about the ways in which IT can be used as a resource "for the freeing of teachers and learners alike from the constraints of the coursebook" and for providing "rapid and flexible access to unlimited information resources." He also warns, though, how, as Wolf (2008) says, that the "multi-tasking, rapidly switching, superficial processing of information might … impair more reflective modes of thinking" (p. 392).

Although there are very few publications reporting research studies of the development and effects of materials for new technologies, some journals now have regular features reviewing new electronic materials (for example, *ELT Journal*) and some experts have written about the potential impact of such materials on language learning. For example, Chapelle (1998, 2001), Chapelle and Lui (2007) and Chapelle and Jamieson (2008) have written about the attitudinal and learning effects of CALL materials on learners. Eastment (1999), Derewianka (2003a, 2003b), Murray (2003), Blake (2008), Reinders and White (2010), Kervin and Derewianka (2011), Motteram (2011), Kiddle (2013), Mishan (2013), and Mishan and Timmis (2015) have written about the development and use of electronic materials for the teaching and / or learning of English. For detailed discussion about these and other publications as well as the principled development of materials for electronic delivery, see Chapter 8.

Perhaps the development that has received the most positive responses is the increase in courses that feature a blended learning approach. In these approaches decisions are made about whether to deliver each section of the course face-to-face or electronically, depending on such pragmatic criteria as cost, availability of expertise, availability of time and learner preference, as well as suitability of methodology (e.g. information is probably best delivered electronically and communicative competence is probably best developed through face-to-face interaction). There are many case studies of such courses in action in Tomlinson and Whittacker (2013), including a course for taxi drivers in Turkey in which the drivers followed up face-to-face classes on their mobile phones and received one-to-one tutorials whilst waiting for customers.

Supplementary Materials

Our early memories of materials for use in language classrooms are of coursebooks rather than supplementary materials (i.e. materials intended to provide additional language experience or instruction). Brian remembers using just a coursebook with his classes in Nigeria in 1966 and Hitomi remembers a similar experience with her classes in Nagoya in the 1980s. We were therefore rather surprised to find out from Daoyi and Zhaoyi (2015) that many series of supplementary readers were published and used in primary and secondary schools in China in the period from 1912–1949. On reflection, this was probably also true of many ESL countries where English was used as a medium of instruction. Brian now remembers that in Zambia, in 1969, senior forms in secondary schools studied English literature as well as English language and all classes had sets of extensive readers to supplement their coursebook.

Extensive readers were popular as supplementary materials in UK language schools in the 1970s and became even more so after the publication of a report on the successful impact on student's language growth of the Fiji book flood (Elley & Mangubhai,

1981). Other extensive reader experiments in the 1980s demonstrated positive effects too, for example in Singapore and in Cameroon (Davies, 1995), and many mainstream publishers developed their own series of graded readers. Brian remembers, at Bell College, Saffron Walden, in the late 1970s, not only using sets of EFL readers but of using a complete library of English literature books for the more advanced learners. In particular he remembers an Argentinian student who was inspired by a classroom activity to read a novel by Graham Green and then to read all his novels in the library. He remembers, too, an action research project in which he found that the only students who made progress in his intermediate level class were those who sought out English outside the classroom through interaction with other students and with local people and / or read English newspapers, magazines and books from the library. For powerful research-based arguments in favor of extensive reading see Day and Bamford (1998), Krashen (2004) and Maley (2008), and go to the Extensive Reading Foundation web site (www.erfoundation.org).

We think that what was beginning to happen at Bell College in the late 1970s and early 1980s with regard to supplementary materials reflected what was beginning to happen around the world. In addition to having a core coursebook, each class had access to other coursebooks, to a set of graded readers, to workbooks, to videos, to a library and to computer activities in the computer lab. In addition, at Bell College we were privileged to have access to a video studio (where Brian remembers his classes scripting, directing and producing videos of poems or stories they had responded to earlier in the week), we involved the students in projects and presentations, and we offered a program of special interest classes in which content rather than language drove the syllabus (e.g. English Through Pottery, English Through Local History, English Through Pub Architecture.). On reflection, students probably spent more time doing supplementary activities than they did using the core coursebook.

As we moved into the 1980s separate skills books became popular, to provide extra focused experience of reading, writing, listening, and speaking (e.g. the Oxford Supplementary Skills Series edited by Alan Maley in 1987 / 88) and a number of communicative activity books provided our students with enjoyable experience of communicating in order to complete a task and achieve a context dependent goal (e.g. Maley, Duff, and Grellet, 1981; Porter Ladousse, 1983). We also experimented with materials that we designed in house to implement such "eccentric" approaches as The Silent Way (Gattengo, 1963; Richards & Rodgers, 2001), Community Language Learning (Richards & Rodgers, 2001), and Suggestopedia (Hooper Hansen, 2011). Our students and those in other privileged language schools around the world certainly had a rich experience of language in use. Students in state schools and colleges had a narrower experience, which was still focused on the use of a core coursebook, but in China, for example, use was made of supporting "activity books, assessment books, skill development books, readers, flashcards and wall charts" as well as "cassette tapes and CDs" (Daoyi & Zhaoyi, 2015, p. 145). Brian remembers a book of communicative activities being written by teachers in Vanuatu for use in both primary classes and examinations (Tomlinson, 1981) and student made puppet theatres and big books being used to supplement the coursebook too. But Hitomi remembers in Japan at that time being still mainly restricted to a core coursebook.

Nowadays more supporting components than ever are being offered with coursebooks, although it is arguable that most of them simply provide additional information and practice rather than enriching the students' language experience as supplementary materials in the 1980s tended to do. *Speakout* (Parsons & Williams, 2011), for example, is accompanied by a teacher's resource book, which contains:

- Detailed teaching notes …
- An extensive bank of photocopiable activities covering grammar, vocabulary and functional language in communicative contexts.
- Mid-course and end-of-course tests …

Also available are Active Teach (containing the student book in digital format, integrated whiteboard software and an answer reveal function) and MySpeakout Lab (including an online learning tool with personalized practice, an automatic gradebook and video podcasts with interactive activities). A number of publishers have expressed their concerns about the cost and inessentiality of all these add-on components and certainly in our travels around the classrooms of the world we rarely see any course add-on components in evidence. We feel quite strongly that the money invested by publishers and therefore by schools in these inessential add-ons could be better invested in providing more experience of the language in use through, for example, extensive readers, authentic videos, and access to newspapers and magazines (a popular resource made use of in China since the 1930s). In our recent review of adult global course-books (Tomlinson & Masuhara, 2013) we complained that "there are even more and more expensive course components" (p. 248) since our equivalent reviews in 2001 and 2008. Currently, though, more and more add-ons are being made available "free" to coursebook users via the Internet. For example, the recently published fourth edition of the coursebook *Headway intermediate* (Soars & Soars, 2016) provides extra grammar practice, vocabulary practice, tests, games and dialogue practice on a freely available web site, https://elt.oup.com/student/headway/int/?cc=gb&selLanguage=en. The newly appointed chief product and marketing officer of a rival company has just announced an intention to focus even more on providing additional wrap around services to support their coursebook delivery. Interestingly the announcement also mentioned developing blended learning courses and international courses as other priorities.

Two methodologies have made a big impact recently in books about methodology, CLIL (content and language integrated learning) and TBLT (task-based language teaching). However, not only have they arguably had very little impact on what happens in mainstream coursebooks (despite claims on blurbs that they do) but they have led to the publication of very few supplementary materials either (one exception being Coyle, Hood, and Marsh, 2010). This is probably for the same reasons that one of our favorite approaches, total physical response (TPR) (see Tomlinson, 1994a) has rarely been implemented in supplementary materials for students. The activities are difficult to transfer to the page and, more importantly, they are best realized in teacher's resource books rather than student textbooks, thus selling only one copy per class rather than 40.

For extensive reviews of coursebooks used in different areas of the world see Tomlinson (2008).

Self-Access Materials

Students seem to have been learning other languages by themselves for as long as languages have been learned. In our experience the most effective way of quickly gaining basic communicative competence seems to be immersion in the target language through, for example, moving to a country where the language is spoken or joining (or forming) a community of speakers of the language. Barker (2010) gives a successful example of forming a community of language speakers at a university in Japan where some students from his classes formed a club whose members always spoke English to each other when they met either inside or outside the university. Brian advised agricultural students at a university in Addis Ababa to do something similar, and soon they went from being laughed at to being joined by students from many different courses.

Immersion involves studying subjects in an L2 and is a potentially successful way of quickly gaining communicative competence in the L2 because of the massive exposure to relevant input and the multiple opportunities for using the target language for communication. However, there is a danger that achieving communicative effect always takes priority over accuracy and that language errors start to fossilize. This is what happened on the Canadian Immersion Programme (Swain & Lapkin, 2005) when English-speaking students studied all their school subjects in French. The students gained the target knowledge in their subjects and made rapid progress in developing fluency and communicative effect in the L2. However, they continued to make basic grammatical errors until language-awareness classes were added to the curriculum. The same thing happened to Schmidt (2001) when he assumed that he would acquire Portuguese from immersion in the language but only really made progress when he realized that he needed to pay attention to language forms too. He used the term "noticing" to label this process of paying attention to language forms encountered during communication and argued persuasively for making use of it in self-access attempts to learn a language. Bolitho and Tomlinson had already come to a similar conclusion with regard to the improvement of accuracy and pragmatic effect at higher levels in their book, *Discover English,* which was first published in 1980 and is still in print today as Bolitho and Tomlinson (2005). This is an activity book intended primarily to help higher level learners to make their own discoveries about how English is used from focused exposure to it. It focuses mainly on sentence-level grammar but its authors have started discussions about supplementing it with *Discover English Discourse.* Unfortunately though, the publishers have resisted this move as the activities are considered to be too open-ended for teachers to accept (i.e. not usable for easy to mark tests and difficult to give feedback to).

In our view many self-access materials still focus on information about and practice in specific language items or language skills which are problematic for the learners and often do not include enough exposure to authentic language in use, enough opportunities for communication, enough experience in making discoveries from authentic encounters with the language or enough material designed to engage the learners affectively and cognitively. This is partly because of the restrictions inherent in self-access study (e.g. nobody to interact with; nobody to monitor production; the perceived need for a marking key) and partly because a focus on forms is what many self-access learners believe is necessary. For a critique of forms-focused self-access materials, a suggested list of principles to humanize self-access materials, and an extended example of "access-self materials" see Tomlinson (2011c). See also Cooker (2008, 2010) who insists that criteria for evaluating self-access materials should be based on such core principles as "the ability to interest and engage learners, to be meaningful and challenging and to have a sustained positive impact" (Cooker, 2008, pp. 128–129). This is echoed and extended by Tomlinson (2010c, pp. 73–81), who proposes that criteria for developing and evaluating self-access materials should be driven by five universal principles of acquisition (e.g. "In order for the learners to maximize their exposure to language in use they need to be engaged both affectively and cognitively in the language experience"), five principles of self-access materials development (e.g. "Provide many opportunities for the learners to produce language in order to achieve intended outcomes rather than to just practice specified features of the language") and seven principles of delivery (e.g. "The materials should aim to help the students to become truly independent so that they can continue to learn the language forever by seeking further contact with it"). He also insists that local criteria should be developed to take into account such factors specific to the learning context as:

- age;
- gender;
- levels;
- purposes for learning the language;
- amount of class learning time;
- estimated time available for self-access;
- previous experience of using self-access materials;
- attitudes to self-access;
- learning-style preferences;
- learner needs;
- learner wants.

We believe that exposure to the language in use, opportunity to use the language, and experience of making self-discoveries can and should be built into self-access programs together with texts and activities that stimulate affective and cognitive engagement. This can be achieved by, for example:

- using a text-driven approach (Tomlinson, 2013b) in which students select a potentially engaging text, respond to it personally, develop their own text (e.g. by answering a letter), make discoveries about a linguistic or pragmatic feature of the core text and then revise their development text making use of their discoveries;
- providing access to an extensive reading / listening / viewing library and offering a menu of postexperience creative tasks to those students who want to do them (Fenton-Smith, 2010);
- stimulating students to look out for English outside the classroom and then to interact with whatever language experience interests them—e.g. joining a Philosophy in Pubs group (Tomlinson, 2014a). See Cooker (2008, 2010) and Tomlinson (2010c, 2011c) for detailed examples of such humanistic self-access activities.

Many institutions now have self-access centers and one that we both think sets a very good example is in Kanda University in Japan. This center provides a very rich access to books, films, television programs, digital materials, skills-based task materials and language focused activity materials, as well as providing such facilities as a proficient speaker available for advice or conversation and advertisements for local places and events in which English will be used.

Publications about Materials Development

As recently as the 1970s and 1980s there were very few publications on materials development. There were a few books on methodology, which contained sections on, or at least reference to, materials (e.g. Moskowitch, 1978; Richards, 1978) but the phrase "materials development" was not used. The process of producing language-learning materials tended to be referred to as materials writing and there was very little discussion of the principles that did or should inform it.

There were a few books and papers at that time on what we now refer to as materials development. Madsen and Bowen (1978) focused on teachers adapting materials and asserted that good teachers are constantly adapting the materials that are available to them. Candlin and Breen (1980) focused on the principles and procedures of evaluating and designing materials. And Cunningsworth (1984) devoted a complete book to the evaluation and selection of materials. However, most references to materials writing / design came in books and articles on language teaching methodology, which illustrated pedagogic methods and approaches with extracts from coursebooks (as Cunningsworth, 1984, does). This was the norm throughout the 1980s, with very few books taking the lead from Cunningsworth's breakthrough (Dubin and Olshtain's, 1986, book on designing language courses; Grant's, 1987, book on making the most of your textbook and Sheldon's, 1987, book on the problems of textbook evaluation and design being conspicuous exceptions). There were some articles on particular aspects of materials development published in the 1970s and 1980s in such professional journals as *ELT Journal* and *Modern English Teacher* but we had to wait until the mid-1990s for further dedicated books on materials development to appear. Both the articles and the books tended to focus on materials development as a practical undertaking. For example, in the United States Byrd (1995) published a book that provided a practical guide for materials writers, in England Cunningsworth (1995) continued his focus on evaluation by publishing a book on how to choose your coursebook and Graves (1996) published a book on teachers in the role of course developers. Tomlinson (1998) marked an important development by discussing the principles and procedures of a number of the important processes of materials development (although Hall, 1995, had already published a chapter on the theory and practice of materials production in Hidalgo, Hall, and Jacobs, 1995, a book focusing on materials writing in Southeast Asia). In Tomlinson (1998) there were chapters on data collection, the process of evaluation, the process of materials writing, the process of materials publication and, perhaps for the first time, there were chapters explicitly concerned with the effective application of theory to practice. This book was published by Cambridge University Press as a collection of papers by presenters at Materials Development Association (MATSDA) conferences and workshops on different aspects of materials development for language learning, events that also stimulated many articles on materials development in various established journals and in the MATSDA journal, *Folio*. The book has now been brought up to date and added to as Tomlinson (2011).

In the 1990s, books on language teaching methodology also gave more attention to applications of methodology to materials development and illustrated the approaches outlined with samples of published materials. A good example of such a book is McDonough and Shaw (2003), which has substantial sections on approaches to materials, on materials adaptation, and on materials evaluation. This book has been brought up to date and expanded with numerous illustrations from contemporary published materials as McDonough, Shaw, and Masuhara (2013).

In 2000, Fenner and Newby published a book on the approaches to materials design currently being implemented in European coursebooks, in 2001 Richards published a book that focused on curriculum development but made frequent reference to materials development and in 2002 McGrath published an important volume on materials evaluation and design. McGrath (2002) is important because it was probably the first book to not only provide systematic applications of theory to the practice of evaluating, adapting and supplementing materials but also to offer principled suggestions for systematizing materials design. Johnson (2003) published a book reporting research which investigated the difference between how expert materials writers wrote materials for a task and how novice writers wrote materials for the same task. Then Tomlinson (2003) published the first book designed to be used as a coursebook on the many teacher-training and postgraduate materials development modules that were now being offered all over the world. It contains chapters on analysis, evaluation, selection, adaptation, principled frameworks for materials development, materials for teaching grammar, vocabulary and the four skills, in-house materials production by institutions and coursebook development on national projects, as well as chapters on such practical aspects of materials development as design and illustration. Practical guidance is also a feature of Tomlinson and Masuhara (2004), a book written in English for inexperienced teachers in South East Asia but since translated into Chinese, Korean, and Portuguese. The book gives advice on design, lay out, illustrations, text selection and writing instructions, and advises and exemplifies how to design, evaluate, and adapt materials in principled and feasible ways. In the early years of this century Jayakuran Mukandan in Malaysia started to run MICELT conferences for Universiti Putra Malaysia. These conferences focused on different aspects and issues of materials development, featured experts in the field from all over the world, gave a chance to large numbers of local researchers to present the results of their studies and attracted audiences of over 500 practitioners from all over Southeast Asia. Some of the papers from these conferences were published and many interesting articles on issues in materials development can be found in Mukundan (2003, 2006, 2008). Also at around this time in the same area of the world the Regional English Language Centre (RELC) in Singapore was inviting experts on materials development to speak at its conferences, and in 2003 RELC held a very well received conference on Methodology and Materials Design in Language Teaching. Some of the papers from this conference on aspects of materials development were then published as Renandya (2003). This approach of encouraging studies of materials development so that the results can be presented at conferences and then published in proceedings has continued with, for example, presentations at five recent MATSDA conferences being turned into chapters for books focusing on the themes of the conferences (Mishan & Chambers, 2010; Tomlinson 2013c, 2016a; Maley & Tomlinson, in press; Masuhara et al., 2017).

From 2006 to 2016, publications on materials development have focused very much on the application of theory to aspects of materials development practice. Tomlinson (2007) is primarily a book about language acquisition but many of its chapters include applications of theory to materials development (e.g. applications of research on recasts in the United Kingdom and Spain, on visual imaging in Japan, Singapore and Spain, on the use of the inner voice in Singapore and the United Kingdom, on comprehension approaches in Singapore and on reticent learners in Vietnam). The contribution of researchers from all over the world has become the norm in materials development and this is also evident in Tomlinson (2008). The book starts with a chapter on the interaction between language acquisition and language-learning materials and then focuses on research evaluating the potential effects of language learning materials in the United Kingdom, in the United States, in Australasia, in Ireland, in Greece, in Central and Eastern Europe, in Africa, in Japan, in South East Asia, in the Middle East, and in South America.

Harwood (2010a) also includes contributions from different areas of the world and explores the issues involved in the principled design, implementation, and evaluation of materials. It includes chapters on, for example, a genre-based approach to the development of materials for teaching writing, on an approach to developing materials that applies content-based approaches for developing reading skills, and on developing materials for community-based adult ESL programs. Tomlinson and Masuhara (2010) reports projects from all over the world in which research has been conducted on the effectiveness of materials designed to apply the principles of, for example, facilitating language acquisition through extensive reading, process, and discovery approaches to the development of writing skills, process drama approaches to developing communicative competence and the use of problem solving approaches. This book signals a new direction in publications on materials in that it focuses exclusively on reports of research projects investigating various aspects of the effects of materials development on both learners and teachers. Gray (2010) also contains references to research but it departs from the current focus on the effectiveness of materials and concerns itself with how the world is represented as affluent, materialistic, Westernized, and aspirational in global coursebooks, and especially with the effects of producing global coursebooks as promotional commodities that portray users of English in very selective ways. Tomlinson (2011), a revised version of Tomlinson (1998), also refers to the increasing body of research data on various aspects of materials development as well as proposing ideas for data collection, for processes of materials development and evaluation and for processes of electronic design and delivery of materials. There are also chapters proposing applications to materials development of such nonmainstream theories as visualization, flexi-materials, suggestopedia and humanistic approaches to developing self-access materials. McGrath (2013) is a similar mix of surveys, proposals and research reports, as is Tomlinson (2013a), a revised version of Tomlinson (2003a). McGrath (2013) introduces a relatively new and now increasingly researched focus on what teachers actually do with their textbooks. Tomlinson (2013a) attempts, in its 561 pages, a similar comprehensive coverage of different aspects of materials development as in its first edition but also includes chapters on such comparatively new areas as materials for ESOL, materials for blended learning, digital materials, and corpus-informed materials. The fact that books on materials development are now being published in revised editions is indicative of the growing demand in the field for such publications. Other examples of this are McDonough, Shaw, and Masuhara (2013) and McGrath (2016, an update of McGrath, 2002).

Most of the recent publication in the field of materials development follow the departure started by Tomlinson and Masuhara (2010) in being mainly focused on the findings of research studies investigating the effects of types of materials on their users (e.g. Maley & Tomlinson, in press; Masuhara et al., 2017). Tomlinson (2013c) explores the application to materials development of the research findings of various relevant areas of applied linguistics, as well as considering the implications of practice for the development of theory. In the first part of each chapter a review is provided of current research findings in the area being focused on and then, in the second part, published materials are evaluated against these research findings and practical applications to materials development are suggested and illustrated. A similar approach is taken in Tomlinson (2016a) but in this book the focus is specifically on the applications of findings and theories from the significant field of second language acquisition research. Another recent publication with a focus on applying theory to practice is Harwood (2014). This is a collection of chapters either proposing applications of theory or reporting on research studies of textbook content, textbook consumption and textbook production. Garton and Graves (2014) also connects theory to practice in materials design and use in its reports of research and application in numerous international settings. The emphasis on applying theory to practice and on reporting the results of materials development research is also evident in two special materials development issues of renowned applied linguistics journals (Tomlinson, 2016b, 2016c) and in recent issues of the MATSDA journal *Folio* (see www.matsda.org), the only journal we know of dedicated to articles on materials development for language learning (though the materials development special interest groups of TESOL in the United States, IATEFL in the United Kingdom and JALT in Japan do publish newsletters and the IATEFL special interest group, MAWSIG, is about to launch a new journal, *ELT Materials Review*).

As of late 2016, the most recently published books we know of on materials development (apart from McGrath's 2016 revised version of McGrath, 2002 and the already mentioned Tomlinson, 2016a) are Mishan and Timmis (2015) and Azarnoosh, Zeraatpishe, Faravani, and Kargozari (2016). Mishan and Timmis is a book that is targeted at TESOL teachers in training or in practice and which aims to provide a practical introduction to the principles of materials development. It encourages a principled and critical approach to teachers when making choices in their evaluation, selection, adaptation and development of materials. Azarnoosh et al. (2016) is a book of chapters commenting on current issues in materials development which reflects the increasing internationalization of research on materials development by being edited by four Iranian academics and containing chapters by researchers from nine different countries.

And now there is this book, the first one to attempt coverage of the theory and practice of materials development to date, as well as recommending principled procedures for all the important processes involved in materials development.

We would like to end this section with a quote from Tomlinson (2012, p. 146), which we both endorse and which we are both encouraging our postgraduate students and our colleagues to respond to:

> The literature on materials development has moved a long way since the early focus on ways of selecting materials to the current focus on the application of theory to practice and practice to theory. But in my view there are certain aspects of materials development which have not yet received enough attention. I would like to read publications exploring the effects on the learners of different ways of using the same materials (for example, as a script versus as a resource; as a sequential course versus as a course for learner navigation; as a core component versus as a supplement). Most of all though I would like to read publications reporting and applying the results of longitudinal studies of the effects of materials on not just the attitudes, beliefs, engagement and motivation of learners but on their actual communicative effectiveness too. For the field of materials development to become more credible it needs to become more empirical. (Tomlinson, 2012, p. 146)

Materials Development Projects

Whilst innovation in materials development has been inevitably restricted by the understandable conservatism of commercial publishers, it has flourished on many national and institutional materials development projects since the mid-1980s. We have both been involved in many such projects and have found them to be very exciting and stimulating both for those involved in developing materials and those involved in using them. Unfortunately, though, many of the products and other benefits of these projects have not survived after key personnel have moved on or after a Minister or director has changed and new (or old) directions have been determined. Very few of these projects have actually been reported on in accessible publications and important lessons have been forgotten. We were both in Indonesia in 2014 and Brian took the opportunity to check how much impact a project that he directed in the 1980s was still having on the schools and teachers of Indonesia. This was the PKG project (By the Teacher for the Teacher), which was innovative in that, in each secondary school, an experimental beginners' English class was taught by teachers who had been trained to teach English in English, to make use of TPR Plus, group work, extensive reading and discovery approaches, and to develop materials in local teams (Tomlinson, 1990). The approach was very popular with students (as evidenced by, for example, attendance records) and very successful (as shown, for example, by the dramatic success of the experimental students in end of the year examinations). But we could find no trace of the PKG in 2014 and neither its methodology nor its materials were being used. Instead teachers seemed to have gone back to lecturing to students about English in Bahasa Indonesia. Very disappointing but not unusual.

We have been involved together in numerous materials development projects. Some of them were aborted because the funds ran out or because of a change of personnel. For example, a very ambitious British Council project developing materials for "leaders" in sub-Saharan Africa got to a stage where materials were successfully trialed in Senegal but then the project was abandoned when British Council officers were transferred and replaced by people with different priorities. A project in Serbia and a very large project in Iran (involving replacing all the official English textbooks) were abandoned before they got going because elections were held and the Minister of Education was replaced. A promising project in Vietnam reached a stage where excellent local materials had been developed by Vietnamese university lecturers but then funds were unavailable to complete the project. And the same thing happened to a similar project to develop materials for English courses in Southeast Asian universities. Fortunately, some of the projects we have been involved in were completed and implemented. For example, in Namibia, 30 teachers from all over the country wrote a text-driven coursebook in 6 days for government secondary schools (Tomlinson, 2013b). We were both involved in a project in which local teachers developed a coursebook for secondary schools in Bulgaria, a project in which a large team from Leeds Metropolitan University and from the University College of St. Mark and St. John, Plymouth combined to develop language improvement courses for English teachers in Ethiopia, a project that developed primary and secondary school materials for China and a project that developed a secondary school course for Singapore. We know that all these materials were published and distributed and that the primary course in China and the secondary course in Singapore were extensively used but we have no idea how effective the materials have been. This is one of the frustrating aspects of being involved in innovative projects. You enjoy the freedom to innovate and you are rewarded by the enthusiasm, skill and increased self-esteem of the local participants but you rarely get a chance to find out what eventually becomes of the projects and are denied a chance to learn from the experience (though see Timmis, 2014 for reflections on his involvement in one of the Chinese projects mentioned above). Also, until recently, it was rare for a rigorous longitudinal evaluation of the effects of materials development projects to be undertaken.

Despite our sometimes-frustrating experience of materials development projects, there is no doubt about it that teacher participation in materials development projects can be enriching both for the materials and for the teachers (Tomlinson, 2014b). There is also no doubt that much of the innovation in materials development has taken place on such projects sponsored by ministries or institutions dissatisfied with the suitability of what is being made available to them by commercial publishers. Unfortunately only a few of these projects have been written up and published. Some of the more innovative of these projects include:

- the CBSE-ELT Project in India in which the College of St. Mark and St. John in Plymouth assisted the Central Board of Secondary Education (CBSE) in facilitating the development of communicative and task-based textbooks;
- a secondary school coursebook in Namibia that was written by 30 teachers in 6 days, which made use of nationwide surveys of student and teacher needs and wants, which contained a number of normally taboo topics (e.g. drug abuse), and which was text driven (Tomlinson, 1995);
- a secondary school textbook project in Bulgaria in which two textbooks were developed by small teams of teachers and then one of them was chosen for publication (a book which focused on helping students to explain Bulgarian culture to overseas visitors) (Tomlinson, 1995);
- an extensive reading project for young learners developed in Hong Kong in 1995 and revised in 2004 (Arnold, 2010);
- an 8-year secondary school coursebook series in Romania written by a team of 14 teachers (Popovici & Bolitho, 2003);
- an institution-specific course developed by a large team of teachers at Bilkent University, Ankara (Lyons, 2003);
- a number of projects producing task-based language teaching materials for teaching Dutch in Belgium (Van den Branden, 2006);
- primary and secondary courses developed by large teams of teachers in Romania, Russia, Belarus, and Uzbekistan (Bolitho, 2008);
- a project in which a selected group of teachers produced materials for Sultan Qaboos University, Muscat to help EAP students develop writing skills through an innovative experiential approach which combined a text-driven approach, a discovery approach and a process approach (Al-Busaidi & Tindle, 2010);
- a project in Northern Arizona University that brought together experts in applied linguistics and chemistry to develop a textbook to help university students to develop discipline specific reading and writing skills (Stoller & Robinson, 2014);
- a British Council project in India (the ELTReP awards scheme) in which first-time researchers studied the effects of pedagogic approaches and materials in Indian schools (with 22 of the studies due to be published online in 2017).

Adapted and expanded from Tomlinson (2012), p. 167.

Currently we know of large-scale materials development projects being undertaken by foreign language resource centers in the United States (http://www.nflrc.org), for example COERLL's open educational resources, CARLA's materials for less-commonly taught languages and CASLS's work on materials creation. We also know that the British

Council and such institutions as NILE (the Norwich Institute for Language Education) are currently involved in materials development projects in such countries as Columbia, Georgia, Kazakhstan, and Russia. Let us hope that some of these projects are evaluated and the results published.

Conclusion

Materials development has come a long way in a comparatively short time and ahead lie exciting possibilities in the development of digital materials, of materials for blended learning, and of research into the actual effectiveness of different types of materials and into how to make the staple coursebook more flexible, more locally appropriate, and more effective in facilitating communicative competence.

This has been a sketch of what has happened in the field of materials development so far. What follows in the rest of this book is our attempt to provide more detail on the main processes and issues of materials as we have experienced them, as they have been reported in the literature and as we feel they can best be proceduralized.

What Do You Think?

1. a) What do you think will happen to the coursebook? Do you think it will continue to be the main way of delivering language courses to students? Do you think it will eventually be replaced by digital materials?
   b) Try to imagine what a coursebook will look like in 20 years' time. What do you think it will contain? Do you think it will be supplemented by extra course components or it will go back to being self-standing?
   c) What do you think are the advantages and disadvantages of replacing global coursebooks with locally produced materials?
2. a) What do you think are the main advantages and disadvantages of digital materials?
   b) What new developments can you envisage in the design and delivery of digital materials?
   c) Do you think most language courses are going to adopt a blended approach in the future? Why?
3. a) What do you think are the main advantages and disadvantages of including extensive reading as part of a language course?
   b) Do you think that published extensive readers should be graded and simplified according to the language level of the target learners?
4. a) What do you think is the most effective way of learning a language through self-access?
   b) Do you think self-access components should be integrated into taught language courses? If so what do you think is the best way of doing this?

Note that the "what do you think?" questions in this and other chapters in this book are obviously not intended as tests but rather as a stimulus to thought and discussion, both through inner speech self-discussions and through conversations with others face to face or via the Internet.

References

Al-Busaidi, S., & Tindle, K. (2010). Evaluating the impact of in-house materials on language learning. In B. Tomlinson & H. Masuhara (Eds.), *Research for materials development in language learning: Evidence for best practice* (pp. 137–149). London: Continuum.

Arnold, W. (2010). A longitudinal study of the effects of a graded reading scheme for young learners in Hong Kong. In B. Tomlinson & H. Masuhara (Eds.), *Research for materials development in language learning: Evidence for best practice* (pp. 37–49). London: Continuum.

Azarnoosh, M., Zeraatpishe, M., Faravani, A., & Kargozari, H. R. (Eds.). (2016). *Issues in materials development*. Rotterdam: Sense.

Barker, D. (2010). The role of unstructured learner interaction in the study of a foreign language. In S. Menon & J. Lourdunathan (Eds.), *Readings on ELT materials IV* (pp. 50–70). Petaling Jaya: Pearson Malaysia.

Blake, R. (2008). *Brave new digital classroom: Technology and foreign language learning*. Washington DC: Georgetown University Press.

Bolitho, R. (2008). Materials used in Central and Eastern Europe and the former Soviet Union. In B. Tomlinson (Ed.), *English language teaching materials: A critical review*. London: Continuum.

Bolitho, R., & Tomlinson, B. (2005). *Discover English*. Oxford: Macmillan.

British Council. (2008). *Teaching English. Course books*. London: Author.

Brown, H. D. (1995). *Principles of language learning and teaching* (3rd ed.). Englewood Cliffs, NJ: Prentice Hall Regents.

Byrd, P. (1995). *Materials writers guide*. Rowley, MA.: Newbury House.

Candlin, C. N., & Breen, M. (1980). Evaluating and designing language teaching materials. *Practical papers in English language education*. Vol. 2. Lancaster: Institute for English Language Education, University of Lancaster.

Chapelle, C. A. (1998). Multimedia CALL: Lessons to be learned from research on instructed SLA. *Language Learning and Technology, 2*(1), 22–34.

Chapelle, C. A. (2001). *Computer applications in second language acquisition*. Cambridge: Cambridge University Press.

Chapelle, C. A., & Jamieson, J. (2008). *Tips for teaching with CALL: Practical approaches to computer-assisted language learning*. White Plains, NY: Pearson Longman.

Chapelle, C. A., & Lui H. M. (2007). Theory and research: Investigation of "authentic" CALL tasks. In J. Egbert & E. Hanson-Smith (Eds.), *CALL environments* (2nd ed., pp. 111–130). Alexandria, VA: TESOL Publications.

Cooker, L. (2008). Self-access materials. In B. Tomlinson (Ed.), *English language learning materials: A critical review* (pp. 110–132). London: Continuum.

Cooker, L. (2010). Some self-access principles. *Studies in Self-Access Learning, 1*(1), 5–9.

Coyle, D., Hood, P., & D. Marsh (2010). *Content and language integrated learning*. Cambridge: Cambridge University Press.

Cunningsworth, A. (1984). *Evaluating and selecting EFL teaching material*. London: Heinemann.

Cunningsworth, A. (1995). *Choosing your coursebook*. Oxford: Heinemann.

Daoyi, L., & Zhaoyi, W. (Eds.). (2015). *English Language education in China: past and present*. Beijing: People's Education Press.

Darici, A., & Tomlinson, B. (2016). A case study of principled materials in action. In B. Tomlinson (Ed.), *Second language acquisition research and materials development for language learning*. New York: Routledge.

Davies, C. (1995). Extensive reading: An expensive extravagance. *ELT Journal, 49*(4), 329–336.

Day, R., & Bamford, J. (1998). *Extensive reading in the second language classroom.* Cambridge: Cambridge University Press.

Derewianka, B. (2003a). Developing electronic materials for language teaching. In B. Tomlinson (Ed.), *Developing materials for language teaching* (pp. 199–220). London: Continuum.

Derewianka, B. (2003b). Designing an on-line reference grammar for primary English teachers. In W. A. Renandya (Ed.), *Methodology and materials design in language teaching* (pp. 44–51). Singapore: SEAMEO.

Dubin, F., & Olshtain, E. (1986). *Course design.* New York: Cambridge University Press.

Eastment, D. (1999). *The internet and ELT.* Oxford: Summertown Publishing.

Elley, W. B., & Mangubhai, F. (1981). *The impact of a book flood in Fiji primary schools.* Wellington and Suva: New Zealand Council for Educational Research and Institute of Education and University of the South Pacific.

Ellis, R. (2016). Language teaching materials as work plans: an SLA perspective. In B. Tomlinson (Ed.), *SLA research and materials development for language learning* (pp. 203–218). New York: Routledge.

Fenner, A., & Newby, D. (2000). *Approaches to materials design in European textbooks: Implementing principles of authenticity, learner autonomy, cultural awareness.* Graz: European Centre for Modern Languages.

Fenton-Smith, B. (2010). A debate on the desired effects of output activities for extensive reading. In B. Tomlinson & H. Masuhara (Eds.), *Research for materials development in language learning: Evidence for best practice* (pp. 50–61). London: Continuum.

Garton, S., & Graves, K. (Eds.). (2014). *International perspectives on materials in ELT.* Basingstoke: Palgrave Macmillan.

Gattegno, C. (1963). *Teaching foreign languages in schools: The silent way.* New York: Educational Solutions Worldwide.

Gilmore, A. (2009). Using online corpora to develop students' writing skills. *ELT Journal, 63*(4), 363–372.

Grant, N. (1987). *Making the most of your textbook.* Harlow: Longman.

Graves, K. (1996). *Teachers as course developers.* Cambridge: Cambridge University Press.

Gray, J. (2010). *The construction of English: Culture, consumerism and promotion in the ELT coursebook.* Basingstoke: Palgrave Macmillan.

Hall, D. (1995). Materials production: Theory and practice. In A. C. Hidalgo. D. Hall & G. M. Jacobs (Eds.), *Getting started: Materials writers on materials writing* (pp. 8–24). Singapore: SEAMEO Language Centre.

Harwood, N. (Ed.). (2010a). *Materials in ELT: Theory and practice.* Cambridge: Cambridge University Press.

Harwood, N. (2010b). Issues in materials development and design. In N. Harwood (Ed.), *Materials in ELT: Theory and practice* (pp. 3–32). Cambridge: Cambridge University Press.

Harwood, N. (Ed.). (2014). *English language teaching textbooks: Content, consumption, production.* Basingstoke: Palgrave Macmillan.

Hidalgo, A. C., Hall, D., & Jacobs, G. M. (Eds.). (1995). *Getting started: Materials writers on materials writing.* Singapore: SEAMEO Language Centre.

Hooper Hansen, G. (2011). Lozanov and the teaching text. In B. Tomlinson (Ed.), *Materials development in language teaching* (pp. 403–413). Cambridge: Cambridge University Press.

Johnson, K. (2003). *Designing language teaching tasks.* Basingstoke: Palgrave Macmillan.

Kervin, L., & Derewianka, B. (2011). New technologies to support language learning. In B. Tomlinson (Ed.), *Materials development in language teaching* (pp. 328–351). Cambridge: Cambridge University Press.

Kiddle, T. (2013). Developing digital language learning materials. In B. Tomlinson (Ed.), *Developing materials for language learning* (pp. 189–206). London: Bloomsbury.

Krashen, S. (2004). *The Power of reading: Insights from the research.* Portsmouth, NH: Heinemann.

Kukulska-Hulme, A., Norris, L., & Donohue, J. (2015). *Mobile pedagogy for English language teaching: A guide for teachers.* London: British Council.

Levy, M. (2012). Technology in the classroom. In A. Burns & J. Richards (Eds.), *The Cambridge guide to pedagogy and practice in second language teaching* (pp. 279–286). Cambridge: Cambridge University Press.

Lyons, P. (2003). A practical experience of institutional textbook writing: product / process implications for materials development. In B. Tomlinson (Ed.), *Developing materials for language teaching* (pp. 490–504). London: Continuum.

Madsen, K. S., & Bowen, J. D. (1978). *Adaptation in language teaching.* Boston: Newbury House.

Maley, A. (2008). Extensive reading: maid in waiting. In B. Tomlinson (Ed.), *English language learning materials: A critical review* (pp. 133–156). London: Continuum.

Maley, A. (2011). Squaring the circle—reconciling materials as constraint with materials as empowerment. In B. Tomlinson (Ed.), *Materials development in language teaching* (2nd ed., pp, 379–402). Cambridge: Cambridge University Press.

Maley, A., Duff, A., & Grellet, F. (1981). *The mind's eye.* Cambridge: Cambridge University Press.

Maley, A., & Tomlinson, B. (Eds.). (in press). *Authenticity in materials development for language learning.* Manuscript submitted for publication. Newcastle upon Tyne: Cambridge Scholars.

Masuhara, H., Haan, M., Yi, Y., & Tomlinson, B. (2008). Adult EFL courses. *ELT Journal, 62*(3), 294–312.

Masuhara, H., Mishan, F., & Tomlinson, B. (Eds.). (2017). *Practice and theory for materials development in L2 learning.* Newcastle upon Tyne: Cambridge Scholars.

McDonough, J., & Shaw, C. (2003). *Materials and methods in ELT: A teacher's guide* (2nd ed.). London: Blackwell.

McDonough, J., Shaw, C., & Masuhara, H. (2013). *Materials and methods in ELT: A teacher's guide* (3rd ed.). London: Blackwell.

McGrath, I. (2002). *Materials evaluation and design for language teaching.* Edinburgh: Edinburgh University Press.

McGrath, I. (2013). *Teaching materials and the roles of EFL/ESL teachers: Practice and theory.* London: Bloomsbury.

McGrath, I. (2016). *Materials evaluation and design for language teaching* (2nd ed.). Edinburgh: Edinburgh University Press.

Mishan, F. (2013). Studies of pedagogy. In B. Tomlinson (Ed.), *Applied linguistics and materials development* (pp. 269–286). London: Bloomsbury.

Mishan, F. (2016). Comprehensibility and cognitive challenge in language learning materials. In B. Tomlinson (Ed.), *SLA research and materials development for language learning* (pp. 166–185). New York: Routledge.

Mishan, F., & Chambers, A. (Eds.). (2010). *Perspectives on language learning materials development*. Berne: Peter Lang.

Mishan, F., & Timmis, I. (2015). *Materials development for TESOL*. Edinburgh: Edinburgh University Press.

Moskowitch, G. (1978). *Curing and sharing in the foreign language class: A sourcebook on humanistic techniques*. Rowley, MA: Newbury House.

Motteram, G. (2011) Coursebooks and multi-media supplements. In B. Tomlinson (Ed.), *Materials development in language teaching* (pp. 303–327). Cambridge: Cambridge University Press.

Mukundan, J. (Ed.). (2003). *Readings on ELT material*. Sedang: Universiti Putra Malaysia Press.

Mukundan, J. (Ed.). (2006). *Focus on ELT materials*. Petaling Jaya: Pearson Malaysia.

Mukundan, J. (Ed.). (2008a). *Readings on ELT materials III*. Petaling Jaya: Pearson Malaysia.

Mukundan, J. (Ed.). (2008b). Multimedia materials in developing countries: The Malaysia experience. In Tomlinson, B. (Ed.), *English language teaching materials: A critical review* (pp. 100–109). London: Continuum.

Mukundan, J. (Ed.). (2009). *Readings on ELT materials III*. Petaling Jaya: Pearson Malaysia.

Murray, D. E. (2003). Materials for new technologies: Learning from research and practice. In W. A. Renandya (Ed.), *Methodology and materials design in language teaching* (pp. 30–43). Singapore: SEAMEO.

Parsons, J., & Williams, D. (2011). *Speakout*. Harlow: Pearson Education.

Pinnard, L. (2016). Looking outward: using learning materials to help learners harness out-of-class learning opportunities. *Innovation in Language Learning and Teaching* [Special issue, guest editor B. Tomlinson], *10*(2), 133–143.

Popovici, R., & Bolitho, R. (2003). Personal and professional development through writing: The Romanian textbook project. In B. Tomlinson (Ed.), *Developing materials for language teaching* (pp. 505–517). London: Continuum.

Porter Ladousse, G. (1983). *Speaking personally*. Cambridge: Cambridge University Press.

Prowse, P. (2011). How writers write: testimony from authors. In B. Tomlinson (Ed.), *Materials development in language teaching* (2nd ed., pp. 151–173). Cambridge: Cambridge University Press.

Reinders, H., & White, C. (2010). The theory and practice of technology in materials development and task design. In N. Harwood (Ed.), *Materials in ELT: theory and practice* (pp. 58–80). Cambridge: Cambridge University Press.

Renandya, W. A. (Ed.). (2003). *Methodology and materials design in language teaching: current perceptions and practises and their implications*. Singapore: RELC.

Richards, J. (1978). *Understanding second and foreign language learning*. Rowley, MA: Newbury House.

Richards, J. (2001). *Curriculum development in language education*. Cambridge: Cambridge University Press.

Richards, J. C., & Rodgers, T. S. (2001). *Approaches and methods in language teaching*. Cambridge: Cambridge University Press.

Salaberry, M. R. (1996). A theoretical foundation for the development of pedagogical tasks in computer mediated communication. *CALICO Journal 14*(1). Retrieved from https://journals.equinoxpub.com/index.php/CALICO/article/view/23391/19396.

Schmidt, R. (2001). Attention. In P. Robinson (Ed.), *Cognition and second language instruction* (pp. 3–32). Cambridge: Cambridge University Press.

Sheldon, L. E. (Ed.). (1987). *ELT textbooks and materials: problems in evaluation and development. ELT documents 126*. London: Modern English Publications and the British Council.

Soars, L., & Soars, J. (2016). *New headway intermediate* (4th ed.). Oxford: Oxford University Press.

Stoller, F. L., & Robinson, M. S. (2014). An interdisciplinary textbook project: Charting the paths taken. In N. Harwood (Ed.), *English language teaching textbooks: Content, consumption, production* (pp. 262–298). Basingstoke: Palgrave Macmillan.

Swain, M., & Lapkin, S. (2005). The evolving sociopolitical context of immersion education in Canada: Some implications for program development. *The International Journal of Applied Linguistics*, *15*(2), 169–186.

Thomas, M., & Reinders, H. (Eds.). (2015). *Contemporary task-based language teaching in Asia*. London: Bloomsbury.

Thornbury, S., & Meddings, L. (2001). Coursebooks: the roaring in the chimney. *Modern English Teacher*, *10*(3), 11–13.

Timmis, I. (2014). Writing materials for publication; questions raised and lessons learned. In N. Harwood (Ed.), *English language teaching textbooks; content, consumption, production* (pp. 241–261). Basingstoke: Palgrave Macmillan.

Tomlinson, B. (Ed.). (1981). *Talking to learn*. Port Vila: Government of Vanuatu.

Tomlinson, B. (1990). Managing change in Indonesian high schools. *ELT Journal*, *44*(1), 25–37.

Tomlinson, B. (1994a). Materials for TPR. *Folio*, *1*(2), 8–10.

Tomlinson, B. (1994b). Pragmatic awareness activities. *Language Awareness*, *3*(3 & 4), 119–129.

Tomlinson, B. (1995). Work in progress: textbook projects. *Folio*, *2*(2), 26–31.

Tomlinson, B. (Ed.). (1998). *Materials development in language teaching*. Cambridge: Cambridge University Press.

Tomlinson, B. (2001). Materials development. In R. Carter & D. Nunan (Eds.), *The Cambridge guide to TESOL* (pp. 66–71). Cambridge: Cambridge University Press.

Tomlinson, B. (Ed.). (2003). *Developing materials for language teaching*. London: Continuum Press.

Tomlinson, B. (Ed.). (2007). *Language acquisition and development: Studies of first and other language learners*. London: Continuum.

Tomlinson, B. (Ed.). (2008). *English language teaching materials: a critical review*. London: Continuum.

Tomlinson, B. (2010a). Principles and procedures of materials development. In N. Harwood (Ed.), *Materials in ELT: Theory and practice* (pp. 81–108). Cambridge: Cambridge University Press.

Tomlinson, B. (2010b). What do teachers think about EFL coursebooks? *Modern English Teacher*, *19*(4), 5–9.

Tomlinson, B. (2010c). Principles and procedures for self-access materials. *Studies in Self-Access Learning Journal*, *1*(2), 72–86.

Tomlinson, B. (Ed.). (2011). *Materials development in language teaching* (2nd ed.). Cambridge: Cambridge University Press.

Tomlinson, B. (2011c). Access-self materials. In B. Tomlinson (Ed.), *Materials development in language teaching* (2nd ed., pp. 414–432). Cambridge: Cambridge University Press.

Tomlinson, B. (2012). Materials development for language learning and teaching. *Language Teaching: Surveys and Studies, 45*(2), 143–179.

Tomlinson, B. (Ed.) (2013a). *Developing materials for language teaching* (2nd ed.). London: Continuum Press.

Tomlinson, B. (2013b). Developing principled frameworks for materials development. In B. Tomlinson (Ed.), *Developing materials for language teaching* (2nd ed., pp. 95–118). London: Continuum Press.

Tomlinson, B. (Ed.). (2013c). *Applied linguistics and materials development.* London: Continuum.

Tomlinson, B. (2014a). Looking out for English. *Folio, 16*(1), 5–8.

Tomlinson, B. (2014b). Teacher growth through materials development. *The European Journal of Applied Linguistics and TEFL* [Special issue: A. Maley (Ed.)], *3*(2), 89–106.

Tomlinson, B. (2015). Developing principled materials for young learners of English as a foreign language. In Bland, J. (Ed.), *Teaching English to young learners—critical issues in language teaching with 3–12 year olds.* London: Bloomsbury.

Tomlinson, B. (Ed.). (2016a). *SLA research and materials development for language learning.* New York: Routledge.

Tomlinson, B. (Guest Ed.). (2016b). *Innovation in Language Learning and Teaching (RILL)* [Special issue on materials development], *10*(2).

Tomlinson, B. (Guest Ed.). (2016c) *European Journal of Applied Linguistics and TESOL* [Special issue on materials development], *3*(2).

Tomlinson, B., Dat, B, Masuhara, H., & Rubdy, R. (2001). ELT courses for adults. *ELT Journal, 55*(1), 80–101.

Tomlinson, B., & Masuhara, H. (2004). *Developing language course materials.* Singapore: RELC Portfolio Series.

Tomlinson, B., & Masuhara, H. (Eds.). (2010). *Research for materials development in language learning: evidence for best practice.* London: Continuum.

Tomlinson, B., & Masuhara, H. (2013). Review of adult ELT textbooks. *ELT Journal, 67*(2), 233–249.

Tomlinson, B., & Whittaker, C. (2013). (Eds.). *Case studies of blended learning courses.* London: British Council.

Van den Branden, K. (2006). *Task-based language education: From theory to practice.* Cambridge: Cambridge University Press.

Wolf, M. (2008). *Proust and the squid.* London: Icon Books.

2

Issues in Materials Development[*]

Introduction

Ever since materials development for language teaching started to be written about there have been a number of issues that have been hotly debated. All of them are still being discussed and none of them has really been resolved. What we aim to do in this chapter is to introduce you to some of these issues by presenting the case both for and against, by presenting our position on each issue, and by inviting you to answer questions for yourself in relation to your own teaching / writing contexts.

Textbooks

The Value of Textbooks

In our experience the textbook is undoubtedly still the main medium for delivering language learning materials but is it, and has it ever been, the best? This is a question that has provoked heated debate in publications since at least the 1980s when Allwright (1981) criticized the ways in which textbooks typically deliver materials and O'Neil (1982) responded with a rigorous defense. Since then there have been numerous contributors to the debate. Some have presented balanced arguments for and against (e.g. Mishan, 2005), some have argued the case for the value of the textbook (e.g. Hutchinson & Torres, 1994; Cunningsworth, 2002), some have been critical of the typical contents and approach of coursebooks (e.g. Phillipson, 1992; Gray, 2002; Maley, 2011; Tomlinson, 2012a, 2012b), and some have been critical of textbooks per se (e.g. Thornbury & Meddings, 2001). Other contributors to the textbook debate include Prabhu (1989); Littlejohn (1992); Richards (1993); Wajnryb (1996); Flack (1999); Bao (2006); Mukundan (2009), and Tomlinson (2014).

The opposition to typical textbooks has had little effect in the classroom as most language teachers seem to continue to use them. For example, a British Council survey (2008) showed that 65% of the teachers they questioned always or frequently used a coursebook and only 6% never used a coursebook. Another survey, this one of teachers attending conferences in Malaysia, the United Kingdom, and Vietnam (Tomlinson,

---

[*]Some of the sections of this chapter are updated revisions of sections in Tomlinson (2012a).

The Complete Guide to the Theory and Practice of Materials Development for Language Learning,
First Edition. Brian Tomlinson and Hitomi Masuhara.
© 2018 John Wiley & Sons, Inc. Published 2018 by John Wiley & Sons, Inc.

2010b), revealed that 92% of the teachers who filled in a questionnaire used a coursebook regularly (many because they were required by their institutions to do so) but that 78% of them were negative about the coursebooks that they were using. A recent study of teachers' attitudes and behaviors in schools in Myanmar and the United Kingdom (Saw, 2016) revealed that only three out of 85 teachers did not use coursebooks, that most teachers used coursebooks, even though they found them uninteresting and not relevant, because they were obliged to do so, and that 81 of the teachers supplemented their coursebooks with other materials to "make lessons more suitable" (p. 268).

You just need to attend any EFL conference and visit any EFL bookshop or any language school staff room to see that EFL / ESL textbooks are still prospering. And, we would argue, you just need to flick through any current coursebook to see that coursebooks might have changed in presentation and in their blurbs but that they remain essentially the same in pedagogic approach (and even sequence) as they were when the debate about the value of textbooks started (see Tomlinson, Dat, Masuhara, & Rubdy, 2001; Masuhara & Tomlinson, 2008; Masuhara, Haan, Yi, & Tomlinson, B., 2008; Tomlinson & Masuhara, 2008; Tomlinson & Masuhara, 2013; Tomlinson, 2014, and Tomlinson, 2016a for evaluations of current coursebooks).

Those in favor of the textbook (and especially of the contains-all coursebook) argue that it is provides an efficient, attractive, time-saving, organized and economical way of supplying the resources that the harassed teachers need to offer their learners security, system, progress and revision, or, as Mishan and Timmis (2015, p. 45) say it so well, it is "a time-saver for the busy teacher and a guide for the inexperienced one." It also helps administrators to gain face validity for their courses, to timetable lessons, and to standardize the teaching in their institutions. Those opposed to the dominance of textbooks (and especially coursebooks) argue that they can disempower both the teacher and the learners by dictating what is done in the classroom (even if this is not the intention of their authors). They also claim that textbooks cater for idealized groups of users and cannot cater for the real needs and wants of their actual users in specific institutions, that they are used mainly to impose control and order (e.g. "OK, class, turn to page 46 of your textbook"—Mukundan, 2009, p. 99), and that they provide only an illusion of system and progress (the units progress in a predetermined, developmental way but often the learners do not). Many of them also claim that, "a coursebook is inevitably superficial and reductionist in its coverage of language points and in its provision of language experience … it imposes uniformity of syllabus and approach, and it removes initiative and power from teachers" (Tomlinson 2001a, p. 67). Another argument that has been put forward against typical textbooks (and especially those from the United Kingdom or United States with prestigious publishers from, for example, Oxford and Cambridge) is that their appearance of authority makes it difficult for teachers or students to challenge or modify them (e.g. Luke, de Castel & Luke, 1989; Dendrinos, 1992; Gray, 2010), though Apple (1992), Hutchinson & Torres (1994), Canagarajah (1993), and Gray (2010) have all demonstrated that some confident and experienced teachers do challenge them. Another argument against the dominance of textbooks is that it is usually administrators, occasionally teachers, but never students who decide which books to use. Consequently textbooks are usually "designed primarily to satisfy administrators and teachers but in doing so often ignore the needs and wants of learners" (Tomlinson 2010b). Brian surveyed administrators, teachers and students in 12 countries for a major British publisher to find out what they wanted from a coursebook. Surprisingly both students and teachers ranked "interesting texts" as the most important requirement and rated grammar well down the scale of importance. However, when the findings were presented in a confidential report to the publisher they were ignored in the development of a new coursebook series, which featured a return to the centrality of grammar and continued to cater mainly for the needs of the administrators who would be deciding whether to buy the series. We wonder how much pedagogic research commissioned by publishers has been ignored and has remained forever confidential because its findings are not what the publishers can afford to hear.

For a more detailed discussion of the arguments for and against textbooks, and for detailed references, see Mishan (2005, 2013) and Mishan and Timmis (2015). For discussion of issues relating to coursebooks, in particular, see Tomlinson (2015a).

Our own view is that the debate about textbooks has been polarized in reviews of the literature. Mishan and Timmis (2015, p. 45), for example, talk about "Factionism" and divide contributors to the debate into "Those arguing in favour of the coursebook" and those who are "anti-coursebook." The reality seems to be that many writers categorized as in favor of coursebooks are writing about the potential benefits of an ideal coursebook whereas those branded as "anti-coursebook" are being critical of the contents and approach of actual coursebooks (as is the case of most of our contributions to the debate). Our own view is that most teachers do need and benefit from textbooks to save time and money and that many teachers really do want to use a coursebook that provides everything they need in one convenient source. Teachers we have met all over the world would be happy and competent to develop their own locally specific materials if only they had the time, resources, and confidence to do so (as was demonstrated during one-week materials writing workshops we have run in Belgium, Botswana, Luxembourg, Malaysia, Mauritius, the Seychelles, Turkey, and Vietnam).

A textbook is capable of achieving all the benefits its proponents say it can but, unfortunately, in our experience very few of them actually do so when made use of in actual classrooms and few (even some of those we have written ourselves) rarely really satisfy the needs and wants of the students in any particular class (though see Hadley, 2014, for claims that a particular global textbook he used with university students in Japan did succeed). In Tomlinson et al. (2001), Masuhara et al. (2008) and Tomlinson and Masuhara (2008, 2013) we have detailed what we appreciate and what we are critical of in current coursebooks. In short, we appreciate the increase in activities encouraging personalization, encouraging learner discovery and helping learners to achieve appropriacy and effectiveness of communication, as well as the use of illustrations to trigger activities rather than just as decorations for the eyes. We are critical of the persistent focus on explicit teaching and practice of language forms, of the insufficiency of rich and meaningful input, of the lack of narrative texts, of the neglect of affective and cognitive engagement, of the dominance of closed exercises (Tomlinson, 2015a), and of the scarcity of opportunities for authentic communication.

Global coursebooks in particular are rarely considered to be sufficiently engaging or relevant for their actual users. "In attempting to cater for all students at a particular age and level global coursebooks often end up not meeting the needs and wants of any student" (Tomlinson, 2012a). What we would both like to see are more localized textbooks and more global textbooks that offer variability and flexibility of use in order to help teachers and students to localize and personalize the materials for themselves. We accept that the cost of developing commercial coursebooks understandably prohibits publishers from taking undue economic risks with innovative materials and we put our hopes for change with institutions and ministries of education that decide to develop their own locally appropriate materials to supplement or replace global coursebooks which have been shown to be locally unsuitable. We would also like to see publishers developing web-based global "coursebooks" that offer opportunities for choice, modification, addition and replacement of texts and tasks (Tomlinson, 2013b) and which facilitate "an ongoing process where materials are refined and even changed throughout the life of a product" (Amrani, 2011, p. 297).

The Need for Published Materials

In order to improve their students' experience of learning English, many institutions and teachers have replaced published materials with "home-made" materials in order to achieve greater local relevance, personalization, and engagement. For example, Lyons (2003) writes about the implications of teachers developing materials to replace global textbooks at Bilkent University in Ankara. Al-Busiadi and Tindle (2010) report on a project at Sultan Qaboos University in Oman in which teachers developed experiential materials for the teaching of writing skills. Jones and Schmitt (2010, p. 225) report on "the development and piloting of discipline-specific vocabulary materials on a CD−ROM software program" at the University of Nottingham. Hewings (2010) reports on the development of in-house teacher-written materials to help students develop academic writing skills at the University of Birmingham. Mason (2010) reports on the effects of delivering a British culture course at the University of Sousse with teacher-developed paper, video and Internet materials. Trabelsi (2010) reports on the process of developing authentic materials at a Tunisian university to replace overseas coursebooks for business students. Troncoso (2010) reports on the effectiveness of his in-house materials for developing intercultural competence for learners of Spanish. These reports mention problems caused by the inexperience of the teachers as materials developers but all conclude that their local materials were more relevant and more potentially engaging than the coursebooks they replaced. Ironically, many of these replacement materials were actually published as books by institutions (e.g. by Bilkent University and by Sultan Qaboos University). Many teachers have also replaced published materials with approaches that do not need the teacher to find or write materials. For example, Tomlinson (2013a) reports how a teacher in a junior secondary school in Jakarta asked a group of students each week to find a potentially engaging reading passage, on which she then based a reading lesson, and then in the next term she gave each group the responsibility for finding a text, writing a lesson plan based on it, and then teaching a reading lesson. Tomlinson (2013a) also mentions a class in the United Kingdom that he got each week to dramatize and video their version of an extract from literature, as well as a class in Vanuatu that spent every lesson for a whole term writing their own novels, with support from their peers and their teacher. Jensen and Hermer (1998) also describe student-initiated activities. Verhelst (2006) reports on task-based activities in Belgium primary schools in which the learners responded to stories and poems by expressing their feelings or representing their versions in clay models. Hae-Ok (2010) recounts an innovative and successful project for which she got permission to replace published materials with a process drama approach in a South Korean secondary school and Mishan (2010) describes how she used a problem-based approach instead of published materials at the University of Limerick.

One movement that aims to free teachers from their dependence on published materials has been the Dogme ELT movement, whose methodology focuses on approaches that are learner-centered and materials-light. Meddings and Thornbury (2009) sets out the core principles of Dogme. The methodology proposed is conversation driven rather than materials driven and focuses on the language that emerges from activities rather than on a predetermined language syllabus. The curriculum is articulated retrospectively and it is likely to be much more relevant to the needs and wants of the learners. However, it is important, in our view, if this approach is used in institutions with a predetermined syllabus, to check before the end of a course that there are no significant gaps between the emerging syllabus and the institutional syllabus. This is also true of those institutions in which our favored text-driven approach is used (see Tomlinson, 2013b).

Our position is that most teachers and students do actually welcome published materials and can gain security, system, and support from them. However, if teachers have sufficient confidence, realize their potential for principled creativity, and are respected by their learners, then freeing a course from dependence on a textbook can actually be more facilitative in providing the personalized, relevant and engaging experience of language in communicative use, the opportunities for noticing how authentic language is used, and the opportunities for engaging in meaningful communication that many textbook authors find difficult to provide for their unknown students. The ideal, we have found, is to base a course on principled selections from different coursebooks and to supplement these with both teacher- and student-developed materials.

Textbooks as Scripts or as Resources?

It is our experience that most textbooks are written as scripts to be followed rather than as resources to be exploited, that inspectors, principals, and heads of departments require the teachers to follow and complete their textbook and that most teachers feel obliged (even if not inclined) to do so. The position of many administrators, parents, teachers, and even students is that textbooks have been developed and published by experts, that they help to standardize and control the teaching, that they ensure that inexperienced teachers know what to do, that they save time for more experienced teachers, and that omitting or changing sections of them would put their users in jeopardy. Therefore, publishers make sure that their textbooks make it clear what the teacher should do in class and how she should do it because they know that this is what most buyers of their books want. But is it what the students want and is it what they need? Textbooks designed as scripts to follow are aimed at idealized groups of stereotypical learners and cannot cater for all the needs and wants of any actual class of learners (especially any class much bigger, more diverse and less resourced than those the authors have experience of teaching).

How teachers actually use their coursebooks has until recently been a neglected area in the literature. However, there is evidence of teachers (especially those with little experience or confidence) following textbooks reverentially. For example, Ball and Feiman-Nermser (1988), Gray (2000) and Tsui (2003) found that novice teachers tended to stick to the textbook script. Be (2003) discovered that the 28 teachers he studied in two secondary schools in Vietnam were using their textbooks as scripts rather than resources regardless of their experience. Chandran (2003) revealed that most of the 60 high school teachers he surveyed in Malaysia used a commercial coursebook most of the time, and Jazadi (2003) found that 67% of high school teachers he surveyed in Lombok, Indonesia, used the Department of Education mandated textbooks most or all of the time. However, there is some evidence that some more confident and / or experienced teachers do actually treat their textbook as a resource rather than a script regardless of the design or origin of the book (e.g. Gray, 2000, 2010; Tsui, 2003). See McGrath (2013) for a summary of research on the use of textbooks by novice and by experienced teachers, and Garton and Graves (2014) for international reports of what teachers do with materials in the classroom.

Menkabu and Harwood (2014) provide a useful survey of the research on textbook use. They report how both Shawyer (2010a, 2010b) and Wette (2010) show how EFL teachers in the same context can vary considerably in how they use a coursebook. Shawyer revealed how 10 highly qualified and experienced teachers working in UK language schools varied from being curriculum transmitters, who followed the coursebook as a script, to curriculum developers who adapted and supplemented the coursebook to match the needs of their students, to curriculum makers who created a curriculum to match their needs analysis of their students and largely abandoned their coursebook. What Menkabu and Harwood (2014) reveal most conspicuously is the role of examinations in determining how a coursebook is used. For example, they report a study by Lee and Bathmaker (2007), which revealed how teachers in Singapore, as well as making the coursebook easier to match their perception of their students as being low level, supplemented their coursebook with practice tests to prepare their students for examinations. They also report a study by Cheng (1997) revealing exam-driven textbook use by teachers in Hong Kong and a study by Pelly and Allison (2000) revealing similar (but reluctant) exam-driven modifications by teachers in Singapore. Such studies accord with our own experience of exam-driven textbook use by teachers in such countries as China, Indonesia, Japan, Malaysia, and Singapore, and with MA dissertation studies of textbook use in China by our students at the University of Liverpool. They also resonate with many of the contributions to Thomas and Reinders (2015), which reveal how teachers weakened task-based language teaching approaches and materials in a number of Asian countries in order to prepare their students for examinations. For further discussion of when, why and how teachers supplement and modify their coursebooks see Chapter 4 (Materials Adaptation) and Chapter 15 (Materials Development Research).

We have both been using (and writing) textbooks as resources throughout our careers and we have found that our students have appreciated and enjoyed this. For example, in Kobe University, Brian was obliged to use a coursebook but did not use all of it and did not follow its sequence. Instead, in the first lesson of the semester, he asked the students in groups to look through the book and then to vote on which unit to start with. Inevitably they chose the unit with the most potentially engaging texts and then followed this same principle in selecting units for the subsequent weeks. In using most units the sequence of activities was changed so that personal response activities and open-ended activities were given precedence over the drill and easy practice exercises that dominated many of the other teachers' classrooms. Some activities were omitted from each unit because they had no potential for affective or cognitive engagement and some whole units were omitted too. Fortunately, although the Department insisted on the use of a coursebook, it did not monitor how it was used. Most teachers are not so lucky and have to or feel obliged to follow their coursebook script. Hitomi, when teaching in a senior high school in Japan, which based its examinations on the coursebook, managed to add her own more engaging materials to the coursebook and bought the time by deleting the least engaging activities. However, one of her colleagues was even more radical and replaced the coursebook with a set of communicative activities. The students and the parents complained and he was not given any examination year classes to teach after that. At Sultan Qaboos University in Oman we were both teaching first year undergraduates and were obliged to use what to us was a tedious and often locally irrelevant coursebook. We both modified and supplemented the coursebook with more communicative and potentially engaging activities and we both deleted the least engaging activities. Yet our students, as well as seeming to enjoy their classes and become more motivated to learn English, performed as well on the numerous institutional tests as those students of teachers who followed the coursebooks as scripts. Unlike Cangarajah (1993) and Yakhontova (2001), we have never encountered persisting student resistance to us using communicative activities instead of the grammar practice exercises that students seem to expect in Asia. We discuss the objectives and rationale for novel activities with our students and invite them to trial them three times. The first experience usually meets resistance, the second less resistance, and the third acceptance, providing the students are affectively and / or cognitively engaged by the activities and a rapport has been established with the students.

We only wish we had conducted research on our classes and measured the actual effects on our students of treating the coursebook as a resource rather than a script.

Pedagogic Approaches

Authenticity of Texts and Tasks

It has been argued that explicit teaching of language through contrived examples and texts helps the learners by focusing their processing energies on the target feature, and this, in our experience, is what most coursebooks typically do. However, many second language acquisition researchers (and teachers) argue that this overprotects the learners, that it contradicts what is known about how languages are acquired, and that it does not prepare them for the reality of language use outside the classroom. Such researchers as Bacon and Finneman (1990), Kuo (1993), Little, Devitt, and Singleton (1989), McGarry (1995), Wong, Kwok, & Choi (1995), Nuttall (1996), Mishan (2005), Gilmore (2007a, 2007b), Rilling and Dantas-Whitney (2009), and Tomlinson (2013a, 2013c, 2016a) argue that authentic materials can provide the rich and meaningful exposure to language in use, which is a prerequisite for language acquisition. Some of them also claim that such exposure can motivate learners, that it can help learners to develop a range of communicative competencies, and that it can enhance positive attitudes towards the learning of a language. Mishan (2005) gives a detailed account of the history of the debate about authenticity and provides a thorough and principled rationale for using authentic materials, as does Trabelsi (2010), who advocates providing university students with materials which are authentic because they "are tailored to the learners' profile and are suitable to the stakeholders' … expectations and demands" (p. 116).

A number of researchers have compared data from corpora of authentic language use with data from coursebooks and have criticized the lack of authenticity of the coursebooks. For example, Cullen and Kuo (2007) surveyed 24 EFL coursebooks and found only a weak match between the findings of spoken corpora and the materials in the coursebooks. Lam (2010) reports how frequent the discourse particle "well" is in the Hong Kong corpus of Spoken English and yet how infrequent it is in the coursebooks used in Hong Kong. Timmis (2010) finds a mismatch between the intuition-based conversations in an EFL coursebook and those in spoken corpora. Tomlinson (2010c) compares how people typically get others to help them do something in authentic interaction (e.g. by using "If you can …") with how textbooks advise learners to do this (e.g. by using the imperative). Cohen and Ishihara (2013) report studies that show how unreliable intuition-based materials are and how underrepresented pragmatic use of the target language is in commercial materials. However, some researchers, such as Widdowson (1984, 2000), Yano, Long and Ross (1994); Day and Bamford (1998), Ellis (1999) and Day (2003) say that authentic materials can cause difficulties for learners (and especially those at lower levels), and they advocate sometimes contriving materials to simplify and focus learning. Widdowson (1984, p. 218), for example, says that "pedagogic presentation of language … necessarily involves methodological contrivance which isolates features from their natural surroundings." Ellis (1999, p. 68) argues for "enriched input," which has been deliberately flooded with examples of a target structure for use in a meaning focused activity. Day (2003, p. 2) attacks the "Cult of Authenticity," says there is no empirical evidence that authenticity facilitates language acquisition, and provides evidence that learners find authentic texts more difficult than simplified or elaborated texts. Ironically, though, he does quote Wong, Kwok and Choi's (1995) powerful endorsement of authentic materials: "In particular, authentic materials can help us to achieve the aims of enriching students' experiences in the learning and use of English, sensitizing them to the use of English in the real world …" (1995, p. 318). Moore (2014) accepts the responsibility of EAP textbook authors to prepare students for reading EAP texts in the real world but argues for helping them by, for example, introducing the content of a long authentic text first of all through short key sentences or by abridging long texts by removing complex examples.

One thing we experimented with on a project in sub-Saharan Africa was to provide three versions of an EAP text for students to choose from in class (one original, one slightly abridged and one made easier through both subtraction and elaboration). Having read one of the texts, the students formed groups in which all the members worked together on the same follow up tasks regardless of which version of the text they had read. Brian trialed the materials in Senegal and found that, contrary to the expectations of the teachers, the students did not all opt to read the easiest looking text. He also found that many students who had chosen one of the "easier" versions went back to read the original text after the follow up activities. Unfortunately, this project, like many materials development projects, was never completed for political and economic reasons, so we did not get the opportunity to find out how valuable this approach was on a pan-African scale.

Prodromou (1992) and Trabelsi (2010) raised the issue of authenticity of materials in connection with the learners' culture. What might be considered authentic in the United Kingdom or the United States might not be considered authentic, for example, in Prodromou's Greece or Trabelsi's Tunisia. What is authentic for one learner might be inauthentic for a different learner in the same context. It is argued that it is not the text or the task that is authentic but the learner's interaction with it. Widdowson (1978) states that a text can be contrived or genuine and its use can be authentic or not. Breen (1985, p. 61) insists on "the authenticity of the learner's own interpretation" and on the authenticity "of the actual social situation of the classroom," and Van Lier (1996, p. 128) asserts that authenticity "is basically a personal process of engagement."

For us an authentic text is one that is produced in order to communicate rather than to teach and an authentic task is one that involves the learners in communication in order to achieve a context based outcome rather than just to practice language or produce output. An authentic text could be produced by a non-native speaker, it could be tailored in order to be comprehensible to a particular level of learner and it might even be a version of an original that has been elaborated to facilitate communication. After all, most interactions in English are between non-native speakers and proficient users of English vary their use of English in relation to the age, topic familiarity, and topic competence of their interactants. In our view an authentic task does not have to be a real-life task but can be a classroom task that involves the learners in replicating real-life skills in order to achieve a linguistic or nonlinguistic outcome (e.g. one member of a group getting the others to draw a replica of a painting she has been shown). Given these definitions, we think that every text that learners encounter should be authentic and that most tasks should be authentic too—otherwise the learners are not being prepared for the reality of language use. We would not argue that authentic texts and tasks are necessarily more interesting or motivating than contrived texts. It all depends on the affective and / or cognitive engagement achieved by interaction with a text and / or a task for the individual learner. But we would argue that the learners need to be prepared for the unpredictable and varied demands of real-life language use and not just for the predictable demands of examinations. We would also argue that materials are only really authentic to learners if they are of value to them. An authentic menu taken from the web site of the Grosvenor Hotel in Chester (where we usually celebrate special occasions) might be of value to students with an interest in fine dining in Western-style restaurants but is unlikely to be valuable to many students in rural areas in Southeast Asia. Implicit in what is said above is that what is considered authentic in design because it is seen as representative of how the target language is typically used might not be perceived as authentic in action or in reflection because the users do not perceive the relevance or value of the materials. The ideal is therefore for the designers to try to ensure that their materials achieve authenticity in design, in use and in reflection (see Chapter 1 for an explanation of these terms).

A recognition of the significance of the debate about authenticity is a conference dedicated to the theme of Authenticity in Materials Development held by the Materials Development Association (MATSDA) at the University of Liverpool on June 18–19, 2016 (see www.matsda.org for details of this and other MATSDA conferences). Many arguments were put forward for and against an insistence on authenticity plus many constructive suggestions for preparing students for the reality of language use. See Maley and Tomlinson (in press) for a publication of chapters based on papers from this conference.

Should Materials be Forms Focused or Form Focused?

Forms-focused materials are those that focus on teaching a predetermined language item or language feature. Typically, the teaching point is selected from a prescribed syllabus which has been developed for a particular type or level of learner and it is taught to the learners explicitly through exemplification, generalization, controlled practice, guided practice, and elicited production. The theory is that, by isolating the teaching point, the learners are being helped to focus, by providing so much concentrated experience the teaching point is being made salient and by gradually increasing the difficulty the learners are being helped to learn. In our experience, most L2 classrooms around the world still feature forms-focused teaching and most L2 coursebooks feature it too. For example, we have just taken the first coursebook we came to in our bookcase, *English unlimited pre-intermediate* (Tilbury, Clementson, Henra, & Rea, 2010). The table of contents specifies the vocabulary, grammar and pronunciation points for each unit together with goals, skills and "Explore" activities, which are connected with these points. For example, the grammar points for Unit 1 are "present simple, past simple, present progressive," the vocabulary points are related to music, deciding what to do, sports, exercises, and interests, and the pronunciation point is word stress. The activities are interestingly personalized but they all focus on one or more of the teaching points, they are mainly practice activities, and none of them involve contextual communication in order to achieve an outcome.

Form-focused materials pay attention primarily to meaning and use. Their texts and activities are chosen for their potential to engage the learners and not to illustrate or provide practice in any particular language item or feature. The learners focus on understanding the meaning of texts and on communicating meaning to others and in doing so they experience a variety of language items and features. Although their focus is on meaning, the students will pay some attention to form either when they are having problems understanding or communicating meaning or when attention is subsequently drawn to a particular form by the materials or their teacher. While PPP (presentation, practice, production) is the most common methodology in forms-focused materials and in most coursebooks, task-based language teaching (TBLT), text-driven approaches and content, and language integrated learning (CLIL) are typical methodologies for form-focused materials. Task-based language teaching provides the learners with a task requiring the achievement of an effective outcome. Text-driven approaches provide the learners with a potentially engaging text to respond to. Content, and language-integrated learning provides the learners with experience of and / or instruction about a content subject (e.g. physics, football, ballet). All three of these approaches are form focused because they concentrate on the creation and understanding of meaning but also encourage attention to form when this could help or interest the learners. Although form-focused approaches (and the three methodologies mentioned above) are advocated by many researchers, very few coursebooks make use of them.

For more information about the principles and procedures of forms-focused and form-focused approaches see Long (1991), Long and Robinson (1998), Ellis, (2001) and Williams (2005), and for more information about the methodologies mentioned in this section see "Methodologies Used in Textbooks" below.

We do not think that you will be very surprised that we favor form-focused materials. They follow an experiential, principled approach in which learners experience language being used for communication and only pay attention to form when doing so helps them to achieve meaning. We have been using such approaches for many years (e.g. Tomlinson & Masuhara, 1994) and we have always found learners to be more engaged and motivated by them than by the typical forms-focused activities of the coursebooks.

Methodologies Used in Textbooks

When we look back at coursebooks published since we started teaching, there have been many changes in the methodologies that coursebooks claim to be using but it seems to us that there has been very little change in the pedagogy they actually use. The blurbs on the back of coursebooks change all the time. In the 1960s, they focused on the direct teaching of the target language without the use of translation or explanation; in the early 1970s they said they were using the situational approach, and in the late 1970s they proclaimed that they were using the new communicative approach. Since then the blurbs have claimed to be following natural, topic-based, theme-based or task-based approaches and most coursebooks today stress that their syllabus is based on the "can do" statements of the Common European Framework. In our opinion, though, since the mid-1970s most coursebooks have actually been and are still using a PPP approach and featuring such low-level, closed-practice exercises as listen and repeat, dialogue repetition and filling in the blanks (Tomlinson, 2015b; Tomlinson, in press). Many researchers have complained that PPP provides only an illusion of language learning, that it is not possible to acquire a language form instantly through such one-off concentrated focus and that there is no theoretical or research based justification for PPP (e.g. Willis & Willis, 2007). Many of them have also proposed more experiential approaches to developing and using language-learning materials. For example, Bolitho (2003), Bolitho & Tomlinson (2005) Bolitho et al. (2003), and Tomlinson (1994, 2007) have proposed a language awareness approach involving learners first experiencing an authentic text holistically and then analyzing it with a view to making discoveries for themselves about language use. Tomlinson (2013b, 2016a) has developed a text-driven approach in which the learners first respond to a potentially engaging text personally before making use of it as a stimulus for language use and a resource for language discovery. "Prabhu (1987), Ellis (1998, 2003, 2011), Van den Branden (2006), Willis (1996) and Willis and Willis (2007) have advocated task-driven approaches in which the 'learners" target is task completion and the teacher's objective is language development" (Tomlinson, 2012a, p. 160). And Masuhara (2006) and Tomlinson (2001b) have suggested using a multi-dimensional approach to materials development in which the learners are helped to make use of sensory imaging, motor imaging and inner speech during their experience and production of language in use. What all these innovative approaches seem to have in common is a move away from discrete teaching points driving instructional material to a focus on language in use. The emphasis is on facilitating learning rather than promoting teaching, an emphasis that most of the plenary and parallel papers have shared at recent MATSDA conferences at Queen's University Belfast, the University of Liverpool and the University of Limerick.

There have been some pedagogical innovations in published materials, especially in the supplementary materials published in the 1970s and 1980s, which featured communicative activities, and in some recently published resource books for teachers. However, most of the innovative core materials we know about have been on projects. We know, for example, of projects that have used Total Physical Response and discovery approaches for young beginners, for example the PKG (By the Teacher for the Teacher) project in Indonesia (Tomlinson, 1995), and of projects that have followed a text-driven approach (Tomlinson, 1995, 2013b), a task-based approach (Prabhu, 1987) or a Content and Language Integrated Learning (CLIL) approach (Eurydice, 2006), and we have been personally involved in the development of published text-driven materials in China, Ethiopia, Oman, Singapore, and Turkey. The most popular approach in the literature at the moment seems to be the task-based approach in which the learners are set tasks in which they use the language at their disposal to achieve linguistic or nonlinguistic outcomes (e.g. arrangements for a trip, an agenda for a meeting, a presentation on a contentious issue, the solution to a problem, a design for a new vehicle). There are many books that outline the theory and procedures of task-based approaches (e.g. Ellis, 2003; Nunan, 2004; Willis & Willis, 2007) and some publications that give advice relevant to materials development for task-based approaches (e.g. Bygate, Skehan & Swain, 2001; Samuda & Bygate, 2008; Masuhara, 2015). After all this time, though, there are very few books that report task-based materials development projects or which exemplify classroom materials. One book that does both is Van den Branden (2006). It includes chapters on developing task materials for beginners (Duran & Ramaut, 2006), for primary and secondary education (Van Gorp & Bogaert, 2006), and for science education and vocational training (Bogaert, Van Gorp, Bultynck, Lanssens, & Depauw, 2006). Another book that reports the development and use of task-based materials is Thomas and Reinders (2015), which contains chapters on the use of task-based materials in many countries in Asia. Foster and Hunter (2016) and Mackey, Ziegler and Bryfonski (2016) consider applications of SLA research to materials for task based learning. However, we know of no currently available coursebook that features task-based materials, despite claims to the contrary. See Mishan (2013) for a critique of a global coursebook claiming to be task based and also for reference to a coursebook that is task based (*Widgets*—Benevides & Valvona, 2008).

Another approach that is popular both in the literature and on projects nowadays is CLIL, an approach in which the learners focus on learning content knowledge and skills (e.g. geography, playing a sport, cultivating crops) while gaining experience of using English. Again, there are many publications focusing on the principles and procedures of CLIL but very few proposing procedures for materials development. One publication that does focus on materials development for CLIL is Coyle, Hood, & Marsh (2010), which includes a chapter on "Evaluating and creating materials and tasks for CLIL classrooms."

Our own preference, you will not be surprised to discover, is the text-driven approach in which a written or spoken text selected for its potential for affective and / or cognitive engagement drives a unit of materials in which readiness activities activate the learners' minds in relation to the text, initial response activities stimulate learner engagement whilst experiencing the text, intake response activities encourage the development and articulation of personal responses, input response activities involve exploration of linguistic or pragmatic features of the text, and development activities invite learners to use language for communication in relation to the core text (Tomlinson, 2013b). Admittedly there is, as yet, little empirical evidence to prove the effectiveness of this and of other experiential approaches, just as there is no published empirical evidence that we know of to prove the effectiveness of PPP or of other typical coursebook approaches, despite Hadley's (2014) claim to the contrary. There are, though, research indications of the effectiveness of text-driven approaches in relation to student engagement, motivation and performance, such as Al-Busaidi and Tindle (2010); McCullugh (2010); Troncoso (2010); Heron (2013, 2016); Darici and Tomlinson (2016). What we need is research to find out which pedagogical approaches to materials development best facilitate language acquisition in the classroom. This would be very challenging because of the difficulty of controlling learner variables, teacher variables, and out-of-class experience of the language but we believe that attempts to achieve it could be very informative, especially if undertaken on a large scale in many different learning contexts.

The Topic Content of Language Learning Materials

Acceptability

Most publishers go out of their way to avoid giving offense and to do so they often supply their authors with lists of taboo topics (e.g. sex, politics, history, geography, drugs, alcohol, pork, balloons), plus guidelines on how to avoid any risk of sexism and racism. Their caution is understandable but unfortunately it often leads to the proliferation of safe, sanitized, and anodyne texts. A number of authors have objected to what they see as sometimes excessive caution (e.g. Wajnryb, 1996; Tomlinson, 2001a) and "they have complained about the unengaging blandness of commercially published materials" (Tomlinson, 2012a, p. 162). Tomlinson (1995) has compared materials in current commercial coursebooks unfavorably with materials published on national projects and especially with the Namibian coursebook *On Target* (1995), in which such provocative (and potentially engaging) topics as marital violence, tourism and drug abuse are included with the permission of the Ministry of Education in response to student requests for such controversial topics in a preliminary questionnaire. Banegas (2011) describes a syllabus being used at a secondary school in Argentina. Syllabus 1 follows a conventional coursebook while Syllabus 2 is "a negotiated syllabus driven by such teacher suggested topics as gay marriage and child abuse and such student suggested topics as divorce and single parenting" (Tomlinson, 2012a, p. 162), which is implemented by making use of a teacher-developed sourcebook of controversial and potentially engaging listening and reading texts. Gray (2010) investigates publishers' documents that prohibit their authors from using dangerous topics such as politics, alcohol, religion and sex which could be offensive, and he also reports interviews he held with publishers in which they defend their censoring of materials in order to match the sensitivities of their potential markets. Gray comments on how the topics that they do permit represent a successful, materialistic, and aspirational EFL world. Waijnryb (1996, p. 291) complains that the EFL world portrayed in coursebooks is too "safe, clean, harmonious, benevolent, undisturbed." Tomlinson (2001a, p. 68), whilst appreciating the need for publishers to be cautious, points out how affective engagement is a vital factor in learning and says "it is arguable that provocative texts which stimulate an affective response are more likely to facilitate learning than neutral texts which do not." This is our position and we have both run many courses in which we have stimulated materials developers (including groups from Iran, Oman and Turkey) to make use of provocative topics and texts that would be both acceptable in their cultures and have the potential for stimulating affective engagement.

Humanizing Materials

Many theorists and practitioners have pointed out how language learning materials focus on the target language and tend to neglect the learner as an individual human being with interests, wants, and talents unrelated to the language being learned. Many of them have stressed the need to humanize language-learning materials, both in their development and in their use in the classroom (e.g. Arnold, 1999; Arnold & Brown, 1999; Maley, 2003, 2008, 2011; Rinvolucri, 2003; Masuhara, 2006, 2007; Tomlinson & Avila 2007a, 2007b; Masuhara et al., 2008; Tomlinson, 2008b, 2013a, 2013c, 2016b; Mukundan, 2009; Hooper Hansen, 2011; McDonough, Shaw & Masuhara, 2013; Ghosn, 2013; Mishan, 2013; Tomlinson & Masuhara, 2013), and there is a popular web journal, originally started by Mario Rinvolucri, which publishes articles proposing ways of humanizing materials development and other aspects of language teaching (*Humanising Language Teaching*: www.hltmag.co.uk). Most of the above authors refer to the literature on learning, on classroom learning, and on SLA, as well as to their own experience in the classroom, and they emphasize the need to help learners of all ages and levels to personalize, to localize, and to make meaningful their experience of the target language, as well as the need for materials to be affectively and cognitively engaging whilst catering for all learning styles. Arnold and Brown (1999), for example, refer to researchers who demonstrate the value of whole-brain learning and they quote Gross (1992, p. 139) who asserts that "We can accelerate and enrich our learning, by engaging the senses, emotions, imagination." Canagarajah (1993) gives examples of the revision of textbook comprehension questions so as to stimulate localized and personalized responses. Tomlinson (2013a) agrees with Berman (1999, p. 2), who says, "We learn best when we see things as part of a recognized pattern, when our imaginations are aroused, when we make natural associations between one idea and another, and when the information appeals to our senses." Tomlinson also calls for humanistic coursebooks that engage affect through personalized activities and which feature imaging activities, inner voice activities, kinesthetic activities and other multi-dimensional activities. Like many other authors, Mukundan (2009, p. 96) is critical of the excessive control imposed by coursebooks and he says that the classroom should be like a jungle "where chance and challenge and spontaneity and creativity and risk work in complementary fashion with planned activity." Hooper Hansen (2011, p. 107) is in favor of helping learners to achieve "a state in which the mind is optimally relaxed and fully expanded" and suggests, for example, using paintings as texts, something we have seen done to great effect in the Norwegian coursebook *Search 10* (Naustdal Fenner & Nordal-Pedersen, 1999). Masuhara (2006) and Tomlinson (2001b, 2013a) propose and exemplify multi-dimensional approaches to language learning in which the learners are encouraged to make use of sensory imaging, motor imaging and inner speech reflection, as well as personal associations, connections and emotions in order to humanize their language-learning experience. You can probably get a sense of what is meant by humanizing from the quotations above. Tomlinson (2013a, p. 139) defines a humanistic coursebook as "one which respects its users as human beings and helps them to exploit their capacity for learning through meaningful experience" and "to connect what is in the book to what is in their minds." He provides many examples of his own efforts to humanize coursebooks and makes suggestions for humanizing without the coursebook, for partial replacement of the coursebook, for humanizing with the coursebook, for localizing coursebooks and for developing humanistic coursebooks.

Many of the authors referred to above are critical of commercially published coursebooks for being insufficiently humanistic. For example, Arnold and Brown (1999, p. 5) say that we need to add "the affective domain" to "the effective language teaching going on in the classroom" in order to make language learning more humanistic. Maley (2011) points out that coursebooks typically predetermine the content, the sequencing of the content, and the procedures for using the content. He suggests using more open and unpredictable process activities such as projects, community language learning, drama, extensive reading and creative writing to give learners opportunities to decide on content and language use for themselves. Masuhara et al. (2008, p. 310) criticize coursebooks for making insufficient use of "engaging and extensive reading and listening texts," for neglecting the opportunities for individual development offered by extensive writing, for not making full use of "the resources of the mind by stimulating multi-dimensional mental responses which are at the same time sensory, cognitive and affective," for not making use of extended projects, for featuring primarily analytical activities and for not stimulating the imagination and creativity of learners. Tomlinson (2013a, pp. 139–140) criticizes coursebooks (including some of his own) for not connecting with the learners' lives and says that many coursebooks concentrate on "the linguistic and analytical aspects of language learning" and fail "to tap the human beings' potential for multi-dimensional processing." He also says they make "insufficient use of the learners' ability to learn through doing things physically, to learn through feeling emotion, to learn through experiencing things in their mind." Tomlinson and Masuhara (2013, p. 247) evaluate six recently published coursebooks and congratulate them for providing a much higher "level of personalization." However they conclude that "there is still too much attention given to grammar at the expense of affective and cognitive engagement, not enough activities for the experientially and kinaesthetically inclined …" Mishan (2013, p. 279) puts forward arguments for humanistic approaches to materials development and refers to a number of resource books for teachers that suggest or provide humanistic approaches for the teacher to use in the classroom. However, she is very critical of coursebooks for concentrating on "bite-sized information chunks" and she says that the "holistic ethos of humanistic approaches is, on the whole, anathema to the modern coursebook culture of instant linguistic gratification." Tomlinson (2013c, p. 17) evaluated a different six current coursebooks and found that "the topics are bland and safe, and are unlikely to stimulate any affective responses," "the learners are rarely asked to think for themselves," and "the learners are rarely asked to be creative." Mishan (2016) criticizes coursebooks for simplifying and sanitizing texts, and thereby compromising comprehensibility, engagement, and cognitive challenge. Tomlinson (2016a) evaluates three recent coursebooks against the criteria of their potential to stimulate affective engagement and their potential to stimulate cognitive engagement and concludes that there is a very weak match with the criteria in all three coursebooks. We know of no publication that finds evidence of humanistic approaches in global coursebooks and of no publication which supports this situation. For a case study of the development and trialing of a unit of humanistic materials see Darici and Tomlinson (2016) and for suggestions and examples of ways of developing and of adapting materials for whole-class "teaching" that match humanistic principles see Tomlinson (2016b). For a recent rationale for the need for such essential goals of a humanistic approach as affective engagement, cognitive challenge, student enjoyment and student self-esteem see Mishan and Timmis (2015).

We take a very strong position on humanistic materials. We believe that, without affective and cognitive engagement, deep processing cannot be achieved and durable acquisition is therefore impossible. We also believe that deep processing is activated by personal involvement as an individual human being and that the only coursebooks that could achieve more than coverage of teaching points are those that follow a humanistic approach to language learning and help the learners to localize the materials and to personalize them, and in doing so to achieve confidence and self-esteem. This is a view based on our considerable experience of developing and using humanistic materials in many different countries and on our understanding of the principles of language acquisition. While our view accords with the similar views of many practitioners and theorists in the literature we have to concede that, as yet, there is no empirical evidence to support (or to negate) this view.

Ideology in Materials

Since the mid-1990s, critical theorists and socio-cultural theorists have attacked the role of English language teaching in a globalization process which they say promotes Western, capitalist, materialistic values. Ferguson (2003) uses the term

"Angloglobalisation" to claim that there is a positive connection between the British Empire, English, and globalization but Phillipson (1992), Pennycook (1994, 1998), Gray (2002) and Block (2006) have been scathingly critical of the apparent link between English and empire. Gray (2010, pp. 16–17) agrees with them and points out how English has become "a form of linguistic capital, capable of bringing a profit of distinction to those speakers with the ability to access it (or more accurately, its socially legitimated varieties), and as an increasingly commodified dimension of labour-power." He draws attention to the global coursebook as an "artefact," a "commodity" that promotes socio-economic norms through its texts, its activities, its values and its illustrations. He analyzes four commercially successful British coursebooks and, for example, concludes that they all celebrate success, individualism, pleasure, social mobility, and materialism. He also examines publishers' guidelines, he interviews publishers, and he concludes that a standardized product is being "delivered through the standardized methodology embodied in the coursebook into the global marketplace—in which all are assumed to want and need exactly the same thing" (p. 138). This he sees mainly as a result of the publishers' tabooing of controversially inappropriate topics and of their insistence on discrete-item approaches in which linguistic content is "made deliverable for teachers in manageable portions and finally made testable by examinations" (p. 137).

Other writers have also written about how the coursebook has become a commodity to be consumed. Tickoo (1995, p. 39) sees textbook writing in a multilingual and multicultural society (such as the one in Singapore) as being determined by different sets of criteria. "Some of them arise from such a society's need to teach the values it wants to foster. Some arise in the desire to make education a handmaiden of economic progress and social reconstruction." Toh (2001) reports and comments on his research findings that the content of coursebooks developed for use in Singapore schools reflects conformity to Western socio-cultural norms. Singapore Wala (2003) considers the coursebook to be a communicative act, "a dynamic artefact that contributes to and creates meaning together with other participants in the context of language teaching" (p. 59). She analyzes coursebooks developed for Singapore and concludes that "a coursebook is not just a collection of linguistic items—it is a reflection of a particular world-view based on the selection of resources" (p. 69).

Holliday (2005) argues that language education is becoming increasingly commodified and that students have become recast as learners and consumers, Bolitho (2008) asserts that textbooks have acquired iconic status as symbols of what is to be aspired to, and Mukundan (2009) talks about the "declared agenda" of the classroom, which involves the teacher being directed by the textbook writer to create a "zoo-like environment, where learners behave like caged animals, performing planned tricks for the animal trainer …" (p. 96). See also Adaskou, Britten, & Fahsi (1990), Alptekin (1993), Zhang (1997), Cortazzi and Jin (1999), Gray, J. (2000, 2010), Gray, F. (2002), and Curdt-Christiansen (2015) for discussion of issues relating to culture and materials development. For a detailed and very useful survey of the literature concerning cultural issues see Mishan and Timmis (2015); for a review of the literature on cultural mismatches between coursebook producers and coursebooks as well as reports of personal experiences of students welcoming potentially engaging innovative methodologies see Tomlinson (2005); and for critical reviews of textbooks used in different areas of the world see Tomlinson (2008a).

In our opinion, it is inevitable that a coursebook will communicate a view of both teaching and learning, a view of the target language and the culture(s) it is used to represent, and the worldview(s) of its producers. This is potentially dangerous as the coursebook is revered in many classrooms as the ultimate authority and there is a risk of its users uncritically accepting the world it portrays as a world to aspire to. However, our experience throughout the world is that teachers and learners are much more critical than they are given credit for and they often find ways to resist the commodity they are being asked to consume. It is also our experience that textbook publishers and writers do not conspire to convert textbook users to their view of the world. They simply (and inevitably) portray the world as they know it and are often unaware of the potential conflict between their views of teaching, of learning, of the target language, and of the target culture, and the views of the textbook users. What we would like to see is activities in coursebooks inviting learners to compare the views represented by the coursebook with those held by their culture and by themselves. This could enrich their experience rather than impoverish it.

This chapter has focused on a number of issues in relation to materials development that divide both theorists and practitioners. For further discussion of these and other issues see Harwood (2010), Mishan and Timmis (2015), Tomlinson (2010a, 2011, 2012a, 2012b) and Azarnoosh et al. (2016). For discussion of the very important issues concerning approaches to the principled development of materials, to the evaluation of materials, to the adaptation of materials, and to the effective development and use of digital materials see the relevant chapters in this volume.

Conclusion

To sum up our position we would like to conclude this chapter by stating what we believe and by inviting you to think about your position in relation to the issues focused on.

We believe that:

- Coursebooks can be helpful to teachers (especially those with little time and / or experience) and they can provide psychological support, a sense of security and system, and a means of revision to students. However, for a coursebook to be really beneficial to students it needs to be self-standing, flexible, localizable, personalizable, humanistic, and designed to facilitate adaptation.
- Published materials can help to facilitate language acquisition (especially those that provide opportunities for extensive reading, listening or viewing, and those that provide texts, illustrations, experiences which teachers and students can make use of to develop locally appropriate activities of their own). However, published materials are not essential and resourceful teachers and students can usefully supplement and even replace them with project-driven, text-driven, task-based, content-based, conversation-based, experience-based, and enquiry-based materials of their own.
- Materials should be designed and used as resources. Teachers and students should be given options to choose from and texts, activities, and approaches should not be imposed on them. This does not mean that teachers and students should not be introduced to potentially useful innovative approaches. It means that if innovations are introduced their rationale should be clearly explained and teachers and students should be invited to trial them, to reflect on them and then to make their own decisions about which texts and which activities to use and how they use them.
- Form-focused approaches that focus initially on meaning and communication and then focus on learning points emerging from this experience should be used in

materials development. Ideally, the students should be helped to make discoveries for themselves rather than be instructed by the teacher or textbook and the learning points should be determined by the teacher (or the students) after experiencing the initial phase—possibly with some assistance from a textbook listing of potential learning points.

- Materials should use authentic texts and authentic tasks that give the learners actual experience of the target language in use. It is important, though, that such texts and tasks should have the potential to engage the learners both affectively and cognitively.
- Open-ended and flexible approaches, which have the potential to cater for individual preferences and to challenge and stimulate everybody using them, should be used in materials development. Our favorite such approach is the text-driven approach but we also make use of task-based, project-based, and CLIL-based approaches in our development of materials.
- Materials developers should be sensitive to the risks of causing embarrassment and offense but their materials should nevertheless make use of controversial (and even provocative) texts and topics to stimulate affective and cognitive engagement—especially if the teachers and the students are given options to select from.
- Materials developers should be aware of cultural differences between their favored approaches and the cultural norms of their target learners but should still make use of such problematic approaches if they believe from their experience and research that they will ultimately benefit the users of their materials. It is important though that the rationale for "new" approaches should be explained to the teachers and the students and that they should be given time to trial and reflect on the value of such approaches. It is also important that the materials are flexible in the sense that they are designed with the potential of being used in different ways (for a discussion and examples of flexibility see Bao, 2015).

What Do You Think?

1. Do you use a coursebook? Why / why not?
2. If you use a coursebook, do you use it as a script or as a resource? Why?
3. If you use a coursebook as a resource, when, why and how do you adapt it?
4. What do you think the ideal coursebook should include and do?
5. Do you develop your own materials? Why / why not?
6. If you develop your own materials when, why and how do you develop them?
7. Do you think that listening and reading texts should be authentic? Why?
8. Do you think that tasks should be authentic? Why?
9. Do you think that materials should be form focused or forms focused? Why?
10. Which of the following approaches (if any) would you use in class (or in your materials)? Why?
    a) Text-driven approaches.
    b) Task-based approaches.
    c) Project-based approaches.
    d) CLIL approaches.
11. Would you use provocative texts and topics in class (or in your materials) ? Why / why not?
12. Would you use an innovative approach which might be culturally problematic?

References

Adaskou, K. D., Britten, D., & Fahsi, B. (1990). Design decisions on the cultural content of a secondary English course for Morocco. *ELT Journal, 44*(1), 3–10.

Al-Busaidi, S., & Tindle, K. (2010). Evaluating the effect of in-house materials on language learning. In B. Tomlinson & H. Masuhara (Eds.), *Research for materials development in language learning: Evidence for best practice* (pp. 137–149). London: Continuum.

Allwright, R. L. (1981). What do we want teaching materials for? *ELT Journal, 36*(1), 5–18.

Alptekin, C. (1993). Target language culture in EFL materials. *ELT Journal, 47*(2), 136–143.

Amrani, F. (2011). The process of evaluation: A publisher's view. In B. Tomlinson (Ed.), *Materials development in language teaching* (2nd ed., pp. 267–295). Cambridge: Cambridge University Press.

Apple, M. (1992). The text and cultural politics. *Educational Researcher, 21*, 4–11.

Arnold, J. (Ed.). (1999). *Affect in language learning*. Cambridge: Cambridge University Press.

Arnold, J., & Brown, H. D. (1999). A map of the terrain. In J. Arnold (Ed.), *Affect in language learning* (pp. 1–24). Cambridge: Cambridge University Press.

Azarnoosh, M., Zeraatpishe, M., Faravani, A., & Kargozari, H. R. (Eds.). (2016). *Issues in materials development*. Rotterdam: Sense.

Bacon, S. M., & Finneman, M. D. (1990). A study of the attitudes, motives and strategies of university foreign language students and their disposition to authentic oral and written input. *Modern Language Journal, 74*(4), 459–473.

Ball, D. L., & Feiman-Nermser, S. (1988). Using textbooks and teachers' guides: A dilemma for beginning teachers and educators. *Curriculum Enquiry, 18*, 401–423.

Banegas, D. L. (2011). Teaching more than English in secondary education. *ELT Journal, 65*(1), 80–82.

Bao, D. (2006). Breaking stereotypes in coursebooks. In J. Mukundan (Ed.), *Readings on ELT materials II* (pp. 70–83). Petaling Jaya: Pearson Malaysia.

Bao, D. (2015). Flexibility in second language materials. *The European Journal of Applied Linguistics and TEFL: Materials in the ELT Classroom: Development, Use and Evaluation* [Guest editor B. Tomlinson], *4*(2), 37–52.

Be, N. (2003). *The design and use of English language teaching materials in Vietnamese secondary schools*. (Unpublished PhD thesis). Victoria University, Wellington, New Zealand.

Benevides, M., & Valvona, C. (2008). *Widgets*. Hong Kong: Pearson Longman.

Berman, M. (1999). The teacher and the wounded healer. *IATEFL Issues, 152*, 2–5.

Block, D. (2006). *Multicultural identities in a global city*. London: Palgrave.

Bogaert, N., Van Gorp, K., Bultynck, K., Lanssens, A., & Depauw, V. (2006). Task-based language teaching in science education and vocational training. In K. Van den Branden (Ed.), *Task-based language education: from theory to practice* (pp. 106–128). Cambridge: Cambridge University Press.

Bolitho, R. (2003). Materials for language awareness. In B. Tomlinson (Ed.), *Developing materials for language teaching* (pp. 422–425). London: Continuum.

Bolitho, R. (2008). Materials used in Central and Eastern Europe and the former Soviet Union. In B. Tomlinson (Ed.), *English language teaching materials: A critical review*. London: Continuum.

Bolitho, R., Carter, R., Hughes, R., Ivanic, R., Masuhara, H., & Tomlinson, B. (2003). Ten questions about language awareness. *ELT Journal, 57*(2), 251–259.

Bolitho, R., & Tomlinson, B. (2005). *Discover English*. Oxford: Macmillan.

Breen, M. (1985). Authenticity in the language classroom. *Applied Linguistics, 6*(1), 60–70.

British Council. (2008). *Teaching English: Course books*. London: Author.

Bygate, M., Skehan, P., & Swain, M. (Eds.). (2001). *Researching pedagogic tasks*. Harlow: Pearson.

Canagarajah, S. (1993). Critical ethnography of a Sri Lankan classroom; Ambiguities in student reproduction through ESOL. *TESOL Quarterly, 27*(4), 601–626.

Chandran, S. (2003). Where are the ELT textbooks? In W. A. Renandya (Ed.), *Methodology and materials design in language teaching* (pp. 161–169). Singapore: SEAMO.

Cheng, L. (1997). How does washback influence teaching? Implications for Hong Kong. *Language and Education, 11*, 38–54.

Cohen, A. D., & Ishihara, N. (2013). Pragmatics. In B. Tomlinson (Ed.), *Applied linguistics and materials development* (pp. 113–126). London: Bloomsbury.

Cortazzi, M., & Jin, L. (1999) Cultural mirrors: materials and methods in the EFL classroom. In E. Hinkel (Ed.), *Culture in second language teaching* (pp. 196–219). Cambridge: Cambridge University Press.

Coyle, D., Hood, P., & Marsh, D. (2010). *Content and language integrated learning*. Cambridge: Cambridge University Press.

Cullen, R., & Kuo, I. C. (2007). Spoken grammar and ELT course materials: a missing link? *TESOL Quarterly, 41*, 361–386.

Cunningsworth, A. (2002). *Choosing your coursebook*. Oxford: Heinemann.

Curdt-Christiansen, X. L. (2015). Striking a balance: Cultural conflicts or cultural adaptation. *The European Journal of Applied Linguistics and TEFL: Materials in the ELT Classroom: Development, Use and Evaluation* [Guest editor B. Tomlinson], *4*(2) 73–92.

Darici, A., & Tomlinson, B. (2016). A case study of principled materials in action. In B. Tomlinson (Ed.), *SLA research and materials development for language learning* (pp. 71–86). New York: Routledge.

Day, R. (2003). Authenticity in the design and development of materials. In W. A. Renandya (Ed.), *Methodology and materials design in language teaching* (pp. 1–11). Singapore: SEAMEO Regional Language Centre.

Day, R., & Bamford, J. (1998). *Extensive reading in the second language classroom*. Cambridge: Cambridge University Press.

Dendrinos, R. (1992). *The EFL textbook and ideology*. Athens: N. C. Grivas Publications.

Duran, G., & Ramaut, G. (2006). Tasks for absolute beginners and beyond: developing and sequencing tasks at basic proficiency levels. In K. Van den Branden (Ed.), *Task-based language education: From theory to practice* (pp. 17–46). Cambridge: Cambridge University Press.

Ellis, R. (1998). The evaluation of communicative tasks. In B. Tomlinson (Ed.), *Materials development in language teaching* (pp. 217–238). Cambridge: Cambridge University Press.

Ellis, R. (1999). Input based approaches to teaching grammar: a review of classroom oriented research. *Annual Review of Applied Linguistics, 19*, 64–80.

Ellis, R. (2001). Investigating form-focused instruction. *Language Learning, 51*(Suppl. 1), 1–46.

Ellis, R. (Ed.) (2003). *Task-based language learning and teaching*. Oxford: Oxford University Press.

Ellis, R. (2011). Macro- and micro-evaluations of task-based teaching. In B. Tomlinson (Ed.), *Materials development in language teaching* (2nd ed., pp. 21–35). Cambridge: Cambridge University Press.

Eurydice (2006). *Content and language integrated learning (CLIL) at schools in Europe.* Brussels: Eurydice.

Ferguson, N. (2003) *Empire.* London: Penguin.

Flack, R. (1999). A problem shared . . . coursebook deficiency disorder: coursebook bore. *Modern English Teacher, 81*(1), 60–61.

Foster, P., & Hunter, A. (2016). When it's not what you do, but the way that you do it: How research into second language acquisition can help teachers to make the most of their classroom materials. In B. Tomlinson (Ed.), *SLA research and materials development for language learning* (pp. 280–292). New York: Routledge.

Garton, S., & Graves, K. (Eds.). (2014). *International perspectives on materials in ELT.* Basingstoke: Palgrave Macmillan.

Ghosn, I. (2013). Language learning for young learners. In B. Tomlinson (Ed.), *Applied linguistics and materials development* (pp. 61–74). London: Bloomsbury.

Gilmore, A. (2007a). Authentic materials and authenticity in foreign language learning. *Language Teaching, 40,* 97–118.

Gilmore, A. (2007b). *Getting real in the language classroom: developing Japanese students' communicative competence with authentic materials* (Unpublished PhD thesis). University of Nottingham, Nottingham.

Gray, J. (2000). The ELT coursebook as cultural artefact: how teachers censor and adapt. *ELT Journal, 54*(3), 274–283.

Gray, F. (2002). The global coursebook in English language teaching, In D. Block & D. Cameron (Eds.), *Globalization and language teaching* (pp. 151–166). London: Routledge.

Gray, J. (2010). *The construction of English: culture, consumerism and promotion in the ELT coursebook.* Basingstoke: Palgrave Macmillan.

Gross, R. (1992). Lifelong learning in the learning society of the twenty first century. In C. Collins & J. Mangieri (Eds.), *Teaching thinking: An agenda for the twenty first century* (pp. 135–143). Hillsdale, NJ: Lawrence Erlbaum.

Hadley, G. (2014). Global textbooks in local contexts: an empirical investigation of effectiveness. In N. Harwood (Ed.), *English language teaching textbooks: Content, consumption, production* (pp. 205–240). Basingstoke: Palgrave Macmillan.

Hae-Ok, P. (2010). Process drama in the Korean EFL secondary classroom: A case study of Korean middle school classrooms. In B. Tomlinson & H. Masuhara (Eds.), *Research for materials development in language learning: Evidence for best practice* (pp. 155–171). London: Continuum.

Harwood, N. (2010). Issues in materials development and design. In N. Harwood (Ed.), *English language teaching materials: theory and practice* (pp. 3–32). Cambridge: Cambridge University Press.

Heron, M. (2013). *To what extent can using affectively engaging texts stimulate motivation in the learner centred classroom?* (Unpublished MA dissertation). Leeds Metropolitan University, Leeds.

Heron, M. (2016). Using affectively engaging texts to stimulate motivation in the learner centred classroom. In M. Azarnoosh, M. Zeraatpishe, A. Faravani & H. R. Kargozari (Eds.). *Issues in materials development* (pp. 159–182). Rotterdam: Sense.

Hewings, M. (2010). Materials for university essay writing. In N. Harwood (Ed.), *English language teaching materials: theory and practice* (pp. 251–278). Cambridge: Cambridge University Press.

Holliday, A. (2005). *The struggle to teach English as an international language.* Oxford: Oxford University Press.

Hooper Hansen, G. (2011). Lozanov and the teaching text. In B. Tomlinson (Ed.), Materials development for language teaching (pp. 403–413). Cambridge: Cambridge University Press.

Hutchinson, T., & Torres, E. (1994). The textbook as agent of change. *ELT Journal, 48*(4), 315–328.

Jazadi, I. (2003). Mandated English teaching materials and their implications for teaching and learning: The case of Indonesia. In W. A. Renandya (Ed.), *Methodology and materials design in language teaching* (pp. 142–160). Singapore: SEAMEO Regional Language Centre.

Jensen, M., & Hermer, A. (1998). Learning by playing: learning foreign languages through the senses. In M. Byram & M. Fleming (Eds.), *Language learning in intercultural perspectives* (pp. 178–192). Cambridge: Cambridge University Press.

Jones, M., & Schmitt, N. (2010). Developing materials for discipline-specific vocabulary and phrases in academic seminars. In N. Harwood (Ed.), *English language teaching materials: theory and practice* (pp. 225–248). Cambridge: Cambridge University Press.

Kuo, C. H. (1993). Problematic issues in ESP materials development. *English for Specific Purposes, 12*, 171–181.

Lam, P. W. Y. (2010). Discourse particles in corpus data and textbooks: the case of well. *Applied Linguistics, 31*(2), 260–281.

Lee, R., & Bathmaker, A. (2007). The use of English textbooks for teaching English to "vocational" students in Singapore secondary schools: a survey of teachers' beliefs. *RELC Journal, 38*(3), 350–374.

Little, B. L., Devitt, L. S., & Singleton, D. (1989). *Learning foreign languages from authentic texts.* Dublin: Authentik Language Learning Resources Ltd.

Littlejohn, A. P. (1992). *Why are ELT Materials the way they are?* (Unpublished PhD thesis). Lancaster University, Lancaster.

Long, M. (1991). Focus on form: A design feature in language teaching methodology. In K. De Bot, R. Ginsberg & C. Kramsch (Eds.), *Foreign language research in cross-cultural perspective* (pp. 39–52). Amsterdam: John Benjamins.

Long, M., & Robinson, P. (1998). Focus on form: Theory, research and practice. In C. Doughty & J. Williams. (Eds.), *Focus on form in classroom second language acquisition* (pp. 15–41). Cambridge: Cambridge University Press.

Luke, C., de Castell, S., & Luke, A. (1989). Beyond criticism: the authority of the school textbook. In S. de Castell, A. Luke & C. Luke (Eds.), *Language, authority and criticism: readings on the school textbook* (pp. 245–260). London: Falmer Press.

Lyons, (2003). A practical experience of institutional textbook writing: product / process implications for materials development. In B. Tomlinson (Ed.), *Developing materials for language teaching* (pp. 490–504). London: Continuum.

Mackey, A., Ziegler, N., & Bryfonski, L. (2016). From SLA research on interaction to TBLT materials. In B. Tomlinson (Ed.), *SLA research and materials development for language learning* (pp. 103–118). New York: Routledge.

Maley, A. (2003). Creative approaches to writing materials. In B. Tomlinson (Ed.), *Developing materials for language teaching* (pp. 183–198). London: Continuum.

Maley, A. (2008). Extensive reading: maid in waiting. In B. Tomlinson (Ed.), *English language learning materials: A critical review* (pp. 133–156). London: Continuum.

Maley, A. (2011). Squaring the circle—reconciling materials as constraint with materials as empowerment. In B. Tomlinson (Ed.), *Materials development for language teaching* (pp. 379–402). Cambridge: Cambridge University Press.

Maley, A., & Tomlinson, B. (Eds.). (in press). *Authenticity and materials development for language learning*. Newcastle upon Tyne: Cambridge Scholars.

Mason, J. (2010) The effects of different types of materials on the intercultural competence of Tunisian university students. In B. Tomlinson & H. Masuhara (Eds.), Research for materials development in language learning (pp. 67–82). London: Continuum.

Masuhara, H. (2006). The multi-dimensional awareness approach to content teaching. In J. Mukundan (Ed.), *Focus on ELT materials* (pp. 1–11). Petaling Jaya: Pearson Longman.

Masuhara, H. (2007). The role of proto-reading activities in the acquisition and development of reading skills. In B. Tomlinson (Ed.), *Language acquisition and development: Studies of learners of first and other languages* (pp. 15–31). London: Continuum.

Masuhara, H. (2015). "Anything goes" in task-based language teaching materials? The need for principled materials evaluation, adaptation and development. *The European Journal of Applied Linguistics and TEFL: Materials in the ELT Classroom: Development, Use and Evaluation* [Guest editor B. Tomlinson], *4*(2), 113–128.

Masuhara, H., Haan, M., Yi, Y., & Tomlinson, B. (2008). Adult EFL courses. *ELT Journal. 62*(3), 294–312.

Masuhara, H., & Tomlinson, B. (2008). Materials for general English. In B. Tomlinson (Ed.), *English language learning materials: A critical review* (pp. 17–37). London: Continuum.

McCullugh, M. (2010) An initial evaluation of a set of published materials for medical English. In B. Tomlinson & H. Masuhara (Eds.), *Research for materials development in language learning* (pp. 381–393). London: Continuum.

McDonough, J., Shaw, C., & Masuhara, H. (2013). *Materials and methods in ELT: A teacher's guide* (3rd ed.). London: Blackwell.

McGarry, D. (1995). *Learner autonomy 4: The role of authentic texts*. Dublin: Authentik Language Learning Resources Ltd.

McGrath, I. (2013). *Teaching materials and the roles of EFL / ESL teachers*. London: Bloomsbury.

Meddings, L., & Thornbury, S. (2009). *Teaching unplugged: dogme in English language teaching*. Peaslake: Delta.

Menkabu, A., & Harwood, N. (2014). Teachers' conceptualization and use of the textbook on a medical English course. In N. Harwood (Ed.), *English language teaching textbooks; content, consumption, production* (pp. 145–177). Basingstoke: Palgrave Macmillan.

Mishan, F. (2005). *Designing authenticity into language learning materials*. Bristol: Intellect.

Mishan, F. (2010). Withstanding washback: thinking outside the box in materials development. In B. Tomlinson & H. Masuhara (Eds.), *Research for materials development in language learning* (pp. 353–369). London: Continuum.

Mishan, F. (2013). Studies of pedagogy. In B. Tomlinson (Ed.), *Applied linguistics and language learning* (pp. 269–286). London: Bloomsbury.

Mishan, F. (2016). Comprehensibility and cognitive challenge in language learning materials. In B. Tomlinson (Ed.), *SLA research and materials development for language learning* (pp. 166–184). New York: Routledge.

Mishan, F., & Timmis, I. (2015). *Materials development for TESOL*. Edinburgh: Edinburgh University Press.

Moore, J. (2014). *How to write EAP materials*. Oxford: ELT Teacher to Writer.

Mukundan, J. (2009). Are there really good reasons as to why textbooks should exist? In J. Mukundan (Ed.), *Readings on ELT materials III*. (pp. 92–100). Petaling Jaya: Pearson Malaysia.

Naustdal Fenner, A., & Nordal-Pedersen, G. (1999). *Search 10*. Oslo: Gyldendal.

Nunan, D. (2004). *Task-based language teaching*. Cambridge: Cambridge University Press.

Nuttall, C. (1996). *Teaching reading skills in a foreign language*. Oxford: Macmillan.

O'Neil, R. O. (1982). Why use textbooks? *ELT Journal, 36*(2), 104–111.

On Target. (1995). Windhoek: Gamsburg Macmillan.

Pelly, C. P., & Allison, D. (2000). Investigating the views of teachers on assessment of English language learning in the Singapore education system. *Hong Kong Journal of Applied Linguistics, 5*, 81–106.

Pennycook, A. (1994). *The cultural politics of English as an international language*. New York: Longman.

Pennycook, A. (1998). *English and the discourses of colonialism*. London: Routledge.

Phillipson, R. (1992). *Linguistic imperialism*. Oxford: Oxford University Press.

Prabhu, N. S. (1987). *Second language pedagogy*. Oxford: Oxford University Press.

Prabhu, N. S. (1989). Materials as support: materials as constraint. *Guidelines, 11*(1), 66–74.

Prodromou, L. (1992). What culture? Which culture? *ELT Journal, 46*(1), 39–50

Richards, J. (1993). Beyond the textbook: the role of commercial materials in language teaching. *Perspective, 5*(1), 43–53.

Rilling, S., & Dantas-Whitney, M. (Eds.). (2009). *Authenticity in the language classroom and beyond: Adult learners*. Alexandria, Virginia: TESOL.

Rinvolucri, M. (2003). *Humanising your coursebook*. Peaslake: Delta Publishing.

Samuda, V. (2005). Expertise in pedagogic task design. In K. Johnson (Ed.), *Expertise in second language learning and teaching* (pp. 230–254). Basingstoke, Palgrave Macmillan.

Samuda, V., & Bygate, M. (2008). *Tasks in second language learning*. New York: Palgrave Macmillan.

Saw, T. S. (2016). *Evaluating the external materials used for cultural elements in ELT course-books through teacher perception of teaching and learning* (Unpublished PhD thesis). University of Essex, Colchester.

Shawyer, S. (2010a). Classroom level curriculum development: EFL teachers as curriculum-developers, curriculum-makers and curriculum-transmitters. *Teaching and Teacher Education, 26*, 173–184.

Shawyer, S. (2010b). Classroom-level teacher professional development and satisfaction: Teachers learn in the context of classroom-level curriculum development. *Professional Development in Education, 36*, 597–620.

Singapore Wala, D. A. (2003). A coursebook is what it is because of what it has to do: An editor's perspective. In B. Tomlinson (Ed.), *Developing materials for language teaching* (pp. 58–71). London: Continuum.

Thomas, M., & Reinders, H. (Eds.). (2015). *Contemporary task-based language teaching in Asia*. London: Bloomsbury.

Thornbury, S., & Meddings, L. (2001). Coursebooks: The roaring in the chimney. *Modern English Teacher, 10*(3), 11–13.

Tickoo, M. (Ed.). (1995). *Language and culture in multilingual societies*. Singapore: RELC Anthology Series

Tilbury, A., Clementson, T., Henra, L. A., & Rea, D. (2010). *English unlimited pre-intermediate coursebook*. Cambridge: Cambridge University Press.

Timmis, I. (2010) Teachers telling tales: Exploring materials for teaching language. In F. Mishan & A. Chambers (Eds.), *Perspectives on language learning materials development* (pp. 63–86). Bern: Peter Lang.

Toh, G. (2001). Primary school English textbooks in Singapore across the decades: An examination of cultural content of the Oxford series, PRP and PETS. In J. Tan, S. Gopinathan, & H. W. Kam (Eds.), *Challenges facing the Singapore education system today*. (pp. 140–157). Singapore: Prentice Hall.

Tomlinson, B. (1994). Pragmatic awareness activities. *Language Awareness, 3.3 and 3.4*, 119–129.

Tomlinson, B. (1995). Work in progress: textbook projects. *Folio, 2*(2), 26–31.

Tomlinson, B. (2001a). Materials development. In R. Carter and D. Nunan (Eds.), *The Cambridge guide to TESOL* (pp. 66–71). Cambridge: Cambridge University Press.

Tomlinson, B. (2001b). Connecting the mind: A multi-dimensional approach to teaching language through literature. *The English Teacher 4*(2), 104–115.

Tomlinson, B. (2005). English as a foreign language: matching procedures to the context of learning. In E. Hinkel (Ed.), *Handbook of research in second language teaching and learning* (pp. 137–154). Mahwah, NJ: Lawrence Erlbaum.

Tomlinson, B. (2007). Teachers' responses to form-focused discovery approaches. In S. Fotos & H. Nassaji (Eds.), *Form focused instruction and teacher education: studies in honour of Rod Ellis* (pp. 179–194. Oxford: Oxford University Press.

Tomlinson, B. (Ed.). (2008a). *English language teaching materials: a critical review*. London: Continuum.

Tomlinson, B. (2008b). Humanising an EAP coursebook. *Humanising Language Teaching 10*(2). Retrieved from www.hltmag.co.uk/index.htm

Tomlinson, B. (2010a). Principles and procedures of materials development. In N. Harwood (Ed.), *Materials in ELT: theory and practice* (pp. 81–108). Cambridge: Cambridge University Press.

Tomlinson, B. (2010b). What do teachers think about EFL coursebooks? *Modern English Teacher, 19*(4), 5–9.

Tomlinson, B. (2010c). Helping learners to fill the gaps in their learning. In F. Mishan & A. Chambers (Eds.), *Perspectives on language learning materials development* (pp. 87–108). Bern: Peter Lang.

Tomlinson, B. (2011). Principled procedures in materials development. In B. Tomlinson (Ed.), *Materials development in language teaching* (2nd ed., pp. 1–31). Cambridge: Cambridge University Press.

Tomlinson, B. (2012a). Materials development for language learning and teaching. *Language Teaching: Surveys and Studies, 45*(2), 1–37.

Tomlinson, B. (2012b). Introduction: Textbooks and materials evaluation. In M. Eisenmann & T. Summer (Eds.), *Basic issues in EFL teaching and learning* (pp. 342–356). Heidelberg: Universitatsverlag Winter.

Tomlinson, B. (2013a). Humanizing the coursebook. In B. Tomlinson (Ed.), *Developing materials for language teaching* (2nd ed., pp. 139–156). London: Continuum.

Tomlinson, B. (2013b). Developing principled frameworks for materials development. In B. Tomlinson (Ed.), *Developing materials for language teaching* (2nd ed., pp. 95–118). London: Continuum.

Tomlinson, B. (2013c). *Applied linguistics and materials development*. London: Bloomsbury.

Tomlinson, B. (2014). Teacher growth through materials development. *The European Journal of Applied Linguistics and TEFL* [Special issue], *3*(2), 89–106.

Tomlinson, B. (2015a). Challenging teachers to use their coursebook creatively. In A. Maley & N. Peachey (Eds.), *Creativity in the language classroom* (pp. 24–28). London: British Council.

Tomlinson, B. (2015b). Key issues in EFL coursebooks. *ELIA*, *15*, 171–180.

Tomlinson, B. (2016a). Achieving a match between SLA theory and materials development. In B. Tomlinson (Ed.), *SLA research and materials development for language learning* (pp. 3–22). New York: Routledge.

Tomlinson, B. (2016b). Applying SLA principles to whole class activities. In B. Tomlinson (Ed.), *SLA research and materials development for language learning* (pp. 33–49). New York: Routledge.

Tomlinson, B. (in press). Making typical coursebook activities more beneficial for the learner. In D. Bao (Ed.), *Creative concerns in ELT materials development: Looking beyond the current design*. Bristol: Multilingual Matters.

Tomlinson, B., & Avila, J. (2007a). Seeing and saying for yourself: The roles of audio-visual mental aids in language learning and use. In B. Tomlinson (Ed.), *Language acquisition and development: Studies of learners of first and other languages* (pp. 61–81). London: Continuum.

Tomlinson, B., & Avila, J. (2007b). Applications of the research into the roles of audio-visual mental aids for language teaching pedagogy. In B. Tomlinson (Ed.), *Language acquisition and development: studies of learners of first and other languages* (pp. 82–89). London: Continuum.

Tomlinson, B., Dat, B., Masuhara, H., & Rubdy, R. (2001). ELT courses for adults. *ELT Journal*, *55*(1), 80–101.

Tomlinson, B., & Masuhara, H. (1994). *Use your English*. Tokyo: Asahi Press.

Tomlinson, B., & Masuhara, H. (2004). *Developing language course materials*. Singapore: RELC Portfolio Series.

Tomlinson, B., & Masuhara, H. (2008). Materials used in the UK. In B. Tomlinson (Ed.), *English language learning materials: A critical review* (pp. 159–178). London: Continuum.

Tomlinson, B., & Masuhara, H. (2013). Adult coursebooks. *ELT Journal*, *67*(2), 233–249.

Trabelsi, S. (2010). Developing and trialling authentic materials for business English students at a Tunisian university. In B. Tomlinson & H. Masuhara (Eds.), *Research for materials development in language learning: Evidence for best practice* (pp. 103–120). London: Continuum.

Troncoso, C. R. (2010) The effects of language materials on the development of intercultural competence. In B. Tomlinson & H. Masuhara (Eds.), *Research for materials development in language learning: Evidence for best practice* (pp. 83–102). London: Continuum.

Tsui, A. (2003). *Understanding expertise in teaching: Case studies of ESL teachers*. New York: Cambridge University Press.

Van den Branden, K. (2006). *Task-based language education: from theory to practice*. Cambridge: Cambridge University Press.

Van Gorp, K., & Bogaert, N. (2006). Developing language tasks for primary and secondary education. In K. Van den Branden (Ed.), *Task-based language education: from theory to practice* (pp. 76–105). Cambridge: Cambridge University Press.

Van Lier, L. (1996). *Interaction in the language curriculum: awareness, autonomy and authenticity*. Harlow: Longman.

Verhelst, M. (2006) A box full of feelings: promoting infant's second language acquisition all day long. In K. Van den Branden (Ed.), *Task-based language education: from theory to practice* (pp. 197–216). Cambridge: Cambridge University Press.

Wajnryb, R. (1996). *Death, taxes and jeopardy: Systematic omissions in EFL texts, or life was never meant to be an adjacency pair*. Plenary paper presented at the 9th ELICOS Conference, Sydney.

Wette, R. (2010). Professional knowledge in action: How experienced ESOL teachers respond to feedback from learners within syllabus and contextual constraints. *System*, *38*, 45–58.

Widdowson, H. G. (1978). *Teaching language as communication*. Oxford: Oxford University Press.

Widdowson, H. G. (1984). *Explorations in applied linguistics 2*. Oxford: Oxford University Press.

Widdowson, H. G. (2000). On the limitations of linguistics applied. *Applied Linguistics*, *21*(1), 3–25.

Williams, J. (2005). Form-focused instruction. In E. Hinkel (Ed.), *Handbook of research in second language acquisition and learning* (pp. 671–691). Mahwah, NJ: Lawrence Erlbaum.

Willis, J. (1996). *A framework for task-based learning*. Harlow: Longman Pearson.

Willis, D., & Willis, J. (2007). *Doing task-based teaching*. Oxford: Oxford University Press.

Wong, V., Kwok, P., & Choi, N. (1995). The use of authentic materials at tertiary level. *ELT Journal*, *49*(4), 318–322.

Yakhontova, T. (2001). Textbooks, contexts and learners. *English for Specific Purposes*, *20*, 397–415.

Yano Y., Long, M. H., & Ross, S. (1994). The effects of simplified and elaborated texts on foreign language comprehension. *Language Learning*, *44*(2), 189–212.

Zhang, W. (1997). A strong cultural component in EFL materials. *Folio*, *4*(1), 38–41.

3

Materials Evaluation

Introduction

Materials evaluation is a procedure that involves attempting to predict or measure the value of the effects of language-learning materials on their users. The macro effects on learners can include the understanding and production of language, the acquisition of language, the development of language skills and the development of communicative competence, whilst the micro effects can include engagement, motivation, self-reflection, self-esteem, autonomy and attitudes toward the target language and towards the learning of it. Teachers are also users of materials and the effects on them can include changes of beliefs, engagement, motivation, investment and teacher development, as well as ease of preparation and delivery. It can even be argued that administrators are users of materials and that the effects they are looking for are standardization and value for money. Interestingly, although the prime users of commercially produced materials are learners their prime buyers are administrators. Brian once did a confidential research project for a major British publisher in which he investigated what the users of coursebooks wanted from the coursebooks they used. He found in the 12 countries he researched that in most institutions the coursebooks were selected by administrators, that in a few institutions the classroom teachers selected the coursebooks and that in no institutions were the textbooks selected by learners. Guess who most commercial coursebooks are designed to appeal to?

Materials evaluation is probably the most written about procedure in the field of materials development. This is not surprising as publishers have always evaluated the materials developed by their authors and teachers have always evaluated materials either explicitly when selecting them or implicitly when using them. What is surprising, as you will see below, is that so little has been published about publisher evaluation and about informal teacher evaluation, and so much has been published about formal evaluation for reviews and for materials selection.

Brian's early experiences of materials evaluation included untrained evaluations of a global coursebook he wanted to make more relevant to his students in Nigeria and then of a coursebook written for Malawi, which was being used in Zambian secondary schools. In Zambia, Brian was teaching in the same secondary school as Rod Ellis and their discontent with the coursebook led them to writing their own series of coursebooks to replace it (Ellis & Tomlinson, 1973, 1974). That series was then selected to be the one and only official coursebook for Zambian secondary schools and it was still in use when

The Complete Guide to the Theory and Practice of Materials Development for Language Learning,
First Edition. Brian Tomlinson and Hitomi Masuhara.
© 2018 John Wiley & Sons, Inc. Published 2018 by John Wiley & Sons, Inc.

we visited Zambia 30 years later. Even though the book does have its strengths, Brian and Rod wish they had had more expertise in materials evaluation when they were writing it and that their publishers and the selection committee had been more rigorously evaluative too.

Hitomi started her teaching career in Japan where there was very little scope for teachers to write replacement coursebooks but she was immediately involved in formal evaluation in order to contribute to a selection of coursebooks and then in informal evaluation in order to make the coursebooks more relevant and engaging for her students. Since then she has gone on to gain considerable experience of evaluation in selecting textbooks, in writing coursebook reviews, and in textbook projects.

When we run courses and workshops for teachers on materials development we always focus on materials evaluation as we think that teachers can learn a lot about materials, about language acquisition, and about their own implicit beliefs through spending time on rigorous evaluations of materials in preparation, as published, and in use. Away from the course, the teachers will not have the time to be so rigorous but being so on a course helps them to be principled when evaluating materials which they are developing, which their colleagues are developing, which they are selecting from, which they are reviewing, which they are adapting, or which they are actually in the process of using. We really wish we had received such training early in our teaching careers.

From our now extensive experience of materials evaluation we would say that an evaluation of language learning materials should attempt to predict or measure whichever of the following effects are relevant to the context of learning in which the materials are being or are going to be used:

- The surface appeal of the materials for the learners. (For example, are the illustrations attractive? Are the sections separated by sufficient white space? Is there an effective use of color?)
- The content appeal of the materials (Do the users like the topic content, the texts, and the activities provided by the materials?)
- The credibility of the materials to learners, teachers and administrators. (Do the materials look as though they are going to meet their needs and wants?)
- The validity of the materials. (Is the learning they attempt to facilitate worth facilitating?)
- The reliability of the materials. (Would the materials have the same effects with different groups of target learners and when "delivered" by different teachers?)
- The ability of the materials to interest both the learners and the teachers.
- The ability of the materials to motivate the learners to use them and the teachers to "deliver" them.
- The ability of the materials to engage the learners affectively and cognitively.
- The degree of challenge presented by the materials (with achievable challenge being the ideal aimed at).
- The relevance of the materials to the learners' lives, needs, and wants.
- The value of the materials in terms of short-term learning (important, for example, for performance on tests and examinations).
- The value of the materials in terms of long-term acquisition and development (of language, of language skills, and of communicative competence).
- The learners' perceptions of the value of the materials.

- The teachers' perceptions of the value of the materials.
- The assistance given to the teachers in terms of preparation, delivery, and assessment.
- The flexibility of the materials (e.g. the extent to which it is easy for a teacher to adapt the materials to suit a particular context—see Bao (2015) for a focus on flexibility of materials).
- The contribution made by the materials to teacher development.
- The match with administrative requirements (e.g. standardization across classes, coverage of a syllabus, preparation for an examination).

Adapted from Tomlinson (2013b), pp. 21–22.

Before deciding which of the effects listed above to measure it would be necessary to consider which of them are relevant to the specific context of use. No two evaluations can be the same, as the levels, needs, wants, experiences, objectives, and out-of-class backgrounds of the learners will differ from context to context. This is obviously true of an evaluation of the value of a coursebook being used with groups of teenagers preparing for an examination in Thailand compared to an evaluation of the same book being used with groups of young adults preparing for a different examination in Peru. The main point is that it is not the materials that are being evaluated but their effect on the people who come into contact with them (including, of course, the evaluators).

In order to measure the value of any of the general effects listed above it would be necessary to specify specific criteria (ideally phrased as questions that are unambiguous and answerable). For advice on how to develop and use such criteria see "The Principles and Procedures of Materials Evaluation that we Recommend," later in this chapter.

Before concluding this introduction we would like to stress that conducting an evaluation is not the same as doing an analysis. Both the objectives and the procedures are different. As we have said, an evaluation makes judgements about the effects of materials on their users. An evaluation can (and should be) structured, criterion referenced, and rigorous but it will always be essentially subjective. In contrast, an analysis focuses on the materials themselves and it aims to be objective in its analysis of them. It "asks questions about what the materials contain, what they aim to achieve and what they ask learners to do" (Tomlinson, 1999, p. 10). So, for example, "Does it provide a transcript of the recorded dialogues?" is an analysis question that can be answered by either "Yes" or "No." "What does it ask the learners to do before listening to a song?" and "which tenses does it teach?" are also analysis questions and can be answered factually. As a result of answering many such questions, a description of the materials can be made that specifies what the materials do and do not contain and what they ask the learners to do. On the other hand, "Are the reading texts likely to engage the learners affectively?" is an evaluation question and can be answered on a cline between "very unlikely" and "very likely." It can also be given a numerical value (e.g. 5 for "very likely"), and, after many evaluation questions have been asked and answered, scores can be calculated that can be used as indicators of the potential value of the materials. For example, a coursebook that scores a total of 80% or more is very likely to be effective but, if it scored a subtotal of only 55% for speaking skills, it would be unlikely to be effective for a class of students whose main objective is to develop their oral communication skills. See Littlejohn (2011) for an example and a discussion of materials analysis and Tomlinson, Dat, Masuhara, & Rubdy (2001), Masuhara, Haan, Yi, & Tomlinson (2008), and Tomlinson and Masuhara (2013) for examples of criterion-referenced and rigorous materials evaluation.

A rigorous analysis of a set of materials can be very useful for finding out, for example, if:

- anything important has been missed out of a draft manuscript;
- the materials match the requirements of a syllabus or of a particular course;
- the materials contain what the teachers believe they should contain;
- the materials ask the students to do what they will have to do in an examination they are preparing for;
- the materials are promising enough to be subjected to a subsequent evaluation.

Analysis seems to be objective because the questions are likely to be given the same answers by each of a large number of analysts. There is only one answer, for example, to the question, "Does the coursebook contain practice tests?" or the question, "Does each unit have a pronunciation section?" However, analysts are inevitably and often overtly influenced by their own ideology and their selections of questions are biased accordingly. For example, the question, "Do the listening texts include different regional accents?" implies that they should do. Analysts also often have a hidden agenda when developing their instruments of analysis. For example, an analyst might ask the question, "Are the reading texts authentic?" in order to provide data to support an argument that EAP coursebooks do not typically help to prepare learners for the realities of academic reading. This is valid if the analysis questions are descriptive and the data that the analysis provides is then subjected to evaluative interpretation. For example, Brian conducted an analysis of 10 lower-level coursebooks (Tomlinson, 1999, p. 10) to provide data to support his contention that such books were typically too limited in their emphasis on language forms, on language practice rather than language use and on low-level decoding skills. His data disclosed that "nine out of the ten books were forms and practice focused and that in these books there were five times more activities involving the use of low-level skills (e.g. pronouncing a word) than there were involving the use of high-level skills (e.g. making inferences)" (Tomlinson, 2013b, p. 23). Brian then made use of his data to put forward a case for making lower level coursebooks more holistic, more meaning focused and better able to contribute more to the learners' development of high-level skills. Yet a different analysis using the same instruments to reveal the same data could use its results to argue that lower level coursebooks were actually helping learners to develop from a confident base of low-level skills. Of course, both arguments would need to present data from an evaluation of the effects of the materials on the learners' development to give credibility to their case.

One problem when looking for advice on evaluation is that many experts writing about materials evaluation mix analysis and evaluation and therefore make it very difficult to use their suggested criteria because, for example, in a numerical evaluation most analysis questions could only be answered by either 1 or 5 on a five-point scale and would thus be weighted disproportionately when combined with evaluation questions, which could yield 2, 3 and 4 as well. For example Mariani (1983, pp. 28–9) includes, in a section on "Evaluate your coursebook," such analysis questions as "Are there any teacher's notes …" and "Are there any tape recordings?" alongside such evaluation questions as "Are the various stages in a teaching unit adequately developed." The two analysis questions could score 5 each (even if the teachers' notes and the recordings were not very useful) and the evaluation question might only score 2—thus giving an undeserved high score of 12 out of 15. Likewise Cunningsworth (1984, pp. 74–79) includes both analysis and evaluation questions in his "Checklist of Evaluation Criteria." He does demonstrate awareness of the problem, though, by saying that "Some of the points can be checked off either in polar terms (i.e. yes or no) or, where we are talking about more or less of something, on a gradation from 1 to 5" (1984, p. 74). Our preference for separating analysis from evaluation is shared by Littlejohn (2011), who puts forward a general framework for analyzing materials (pp. 182–198), which he suggests should be used before evaluating materials and making decisions about them. He proposes a model, which is sequenced as follows:

- Analysis of the target situation of use.
- Materials analysis.
- Match and evaluation (determining the appropriacy of the materials to the target situation of use).
- Action.

This is a model that has been used by many of our postgraduate students in their detailed investigations of the value of specific materials in specific contexts of learning but it is dauntingly detailed and demanding for busy teachers wanting, for example, to make quick but principled decisions about the selection and / or adaptation of coursebooks. McDonough, Shaw, and Masuhara (2013) offer a similar but less daunting model designed to be useful to teachers without demanding too much time and expertise. Their model has two stages: an initial one, which involves an "external evaluation that offers a brief overview of the materials from the outside (cover, introduction, table of contents)" (p. 53) and a subsequent one that involves a criterion-referenced "internal evaluation."

What the Early Literature Tells Us about Materials Evaluation

Establishing Criteria and Developing Evaluation Instruments

Materials evaluation dominated much of the early literature on materials development. The publications were essentially practical and mainly attempted to help teachers to develop criteria for evaluating and selecting coursebooks. For example, in the 1970s Tucker (1975) put forward a four-component scheme for measuring the internal and external value of beginners' textbooks; Davison (1976) proposed a five-category scheme for the evaluation and selection of textbooks, and Dauod and Celce-Murcia (1979) supplied check lists of criteria for teachers to use in evaluating coursebooks. Candlin and Breen (1980) proposed criteria for evaluating materials and, uniquely at the time, also proposed the use of these criteria when developing the materials—something we strongly believe in and which we insist on when working on materials-development projects. Rivers (1981) shared her categories and criteria for evaluating materials; Mariani (1983) focused on evaluation for supplementation; Williams (1983) focused on how to develop criteria for textbook evaluation, and Cunningsworth (1984, pp. 74–79) provided the most detailed checklist so far of evaluation criteria to be used "as an instrument … for evaluating teaching material" (p. 74). Breen and Candlin (1987) published a principled guide that was intended unusually for both evaluators and producers of materials and then Sheldon (1987, 1988) also suggested principled criteria that could be used for both evaluating and developing textbook material. Skierso (1991) provided probably the most detailed and comprehensive checklist of criteria for textbooks and for teachers' books by combining criteria from a number of publications. Cunningsworth

(1995), Harmer (1991, 1998), Roberts (1996), Ur (1996), Brown (1997), Hemsley (1997) and Gearing (1999) also proposed their own checklists for use when evaluating materials. At that time anybody who wanted to do an evaluation had so many different sources to go to for advice and criteria. Unfortunately many of the checklists of evaluation criteria in the literature were specific to the context of learning and the purpose for evaluation that the writer had in mind. Many also were informed by the specific pedagogic beliefs and prejudices of their authors, and few could be transferred to other contexts without considerable modification. In addition, many authors simply provided their list without justifying the principles behind it and without giving advice to the reader on how to develop their own context relevant criteria. There were some exceptions, though, with, for example, Mathews (1985) insisting that any evaluation should work from and consistently relate to a specification of the teaching situation; Cunningsworth (1995) stressing the importance of developing criteria relevant to the actual target learners, and Byrd (2001) emphasizing the need for criteria to relate to the fit between the textbook and the curriculum, students, and teachers.

In the early literature there was no attempt to establish what evaluation criteria should and should not do. Checklists were just presented without any rational or theoretical justification. It was not until 2004 that Tomlinson and Masuhara (2004, p. 7) proposed the following questions for evaluating evaluation criteria:

- "Is each question an evaluation question?" (as opposed to an analysis question inviting a factual or yes / no answer).
- "Does each question only ask one question?" (and therefore does not include "and").
- "Is each question answerable?" (i.e. not so large and vague that nobody can answer it).
- "Is each question free of dogma?" (i.e. it does not assume or impose a methodology).
- "Is each question reliable in the sense that other evaluators would interpret it in the same way?"

We (and our students on materials development courses) have found that very few of the lists of criteria published in the early literature satisfy the above criteria and most of them are not generalizable or transferable, despite sometimes appearing to be so. Tomlinson (2012, pp. 147–148) gives the following examples of criteria from the literature, which do not match the criteria suggested in Tomlinson and Masuhara (2004):

- "Are there any materials for testing?" (Cunningsworth 1984) is an analysis question in the same checklist as such evaluation questions as, "Are the learning activities in the course material likely to appeal to the learners …?"
- "Is it attractive? Given the average age of your students, would they enjoy using it?" (Grant, 1987, p. 122) contains two questions in one criterion.
- "Does the writer use current everyday language, and sentence structures that follow normal word order?" (Daoud & Celce-Murcia 1979, p. 304) contains two questions and both are unanswerable without a data analysis of both a corpus of current language and the complete script of the materials. "To what extent is the level of abstractness appropriate?" (Skierso, 1991, p. 446) is another example of a criterion that is too large and vague to be answerable.
- "Are the various stages in a teaching unit (what you would probably call presentation, practice and production) adequately developed?" (Mariani, 1983, p. 29) is dogmatic in insisting on the use of a PPP approach.

- "Is it foolproof (i.e. sufficiently methodical to guide the inexperienced teacher through a lesson?" (Dougill, 1987, p. 32) is unreliable in that it can be interpreted in different ways by different evaluators.

Reporting Evaluations

The focus of much of the literature on materials evaluation is on the principles and procedures of conducting evaluations. There are some publications, though, which report on the effectiveness of materials. There are many journals that have had for a long time regular predictive reviews of recently published materials, for example *ELT Journal, Practical English Teaching, Modern English Teacher, English Teaching Professional, Folio, The Language Teacher, TESOL Journal* and *RELC Journal.* Some of them also include post-use reviews of materials. For example, *Modern English Teacher* includes a section titled "A Book I've Used," which consists of reviews by practitioners of their use of a recently published textbook and the IATEFL special interest group MAWSIG is about to launch *ELT Materials Review*, a journal that will provide rigorous post-use evaluations of published materials. Most journal reviews are of specific textbooks or courses but *ELT Journal*, for example, also publishes survey reviews of a number of current textbooks of the same subgenre. For example, Tomlinson et al. (2001) is a review of eight currently popular UK coursebooks for adults in which four reviewers from different cultural backgrounds independently subjected each course to a rigorous evaluation using the same 133 criteria. A similar review was published by Masuhara et al. (2008), in which they subjected eight coursebooks for adults to a rigorous criterion referenced review. Interestingly the two reviews came to similar conclusions. They both welcomed the attempts to personalize and humanize the coursebooks and both were critical of the expensive and unwanted increase in the number of components of coursebooks, of the neglect of literature as a source of potentially engaging texts, of the lack of intelligent content at lower levels, of the neglect of extensive reading and listening and of "the scarcity of real tasks which have an intended outcome other than just the practice of language forms" (Masuhara et al., 2008, p. 310). Other survey reviews that have appeared in *ELT Journal* include Tribble (2009) on resources for teaching academic writing, McDonough (2010) on materials for English for specific purposes, Wilson (2010) on materials for IELTS preparation and Tomlinson and Masuhara (2013) on current coursebooks for adults.

This is a very short section because, until recently, not much has been published that reports the conduct and results of evaluations of actual materials. However, see the section reporting evaluations further below for outlines of recently published reports of evaluations in action.

What the Current Literature Tells Us about Materials Evaluation

Establishing Criteria and Developing Evaluation Instruments

Since the turn of the century there has been a move away from the presentation of checklists for the reader to use (though to our regret we find that many postgraduate students still prefer to use published checklists rather than generate their own context relevant criteria). We have often been asked to publish evaluation checklists but we have always declined because we believe that no checklist can ever be transferable from one evaluation context to another, that any checklist inevitably reflects the pedagogic beliefs of its designer(s), and that a published checklist is inevitably invested with an authority it might not deserve but which might attract teachers and students to use it uncritically and inappropriately in their evaluations.

Tomlinson (2003) prefers to outline a process for generating principled criteria rather than present a ready-made but unrealistic set of criteria for all contexts. He is insistent that evaluators need to develop their own criteria which take into account the context of their evaluation and the beliefs of all the evaluators. He describes, justifies, and exemplifies ways of developing principled criteria and risks annoying postgraduate and other evaluators by not providing checklists for others to use. He also echoes Candlin and Breen (1980) by advocating that evaluation criteria should be developed before materials are produced and that these criteria should be used to make decisions about the approach, procedures and activities and to evaluate them whilst they are being developed, after they have been developed and after they have been trialed. We have always followed this procedure on textbook projects we have been involved in (e.g. in China, Ethiopia, Singapore and sub-Saharan Africa) but often the final project is evaluated by "experts" flown in by the sponsor who then use their own impressions or checklist to evaluate the materials.

Tomlinson (2003) makes what for him is a significant distinction between universal criteria and local criteria. He defines universal criteria as criteria that can be used to evaluate any materials for any learner anywhere. To develop these criteria he suggests that evaluators should generate a list of beliefs that they hold about how second or foreign languages are most effectively acquired (based on their reading, research and experience) and then to transform these beliefs into criteria for evaluating materials— for example, "I believe that learners need to be affectively engaged" becomes "Are the materials likely to achieve affective engagement?" In contrast to universal criteria, local criteria are those which are specific to the context in which the materials are being (or are going to be) used and that they are best developed by first specifying a profile of the target context. He also recommends a procedure for generating evaluation criteria to be used for the development, the ongoing monitoring and the eventual evaluation of materials (pp. 27–33)—a procedure that was used in Tomlinson et al. (2001) and later in Masuhara et al. (2008) and Tomlinson and Masuhara (2013) for evaluating coursebooks, as well as on a number of materials development projects led by Leeds Metropolitan University in, for example, China, Ethiopia and Singapore. We will describe this procedure in detail later in this chapter when giving our personal recommendations for evaluation.

Tomlinson (2003, p. 16) says (as we stressed earlier in this chapter) that evaluation is inevitably subjective, that it "focuses on the users of the materials" and that it attempts to measure the potential or actual effects of the materials on their users. In contrast, analysis focuses on the materials and aims to discover what they contain, what they ask learners and teachers to do and what they say their objectives are. He makes the point that materials analysis attempts to provide an objective account of materials but the analyst's choice of questions to ask is usually subjective and there is often a hidden agenda that it is hoped the resultant data will support. Littlejohn (2011, p. 181) makes a similar distinction when he says that analysis is concerned with materials "as they are" and "with the content and ways of working that they propose," and that analysis is not concerned with "how effective materials may be in achieving their aims." He also says that it is useful to do an analysis of a set of materials first so as to discover the extent of their match with the target context of use and then, if there is sufficient match, to do an evaluation in order to predict the likely effects of the materials on their intended users. Byrd (2001) makes a very different distinction between evaluation and analysis of textbooks when she talks about evaluation for selection of materials and analysis for their implementation. As we have said above, the literature often confuses materials analysis with materials evaluation and uses the terms as though they are interchangeable. For example, Mariani (1983, pp. 28–29) includes in a section on "Evaluate your coursebook" such analysis questions as "Are there any teacher's notes?" and Cunningsworth (1984, pp. 74–79) includes both analysis and evaluation questions in his "Checklist of Evaluation Criteria."

In recent years a number of other writers have put forward principled frameworks for materials evaluators to make use of rather than providing checklists for them to follow. McGrath (2002, p. 31) distinguishes between "general criteria (i.e. the essential features of any good teaching-learning material)" and "specific (or context related) criteria," a distinction similar to the one made by Tomlinson (2003) between universal and local criteria. For coursebook selection McGrath outlines a procedure that includes the following sequential stages: materials analysis, first-glance evaluation, user feedback, close analysis, and evaluation with situation-specific checklists and then selection. McDonough and Shaw (2003, p. 61) suggest an approach in which the evaluators first conduct an external evaluation "that offers a brief overview from the outside" and then carry out "a closer and more detailed internal evaluation." They give practical advice on how to conduct both types of evaluation and discuss factors to consider when developing criteria. They also stress that the four main considerations when deciding on the suitability of materials are usability, generalizability, adaptability, and flexibility. McDonough, Shaw, and Masuhara (2013) update and develop this practical advice further. Riazi (2003) provides a useful critical survey of textbook evaluation schemes from 1975 onwards in which he points out how ephemeral many of the criteria are because they were based on pedagogic approaches that were favored at the time of publication. In his conclusion he wisely supports Cunningsworth (1995) in insisting on the importance of collecting data about the context of learning before starting any evaluation and he outlines a procedure that includes a survey of the teaching / learning situation, a neutral analysis (we wonder if this is actually possible), a belief-driven evaluation, and then the selection. Other writers who have offered principled advice on how to develop evaluation criteria include Wallace (1998), who suggests 12 "criterion areas" for materials evaluation, and Rubdy (2003), who proposes and exemplifies an interactive model of evaluation combining psychological validity, pedagogical validity and process / content validity. Tomlinson and Masuhara (2004) propose a principled evaluation procedure for inexperienced, unqualified teachers, a procedure that we will outline in detail in our final section of this chapter and which has been reproduced in Korean and Portuguese translations of the book and in a version published in China (Tomlinson & Masuhara, 2007). McCullagh (2010) also reports on a principled procedure that she used to evaluate materials developed for use with non-native speaker medical practitioners.

Evaluation and selection of learning materials: A guide. (2008) is an unusual publication. This is a booklet specifically published for language teachers in Prince Edward Island, Canada instructing them how to evaluate and select from the learning materials available to them. It is unusual in that it is very well-informed, very principled, very thorough, very coherent but very prescriptive in its insistence that "The overall goal must be to support the learning outcomes of the curriculum. The consideration of curriculum fit must be applied rigorously to all mediums of presentation" (p. 1).

Mukundan and Ahour (2010) very usefully review 48 evaluation checklists from 1970 to 2008 and are critical of most of them for being "too demanding of time and expertise to be useful to teachers, too vague to be answerable, too context bound to be generalizable, too confusing to be useable and too lacking in validity to be useful" (Tomlinson, 2012, p. 148). They assert that a framework for generating flexible criteria would be more useful than detailed and inflexible checklists and also that more attention should be given to retrospective evaluation than to predictive evaluation in order to help teachers to evaluate the effects of the materials they have used so as to be able to make informed modifications the next time they use them. This is a point which is also made by Tomlinson (2003, 2013b) and by Ellis (2011), and which we constantly make to teachers, to project sponsors and to publishers. Mukundan and Ahour (2010) also advocate what they call a "composite framework" for evaluation consisting of multiple components and including computer analysis of the script of the materials (focusing in the examples they give on vocabulary load or on recycling). Mukundan has campaigned against the exclusive use of predetermined checklists for many years and in Mukundan (2006) he describes the use of a composite framework, which combines the use of checklists, of reflective journals and of concordance software, to evaluate locally published ELT textbooks in Malaysia.

In recent years, publications have focused much less on materials evaluation and much more on principled ways of developing and using materials. Mishan and Chambers (2010), for example, contains no chapters on materials evaluation and neither does Harwood (2010). Both books focus very much on principles and procedures for developing materials for different purposes and for different types of learners. Tomlinson (2011), however, does contain a section on materials evaluation. In it, Littlejohn (2011) updates, develops, and exemplifies his influential (1998) framework for analyzing materials and adds sections on postanalysis evaluation and use of materials. One of the points he stresses is how empowering it can be for teachers to use his framework. Whilst acknowledging that Littlejohn's framework has been very useful for researchers and postgraduate students and is frequently cited in the literature it does seem to us to be rather demanding of time and expertise to be a practical tool for busy teachers.

In Tomlinson (2011), Ellis (2011) reviews principles and procedures for researcher-led macro-evaluations of task-based approaches and then focuses on practical procedures for teacher-led micro-evaluations of task-based approaches that provide teachers with useful information, contribute to teacher development and can inform macro-evaluations. In another contribution to Tomlinson (2011) Masuhara (2011) updates and develops her often-cited (1998) chapter on what teachers really want from coursebooks. She investigates teacher needs and teacher wants. Then she suggests ways in which teachers can improve their evaluation and development of published materials as well as their own ability to use materials in the ways they think are most effective for their students, whilst empowering themselves and contributing to their own teacher development. She also reports improvements she has noticed since 1998 in the inclusion of teachers in the process of evaluating and developing materials. In the final chapter of the evaluation section of Tomlinson (2011), Amrani (2011) reports on current practice in publisher evaluation of materials. She reveals that publishers rarely subject all their materials to time-consuming piloting nowadays (see Roxburgh, 1997, and Singapore Wala, 2013a, for their views on the importance of piloting) and instead they use selective piloting of sections; they have the materials predictively evaluated by focus groups and they use reviewers, questionnaires, panels of experts, and editorial visits. She also reveals that development times for a course have been cut down from 7 years to 3 years since Donovan (1998) wrote about the processes of publisher evaluation, and that publishers evaluate materials primarily in order to identify customer expectations, to check the match of a specific section with its objectives and to "see how the scope and sequencing work in terms of a fuller syllabus" (Amrani, 2011, p. 273). Amrani predicts that post-use evaluation will increasingly inform future materials development and that "evaluation will become less of a clear cut stage prior to publication and be more of an ongoing process where materials are refined and even changed throughout the life of a product" (p. 295). We hope her predictions come true and we applaud the apparent thoroughness of the evaluation procedures she reports. However, we are a little concerned that much of the current publisher evaluation depends on the views of teachers and "experts" willing to contribute, that so little of it seems to be of the actual effects of materials in and after use, and that none of it seems to include feedback from learners.

McGrath (2013) makes similar points to ours above by stressing the importance of in-use and post-use evaluation and of the inclusion of learners in the evaluation process. In a very useful section on How Teachers Evaluate Coursebooks (pp. 106–126), McGrath reports studies of how coursebooks are evaluated and selected. Many of the studies report how teachers think they should be responsible for the evaluation and selection of coursebooks but that in most cases (even if teachers are consulted) the decisions are taken by administrators or heads of department—sometimes influenced by publishers' offers. However, McGrath reports a very encouraging study of a Swedish secondary school (Fredriksson & Olsen, 2006), which narrates a progression from teachers being influenced by another school and by an author in their selection of textbooks to teachers piloting a book in two classes before evaluating it and making a decision. He also reports a study in Taiwan (Wang, 2005) in which teachers who had been given a checklist to use in selecting their own textbook reflected on the process. In McGrath (2013) there is a subsection (p. 117–125) that provides a critical review of studies of teachers' own criteria. The actual criteria seem to depend on contextual circumstances and range from very teacher-centered criteria such as survival from inexperienced, overworked teachers to more learner-centered criteria such as student motivation from more experienced and confident teachers. McGrath (2013) looked for evidence of in-use and post-use teacher evaluation of materials but, disappointingly, only found two: Law's (1995) study of Hong Kong teachers and Fredriksson and Olsen's (2006) study in Sweden. However there are studies of teacher in-use and post-use evaluation of materials in Tomlinson and Masuhara (2010)—Al-Busaidi and Tindall (2010), Pryor (2010), Stillwell, McMillan, Gillies, and Waller (2010), and Stillwell, Kidd et al. (2010). For information about these studies see our section on "Reporting Evaluations" below.

McDonough, Shaw, and Masuhara (2013) contains a section on evaluation that accepts that there is no "agreed set of procedures or criteria for evaluation" (p. 52) but puts forward a "model for hard-pressed teachers or course planners that will be brief, practical to use and yet comprehensive in its coverage of criteria" (p. 52). This model is in two stages: (1) "an external evaluation that offers a brief overview from the outside (cover, introduction, table of contents)" (p. 53) which is used to eliminate materials which do not match the content and approach needed for the target learners; (2) "a closer and more detailed evaluation" (p. 53) of materials that have been found in stage (1) to match the requirements of the target context of learning. After stage (2), decisions are made about the usability, generalizability, adaptability, and flexibility of the materials.

In Tomlinson (2013a) there are two chapters on evaluation. Tomlinson (2013b) looks in detail at the principles that can inform materials development and considers, in particular, principles deriving from the evaluators' theories of learning and teaching, from learning theory, from SLA research, and from his own experience and research. He then says what he thinks can be predicted in pre-use evaluation, can be observed in whilst-use evaluation, and can be measured in post-use observation as well as suggesting effective ways of doing so. He also reviews standard approaches to materials development and suggests the following criteria for evaluating evaluation checklists and lists of criteria:

- Is the list based on a coherent set of principles of language learning?
- Are all the criteria actually evaluation criteria or are they criteria for analysis?
- Are the criteria sufficient to help the evaluator to reach useful conclusions?
- Are the criteria organized systematically (for example, into categories and subcategories that facilitate discrete as well as global verdicts and decisions)?
- Are the criteria sufficiently neutral to allow evaluators with different ideologies to make use of them?
- Is the list sufficiently flexible to allow it be made use of by different evaluators in different circumstances? (Tomlinson, 2013b, p. 36)

Finally Tomlinson proposes a procedure to use in "major" evaluations and a reduced version of it for use in less formal evaluations where saving time is important. These procedures involve the evaluators developing their own universal criteria by brainstorming their beliefs about what facilitates language acquisition and development and their own local criteria by profiling the target context of learning. We will provide more details about these procedures in the final section of this chapter.

The second chapter on evaluation in Tomlinson (2013b) focuses on the role of feedback in the process of developing and publishing a coursebook. In it, Singapore Wala (2013) reviews the literature on such feedback (and especially on the role of teachers in providing feedback) and considers the issue of whose feedback to include, so as to satisfy all the stakeholders in the process. She then focuses on the case of Singapore and details the various feedback processes that were built into the development of a coursebook to match the requirements of a new Ministry of Education syllabus. These included feedback from teachers about existing materials, feedback from teachers who trialed sample units in target schools, feedback from the Curriculum Development Planning Division and feedback from various "feedback loops" (p. 82) that had been incorporated in the materials-development process. In her conclusion, Singapore Wala focuses on the tension between feedback from curriculum developers who work with ideals and abstracts and are located in the future and feedback from teachers who work with students in classrooms and are located in the present.

Tomlinson (2013c) focuses on the application of applied linguistics research and theory to the development of materials. None of the chapters focus on evaluation directly but Tomlinson (2013d) develops a number of principles for facilitating language acquisition and then makes use of 10 of them as criteria for evaluating six current global coursebooks. He found, for example, that all six books achieved low ratings for affective engagement, utilization of the resources of the brain, opportunities for language use, catering for the individual and focus on meaning, and that none of them made any use of nonlinguistic communication. Five of these six coursebooks (plus one other) are evaluated in Tomlinson (2013e) against findings from classroom research and the conclusion is that there is a very weak match between the six books and "what we have learned from classroom research" (p. 53). These coursebooks are also evaluated in Kennedy and Tomlinson (2013), this time against typical requirements of language policy and planning. It was found that the books were likely to foster critical thinking and to contribute to educational development (a very important contribution for coursebooks to make in our view) but that they were all catering more for "students from middle class families in urban areas than to students from working class families in rural areas" (p. 262).

Harwood (2014) does not focus on issues and procedures of materials evaluation but it does contain some chapters that report on studies which involved evaluation and these will be outlined in our section on reporting evaluations below.

Mishan and Timmis (2015) includes a chapter on "Evaluation and Adaptation." It supports Tomlinson's (2003; 2013b) insistence on principled and systematic evaluation and says (p. 57) that this is important because "in some contexts, materials will constitute the main exposure which learners have to the TL," because, as Sheldon (1988) says "materials potentially represent a significant professional, financial and / or political investment" and because "materials evaluation can be a powerful professional development activity." We would certainly agree with these reasons and would add that involving teachers in materials evaluation, selection, and adaptation can empower and enhance them as participants in a decision-making process. In their chapter, Mishan and Timmis (2015) focus on the what, when, how and who of evaluation. In doing so they very much echo points made by Tomlinson (2003) and McGrath (2002, 2013) but add a useful exemplification of how to word the same criterion differently for pre-use, whilst-use and post-use evaluation, a caution about the difficulty of distinguishing between the effects of the materials and the effects of the teacher in whilst-use evaluation, and useful summaries of what the literature says about practical and economic ways of achieving teacher and learner evaluation of materials.

Nimehchisalem and Mukundan (2014) advocate explicit, criterion-referenced evaluation for all but very experienced teachers who are capable of applying their principles in implicit, impressionistic evaluation. They are critical of most published checklists for being insufficiently valid, reliable, economical or practical. They refer to the ELT Textbook Evaluation Checklist, which was stimulated by the evaluation of 48 checklists in Mukundan and Ahour (2010) and developed by Mukundan, Hajimohammadi and Nimehchisalem (2011a). Nimehchisalem and Mukundan (2014) report on a revised version of the ELT Textbook Evaluation Checklist that was produced following qualitative and quantitative evaluations of the original plus feedback from three renowned experts in the field. Before reporting on their revised version they provide a useful evaluation of the literature in which they focus on valid principles and prerequisites proposed by various researchers but also comment on how many published checklists have failed to heed the warnings of Ur (1996) and Littlejohn (1998) as well as the pitfalls listed by Tomlinson (2003), which they summarize as "(1) confusion over evaluation and analysis questions, (2) multiple questions in one item, (3) extended, unclear and unanswerable items, (4) dogmatic questions and finally (5) items that may be interpreted in different ways by various evaluators"—Nimehchisalem and Mukundan (2014, p. 764).

The evaluation of the ELT Textbook Evaluation Checklist by the three experts led to a number of suggestions for additions to the checklist. Some of these were disregarded in the interests of economy or because of existing coverage but the following additions were made: (1) "A note was … added to the beginning of the checklist which instructed evaluators to disregard the sections that they found irrelevant to their present context"

(p. 768); (2) "The book is supported by other materials like review and test units" (p. 768) was added as a criterion. "Various listening contexts such as formal vs. informal contexts are considered" was added (p. 768). A numerical interpretation guide was added to the end of the checklist. In addition, a number of items were removed because they were considered redundant or unfair and a number of items were modified because they were too general or ambiguous. The result of the revisions is a robust, comprehensive checklist that (unlike most checklists) is flexible enough to be used in different learning contexts. However, we would make some criticisms of it for mixing evaluation and analysis criteria and for sometimes having two different criteria embedded in one. What we would really praise the authors for is subjecting their checklist to numerous ongoing evaluations and then making considered revisions to their checklist. This process of constant revision is one we followed in revising our criteria in Tomlinson et al. (2001), Masuhara et al. (2008), and Tomlinson and Masuhara (2013), and one we would insist on for any checklist or set of criteria. We would also urge evaluators not to follow a published checklist blindly but to develop their own context specific lists or to adapt the most appropriate published checklist to fit the characteristics of the learning context and the principles of the evaluators.

Richards (2014) includes a section on evaluation in his chapter on the ELT textbook. Its main contribution to the field is to stress the need always to relate evaluation and selection to the target context of learning and in particular when selecting a textbook to consider:

Institutional factors such as:

- the type of curriculum and tests in place in the school;
- organizational structure of the institution;
- length and intensity of the English course(s);
- cost of the book and its availability;
- resources in place, such as whiteboards, computers, or self-access facilities;
- support available to prepare new teachers for the use of textbooks;
- classroom conditions such as class size or seating arrangements.

Teacher factors such as:

- proficiency in English;
- level of training and teaching experience;
- familiarity with different methodologies;
- attitudes towards use of textbooks;
- preferred teaching styles.

Learner factors such as:

- "learners" needs and aims;
- proficiency level;
- language learning experience;
- age range;
- interests;
- cultural background;
- language background;
- occupations;
- preferred learning styles. (Richards, 2014, 28–29)

Whilst this is a useful list of factors to consider there is a danger that it could end up constraining choice to the extent that the decision is always taken to carry on using what has always been used and to avoid any risks. We always prefer to start by considering universal criteria first (Tomlinson, 2013b) and then local criteria next, to highlight the need for a match with learning principles. We have found that learners in particular are far more adaptable to the new providing that it offers something of potential value to them (Tomlinson, 2005). Richards (2014) also has a useful list of ways of recording information for whilst-use evaluation (but does not include ways of measuring and recording information about learner performance) but in relation to post-use evaluation he only offers "Post-use evaluation provides information that will help decide if the book will continue to be used" (p. 33) without saying how the information can be gained.

Tomlinson (2016) focuses on SLA research and materials development. Whilst the focus is on applying SLA research findings to the development of materials there are some chapters that feature the development and application of evaluation criteria. For example, Tomlinson (2016) develops criteria from SLA theory and then applies them to the evaluation of samples of materials. Nakata and Webb (2016) develop criteria for evaluating vocabulary exercises and then use them to evaluate typical coursebook vocabulary exercises, and Boers and Strong (2016) develop criteria for evaluating collocation exercises and then use them to evaluate collocation exercises from language-learning materials.

Reporting Evaluations

Many micro-evaluations of actual materials are conducted for sponsors of projects or for publishers and are inevitably confidential. Brian, for example, has conducted confidential micro-evaluations and macro-evaluations for the British Council, for Cambridge University Press, for Disney Publications, for Microsoft, and for publishers in Iran and Malaysia. And we were both recently involved in an evaluation for the University of Cambridge. There are some reports of evaluations of materials in action scattered throughout the published literature but, until recently, they have rarely been collected in one volume or issue. This is a point made by Ellis (2011, p. 234), who says that such micro-evaluations are "often seen as too localized and too small scale, and so theoretically uninteresting." However, in Tomlinson (2008) there are reports of macro-evaluations of current materials for young learners, for self-access learning, for EAP and for general English, as well as of nine evaluations of materials currently used in different parts of the world. In addition, there are reports of micro-evaluations of materials in action in Mukundan (2006a), Harwood (2010), Tomlinson and Masuhara (2010), McGrath (2013), Harwood (2014) and Tomlinson (2016).

Very little has been published on the ongoing process of evaluating commercial materials in production. However, Donovan (1998) has written on and exemplified the process of piloting commercial coursebooks prior to their publication. He discusses the issues involved when deciding what is to be piloted, who should pilot it, and how it should be piloted and he illustrates the processes of piloting with many examples provided by pilots of Cambridge University Press coursebooks. He also discusses in detail what the benefits and pitfalls are of piloting. He strongly advocates the use of piloting as a very effective way of obtaining feedback on the actual rather than just the predicted effectiveness of materials in development but he also prophesizes that the increasing expense involved and the decreasing time available might result in publishers reducing their use of piloting. And he was right. Thirteen years later Amrani (2011) reported that commercial publishers (including Cambridge University Press) no longer used piloting as their main means of gaining feedback on the appeal and effectiveness of the materials they are developing. Now they use more economical ways, such as commissioning pre-use reviews from experienced teachers and academics, gaining feedback from invited focus groups, from questionnaires, from invited panels of experts, from editorial and writer visits to classrooms, from desk research and from competitor analysis. All these ways might be quick and cost-effective indications of the potential value of the product but, in our view (and that of Singapore Wala, 2013a) they are no substitute for rigorous piloting. Amrani does regret the inevitable reduction of piloting and does discuss the benefits and problems of the other ways of evaluating materials in development. In her conclusion she looks to the future of publisher evaluation of materials and predicts that "Increasingly post-publication review will inform future materials development" (Amrani 2011, p. 295). We would certainly welcome more postpublication evaluations but the main focus of publishers' in- and post-production evaluations will understandably be on how they can gain feedback that will increase the sales of revised or future coursebooks. This is a point made by Bell and Gower (2011), who discuss the compromises that are inevitable during the ongoing process of producing a global coursebook and by Singapore Wala (2013a, 2013b), who focuses on evaluation, and especially on piloting, when providing publisher perspectives on the whole process of publishing a commercial coursebook from conception to postpublication feedback.

We cannot expect piloting (or any other means of evaluating materials in development) to be able to provide valid and reliable evidence of the effectiveness of the materials in relation to the language acquisition and development of their users. This would involve longitudinal measurement of post-use effects and would really require the expertise, time, and funding that only a consortium of universities and publishers could provide. Remarkably such evaluations are frequently attempted by MA and PhD students throughout the world (for example, we have just supervised numerous such evaluation studies at the University of Liverpool) but they are not often reported in the literature. One exception is Ellis (2011) who reports on three micro-evaluations of the effectiveness of task-based materials conducted by MA students at the University of Auckland. Another exception is Barnard (2007) who reports an extensive PhD study of the effectiveness of comprehension-based materials in the teaching of Bahasa Indonesia to beginners at the National University of Singapore. Other postgraduate micro-evaluations are reported in McGrath (2013) and Harwood (2014), and, as we mentioned earlier, a new journal, *ELT Materials Review*, is about to be launched by the Materials Writers Special Interest Group (MAWSIG) of IATEFL (the International Association of Teachers of English as a Foreign Language), which will publish detailed and rigorous post-use evaluations of the effectiveness of published materials.

An interesting recent development has been the establishment of an online evaluation tool by the Materials Development and Evaluation Research Unit at Universiti Putra Malaysia, the host of the many MICELT conferences organized by Jayakuran Mukundan in recent years. This evaluation tool (www.elt-tec.com) has been developed by Jayakuran Mukundan, Almaz Hong Siaw Swin, Ng Yu Jin, and Vahid Nimehchisalem so that users can access a generic checklist to use in the evaluation of coursebooks and can then compare their evaluation of a course with those of users of the course in countries all over the world. It can also be used by publishers to evaluate their courses prior to publication.

The Principles and Procedures of Materials Evaluation Which We Recommend

When Developing Materials

Most course materials are developed to match a predetermined syllabus but very few are developed in accordance with a predetermined set of principled criteria. In our view this is why some of them achieve coverage of language items and language skills but are less successful in facilitating language acquisition and development. From our experience of developing materials to match criteria we would recommend to all materials writers (whether they are developing materials for their own class, for an institution, for a Ministry of Education or for a commercial publisher, and whether they are developing print or digital materials) that they make use of the set of procedures outlined below.

1. **Establish a team** (even if there are only two of you) so that beliefs can be shared and debated.
2. **Brainstorm your beliefs** by first of all individually listing at random what you believe best facilitates language acquisition and development and then by comparing the lists and producing a new list of commonly held beliefs. At the second stage we would recommend writers trying to justify their beliefs which are not commonly held by the team before the final list is compiled. Here is a small sample taken from our long random list of commonly held beliefs:
   We believe that language acquisition and development is best facilitated by:
   - exposing learners to the target language in use;
   - ensuring that the learners' exposure is rich in quantity, quality and variety;
   - ensuring that the learners' exposure is meaningful to the learners;
   - ensuring that the learners' exposure is related to their lives, interests, needs and wants;
   - ensuring that the learners' exposure is contextualized;
   - ensuring that the learners' exposure is comprehensible to the learners;
   - engaging the learners affectively;
   - engaging the learners cognitively;
   - providing the learners with opportunities to use the target language for meaningful communication;
   - providing the learners with opportunities to make discoveries about how the target language is used.
3. **Categorize your beliefs** by grouping them under headings. Here is a small sample of our category headings:
   - exposure to written language;
   - exposure to spoken language;
   - written communication;
   - spoken communication;
   - language content;
   - topic content;
   - skills content;
   - motivation.

4. **Convert your beliefs into universal criteria** by turning them into questions that attempt to predict the likely effects of the materials on their users. When doing this make sure that each question:
    - is answerable;
    - only has one answer;
    - is evaluative and not analytical;
    - is valid;
    - is useful.
  Here is a small sample of our universal criteria:

  Reading Texts
    To what extent are the texts likely to:
    - Expose the learners to language in authentic use?
    - Expose the learners to language in typical use?
    - Expose the learners to language which is meaningful to them?
    - Expose the learners to language which is comprehensible to them?
    - Expose the learners to language which relevant to their lives?
    - Expose the learners to language which is relevant to their needs?
    - Expose the learners to language which is relevant to their wants?
    - Expose the learners to language which is recycled at intervals?
    - Interest the learners?
    - Engage the learners affectively?
    - Engage the learners cognitively?
    - Motivate the learners to read outside the course?
  Note that:
    - We would say that all 12 of these criteria are important for the selection or development of reading texts for any materials development. Other criteria could be added for larger projects such as the development of a global coursebook (for example, to what extent are the texts likely to have immediate appeal to a wide variety of learners?).
    - A similar set of criteria could be developed in relation to the predicted effects on teachers in the target context of learning and another could be developed in relation to administrators.
5. **Develop a set of local criteria** by first creating a profile of the learning context of the target learners and then deriving criteria from it. In the profile, information should be provided, for example, about the age, gender, language level, motivation, reasons for learning the language, needs, wants and interests of the learners, the qualifications, experience, age, preferred teaching styles, and workload of the teachers, and the duration, intensity and targets of the course(s). This is obviously easier to do when writing for your own class or institution than it is for a national and (especially) for a global coursebook. To provide an informative profile for the latter types of books, research, observational visits and questionnaires are necessary and flexibility becomes the most important criterion. For example, when developing a national coursebook for Namibia (*On Target*, 1994), questionnaires were administered to students and to teachers throughout the country and very useful information was gathered (especially about the students' preference for narrative texts and for serious and provocative topics such as drug abuse and domestic violence). Here

are some examples of local criteria for 15-year-old students at state high schools in Indonesia:

Listening Texts

To what extent is the topic content of the listening texts likely to:

- Be acceptable in a Muslim community?
- Achieve sufficient topic familiarity for 15-year-old students in Indonesia?
- Be relevant to the lives of 15-year-old students in Indonesia?
- Stimulate affective responses from 15-year-old students in Indonesia?
- Stimulate 15-year-old students in Indonesia to think?
- Stimulate 15-year-old students in Indonesia to communicate their views?
- Appeal to both male and female 15-year-old students in Indonesia?
- Appeal to students in both rural and urban areas of Indonesia?
- Be of educational value to 15-year-old students in Indonesia?
- Motivate 15-year-old students in Indonesia to look out for English outside their classroom?

It might seem strange to develop universal criteria before local criteria (i.e. criteria for any learner anywhere before criteria for the target learning context) but we have found that focusing on local criteria first can lead to a neglect of vitally important principles of language acquisition and can lead to the development of materials that appear to be locally relevant but which do not actually help learners to acquire and use the target language.

6. **Develop a set of medium specific criteria** by first listing important aspects of the medium being used and then deriving criteria from them. For example, for paper materials you would list aspects of design, layout, instructions and illustrations (see Chapters 13 and 14). These aspects could also be important for digital materials but you would also need to focus on aspects of individualization, navigation, and interactivity (see Chapter 14). Here are some examples of medium specific criteria for paper materials in Indonesia:

Illustrations

To what extent are the illustrations likely to:

- Help the students to understand the language connected to the illustrations?
- Help the students to use the target language for communication?
- Help the students to do activities connected to the illustrations?
- Be acceptable in a Muslim community?
- Achieve sufficient familiarity for 15-year-old students in Indonesia?
- Be relevant to the lives of 15-year-old students in Indonesia?
- Stimulate affective responses from 15-year-old students in Indonesia?
- Stimulate 15-year-old students in Indonesia to think?
- Appeal to both male and female 15-year-old students in Indonesia?
- Appeal to students in both rural and urban areas in Indonesia?

Note that, as with many other categories and subcategories, it would be useful to ask analysis questions before doing an evaluation. For example, are the illustrations intended to be functional or just decorative?

7. **Combine the three sets of criteria** in a way which will make it easy to use them. We would advise the use of a table for each category and subcategory with the following headings:

Category –
Sub-category –

Criterion	Grade[a]	Comment[b]

[a] We would recommend using a five-point scale with a criterion achieving 4 or 5 in order for it to be considered as successfully achieved.

[b] The comment column can be used to record reasons and examples justifying the grade as well as suggestions for modifications that could lead to a higher grade.

When you have made use of the above set of procedures you will have a set of principled criteria that you can use both to drive the development of your materials and (with some additions and modifications) to evaluate them during and after their development.

In this chapter we have focused on developing criteria prior to starting to write your materials. In Chapter 4 we will be focusing on evaluating materials prior to adapting them and in Chapter 5 we will be focusing on principled ways of actually developing materials.

When Reviewing Materials

If you are reviewing your team's materials during their development it is important that you make use of the criteria you developed prior to starting to write them. It is also important that you review the materials that you have written and that other members of the team review them too. For example, when *On Target* (1994) was being written by a team of 30 writers in Namibia, each mini-team of three wrote a first unit. Each mini-team then reviewed all the other mini-team's units and the best one (i.e. the one considered by the most mini-teams to be the most likely to be effective with the target users) was determined and then modified in relation to feedback from the mini-teams. Each mini-team was then made responsible for writing a unit and for periodically reviewing another mini-team's unit. Use was made during and after the writing of a unit of the monitoring mini-team's comments as well as of criterion referenced feedback from advisors.

When reviewing your materials you will inevitably find that some criteria questions are not answerable, not valid or not useful and you will decide to delete or modify them. You might also decide to add criteria that occur to you during the evaluation process. This ongoing, organic development of evaluation criteria is an important aspect of the evaluation process and is one of the many reasons why you can never just take a checklist from the literature and use it to evaluate any materials.

If you are reviewing materials whose writing you have not participated in we believe it is important to use whatever criteria (if any) which have been developed specifically for those materials by their writers or by the journal or publisher. If no evaluation criteria have been developed then we think you should develop criteria yourself which are specific to the materials you are evaluating and then ask the writers or sponsor if they are appropriate. If you are reviewing materials as part of a research project we would recommend developing a set of materials specific criteria and then having your criteria evaluated before use by experts with experience of evaluation.

When developing criteria to drive the writing of a course of materials we believe you need a thorough and detailed set of criteria. This is a time-consuming, demanding but necessary process. Obviously though you would not need as many criteria if you were developing supplementary materials for your own class or if you were writing a brief review for a journal.

When Trialing Materials

Despite what Amrani (2011) says about publishers no longer relying on trialing for feedback we hope that the practice of trialing materials before their final publication will continue, as we think it is the most reliable way of gaining information about the effectiveness of the materials for their users. Trialing depends on the good will of the teachers invited to trial the materials and therefore asking them to conduct a multi-criteria evaluation is out of the question. We believe, though, that it is very important that revised versions of a selection of the most important evaluation questions developed during the pre-writing evaluation are used rather than asking the vague, general questions about teacher and learner attitudes, which we have sometimes experienced in trialing. One way of achieving coverage of as many criteria as possible is to give different evaluation questions to different groups of teachers so as not to place too great a demand on their time.

When Selecting Materials

We find that after so many years of evaluating materials we can informally apply our most important criteria to the selection of materials but we would strongly recommend, in any selection procedure for an institution or especially for a nation, that a formal criterion referenced procedure is followed. In our view this means going through the seven-stage procedure recommended for writing and evaluating materials above and comparing the grades and comments for each book evaluated before making a selection.

When Adapting Materials

We believe that formal adaptations for an institution or nation require the formal seven-stage evaluation procedure prior to decisions about adaptation. In such cases, it is important that suggestions for adaptation are included in the comments column of the evaluation table. However, many adaptations are made on the spur of the moment by teachers who realize that a unit of materials they are being asked to use is unlikely to be effective for a particular class. In such a case we would recommend that the following questions are asked and then modifications are made:

To what extent are the materials likely to:

- Expose the learners to the language in use?
- Be relevant to the lives of the learners?
- Engage the learners affectively?
- Engage the learners cognitively?
- Provide opportunities for the learners to make discoveries about the target language is typically used?
- Provide opportunities for the learners to use the target language for purposeful communication?

Some of our best lessons have resulted from asking these questions of a unit of material and then making last-minute modifications to how we intend to use it (sometimes even on the stairs on the way to the classroom).

For suggestions and examples of informal and impromptu adaptations see Chapter 4, "Materials Adaptation," in this volume.

When Using Materials

It can be very revealing to evaluate materials as they are being used either as a teacher using the materials with a class or as an observer watching materials being used. Obviously we cannot observe acquisition taking place and there are many criteria from a pre-use evaluation which would not be answerable in a whilst-use observation. However, in our view we can observe, for example, the extent to which the learners:

- can follow the instructions without help;
- can understand the "texts" without help;
- can do the activities without help;
- are motivated to experience the "texts";
- are engaged by the "texts";
- are motivated to do the activities;
- are engaged by the activities.

Each of the above capabilities needs breaking down into specific questions to focus and facilitate a whilst-use evaluation. For example,

- What approximate percentage of the learners seem to have completed the activity?
- What approximate percentage of the learners seem to have completed the activity successfully?

Of course, one major difficulty in observing materials in use is separating evaluation of the materials from evaluation of how the teacher is using them. For example, there might be a number of authentic texts in a unit with great potential for exposure to the target language in use but the teacher only uses one of them and spends most of the lesson doing the drills and artificial exercises from the unit. Or the teacher might add a really interesting readiness activity before asking the students to read a text with the result that the students are affectively engaged whilst reading it. Our advice is that it is best for you or the teacher you are observing to keep to the unit as it is if your main aim is to evaluate the effectiveness of the materials rather than the effectiveness of the teacher's use of the materials (unless of course the latter is a research focus). We would advise a narrow focus when evaluating materials in use as it is very difficult to notice many different effects at the same time and a narrow focus helps in noticing and recording in greater detail and with more rigor. For example, the focus could be engagement during a task and the observer could use the following questions to "measure" the effectiveness of the materials for the learners:

To what extent did the learners:

- Stay on task?
- Maintain eye contact with the "texts" they were asked to read or watch as part of the task?
- Maintain eye contact with each other during oral communication phases of the task?

- Maintain proximity to the materials during "text" phases of the task?
- Maintain proximity with each other during oral communication phases of the task?
- Volunteer contributions during pair or group phases of the task?
- Volunteer contributions during plenary phases of the task?

After Using Materials

Post-use (or retrospective) evaluation of the effect of materials is the most revealing form of materials evaluation but it is also the least common. This is probably because such an evaluation is inevitably time consuming and demanding of expertise. It is also difficult to make reliable and valid because of the problem of ensuring that the effects measured are as a result of the materials rather than, for example, the teacher's use of them or the learners' subsequent experience of the target language in use. In order to gain results of any significance the evaluation would have to be on a large scale, involve many teachers with a variety of backgrounds and pedagogic inclinations, involve learners with a variety of objectives and motivations, have access to information about exactly what the teachers and learners did while using the materials and also record the learners' out-of-class and after-course experience of English. Publishers could undertake such evaluations but the cost could be high both of conducting the evaluation and of modifying materials already published. Consortia of universities and publishers could undertake such evaluations and it is our hope that they will.

Pre-use and whilst-use evaluations can legitimately and usefully predict and measure the attitudes of the users towards the materials being evaluated as positive attitudes would be potential indicators of likely successful effects. However, we believe that post-use evaluations should focus wherever possible on the actual capabilities of the learners who have used the materials either in relation to general ability to use the target language for communication or with reference to the specific performance targets which the materials were being used to help them attain (e.g. getting a good grade on the IELTS examination; being able to study architecture successfully in the medium of the target language; being able to use English safely and effectively as an airline pilot). Quite often, though, in the few published post-use evaluations we have read, the instruments of measurement have not achieved sufficient validity to justify the claims of the evaluators. For example, Hadley (2014, p. 230) claims to have demonstrated empirically that global textbooks "can play an important role in helping … second language learning." But this claim is based on a study in which a particular global coursebook was used with learners in Japan who were shown to have increased their scores on the coursebook placement test, which consisted of "70 multiple choice items divided into three sections that assess listening … reading … and grammatical knowledge" (p. 222). Can such a placement test provide a valid test of language learning? It certainly cannot be a valid test of communicative competence.

Potentially valid ways of measuring performance effects in our opinion include:

- using the results of performance tests that assess real-life capabilities (ideally administered prior to the use of the materials, immediately after their use and after a gap in time to allow for the delayed effect of language acquisition);
- receiving evaluative feedback from observers of the learners' postcourse use of the target language (e.g. from lecturers on an architecture course; from managers of hotels

the learners are working in; from the learners' self-evaluation of their communicative competence);

- shadowing learners to observe their postcourse use of the target language (e.g. sitting in on lectures; videoing on-job performance; observing presentations);
- "participating" in postcourse communication with the learners (e.g. e-mailing office workers; phoning hotel receptionists; soliciting blogs).

These procedures are obviously time consuming and demanding of personnel and expertise and cannot always be undertaken. Although not as valid and reliable as performance measurements, the following procedures could also give useful indications of the effectiveness of a set of materials:

- Getting learners to rate themselves from 1–5 on a list of capabilities at the beginning of a course, in the middle of the course, at the end of the course, and (if possible) after a delay.
- Getting learners to rate their peers from 1–5 on a list of capabilities at the beginning of a course, in the middle of the course, at the end of the course, and (if possible) after a delay.
- Getting teachers to rate their students from 1–5 on a list of capabilities at the beginning of a course, in the middle of the course, at the end of the course, and (if possible) after a delay.

Our recommendations in this section might seem rather absolute but they are based on our experience of over 40 years of writing and of evaluating materials developed for the global market and also specifically for Belgium, Botswana, Bulgaria, China, Ethiopia, Indonesia, Iran, Japan, Luxembourg, Malaysia, Mauritius, Morocco, Nigeria, Oman, Singapore, Vanuatu, Vietnam, and Zambia. We hope that we have learned from what we achieved and from the mistakes we made.

Conclusion

The length of this chapter reflects the prominence of materials evaluation in the literature on materials development and the fact that it is the one aspect of the field which most concerns (and ideally involves) learners, teachers, writers, publishers and researchers. We hope we have made our views clear in this chapter. In summary they are that:

- Evaluation needs to be systematic, rigorous and criterion referenced.
- Evaluation should be of the effects of materials on their users and not of the materials themselves.
- Pre-use evaluation can be useful but in-use and especially post-use evaluation is potentially more reliable and informative.
- The criteria for evaluating materials should ideally be developed prior to the writing of the materials and should then be used to evaluate them whilst they are being developed and after their completion.
- Materials evaluation should feature in both pre-service and in-service teacher training courses both to help the participants to develop awareness and expertise and to empower them as informed and thinking professionals.

- Teachers (and learners) should be helped to develop their own criteria for evaluating materials and should not be made to use externally imposed criteria developed by "experts."
- Published materials should be evaluated by learners and teachers whilst and after being used in typical target classrooms.
- Digital materials should be evaluated by learners and teachers whilst and after being used by individuals and by groups. (See Chapter 7 for evaluations of digital materials and ways of using the internet for the evaluation of materials.)

What Do You Think?

1. Do you think learners should be involved in materials evaluation? If so, why do you think they should be involved and when and how should they be involved?
2. Do you think that you have the awareness and expertise to conduct a materials evaluation? If not, what do you think you need to do in order to gain this awareness and expertise?
3. What do you think are the most effective ways of gaining post-use information about the effects of a set of materials on their users? For each way, say what you think are the advantages and the potential problems.
4. Do you agree that criteria need to be developed prior to the writing of materials and then used to drive the development of the materials and the evaluation of them during and after their development. Why / why not?
5. What do you think the advantages and disadvantages are of developing evaluation criteria:
   - by yourself?
   - in a small team?
   - in a large team?

Tasks

1. Take a unit of materials from a coursebook or from the web, decide upon a group of target learners and then make use of our suggested procedures in "The Principles and Procedures of Materials Evaluation that We Recommend" above to:
   - develop 10 universal criteria;
   - develop five local criteria;
   - use your universal and local criteria to conduct an evaluation of the unit.
2. Set yourself a mini-materials development task (e.g. a reading activity for a specific class). Before starting to develop the materials:
   - revise your ten universal criteria from Task 1 above;
   - develop five local criteria;
   - use your universal and local criteria to develop, monitor and revise your materials;
   - if possible, devise a focused whilst-use evaluation instrument and use it to evaluate your materials while they are being used;
   - if possible, devise a post-use evaluation instrument and use it to evaluate your materials after they have been used.

References

Al-Busaidi, S., & Tindall, K. (2010). Evaluating the impact of in-house materials on language learning. In B. Tomlinson & H. Masuhara (Eds.), *Research for materials development in language learning: Evidence for best practice* (pp. 137–149). London: Continuum.

Amrani, F. (2011). The process of evaluation: A publisher's view. In B. Tomlinson (Ed.), *Materials development in language teaching* (2nd ed., pp. 267–295). Cambridge: Cambridge University Press.

Bao, D. (2015). Flexibility in second language materials. *The European Journal of Applied Linguistics and TEFL: Materials in the ELT Classroom: Development, Use and Evaluation* [Guest editor B. Tomlinson], *4*(2), 37–52.

Barnard, E. S. (2007). The value of comprehension in the early stages of the acquisition and development of Bahasa Indonesia by non-native speakers. In B. Tomlinson (Ed.), *Language acquisition and development: Studies of first and other language learners* (pp. 187–204). London: Continuum.

Bell, J. & Gower, R. (2011). Writing course materials for the world: a great compromise. In B. Tomlinson (Ed.), *Materials development in language teaching* (pp. 135–150). Cambridge: Cambridge University Press.

Boers, F., & Strong, B. (2016). An evaluation of textbook exercises on collocations. In B. Tomlinson (Ed.), *SLA research and materials development for language learning* (pp. 139–152). New York: Routledge.

Breen, M., & Candlin, C. (1987). Which materials? A consumer's and designer's guide. In L. E. Sheldon (Ed.), *ELT textbooks and materials: problems in evaluation and development.* London: Modern English Publications and the British Council.

Brown, J. B. (1997). Textbook evaluation form. *The Language Teacher, 21*(10), 15–21.

Byrd, P. (1995). *Materials writers guide.* Rowley, MA: Newbury House.

Byrd, P. (2001). Textbooks: evaluation for selection and analysis for implementation. In M. Celce-Murcia (Ed.), *Teaching English as a second or foreign language* (3rd ed., pp. 415–427). Boston, MA: Heinle & Heinle.

Candlin, C. N., & M. Breen (1980). Evaluating and designing language teaching materials. *Practical papers in English language education* (Vol. 2). Lancaster: Institute for English Language Education, University of Lancaster.

Cunningsworth, A. (1984). *Evaluating and selecting EFL teaching material.* London: Heinemann.

Cunningsworth, A. (1995). *Choosing your coursebook.* Oxford: Heinemann.

Daoud, A. M., & Celce-Murcia, M. (1979). Selecting and evaluating a textbook. In M. Celce-Murcia & L. McIntosh (Eds.), *Teaching English as a second or foreign language* (pp. 302–307). New York: Newbury House.

Davison, W. (1976). Factors in evaluating and selecting texts for the foreign language classroom. *English Language Teaching, 30*(4), 310–314.

Donovan, P. (1998). Piloting—a publisher's view. In B. Tomlinson (Ed.), *Materials development in language teaching* (pp. 149–189). Cambridge: Cambridge University Press.

Dougill, J. (1987). Not so obvious. In L. E. Sheldon (Ed.), *ELT textbooks and materials: Problems in evaluation and development.* London: Modern English Publications and the British Council.

Dubin F., & Olshtain, E. (1986). *Course design*. New York: Cambridge University Press.

Ellis, R. (2011). Macro—and micro-evaluations of task-based teaching. In B. Tomlinson (Ed.), *Materials development in language teaching* (pp. 21–35). Cambridge: Cambridge University Press.

Ellis, R., & Tomlinson, B. (1973). *English through situations*. Book 1. Lusaka: Longman Zambia.

Ellis, R., & Tomlinson, B. (1974). *English through situations*. Books 2 & 3. Lusaka: Longman Zambia.

Evaluation and selection of learning materials: A guide. (2008). Charlottetown, Prince Edward Island: Department of Education.

Fredriksson, C., & Olsen, R. (2006). *English textbook evaluation; An investigation into the criteria for selecting English textbooks*. Retrieved from https://dspace.mah .se/bitstream/handle/2043/2842/CeciliaFredriksson%2bRebeccaOlsson%5b1%5d.pdf? sequence=1&isAllowed=y

Gearing, K. (1999). Helping less-experienced teachers of English to evaluate teachers' guides. *ELT Journal, 53*(2), 122–127.

Grant, N. (1987). *Making the most of your textbook*. Harlow: Longman.

Hadley, G. (2014). Global textbooks in local contexts: An empirical investigation of effectiveness. In N. Harwood (Ed.), *English language teaching textbooks: Content, consumption, production* (pp. 205–238). Basingstoke: Palgrave Macmillan.

Harmer, J. (1991). *The practice of English language teaching*. Harlow: Longman.

Harwood, N. (Ed.). (2010). *Materials in ELT: Theory and practice*. Cambridge: Cambridge University Press.

Harwood, N. (Ed.). (2014). *English language teaching textbooks: Content, consumption, production*. Basingstoke: Palgrave Macmillan.

Hemsley, M. (1997). The evaluation of teachers' guides – design and application. *ELTED, 3*(1), 72–83.

Kennedy, C., & Tomlinson, B. (2013). Implementing language policy and planning through materials development. In B. Tomlinson (Ed.) (2013). *Applied linguistics and materials development* (pp. 255–268). London: Bloomsbury.

Law, W. H. (1995). *Teachers' evaluation of English textbooks: An investigation of teachers' ideas and current practices and their implications for developing textbook evaluation criteria* (Unpublished M.Ed. dissertation). University of Hong Kong, Hong Kong.

Littlejohn, A. (1998). The analysis of language teaching materials: Inside the Trojan Horse. In B. Tomlinson (Ed.), *Materials development in language teaching* (pp. 190–216). Cambridge: Cambridge University Press.

Littlejohn, A. (2011). The analysis of language teaching materials: Inside the Trojan Horse. In B. Tomlinson (Ed.), *Materials development for language teaching* (2nd ed., pp. 179–211). Cambridge: Cambridge University Press.

Mariani, L. (1983). Evaluating and supplementing coursebooks. In S. Holden (Ed.), *Second selections from Modern English Teacher* (pp. 17–21). Harlow: Longman.

Masuhara, H. (1998). What do teachers really want from coursebooks? In B. Tomlinson (Ed.), *Materials development in language teaching* (pp. 239–260). Cambridge: Cambridge University Press.

Masuhara, H. (2011). What do teachers really want from coursebooks? In B. Tomlinson (Ed.), *Materials development in language teaching* (2nd ed., pp. 236–266). Cambridge: Cambridge University Press.

Masuhara, H., Haan, M., Yi, Y., & Tomlinson, B. (2008). Adult EFL courses. *ELT Journal*, *62*(3), 294–312.

Mathews, A. (1985). Choosing the best available textbook. In A. Mathews, M. Sprat & L. Dangerfield (Eds.), *At the chalkface* (pp. 202–206). London: Edward Arnold.

McCullugh, M. (2010). An initial evaluation of a set of published materials for medical English. In B. Tomlinson & H. Masuhara (Eds.), *Research for materials development in language learning* (pp. 381–93). London: Continuum.

McDonough, J. (2010). English for specific purposes: a survey review of current materials. *ELT Journal*, *64*(4), 467–477.

McDonough, J. & Shaw, C. (2003). *Materials and methods in ELT: A teacher's guide* (2nd ed.). Chichester: Wiley-Blackwell.

McDonough, J., Shaw, C., & Masuhara, H. (2013). *Materials and methods in ELT: A teacher's guide* (3rd ed.). Chichester: Wiley-Blackwell.

McGrath, I. (2002). *Materials evaluation and design for language teaching*. Edinburgh: Edinburgh University Press.

McGrath, I. (2010). *Teaching materials and the roles of EFL/ESL teachers: Practice and theory*. London: Bloomsbury.

McGrath, I. (2013). *Teaching materials and the roles of EFL/ESL teachers*. London: Bloomsbury.

Mishan, F. & Chambers, A. (Eds.). (2010). *Perspectives on language learning materials development*. Bern: Peter Lang.

Mishan, F. & Timmis, I. (2015). *Materials development for TESOL*. Edinburgh: Edinburgh University Press.

Mukundan, J. (2006). Are there new ways of evaluating ELT coursebooks? In J. Mukundan (Ed.), *Readings on ELT materials II* (pp. 170–180). Petaling Jaya: Pearson Malaysia.

Mukundan, J., & Ahour, T. (2010). A review of textbook evaluation checklists across four decades (1970–2008). In B. Tomlinson & H. Masuhara (Eds.), *Research for materials development in language learning: Evidence for best practice* (pp. 336–352). London: Continuum.

Mukundan, J., Hajimohammadi, R., & Nimehchisalem, V. (2011). Developing an English language textbook evaluation checklist. *Contemporary Issues in Education Research*, *4*(6), 21–27.

Nakata, T., & Webb, S. (2016). Vocabulary learning exercises: Evaluating a selection of exercises commonly featured in language learning materials. In B. Tomlinson (Ed.), *SLA research and materials development for language learning* (pp. 123–138). New York: Routledge.

Nimehchisalem, V., & Mukundan, J. (2014). Refinement of the English language teaching textbook evaluation checklist. *Pertanika Journal of Social Sciences and Humanities*, *23*(4), 761–780.

On Target. (1994). Windhoek: Gamsburg Macmillan.

Pryor, S. (2010). The development and trialling of materials for second language instruction: A case study. In B. Tomlinson & H. Masuhara (Eds.), *Research for materials development in language learning: Evidence for best practice* (pp. 207–223). London: Continuum.

Riazi, A. M. (2003). What do textbook evaluation schemes tell us? A study of the textbook evaluation schemes of three decades. In W. A. Renandya (Ed.), *Methodology and materials design in language teaching: Current perceptions and practices and their implications* (pp. 52–68). Singapore: RELC.

Richards, J. C. (2014). The ELT textbook. In S. Garton & K. Graves (Eds.), *International perspectives on materials in ELT* (pp. 19–36). Oxford: Palgrave Macmillan.

Rivers, W. M. (1981). *Teaching foreign-language skills.* Chicago: Chicago University Press.

Roberts, J. T. (1996). Demystifying materials evaluation. *System, 24*(3), 375–389.

Roxburgh, J. (1997). Procedures for the evaluation of in-house EAP textbooks. *Folio, 4*(1), 15–18.

Rubdy, R. (2003). Selection of materials. In B. Tomlinson (Ed.), *Developing materials for language teaching* (pp. 37–57). London: Continuum.

Sheldon, L. E. (Ed.). (1987). *ELT textbooks and materials: Problems in evaluation and development.* London: Modern English Publications and the British Council.

Sheldon, L. E. (1988). Evaluating ELT textbooks and materials. *ELT Journal, 42*(4), 237–246.

Singapore Wala, D. A. (2013a). Publishing a coursebook: The role of feedback. In B. Tomlinson (Ed.), *Developing materials for language teaching* (2nd ed., pp. 63–88). London: Bloomsbury.

Singapore Wala, D. A. (2013b). The instructional design of a coursebook is as it is because of what it has to do: An application of systemic functional theory. In B. Tomlinson (Ed.), *Developing materials for language teaching* (2nd ed., pp. 119–138). London: Bloomsbury.

Skierso, A. (1991). Textbook selection and evaluation. In M. Celce-Murcia (Ed.), *Teaching English as a second or foreign language* (pp. 432–453). Boston: Heinle & Heinle.

Stillwell, C., Kidd, A., Alexander, K., McIlroy, T., Roloff, J., & Stone, P. (2010). Mutual benefits of feedback on materials through collaborative materials evaluation. In B. Tomlinson & H. Masuhara (Eds.), *Research for materials development in language learning: Evidence for best practice* (pp. 257–272). London: Continuum.

Stillwell, C., McMillan, B., Gillies, H., & Waller, T. (2010). Four teachers looking for a lesson: Developing materials with lesson study. In B. Tomlinson & H. Masuhara (Eds.), *Research for materials development in language learning: Evidence for best practice* (pp. 237–250). London: Continuum.

Tomlinson, B. (1999). Developing criteria for materials evaluation. *IATEFL Issues 147,* 10–13.

Tomlinson, B. (2005). English as a foreign language: Matching procedures to the context of learning. In E. Hinkel (Ed.), *Handbook of research in second language teaching and learning* (pp. 155–174). Mahwah, NJ: Lawrence Erlbaum.

Tomlinson, B. (2003). Materials evaluation. In B. Tomlinson (Ed.), *Developing materials for language teaching* (pp. 15–36). London: Bloomsbury.

Tomlinson, B. (ed.) (2008). *English language teaching materials: a critical review.* London: Continuum.

Tomlinson, B. (Ed.). (2011). *Materials development in language teaching* (2nd ed.). Cambridge: Cambridge University Press.

Tomlinson, B. (2012). Materials development for language learning and teaching. *Language Teaching, 45*(2), 143–179.

Tomlinson, B. (Ed.). (2013a). *Developing materials for language teaching* (2nd ed.). London: Bloomsbury.

Tomlinson, B. (2013b). Materials evaluation. In B. Tomlinson (Ed.), *Developing materials for language teaching* (2nd ed., pp. 21–48). London: Bloomsbury.

Tomlinson, B. (Ed.). (2013bc). *Applied linguistics and materials development.* London: Bloomsbury.

Tomlinson, B. (2013d). Second language acquisition and materials development. In B.

Tomlinson (Ed.), *Applied linguistics and materials development* (pp. 11–30). London: Bloomsbury.

Tomlinson, B. (2013e). Classroom research of language classes. In B. Tomlinson (Ed.), *Applied linguistics and materials development* (pp. 11–30). London: Bloomsbury.

Tomlinson, B. (Ed.). (2016). *SLA research and materials development for language learning.* New York: Routledge.

Tomlinson, B., Dat, B., Masuhara, H., & Rubdy, R. (2001). EFL courses for Adults. *ELT Journal, 55*(1), 80–101.

Tomlinson, B., & Masuhara, H. (2004). *Developing language course materials.* Singapore: RELC.

Tomlinson, B., & Masuhara, H. (2007). *Developing language course materials.* Beijing: People's Educational Press.

Tomlinson, B., & Masuhara, H. (Eds.). (2010). *Research for materials development in language learning: Evidence for best practice.* London: Continuum.

Tomlinson, B., & Masuhara, H. (2013). Adult coursebooks. *ELT Journal, 67*(2), 233–249.

Tribble, C. (2009). Writing academic English—a survey review of current published resources. *ELT Journal, 63*(4), 400–417.

Tucker, C. A. (1975). Evaluating beginner textbooks. *English Teaching Forum, 13*, 335–361.

Ur, P. (1996). *A course in language teaching: Practice and theory.* Cambridge: Cambridge University Press.

Wallace, M. J. (1998). *Action research for language teachers.* Cambridge: Cambridge University Press.

Wang, L. Y. (2005). *A study of junior high school English teachers' perceptions of the liberalization of the authorized English textbooks and their experience of textbook evaluation and selection* (Unpublished MA dissertation). National Yunlin University of Science and Technology, Douliu City, Taiwan.

Williams, D. (1983). Developing criteria for textbook evaluation. *ELT Journal, 37*(3), 251–255.

Wilson, J. (2010). Recent IELTS materials. *ELT Journal, 64*(2), 219–232.

4

Materials Adaptation

Introduction

Definition of Adaptation

Materials adaptation is a general term for the process that involves making changes to existing materials to better suit specific learners, teachers and contexts for the purpose of facilitating effective learning. This may mean reducing mismatches between materials, learners, teachers and contexts or making fuller use of the potential value of existing materials.

Scope and Range of Adaptation

Adaptation may manifest itself in wide-ranging ways, depending on the agent of change (who), the reasons (why), the objectives (what for), and the timing. On the one hand, adaptation may be very small in scale as in a teacher's intuitive, spontaneous, and reactive actions in a particular class. For example, a teacher tries to make a text on the topic of daily routine in a Japanese junior high-school coursebook more engaging and learnable by inviting students to mime while the teacher reads it: "Everyday Becky wakes up at 6:30 in the morning. She stretches her arms and rubs her eyes and she yawns" (an extract from Islam and Mares, 2003, p. 93). Adaptation may involve more deliberate actions involving student contributions, as in Ottley (2016). On starting a new job in Iraqi-Kurdistan, he wanted to know what might interest his class of students consisting of Muslims and Christians, Sunnis and Shi'ites, Kurds from Iraq, Iran and Syria, and Arabs. So he invited a representative sample of students to come to an informal forum meeting. Based on the discussion, he added, replaced and supplemented the commercial EAP coursebook by a major international publisher that he was expected to use. On the other hand adaptation could take place as a more systematic, collaborative and long-term project at an institutional or larger national or international level. For example, the Language Centre at Sultan Qaboos University in the Sultanate of Oman initially evaluated its existing commercial course materials and tried to adapt them to better suit its curriculum and its student needs. In this case, it is interesting to note that adapting existing materials meant making time-consuming fundamental and extensive changes that could possibly threaten the coherence of the course. Consequently, they decided to discard the original materials and launched a project to develop in-house materials

The Complete Guide to the Theory and Practice of Materials Development for Language Learning,
First Edition. Brian Tomlinson and Hitomi Masuhara.
© 2018 John Wiley & Sons, Inc. Published 2018 by John Wiley & Sons, Inc.

from scratch. Their materials development project is reported in Al-Busaidi and Tindle (2010).

The Growing Significance of Adaptation: Is Adaptation a Necessity or an Option?

How significant is materials adaptation? Our answer to this question has always been "Very significant" but we now need to rephrase our response as "phenomenally significant." Traditionally, materials adaptation has been known as small changes that a lot of teachers make in some form or another which are not well studied or supported in the literature or in training courses (see the state-of-the art review by Tomlinson, 2012 for an overview).

In our critical review of the up-to-date literature on adaptation and teacher use of materials, we have found overwhelming evidence to support the fact that adaptation has become a necessity rather than an option in most cases, whether the coursebooks are commercially produced or are nationally / institutionally tailored.

What brought about this heightened necessity for adaptation? We need to look at the two major paradigm shifts that have been taking place since the mid-1990s. One of them is the division between materials producers and users and the other is ownership of "English."

Paradigm Shift 1: Division between Materials Producers and Users

The global demands of ELT and the proliferation of ESL / EFL commercial coursebooks in the 1980s deepened the division between professional materials producers of "global courses" and their users. As a result, Masuhara (1998, revised 2011, pp. 248–249) points out that the major parts of coherent course design seem to have been, in effect, taken over by materials producers (i.e. writers and publishers). Needs analysis seems to have been replaced by publishers' market research (note that financial feasibility and profitability are the main driving forces), syllabus design is manifested as a course map devised by writers / publishers and selection of methodology is embodied in activities and instructions. The only influence actual material users (i.e. administrators, teachers and learners) have is through selection of a ready-made coursebook and / or through teachers' or learners' flexible use of it (e.g. adaptation, supplementation). As Forman (2014, p. 72) puts it, after reviewing the relevant literature, "For the majority of foreign language teachers and students across the globe, the textbook is the curriculum" (for confirmation, see Guerrettaz & Johnston, 2013; Garton & Graves, 2014; Richards, 2014). The division between materials producers and users creates a mismatch between the materials and the target users' needs and wants, their curriculum, syllabus and preferred methodology. At the moment, there is "geographical, cultural and linguistic distance between the producers of many coursebooks and the people who use them" (Tomlinson and Masuhara, 2010, p. 414). The bigger the distance the more likely the mismatch.

There is a crucial unanswered question here: who oversees the coherence and consistency of course design and curriculum implementation in terms of validity and reliability of language learning when there is a chasm between the material producers and users? In a traditional course design, materials were considered last as the result of educational deliberation, the present reality, however, is that materials exist first in the market regardless of the fit to the users' social contexts, curriculum, teachers' or learners' needs and wants. Guerrettaz and Johnston (2013), gained their carefully triangulated multiple data from a study of an intensive ESL grammar course at a mid-Western public university in the United States and demonstrate that class materials do constitute the primary source of the curriculum and also that "83% of the classroom discourse was related to the materials" (Guerrettaz & Johnston, 2013, p. 785)—with discourse being, of course, a potential major source of language acquisition and educational development. If such evidence was supported by more studies, the accountability of the coursebook-based curriculum would have to be scrutinized in terms of its educational validity and effectiveness.

Some users may take the initiative in making flexible use of coursebooks as resources in order to retain their control over teaching and learning (e.g. Gray, 2000; Wette, 2009; Bolster, 2014, 2015). In some countries, the ministry of education develops and provides the national textbooks and in other countries there is a strict authorization process so materials producers have to adhere strictly to guidelines (Mukundan, 2008; Richards, 2014; Loh & Renandya, 2016). But there are studies that show how teachers tend to revere the impressively produced commercial coursebooks by international publishers and rigidly use them as a script (Bacha, Ghosn, & McBeath, 2008). The Dogme argument (Thornbury, 2005; Meddings and Thornbury, 2009), in which Thornbury advocates the teachers' independence from ready-made coursebooks, could be described as an attempt to restore the broken link in course design and as teachers regaining the control over the whole process of ensuring effective teaching and learning.

Paradigm Shift 2: Global English for a Multiplicity of Cultures

The second paradigm shift behind the unprecedented need for adaptation is the surge of English as an international language (EIL) across the globe. Masuhara, Mishan, and Tomlinson (2017) collected 16 studies conducted by teachers and researchers on their materials evaluation, adaptation and development practice from 12 countries (i.e. Australia, Cyprus, Egypt, Hong Kong, Iran, Ireland, Italy, Lebanon, Oman, Russia, the United Kingdom, Vietnam). What these reports provide is startling evidence of how the global expansion of EIL and available technologies are resulting in a phenomenal diversity of teaching situations and learner needs (e.g. English for firefighter training in Vietnam; the use of social media and online resources in order to develop learner-generated materials in Italy). The ongoing advancement of technology seems to accelerate diversification of delivery modes of language learning—e.g. blended learning, M-learning, individualization of learning (Kern, 2013; Mishan, 2013; Tomlinson & Whittaker, 2013). Garton & Graves (2014) with 15 studies from nine countries also identify such tendencies in materials development.

What the adaptation studies in Garton and Graves (2014) and Masuhara et al. (2016) provide is plenty of evidence for the wide-ranging, complex and dynamic reality of teaching EIL and the teachers' efforts to adjust coursebooks for their learners by adaptation or to develop their own materials.

Graddol (2006) noted, "The new language which is rapidly ousting the language of Shakespeare as the world's lingua franca is English itself—English in its new global form." One of his future projections in 2006 included, "Native-speaker norms are becoming less relevant as English becomes a component of basic education in many countries." Pennycook (2010, p. 685) describes the current situation of English being used around the world as English as a "translingua franca" in which speakers from different localities negotiate meaning using the semiotic resources available to them at the time (see also Canagarajah, 2007). In this era of "world Englishes" (Kirkpatrick, 2010), the aura of the socio-economical, educational, cultural hegemony of the native speaker of English "inner circle" (as described in Kachru, 1992) seems to have faded somewhat for the learners who want to learn English as a basic skill to enhance advancement in their own environment for their global or local aspirations. See Saraceni (2015) for an insightful and provocative investigation of the impact of the increase in use and status of "world Englishes."

The production of a coursebook requires "a large investment of time, effort, and financial resources by authors and publishers" (Richards, 2014, p. 20). Amrani (2011, p. 271) explains from a publisher's point of view, "an error . . . for a publisher . . . is more likely to be a significant loss of venue and, potentially, jobs". The ELT coursebook market has become so global, diverse and dynamic that it would be a physical and economic impossibility for any materials producers to conduct market research (unless it is projected to be financially viable) or to even consider a new project for particular target users.

Shin, Eslami, & Chen (2011) analyzed seven series of internationally distributed ELT textbooks. Their study shows that even though cultural aspects were proportionally diverse in each textbook series, native speakers' cultural content and the ideologies underlying it still dominate most textbooks. They also found that cultural presentation still largely remains at the traditional knowledge-oriented level and does not engage learners in deep levels of reflection.

It is not difficult to find studies that report shortcomings of cultural representations in commercially available materials (e.g. Ghosn, 2013; Forman, 2014; Messekher, 2014; Ottley, 2014; Tasseron, 2017). Forman (2014), for example, describes how highly qualified and experienced Thai teachers felt uneasy using global coursebooks "published by Western companies which embrace Western values, are monolingual in English, and are marketed in non-Anglophone as well as Anglophone contexts" (Forman, 2014, p. 75) and gives an example:

> In terms of content, this particular textbook, in common with many others on the market, promotes various individualistic, aspirational, and Western discourses. In the episodes examined here, these included travelling, consuming, and complaining—all of which were not only largely irrelevant to Thai and presumably many other students' lives, but in some cases ran directly counter to cultural expectations. (Forman, 2014, p. 85)

Bell and Gower (1998; revised version 2011, p. 137) clarify from the materials writers' perspectives that the term "global coursebook" is misleading when it "really means a coursebook for a restricted number of teaching situations in many different countries rather than all teaching situations in all countries." They go on to explain what may lie behind the fierce arguments for and against the so-called "global coursebook: the all-singing, all-dancing, glitzy (expensive) multimedia package with a dedicated web site of extras, usually produced in a native-speaker situation but destined for the world with all the language in the book (including rubrics) in the target language" (Bell & Gower, p. 137).

Bell and Gower (2011) also show their full awareness of a potential cultural mismatch if the material written in one context is adopted inappropriately in another context by the decision makers and / or misused in practice. They therefore advocate flexible use through adaptation or supplementation to make the materials more appropriate for local contexts. Harmer (2001, p. 8) explains how coursebooks are intended to be used:

> coursebooks like any lesson plan . . ., are proposals for action, not instructions for use. Teachers look at these proposals and decide if they agree with them, if they

want to do things in the way the book suggests, or if, on the contrary, they are going to make changes, replacing things, modifying activities, approaching texts differently, or tackling a piece of grammar in a way which they, through experience know to be more effective . . . (Harmer, 2001, p. 8)

Richards (2014) emphasizes how materials producers are trying to be sensitive to cultural appropriacy:

textbooks today are much more culturally sensitive than their predecessors. Publishers and writers seek to ensure that their textbooks reflect progressive and politically acceptable values. Efforts are made to avoid social bias and ethnocentrism, and to reflect universal human concerns, needs, and values in their content. Often guidelines are provided for authors. Part of one publisher's guidelines suggests maintaining a 50–50 balance between the sexes: numerically and in terms of the significance and prominence of the activity illustrated; within schools and across the series, to aim for a gender-neutral style of illustration; to use illustrations that include all physical types, with occasional evidence of physical disability; and to avoid images with a stereotypical association. (Richards, 2014, p. 27)

An alternative approach to cultures is suggested by Benjamin (2015):

When used to describe EFL materials in the Middle East, the phrase "culturally appropriate" often means that the materials do not risk offending Islamic beliefs. However, Middle Eastern learners have other shared interests and activities, and are proud of their heritage and national treasures just as any other group of learners would be. In short, delivering culturally appropriate EFL classes to Muslims involves realising and embracing the fact that they enjoy a rich and diverse culture alongside Islam, and tapping in to the distinctive characteristics and activities that motivate Muslim learners and give them their desire to learn. (Benjamin, 2015, p. 30)

Ottley (2016) shares a similar positive view on cultural engagement and shares some concrete examples of how an outsider teacher like himself was able to offer valuable language support using culturally relevant adapted or developed materials through collaboration with his local students. Ghosn (2013) provides empirically supported arguments for using stories with universal themes to be incorporated into primary school materials to facilitate language acquisition in a meaningful and relevant way regardless of local cultures.

What is noteworthy is that local teachers are likely to have different views on materials with socioculturally or ideologically sensitive contents (e.g. Tasseron, 2017, from the Sultanate of Oman; Bosompen, 2014, from Ghana with multicultural, multiethnic, and multireligious contexts). Scotland (2014) discusses the conflict between the local culture and the Western teachers' cultures, which affected the teachers' professional identity in Qatar, and describes how these Western teachers took varied actions for resolution.

The gaps between commercial coursebooks and the realities of learning EIL in various parts of the globe seem to be one of the major reasons compelling the teachers consciously or subconsciously to adapt and or supplement commercially published materials or develop their own materials.

We strongly argue that adaptation should be given far more significance and support from authorities, teacher educators, researchers, curriculum developers and other stakeholders. It is promising, though, that there seems to be growing awareness of the pivotal role that materials play in various fields such as education, curriculum development, EIL, world Englishes, and cultural studies.

Who Does Adaptation?

A growing number of publications, conference presentations and some international teacher development courses (e.g. CELTA, DELTA) seem to focus on adaptation conducted by teachers. This probably is a reflection of the reality that teachers around the globe are striving daily to prepare and deliver appropriate teaching to multilevel students in their diverse situations.

Before we begin our exploration of teacher adaptation, it may be worth noting that there are cases in which other agents initiate or participate in adaptation. For example, Saraceni (2013) advocates providing learners with an important role in adapting materials and proposes ways of helping them to become able to do so. Such an approach seems to offer a more direct alternative way of incorporating learner needs and wants, bypassing the reported problems associated with needs analysis studies (e.g. learners' impressionistic, contradictory and often elliptical responses that are difficult for researchers to interpret). It is reassuring to see a gradually increasing number of publications on learner contributions to materials evaluation, adaptation, and development. For example, McGrath (2013) refers to some studies on Southeast Asian learners' reactions to being involved in developing materials or using learner-devised materials in his chapter on "learner perspectives." Cases of collaboration between learners and teacher-materials writers are reported in Jolly and Bolitho's (2011) account of how a group of materials writers trialed and adapted their materials incorporating learner feedback as part of the materials development process. Edwards and Burns (2015) show how their action research, incorporating students' needs and feedback when adapting assessment as well as materials, led to improvements in the curriculum of Australian English-language intensive courses for overseas students.

Other agents for adaptation could be materials writers, publishers, regional educational boards or ministries of education in various countries. Santos (2015) describes what led to the revision of her original coursebook and how she conducted its adaptation, supplementation and development (see also Feak & Swales, 2014). Both Amrani (2011) and Singapore Wala (2013) provide publishers' perspectives on how evaluation of manuscripts through trialing and feedback lead to publisher / writer adaptation during the production process. In our own experience of various materials development consultancies, some publishers use adaptation on a large scale. They request materials writers to produce a prototype English language teaching course for roughly specified target users (e.g. young adults in Spain) with an intention of adapting it for different regions later (López Barrios, & Villanueva de Debat, 2006, report such a case in Argentina). On an even larger scale, some ministries of education are interested in adapting an existing coursebook so that the content will be better suited for their cultures and their curriculums.

Overview of This Adaptation Chapter

We have been working with many teachers around the world through numerous materials development courses (e.g. MAs, short courses for national and international clients, including Ministries of Education), conferences and institutional, national and international consultancies. What we have found was that teachers seem to adapt their materials all the time before, during and after teaching in diverse contexts. What these teachers have told us includes that they:

- often feel the need to improve the given materials for their specific learners and contexts;
- feel frustrated as they tend to have little freedom, time, expertise or energy to adapt materials;
- have varied feelings and attitudes toward their own adapted materials according to their beliefs, confidence and teaching experience;
- do not seem to be able to find a lot of publications on adaptation;
- have not been given much training, if at all, in adaptation;
- fear that by adapting existing materials they may be interfering with the coherence of courses which, they believe, have been carefully prepared by experts, endorsed by the authorities and presented to students and parents.

Do teachers adapt materials? Why do teachers adapt / not adapt materials? What do teachers adapt materials for? How do they go about adaptation? How do we know that their adaptations are valid and effective? What kinds of resources on adaptation are available?

In this chapter we will explore these questions by critically evaluating the literature, including the growing number of empirical research studies on teacher use of materials. We will consider issues and try to identify principles and systematic procedures for materials adaptation. Lastly, we will provide some examples of adaptation that we believe to be principled, effective and verifiable.

What the Literature Tells Us about Materials Adaptation

In this chapter, we have taken a different approach in exploring adaptation compared to the existing literature, which mainly focuses on the principles and procedures of adaptation (e.g. McGrath, 2002, 2013, 2016; McDonough, Shaw, & Masuhara, 2013; Tomlinson, 2013b; Mishan & Timmis, 2015). All the books above are based on the authors' rich experience of working with teachers and researchers and they are very valuable resources. Our decision reflects the recent call for making more systematic exploration of research that investigates teacher adaptation of materials.

In selecting samples of teacher adaptation research, we have consulted the most recent and the most cited publications on materials development (e.g. Tomlinson, 1998, 2003, 2008, 2011, 2013a, 2013b, 2016; McGrath, 2002, 2013, 2016; Gray, 2010, 2013; Harwood, 2010, 2014; Tomlinson & Masuhara, 2010; McDonough et al., 2013; Garton & Graves,

2014; Mishan & Timmis, 2015). We have also conducted journal surveys using large databases (e.g. EBSCO host) and we have searched past issues of *Folio* (the Journal of the Materials Development Association), the *IATEFL Materials Writers' Special Interest Group Newsletter*, and the *Humanistic Language Teaching* magazines archives. In our search for studies focusing on adaptation, we have reconfirmed that:

> Teachers are ultimately in a crucial position in language teaching and learning because they are the ones that realize curricula, syllabuses, methodology and materials in classrooms. Teachers play central roles in materials development— for they are the ones who select materials (or, at least, have some influence in the selection process) who actually teach the materials and who adapt and develop materials. (Masuhara, 2011, p. 238).

Adaptation is part of what a teacher does in and out of classroom and the literature on materials adaptation so far has tended to discuss what are considered to be principles and procedures of adaptation such as deletion, addition, reduction, modification, replacement etc. (e.g. Cunningsworth, 1985; McGrath, 2002; Islam & Mares, 2003; McDonough et al., 2013) but which we would now prefer to refer to as techniques. However, we have realized that adaptation also has wider implications for overall curriculum development and implementation. There is cross-sectional and interdisciplinary potential between materials development studies and those of teachers' practice in classrooms in curriculum development and teacher education (Harwood, 2014, p. 195 refers to rich research resources in "main stream education" in nonlanguage subjects). Though the focus is more on curriculum realization, the relationship between materials and the teacher is being explored in recent studies (Wette, 2009; Shawer, 2010; Guerrettaz & Johnston, 2013). We also see the studies of teacher beliefs and of teacher education as very relevant when we discuss why and how teachers adapt materials.

We have tried to mainly select very recent classroom empirical studies on adaptation and teacher use at different levels in different regions of the world (see McGrath, 2013, for other reviews). Through our review, we intend to extract some universal issues that emerge from specific contemporary adaptation studies in different contexts. By doing so, we aim to evaluate the existing literature on adaptation so as to make further attempts in establishing links between practice and research regarding materials adaptation.

Do Teachers Actually Adapt Teaching Materials?

What do teachers actually do with their materials? We will look at adaptation studies conducted at university (Studies 1–6), secondary school (Study 7) and primary school (Study 8) levels.

Study 1: Shawer (2010)—A Research Study Conducted in Colleges in the United States

Shawer studied the adaptation practices of 10 experienced (3 to 20 years) native teachers who teach English to international students in three colleges in the United States. His research methods include pre-observation and post-observation interviews (3–10 minutes per session), observations (9–26 times per teacher), general and group interviews (65–95 minutes), matching of teacher planning, actual teaching and student input.

Shawer, based on his analyses of multiple data, identifies three categories of teachers according to the degree of adherence to the curriculum materials (i.e. textbooks, workbooks and teachers' guides in addition to any software and audio-visual materials). The first are "curriculum makers," who conduct needs assessment, select topics, and organize content. They use multisources rather than a single textbook and create a lot of their own materials, though they may occasionally make use of some topics or activities from textbooks as resources. The description of "curriculum makers" reminds us of Thornbury's Dogme arguments (Thornbury, 2005) in which he advocates teachers' independence from coursebooks. "Curriculum developers" adapt textbooks to make them appropriate for their students. If they think the textbooks are not satisfactory they subtract or supplement by using their own materials but not so extensively as curriculum makers. "Curriculum transmitters" rely solely on curriculum materials, unit by unit, page by page exactly as the guide instructs.

Out of 10 teachers in Shawer's study, five of them were curriculum makers, three of them, curriculum developers and two curriculum transmitters.

What surprised us in this study is that, contrary to wide beliefs, experience, gender and institutional control did not seem to affect how much these English as L1 teachers adhere to the curriculum (see the participant demographics on p. 177 of Shawer, 2010). For example, the two curriculum-transmitters (one male, one female) were textbook-bound even though they had "good training and experience" (Shawer, 2010, p. 182) and had freedom regarding the use of the textbook compared with the curriculum makers or developers who worked in "a context that imposed restrictions through prescribing and strictly monitoring the teaching of a textbook" (Shawer, 2010, p. 177).

Study 2: Grammatosi and Harwood (2014)—A University in the United Kingdom

A carefully designed case study with triangulation of multiple data (10 × 50-minute observations, pre-observation and post-observation interviews and artefact analyses of lesson plans and the teacher's own materials). The English as L1 speaker teacher in focus is experienced and qualified (12 years with overseas experience and CELTA) and teaches a presessional EAP course in a language center in a university in the United Kingdom. This study offers how a particular teacher plans his lessons through use / nonuse of the commercial ELT textbook chosen by the director and what factors affect his decisions.

In this study, the teacher might be categorized as a potential "curriculum maker" in Shawer's term. This teacher describes his normal self, however, as more of a "curriculum developer" and explains that he had to compensate more due to the mismatch between the coursebook that the Director assigned to him against his wishes and what he wanted to use.

This case reminds us that teachers may have teaching style preferences but may take different approaches and strategies depending on the situation (e.g. mandated textbook, students' level, the teacher's perceived learner preferences, the teacher's repertoire).

Study 3: Guerrettaz and Johnston (2013)—A University in the United States

> This a methodologically rigorous and informative case study that investigates how an L1 teacher uses a popular commercial grammar textbook (i.e. *Understanding and using English grammar* by Azar, 2001) in an ESL advanced class as a part of a university intensive course in the United States. Multiple data sources included observation (approximately 14 hours, twice weekly throughout the seven weeks of class), artefacts analyses (e.g. textbook, syllabus, attendance, daily plans, quizzes and tests offered by the textbook, all documents from the course web site, materials, assignments), transcripts of audio-recordings of classes, interviews, and focus groups, as well as analysis of the classroom discourse focused around these activities.

The analyses revealed that materials played a central role in the curriculum, classroom discourse, and language learning: "The materials constituted the primary source for the organization of curriculum, including the nature and sequence of content" (Guerrettaz and Johnston, 2013, p. 792). The various data seemed to provide convincing evidence that the textbook was accepted by the teacher and the learners as "an arbiter of validity" (Guerrettaz and Johnston, 2013, p. 784) and "the textbook alone constitutes the legitimate curriculum" and "a sense of semilegitimacy about the supplementary materials". The teacher's use of quizzes and tests provided by the textbook "had a strong bearing on the learning goals, which further increased the importance of the materials in the classroom ecology" (Guerrettaz and Johnston, 2013, p. 785).

This teacher is likely to be categorized as a "curriculum transmitter" in Shawer's term. Just like the two curriculum transmitters in Shawer's (2010) Study 1, this native speaker teacher in Study 3 was aware of the options of adaptation and supplementation based on many years of teaching experience. A note of caution is required here, however, as this Study 3 was conducted when it was this teacher's first time to use the textbook. He may have let the grammar textbook with a reputation function as the curriculum in this study but he might decide to add his own materials next time, thus becoming a curriculum developer.

In general, the classroom discourse data revealed a tendency in which controlled grammar activities resulted in "impoverished" (p. 787) teacher–learner exchanges whereas more open-ended activities led to more meaningful learner exchanges and class discussions (there are similar results in various studies in Ghosn, 2013). Occasionally there were moments when the teacher and the learners had relaxed, resulting in lively and meaningful interactions (e.g. Extract 2 and Extract 4). Guerrettaz and Johnston (2013, p. 788) note that "richer language use arose when the affordances offered by the materials provided learners with opportunities to relate them to their own lives and experiences, or allowed them to bring their specific language learning concerns to the table." Such interactions are the kind that is described to facilitate the learners' linguistic development in the SLA literature (Ellis, 2016). Such classroom interactions, however, were incidental on two accounts: the textbook activities were not intentionally designed to induce such interactions; the teacher did not plan such interaction, either—though he did let the conversation develop, perhaps more from genuine human interest, than pedagogic intent.

What does this case study of one teacher tell us about adaptation? Let us reflect upon Guerrettaz and Johnston's (2013) case study in Study 3 from the perspective of adaptation:

1. How much and how often did the textbook provide genuine language acquisition and development opportunities (like Extract 4) in relation to grammar use and recognition (i.e. the purpose of the grammar class)?
2. Why did the teacher let the textbook function as the grammar curriculum in his attempt to achieve the purpose of his class?
3. Why did the teacher use the quizzes and tests provided in the textbook as the tools to assess learner achievement?
4. Did the learners develop the ability to use and recognize grammar?

Question 1 above relates to the issue of effectiveness of a textbook and of validity of a textbook becoming the curriculum (see our arguments earlier in this chapter on the growing significance of adaptation). Question 2 above brings forth the issue of teachers' responsibility and accountability, knowledge, beliefs, and skills as a curriculum mediator and realizer. Question 3 reminds us of the power of assessment and its washback on teaching and learning. Question 4 is an issue of effectiveness of materials in teaching and learning—the ultimate target of language learning materials development and curriculum implementation.

As regards issue 1 (i.e. the effectiveness of a textbook and the validity of a textbook becoming the curriculum), the data did not provide strong support for the textbook activities leading to lively classroom interactions as recommended in SLA literature. By using the accompanying quizzes and exam as the targets (issue 3, i.e. the power of assessment and its washback on teaching and learning), this experienced L1 teacher seemed to have let the textbook determine the syllabus, sequence and pace (issue 2, i.e. teachers' responsibility and accountability, knowledge, beliefs and skills as curriculum mediator and realizer). Can we equate the learners' high scores in the textbook quizzes and exam with fulfilment of the purpose of the course—i.e. "to promote students' ability to use and recognize grammatical structures" (p. 783)? In other words, have the 18 adult students (age 19–44) learned the kinds of grammar knowledge and skills that will enable them to advance in their American University degree studies as a result of attending this course with "fifty minutes a day, five days a week, for seven weeks" (p. 783)?

Ultimately, one of the major aims of a language teaching curriculum is to facilitate the language acquisition and development that the learners have invested their time and money in. Adaptation is a way in which teachers as curriculum implementers can ensure that materials contribute in fulfilling this target. We asked one fundamental question earlier in this chapter: Who oversees the coherence and consistency of course design and curriculum implementation in terms of the validity and reliability of language learning when there is a chasm between the material producers and users? This Guerrettaz and Johnston (2013) case study demonstrates how significant a role a textbook can play, "reaching into every major aspect of classroom life" (p. 792), alerting us to the fact that the responsibility for valid learning and teaching rests not only with teachers but also with materials developers, administrators, curriculum developers and policy makers.

Study 4: Bolster (2014 and 2015)—A Branch of a UK University in China

This study involves 18 experienced (5–30 years) and well qualified (78% MA holders); professional certificates including CELTA, DELTA, PGCE) native / near native EAP teachers in a foundation year program at the overseas branch campus of the University of Nottingham Ningbo, China (UNNC). One of the research questions is whether experienced teachers adapt published materials and, if so, to what extent?

The analysis of the pre-lesson questionnaire, which asks about teachers' plans, reveals that all of the teachers expressed their intention of adaptation to varying degrees. The highest scorer in terms of adaptation among the 18 teachers would make changes to all the 8 activities (100%) whereas the least would make 25% changes. "The mean and median of how much teachers adapted were 64.5 and 62.5% respectively" (Bolster, 2015, p. 17). Most teachers in this study seem to be "Curriculum Developers" in Shawer's (2010 see Study 1 above) term.

The teachers' attitude toward the coursebook was generally positive—"Most teachers appreciate having a core textbook to give them guidance and save them some lesson preparation time." They also seem to support the weak anticoursebook viewpoint summarized in Harwood (2005) in that they are critical but appreciate the textbook as a provider of structure and reference for the learners and they believe that the coursebook "syllabus should be flexible enough to allow the local teacher to input additional locally appropriate content" (p. 154).

Bolster's (2014 and 2015) study provides insights into experienced teachers' adaptation approaches and their rationales. She provides very interesting discussions on which activities attract more adaptation and on how a coursebook could offer a system for flexibility for localization and personalization.

Study 5: Tasseron (2017)—University in the Sultanate of Oman

This study, which focuses on how teachers use *New cutting edge elementary and pre-intermediate*, took place in a college in the Sultanate of Oman with 95 teachers from various countries including Oman, several Middle Eastern countries, India, Pakistan, the Philippines, the United Kingdom, Canada, South Africa, and the United States. Tasseron used a 44-item questionnaire (return rate 32%) on the grammar sections in the coursebook, observation (one session each for six lecturers), semistructured interviews with five out of the observed six lecturers and materials evaluation. His choice of these components is because of the importance given in the Middle East to prescriptive grammar.

Tasseron reports that most teachers claimed that they used the grammar components consistently and adhered closely to the coursebook script in their lessons. In observations and interviews with six lecturers, however, he found that lecturers made consistent use of additional materials such as worksheets they had prepared and grammar practice activities in conjunction with the coursebook. The lecturers said that they wanted to provide their learners with additional opportunities to practice what had been taught, adding variation to the lessons and providing content more relevant to the Omani context. It was noteworthy that in responses to cultural content in the global ELT coursebooks, the teachers' views ranged from open minded to censorious.

Study 6: Bosompem (2014)—A University in Ghana

This study took place in a Ghanaian government-run tertiary institution on the theme of "how teachers adapt materials, their rationale and their attitudes towards the practice" (p. 108). It involved altogether 16 teachers with university degrees and with or without formal teacher training (which is not compulsory in Ghana). Twelve of those who responded to the questionnaire had teaching experience ranging from 6.5 months to 10 years. Four interviewees had teaching experience of 2–7 years.

Bosompem provides the background information to situate her study. In Ghana, English is an official language and the medium of instruction in schools, reflecting the country's awareness that " the effectiveness of English language teaching, learning, and use determines whether the country's education will succeed or fail" (Bosompem, 2014, p. 104). The "textbook assumes a pivotal role in English language education" (p. 104) as there is "limited opportunities to encounter authentic spoken or written materials" (p. 104). "Although the classroom teacher is the direct user of the books, selection usually goes beyond them to involve the Ministry of Education, institutional and departmental heads, and even fellow teachers" (p. 105).

Did Ghanaian teachers adapt their textbooks? Bosompem found out that 10 out of 12 teachers had positive attitudes to teacher adaptation, acknowledging that it is inevitable due to the diversity of teaching contexts (e.g. students' reading ability). "Nine teachers endorsed adaptation as a legitimate teaching practice that needs no authorisation and nine encouraged teachers to do it with confidence" (p. 110).

It is noteworthy that the teachers' accounts of their practice, Bosompem found out, were not always in line with their attitudes to adaptation. For example, three teachers respectively with 6.5 months, 2 years and more than 10 years of teaching experience said, "they never intentionally made changes to the content of the textbook." The two teachers thought the textbook (written by Ghanaians and Nigerians) was appropriate and therefore needed no adaptation. One of the alleged nonadapters with more than 10 years of experience, however, did say in another part of the questionnaire, "he would 'leave the contents as they are but look for addition elsewhere to supplement'. This may imply that he is not aware that supplementation is a form of adaptation" (Bosompen, 2014, p. 110).

Bosompem's study (2014) provides insights into some teachers' reluctance to adapt, which is a significant issue and yet has been overlooked in the literature. An interviewee with three years of teaching experience explains the reason behind his reservation: "the absence of a formal directive by the school authorities". As part of the school's mentoring scheme, he had observed his mentor teacher adapting the textbook. But, as no one officially authorized making changes to the textbook when necessary, he felt that adaptation was for experienced teachers only. Another interviewee with 2 years of experience said that understudying is different from being coached about materials adaptation. Without training on adaptation she lacked confidence and felt apprehensive about the possible negative outcomes of her adaptations on her lessons and her students. Another interviewee with 7 years of experience recalled that he "not only feared making changes at the initial stages of his teaching career," but "also felt guilty challenging the authority of the book writers and that of the leaders who gave me the books for my lessons" (p. 112).

Adaptation seems to be associated with a feeling of "semi-illegitimacy" as it "deviates" (the words used by an experienced L1 teacher in the United States in Guerrettaz & Johnston, 2013, p. 785) from the mandated textbook that in many cases somebody in authority has selected. Shawer (2010, pp. 174–175) discusses "curriculum fidelity" studies at length. He says that the top-down "transmission model promotes neither the interaction between prior and new knowledge nor the conversations that are necessary for internalization and deep understanding." He describes a more recent "curriculum development" model in which local needs and wants are recognized and the positive role of adaptation is acknowledged. He also explains about "curriculum enactment" in which teachers and learners jointly create a process curriculum—a more constructivist approach (see Wette, 2009, for an example of ESOL courses in New Zealand).

The ambivalent feeling surrounding adaptation may also come from the nonpolitical and common place practice of standardization between the teaching team or, more significantly, having to cover the syllabus content in time for an exam. The students, parents and school authorities could reprimand teachers if exam results were not as high as expected as a result of "deviation." Such an undercurrent seems to exist to varying degrees in the six studies above and is probably applicable to the majority of educational institutes regardless of the kind (e.g. secondary schools, foundation course in universities, language schools) or countries. The seeming contradiction between responses in questionnaires and in interviews noted in Bosompen (2014) and Tasseron (2017) may be that teachers may feel obliged to publically proclaim or be seen to observe adherence to the coursebooks. It is possible that teachers may be adapting consciously or inadvertently by, for example, adding, deleting and supplementing out of concern for the students based on their perceptions of their students' level, interests and sociocultural contexts. Or it could be that teachers may prefer to adhere very closely to the coursebook as nonadaptation is a safer option. They would not like to offend their employers or inspectors. They tend to have a heavy teaching and marking workload, to teach large classes and to lack formal teacher education and confidence in the target language. Their reverence towards coursebooks (e.g. Zacharias, 2005) may not be a blind one but it may be the result of not having strong alternatives that seem to be preferable in content, appearance and availability.

If we consider adaptation as part of curriculum realization, it becomes an issue for governments, local educations and institutions as well as for teachers. Mukundan (2008) explains how school coursebooks are developed and distributed by the government in Malaysia. They are designed to carry an agenda fostering nationhood, citizenship and good values. The problem is, Mukundan (2008, p. 19) points out, that the adolescent learners may not feel fully engaged with the constant diet of these government ideals embodied in specially written dialogues and texts. This situation creates a dilemma among the teachers between their conflicting duties as curriculum mediators who deliver government messages and as facilitators of language acquisition, which requires learner engagement and motivation. The former duty as a messenger discourages adaptation but the latter requires adaptation. From the government point of view, officials may feel apprehensive about publically authorizing adaptation by the teachers without reassurance of the state agenda being disseminated. The teachers are left with a dilemma.

One teacher in Bosompem (2014, p. 111) suggests "a sensitisation programme to educate novice and newly employed teachers on how to use and adapt materials." He also proposes that such teachers should be specifically made aware that adaptation is a legitimate and integral part of language teaching and so does not need any authorisation." Bouckaert (2015) and Yan (2007) argue for the value of including materials evaluation, adaptation and development as part of preservice training. We will discuss teacher education after we look at the next study.

Study 7: Abdel Latif (2017)—Secondary Schools in Egypt

This study investigates how grammar teaching materials (i.e. *Hello! English for secondary schools* by Haines and Dallas, 2008) are used in the classroom and what teachers' beliefs lie behind such use. It was conducted in six general secondary schools in Greater Cairo in Egypt involving 12 Egyptian female (n = 5) and male (n = 7) teachers with varied teaching experience (10–30 years). All the teachers had a BA degree in either English language teaching or English literature and linguistics. The methods include classroom observation (two classes per teacher; naturalistic observation; audio-taped recordings; field notes) and semistructured interviews (the teachers' views on the materials, their attitudes towards teaching each type of activity, the rationale for their beliefs, attitudes and grammar teaching practices, and their conceptions of good grammar teaching materials). The classroom observation data was analyzed in terms of the time the teachers allocated to teaching grammar using the textbook materials as well as the frequencies of the textbook grammar activity types they taught.

The analyses of the observation data revealed that firstly the teachers spent a much longer time (68.3% of a class period) on grammar explanations on the board than the time taken working with the textbook grammar activities (31.7% of all the activities). The data seem to provide evidence that the 12 teachers preferred to teach grammar using their own instructional scenarios and self-designed activities rather than using textbook materials. Secondly, according to the analyses of frequency of grammar activities taught, the 12 teachers omitted nearly half of the textbook grammar activities. The teachers tended to neglect the main inductive and communicative activities. The interview data revealed two influential factors: teachers' beliefs on what should be taught in English lessons and how it should be taught, and examination washback. Those teachers seemed to independently agree that good grammar teaching materials should:

- be well organized and present grammar deductively;
- add to students' grammar knowledge in a concrete way;
- foster the teacher's active role.

Abdel Latif (2017) noticed a strong washback effect of the examination. The lack of an oral component in their examination system meant that teachers paid more attention to grammar teaching than to oral communicative activities. The teachers favored the workbook more than the student book as the former provided more grammar controlled activities that match the final-year examination papers.

Four major issues seem to emerge from this study: teacher beliefs, material and its use, exam washback and teacher education. In both Tasseron's study in an Omani College (see Study 5 above) and Abdel Latif's studies in Egyptian secondary schools (Study 7), the dominant teachers' approach seems to be teaching explicit knowledge in a deductive way and setting grammar practice as homework. A similar phenomenon is reported across Middle Eastern and Gulf countries (e.g. Al-Issa, 2007; Bacha et al., 2008). The teachers in both studies 5 and 7 above blame the exams as one of the major reasons. The coursebooks used in both studies, on the other hand, claim to offer a multi-syllabus including communication skills as well as language work. The teachers in both studies seem to value the grammar sections of student books and make even fuller use of workbooks that offer explicit practice of taught grammar items.

There seem to be mismatches between the teacher practice (and examination systems) in Study 5 and Study 7 and their respective nation's preferred directions in official documents, course materials and language learning theories.

Euromonitor International compiled a report for the British Council on "The Benefits of the English Language for Individuals and Societies: Quantitative Indicators from Algeria, Egypt, Iraq, Jordan, Lebanon, Morocco, Tunisia and Yemen" (Euromonitor International, 2012). According to the report:

> Although each of them has distinctive geographical and cultural differences, they are all seeking to develop their economies and create better living standards and improved social conditions for their inhabitants. One of the most important ways they are trying to achieve this is through the improvement of English language skills at all levels. Each of the governments regard this as an essential part of achieving growth, by giving domestic companies a competitive edge in the global economy as well as attracting investment from abroad. (Euromonitor International, 2012, p. 8)

The report continues to describe the aspirations of the younger generations in relation to English language learning (Euromonitor International, 2012):

> The English language is set to become even more popular in the long term across the region due to increased interest from the younger population in particular. Most young people in the region have a very clear understanding of the importance of English proficiency and its role in helping them to gain employment with multinational companies either within their country or abroad, with employment in international economic hubs such as the United Arab Emirates a typical target. Private language training centres play a central role in helping these individuals improve their English language skills. (Euromonitor International, 2012, p. 8)

The report (Euromonitor International, 2012), based on their quantitative research data, explains that:

> one of the primary reasons this group [younger population] wish to improve their English skills is to more actively immerse themselves in online social networking, which is primarily conducted in English. A strong level of English is also seen as essential in order to access the best higher education opportunities and ultimately enhance career prospects. (Euromonitor International, 2012, pp. 8–9)

In the case of Oman, Al-Issa (2007, p. 200) explains that "…people in Oman learn English for communicative purposes and that functional knowledge of English is important for travelling, pursuing higher education, finding a white-collar job, science and technology acquisition and cultural analysis and understanding". He then quotes Al-Balushi (1999: 4) who describes the current teaching practice in that "teaching methodology still tends to be very formal and emphasizes a largely passive role for students with an emphasis on rote learning" (Al-Issa, 2007, p. 201).

We wonder if the policy makers, institutions and teachers are aware of the discrepancy between what this report says and the reality of ELT in their countries? We also wonder what the learners' views about it are.

Regarding materials, Tasseron (2017) in Study 5 conducted an evaluation of course-books and found that the content and approaches of a global course do not seem to accord with current SLA literature (see concise summaries of current SLA thinking in Ellis, 2016, p. 204 and in Tomlinson, 2013a, pp. 11–29).

On the topic of material use, Graves and Garton (2014, p. 275) speculate that "the effective use of materials depends on the teacher's understanding of the materials, on the fit with their beliefs, expertise, and experience, and on their ability to adapt the materials to their particular learners." The 12 Egyptian secondary school teachers in Abdel Latif (2017) may have 10–30 years of experience but seem short of expertise in terms of being aware of the directions of ELT in their own country. They might benefit from teacher development systems in which they are given opportunities to reflect on their own practice in the light of relevant and up-to-date SLA theories. The selector of the materials as well as the teachers would benefit from experiencing materials analysis, evaluation, adaptation and development so that they would be able to understand the reasoning behind materials in relation to theories and make appropriate adaptations.

In the next study, washback from exams comes up again in relation to teacher use and adaptation of materials.

Study 8: Loh and Renandya (2016)—Primary Schools in Singapore

This research investigates the perceptions and practices of EL teachers under Strategies for English Language Learning and Reading (STELLAR), a national literacy reform program, which is the most comprehensive and extensive literacy reform that affects all six levels in the primary education sector in 49 years since Singaporean independence in 1965.

Loh and Renandya provide background information for this curricular innovation. They provide various official documents both in hard copies and online that show the government view that English should be given the utmost importance to ensure the economic survival of Singapore and that they consider English to be the language of business, science, diplomacy and academia. The primary aims of the STELLAR program are to strengthen the primary students' oral language, grammar and reading skills—"through an employment and a structured combination of research-based teaching strategies, the STELLAR program advanced a systematic way of bringing together a vast array of teaching approaches and strategies in the language curriculum" (Loh & Renandya, 2016, p. 96). The approaches include shared reading; the text-driven approach; the language experience approach; sustained silent reading; a writing process cycle. There were a lot of

supporting systems for teachers and schools such as professional development opportunities, mentor allocation in each school, as well as STELLAR funding for resourcing necessary materials in all the schools.

This research was conducted with methodological rigor. Purposeful sampling was
used to select the two schools (namely: Singa School and Pura School), the former out
of 134 government schools and the latter out of 41 government-aided schools (Ministry of Education, 2015). The government schools were established in the mid-1990s
whereas the government aided schools are so called "branded schools," originally established in the 1940s to educate children from Chinese clans, well funded and resourced
with track records of numerous awards to acknowledge academic and sporting
excellence.

The teachers in the two sampled schools were carefully matched in terms of number,
gender, age, experience and three ethnic groups (Chinese, Malay and Indian).

The research methods: 1st stage: questionnaire; 2nd stage: observations of the two
teachers from each school (25 lessons in Singa Primary school; 21 lessons in Pura Primary School), artefact analyses (for two units of the school's EL curriculum i.e. lesson
plans, teaching resources, school-based curriculum plans, school worksheets, teacher-
prepared worksheets), and two rounds of semistructured interviews (transcribed and
checked), based on the lesson observations and artefact analysis. The questionnaire
investigated firstly perceptions of adequacy of the materials and resources and secondly
teachers' practice in terms of how the teachers adapted the materials.

The data revealed a high satisfaction rate for the materials and the implementation support materials (high 70–80%) in both schools. The teachers in both schools also appreciated that the STELLAR program was flexible rather than restrictive.

> More than 90% of the teachers in both schools view adaptations as crucial for
> the acceptance and efficacy of the curriculum. Teachers in both schools make
> adaptations to both the methods recommended and the materials given, so as
> to meet the needs of the diverse learners in their classrooms. (Loh & Renandya,
> 2016, p. 107)

Loh and Renandya (2016) did find that there were distinctive differences between the
two schools in terms of approaches to adaptation. Singa (the government school) teachers were actively involved with the new program. They added and expanded the materials to enhance their effects and add innovative elements to the original materials. The
teachers in Pura (the government-aided school), on the other hand, were restricted in
their use of the STELLAR materials as the school had its own parallel exam preparation syllabus and the teachers had to manage and complete both the national (i.e. the
STELLAR) and school-based curricular requirements. Clearly, exam washback affected
the Pura teachers.

We discussed earlier why some teachers might feel guilty toward adaptation in relation
to Bosompem (2014) in Study 6. We also considered the perspectives of curriculum
planners, administrators and institutions that expect curriculum fidelity for the sake
of quality assurance and standardization. There is a dynamic tension between teacher
adaptation and curriculum implementation.

Loh and Renandya (2016) argue that:

> Making adjustments or changes to the curriculum should not be viewed as a deficiency, nor should it be treated as taboo. When teachers make adaptations to the guidelines or materials, in general, they do so because they want to optimize the learning experience of their pupils (Loh and Renandya, 2016, pp. 106–107)

How do curriculum planners, administrators and institutions know that teachers are making valid adaptations that enact the curriculum? In Tasseron (2017) Study 5 and in Abdel Latif (2017) Study 7, teachers' strong beliefs about direct grammar teaching for the exam overruled learning theories or national objectives. Loh and Renandya emphasize the importance of teacher education:

> Should we not then ensure that teachers are equipped to make adaptations in a principled way, rather than a haphazard way? Hence, in-service professional development activities should include courses to guide teachers to "reflect upon their own practice and identify principles and systematic procedures for materials adaptation" (Tomlinson & Masuhara, 2004, p. 11). With teachers having a better understanding of what goes into the considerations of materials adaptation, curriculum planners would then be more amenable and accepting of their curriculum being adjusted and modified by teachers. (Loh & Renandya, 2016, p. 107)

Adaptation is a way in which teachers transmit, develop and make curricula. It would be in the interest of both the authorities and the teachers for resources and professional development to be provided to facilitate teacher adaptation.

Any curriculum reform or innovation requires careful implementation plans. Top-down, one-way imposition tends to cause a lot of confusion, damage and resistance and there is a lot of literature on this (e.g. see McDonough et al., 2013, Chapters 1 and 11 regarding the debate for and against communicative language teaching; Craig, 2006 and Menken, 2008 for cases in the United States; Loh, 2010 for primary reform in Singapore). Bosompen (2014) reports that:

> Some Ghanaian teachers, particularly in rural areas, have actually rejected textbooks prescribed by school authorities because "the books were not aligned with the children's reading ability" . . . and "the teachers did not have the skills to adapt the books to the children's skill levels". The teachers reverted to writing on the chalkboard since that was the medium of reading and writing familiar to them. (Bosompen, 2014, p. 105)

Loh and Renandya (2016) recall a very similar case in relation to the previous Singaporean government initiative in 2001:

> changes will occur in any implementation, due to the fact that implementers are humans with different sets of beliefs and experiences. This was what happened when the MOE implemented the EL syllabus 2001—the teachers' "expertise and ability to work with the new curriculum was not sufficiently considered," and

hence, they "reinterpreted the curriculum based on their own previous teaching experiences and their understandings of their students' needs" (Christison & Murray, 2014, p. 55). Teachers as the main stakeholders of curriculum change implementation must be engaged during implementation, because they are the ones who will enact the curriculum. (Loh & Renandya, 2016, p. 106)

Loh and Renandya inform us how the Singaporean government's new primary STELLAR program is accompanied by an in-service professional development scheme and by countrywide mentoring and grouping support systems, which are more interactive, not top-down, rigid or evaluative. The ongoing evaluation of the 6-year implementation of the new program so far seems to indicate positive changes taking place with innovative adaptations that enhance the STELLAR principles.

Adaptation—Practice and Theory

At the beginning of the chapter we asked various questions. We will now consider each of them in the light of existing literature and of the eight teacher adaptation studies.

Do Teachers Adapt Materials? Is Adaptation Necessary?

McGrath (2013), based on his literature survey, summarized that textbook writers, teacher educators and other commentators all recommend that teachers adapt materials, be they given materials or self-sourced ones. Ur (2015), on the other hand, states on the basis of her teaching career that coursebooks, especially tailor-made ones, tend to be well written if they are developed by experienced writers. She argues that such coursebooks are convenient and time saving for busy teachers, can facilitate teachers' professional development, and allow teachers' creativity to emerge, and therefore do not require extensive adaptation. She proposes a set of "generic" techniques that she thinks help teachers make small and practical adaptation of prescribed coursebooks.

Studies 1–8 in this chapter have revealed that most, if not all, of the teachers do feel the urge to adapt and some go ahead while some hesitate or choose not to adapt. Study 8 by Loh and Renandya (2016) shows that more than 90% of the teachers considered adaptations to be crucial to make the materials suit the learners, the context and their beliefs even though the given materials were tailor made, well informed and well written.

We argued earlier in this chapter that adaptation has become even more necessary because of the role divisions between commercial coursebook producers and users. The spread of global English as a lingua franca has made adaptation even more significant and necessary. As seen in the reviewed studies 4–8 respectively from China, Oman, Ghana, Egypt and Singapore, English is considered as one of the basic skills like literacy—a key to survival in global commerce, science, technology and academia. Such a view is motivating learners from various countries to go to study in the United States, in Australia, in New Zealand and in the United Kingdom as in Studies 1, 2 and 3.

Study 3 (Guerrettaz & Johnston, 2013) provides concrete evidence that the coursebook IS functioning as the curriculum and is controlling learning, teaching and assessment. Such a phenomenon, if confirmed in other studies, has considerable implications for researchers and for all the stakeholders of curriculum development (e.g. policy makers, institutions, teachers, assessors, teacher developers, learners, family, society). The validity and effectiveness of the selected coursebook is crucial (See Chapter 3 "Evaluation" in this book). How teachers use it and their expertise are even more so: i.e. teachers' responsibility and accountability, knowledge, beliefs, and skills as curriculum mediators and realizers. The power of assessment and its washback on teaching and learning has been discussed widely in the literature and yet Studies 3, 5, 7 and 8 clearly indicate that the same problems exist: the curriculum goal has been reduced to achieving pass scores in exams rather than achieving linguistic, strategic, and educational targets. The exam backwash would be fine if there were coherence between assessment, learning and teaching in relation to global English as a means of communication as is indicated in official documents. Judging from the teachers' accounts in the Studies 3, 5 and 7, their quizzes or exams require mainly discrete grammar knowledge with some reading and writing skills.

Why Do Teachers Adapt Materials? What For?—The Reason and Purpose of Adaptation

"Why do teachers adapt materials? It all starts with the teacher intuitively feeling. 'Mmm, something is not quite right'" (Tomlinson and Masuhara, 2004, p. 12). Such a feeling may have been sparked off by the students' reactions or lack of reactions when the teacher started a new unit. What is the reason (i.e. why)? The students are feeling sleepy after lunch on a hot day? Could it be the topic of the unit is irrelevant to the students' lives? The text is not engaging? The activities in the textbook are too mechanical to be cognitively challenging? All these are possible reasons for adaptation.

So the teacher may decide on the spot to add an anecdote about a student to personalize and to localize the topic. She could replace the one-word gap-filling activity in the text with an open-ended completion task so that the students could creatively write what the heroine or hero is going to say next and develop the story. The teacher's adaptation here has purposes (i.e. what for?) such as making the topic relevant through localization and personalization. The teacher is also trying to make the activities stimulating, engaging, creative, and fun.

The reasons for and purposes of adaptation are like a flip of a coin. The former focuses on what needs improving, the latter targets improvements, as was exemplified in the last two paragraphs.

Experts have listed and explained possible reasons and / or suggested purposes of adaptation (e.g. Mishan and Timmis, 2015 provide a brief summary of the major lists of past literature including McGrath, 2002, 2013; Islam & Mares, 2003; McDonough et al., 2013; Saraceni, 2013 and Tomlinson & Masuhara, 2004; see also McGrath, 2016). They are all useful references based on authors' experience in research, pedagogy and materials development experience. The list of reasons and purposes of adaptation, however, could be endless as each author puts slightly different labels on intertwined phenomena and gives prominence to certain aspects. If we focus on the main factors that spark off various reasons and purposes, however, we could narrow it down to a manageable list that could then be subcategorized when necessary. We have refined the five factors identified by Tomlinson and Masuhara (2004, p. 12) and added examples from actual adaptation studies:

- Teaching environment (national, regional, institutional, cultural levels, etc.). For example, in Loh and Renandya (2016) in Study 8, the Pura schoolteachers in Singapore had to cover an institutional test-orientated syllabus as well as the national primary

STELLAR program in alternate weeks. As a result of the two (not-entirely compatible) demands, the teachers had to face time constraints (i.e. reason for adaptation), which resulted in adaptations that helped manage reasonable coverage of materials for both syllabi (i.e. purpose for adaptation). In the case of Study 5 by Tasseron (2017) in Oman and in Study 7 in Egypt by Abdel Abdel Latif (2017), the exams (i.e. reason) resulted in adapting the communicative coursebook into explicit and deductive grammar teaching materials for exam preparation (i.e. purpose). In relation to materials with socioculturally or ideologically sensitive contents (i.e. reason), different teachers adapted for different purposes. One teacher reported skipping sections in order to avoid potential problems (i.e. purpose), other teachers used controversial issues for group discussion (i.e. purpose) or provided opportunities to learn from other cultures for the sake of raising cultural awareness (i.e. purpose).

- Learners (age, language level, prior learning experience, learning styles, etc.). For example, in Bosompem (2014, pp. 114–115), in Study 6, six out of 16 Ghanaian teachers felt that the students' prior experience and knowledge were not exploited by the textbook (i.e. reason). One teacher therefore added "detailed explanation in order to bring them on board"—perhaps to make the text more relevant to the students (i.e. purpose). Another teacher "creates and integrates engaging contents"—perhaps in order to achieve learner engagement (i.e. purpose) by replacing the text with his own. Two teachers made modifications to "exploit students' experience and creativity" (i.e. purpose). Bosompem (2014, p. 113) in Study 6 also reports, "'the level of the students' and 'the standard of the learners' are the basis for adapting textbooks for many teachers" (i.e. reason). Therefore the teachers took measures to make the language and cognitive demands of the materials become challenging but achievable (i.e. purpose).
- Teachers (personality, teaching styles, belief about language learning and teaching, etc.). For example, Bosompem (2014, p. 114) mentions a teacher "who makes adaptations because his 'teaching styles' are different from those found in the textbook" (i.e. reason) to solve the conflict between the methodological differences (i.e. purpose). She also reports how "Teachers in this study said they make changes to 'spice the lesson with varieties' [i.e. purpose] …, to make 'the lesson interesting' [i.e. purpose] …, to make 'teaching and learning fun and easier' [i.e. purpose] …, and 'to enrich students' awareness and experience' [i.e.purpose] . . ." In the case of Abdel Latif (2017) the Egyptian secondary school teacher believed in the teacher's central role in teaching but the communicative coursebook incorporated pair and group communication activities in which the teacher's role is that of facilitator of learner–learner interactions (i.e. reason). Therefore, it was decided to use more than half of the lesson time giving a lecture using the board in order to satisfy both the teachers' and learners' expectations (i.e. purpose).
- Course (objectives, syllabus, intended outcomes, etc.). For example, in Grammatosi and Harwood (2014) in Study 2 in a UK university the teacher felt that the book selected by the director was not suitable for the learners (i.e. reason) based on his experience and perception. So, he made some use of the textbook framework as the syllabus but made liberal changes with a lot of use of his own materials and multisourced "textbook cherry-picked" materials to achieve the objectives of the EAP course more effectively (i.e. purpose).
- Materials (texts, tasks, activities, visuals, teacher book, multimedia extras, etc.). For example, in Bolster's study (2014 and 2015) in Study 4 in a foundation year program in

China, 18 experienced teachers thought that the textbooks suffered from such inadequacies as "out of date topic" and "boring repetition" (i.e. reason); therefore they made changes to make the topics more interesting and they personalised other perceived inadequacies of the textbook (Bolster, 2015, p. 18).

All the eight studies provided ample evidence of how teachers are trying their best to help the students based on their beliefs of how teaching and learning should take place (e.g. encouraging personalization, localization, engagement, practice) and their perceptions of the benefit of the students (e.g. level, interest, relevance, high scores in exams).

We would encourage further pursuit of validity in future studies in relation to reasons and purposes of adaptation by examining whether:

- teachers' beliefs are supported by professional development that encourages self-reflection and validation through critical appreciation of the relevant literature;
- learner factors are based on actual data from the learners rather than based on teachers' perceptions;
- there is coherence between five factors (i.e. environment, course, materials, teachers and learners).

How Do Teachers Adapt Materials?—Procedures and Techniques of Adaptation

It is interesting to note that procedures of adaptation often seem to be overshadowed or even overlooked in the literature on materials adaptation and in the studies we have looked at. The discussion tends to focus on reasons for and objectives of adaptation and then move onto techniques (e.g. addition, deletion).

Mishan and Timmis (2015, pp. 67–68) advocate the importance of principled procedures and contrast this with a few common examples of "ad hoc adaptation" (e.g. a teacher asking other teachers for a good replacement activity at the last minute). Loh and Renandya (2016, p. 107) argue for teacher education that helps teachers who are making adaptations "in a haphazard way."

Tomlinson and Masuhara (2004) recommend the following procedures that are designed to help the teachers make their adaptations principled:

- Step 1. Profiling of teaching contexts (e.g. learner needs, course objectives).
- Step 2. Identifying reasons for adaptation.
- Step 3. Evaluating the existing materials.
- Step 4. Listing objectives for adaptation.
- Step 5. Adapting.
- Step 6. Teaching (Steps 3–7 are cyclical).
- Step 7. Revising.

Going through this sequence would be best done as a collaborative task as a part of an in-service professional development program (see Masuhara, 2006 for detailed discussion of how each step relates to teacher development). The teachers can actually use their coursebook units and adapt them for subsequent use. Many teachers may think Step 1 to be redundant as they believe that they know their learners and teaching context very well. In our experience, this step is crucial. For example, considering the national directives and curriculum objectives for ELT might have helped the Omani and Egyptian teachers in Studies 5 and 7 to reflect upon the reasoning behind the materials and upon their own practice.

Step 3 requires teachers to articulate a few crucial evaluation criteria (see Chapter 3 in this book). Using this procedure the experienced L1 curriculum transmitter teacher in Study 3 may have realized that mechanical exercises in the grammar textbook were not satisfying SLA principles. The experienced L1 EAP teacher in Study 2 may find himself become even clearer in articulating the justifications behind his adaptation in relation to learning theories and learners. The cyclical nature of suggested materials adaptation procedures can also easily be turned into action research.

Regarding the techniques of adaptation, McGrath (2013, pp. 63–65) makes an attempt to standardize the nagging inconsistencies of terms used for action among eight oft-cited publications for the sake of consistency between adaptation studies.

In the eight studies we looked at, for example, Bolster (2014 and 2015) in Study 4 used categories and explanations from Islam and Mares (2003) that were based on McDonough and Shaw (1993) and Cunningsworth (1995). Bosompem (2014) in Study 6 used various categories from McGrath (2002) and McDonough and Shaw (2003). Loh and Renandya (2016) in Study 8 used the categories in Tomlinson and Masuhara (2004). Shawer (2010) in Study 1 created some more subcategories based on his data.

As the amount of research on materials adaptation is gradually increasing, it may make sense to try to standardize terms for major categories and subcategories.

We strongly argue that it is vital that adaptation is accepted as an intuitive, organic, dynamic but principled creative process that is stimulated by the teachers' motivation to provide the best teaching input and approaches for specific learners in a specific context with specific learning objectives. We would discourage the prescribed use of techniques or advice as this could be counteractive or even damaging to teachers' creativity. Discussion of categories of techniques may come in useful though if we want to investigate why and how teachers go about adapting materials (see Masuhara, 2011 for an extensive discussion of possible research on teacher use).

What Kinds of Resources on Adaptation Are Available?—Teacher Education and Literature

According to Graves and Garton (2014, p. 275), the contributors to their edited book pointed out "the paucity of courses in materials design and evaluation in teacher preparation programmes." Graves and Garton (2014) argue that such teacher professional development courses should weave analysis of coursebooks and how to use and adapt them into core areas such as second language acquisition, methodology and linguistics, an approach we would endorse and have advocated. They recommend experiential approaches so that the course participants can actually adapt the materials rather than just learning about adaptation. McGrath (2013, p. 219) seems to share a similar view in saying "Teacher education has a vital part to play in shaping teachers' attitudes and developing their abilities, and a carefully designed, contextually sensitive and practice-based approach to teacher education in materials evaluation and design …could make a real difference" (see also his discussion on pre- and in-service courses on pp. 89–92). We also use experiential approaches and make use of contextualized simulations in which the trainee teachers have to adapt materials for a specific learning context. We usually act as informants who provide information about the learning context when asked and we act as facilitators in the eventual evaluation of the adapted materials (Tomlinson and Masuhara, 2013).

We welcome more voices joining in what we have been advocating for a long time through our work and through MATSDA (the Materials Development Association, www.matsda.org) (Tomlinson, 1998 and 2011; McDonough et al., 2013; Tomlinson, 2003, 2013a and 2013b). Masuhara (2006) describes step by step how materials adaptation tasks can lead to teacher development of the kind advocated by Graves and Garton (2014). Tomlinson and Masuhara (2003 and revised version in 2013), for example, report how they used simulation and problem-solving approaches to materials adaptation and development in MA courses and pre-service and in-service professional development courses. In such courses, the participants actually:

1. Analyze the specific needs of specified learners in specified learning contexts.
2. Consider appropriate methodology that is validated by experience and by SLA research and theory.
3. Develop evaluation criteria for materials being used in the target learning context.
4. Evaluate a unit of a coursebook against the criteria in three above.
5. Adapt the materials for the specific learners and context.
6. Trial the materials and evaluate their effectiveness.

In order to accomplish each stage, they consult the relevant literature with a clear focus in relation to the specific target learners and contexts. This affords critical understanding and self-reflection. As the simulated tasks are often done collaboratively, the participants have to articulate and justify their beliefs and learn from each other.

There seems to be a growing awareness of the value of materials evaluation, adaptation and development during preservice training. Canniveng and Martinez (2003) discuss the shortcomings of traditional prescriptive teacher training and how materials development tasks can create opportunities for self-reflection and for nurturing real-life skills required for teachers. Tan (2006, p. 207) reports how student teachers can be helped to become "teacher as researcher" and "teacher as reflective practitioner" through materials development experience.

Bouckaert (2015, p. 10), as part of her report on student teachers' views on materials development, refers to the Dutch survey (Stichting Leerplan Ontwikkeling, [Netherlands Institute for Curriculum Development] SLO, 2012) that revealed that nearly 80% of secondary school teachers sometimes or often develop materials as an addition to the coursebook. Yan (2007) reports on how student teachers adapted materials and what effects they found on the learners.

Minor Adaptation

Minor adaptations can have a major effect. By that we mean that a very small change to a unit of materials made before or even during a lesson can have a significant impact on the engagement, motivation and on-task attention of the learners. Sometimes we have planned such changes well in advance to achieve a greater match between the materials and the learners, sometimes we have made the changes in our heads on the way to a classroom because we cannot face the tedium threatened by some of the activities and sometimes we have made the changes during a class because we can see that the learners are bored. For example, on the stairs on the way to cover a lesson for a teacher the idea came of getting students to act out a potentially engaging text about an old lady who robbed a bank instead of getting them to answer the comprehension questions in the coursebook. Then the idea came of getting them to act out the first scene of a film version of the event narrated by the teacher and then to skim the written text in the book and take part in a group competition in which they took it in turns to articulate differences between the film and what happened in real life (see Tomlinson, 2007 for subsequent developments which changed the minor adaptations into major ones). We like to think that most of our minor changes have been principled in the sense that they are informed by what we believe can best facilitate language acquisition and development (including making the lesson more interesting for us as teachers). It is not always easy to make such changes (especially at the last minute) and we believe that teachers should be helped to develop the awareness, expertise and confidence to do so as part of their initial training and their in-service development.

Tomlinson (2015) reports an experiment at a university in Columbia in which he challenged teachers in training to make adaptations to a coursebook unit to suit a specific target learning context. He then trained them to think more creatively and to turn closed activities into open activities and then found that in postworkshop adaptations to a coursebook unit the participants were far more creative and focused on opening up activities to make them more open-ended, engaging and challenging. In this chapter, Tomlinson gives many examples of minor adaptations with the potential for engagement and challenge. For example, the students perform dialogues in character. For instance, in a dialogue in which A is a salesman in a shoe shop and B is the customer, A is told that he is the ex-husband of B and has not seen her since the divorce. Or in a dialogue in which A asks B how to operate her new office computer, B is told that he is in love with A but she does not know this.

Tomlinson (in press) also gives many examples of minor changes that could make coursebook activities more engaging and challenging and which could open up the many closed questions he found in his review of global and Asian coursebooks. For example, the students act out a text from the coursebook as the teacher reads it aloud as dramatically as possible. For instance, before reading aloud a Korean folk tale about a hard-working but poor farmer and his lazy, greedy and rich brother the teacher divides the class into two halves and tells one half to act out what the hard-working brother does as the teacher reads it and the other half to act out what the lazy brother does.

After this dramatization of the text the teacher asks the true / false questions from the coursebook as personal questions to the brothers. For example, instead of saying, "X was lazy? True or false?" the teacher says to the students representing one of the brothers, "You were lazy, weren't you? Why?"

The students then in groups rewrite the story so that the true answers become false and vice versa (Tomlinson, in press).

Other writers who have suggested and exemplified minor changes include Ur (2015) and Timmis (2016). Timmis suggests small "single-line" extensions to coursebook dialogues so as to "enliven" them (p. 149) as well as such other modifications as changing the mood, changing the cast, changing the register and unscripting the dialogue so as to achieve more engagement and greater plausibility. Ur suggests ways of making adaptations that make use of "ready-made exercises," require minimal preparation and are simple in "preparation and administration" (p. 11). She describes and exemplifies such activities as "varying checking procedures," "varying instructions," deleting options and deleting "one column of a 'matching' exercise" (pp. 12–13) and she does so in order to "increase the learning value" and "learner interest" as well as making "the exercise accessible and useful to students at different levels in a heterogeneous class" (p. 11).

The Principles and Procedures of Materials Adaptation that We Recommend

We would advocate making adaptations when materials do not (or are unlikely to):

- match the needs of the target learners;
- match the wants of the target learners;
- make relevant connections with the learners lives;
- stimulate affective engagement;
- stimulate cognitive engagement;
- provide achievable challenges;
- provide exposure to language in use;
- provide opportunities to use the target language for communication;
- provide opportunities for learners to notice and make discoveries about how the target language is typically used;
- provide enough varied recycling.

If one or more of these deficiencies is suspected or discovered when evaluating materials selected for use (or when preparing to teach or even when teaching the materials) we would recommend:

- articulating objectives for the adaptation (e.g. to connect the text to the learners' lives);
- making the adaptations in the least demanding but most potentially effective way (e.g. adding a readiness activity in which the teacher gets the learners to think about events in their lives which the learners might then visualize when reading the text);
- teaching the adapted materials (or observing them taught);
- evaluating the adaptations against the intended objectives;
- revising the adaptations if necessary for subsequent use.

An Example of an Adaptation

Target Learners

A group of non-native speaking doctors recently arrived in an English speaking country. They are doing a language support course whilst also working as doctors. Their level of English varies considerably but they are all united in their reluctance to attend the course.

Coursebook

McCullagh, M. and Wright, R. (2008). *Good practice: Communication skills in English for the medical practitioner.* Cambridge: Cambridge University Press.

This is an excellent coursebook for medical students (who will have to pass an examination in English) and for non-native speaking doctors seeking work in an English speaking environment.

Unit for Adaptation

Unit 9—Breaking Bad News.
   Case study: disregarding a constraint (pp. 91–92).

Reasons for Adaptation

This unit makes use of a text that has great potential for affective engagement. However:

- The text is quite long and some of the language would be demanding for many of the less proficient members of the group (e.g. "The lungs had left-sided rales . . . The chest radiograph showed a large infiltrate on the left and what I feared was a mass").
- There is no readiness activity to activate the minds of the doctors in relation to the topic of the text, just an instruction to "Read this article, identify the constraint and decide whether the doctor is justified in his actions. Discuss with the rest of the group."
- The postreading activities consist of conventional and typical coursebook exercises requiring individuals to match and to categorize (probably at the insistence of the publisher and in order to prepare the students for examinations). These activities are unlikely to engage and motivate this reluctant group of learners.
- There are no activities requiring the learners to interact (the most pressing need of this group) or to think for themselves (one of the few activities this group do enjoy).

Objectives of the Adaptation

- To maximize the potential for affective engagement of the text.
- To motivate the learners to think and to interact.
- To present all the learners with an achievable challenge.

The Adaptation

A Time to Listen

1. Please get into groups of three.
2. One of you is a doctor, one is a patient and one is an observer.
3. If you are the patient you are going to tell the doctor what is wrong with you.
4. If you are the observer do the task you are given (the teacher gives the observers the instruction, "Time how long it takes before the doctor interrupts the patient").
5. Listen to what happened when a doctor decided not to interrupt a patient (the teacher summarizes what is reported in *A time to listen* (Barr, 2004), focuses on the problems caused by doctors prematurely interrupting patients—and especially on the case of the old lady whose cancer was only revealed because the doctor let her talk for 22 minutes—and concludes by reading aloud a quote from the old lady, "Oh, don't worry about all that. I've had a good life. But I just wanted you to know—this is the best doctor visit I've ever had. You're the only one who ever listened to me").
6. Read the text *A time to listen* and as you read it try think of a way of allowing patients enough time to talk about their problem without creating long queues of patients waiting to see the doctor.

---

7. Write a letter to your hospital authority telling them about your idea in 6 above. You can do this individually, in pairs or in a small group.
8. Show your letter to another individual, pair or group and ask them for suggestions for improvement.
9. Compare your letter with the one your teacher gives you.
10. Revise your letter making use of the suggestions from 8 and what you've learned from the letter you looked at in 9.

Conclusion

- Adaptation is an inevitable and necessary procedure to ensure a match between materials and learners.
- Coherence needs to be achieved between curriculum development, materials development, assessment and teacher education. It is difficult and rare for adaptations to be made to curricula or assessment procedures so often adaptations need to be made to materials and to teacher education.
- To conduct valid adaptations, teachers need support in terms of acknowledgment, encouragement and guidance, as well as the provision of pre-service and in-service teacher education and the facilitation of classroom research and materials development.
- Teacher education would benefit from an experiential materials evaluation, adaptation and development component in which teachers are helped to become reflective teachers, researchers and materials developers.

What Do You Think?

1. Do you think learners should be involved in materials adaptation? If so, why do you think they should be involved and when and how should they be involved?
2. Do you think that you have the awareness and expertise to conduct a materials adaptation? If not, what do you think you need in order to gain this awareness and expertise?
3. What do you think are the most effective ways of measuring the effects of a set of adapted materials on their users? For each way, say what you think are the advantages and the potential problems.
4. Do you agree that criteria need to be developed prior to the writing of materials and then used to drive the development of the materials and the adaptation of them during and after their development? Why/why not?

Tasks

1. Pick a unit from a coursebook at random.
    a) Compile a profile of a target learning context for which the unit might be suitable.
    b) Develop 10 universal criteria and five local criteria (see Chapter 3) for evaluating the unit.

c) Carry out a criterion referenced evaluation of the unit giving a grade out of 5 for each criterion and commenting on any criterion which achieved 2 or less.

d) Develop an adaptation of the first two pages of the unit so as to improve the score for those criteria evaluated as 2 or less.

2. From the same coursebook you evaluated in 1 above:

a) Select three activities which you think are unlikely to engage and challenge the target students in your profile in 1 above.

b) For each activity suggest a small change that could make it more engaging and challenging for the students.

Further Reading

McGrath, I. (2016). *Materials evaluation and design for language teaching* (2nd ed.). Edinburgh: Edinburgh University Press.

References

Abdel Latif, M. M. (2017). Teaching grammar using inductive and communicative materials: Exploring Egyptian EFL teachers' practice and beliefs. In H. Masuhara, F. Mishan, & B. Tomlinson (Eds.), *Practice and theory for materials development in L2 learning* (pp. 275–289). Newcastle upon Tyne: Cambridge Scholars.

Al-Balushi, O. A. (1999). *The Internet and Omani students' language learning problems: A critical study* (Unpublished MA dissertation). Sultan Qaboos University, Muscat.

Al-Busaidi, S., & Tindle, K. (2010). Evaluating the impact of in-house materials on language learning. In B. Tomlinson, & H. Masuhara (Eds.), *Research for materials development for language learning—evidence for best practice* (pp. 137–149). London: Continuum.

Al-Issa, A. (2007). The implications of implementing a "flexible" syllabus for ESL policy in the sultanate of Oman. *RELC Journal: A Journal of Language Teaching and Research*, *38*(2), 199–215.

Amrani, F. (2011). The process of evaluation: A publisher's view. In B. Tomlinson (Ed.), *Materials development in language teaching* (2nd ed., pp. 267–295). Cambridge: Cambridge University Press.

Azar, B. S. (2001). *Understanding and using English grammar: Student book with answer key.* New York: Pearson.

Bacha, N., Ghosn, I. & McBeath, N. (2008). The textbook, the teacher and the learner: A Middle East perspective. In B. Tomlinson (Ed.), *English language learning materials—A critical review* (pp. 281–299). London: Continuum.

Bell, J., & Gower, R. (1998). Writing course materials for the world: A great compromise. In B. Tomlinson (Ed.), *Materials development in language teaching* (1st ed., pp. 116–129). Cambridge: Cambridge University Press.

Bell, J., & Gower, R. (2011). Writing course materials for the world: A great compromise. In B. Tomlinson (Ed.), *Materials development in language teaching* (2nd ed., pp. 135–150). Cambridge University Press: Cambridge.

Benjamin, P. (2015). Cultural appropriacy in materials adaptation: Do we need to walk on eggshells? *Folio 16*(2), 30–35.

Bolster, A. (2014). Materials adaptation of EAP materials by experienced teachers (Part I). *Folio, 16*(1), 16–22.

Bolster, A. (2015). Materials adaptation of EAP materials by experienced teachers (Part II).*Folio, 16*(2), 16–21.

Bosompem, L. G. (2014). Materials adaptation in Ghana. In S. Garton & K. Graves (Eds.), *International perspectives on materials in ELT* (pp. 104–120). Basingstoke: Palgrave Macmillan.

Bouckaert, M. (2015). Perspectives on ELT materials development: Student teachers' voices. *Folio, 16*(2), 9–15.

Canagarajah, S. (2007). Lingua Franca English, Multilingual communities, and language acquisition. *Modern Language Journal, 91*(5), 923–939

Canniveng, C., & Martinez, M. (2003). Materials development and teacher training. In B. Tomlinson (Ed.), *Developing materials for language teaching* (1st ed., pp. 479–489). London: Continuum.

Christison, M. A., & Murray, D. E. (2014). *What English language teachers need to know. Volume III: Designing curriculum*. New York: Routledge.

Craig, C. J. (2006). Why is dissemination so difficult? The nature of teacher knowledge and the spread of curriculum reform. *American Educational Research Journal, 43*(2), 257.

Cunningsworth, A. (1985). *Evaluating and selecting EFL teaching materials*. Oxford: Heinemann.

Cunningsworth, A. (1995). *Choosing your coursebook*. Oxford: Heinemann.

Edwards, E., & Burns, A. (2015). Action research to support teachers' classroom materials development. *Innovation in Language Learning and Teaching, 10*(2), 106–120.

Ellis, R. (2016). Language learning materials as work plans: An SLA perspective. In B. Tomlinson (Ed.), *SLA research and materials development for research* (pp. 203–218). New York: Routledge.

Euromonitor International. (2012). *The benefits of the English language for individuals and societies: Quantitative indicators from Algeria, Egypt, Iraq, Jordan, Lebanon, Morocco, Tunisia and Yemen*. London: Euromonitor International.

Feak, C. B., & Swales, J. M. (2014). Tensions between the old and the new in EAP textbook. In N. Harwood (Ed.), *English language teaching textbooks—content, consumption, production* (pp. 299–319). Basingstoke: Palgrave Macmillan.

Forman, R. (2014). How local teachers respond to the culture and language of a global English as a foreign language textbook. *Language, Culture and Curriculum, 27*(1), 72–88.

Garton, S., & Graves, K. (2014). *International perspectives on materials in ELT*. Basingstoke: Palgrave Macmillan.

Ghosn, I. (2013). *Storybridge to second language literacy: The theory, research, and practice of teaching English with children's literature*. Charlotte, NC: Information Age Publishing, INC.

Graddol, D. (2006). *English next—why global English may mean the end of "English as a foreign language."* London: The British Council.

Grammatosi, F. & Harwood, N. (2014). An experienced teacher's use of the textbook on an academic English course: a case study. In N. Harwood N (Ed.), *English language teaching textbooks: Content, consumption, production* (178–204). Basingstoke: Palgrave Macmillan.

Graves, K., & Garton, S. (2014). Materials in ELT: Looking ahead. In S. Garton, & K. Graves (Eds.), *International perspectives on materials in ELT* (pp. 270–279). Harlow: Palgrave Macmillan.

Gray, J. (2000). The ELT coursebook as cultural artefact: How teachers censor and adapt. *ELT Journal, 54*(3), 274–283.

Gray, J. (2010). *The construction of English: Culture, consumerism and promotion in the ELT global coursebook.* Basingstoke: Palgrave Macmillan.

Gray, J. (Ed.). (2013). *Critical perspectives on language teaching materials [Electronic book].* Basingstoke: Palgrave Macmillan.

Guerrettaz, A. M., & Johnston, B. (2013). Materials in the classroom ecology. *Modern Language Journal, 97*(3), 779–796.

Haines, S., & Dallas, D. (2008). *Hello! English for secondary schools.* The Egyptian International Publishing Company Longman.

Harmer, J. (2001). Coursebooks: A human, cultural and linguistic disaster. *Modern English Teacher, 10*(3), 5–10.

Harwood, N. (2005). What do we want EAP materials for? *Journal of English for Academic Purposes, 4*(2), 149–161.

Harwood, N. (Ed.). (2010). *English language teaching materials—theory and practice.* Cambridge: Cambridge University Press.

Harwood, N. (Ed.). (2014). *English language teaching textbooks—content, consumption, production.* Basingstoke: Palgrave Macmillan.

Islam, C., & Mares, C. (2003). Adapting classroom materials. In B. Tomlinson (Ed.), *Developing materials for language teaching* (pp. 86–100). London: Continuum.

Jolly, D., & Bolitho, R. (2011). A framework for materials writing. In B. Tomlinson (Ed.), *Materials development in language teaching* (2nd ed., pp. 107–134). Cambridge: Cambridge University Press.

Kachru, B. B. (1992). World Englishes: approaches, issues and resources. *Language Teaching, 25*(1), 1–14

Kern, N. (2013). Blended learning: Podcasts for taxi drivers. In B. Tomlinson, & C. Whittaker (Eds.), *Blended learning in English language teaching: Course design and implementation* (pp. 131–139). London: The British Council.

Kirkpatrick, A. (Ed.). (2010). *The Routledge handbook of world Englishes.* Abingdon: Routledge.

Loh, J. (2010). Reflecting, shaking and being shook: Resistance in a primary classroom. *English Language Teaching: Practice and Critique, 9*(3), 160–168.

Loh, J., & Renandya, W. A. (2016). Exploring adaptations of materials and methods: A case from Singapore. *The European Journal of Applied Linguistics and TEFL,4*(2), 93–111.

Lopez Barrios, M., & Villanueva de Debat, E. (2006). Minding the needs of the Argentine learner: Global textbooks and their adapted versions for the local context. *Folio, 10*(2), 14–16.

Masuhara, H. (1998). What do teachers really want from coursebooks? In B. Tomlinson (Ed.), *Materials development in language teaching* (1st ed., pp. 239–260). Cambridge: Cambridge University Press.

Masuhara, H. (2006). Materials as a teacher development tool. In J. Mukundan (Ed.), *Readings on ELT materials II* (pp. 34–46). Petaling Jaya: Pearson Malaysia.

Masuhara, H. (2011). What do teachers really want from coursebooks? In B. Tomlinson (Ed.), *Materials development in language teaching* (2nd ed., pp. 236–266). Cambridge: Cambridge University Press.

Masuhara, H., Mishan, F., & Tomlinson, B. (Eds.). (2017). *Practice and theory for materials development in L2 learning.* Newcastle upon Tyne: Cambridge Scholars.

McDonough, J. & Shaw, C. (1993). *Materials and methods in ELT.* Oxford: Blackwell.

McDonough, J. & Shaw, C. (2003). *Materials and methods in ELT* (2nd ed.). Oxford: Blackwell.

McDonough, J., Shaw, C., & Masuhara, H. (2013). *Materials and methods in ELT* (3rd ed.). Chichester: Wiley.

McGrath, I. (2002). *Materials evaluation and design for language teaching*. Edinburgh: Edinburgh University Press.

McGrath, I. (2013). *Teaching materials and the roles of EFL / ESL teachers*. London: Bloomsbury.

McGrath, I. (2016). *Materials evaluation and design for language teaching* (2nd ed.). Edinburgh: Edinburgh University Press.

Meddings, L., & Thornbury, S. (2009). *Teaching unplugged: Dogme in English language teaching*. Peasdale: Delta.

Menken, K. (2008). *English learners left behind: Standardized testing as language policy*. Clevedon: Multilingual Matters Ltd.

Messekher, H. (2014). Cultural representations in Algerian English textbooks. In S. Garton & K. Graves (Eds.), *International Perspectives on materials in ELT* (pp. 69–86). Basingstoke: Palgrave Macmillan.

Ministry of Education (2015). *List of primary schools by planning area*. Retrieved from http://moe.gov.sg/education/admissions/primary-one-registration/listing-by-planning-area/

Mishan, F. (2013). Demystifying blended learning. In B. Tomlinson (Ed.), *Developing materials for language teaching* (2nd ed., pp. 207–224). London: Bloomsbury.

Mishan, F., & Timmis, I. (2015). *Materials development for TESOL*. Edinburgh: Edinburgh University Press.

Moor, P., Cunningham, S., & Eales, F. (2005). *New cutting edge elementary*. Harlow: Pearson Longman.

Mukundan, J. (2008). Agendas of the state in developing world English language textbooks. *Folio*, *12*(2), 17–19.

Nation, I. S. P., & Macalister, J. (2010). *Language curriculum design*. New York: Routledge.

Ottley, K. (2014). Please read the text on page seven: It has nothing to do with you. *Folio*, *16*(1), 12–14.

Ottley, K. (2016). Why one-size-fits-all is not fit for purpose. In B. Tomlinson (Ed.), *SLA research and materials development for language learning* (pp. 268–279). New York: Routledge.

Pennycook, A. (2010). The future of Englishes: one, many or more? In A. Kirkpatrick (Ed.), *The Routledge handbook of world Englishes* (pp. 673–687). Abingdon: Routledge.

Richards, J., C. (2014). The ELT textbook. In S. Garton, & K. Graves (Eds.), *International perspectives on materials in ELT* (pp. 19–36) Basingstoke: Palgrave Macmillan.

Santos, D. (2015). Revising listening materials: What remains, what is changed and why. *The European Journal of Applied Linguistics and TEFL,4*(2), 19–36.

Saraceni, C. (2013). Adapting courses: A personal view. In B. Tomlinson (Ed.), *Developing materials for language teaching* (2nd ed., pp. 49–62). London: Bloomsbury.

Saraceni, M. (2015). *World Englishes: A critical analysis*. London: Bloomsbury.

Schrampfer Azar, B. (2001). *Understanding and using English grammar* (3rd ed.). New York: Pearson Education.

Scotland, J. (2014). Operating in global educational contact zones: How pedagogical adaptation to local contexts may result in the renegotiation of the professional identities of English language teachers. *Teaching and Teacher Education*, *37*, 33–43.

Shawer, S. F. (2010). Classroom-level curriculum development: EFL teachers as curriculum-developers, curriculum-makers and curriculum-transmitters. *Teaching and Teacher Education,26*, 173–184.

Shin, J., Eslami, Z. R., & Chen, W. (2011). Presentation of local and international culture in current international English-language teaching textbooks. *Language, Culture and Curriculum, 24*(3), 253–268.

Singapore Wala, D. A. (2013). Publishing a coursebook: The role of feedback. In B. Tomlinson (Ed.), *Developing materials for language teaching* (2nd ed., pp. 63–87). London: Bloomsbury.

Tan, B. T. (2006). Student-teacher-made language teaching materials—A developmental approach to materials development. In J. Mukundan (Ed.), *Focus on ELT materials* (pp. 207–227). Petaling Jaya: Pearson Malaysia.

Tasseron, M. (2017). How teachers use the global ELT coursebook. In H. Masuhara, F. Mishan, & B. Tomlinson (Eds.), *Practice and theory of materials development in L2 learning* (pp. 290–311). Newcastle upon Tyne: Cambridge Scholars.

Thornbury, S. (2005). Dogme: Dancing in the dark? *Folio, 9*(2), 3–5.

Timmis, I. (2016). Humanising coursebook dialogues. *Innovation in Language Learning and Teaching, 10*(2), 144–153.

Tomlinson, B. (Ed.). (1998). *Materials development in language teaching* (1st ed.). Cambridge: Cambridge University Press.

Tomlinson, B. (Ed.). (2003). *Developing materials for language teaching*. London: Continuum.

Tomlinson, B. (2007). The value of recasts during meaning focused communication, 1. In B. Tomlinson (Ed.), *Language acquisition and development: Studies of learners of first and other languages* (pp. 141–161). London: Continuum.

Tomlinson, B. (Ed.). (2008). *English language learning materials—A critical review*. London: Continuum.

Tomlinson, B. (Ed.). (2011). *Materials development in language teaching* (2nd ed.). Cambridge: Cambridge University Press.

Tomlinson, B. (2012). Materials development for language learning and teaching. *Language Teaching, 45*(2), 143–179.

Tomlinson, B. (Ed.). (2013a). *Applied linguistics and materials development*. London: Bloomsbury.

Tomlinson, B. (Ed.). (2013b). *Developing materials for language teaching* (2nd ed.). London: Bloomsbury.

Tomlinson, B. (2015). Challenging teachers to use their coursebook creatively. In A. Maley & N. Peachey (Eds.), *Creativity in the language classroom* (pp. 24–28). London: The British Council.

Tomlinson, B. (Ed.). (2016). *SLA research and materials development for language learning*. New York: outledge.

Tomlinson, B. (in press). Making typical coursebook activities more beneficial for the learner. In D. Bao (Ed.), *Creative concerns in ELT materials development: Looking beyond the current design*. Bristol: Multilingual Matters.

Tomlinson, B., & Masuhara, H. (2003). Simulations in materials development. In B. Tomlinson (Ed.), *Developing materials for language teaching* (pp. 462–478). London: Bloomsbury.

Tomlinson, B., & Masuhara, H. (2004). *Developing language course materials*. Singapore: SEAMEO Regional Language Centre.

Tomlinson, B., & Masuhara, H. (Eds.). (2010). *Research for materials development in language learning: Evidence for best practice*. London: Continuum International Publishing Group.

Tomlinson, B., & Masuhara, H. (2013). Simulations in materials development. In B. Tomlinson (Ed.), *Developing materials for language teaching* (2nd ed., pp. 501–519). London: Bloomsbury.

Tomlinson, B., & Whittaker, C. (Eds.). (2013). *Blended learning in English language teaching: Course design and implementation*. London: British Council.

Ur, P. (2015). Using the coursebook: A teacher's perspective. *The European Journal of Applied Linguistics and TEFL, 4*(2), 5–17.

Wette, R. (2009). Making the instructional curriculum as an interactive, contextualized process: Case studies of seven ESOL teachers. *Language Teaching Research, 13*(4),337–365.

Yan, C. (2007). Investigating English teachers' materials adaptation. *Humanising Language Teaching, 9*(4). Retrieved from http://www.hltmag.co.uk/Jul07/index.htm

Zacharias, N. T. (2005). Teachers' beliefs about internationally-published materials: A survey of tertiary English teachers in Indonesia. *RELC Journal, 36*(1), 23–37.

5

The Development of Materials

Introduction

It has always interested us that a massive amount of time and money is spent on training teachers but very little is spent on training the writers of the materials which the teachers use. We have run weekend MATSDA workshops that focused on the writing of specific types of materials (e.g. extensive readers, materials for EAP and materials for beginners) and we ran an MA dedicated to materials development for language learning, first at the then University of Luton and later at the then Leeds Metropolitan University. This MA course helped many of its graduates to begin careers in publishing, to become successful materials writers, or to pass on their knowledge, awareness, and skills to students on postgraduate or teacher training courses. This MA has been cloned by IGSE (the International Graduate School of English) in Seoul, an institution that is associated with one of the leading publishers in South Korea, which offers outstanding graduates positions in their company. Unfortunately, as far as we know, they are now the only institution offering a dedicated postgraduate course in materials development. There are many universities that offer postgraduate modules in materials development (for example, we have run such modules at Anaheim University, at Bilkent University in Ankara, at the University of Liverpool, at the National University of Singapore and at NILE in Norwich), and most teacher training courses do include a mini-course on materials development. However, we know of no course currently being offered to train materials developers who have been contracted by publishers or by ministries to write materials for publication. Providing such courses could, in our view, considerably improve the quality of both the print and digital materials available for teachers to use.

How Writers Write

Considering how important and frequent the materials writing process is, there are surprisingly few accounts in the literature of how materials writers actually go about the process of writing their materials. What we find really interesting in the few reports that have been published is that most writers reveal that their writing relies heavily on retrieval from repertoire (i.e. they use activities they have used many times before), on cloning other writers' successful publications and on spontaneous "inspiration." As we will reveal below, this is not how we write our materials and it is not how we have trained

The Complete Guide to the Theory and Practice of Materials Development for Language Learning,
First Edition. Brian Tomlinson and Hitomi Masuhara.
© 2018 John Wiley & Sons, Inc. Published 2018 by John Wiley & Sons, Inc.

teachers to write materials in workshops in, for example, Belgium, Botswana, Luxembourg, Mauritius, Malaysia, the Seychelles, Spain, Turkey, and Vietnam.

Hidalgo, Hall, and Jacobs (1995) published accounts of how a number of materials writers in Southeast Asia wrote materials for projects or publication. In their introduction, the editors give a fascinating account of how their book was written and they reveal the guide that the 20 writers were given. Most of the 21 questions were about practical matters (e.g. "Did you use computers?" (p. xi)) but 21 included "What overall principles do you believe to be of the greatest relevance to authors in the Philippines or elsewhere in SE Asia?" (p. xi). In the revised guidelines written after the writers submitted their drafts, the writers were asked to highlight "Key principles which apply to a range of situations and students" (xiii). Although (as we will reveal below) some of the writers, in their published accounts, refer to being influenced by principles of language acquisition, many of them focused more on decisions about the book syllabus and exercise types (e.g. Richards, 1995), on developing objectives (e.g. Sundara Rajan, 1995), on deciding which pedagogic approach(es) to use (e.g. Pascasio, 1995), and on providing a detailed account of what the writers actually did from conception to publication of the materials. Many of them also reported how they replicated previous materials they had written, made use of activity types that had "worked" for them before and relied heavily upon creative inspiration at the time of writing.

The experienced materials writers invited to contribute accounts of how they typically write their materials to Prowse (1998) report similar approaches to the writers in Hidalgo, Hall, and Jacobs (1995). They tend to focus on the creative process and stress, for example, the importance of thinking as you write, of how, "Ideas come to you at any time" during collaboration (p. 130), of thinking about their materials whilst doing something else, of trying out ideas and writing many drafts and of being inspired. Some of the writers refer to prior planning and (as just like many of the writers in Hidalgo, Hall, and Jacobs, 1995) of thinking about objectives and of the target learners. However, none of them refers to developing a principled framework or establishing principled criteria before starting to write. It seems from the two publications about the process of writing materials referred to here that materials writers are very much influenced by existing conventions, by typical topics, by typical activity types, and by typical teaching points, and that not much thought is given to whether or not these accepted conventions are likely to facilitate language acquisition and development. Obviously, this is not true of all materials writers but we have experienced working on projects where full time materials writers have immediately thought about where they can insert a multiple-choice activity or a fill in the blank activity or a sentence completion activity rather than thinking about whether these conventional activities are likely to lead to beneficial outcomes for the learners. Whilst we understand the importance of materials achieving face validity we have been critical of the overreliance on conventional coursebook activities (Tomlinson, Dat, Masuhara, & Rubdy, 2001; Masuhara, Haan, Yi, & Tomlinson, 2008; Tomlinson & Masuhara, 2013 and Tomlinson, 2016b) on the grounds that they lack theoretical and research justification. Tomlinson (2016b) proposes research projects to evaluate the contribution of such conventional activities as multiple choice, fill in the blank, sentence completion, sentence transformation and dialogue repetition to language acquisition and development.

Johnson (2003) focused on how expertise is manifested in task design. He studied the literature on task-based teaching but could find nothing that revealed the procedures which writers follow in actually writing a task. So he set up an experiment at the

University of Lancaster in which eight expert materials writers and eight novice materials writers were asked to "design an activity involving the function of describing people" (p. 4). He asked the writers to think aloud as they were designing their task. Their "concurrent verbalizations" were recorded and later analyzed. Not surprisingly, they revealed that the experts all wrote their materials in very different ways from the novices. The experts, for example, envisaged possibilities in concrete detail (presumably through visualization as we do), were prepared to abandon tasks they had spent time developing (something we both find very difficult to do), designed in opportunistic ways (we like to believe we tend to design in principled ways but are prepared to be opportunistic too), instantiated as they wrote (as we do), showed learner / context sensitivity (as we hope we do), and used repertoire a lot (we are not sure if we do this as we try to repeat principled stages but manifest them in different ways). Interestingly there was no explicit reference by the experts to theory driven principles (something we do articulate explicitly before starting to write). This lack of reference to principles is true also of Prowse (2011), in which he revisits his report of how writers write from Prowse (1998) and adds the reflections of a number of writers of recently published coursebooks on how they typically set about writing their materials. As in Hidalgo, Hall, and Jacobs (1995) and Prowse (1998) these writers also focus on the creative, inspirational, instantaneous aspect of materials writing ("coursebook writing is a creative rather than a mechanical process" (p. 173)) and on making considerable use of their prior experience of teaching and of writing. Again, none of these writers refers to making use of principled frameworks or criteria. Our own preference (which we will elaborate later in this chapter) is for "an approach to materials writing in which the ongoing evaluation of the developing materials is driven by a set of agreed principles, both universal principles applicable to any learning context anywhere and local criteria specific to the target learning context(s)" (Tomlinson, 2012, p. 153).

Hadfield (2014) provides a detailed account of how she wrote activities for *Motivating Learning* (Hadfield & Dornyei, 2013). First, though, she reviews the literature on how writers write (the same publications we have referred to above plus Sundara Rajan's (1995) report of a five-stage procedure) and discovers a tension between the "recursive and messy process" (p. 323) reported by writers and the "orderly, linear progression" "governed by a system of frameworks and principles" (p. 323) that seems to be advocated by the theorists. One theorist referred to by Hadfield though concludes that, "Task design is a complex, highly recursive and often messy process" that does not "entail orderly progressions through checklists of guiding principles" (Samuda, 2005, p. 243). We would consider ourselves both theorists and practitioners and when we write materials we are guided by explicit task-specific principles and by a flexible framework but we also make full use of the resources of the word processor to jump backwards and forwards, to delete, to modify, and to add. Because we typically follow a text-driven framework, most of our ideas are stimulated by the core text we are using to drive the unit rather than any predetermined activity types. So it is both a principled and an organic process.

In order to achieve a complete account of her writing process, Hadfield kept a log as she was writing the activities for *Motivating Learning*. On p. 334 she summarizes the processes recorded in the log in a table that is divided into sub-processes (e.g. "Generating Ideas") and micro-processes (e.g. "brainstorming"). The sub-processes she lists are "Generating Ideas," "Dialoguing" (with herself as a teacher or a student), "Imagining Scenario" (i.e. visualizing the activity in action in the classroom), "Scoping Materials" (i.e. sketching an outline), "Trying Out" ("on self or others"), "Writing Materials," and "Writing Rubrics." Hadfield gives examples of these processes at work in developing her materials and then in her conclusion decides that her approach was usefully "chaotic" but "ordered" too. She also emphasizes the need for "flexibility and responsiveness" (p. 347), for constantly asking yourself questions (e.g. "Does this involve any issues and problems?" (p. 349) and in particular for making use of a "tacit framework of principles" (p. 253) to inform decisions. The processes that Hadfield followed in developing her materials were obviously useful and would be worth replicating for novice writers. However, you cannot teach materials writing. What we do on our courses is to raise awareness of the principles of language acquisition and of classroom learning, to help participants to both refine their tacit frameworks and to develop explicit principles, criteria, and frameworks. The messy, chaotic and inspirational processes are then enhanced by monitored experience of actually developing materials, an experience which also helps to modify both tacit and explicit principles. You can only eventually become an effective materials developer by actually developing materials and through reflection, self-evaluation and constructive criticism.

Principled Development of Materials

Despite the typical reliance on repertoire and inspiration reported above, there are some writers who do report establishing principles prior to writing.

In Hidalgo, Hall, and Jacobs (1995) there are some writers who do advocate principled approaches to materials development. Flores (1995, pp. 58–59), for example, reports on the use of the principles of focusing on language use, communicative needs, integrated skills, school subject needs and the development of aesthetic appreciation through literature in order to drive the writing of a textbook in the Philippines. Penaflorida (1995, pp. 172–179) provides a narrative of how she used the six principles of materials design previously specified by Nunan (1988) to help her to contribute to the writing of an ESP textbook. The principles were adherence to the curriculum, authenticity of text and task, stimulus for interaction, attention to form, and skills development. From the very start of his article Hall (1995: 8) insists that "the crucial question we need to ask" is, "How do we think people learn languages?" He outlines his own beliefs about language learning and teaching and exemplifies the application of the principles that he thinks should "underpin everything we do in planning and writing our materials" (Hall, 1995, p. 8). His basic principles are the need for students to communicate, the need for long-term goals, the need for authenticity, and the need for student centeredness—principles not always prioritized in the development of commercial coursebooks.

Tomlinson (1998b, pp. 5–22; 2011b) proposes 15 principles for materials development, which derive from second language acquisition research and from his experience, and which we will discuss in detail in Chapter 8. A number of other writers outline principled approaches to developing L2 materials in Tomlinson (1998a, 2011a). For example, Bell and Gower (1998, 2011) discuss the need for authors to make principled compromises to meet the practical needs of teachers and learners and to match the realities of publishing materials, as do Mishan and Timmis (2015), and they articulate 11 principles that guided their writing of a commercially published coursebook but which were not always easy to follow. Some of these relate to what they believed would help students to acquire communicative competence in English (e.g. being exposed to natural language, learning to learn, working things out for themselves, and being engaged by the content) and others relate to their approach to the writing of the materials (e.g. flexibility, from text to language, integrating the skills and providing a balance of approaches). One interestingly different principle was that of gaining professional respect through their writing. This is a principle we have found to be difficult to achieve given the compromises that have to be made with publishers determined to achieve the face validity that they believe is necessary to sell their books and with sponsors anxious not to deviate from the curriculum or from the expected norms. We have sometimes gone too far in making compromises and are quite embarrassed by what was published in our names. And sometimes we have actually withdrawn from projects that we were no longer willing to put our names to or have been dropped by publishers or sponsors frightened that our "radical" approaches would threaten the success of their projects. Edge and Wharton (1998, pp. 299–300) talk about the "coursebook as ELT theory" and as a "genre whose goal is a dialogue about principle via suggestions about practice," and they stress the need to develop coursebooks so they can be used flexibly in order to capitalize on "teachers' capacity for creativity." Maley (1998, 2011) also stresses the importance of designing materials to be used flexibly (as does Bao, 2015) who provides a list of practical suggestions for designing flexibility. Maley offers practical suggestions for "providing greater flexibility in decisions about content, order, pace and procedures" (1998, p. 280), which include ways in which teachers can supplement and adapt materials to make them more flexible and ways in which materials writers can design their materials so that teachers and students in different contexts can use them in a variety of ways. For the teachers he focuses on such process options as project work, drama and creative writing which "will generate" their "own content and learning activities" (p. 383). For the materials writers he especially recommends "flexi-materials," which consist of a set of "raw" texts together with a "set of generalizable procedures … which may be applied to any / all of the texts in any combination" (p. 386). A similar approach is advocated in the language through literature activity book *Openings* (Tomlinson, 1994b) in which Part 1 consists of extracts from contemporary world literature and Part 2 consists of a menu of suggested activities to select from for each text. The book was critically acclaimed and was popular with the students we used it with in Japan and Singapore but it did not sell very well (possibly because it did not achieve face validity). Also in Tomlinson (1998a, 2011a) Jolly and Bolitho (1998, 2011) advocate a principled, practical and dynamic framework for materials development by teachers which has since been made use of by many postgraduate students in their research. This framework is intended to stimulate an organic and recursive process of materials development and involves identification of student needs, exploration of these needs, contextual realization of materials, pedagogical realization of materials, production of materials, student use of materials and evaluation of materials against agreed objectives.

A usefully detailed review of the literature on criteria and principles for materials development is provided by McGrath (2002, pp. 152–161) who reviews the relevant literature from Methold (1972), who stressed the importance of recycling and of localization, up to Tomlinson (1998b) and his focus on principles of language acquisition. As well as reporting on recommended procedures for materials development, McGrath also reviews the literature on principled frameworks and on procedures for developing units of materials. In doing so he focuses, in particular, on the theme or topic-based approach (Nunan, 1991), the text-based approach (Hutchinson & Waters, 1987) and the storyline approach (Nunan, 1991; Young, 1980).

Tan (2002) focuses on the role that corpus-based approaches can and should play in language teaching and contains chapters in which corpus linguists and practitioners from around the world report and discuss the effects that the use of corpora have had in, for example, the teaching of vocabulary, the teaching of fixed expressions, the conversation class, the teaching of writing and the teaching of collocation. O'Keefe, McCarthy, and Carter (2007) reveal how, in their experience, corpora can be utilized in the development of classroom activities and focus on such language features as chunks, idioms, grammar and lexis, grammar, discourse, and pragmatics, listenership and response, relational language, and language and creativity. McCarten and McCarthy (2010) (who have authored corpus informed coursebooks) focus on ways in which coursebooks can make use of corpora and describe and exemplify their approach to "bridging the gap between corpus and course book" (p. 11) in relation to the teaching of conversation strategies. Gilmore (2009) and Farr, Chambers, and O'Riordan (2010) advocate principled ways of using corpora as resources for the teaching of languages and Willis (2011) exemplifies a number of ways in which both teachers and students can develop and make use of corpora of their own. This is something we have been doing for many years in our language awareness materials. We often start units by asking students to brainstorm the use of particular language features (e.g. "In case of," "Not now …," the articles, modal verbs, ways of getting people to do things for you). Then we provide experience of this feature in action in a potentially engaging text, the students are asked to respond personally to the content of the text and then to develop (usually in groups) a similar text of their own (e.g. "Rewrite the story so that it is about a girl in Oman"). Then they explore the use in the text of the particular feature they focused on at the beginning of the unit. Finally, they revise their text making use of their discoveries. For homework they find and record samples of the focused feature in use and bring them to class for the next lesson. In that lesson they share their samples and develop a mini-corpus of the feature, which they copy into their corpus file and add to every time they come across other samples of the feature in use. There is an example of this approach in Tomlinson (2010b), which also points out some of the inevitable limitations of corpora and proposes ways of supplementing the information gained from them through author, teacher and learner research. Timmis (2013a) focuses on the use of corpora in developing materials for the development of oral communicative competence. In doing so he makes a very revealing comparison between the texts, language selection, and methodology of a coursebook informed by corpora (*Touchstones*—McCarthy, McCarten, & Sandford, 2006) and one whose lead author has deliberately ignored corpus findings and has preferred to rely on his own intuitions to script typical conversations (*Innovations*—Dellar & Walkley, 2005). Timmis (2013a) prefers a third way in which teachers are enabled to "be 'systematic opportunists'" by acquainting them with spoken language research findings and equipping them with the methodological tools to focus on spoken language" (p. 89), which is featured in listening texts or in classroom conversations. Timmis (2015) provides a detailed consideration of how corpus linguistics can and should inform (but not drive) the development of materials for language learning, as does Mishan and Timmis (2015). Interestingly, Douglas (2012) analyzed six popular global coursebooks, interviewed some of their writers and editors, and found very little evidence (with one notable exception) of publishers and materials writers making use of the information about the use of English currently provided in accessible corpora. One of her conclusions was that it would help if the data collected by corpus linguists related to language use more likely to be of interest to students.

One publication that does focus very much on principles and procedures of materials development is Tomlinson (2003a).It includes, for example, contributions on a principled procedure for writing a coursebook (Mares, 2003), principled frameworks for materials development (Tomlinson, 2003c), which we will discuss in detail below, creative approaches to writing materials (Maley, 2003), ways of humanizing the coursebook (i.e. maximizing its relevance and value to the individual human beings using it) (Tomlinson, 2003d), and on the principled and purposeful use of simulations in materials development for teacher development (Tomlinson & Masuhara, 2003).

Tomlinson (2008a) provides critical reviews of ELT materials in use in different parts of the world and most of its chapters make use of principles and procedures of materials development as criteria in their evaluations. It also contains an Introduction on "Language acquisition and language learning materials" (Tomlinson, 2008b), which suggests ways of applying accepted theories of language acquisition to materials development. The principles suggested include:

- the language experience needs to be contextualized and comprehensible;
- the learner needs to be motivated, relaxed, positive and engaged;
- the language and discourse features available for potential acquisition need to be salient, meaningful and frequently encountered;
- the learner needs to achieve deep and multi-dimensional processing of the language (Tomlinson 2008b, p. 4).

Another book that focuses on principles of materials development is Harwood (2010a). In the introduction, Harwood (2010b) discusses the issues involved in matching materials to the TESOL Curriculum and the issues involved in the content analysis of materials. He also contributes a very useful review of recent accounts by writers of "the design process" (p. 13). He is especially interested (as we are) in Johnson (2003) but also refers (as Hadfield, 2014, does) to Samuda's (2005) report of the "complex, highly recursive and often messy process" (p. 243) of task design as well as to Richard's (2006) account of how reading the current literature on the listening skill helped him to change his approach to developing listening materials. In his review, Harwood agrees with Richards' (2006, p. 23) point that language materials should not only be shaped by research but need to be made suitable for the contexts in which they will be used. Also in Harwood (2010a) there are contributions, for example, by Ellis (2010) on the interaction between second language research and language-teaching materials, by Reinders and White (2010) on making use of the theory and practice of technology in materials development, by Tomlinson (2010a) on his principles of effective materials development and by Benesch (2010) on critical praxis as materials development. There are also reports of principle informed / driven materials development in action. For example, Evans, Hartshorn, and Anderson (2010, p. 152) report on how they follow "a theoretical framework for the development of ELT reading materials" at Brigham Young University in the United States where they apply their curricular principles of responsiveness, cohesion, and stability when developing content-based reading materials for non-native speaking students being prepared to study undergraduate courses in a variety of subjects. Other contributions reporting principled materials development in action in Harwood (2010a) include:

- Jones and Schmitt's (2010) account of developing a listening and language awareness course for EAP students informed by their needs analysis of what non-native speaker students typically need to do in their subject studies at the University of Nottingham and by recent research into vocabulary acquisition.

- Hewings' (2010) report of how materials training EAP students at the University of Birmingham to write academic essays were driven by theories of contextualization, writer's voice, argument, and genre analysis.
- Harwood's (2010b) description of how he developed materials to help EAP students to cite accurately and effectively by using what he calls a critical pragmatic approach in which models are provided both for potential emulation but also for student evaluation as to their value as models for their own needs.

Tomlinson and Masuhara (2010) consists of reports on recent research on materials development from around the world, many of which evaluate the application of theoretical principles of language acquisition to the practice of materials development. For example, Ghosn (2010) reports the results of her research project in Lebanon, which compared language performance by young learner beginners of English who followed a communicative course with equivalent learners who followed a story-based course. The latter gained significantly higher scores on reading comprehension, on mathematics vocabulary, on science vocabulary and on social studies vocabulary. Fenton-Smith (2010) claims beneficial effects on Japanese university students' engagement and motivation from selecting from a menu of post-extensive reading output activities requiring creativity and / or critical thinking. Troncoso (2010) reveals the value of text-driven materials for the teaching of Spanish in a UK university. Al-Busaidi and Tindle (2010) demonstrate the effectiveness of in-house writing materials designed to follow innovative experiential approaches at Sultan Qaboos University in Oman. Park (2010) describes how effective process drama materials were in a Korean middle school classroom. Mishan (2010) reports very positive effects of following a problem solving approach with students at the University of Limerick and McCullagh (2010) evaluates the effectiveness of her published materials, which follow an experiential approach in helping overseas doctors and non-native speakers to communicate in English in the United Kingdom.

Tomlinson (2011a) is the second edition of Tomlinson (1998a) and it includes an updated version of the introduction, which again proposes the application of commonly agreed principles of second-language acquisition to the development of language learning materials. It also contains updated versions of most of the original chapters and many of these chapters have a greater focus on the application of principles than they did previously. For example, Hooper Hansen (2011), explores the principles that informed materials produced and inspired by Lozanov. Maley (2011) investigates the principles behind his suggestions for materials designed to empower teachers. Masuhara (2011) derives principles from her analysis of the materials needs and wants of teachers, and Tomlinson (2011c) examines the principles driving his materials, which stimulate learners to make use of visual imaging. In addition the book contains a number of new chapters, including one by Reppen (2011), who provides a critical overview of the literature on the application of principles to the development of corpora informed classroom materials, as well as chapters by Motteram (2011) and by Kervin and Derewianka (2011) on developing principled and effective learner materials for electronic delivery.

Tomlinson (2013a) is the second edition of Tomlinson (2003a). It contains updates on many of the original chapters plus, for example, additional chapters on principled approaches to developing digital materials (Kiddle, 2013), blended learning materials

(Mishan, 2013), reading materials for young learners (Rixon, 2013), materials for refugee children (Ghosn, 2013a), materials for ESOL learners (Haan, 2013) and materials for developing writing skills (Hyland, 2013), as well as a chapter on ways of using corpora to contribute to the development of materials (Timmis, 2013b).

Tomlinson (2013d) explores the connection between applied linguistics theory and materials development and begins with a chapter by Tomlinson (2013e), which focuses in particular on the lack of match between SLA theory and materials development practice (a chapter that is discussed in more detail in Chapter 8 of this volume). Each chapter focuses on a particular aspect of applied linguistics and evaluates the match between current theory and current materials development practice, as well as suggesting and exemplifying ways of achieving a closer match. For example, there is a chapter by Ghosn (2013b) on the mismatch between what we know helps young learners to acquire an L2 and what materials typically require them to do (see also Chapter 10 in this volume), a chapter by Cohen and Ishihara (2013) on the mismatch between what we know about pragmatic competence and how materials typically try to help learners acquire it, and a chapter about we know about the acquisition or oral communicative competence in an L2 and the ways in which textbooks use to try to help learners achieve it (Burns & Hill, 2013). In a similar way Tomlinson (2016a) investigates the match between second language acquisition research and materials for L2 learning and contains, for example, chapters on brain studies and materials for language learning (Masuhara, 2016), on applying SLA principles to whole class activities (Tomlinson, 2016b), on an evaluation of textbook exercises on collocations (Boers & Strong, 2016) and on corpus-based materials development for teaching and learning pragmatic routines (Bardovi-Harlig & Mossman, 2016).

McGrath (2013) focuses, in particular, on the roles of teachers and learners in the evaluation, selection, adaptation, and classroom use of learning materials but it also contains an introductory session on the "theory" of materials development which includes a chapter on "publisher and coursebook writer perceptions." This chapter considers the process of the development of coursebooks from commissioning to publication and in doing so touches on the publisher and writer research which is typically undertaken prior to the development of a coursebook. Not surprisingly publisher research is focused on market analysis and on discovering gaps in the market. Rather disappointingly, writer research seems to be focused mainly on publisher and market expectations, though McGrath does mention writers consulting "the professional literature"(p. 32) and gives an example of Richards (1995) talking about looking at the literature on conversation strategies when planning his conversation books (for further discussion of the process of publishing materials see Chapter 6 in this book).

Harwood (2014) starts by focusing on textbook content and textbook consumption but ends with a section on textbook production. In it there are accounts of contributing to a national textbook project (Timmis, 2014) and to an institutional textbook project (Stoller & Robinson, 2014), a reflection on the process of revising an EAP textbook (Feak & Swales, 2014) and a detailed report of the processes involved in designing the tasks for a textbook (Hadfield, 2014). Timmis reports how feedback from the publisher caused him to effect a compromise between the principles established by the writing team prior to developing the materials and the conventional expectations of the publisher, the sponsor, and the Ministry of Education. In retrospect, he considers the compromises made to be reasonable and accepts the importance of achieving "teacher plausibility" (Prabhu, 1990). We worked on the same project as Timmis reports and our view was that most of the compromises were to be expected and were acceptable but that some of them compromised the communicative approach requested by the sponsors when we negotiated the contract for the project (e.g. the amount of explicit grammar instruction ultimately required). On a similar project for the same sponsor in the same country we had to make substantial changes to our coursebooks in response to feedback from prestigious academic advisors but when the books went to the Ministry of Education for approval the senior official there expressed his disappointment that the books were so conventional as he knew we were involved in writing them. We then had to reinsert some of our discarded innovations in response to requirements for publication from the Ministry. Timmis seems to be of the view that the writers should anticipate feedback and should plan principled compromises when developing the materials. It is very much our view that we should start with a coherent set of principles and a principle-driven flexible framework and then make acceptable compromises when required to do so. In our experience, if you start with compromises you will have to make even more compromises as you proceed and you can end up being responsible for an incoherent, unprincipled set of materials.

In their account of the development of an institutional EAP textbook, Stoller and Robinson (2014) "depict the following steps in the textbook-development process: i) articulating priorities and principles; ii) scaffolding the instructional approach; iii) selecting target genres, compiling corpora with full-length text exemplars, and analyzing them using tools from corpus linguistics and discourse, genre, and move analysis; iv) converting analytical findings into instructional materials; v) piloting and assessing materials; using feedback to improve materials" (p. 262). They stress that the sequence is not always used in a linear fashion and that each stage influences and informs the others. We very much appreciate this procedural framework as it bases its content on analysis of authentic, targetlike texts, like Jolly and Bolitho (2011) and Mishan and Timmis (2015); recursive use is made of the framework and, like Mishan and Timmis (2015), the framework starts with an articulation of guiding principles and includes the vital stage of piloting.

Feak and Swales (2014) also include an important stage of "analysing the language of target genres" (p. 294) and of engaging in "systematic piloting" and making use of "insights gained to improve materials, even if that signifies major changes" (p. 294). They also emphasize the importance of being willing to abandon materials (as does Johnson, 2003) and to be willing to "write, re-write and re-write again" (p. 294.). Hadfield (2014) also stresses the importance of being willing to abandon and to revise, as well as the value of internal "dialoguing and imagining the classroom scenario" (p. 353).

Mishan and Timmis (2015) devote a chapter to "Materials Design: From Process to Product" in which they propose an "Idealised Sequence" (p. 164). This involves materials developers working through the following stages:

1. Statement of beliefs.
2. Needs analysis.
3. Aims and objectives.
4. Syllabus design.
5. Drafting.
6. Piloting.
7. Production.
8. Revision.

The authors stress that, in reality, this sequence can be applied in a recursive rather than linear way and that the writer can go back and revise their statement of beliefs and / or their aims and objectives. What we particularly like about this sequence is that it is principled in that it is driven by beliefs, discovered needs and specifications of targets rather than, as in many of the projects we have been invited to participate in, by a predetermined syllabus (the syllabus is not designed until stage 4). We also like the fact that the materials are piloted before production (a procedure that Amrani (2011) reports is less prevalent these days in commercial publication because of its demands on time and finance).

Macalister (2016) argues, as we do, that for many teachers the coursebook is the curriculum and that very often this is an "unexamined curriculum" (p. 41), which does not lead to successful learning outcomes because it does not help the teacher to apply principles deriving from "research and theory about best practice in language teaching and learning" (p. 41). Macalister examines classroom practices in relation to coursebooks and the relation between coursebook publication and research based principles and he "examines and exemplifies principles teachers can apply to ensure that their classroom practice is better informed by research and theory than it would be if they relied on the coursebook alone" (p. 41). These principles are the fluency principle, the frequency principle, the interference principle and the principle of the four strands (Nation, 2007), "an approach to curriculum design that advocates that a language course should have a balance between the four strands of meaning-focused input, meaning-focused output, language-focused learning, and fluency development" (Macalister, 2016, p. 45).

Other publications with something valuable to say about principled materials development include Byrd (1995), Richards (1995, 2001), Fenner and Newby (2000), Tomlinson and Masuhara (2004), Mishan (2005), Mukundan (2006), and Mishan and Chambers (2010), McDonough, Shaw, and Masuhara (2013). Teacher's books for coursebooks also often articulate a rationale for their material or the authors discuss the principles that informed them when writing their materials. For example, the *global intermediate teacher's book* (Clandfied & Robb Benne, 2011) contains 12 short essays by experts on topics relevant to the use of the coursebook (e.g. "Blended learning," "Class-centered learning," "Images and critical thinking").

There has certainly been a welcome move, since the mid-1990s, away from treating materials development as a purely practical and atheoretical undertaking to assuming that it should at least be informed by research and theory. In many cases, the findings and theories question the validity of current materials development practice but publishers and materials developers are unlikely to risk losing face validity through making radical changes to their approach to the content and pedagogy of their products.

Practical Guidance to Writers in the Literature

There are very few publications offering practical guidance to materials writers on how to develop effective materials. However, Byrd (1995) provides advice to materials writers, as does Nunan (1988, 1989). Johnson (2003) gives his informed opinion on the expertise needed to be a good task designer and Spiro (2006) provides advice on how to become a second language story writer. Tomlinson (2003c, 2013b) proposes a flexible text-driven framework for developing materials and puts forward ways of ensuring that materials are humanistic (2003d, 2013c), and Tomlinson and Masuhara (2004) provide practical advice on evaluating, adapting and developing materials, on writing instructions, on using illustrations and on layout and design. Coyle, Hood, and Marsh (2010) give detailed advice on how to develop materials for content and language integrated learning and both Van Avermaet and Gysen (2006) and Duran and Ramaut (2006) give advice on writing tasks for young learners. *Folio*, the journal of MATSDA (the Materials Development Association) has been publishing articles providing information, advice and stimulus to materials writers twice a year since 1993. For example in volume *8*(1 / 2), Rinvolucri (2003) provides practical suggestions for creative materials design and Srinivas (2003) describes a principled approach to involving teachers on a materials development project in India, and in volume *16*(2) Bolitho (2015) gives some principled and practical advice on writing coursebooks.

An interesting new publishing initiative is ELT Teacher 2 Writer, a company based in Oxford, United Kingdom. Amongst other things the company publishes eBooks that train teachers in the "craft and skills of ELT writing." As they say on their web site http://www.eltteacher2writer.co.uk/about-elt-teacher-2-writer, "There are training courses for writers of fiction and poetry, so why not ELT materials?" There are 21 published modules and eight forthcoming modules as of January 2017.

A recently formed IATEFL special interest group does now provide practical advice to materials writers and teachers on aspects of materials development. MaWSIG (the Materials Writing Special Interest Group) is responsible for conferences, workshops, webcasts, blogs and newsletters that offer information and advice useful to anyone writing or intending to write materials for language teaching. For example, in December 2015 there were blogs on Getting Started as a Materials Writer by Sandy Mullins and on Writing for Digital … Without Losing the Spark of Creativity by Jeremy Day. At the MAWSIG Conference in London in February 2016 there were sessions on, for example, Working in a Digital Space, Writing Skills for Effective Twenty-First Century Materials and Emerging New Pedagogies: Should We Change the Way We Design Materials?

Recommendations for Developing Materials

After more than 40 years' experience of developing, evaluating, reviewing, using, and researching materials for language learning we are now very clear about our preferred approaches.

Working as a Team

We have developed materials as single authors, in pairs, in small teams and in large teams. As a single author you can enjoy the luxury of doing it your way but this can be a problem too. You are questioned, advised, and sometimes commanded by your editor but you are not pushed, challenged or stimulated by a like-minded practitioner. In our experience, after a while you begin to lose impetus, energy and inspiration and nearing the end of the book your exhausted aim can become just to get it finished. Writing in pairs can be more stimulating and supportive but often differences become irreconcilable and you can still get exhausted nearing the end. Working in a small team overcomes many of the problems mentioned so far but we have found that if members of a small team feel their views and ideas are being ignored they can become resentful (especially if they are prestigious academic or a very experienced materials writers) and the harmony of the team is disrupted. This has happened to us on projects and we have spent time reassuring our disgruntled colleague(s) of their value to the team that could have been more profitably devoted to the development of materials. We have found that working with large teams (with six or preferably more members) is the most efficient and effective way of developing materials, particularly if the teams contain a spread of age, experience, and expertise, if they are stimulated first by facilitators, if they are working to commonly agreed principles and frameworks and, especially, if they are working together in a congenial place (rather than at a distance) where they can get to know and respect each other whilst developing a sense of collegiality and comradeship. When such conditions prevail, materials can be developed very quickly and the initial enthusiasm and energy can be maintained. Members of the team can be stimulated by the ideas and samples of good practice of their colleagues, a collective pride soon develops that drives and sustains the team and problems and weaknesses can be overcome by colleagues and facilitators without undue attention and loss of face. We have worked in or with large teams on projects developing coursebooks for primary and secondary schools in China, for teacher language improvement in Ethiopia, for a university in Turkey, and for secondary schools in Namibia. We have also worked with large teams in one-week workshops at which materials were developed for national use in Botswana, Indonesia, Malaysia, Mauritius, Seychelles, and Vietnam and for institutional use in Belgium, Hong Kong, Luxembourg, and Vietnam. We are not claiming that all the materials developed by these large teams were amazingly effective but in most cases the innovative materials that were developed were popular with students and were considered to be effective in helping them to become more communicatively competent. An interesting example of large team materials development was on the PKG (By the Teacher for the Teacher) program, a nationwide World Bank in-service teacher development project in Indonesia (Tomlinson, 1990) during which communicative materials making use of TPR Plus (Tomlinson, 1994a) extensive reading and discovery approaches (Tomlinson, 1994c; Bolitho et al., 2003) were developed by instructors at national workshops and by teachers at coffee afternoons in their homes. Not only were the materials incredibly popular with the secondary school students in the one class per school that participated in the project (e.g. these classes had much lower absentee rates than the others) but the students even performed a lot better on end-of-year traditional examinations.

Another interesting example was the writing of the Namibian secondary school coursebook *On target* (1995). Thirty teachers from all over Namibia came to Windhoek for six days. Some were young and inexperienced, some were very experienced, all were enthusiastic volunteers, and most had some sort of expertise to offer (e.g. a chief examiner, a dramatist, a poet, a musician, an artist). In 6 days they wrote initial drafts of a complete coursebook by dividing into teams, following an agreed and flexible text-driven framework (Tomlinson, 2013b), sharing their drafts and revising them after feedback from advisors and by a monitoring team. The result was an innovative and communicative coursebook, which was considered to be a great improvement on its predecessor, and very proud teachers who not only had enhanced their skills and self-esteem but could not wait to help train teachers to use the materials back in their regions. Not everybody was happy though. The editors pointed out the many mistakes and the improvements they had to make, as did the prestigious academics, who sometimes monitored the materials produced at national workshops on the PKG program in Indonesia.

Our preference then is for materials to be developed in large teams and our advice to maximize the likelihood of success is to:

- recruit 20 or more team members;
- recruit only enthusiastic volunteers;
- recruit mainly teachers (who have skills and insights to both offer and to gain) rather than academics (who have reputations as experts to protect);
- ensure a mix of ages, skills and experience;
- get the team to write its materials together in the same place rather than at a distance;
- appoint an experienced leader who can stimulate the writers and help to establish principles and a flexible framework on the first day before becoming a member of a small advisory / monitoring team (as was done on the Namibian project described above).

For other observations on writing materials in a large team see Popovici and Bolitho (2003) and Lyons (2003), and for endorsements of "local authors" writing "materials for their own context" and for "team authoring," which is likely to result in rich materials in terms of ideas, thinking styles, flexibility, and understanding—see Bolitho (2015, p. 7).

Articulating Principles

After assembling the team of writers the next step is to articulate the principles which you intend to drive your materials. This is best done by brainstorming individually, then sharing and justifying your principles, then agreeing together on a common set of principles and then converting the principles into criteria (as in Chapter 3) to be used both in the development and the evaluation of the draft materials.

As we said in Chapter 3 we find it useful to agree on both universal criteria (i.e. for any learner anywhere) and local criteria (i.e. for the specific target context of learning). We recommend starting with universal criteria to make sure that you do not get obsessed with meeting local expectations or examination requirements at the expense of vital prerequisites for language acquisition. Here is a small sample of the criteria we developed for a materials development project from agreed principles and from a profile of the target context of learning. The materials were intended for first-year students at an English medium university in Turkey who had good examination scores in English but struggled to communicate effectively in both informal and formal oral and written communication.

A Sample of our Universal Criteria

The materials should:

- expose the learners to authentic samples of oral English in use;
- expose the learners to authentic samples of written English in use;
- require the learners to use English for purposeful communication;
- require the learners to participate in authentic interaction in English;
- encourage learners to seek experience of communication in English outside the classroom;
- provide opportunities for the learners to make discoveries for themselves about how English is used for communication;

- be affectively engaging;
- be cognitively engaging;
- provide achievable challenges to all the learners;
- expose the learners to a variety of text types;
- expose the learners to a variety of task types;
- recycle texts for different purposes;
- provide learners with a choice of texts;
- provide learners with a choice of tasks.

A Sample of our Local Criteria

The materials should:

- be meaningful to young adult Turkish students;
- be relevant to young adult Turkish university students;
- respect young adult Turkish students as intelligent individuals;
- prepare young adult Turkish university students for academic communication in English;
- prepare young adult Turkish university students for social communication in English;
- be respectful to Turkish culture.

Making Use of Frameworks

We have found that taking time to decide on principled and flexible frameworks prior to starting to write the materials not only helps to achieve coherence and consistency but actually saves the writers time once they have got used to making use of the framework(s). We have found the following frameworks to be very useful for the achievement of these purposes, with text-driven frameworks being our preferred choice.

Text-Driven Frameworks

In a text-driven approach a core written / spoken / visual text is used to drive the unit of materials instead of predetermined teaching points. What the learners and the teacher do is determined organically by interaction with the text rather than by a syllabus or content map. This means that an authentic text that is likely to be meaningful, affectively engaging and cognitively engaging can be chosen rather than a text that has been contrived or selected to illustrate teaching points regardless of its likely appeal to the learners.

Our preferred materials-development framework is as follows:

1. **Select a core text** suitable for the target learners (ideally from a bank of potentially engaging texts built up over a period of time—many years in our case).
2. **Experience the text** again as a reader / listener / viewer rather than as a materials developer looking for teaching points.
3. **Reflect on your experience of the text** and in particular on what was happening in your mind so that you can create a similar experience for your learners to replace their likely inclination to study a text word by word.
4. **Create a readiness activity** that could activate the learners' minds in relation to the topic, theme, setting, etc., of the core text. For example, a readiness activity for a poem

in which a Ugandan woman complains about her husband could be for the learner to think about what women typically complain about in their society or to predict what the Ugandan woman might be complaining about. A readiness activity for a story which is set on a beach could be for the learner to visualize and then maybe draw a beach they know from actual or vicarious experience. A readiness activity for an extract from a contemporary film about Little Red Riding Hood could be for the learner to tell themselves the story they know about Little Red Riding Hood. A readiness activity is primarily an individual mental activity which the learner can relate to when they experience the text (just as when using our L1 we automatically relate a text we are experiencing to our own previous life experience). However, sometimes it can be interesting for the learners to compare their mental experiences with other students before going on to experience the text.

5. **Create an initial response activity** that could help the learners to experience the text holistically rather than to start decoding it word by word as soon as they encounter it. Examples of initial response activities would be:
   - As you read the poem note in your mind the different complaints which Lawino makes about her husband Ocol.
   - As you listen to the story try to see pictures in your mind of the beach in the story and of what happens on it.
   - As you watch the extract from the film talk to yourself about the similarities and the differences between your version of Little Red Riding Hood and the version in the film.

6. **Create an intake response activity** that helps the learners to deepen and articulate their personal responses to the text. Examples of intake response activities would be:
   - From the evidence in the poem do you think that Lawino is right to complain about her husband? Why?
   - Why do you think the "strange creatures" selected that man and that woman to take back to their ship?
   - Which version of the story of Little Red Riding Hood do you prefer? Yours or the one in the film? Why?

   There are no right or wrong answers to these questions and lively discussion can often ensue when learners share their responses in pairs or groups and with the whole class. These discussions are often most productive if there is disagreement and if the learners are encouraged to go back to the text to justify their responses.

7. **Create a development activity** in which the learners use the core text as a spring board to meaningful language production of their own. Examples of development activities would be:
   - Write a poem in which Ocol complains about his wife Lawino.
   - In groups write They Came from the Sea Part 2. Start your story, "Next week the same thing happened again." If you like you can brainstorm your story first by making it up as a circle story in which you take it in turns to contribute the next sentence as quickly as you can.
   - As a group write and then practice acting out a film script in which Little Red Riding Hood visits the place where you live.

8. **Create an input response activity** in which the learners return to the text to deepen their understanding of it or to make discoveries about how language is used in it. Examples of input response activities would be:

- In groups, identify the language structures and vocabulary that Lawino uses to make her complaints. Then see if you can make generalizations about the language of complaints. For homework, try to find other examples of the language of complaints and then next week in your group try to make generalizations about different ways of making complaints.
- Read "They Came from the Sea," Part 1, again. Then underline all the examples of the simple past tenses once and all examples of the past continuous twice. Then discuss in groups the differences in the story between the two tenses both in form and in function. For homework try to find other examples of the simple past and of the past continuous and bring them to class next week when you'll look for other differences between the two tenses.
- In the extract from the film that you watched why did Little Red Riding Hood wear a red hood, why did she get the wolf to pick flowers and why did she pretend to be her grandma?

9. **Create instructions** (see Chapter 16) **to get the students to revise the product of the development activity**, which they did in 7 above. For example:
   - Make use of the discoveries you have made about the language of complaint to help you to revise your poem about the complaints of Ocol.
   - Make use of the discoveries you have made about the simple past and the past continuous to help you to revise your story about what happened "the following week."
   - Make use of your answers to the questions about why Little Red Riding Hood did certain things in the film to help you to make her as cunning as possible in your film script about her coming to your area.

The framework above can be used flexibly with, for example, one of the stages receiving most of the time and attention, with some of the stages being omitted or with some of the stages being used in a different sequence (e.g. the input response activity before the first development activity).

In order to maximize the likelihood of learner engagement it is very important that the core texts are selected for their potential to engage the learners affectively and cognitively rather than because they exemplify a predetermined teaching point. Ideally the texts and tasks determine the syllabus but, provided the learners are exposed to a variety of genres (e.g. short stories, conversations, instructions for using a machine) and a variety of text types (e.g. narrative, justification, persuasion) we have found that text-driven approaches can be used to cover a syllabus. On the *On target* (1995) project in Namibia, the writers were told to forget the new curriculum and to focus on engagement. Every night, though, Brian compared what had been produced with what was expected to be covered in terms of language and skills in the curriculum, which he had attached to his hotel wall. He ticked off all the matches he discovered and by the evening of the penultimate day he was delighted (but not really surprised) to find that there was at least a 90% match. He listed language items and skills that had not been covered, got a senior Ministry official to agree that some of them were not really essential, and asked the writers the next day to try to include some of the remaining ones "naturally" in their unit.

See Tomlinson (2013b) for further articulation, justification, and exemplification of text-driven approaches and Al-Busaidi and Tindle (2010), McCullagh (2010), Troncoso (2010), Darici and Tomlinson (2016) and Heron (2016) for reports of text-driven approaches in action.

We also believe very strongly in the value of using TPR Plus frameworks to develop materials. TPR (Total Physical Response) is a comprehension method developed originally by James Ascher (Ascher, 1996; Richards & Rodgers, 2014) to teach beginners by initially getting them to respond physically to L1 oral instructions from their teacher (e.g. "Touch your left foot with your right hand") and not requiring them to speak in the target language until they have acquired enough language to be ready to do so. TPR Plus (Tomlinson, 1994a) is an approach developed on the PKG program in Indonesia (Tomlinson, 1990, 1995). Like Ascher's TPR, it involves the learners responding physically to what the teacher tells them but, instead of being only for beginners and being restricted to random responses to commands in the imperative, it can be used at any level to introduce "new" language, the teacher's utterances connect to build a coherent text (e.g. a story, a song, a recipe, a report of an event, an account of a process, instructions for a game, instructions for painting a mural or assembling a human sculpture) and the learners can be exposed to all verb forms. On the PKG project in Indonesia, for example, students were exposed in 6 weeks to all the language items on the syllabus for that year and could respond to them with understanding. Examples would be students at an elementary level acting out a story from the teacher's narrative that contrasted the use of the past continuous and the simple past or students at an intermediate level miming the process of sewing, cultivating and harvesting a crop whilst responding to passives (e.g. "The seeds are sown at the end of the dry season in shallow channels which have been dug in the soil") and responding to infinitives (e.g. "If the rains come early the channels need to be covered to stop the seeds being washed away"). Sometimes a language-awareness activity is included in the lesson (Islam, 2003) involving the students in making and articulating (in their first language at lower levels) discoveries about a linguistic feature of the input they have acting out (e.g. about the sentence position and form of Japanese verbs after acting out a song in which they raise, lower, clench, open, and clap their hands).

A typical framework for a TPR Plus lesson would be:

1. **A readiness activity** (e.g. the students visualize and then draw a beach they know whilst the teacher moves around describing their drawings in the target language).
2. **A narrative to mime activity** (e.g. the teacher tells a story about strange creatures coming to a beach and taking prisoners back to their ship whilst the students act as people on the beach or as strange creatures).
3. **A language awareness activity** (e.g. the teacher repeats the story, shows sample sentences on power point slides, invites the students to explore a feature of the text in their L1, such as the switch from past continuous to simple past when the action started, and then summarizes in the L2 what the learners say).
4. **A development activity** (e.g. the students in large groups develop a mime continuation of the story).
5. **A performance activity** (e.g. the students act out their continuation of the story whilst the teacher adds an oral narrative in the target language).
6. **An extensive reading activity** (e.g. the students are given in their next lesson a written narrative of the original story and of their continuation of it).

We have also used task-based frameworks based on strong versions of TBLT (Task-Based Language teaching) in which there is no explicit teaching of language either prior to or after the learners doing the task but rather responsive "teaching" when requested during task performance and learner discovery activities after task completion

(Tomlinson, 2013b). We also like to set tasks involving responding to texts as we feel that many of the text-free tasks used as examples in the literature on text-based approaches might be useful in doing controlled experiments but are trivial and unlikely to engage learners in a classroom (e.g. spot the difference, telling a story from a picture and following directions on a map). For more information about TBLT see Ellis (2003), Van den Branden (2006), Willis and Willis (2007), Long (2014), and Richards and Rodgers (2014).

Both TPR Plus and TBLT approaches can be used to cover an imposed syllabus (as we had to do on the PKG program in Indonesia) but it is easier to be creative and coherent if there is no compulsion to follow a predetermined sequence of teaching points. However our preference, as with the text-driven approach, is for a syllabus to derive organically from the texts and tasks and for the focus to be put on engaged exposure and use rather than on learning. In our view students are more likely to acquire language they have been engaged by than language which they have been obliged to study. And, in any case, we have never seen any evidence that learning in order a predetermined sequence of language points is in any way facilitative of language acquisition.

Following Systematic Procedures for Materials Development

Just like Jolly and Bolitho (2011), Stoller and Robinson (2014) and Mishan and Timmis (2015), we believe in using a systematic sequence of procedures recursively with each stage informing and interacting with other stages and with the writers primed to be ready to be to be opportunistic by making full use of the capabilities of the word processor to focus on whatever comes forcefully to mind regardless of its supposed place in the sequence of procedures or activities. Here is our recommended sequence of procedures in an idealized linear form:

1. Brainstorm your principles of language acquisition.
2. Use your principles to develop a set of universal criteria for the development and evaluation of your unit.
3. Write a brief profile of your target learners.
4. Use your profile to develop a set of local criteria for the development and evaluation of your unit.
5. Use your criteria to decide on a flexible framework to drive your units of material.
6. Use your framework to develop an initial draft of a unit.
7. Use your criteria to evaluate your unit.
8. If possible show your criteria and your unit to a colleague and invite their feedback.
9. Revise your unit.
10. Use your unit with a class.
11. Evaluate your unit again in the light of student responses to it.
12. Revise your unit again.
13. Evaluate the procedure you used to develop your materials and make any modifications you think will improve it before developing other units of materials. Ideally use procedures 6–11 when developing initial drafts of your other units and then pilot batches of your revised drafts with classes representative of your target students.

Obviously, time and resources might not allow for every procedure to be made use of. Even so we would say that procedures 1–8 were essential and we would strongly recommend to publishers and to Ministries of Education that all the procedures are followed.

Of course, you might just be developing occasional materials by yourself to use with your classes rather than working with colleagues to develop a course. If this is the case, we would still recommend following the above procedures and we would strongly recommend showing a draft to a respected colleague as well as immediate criterion-referenced evaluation and revision of your materials after first using them with a class.

Conclusion

We have told you what we know, what we think and what we recommend. Of course, there are many other valuable contributions to knowledge, thought, and proceduralization in the literature and on the web. We hope that you will consult and consider these contributions too and then decide what you think and what you want to do.

What Do You Think?

The following questions are not designed to test you but to stimulate thought about what has been said in this chapter. You can either answer them by talking to yourself in your inner voice or you can discuss them with colleagues or fellow students face to face or on social media.

1. Do you think you should base your materials on predetermined teaching points or let learning points emerge from a core text or task? Why?
2. Do you think that developing a framework before starting to write materials is useful? Why?
3. Would you prefer to write materials by yourself, in a pair, in a small team or in a large team? Why?
4. Do you think that teachers with no experience of developing materials should be encouraged to write materials for their students? Why?
5. Do you think that materials writing teams should be made up primarily of teachers, of experienced materials developers or of academics specializing in language acquisition? Why?
6. Think of materials which have impressed you as being likely to facilitate the development of communicative competence for learners using them? What do you remember as being distinctive about them?

Task

Decide on your target learners and then make use of the following procedure to develop a unit of materials for classroom use with them (ideally in a team but by yourself if necessary or preferred):

1. Brainstorm your principles of language acquisition.
2. Use your principles to develop a set of universal criteria for the development and evaluation of your unit.

3. Write a brief profile of your target learners.
4. Use your profile to develop a set of local criteria for the development and evaluation of your unit.
5. Use your criteria to decide on a flexible framework to drive your unit of materials.
6. Use your framework to develop an initial draft of your unit.
7. Use your criteria to evaluate your unit.
8. If possible show your criteria and your unit to a colleague and invite their feedback.
9. Revise your unit.
10. Use your unit with a class.
11. Evaluate your unit again in the light of student responses to it.
12. Revise your unit again.
13. Evaluate the procedure you used to develop your materials and make any modifications you think will improve it before developing another unit of materials.
14. You could write up your experience as an article for the MATSDA journal *Folio* or do a presentation on it at a MATSDA conference (see www.matsda.org).

Further Reading

Harwood, N. (Ed.). (2014). *English language teaching textbooks: Content, consumption, production*. Basingstoke: Palgrave: Macmillan.
McGrath, I. (2013). *Teaching materials and the roles of EFL/ESL teachers: Practice and theory*. London: Bloomsbury.
Mishan, F. & Timmis, I. (2015). *Materials development for TESOL*. Edinburgh: Edinburgh University Press.

References

Al-Busaidi, S., & Tindle, K. (2010). Evaluating the effect of in-house materials on language learning. In B. Tomlinson & H. Masuhara (Eds.), *Research for materials development in language learning: Evidence for best practice* (pp. 137–149). London: Continuum.
Amrani, F. (2011). The process of evaluation: a publisher's view. In B. Tomlinson (Ed.), *Materials development in language teaching* (2nd ed., pp. 267–295). Cambridge: Cambridge University Press.
Ascher, J. (1996). *Learning another language through actions* (5th ed.). Los Gatos, CA: Sky Oaks Productions.
Bao, D. (2015). Flexibility in second language materials. *The European Journal of Applied Linguistics and TEFL: Materials in the ELT Classroom: Development, Use and Evaluation* [Guest editor B. Tomlinson], *4*(2), 37–52.
Bardovi-Harlig, K., & Mossman, S. (2016). Corpus-based materials development for teaching and learning pragmatic routines. In B. Tomlinson (Ed.), *SLA research and materials development for language learning* (pp. 250–267). New York: Routledge.
Bell, J., & Gower, R. (1998). Writing course materials for the world: A great compromise. In B. Tomlinson (Ed.), *Materials development for language teaching* (pp. 116–129). Cambridge: Cambridge University Press.

Bell, J., & Gower, R. (2011). Writing course materials for the world: A great compromise. In B. Tomlinson (Ed.), *Materials development for language teaching* (2nd ed., pp. 135–150). Cambridge: Cambridge University Press.

Benesch, S. (2010). Critical praxis as materials development: responding to military recruitment on a U.S. campus. In N. Harwood (Ed.), *English language teaching materials: theory and practice* (pp. 109–128). Cambridge: Cambridge University Press.

Boers, F., & Strong, B. (2016). An evaluation of textbook exercises on collocations. In B. Tomlinson (Ed.), *SLA research and materials development for language learning* (pp. 139–152). New York: Routledge.

Bolitho, R. (2015). Language textbooks and materials: A way and ways. *Folio, 16*(2), 4–7.

Bolitho, R., Carter, R., Hughes, R., Ivanic, R., Masuhara, H., & Tomlinson, B. (2003). Ten questions about language awareness. *ELT Journal 57*(2), 251–59.

Burns, A., & Hill, D. (2013). Teaching speaking in a second language. In B. Tomlinson (Ed.), *Applied linguistics and materials development* (pp. 231–248). London: Bloomsbury.

Byrd, P. (1995). *Materials writers guide.* Rowley, MA: Newbury House.

Clandfield, L., & Robb Benne, R. (2011). *Global intermediate teacher's book.* Oxford: Macmillan.

Cohen, A. D., & Ishihara, N. (2013). *Pragmatics.* In B. Tomlinson (Ed.), *Applied linguistics and materials development* (pp. 113–126). London: Bloomsbury.

Coyle, D., Hood, P., & Marsh, D. (2010). *Content and language integrated learning.* Cambridge: Cambridge University Press.

Darici, A., & Tomlinson, B. (2016). A case study of principled materials in action. In B. Tomlinson (Ed.), *Second language acquisition research and materials development for language learning* (pp. 71–86). New York: Routledge.

Deller, H., & Walkley, A. (2005). *Innovations.* London: Thomson / Heinle.

Douglas, J. (2012). *How are corpora of spoken English exploited for lexical items in materials development for General English coursebooks at upper intermediate level?* (Unpublished MA dissertation). Norwich Institute for Language Education/Leeds Metropolitan University, Norwich/Leeds.

Duran, G., & Ramaut, G. (2006). Tasks for absolute beginners and beyond: Developing and sequencing tasks at basic proficiency levels. In K. Van den Branden (Ed.), *Task-based language education: from theory to practice* (pp. 47–75). Cambridge: Cambridge University Press.

Edge, J., & Wharton, S. (1998). Autonomy and development: living in the materials world. In B. Tomlinson (Ed.), *Materials development in language teaching* (pp. 295–310). Cambridge: Cambridge University Press.

Ellis, R. (Ed.) (2003). *Task-based language learning and teaching.* Oxford: Oxford University Press.

Ellis, R. (2010). Second language acquisition research and language teaching materials. In N. Harwood (Ed.), *Materials in ELT: theory and practice* (pp. 33–57). Cambridge: Cambridge University Press.

Evans, N. W., Hartshorn, K. J., & Anderson, N. J. (2010). A principled approach to content-based development for reading. In N. Harwood (Ed.), *Materials in ELT: theory and practice* (pp. 131–156). Cambridge: Cambridge University Press.

Farr, F., Chambers, A., & O'Riordan, S. (2010). Corpora for materials development in language teacher education: underlying principles and useful data. In F. Mishan & A. Chambers (Eds.), *Perspectives on language learning materials development* (pp. 33–62). Bern: Peter Lang.

Feak, C. B., & Swales, J. J. M. (2014). Tensions between the old and the new in EAP textbook revision: A tale of two projects. In N. Harwood (Ed.), *English language teaching textbooks; content, consumption, production* (pp. 299–319). Basingstoke: Palgrave Macmillan.

Fenner, A., & Newby, D. (2000). *Approaches to materials design in European textbooks: Implementing principles of authenticity, learner autonomy, cultural awareness.* Graz: European Centre for Modern Languages.

Fenton–Smith, B. (2010). A debate on the desired effects of output activities for extensive reading. In B. Tomlinson & H. Masuhara (Eds.) *Research for materials development in language learning: evidence for best practice* (pp. 50–61). London: Continuum.

Flores, M. M. (1995). Materials development: A creative process. In A. C. Hidalgo, D. Hall, & G. M. Jacobs (Eds.), *Getting started: materials writers on materials writing* (pp. 57–66). Singapore: SEAMEO Language Centre.

Ghosn, I. (2010). Five year outcomes from children's literature-based programmes v programmes using a skills-based ESL course – The Matthew and Peter effects at work? In B. Tomlinson & H. Masuhara (Eds.), *Research for materials development in language learning: Evidence for best practice* (pp. 21–36). London: Continuum.

Ghosn, I. (2013a). Developing motivating materials for refugee children: From theory to practice. In B. Tomlinson (Ed.), *Developing materials for language teaching* (pp. 247–268). London: Bloomsbury.

Ghosn, I. (2013b). Language learning for young learners. In B. Tomlinson (Ed.), *Applied linguistics and materials development* (pp. 61–74). London: Bloomsbury.

Gilmore, A. (2009). Using online corpora to develop students' writing skills. *ELTJ, 63*(4), 363–372.

Haan, N. (2013). Mining the L2 environment: ESOL learners and strategies outside the classroom. In B. Tomlinson (Ed.), *Developing materials for language teaching* (pp. 309–332). London: Bloomsbury.

Hadfield, J. (2014). Chaosmos: Spontaneity and order in the materials design process. In N. Harwood (Ed.), *English language teaching textbooks: Content, consumption, production* (pp. 320–359). Basingstoke: Palgrave Macmillan.

Hadfield, J., & Dornyei, Z. (2013). *Motivating learning.* Harlow: Pearson.

Hall, D. (1995). Materials production: theory and practice. In A. C. Hidalgo, D. Hall & G. M. Jacobs (Eds.), *Getting started: materials writers on materials writing* (pp. 8–24). Singapore: SEAMEO Language Centre.

Harwood, N. (Ed.) (2010a). *Materials in ELT: Theory and practice.* Cambridge: Cambridge University Press.

Harwood, N. (2010b). Research-based materials to demystify academic citation for post-graduate students. In N. Harwood (Ed.), *Materials in ELT: theory and practice* (pp. 301–320). Cambridge: Cambridge University Press.

Harwood, N. (Ed.). (2014). *English language teaching textbooks: Content, consumption, production.* Basingstoke: Palgrave: Macmillan.

Heron, M. (2016). Using affectively engaging texts to stimulate motivation in the learner centred classroom. In M. Azarnoosh, M. Zeraatpishe, A. Faravani & H. R. Kargozari (Eds.), *Issues in materials development* (pp. 159–182). Rotterdam: Sense.

Hewings, M. (2010). Materials for university essay writing. In Harwood, N. (Ed.), *Materials in ELT: theory and practice* (pp. 251–278). Cambridge: Cambridge University Press.

Hidalgo, A. C., Hall, D., & Jacobs, G. M. (Eds.) (1995). *Getting started: Materials writers on materials writing.* Singapore: SEAMEO Language Centre.

Hooper Hansen, G. (2011). Lozanov and the teaching text. In B. Tomlinson (Ed.), *Materials development in language teaching* (2nd ed., pp. 403–413). Cambridge: Cambridge University Press.

Hutchinson, T., & Waters, A. (1987). *English for specific purposes: A learning-centred approach*. Cambridge: Cambridge University Press.

Hyland, K. (2013). Materials for developing writing skills. In B. Tomlinson (Ed.), *Developing materials for language teaching* (pp. 391–406). London: Bloomsbury.

Islam, C. (2003). Materials for beginners. In B. Tomlinson (Ed.), *Developing materials for language teaching* (pp. 256–274). London: Continuum.

Johnson, K. (2003). *Designing language teaching tasks*. Basingstoke: Palgrave Macmillan.

Jolly, D., & Bolitho, R. (1998). A framework for materials writing. In B. Tomlinson (Ed.), *Materials development for language teaching* (pp. 90–115). Cambridge: Cambridge University Press.

Jolly, D., & Bolitho, R. (2011). A framework for materials writing. In B. Tomlinson (Ed.), *Materials development for language teaching* (2nd ed., pp. 107–134). Cambridge: Cambridge University Press.

Jones, M., & Schmitt, N. (2010). Developing materials for discipline-specific vocabulary and phrases in academic seminars. In N. Harwood (Ed.), *Materials in ELT: theory and practice* (pp. 225–248). Cambridge: Cambridge University Press.

Kervin, L., & Derewianka, B. (2011). New technologies to support language learning. In B. Tomlinson (Ed.), *Materials development for language teaching* (2nd ed., pp. 328–351). Cambridge: Cambridge University Press.

Kiddle, T. (2013). Developing digital language learning materials. In B. Tomlinson (Ed.), *Developing materials for language teaching* (pp. 189–206). London: Bloomsbury.

Long, M. (2014). *Second language acquisition and task-based language teaching*. New York: Wiley-Blackwell.

Lyons, P. (2003). A practical experience of institutional textbook writing: product / process implications for materials development. In B. Tomlinson (Ed.), *Developing materials for language teaching* (pp. 490–504). London: Continuum.

Macalister, J. (2016). Applying language learning principles to coursebooks. In W. A. Renandya & H. P. Widodo (Eds.), *English language teaching today: linking theory and practice* (pp. 41–51). New York: Springer.

Maley, A. (1998). Squaring the circle—reconciling materials as constraint with materials as empowerment. In B. Tomlinson (Ed.), *Materials development for language teaching* (pp. 279–294). Cambridge: Cambridge University Press.

Maley, A. (2003). Creative approaches to writing materials. In B. Tomlinson (Ed.), *Developing materials for language teaching* (pp. 183–198). London: Continuum.

Maley, A. (2011). Squaring the circle—reconciling materials as constraint with materials as empowerment. In B. Tomlinson (Ed.), *Materials development for language teaching* (2nd ed., pp. 379–402). Cambridge: Cambridge University Press.

Mares, C. (2003). Writing a coursebook. In B. Tomlinson (Ed.), *Materials development for language teaching* (2nd ed., pp. 130–140). Cambridge: Cambridge University Press.

Masuhara, H. (2011). What do teachers really want from coursebooks? In B. Tomlinson (Ed.), *Materials development for language teaching* (2nd ed., pp. 236–266). Cambridge: Cambridge University Press.

Masuhara, H. (2016). Brain studies and materials for language learning. In B. Tomlinson (Ed.), *SLA research and materials development for language learning* (pp. 23–32). New York: Routledge.

Masuhara, H., Haan, N., Yi, Y., & Tomlinson, B. (2008). Adult EFL courses. *ELT Journal, 62*(3), 294–312.

McCarten, J., & McCarthy, M. (2010). Bridging the gap between corpus and course book: The case of conversation strategies. In F. Mishan & A. Chambers (Eds.), *Perspectives on language learning materials development* (pp. 11–32). Bern: Peter Lang.

McCarthy, M., McCarten, J., & Sandford, H. (2006). *Touchstone*. Cambridge: Cambridge University Press.

McCullugh, M. (2010) An initial evaluation of a set of published materials for medical English. In B. Tomlinson & H. Masuhara (Eds.), *Research for materials development in language learning* (pp. 381–393). London: Continuum.

McDonough, J., Shaw, C., & Masuhara, H. (2013) *Materials and methods in ELT: A teacher's guide* (3rd ed.). Chichester: Wiley-Blackwell.

McGrath, I. (2002). *Materials evaluation and design for language teaching*. Edinburgh: University of Edinburgh Press.

McGrath, I. (2013). *Teaching materials and the roles of EFL/ESL teachers: Practice and theory*. London: Bloomsbury.

Methold, K. (1972). The practical aspects of instructional materials preparation. *RELC Journal, 3*(1), 88–97.

Mishan, F. (2005). *Designing authenticity into language learning materials*. Bristol: Intellect.

Mishan, F. (2010). Withstanding washback: thinking outside the box in materials development. In B. Tomlinson & H. Masuhara (Eds.), Research for materials development in language learning (pp. 353–369). London: Continuum.

Mishan, F. (2013). Demystifying blended learning. In B. Tomlinson (Ed.), *Developing materials for language teaching* (pp. 207–224). London: Bloomsbury.

Mishan, F., & Chambers, A. (Eds.) (2010). *Perspectives on language learning materials development*. Bern: Peter Lang.

Mishan, F., & Timmis, I. (2015). *Materials development for TESOL*. Edinburgh: Edinburgh University Press.

Motteram, G. (2011) Coursebooks and multi-media supplements. In B. Tomlinson (Ed.), *Materials development for language teaching* (2nd ed., pp. 303–327). Cambridge: Cambridge University Press.

Mukundan, J. (Ed.). (2006). *Focus on ELT materials*. Petaling Jaya: Pearson Malaysia.

Nation, I. S. P. (2007). The four strands. *Innovation in Language Learning and Teaching, 1*(1), 1–12.

Nunan, D. (1988). Principles for designing language teaching materials. *Guidelines, 10*, 1–24.

Nunan, D. (1989). *Designing tasks for the communicative classroom*. Cambridge: Cambridge University Press.

Nunan, D. (1991). *Language teaching methodology*. Hemel Hempstead: Prentice Hall.

O'Keefe, A., McCarthy, M., & Carter, R. (2007). *From corpus to classroom: language use and language teaching*. Cambridge: Cambridge University Press.

On target. (1995). Windhoek: Gamsburg Macmillan.

Park, H. (2010). Process drama in the Korean EFL secondary classroom: a case study of Korean middle school classrooms. In B. Tomlinson & H. Masuhara (Eds.), *Research for materials development in language learning* (pp. 155–171). London: Continuum.

Pascasio, E. M. (1995). Experiencing language: A response to the Philippine bilingual policy. In A. C. Hidalgo, D. Hall & G. M. Jacobs (Eds.), *Getting started: materials writers on materials writing* (pp. 82–94). Singapore: SEAMEO Language Centre.

Penaflorida, A. H. (1995). The process of materials development: A personal experience. In A. C. Hidalgo, D. Hall & G. M. Jacobs (Eds.), *Getting started: materials writers on materials writing* (pp. 172–186). Singapore: SEAMEO Language Centre.

Popovici, R., & Bolitho, R. (2003). Personal and professional development through writing: The Romanian textbook project. In B. Tomlinson (Ed.), *Developing materials for language teaching* (pp. 505–517). London: Continuum.

Prabhu, N. (1990). There is no best method—why? *TESOL Quarterly, 24*, 161–176.

Prowse, P. (1998). How writers write: testimony from authors. In B. Tomlinson (Ed.), *Materials development in language teaching* (pp. 130–145). Cambridge: Cambridge University Press.

Prowse, P. (2011). How writers write: Testimony from authors. In B. Tomlinson (Ed.), *Materials development in language teaching* (2nd ed., pp. 151–173). Cambridge: Cambridge University Press.

Reinders, H., & White, C. (2010) The theory and practice of technology in materials development and task design. In N. Harwood (Ed.), *Materials in ELT: theory and practice* (pp. 58–80). Cambridge: Cambridge University Press.

Reppen, R. (2011). Using corpora in the language classroom. In B. Tomlinson (Ed.), *Materials development for language teaching* (2nd ed., pp. 35–50). Cambridge: Cambridge University Press.

Richards, J. C. (2001). *Curriculum development in. language education.* Cambridge: Cambridge. University Press.

Richards, J. C. (1995). Easier said than done: An insider's account of a textbook project. In A. C. Hidalgo, D. Hall & G. M. Jacobs (Eds.), *Getting started: materials writers on materials writing* (pp. 95–135). Singapore: SEAMEO Language Centre.

Richards, J. (2006). Materials development and research—making the connection. *RELC Journal, 37*(1), 5–26.

Richards, J. C., & Rodgers, T. S. (2014). *Approaches and methods in language teaching* (3rd ed.). Cambridge: Cambridge University Press.

Rinvolucri, M. (2003). Humanistic criteria in materials design and exploitation. *Folio, 8*(1/2), 21–23.

Rixon, S. (2013). Author's knowledge, rationales and principles: Steady-flow through or stuck in the publishing pipeline? The case of early reading with young learners. In B. Tomlinson (Ed.), *Developing materials for language teaching* (pp. 229–246). London: Bloomsbury.

Samuda, V. (2005). Expertise in pedagogic task design. In K. Johnson (Ed.), *Expertise in second language learning and teaching* (pp. 230–254). Basingstoke: Palgrave Macmillan.

Spiro, J. (2006). Becoming a second language story writer. In J. Mukundan (Ed.), *Focus on ELT materials* (pp. 47–60). Petaling Jaya: Pearson Malaysia.

Srinivas, R. (2003). Teacher involvement in textbook preparation in India. *Folio, 8*(1/2), 38–40.

Stoller, F. L., & Robinson, M. S. (2014). An interdisciplinary textbook project: Charting the paths taken. In N. Harwood (Ed.), *English language teaching textbooks; content, consumption, production* (pp. 241–261). Basingstoke: Palgrave Macmillan.

Sundara Rajan, B. R. (1995). Developing instructional materials for adult workers. In A. C. Hidalgo, D. Hall & G. M. Jacobs (Eds.), *Getting started: Materials writers on materials writing* (pp. 187–208). Singapore: SEAMEO Language Centre.

Tan, M. (Ed.). (2002). *Corpus studies in language education.* Bangkok: IELE Press.

Timmis, I. (2013a). Spoken language research: The applied linguistics challenge. In Tomlinson, B. (Ed.), *Applied linguistics and materials development* (pp. 79–94). London: Bloomsbury.

Timmis, I. (2013b). Corpora and materials: Towards a working relationship. In B. Tomlinson (Ed.), *Developing materials for language teaching* (pp. 461–474). London: Bloomsbury.

Timmis, I. (2014). Writing materials for publication; questions raised and lessons learned. In N. Harwood (Ed.), *English language teaching textbooks; content, consumption, production.* (pp. 241–261). Basingstoke: Palgrave Macmillan.

Timmis, I. (2015). *Corpus linguistics for ELT: Research and practice.* Abington: Routledge.

Tomlinson, B. (1990). Managing change in Indonesian high schools. *ELT Journal, 44*(1), 25–37.

Tomlinson, B. (1994a). Materials for TPR. *Folio, 1*(2), 8–10.

Tomlinson, B. (1994b). *Openings. Language through literature: An activities book (New Edition).* London: Penguin.

Tomlinson, B. (1994c). Pragmatic awareness activities. *Language Awareness, 3*(3 and 4), 119–129.

Tomlinson, B. (1995). Work in progress: Textbook projects. *Folio, 2*(2), 26–31.

Tomlinson, B. (Ed.). (1998a). *Materials development in language teaching.* Cambridge: Cambridge University Press.

Tomlinson, B. (1998b). Introduction. In B. Tomlinson (Ed.), *Materials development in language teaching* (pp. 1–24). Cambridge: Cambridge University Press.

Tomlinson, B. (Ed.). (2003a). *Developing materials for language teaching.* London: Continuum Press.

Tomlinson, B. (2003b). Materials evaluation. In B. Tomlinson (Ed.), *Materials development for language teaching* (2nd ed., pp. 15–36). Cambridge: Cambridge University Press.

Tomlinson, B. (2003c). Developing principled frameworks for materials development. In B. Tomlinson (Ed.), *Materials development for language teaching* (2nd ed., pp. 107–129). Cambridge: Cambridge University Press.

Tomlinson, B. (2003d). Humanizing the coursebook. In B. Tomlinson (Ed.), *Materials development for language teaching* (2nd ed., pp. 162–173). Cambridge: Cambridge University Press.

Tomlinson, B. (Ed.). (2008a). *English language teaching materials: A critical review.* London: Continuum.

Tomlinson, B. (2008b). Language acquisition and language learning materials. In B. Tomlinson (Ed.), *English language teaching materials: A critical review* (pp. 3–14). London: Continuum.

Tomlinson, B. (2010a). Principles and procedures of materials development. In N. Harwood (Ed.), *Materials in ELT: Theory and practice* (pp. 81–108). Cambridge: Cambridge University Press.

Tomlinson, B. (2010b). Helping learners to fill the gaps in their learning. In F. Mishan & A. Chambers (Eds.), *Perspectives on language learning materials development* (pp. 87–108). Bern: Peter Lang.

Tomlinson, B. (Ed.). (2011a). *Materials development in language teaching.* (2nd ed.) Cambridge: Cambridge University Press.

Tomlinson, B. (2011b). Principled procedures in materials development. In B. Tomlinson (Ed.), *Materials development in language teaching.* (2nd ed., pp. 1–31). Cambridge: Cambridge University Press.

Tomlinson, B. (2011c). Seeing what they mean: Helping L2 readers to visualise. In B. Tomlinson (Ed.), *Materials development for language teaching* (2nd ed., pp. 357–378). Cambridge: Cambridge University Press.

Tomlinson, B. (2012). Materials development for language learning and teaching. *Language Teaching: Surveys and Studies, 45*(2), 143–179.

Tomlinson, B. (Ed.) (2013a). *Developing materials for language teaching* (2nd ed.). London: Bloomsbury.

Tomlinson, B. (2013b). Developing principled frameworks for materials development. In B. Tomlinson (Ed.), *Developing materials for language teaching* (2nd ed., pp. 95–118). London: Bloomsbury.

Tomlinson, B. (2013c). Humanising the coursebook. In B. Tomlinson (Ed.), *Developing materials for language teaching* (2nd ed., pp. 139–156). London: Bloomsbury.

Tomlinson, B. (Ed.). (2013d). *Applied linguistics and materials development*. London: Bloomsbury.

Tomlinson, B. (2013e). Second language acquisition and materials development. In B. Tomlinson (Ed.), *Applied linguistics and materials development* (pp. 11–30). London: Bloomsbury.

Tomlinson, B. (Ed.) (2016a). *SLA research and materials development for language learning*. New York: Routledge.

Tomlinson, B. (2016b). Applying SLA principles to whole class activities. In B. Tomlinson (Ed.), *SLA research and materials development for language learning*. New York: Routledge.

Tomlinson, B., Dat, B., Masuhara, H., & Rubdy, R. (2001). ELT courses for adults. *ELT Journal, 55*(1), 80–101.

Tomlinson, B., & Masuhara, H. (2003). Simulations in materials development. In B. Tomlinson (Ed.), *Materials development for language teaching* (2nd ed., pp. 462–478). Cambridge: Cambridge University Press.

Tomlinson, B., & Masuhara, H. (2004). *Developing language course materials*. Singapore: RELC Portfolio Series.

Tomlinson, B., & Masuhara, H. (Eds.). (2010). *Research for materials development in language learning: evidence for best practice*. London: Continuum.

Tomlinson, B., & Masuhara, H. (2013). Adult coursebooks. *ELT Journal, 67*(2), 233–249.

Troncoso, C. R. (2010.) The effects of language materials on the development of intercultural competence. In B. Tomlinson & H. Masuhara (Eds.), *Research for materials development in language learning: Evidence for best practice* (pp. 83–102). London: Continuum.

Van Avermaet, P., & Gysen, S. (2006). From needs to tasks: Language learning needs in a task-based approach. In K. Van den Branden (Ed.), *Task-based language education: From theory to practice* (pp. 17–46). Cambridge: Cambridge University Press.

Van den Branden, K. (2006). *Task-based language education: From theory to practice*. Cambridge: Cambridge University Press.

Willis, J. (2011). Concordances in the classroom without a computer: assembling and exploiting concordances of common words. In B. Tomlinson (Ed.), *Materials development in language teaching* (2nd ed.) (pp. 51–77). Cambridge: Cambridge University Press.

Willis, D., & Willis, J. (2007). *Doing task-based teaching*. Oxford: Oxford University Press.

Young, R. (1980). Modular course design. In *Projects in materials design. ELT Documents Special* (pp. 222–231). London: British Council.

6

The Process of Publishing Coursebooks

Introduction

In Chapter 5 we explored various approaches, principles, and procedures that materials writers could employ in developing language learning materials. In this chapter we widen our scope to include all the collaborators who help shape ELT materials into published forms, whether print or digital. Publishing requires collaboration between many people who have different roles and agendas. Who are the stakeholders? How does collaboration take place? What kind of stages do materials go through? What happens to the materials? What are the issues in each procedure? As was evidenced in Chapter 4, "Adaptation," textbooks (and sometimes, these days, digital courses) often work as the curriculum, determining the content, sequence, and quality of learning. We believe that it is vital for everyone who is involved in learning and teaching to understand how these important materials are shaped into publication. Because publishing practices change rapidly and vary according to types of materials, we have tried to highlight in this chapter the most recent accounts by those who are directly involved in publishing (e.g. McGrath, 2013, and Mishan and Timmis, 2015, which each have a chapter on the publishing of materials), plus some reference where relevant to past practice.

Kinds of Textbooks

By "textbook" we mean any published set of paper materials that is used on a learning program in order to promote learning. There are many kinds of textbook available. Richards (2014, p. 20), in his chapter "ELT textbooks," provides a list of common kinds of material for English language teaching:

- coursebooks for international markets;
- materials for specific age groups—children, teenagers, adults;
- materials for specific skills—reading, writing, listening, speaking;
- materials for specific purposes—academic study, travel, business, law, engineering;
- materials for exam preparation—TOEFL, TOIEC, IELTS, KET;
- reference materials—dictionaries and grammars;
- self-study materials;
- readers.

The Complete Guide to the Theory and Practice of Materials Development for Language Learning, First Edition. Brian Tomlinson and Hitomi Masuhara.
© 2018 John Wiley & Sons, Inc. Published 2018 by John Wiley & Sons, Inc.

Which kind of textbooks in the list above are you most familiar with? We will discuss materials for different age groups in Chapters 10 and 11; for skills in Chapter 9 and for different purposes and levels in Chapter 12.

Among those different kinds of textbooks above, the most widely used around the world seems to be the coursebook (Richards, 2014; Tomlinson, 2010; Tomlinson, 2015) and it is the publication of coursebooks that we are going to focus on in this chapter (though many of our points are relevant to other types of print materials and to digital materials too). Coursebooks are typically a package that contains more or less everything that the teachers and learners may need for learning at each level. Tomlinson (2015, pp. 172–173) divides coursebooks further into three categories: global coursebooks, adapted coursebooks and local coursebooks. We would now add an extra category of transplanted coursebooks.

Global Coursebooks

So-called "global coursebooks" are produced by commercial publishers, often for targeted regional markets initially but then sold on the international market (for more discussion see Chapter 4, "Adaptation," specifically in the section titled "Paradigm Shift 2: Global English for Multitudes of Cultures"). Contemporary global coursebooks are designed to be visually appealing to attract custom (for details see Chapter 13, "Visuals, Design and Layout") with magazine-like photos and illustrations on glossy paper. Their titles often make no reference to English language teaching but promise international experience of the English speaking world. To keep up with various unpredictable demands from diverse learners in different contexts worldwide, the publishers have been offering multistrand syllabuses (i.e. language, skills, communicative functions and whatever is topical in ELT around the time of publishing— e.g. cross-curricular Content and Language Integrated Learning (CLIL); life skills and critical thinking). Nowadays, more and more multicomponents such as digital and online materials are being added, as Richards (2014, p. 20) explains:

> Textbooks have multiple components such as workbooks, an assessment package, DVDs and CD-ROMs, and additional resources for teachers and students. Digital components are used increasingly, such as an e-book, online workbooks, and options for varying levels of blended use.

Such multicomponent coursebooks require a large investment of time, effort, and financial resources by authors and publishers. In other words, coursebook production, though potentially lucrative (McGrath, 2013, p. 30), is typically competitive and high risk.

Adapted Coursebooks

Adapted coursebooks are local versions of global coursebooks either adapted by the original international publisher to suit a particular market or adapted by local experts for a ministry, institution, or publisher with the permission of the international publisher. They are often more locally relevant and less expensive than their global originals but may also be considered less relevant to local requirements than tailor-made local equivalents.

Local Coursebooks

Local coursebooks are produced for a specific national, regional, or institutional location by a ministry of education, regional education bureau, institution or publisher.

In the case of national textbooks, such as those used in public schools, the Department of Education may initiate a materials writing project, employ a team of writers, or commission publishers to recruit writers to develop a coursebook that suits the national curriculum and guidelines (see Mukundan, 2008 for an example of a secondary coursebook produced and distributed by the Malaysian government; Popovici and Bolitho, 2003 for a Romanian secondary school project; Tomlinson, 1995 for various local projects). The driver behind the projects may be regional government branches. For example, we were invited by the Guangzhou educational bureau to lead a local team to develop primary and secondary school textbooks for Guandong province. Those books were later submitted for government approval to be widely marketed all through China.

In other cases, the Ministry of Education publishes a national curriculum and guidelines and invites local commercial publishers to produce textbooks to match them. The Ministry requires all the publishers to submit their coursebooks to go through approval processes. Only books that have been approved by evaluators from the Ministry of Education can be used in the schools (e.g. Japan, Korea; see Singapore Wala, 2003a, 2003b and 2003 for details of the approval process in Singapore).

Local education bureaus may establish additional processes for further reviewing and adopting in their school districts. For example, a local education bureau may publish a list of approved coursebooks from which schools in the district can choose one for adoption.

Sometimes institutions decide to produce and publish materials themselves. We have been involved with such projects in Sultan Qaboos University in Oman and in Bilkent University in Turkey, and Stoller and Robinson (2014) describe a case of Content and Language Integrated Learning (CLIL) at a university in the United States. The main strength of local coursebooks is their potential for direct relevance to the students, teachers and contexts.

Transplanted Coursebooks

A transplanted coursebook is one that was originally developed for a particular institution or region (i.e. a local coursebook) but has been adopted for use in a different institution or region. Such adoptions are usually the result of the lack of an appropriate coursebook and an appreciation of the potential value of the coursebook being transplanted. Obviously, though, the transplant will be less relevant in its new environment and will need to be adapted to achieve effective use.

Designing coursebooks so that they can be localized or transplanted would obviously increase the potential value of any coursebook. This could easily be achieved by producing an e-version of the coursebook, which could be sold for potential adapters to download, modify and print off for distribution. It could also be sold as a digital course with a menu of illustrations, texts and tasks to select from for each unit.

The Development Process of Coursebooks

The following stages seem to commonly feature in developing coursebooks, though we have found some variations in the literature we have consulted (for similar attempts to explore the publishing process, see Chapter 2 in McGrath, 2013, and Chapter 9 in Mishan and Timmis, 2015).

Stage 1: Planning

This is the stage in which all the fundamental planning takes place. The main crucial factors to be considered seem to include:

- contexts (e.g. political and educational agendas, government policies and legislation, socio-economic demands, syllabuses, examinations);
- target users (e.g. decision-making administrators, teachers, and students);
- the rationale for producing a new course or revised course (e.g. target country adopting a new curriculum, problems with the existing materials, new approaches, a gap in the market);
- logistics for production (e.g. funding, budget, staffing, time available).

Stage 2: Establishing a Writing Team and Principles

This seems to be the stage in which a core working team is developed and principles and procedures are agreed upon in relation to:

- the selection of editors and editorial assistants;
- (theoretical rationales);
- ideals, aims and objectives of the materials;
- reality checks (e.g. management of innovation: balance of familiar versus new to get the teachers on board);
- selection of team members;
- guidance for the writers.

Stage 3: Drafting and Feedback

Some samples are drafted and evaluated, and feedback is given. Feedback could also take place at other stages in various forms for different purposes. For example:

- evaluation of a sample unit by the core team (at an early stage to establish a working framework and a norm);
- internal and external reviewers (at any stage as necessary);
- piloting, classroom observation and feedback (after a reasonably finished draft is ready);
- focus-group discussions.

Stage 4: Production

This stage requires involvement of different kinds of professionals such as artists and technical experts like web designers and audio mixers as necessary.

Stage 5: Post-production

This stage may involve:

- reviewing of the completed coursebook;
- post-use evaluation;
- visits, classroom observation and other research.

We will now look at what happens in the case of global coursebooks at each production stage. We will then discuss the differences in production between global and local coursebooks.

Global Coursebooks

Donovan (1998), Amrani (2011), and Aitchison (2013) provide publishers' accounts of how global coursebooks are developed based on their extensive experience of working in different roles on various projects for different publishers. Their testimonies reveal remarkable changes in international ELT publishing from the 1980s, through the late 1990s, to the present. Amrani (2011, p. 267) points out, updating what is reported in Donovan (1998) regarding publishing practices around the late 1990s, that "… in 1998, the world of ELT and specifically ELT publishing was a very different place." For example, Aitchison (2013) describes how severe the competition has now become:

> These days, as the ELT industry has matured, there are hundreds, maybe thousands, of ELT products available—the vast majority of them well-made, attractive, and effective products. Competition between publishers to sell their products has become fierce and the inevitable outcome of this crowded marketplace is that each individual product sells less than it would have done a few years ago. One of the consequences of this competition is the need for new courses to be launched in their entirety. When customers have dozens of equally effective coursebooks to choose from, they are not prepared to wait for all the levels and supporting components to dribble out from the publisher over the course of many months or even years. They want them all now, ready for the first day of class. (Aitchison, 2013, Section 4: "Getting Paid for your Writing")

Publishers not only have to get all the levels for a course, including supplementary materials, ready at the same time, but the time available for development cycles is shortening. Donovan (1998) commented on the increasing speed with which writers and publishers had to work. Fourteen years later, Amrani (2011) describes how:

> Most ELT publishers now develop new materials every year. Whereas in the early 1990s a development time of seven years for a course from concept to launch was not unheard of most publishers are now working to development cycles of only two or three years. (Amrani 2011, p. 268)

Competition, a short development period for all the components and huge investment costs significantly influence the publishing of global coursebooks and their challenges seem to influence every production stage.

Global Coursebooks—Stage 1: Planning

Both Aichison (2013) and Amrani (2011) agree that publishers plan and control projects very carefully because an error of judgement "for a publisher it is … likely to be a significant loss of revenue and, potentially, jobs" (Amrani, 2011, p. 271). Aitchison (2013) explains:

> Publishing companies typically decide years in advance what type of materials they want to publish, and by when. These decisions are primarily based on fulfilling the company's strategic and financial goals. All the established ELT publishing companies, even the not-for-profit university presses, are run as businesses with all the financial analysis and strategic planning that any multimillion dollar company requires to operate effectively. Exactly what they choose to publish to fulfill their goals and meet the requirements of their shareholders or owners will be based upon a number of factors such as strategic decisions about which regions or educational sectors they are going to focus on, the results of research into educational trends, predictions about changes in educational legislation made by governments around the world, and so on. Likewise, publishers keep a close eye out for rising trends in pedagogy or classroom practice, such as the current interest in corpus-informed materials or in content-based instruction commonly known as CLIL (content and language integrated learning) and may decide they need to publish materials that respond to the trend. (Aitchison, 2013, Section "Making a Contact with a Publisher")

In short, publishing "is about developing materials which offer the highest possible return on investment without compromising essential minimum customer expectations" (Amrani, 2011, p. 273).

What motivates publishers? What comes through from the literature (Aitchison, 2013; Amrani, 2011; Donovan, 2011; McGrath, 2013) is that publishers seem to want a coursebook that:

- responds to current and future market trends;
- promises the highest possible returns;
- helps them to attract or maintain their reputations as leaders in materials development;
- matches the needs and wants of the widest possible number of users;
- is versatile enough to be adapted easily;
- offers quality in terms of language learning;
- offers the right balance between familiarity and innovation;
- competes well against existing publications.

The list above seems to carry inherent conflicts. For example, if a coursebook is written to match the needs and wants of the widest possible users, then there is a risk of trying to please everyone and satisfying no one (e.g. the content may be perceived as safe, bland and irrelevant for specific users). On the other hand, if a coursebook tries to cater for particular types of learners in specific contexts, it may achieve a high satisfaction rating in a narrow market but could cause financial problems because the market is not large enough to be made profitable.

Who are the Stakeholders at this Planning Stage?

According to Aitchison (2013), Section 8 "Editorial Job Titles and Main Responsibilities"), those that are involved in the decision making of ELT projects seem to include the publishing director, publishers and development editors. The publishing director sets "the publishing strategy for the company or division, and oversees the entire editorial department" as well as managing a list of products, overseeing conceptualization of major courses and managing teams of publishers and development editors. Note here that actual writers and end users are not included in this very first stage of planning.

Market Research

Market research seems to have become an important aspect of decision making in the planning stage as Aitchison (2013) explains:

> Most ELT publishers have market research departments and employ up-to-date research techniques to better understand what to publish and how to promote their products. The investment required to produce today's ELT courses is too great to do without the type of thorough and comprehensive understanding of customers that market researchers can provide. (Aitchison, 2013, Section 9: "Suggested Response to Tasks")

McGrath (2013, p. 31) summarizes what market research is for:

> Broadly speaking, then, market analysis indicates whether there is a large enough potential market for a book to make its publication potentially profitable and what the nature of that market is likely to be. The wider that potential market is, the better, of course. (McGrath, 2013, pp. 31–32)

What does market research reveal? According to Amrani (2011, p. 271), "Publishers have access to information about the learning context, class sizes, the syllabus and other hard facts from education ministries, exam boards, local teacher training colleges and local sales offices, who have built up market profiles over many years."

What the statistics and hard facts do not reveal, however, seems to be finer details of the end users (i.e. teachers and students). We have had experience of undertaking confidential research for a major publisher in 12 countries around the world on what students and teachers want from coursebooks. Our findings were very different from those of the market researchers and sales teams, so our findings were basically ignored when a new coursebook was developed. Which, of course, raises the interesting question of who are more reliable, those stakeholders who tell the publishers what they want from coursebooks or those who tell independent researchers what they want?

Amrani (2011) describes the challenges in developing materials for unknown users:

> A publisher is normally preparing materials for unknown classes of students … In fact, in many cases these will be lots of different types of classes with different expectations and different previous knowledge of language, culture and technology. The materials will be used in different educational contexts, from those where the teachers always leads from the front to those where the approach is student-centered and student autonomy is encouraged. However, publishers do not have

the same level of information about students as individuals. Even when materials are evaluated for a specific narrow market, such as the state sector version in a small country, the students still represent an anonymous end user. The publisher can only make educated guesses as to student likes and dislikes. Particularly with schoolbook materials developed for specific ages, this can be a highly complex area. What works with a 14-year-old in one country may well not work in another; not because the linguistic aim and task are intrinsically wrong, but simply because the local cultural approaches to literacy or skills development may be valued differently; or the artwork proposed is considered too adult or childish. This can impact on student motivation and engagement with the materials. (Amrani, 2011, p. 271)

Amrani (2011) says that market research of materials has evolved and dialogue with teachers has increased in importance, and describes a number of research methods that publishers use at different stages of materials production. She claims that at least three different methods are used to assess the same materials or feature and the results are triangulated or cross-referenced to establish the main issues. In this way, she points out, publishers can retain wider perspectives and are more likely to identify recurrent issues that need prioritizing. The kinds of market research described in Amrani (2011) are as follows (see pp. 274–295 for a detailed explanation of procedures and for insightful critiques):

1. Piloting. Piloting involves trialing parts of the draft materials in actual classrooms in collaborating institutions (see Donovan, 1998 for interesting discussions and observations; Amrani, 2011, pp. 274–276 for a more up-to-date account). This is an informative way of evaluating materials through use. There is also a possible bonus for promotion by gaining trust and establishing links with prospective buyers. Amrani (2011) explains, however, that due to the time constraints of the short development period and other logistical problems, piloting is no longer a major method of gaining feedback on global coursebooks.
2. Reviewing. This is a method extensively used currently by most publishers at different stages of a materials development project for different purposes with different reviewers (e.g. experienced teachers, experts, academics). The reviewers are sent samples of the material and questions for them to respond to.
3. Focus groups. A facilitator (e.g. a market research professional or an experienced editor) conducts a face-to-face small group meeting with selected people with a specific profile.
4. Questionnaires. This is a popular method as it is the easiest and most cost effective. It can be undertaken in a short time and yields the largest number of responses (see Masuhara, 2011 for discussion of the pros and cons of such questionnaires). An online survey such as SurveyMonkey.com is often used.
5. Expert panels. "Some publishers appoint a specially selected panel of experts to review materials and advise on current trends. They may meet regularly face-to-face for mini-conferences, perhaps annually or twice a year. Panel experts would normally be selected not just for their prominence and experience in specific areas [such as grammar, examinations, adult education] but also so that a wide range of geographical areas were represented … Having a panel means that a publisher can develop very specific briefs for potential authors before any materials are actually commissioned." (Amrani, 2011, p. 292—the addition in brackets is ours)

6. Cooperation with academics and materials developers on research projects "… publishers sometimes work in cooperation with academics or materials developers on research projects"—e.g. the use of technology with ELT materials in adult classes with the Manchester University Department of Education and the English Profile Project (www.englishprofile.org) with the University of Cambridge (both the description and the examples are from Amrani, 2011, p. 292).
7. Editorial visits and classroom observation. "Publishers send editors around the world to observe students in a cross-section of different classrooms using both their own and competitor materials" (Amrani, 2011, p. 293).
8. Desk research and competitor analysis:

> Publishers regularly visit the Internet to see what is new. In particular they will look at other publishers' web sites and analyze the strengths and weaknesses of the competition. Publishers also like to access specialist sites to monitor what is new in terms of training and materials development, such as: The British Council, JALT, IATEFL, TESOL, MATSDA, ELT Journal. (Amrani, 2011, p. 293)

Our Observations on Publishers' Research

The list of research methods explained by Amrani (2011) is impressive. It is noticeable, however, that none of the research methods really lead to identifying Amrani's concern about information about the end users, especially from the students. Instead, what prevails seems to be the perceptions and opinions of experts, regional representatives, highly motivated teachers from regular piloting institutions (e.g. the British Council schools; customer schools for the local publisher's representatives). Both Donovan (1998) and Amrani (2011) stress how difficult it is to collect representative samples of end users. Viney (2007; see https://peterviney.wordpress.com/ for his interesting blogs) points out how the four big British ELT publishers (i.e. Cambridge University Press, Macmillan, Oxford University Press, Pearson Longman) tend to involve much the same group of people in their research, resulting in all of them reaching more or less the same conclusions. His view, based on his experience, is that:

> the people who will give an articulate pilot report are an elite, and it's near impossible to pilot to a broad enough base of teachers. As a result, we've seen twenty years of publishers competing to clone the same successful textbook. (Viney, 2007, p. 33)

Viney (2007) also provides an interesting but somewhat sobering anecdote:

> A few years ago, I was talking to a director of studies in Europe who discussed the great variety of courses her school ran; early teenagers boosting their school lessons, housewives, retirees, job seekers, business people, exam preparation, first year university students, technical courses, travel and tourism etc. I asked her which textbooks she had selected. Her answer was just one (one size fits all). They used the same series for every class because teachers found it more convenient. I asked if that one course was more suited to the more academic groups, and she said that it was. The less academic groups didn't have the English or the confidence to complain. The more academic groups did. The tendency to "one size fits all" has got worse. It suits publishers. (Viney, 2007, p. 33)

Buying one coursebook series for all courses saves expense in institutions, creating a potential win-win situation between buyers and suppliers. Obviously, Viney's report is an anecdote and we need tightly controlled systematic studies to make any generalization. It is not difficult, however, to imagine a scenario in which the same director offers piloting or reviewing. What kind of feedback would she be giving to represent what teachers and students need and want? She must be, potentially, a very good customer as she might make a considerable bulk order of one coursebook at certain intervals. As a regular customer, there is a fair possibility that she is recognized by the local publisher's representative. If she is cooperative and very articulate and shows understanding of current ELT trends and theories she might even be asked to be a regular reviewer. Both publishers and this director mean well and they are doing their best in their roles. Learners, however, seem to be left out in this hypothetical case. We have recently had experience though of learners' views. When visiting a well-respected language school in the United Kingdom we were told by the director of studies that the students (mainly students from the Middle East preparing for examinations to give them access to UK academic institutions) preferred to use the same coursebook series as they progressed through the levels and that they preferred a coursebook that provided them with explicit presentation and practice of grammatical structures as this would help them pass their examinations. However, in a British Council series of research papers from East India, which Brian is in the process of editing, Modugala (in press) reports on feedback from 30 "seventh grade students (14 boys and 16 girls) of a government aided school in Karnataka, India" who, in a student evaluation of their coursebook, were strongly of the opinion that they "wanted activities as opposed to language practice exercises," that they wanted a lot more opportunities for listening and speaking, that there was "too much grammar" in their coursebook, and that they preferred to focus on one skill at a time rather than all of them together (i.e. integrated skills). All of these are views that would probably surprise the publishers of their coursebook who had presumably based their publishing plan on market research and feedback from teachers.

We have closely observed publishers' market research (both as writers on coursebook teams and as researchers) and we appreciate the publishers' professionalism and their efforts in trying hard to deliver quality whilst understandably pursuing their business interests. It is understandable and, in fact, in our interest that publishers sustain and develop themselves as we need publishers to produce textbooks.

From an educational point of view, however, it becomes a critical issue when business objectives do not coincide with pedagogic ones. For example, clear and valid learner specifications based on needs analyses and other measures constitute the very foundation of course design and materials development (Long, 2005; Masuhara, 2011)—for example, identifying aims and objectives; selecting core texts; deciding on methodology. Such clear learner specifications, however, would be difficult to obtain by publishers who do not have direct access to learners, especially when the ELT world is diversifying and expanding (see section "Paradigm Shift 2: Global English for Multitudes of Cultures" in Chapter 4, "Adaptation"). Moreover, precise specifications of a particular group of learners would result in narrowing the market, which would be counterproductive from a business point of view. However, a greater attempt to elicit feedback from learners could actually increase both the quality and the profitability of coursebooks. This could certainly be achieved by publishers building feedback mechanisms into the digital add-on components of their coursebooks.

The growing criticisms against coursebooks not fitting the learners' social, cultural and educational contexts are noted in Chapter 2, "Issues in Materials Development" and in Chapter 4, "Adaptation." Such considerable expressions of dissatisfaction toward global coursebooks seem to us to stem from this very core conflict between the publishers' business need to set a broad target to ensure large enough markets to sustain a huge coursebook enterprise and the educators' need for a better fit between the materials and particular learners and contexts.

This leaves the question of "who conducts the needs analysis and decides on the aims and objectives for the users?" Our investigation of the literature in Chapter 4, "Adaptation," reveals that materials users (i.e. educational administrators, teachers and students) take it for granted that systematic needs analysis and articulation of aims and objectives have been undertaken by the materials producers.

Global Coursebooks—Stage 2: Establishing Writing Team and Principles

Aichison (2013) starts her book on "How ELT Publishing Works" by emphasizing the vital role that materials writers play:

> Educational content can now be effectively delivered digitally via computers, tablets and smartphones, with all the added advantages of immediate feedback, rich multimedia support, and automatic grading functionality. However, even though the delivery medium may be changing from printed pages to pixels on a screen, the principles underlying materials writing remain the same. Materials need to follow certain syllabuses, present language accurately and clearly, and, above all, engage and motivate students. No computer can ever be programmed to write a motivating and fun activity, nor work out how to present a complex grammatical structure in ways that a struggling student can understand. Only writers can do this, and that is why, however much the medium of delivery may change, the writer remains an indispensable part of the publishing process. (Aitchison, 2013, "Introduction")

How Do Publishers Recruit Writers?

McGrath (2013) provides a chapter on publisher and coursebook writer perspectives in which he summarizes publishers' general approaches to commissioning a coursebook:

> While they remain open to approaches (unsolicited proposals) from prospective writers of other types of materials, as far as coursebooks are concerned, the major publishers at least tend to play safe by commissioning new series from writers they know or—as a less expensive option—publish new editions of popular series. (McGrath, 2013, p. 30)

From the publisher's point of view, Aitchison (2013) explains:

> Many people who have not yet been personally involved in the publishing industry imagine that the way to get published is to send a manuscript to all the potential publishers, then sit back and wait for an editor to call you to tell you that they liked your work and their company is going to publish it. I certainly thought this was how it worked before I became an editor. Then I found out that in reality, it is

very unusual for an ELT publishing company to accept manuscripts that arrive out of the blue like this. The real situation is almost always the reverse—publishing companies first decide what they want to publish, and only then do they commission writers to write according to their specific instructions. (Aitchison, 2013, "section 1: Making Contact with a Publisher")

What Do Publishers Look For from Prospective Materials Writers?

Aitchison (2013, section 9, "Suggested responses to tasks") says, "It is not essential to have higher degrees to write for an ELT publisher. Typically, publishers find that actual teaching experience is more closely correlated to writing success than academic qualification."

Publishers are looking for materials writers who have relevant and successful teaching experience, especially if the experience is in target sectors, regions or countries. It also helps if writers initially offer the kinds of help that publishers appreciate—e.g. participating in a pilot scheme, making their classes available for observation, responding to questionnaires, becoming reviewers. Amrani (2011) says:

> Many teachers and academics who start out by answering questionnaires or working on a pilot go onto become regular reviewers. Proven reviewers who have shown they have a good writing style and a comprehensive understanding of ELT and a particular aspect or market in it are often approached to write web materials or teacher's books or supplementary materials. If they do that successfully, they can find themselves being asked to tender as an author for bigger projects. It should be pointed out that it is more likely to be those reviewers who show an objective critical analysis of the materials and are prepared to point out things that could be improved, backed up with informed argument, who are more likely to be approached. Materials evaluation is one of the main sources for publishers finding new prospective writers and being alerted to new ideas. (Amrani, 2011, p. 294)

An example can be seen in Clandfield (2013). He is a multiple award-winning coursebook author with an active presence online and in journals in ELT. He explains how he started as a regular contributor of materials in onestopenglish (http://www.onestopenglish.com/), a teacher resource site created by Macmillan Education. Clandfield then became one of the authors of the *Straitforward* series, and then the lead author of a global series (both from Macmillan Education). His works are regularly shortlisted for ELTons awards by the British Council (according to the British Council web site, the only international award that recognizes and celebrates innovation in English language teaching (ELT)), and he is sponsored by Cambridge University Press.

Who are the Stakeholders in this Second Stage of "Establishing Writing Teams and Principles"?

According to Aitchison (2013, section 8: "Editorial Job Titles and Main Responsibilities"), the main stakeholders at this stage seem to be various editors:

The publisher / commissioning editor / acquisitions editor / sponsoring editor (different names but more or less a similar role) "commissions new projects and ensures their successful conceptualization." (S)he works closely with the overseas development editor, who "works closely with a writer to guide him / her as they write and rewrite their manuscript, edits material, and gives feedback to writers."

The managing editor "project-manages multiple components / projects focuses on schedules and budgets though also typically has content expertise." (S)he "manages the work of freelance editors working on their projects." The project manager is "responsible for creating and managing complex schedules for multiple components / projects."

Our Observations on Stage 2 in Relation to Establishing a Writing Team

We can see how the publishers do their overall planning. The first stage is decision making by the top management team in the ELT section of the publishers. The second stage seems to be operationalization by the middle management of the publishers. The main authors (perhaps on a royalty contract) do feature in the second planning stage if they have won the tender. Even then, they only seem to be able to add some ideas to the fixed framework and given briefs. The rest of the writers working on multicomponent materials seem to be freelancers on fee-based contracts and they do not seem to have much say in this planning stage.

Aitchison (2013, section 4: "Getting Paid for Your Writing Work") mentions how the author payment system is changing. As has been mentioned in this chapter before, the customers want to buy the whole set ready made. This means that coursebook writing requires a large writing team these days, as can be noticed on the cover of coursebooks with many different names. For example, one working model may be that the main author(s) leads the team in terms of overall concepts and structures. They may be working on the core student coursebook(s) for the other writers to follow. There are freelance writers who may be working on the teacher's book. Some other freelance writers may be writing workbooks or digital materials. Most of the freelance writers will be working on a fee basis, selling off their copyright to the publishers. In this way, publishers have the right to use bits and pieces in any way necessary, for example developing a bank of activities that can be used for digital materials or for workbook exercises in response to specific requests or feedback from different markets. This means that writers must be able to keep to schedules.

It may be inevitable for smooth project management to establish a writing system that suits the publishing schedule. We do wonder, though, how coherence and quality is ensured in terms of the learning experience when the work is so subdivided. It must also be rather challenging for contemporary fee-based writers to find ways of keeping the creativity and inspiration that was reported to matter a lot to the authors in the late 1990s (Prowse, 1998).

What are the Guiding Principles Underlying the Coursebooks?

Amrani (2011) explains how much of the course design is predetermined:

> Course content, approach and task design is often already established by exam syllabuses guidelines or standards such as the Common European Framework. This means that publishers have less of a free hand than previously as there are clearly defined international market expectations that they now need to work within to secure course adoptions. (Amrani, 2011, p. 268)

She also describes the brief that is given to authors before any writing starts:

> The brief for a project is always based on a needs analysis or what publishers normally call "the must haves list" … The "must haves lists" used by commissioning editors for courses are normally generated from a generic list which is continually evolving. The "must have list" [sic] is tailored to each individual project, rather than a new one being started from scratch each time. (Amrani, 2011, p. 270)

This author brief "must haves list" seems to be a compilation of information gained through various types of market research (e.g. expert panels' comments, reviewers' comments, local representatives' information about the target users). Amrani (2011, p. 270) says these "must haves" are used as universal and local criteria for ongoing criterion-referenced evaluation by the authors and the editorial team. We advocate strongly in Chapter 3, "Evaluation," that learning principles be placed as a priority in all the criteria, be it universal, local or media-related. Those "must haves lists" are, understandably, not publically made available apart from a widely known list of cultural taboos to avoid in coursebooks: PARSNIP (Politics, Alcohol, Religion, Sex, Narcotics, Isms, Pork), though actual application would vary depending on the target groups (Chapter 6 in Gray, 2010, discusses regulation of content in details). We remember once on a project (we think in Singapore) not being allowed to make reference to balloons.

Clandfield (2013) provides a glimpse of what writers are advised:

> A common starting point is to look at books that sell well in the target market. Remember, you don't always have to reinvent the wheel when you write a new book. Teachers aren't necessarily looking for books that are innovative in all possible ways. The syllabuses in the existing titles may work very well, and as the author of a new book, you'd be well advised to stick with certain tried-and-tested features, and concentrate on introducing one or two new features that set you apart from the competition in ways that make a positive and welcome difference. (Clandfield, 2013, section 12: "Publishers and Co-authors")

Our Observations on Stage 2 in Relation to "Principles Underlying the Coursebooks"

We wonder what exactly are the "exam syllabus guidelines" that Amrani (2011, p. 268) refers to when she says, "Course content, approach and task design is often already established by exam syllabus guidelines or standards such as the Common European Framework"? Research in second language acquisition and language learning studies (see Chapter 8; Ellis, 2016; Tomlinson, 2016) seems to support that providing explicit knowledge about the language and overt practice in manipulating its structures (e.g. the PPP approach) does not cultivate the ability to be able to use language for communication. Even if the learners spend hundreds of hours on gap fill and matching exercises, they will not acquire or develop the language competence to express themselves. But such arguments seem to fall short when the publishers' priority is to reassure the potential buyers (i.e. administrators, teachers and students) that the coursebook covers the syllabus and the specified language items likely to be tested in the examination. The Common European Framework is designed for free movement for educational and work purposes within the countries belonging to the European Union. Are the coursebooks based on the "can do" statements in the Common European Framework of Reference applicable for learners of English as a foreign language in remote schools in China, India or Iran or in primary schools in Spain?

"Tried and tested features" seem to mean what has been selling—i.e. the "multistrand syllabus." Unless alternative "tried and tested features" attract huge sales, publishers are not likely to take risks. No wonder all the coursebooks look somewhat similar. Criterion-referenced evaluations of adult courses in 2001 (Tomlinson, Bao, Masuhara, & Rubdy, 2001), 2008 (Masuhara, Haan, Yi, & Tomlinson, 2008) and 2013 (Tomlinson & Masuhara, 2013) found that the same PPP method is used even though it is more of a teaching procedure rather than an approach that seems to be in line with current learning theories such as Task-based or Experiential Learning (Ellis, 2016; Tomlinson, 2016).

Global Coursebooks Stage 3: Drafting and Feedback

How do Authors Write?

When publishers approach writers, they seem to give them briefs about target contexts, learners, and the "must haves list" and invite them to put in their proposal for tender. Clandfield (2013) provides a useful guide for coursebook writers on "How to plan a book" as follows:

1. examine what elements make up a modern coursebook
2. explore syllabuses for language learning courses and how these are translated into a book
3. look at what is hot in syllabus design right now
4. provide […] guidance on planning a language course syllabus and how to plan individual units of study in a book
5. provide […] guidance on designing a sequence of tasks or activities within a unit of study
6. explore what the books of the future might hold.
   (Clandfield, 2013, section 1: "Aims")

The main part of a leading authors' role seems to be in planning a syllabus (e.g. a course map) and in considering how the required components (e.g. language, skills, functions and some new elements) fit into the space according to the briefs in the most imaginative way possible within the constraints. Given this situation, Clandfield's advice is helpful for aspiring coursebook writers but is unlikely to lead to the development of principled and effective materials.

As an anecdote, we know a well-known experienced materials writer who is now a well-respected editor for a major publisher. When he was writing coursebooks as an occupation in the early 1990s, we described him as a materials developer. His response was that he does not "develop" materials. He preferred to be called a materials "craftsman" who puts all the pieces together skillfully according to the briefs he receives and creates the best possible learning materials within the constraints imposed on him. In Chapter 5, we discuss how professional materials writers write. The majority of them seem to have a repertoire of activities and spend a lot of time planning which set activities fit better for a particular purpose. Presumably this is what "our" materials craftsman did.

Just as the operational model of the publishers has changed since the mid-1990s, how authors work seems to have changed too. Coursebooks used to mean printed hard copy and the authors were paid royalties, often 10% per copy, of the sum received (see Aitchison, 2013, section 4: "Getting Paid for Your Writing Work"). With this arrangement, there seemed to be more incentive to produce long-lasting series. There seem to have been more time and space for the writers to set up their own principles (Bell and Gower, 1998, and revised version, 2011) based on their considerable experience in classrooms and in ELT academic and professional backgrounds. Prowse (1998, and revised version, 2011) provides testimonials from well-published coursebook writers. Despite the challenges from publishers, users (e.g. institutions, teachers, learners), reviewers, and criticisms, the authors say that coursebook writing is a creative process and they strive for the best possible learning outcomes for the teachers and learners so they can retain their professional pride. Prowse (2011, p. 166) also mentions his experience of how the publishers made sure the author and editors make repeated visits to typical schools in different target regions, observe many classes, have meetings with teachers, educational advisors, planners, and teacher trainers in target countries. Is this still the case in contemporary coursebook writing with such tight production schedules and subdivisions of work?

As for unit design, Clandfield (2013), in section 9, "Planning a Unit or Lessons," sets an interesting task. After describing three approaches in organizing a unit, he asks the readers to plan a lesson in each sequence. He provides the language points, text, and outcomes (e.g. "Students will be able to describe symptoms and communicate a problem to get medicine in a pharmacy," i.e. a task with a nonlinguistic real-life outcome):

1. Choose language points→source text→exercises→outcome.
2. Source text→choose language points→exercises→outcome.
3. Outcome→choose language points→source text→ exercises.

Note that each sequence influences what happens next. For example, if you choose 1, choosing language points, you will be looking for texts that provide contexts for the specified language points.

Clandfield (2013) says in the Section Task commentary, "Often the most exciting lessons to write in my experience are ones that begin with a text or topic …" The power of texts inspiring materials developers, teachers and learners is acknowledged in various authors' comments in Prowse (1998, and 2011). Tomlinson (2003, and revised 2013a) proposes a text-driven approach to materials development (see also Chapter 5 in this book) and provides a theoretical and practical rationale for an approach in which the syllabus is created by a bank of potentially engaging written, spoken, and visual texts, which cover many genres and text types.

What Kinds of Feedback Do the Writers Receive?

Clandfield (2013) describes the authors' frustrations. He is aware of and interested in the latest studies in language, language teaching, and language learning. He gives examples of how he appreciates various insights from corpus linguistics, studies of English as a lingua franca and learning theories and how he makes use of them in his materials. But he is also aware of the constraints:

> As if thinking about the frequency, teachability, learnability and complexity of items to include in a syllabus was not enough, there is also the issue of what teachers are accustomed to. The role of tradition (or teachers' expectations) in what goes in to language courses is also very strong. It is possibly for this reason more

than anything else that any language course that hopes to be successful commercially tends to follow what the majority of other courses do in terms of syllabus design.

While critics of Coursebooks may argue that this is done out of laziness or lack of imagination, it is more often the case that deviations from what teachers are accustomed to are met with strong resistance, even before a book reaches the publication stage (that is, when it is being trialled [*sic*] or sent to reviewers). This is especially the case with grammar or lexis. (Clandfield, 2013, Section Tradition and Dilemmas in Syllabus Design)

In Chapter 3 we report cases in Egypt, Oman and in Singapore of how teachers prefer traditional grammar teaching due to their beliefs and their perception of what examination preparation should be. Bell and Gower (1998, and revised version, 2011), authors in Prowse (1998, and revised version, 2011), Timmis (2014) and Aitchison (2013) describe various challenges and compromises materials writers have to make. We have written numerous coursebooks ourselves. In one of our projects, after having already rewritten the drafts many times, we were asked to make changes at a much later stage to satisfy the inspectors' comments. We argued that our materials realized all the innovations recommended in the guidelines developed by the government curriculum development teams and that rewriting according to the inspectors would go against the new curriculum. Our negotiation resulted in later discovering that the final published coursebooks contained materials that we had not written. The editors seemed to have gone ahead and made some changes themselves or employed ghost writers so that the final product would satisfy the textbook inspectors in the Ministry of Education (rather than the curriculum developers in the same Ministry).

Zemach (2006) provides an editor's advice to prospective writers based on her experience of being a writer and editor. Zemach and Viney (2007, p. 26) also provides an interesting "Author Test" in which different authors are asked to respond to editors' requests such as "Unfortunately, feedback from our Turkish and Middle Eastern markets is indicating that the reading in Chapter 3… isn't really appropriate … I think we need to replace …" How would you respond if you were a materials writer. Viney's answers show in a personal and humorous way how publishing works. Bell and Gower (2011), Feak and Swales (2014) and Santos (2015) also describe how authors and publishers renegotiate during revision.

Our Observations on Stage 3: Drafting and Feedback

Based on his survey (2010), Tomlinson (2015) speculated on "What makes an effective coursebook?" He identifies the typical stakeholders and their wants as follows:

- publishers want a book that sells well and is considered to be of high quality;
- writers want a book that sells well and which enhances their reputation;
- administrators want a book that helps them to standardize and timetable teaching and which helps to prepare students for their examinations;
- teachers want a book which is easy to plan for and use, which appeals to their students, and that helps to prepare their students for their examinations;
- students want a book that is relevant to their needs and wants, which engages them, and which helps to prepare them for their examinations;

- practitioners who write about materials development want a book which matches what research and observation tells us is most likely to help learners to understand and use language effectively (e.g. Harwood, 2014; Tomlinson, 2013b, 2016).

Tomlinson (2015, p. 174) claims, "The ideal coursebook would be one that satisfies all the above requirements. Very few coursebooks, if any, have achieved this, but I know of locally published coursebooks in Namibia and in Norway which have come close."

Global Coursebooks Stage 4: Production

The writers' manuscripts, after various revisions, are passed back to the publishers. Aitchison (2013) describes how manuscripts are shaped into the final published product. In Chapter 13 of this volume, "Visuals, Layout and Design," authors such as Hill (2013), Prowse (2011) and ourselves point out that the visuals, layout, and design of coursebooks do not always match their pedagogical intentions. Aitchison (2013, section 2, "What to Expect on a Writing Project") explains that, due to budget and time constraints, writers are no longer involved in the production stage. Instead, graphic designers, copy editors, marketers and production editors complete this stage. Again, business purposes and educational purposes often do not coincide, as we have often found out to our cost when first seeing published illustrations, which, for example, contradict what it says in a text or what our instructions ask learners to do.

Once the manuscripts are in this stage, it becomes very difficult to make changes. IATEFL Materials Writing Special Interest Group Newsletter Issue 01 includes an article by Amrani (2014) entitled, "Ten things your editor never wants to hear you say." Most of the 'things' are writers asking if the publishers can make minor changes. Once the digital templates are created and layout completed it is best assumed that there will be no turning back.

Global Coursebooks Stage 5: Post-production

Marketing and promotion have been taking place all through the writing process in the form of market research in different guises: for example, piloting, reviewing, focus group meetings, author and editor visits to the target countries and publisher sponsored author presentations at international and national conferences. The sales figures and feedback from the buyers inform subsequent publications.

In relation to marketing and adoption, Bell and Gower (2011) point out that the term "global coursebooks" is misleading in a sense that they really are written for a restricted number of teaching situations in many different countries rather than all teaching situations in all countries. Some criticisms against coursebooks being inappropriate for specific contexts may be avoided by careful marketing and discernable adoption by the users.

Our Observations on the Production Process of Global Coursebooks

In our exploration of the production stages of global coursebooks, what has emerged seems to us to be how constraining global coursebook production seems to have become. Coursebooks have become very expensive to produce and to buy and therefore very restrictive for authors and perhaps for publishers too. There is a growing awareness of the importance of theoretical validity in learning materials but innovations that could surprise the majority of the potential markets are too risky for publishers to take a chance on. The production cycle is getting shorter. The markets have globally expanded and diversified. Some markets demand digital materials with the latest technology whereas others only want traditional print materials. Balancing between production costs and profit seems to be incredibly difficult when markets are so diverse. Criticisms of the coursebook per se and of specific coursebooks seem to be increasing but the demand for printed coursebooks is still high worldwide.

To break away from this rather stagnant situation, some countries and institutions have gone ahead to create local coursebooks that are directly relevant to their teachers and learners in their contexts as we will see in the next section. Before we move on from global coursebooks, Clandfield (2013) contemplates the future of global coursebooks. He argues that the concept of "book" is changing. He lists possible future directions of coursebooks:

- The book looks essentially the same but is made for reading on a digital device (for example, in a PDF format).
- The book looks essentially the same but is read on a digital device with embedded audio and / or video.
- The book looks essentially the same but is read on a digital device and has interactive exercises as well as embedded audio and video.
- The book no longer looks like a book but is divided into units of work which can be downloaded individually, or mounted on a virtual learning environment.
- The book no longer looks like a book but is packaged instead as an app. The content of the app changes over time, with regular updates and extensions.
- The book no longer looks like a book but is a subscription-based web site. There is an overall syllabus, but the contents change over time. (Clandfield, 2013, section 14, "Planning the Book of the Future")

Pay-as-you go coursebooks could potentially create market demand. Having separate modules of coursebooks online could let the users pick and mix what they want and the sales records could be an interesting indicator in market research. Such stand-alone modules are much more economical as printing, storage, and distribution costs can be reduced. We can already see some changes in publishing practice. For example, English 360 http://english360.com/aboutus/ offers a blended learning platform in which teachers can select the materials and only pay when they start to use the materials with their students (N.B. the materials are provided by Cambridge University Press). *English 360* won the David Riley Award for Innovation by BESIG, the Business English Special Interest Group of IATEFL in 2010 and was shortlisted for the ELTon awards in 2011. Teacher2writer (http://www.eltteacher2writer.co.uk/about-elt-teacher-2-writer) publishes ebooks and also offers training modules for teachers who want to learn how to become materials writers. Their sales are on demand and online—just a click away. No office space or personnel are required. In 2004, we were involved in a teacher language-improvement project run by the British Council and the Ethiopian government. The materials we developed were sent in eform for the government to print and distribute. In this way, cost and distribution problems can be reduced.

We welcome these new developments as potential ways in which materials producers and users can communicate better and achieve a closer match between demand and supply. We must remember, though, that availability of technology is still limited to those who have easy and reliable access to technology and are digitally literate enough to take advantage of such online publishing and consumption. Realistically, the majority of learners and teachers globally might benefit more from teacher development programs for adaptation (see Chapter 4 Adaptation and Tomlinson, in press, for how typical coursebook closed exercises such as gap fill can be turned into more communicative open activities that are potentially much more engaging).

Local Coursebooks

Local coursebooks at national and institutional levels seem to bypass various challenges in developing global coursebooks. For example, global coursebook publishers have to:

- ensure a financial return as large as possible for their investment;
- find out about the target markets and the end users;
- make efforts so as to obtain representative feedback through reviews, visits, observation and piloting in various stages from the planning to production stages;
- try to understand local cultures and practices;
- try to predict teacher and student reactions to texts and activities;
- find, if possible, appropriate writers with relevant experience of the target areas.

In the case of national textbooks led by a Ministry of Education, on the other hand, the materials development team can prioritize educational goals without commercial pressure (see Mukundan, 2008 for an account of a secondary coursebook produced and distributed by the Malaysian government; Popovici and Bolitho, 2003 for a Romanian secondary school project, Tomlinson, 1995 for textbook projects in Morocco, Bulgaria, and Namibia). The goals in these national projects are educational—e.g. achieving specified learning effects and satisfying the national agenda for establishing the basic literacy skills of English as a lingua franca. Ministry-led coursebook project team members usually have relevant local knowledge and direct access to teachers and learners. The writers can try out samples and receive direct feedback in various forms as required. Institution-based coursebook projects are similar but have even more flexibility in how the project is run (see Al-Busaidi, & Tindle, 2010; Stoller & Robinson, 2014). In all cases of local coursebooks, a very coherent course design process is followed (see section "The Development Process of Coursebooks" in this chapter).

For us, probably the biggest advantage that local coursebook production enjoys is the possibility of doing needs and wants analyses rather than just market research. For example, the writers of a writing skills course for first-year students at Sultan Qaboos University in Oman were able to find out what writing skills the students would need in their subsequent subject course and what interested and motivated them (Al-Busaidi & Tindle, 2010) and prior to the writing of a new secondary school course for Namibia (*On* target, 1995; Tomlinson, 1995) questionnaires were distributed all over Namibia to find out what students wanted to read, listen to, write, and talk about and what teachers thought they needed (see "Factors That We Believe Will Help Successful Development of a Coursebook" below for more details).

Coursebook projects in Singapore illustrate interesting issues in considering possible future changes in Ministry led curriculum implementation and materials development (Singapore Wala, 2003a, 2003b, 2003; Loh & Renandya, 2015). The government used to develop materials in collaboration with publishers—i.e. Ministry-led national coursebooks. Then, in 1998, the Ministry announced that the production of textbooks and instructional packages would be devolved to publishers (Singapore Wala, 2003a, 2003b, 2013). In 2006, a new national literacy reform program for primary level called Strategies for English Language Learning and Reading (STELLAR) was launched. The STELLAR program does not use conventional textbooks in a traditional sense. Instead of textbooks students are taught with student-centered approaches such as Shared Reading, the Language Experience Approach, Silent Reading, and text-driven approaches with accompanying teacher development programs and financial and mentor support for schools.

Factors that We Believe will Help Successful Development of a Coursebook

We have been involved in numerous international, national, regional and institutional coursebooks development projects. The most successful project from our point of view so far is the Namibian Project in which *On target* was developed by 30 teachers from all over the country in 6 days in a room in Windhoek (see Tomlinson, 1995 for his account of the Namibian project; see also the Recommendations for Developing Materials section in Chapter 5). We think that the following factors contributed to its success and that they could be applied to other coursebook projects.

Factors that Contributed to the Success of *On target*:

1. Meeting the interests of all the stakeholders. The Namibian project was initiated by the Ministry of Basic Education and Culture. The stakeholders were the government, learners, teachers from all over the country, language specialists, assessors, sponsors (e.g. NAMAS the Namibia Association of Norway), consultants and publishers. *On target* was literally a coursebook for the country. It served the government's educational, political, social and economic agenda in an open and thought-provoking way. Learners' needs and wants analyses were conducted before the writing began and their findings were fully incorporated into the materials. The teachers and learners had a direct say during the piloting stages. Assessors, inspectors and publishers as well as teachers collaborated during the writing of the materials. It made commercial sense to the publisher because the book would be sold to all the secondary schools in Namibia.

2. Coherence between the coursebooks and examinations. One of the main reasons that teachers refuse innovation is because they feel that they need to prepare the students to pass their exams. Often exam questions involve conventional testing techniques such as gap fill and completion exercises. If examinations routinely require task completion (Ellis, 2009; Van den Branden, Bygate, & Norris, 2009; Masuhara, 2015), teachers are likely to request more task-based activities in coursebooks. A lot of assessors were in the writing team in the Namibian case and correspondence was achieved between the coursebook and the examinations, as it was in Vanuatu where a task-based primary school leaving examination was introduced and a coursebook of sample tasks was developed by teacher trainers and teachers (Tomlinson, 1981).

3. Teacher education through materials development and use. On the *On target* project, teacher development was achieved through materials development (see Popovici & Bolitho, 2003). The teacher writers understood the learning principles that informed the units and therefore they could use the materials well and explain or demonstrate the materials to other teachers back in their regions.

4. International and local collaboration. *On target* was developed as a collaboration between the Ministry of Education in Namibia, the British Council, a local branch of a major international publisher (Gamsburg Macmillan) and a number of overseas consultants. A considerable number of other countries have also been involved in developing their own new English textbooks (see Tomlinson, 1995; Bolitho, 2008) to meet the contemporary needs of the country, the teachers, and the learners. This is also the case with a number of large institutions. (See Al-Busaidi & Tindle, 2010 for a report of the development of a new textbook in the English Language Centre in Sultan Qaboos University; Stoller and Robinson, 2014.) What those countries and institutions request is theoretical and practical co-leadership in materials development. Bolitho (2008), in reflecting upon various national textbook projects in Central and Eastern Europe, suggests collaboration between local and UK publishers: Partnerships between local and British publishers can be mutually beneficial if handled sensitively. Local publishers for example, get access to authentic material, photo libraries, copy right clearance and native-speaker desk-editor expertise, while UK publishers can draw on in-country expertise in graphic design, market knowledge and distribution, and can benefit from low printing costs. Where this kind of partnership has worked well as in Russia, for example, production standards have been raised, to the advantage of everyone concerned (Bolitho, 2008, p. 221).

Zacharias (2005) provides a list of reasons why Indonesian teachers prefer internationally published materials. It includes professional finish (e.g. no spelling mistakes), reliable availability because of strong distribution networks, and a strong presence on the Internet.

5. No divisions or distance between materials producers and users. On the Namibian project, a team of 30 teachers, specialists, assessors, and publishers wrote the first draft of the materials in a one-week workshop led by Brian as an invited consultant. The participants found participation in the development process to be very stimulating and receiving feedback from peers and experts to be extremely educational (see Popovici & Bolitho, 2003, for similar reflections). The writer teachers then went back to their schools in all the districts and piloted the materials. Students and teachers provided feedback and revisions were made by a team of editors.

6. Acknowledgment and support from the government. Government-led materials development has the advantage that the materials developers can consult government representatives during the writing process. This is what happened on the Namibian project with Ministry of Education officials present throughout the writing workshops.

7. Universal and local relevance. The Namibian government wanted the materials to provide opportunities to explore issues and to develop critical thinking skills. The students in their questionnaire responses wanted to discuss such locally relevant topics as tourism, pollution, AIDS and drug abuse and the Ministry of Education officials were happy to allow such normally taboo topics to be included as part of their hidden agenda of educational development. The writing team was mixed in terms of age, nationality, first language, experience and tribe and their materials presented different views and perspectives using a text-driven approach in cognitively and affectively engaging ways—a different approach in dealing with a hidden agenda from the more prescriptive approach in Malaysia (Mukundan, 2008).

8. Cutting down production costs without losing quality. The physical appearance of the student book and the teacher's guide for *On target* was very modest. This helped reduce the production costs. However, the texts, activities, and black-and-white visuals, the layout and the design are of high quality in that they are relevant to the learners' lives and the texts and visuals were coherently connected—in contrast to some of the problem samples in Chapter 13, "Visual Layout and Design."

The Namibian project took place a long time ago but it does not end there. One of the core leaders of the Namibian project was a Norwegian editor. She went back home and was instrumental in creating another excellent coursebook series for teenagers—the original *Search* and the revised version *Searching* (Fenner & Nordal-Pedersen, 2006).

Conclusion

Coursebooks function as the curriculum in many teaching situations and the quality of coursebooks plays a significant role in determining the success of the learning experience. By carefully following publishers' accounts of the development of global coursebooks we have found out why global coursebooks are what they are. However, business success depends on market responses. If demands change the publishers' products will change. If teachers and students are dissatisfied with the global coursebooks they are being obliged to use (as research and our experience seems to show) then finding ways of expressing this dissatisfaction is essential if publishers are to be made to feel that they might better satisfy market demands by making changes to their products. For us it is essential that the demand drives the market rather than the market drives the demand.

In this chapter, we have also identified the strengths of developing local materials. Taking the case of the Namibian textbook project as a model, we have considered factors that may be applicable to any textbook project. For the majority of teachers globally, however, their day-to-day use of coursebooks is what matters. Not all countries and institutions are able to develop materials on their own. In this case, adaptation seems to become even more crucial in making materials more relevant, effective, and motivating for our learners and there is definitely a case for publishers to develop their global coursebooks so as to achieve maximum flexibility and help teachers to adapt them (see Chapter 4, "Adaptation").

What Do You Think?

1. Are you happy with the coursebook you are using? Why?
2. What kinds of improvement would you like to make to the coursebook? How would you make such improvements?
3. Imagine that a coursebook representative is going to visit your school. What would you like to say to the representative?
4. Imagine that you are in charge of a textbook development project. How would you go about developing the project?
5. In this chapter different kinds of textbooks are listed. Which one is most relevant for you? Why?

Task

Find some closed exercises from your coursebooks. Try to change them so they become open. For example, after reading a text, there are comprehension questions. There is a correct answer to each question. Can you change the questions so that there is no right answer and the question is so interesting that students would want to go back to the text to discover answers?

Which do you think would be more useful for the students the closed exercises or the open activities? Why do you think there are so many closed exercises in published coursebooks?

Further Reading

Clandfield, L. (2013). *How to plan a book* (Kindle ed.). Oxford: Teacher2Writer.
McGrath, I. (2013). *Teaching materials and the roles of EFL/ESL teachers: Practice and theory*. London: Bloomsbury.
Mishan, F., & Timmis, I. (2015). *Materials development for TESOL*. Edinburgh: Edinburgh University Press.

References

Aitchison, J. (2013). *How ELT publishing works* (Kindle ed.). Oxford: ELT Teacher 2 Writer.
Al-Busaidi, S., & Tindle, K. (2010). Evaluating the impact of in-house materials on language learning. In B. Tomlinson, & H. Masuhara (Eds.), *Research for materials development for language learning—evidence for best practice* (pp. 137–149). London: Continuum.
Amrani, F. (2011). The process of evaluation: A publisher's view. In B. Tomlinson (Ed.), *Materials development in language teaching* (2nd ed., pp. 267–295). Cambridge: Cambridge University Press.
Amrani, F. (2014). Ten things your editor never wants to hear you say. *IATEFL Materials Writing Special Interest Group Newsletter, 1*. Retrieved from http://free.yudu.com/item/details/1801448/Building-Materials-IATEFL-Materials-Writing-SIG-Newsletter-Issue-01
Bell, J., & Gower, R. (1998). Writing course materials for the world: A great compromise. In B. Tomlinson (Ed.), *Materials development in language teaching* (1st ed., pp. 116–129). Cambridge: Cambridge University Press.
Bell, J., & Gower, R. (2011). Writing course materials for the world: A great compromise. In B. Tomlinson (Ed.), *Materials development in language teaching* (2nd ed., pp. 135–150). Cambridge University Press: Cambridge.
Bolitho, R. (2008). Materials used in Central and Eastern Europe and the former Soviet Union. In B. Tomlinson (Ed.), *English language learning materials: A critical review* (pp. 313–322). London: Continuum.
Clandfield, L. (2013). *How to plan a book* (Kindle ed.). Oxford: Teacher2Writer.
Donovan, P. (1998). Piloting—a publisher's view. In B. Tomlinson (Ed.), *Materials development in language teaching* (1st ed., pp. 149–189). Cambridge: Cambridge University Press.
Ellis, R. (2009). Task-based language teaching: Sorting out the misunderstandings. *International Journal of Applied Linguistics, 19*(3), 221–246.

Ellis, R. (2016). Language teaching materials as work plans: An SLA perspective. In B. Tomlinson (Ed.), *SLA research and materials development for language learning* (pp. 203–218). Oxford: Routledge.

Feak, C. B., & Swales, J. M. (2014). Tensions between the old and the new in EAP textbook. In N. Harwood (Ed.), *English language teaching textbooks—content, consumption, production* (pp. 299–319). Basingstoke: Palgrave Macmillan.

Fenner, A., & Nordal-Pedersen, G. (2006). *Searching 8, 9, 10*. Oslo: Gyldendal Norsk Forlag ASA.

Gray, J. (2010). *The construction of English: Culture, consumerism and promotion in the ELT global coursebook*. Basingstoke: Palgrave Macmillan.

Harwood, N. (Ed.). (2014). *English language teaching textbooks—content, consumption, production*. Basingstoke: Palgrave Macmillan.

Hill, D. A. (2013). The visual element in EFL coursebooks. In B. Tomlinson (Ed.), *Developing materials for language teaching* (pp. 174–182). London: Continuum.

Loh, J., & Renandya, W. A. (2015). Exploring adaptations of materials and methods: A case from Singapore. *The European Journal of Applied Linguistics and TEFL, 4*(2), 93–111.

Long, M. H. (Ed.). (2005). *Second language needs analysis*. Cambridge: Cambridge University Press.

Masuhara, H. (2011). What do teachers really want from coursebooks? In B. Tomlinson (Ed.), *Materials development in language teaching* (2nd ed., pp. 236–266). Cambridge: Cambridge University Press.

Masuhara, H. (2015). "Anything goes" in task-based language teaching materials?—the need for principled materials evaluation, adaptation and development. *The European Journal of Applied Linguistics and TEFL, 2*, 113–127.

Masuhara, H., Haan, N., Yi, Y., & Tomlinson, B. (2008). Adult EFL courses. *ELT Journal, 62*, 294–312.

McGrath, I. (2013). *Teaching materials and the roles of EFL/ESL teachers*. London: Bloomsbury.

Mishan, F., & Timmis, I. (2015). *Materials development for TESOL*. Edinburgh: Edinburgh University Press.

Modugala, M. (in press). Listening to children's perceptions and experiences of English language teaching material. In B. Tomlinson (Ed.), *Papers from the British Council English Language Teaching Research Partnership Award Project*. New Delhi: British Council.

Mukundan, J. (2008). Agendas of the state in developing world English language textbooks. *Folio, 12*(2), 17–19.

On target. (1995). Grade 10 English Second Language Learner's Book. Windhoek: Gamsburg Macmillan.

Popovici, R., & Bolitho, R. (2003). Personal and professional development through writing: The Romanian textbook project. In B. Tomlinson (Ed.), *Developing materials for language teaching* (1st ed., pp. 505–517). London: Continuum.

Prowse, P. (1998). How writers write: Testimony from authors. In B. Tomlinson (Ed.), *Materials development in language teaching* (1st ed., pp. 130–145). Cambridge: Cambridge University Press.

Prowse, P. (2011). How writers write: Testimony from authors. In B. Tomlinson (Ed.), *Materials development in language teaching* (2nd ed., pp. 151–173). Cambridge: Cambridge University Press.

Richards, J. C. (2014) The ELT textbook. In S. Garton, & K. Graves (Eds.), *International perspectives on materials in ELT* (pp. 19–36) Palgrave Macmillan.

Santos, D. (2015). Revising listening materials: What remains, what is changed and why. *The European Journal of Applied Linguistics and TEFL 4*(2), 19–36.

Singapore Wala, D. A. (2003a). A coursebook is what it is because of what it has to do: Editor's perspective. In B. Tomlinson (Ed.), *Developing materials for language teaching* (1st ed., pp. 58–71). London: Continuum.

Singapore Wala, D. A. (2003b). Publishing a coursebook: Completing the materials development cycle. In B. Tomlinson (Ed.), *Developing materials for language teaching* (1st ed., pp. 141–161). London: Continuum.

Singapore Wala, D. A. (2013). Publishing a coursebook: The role of feedback. In B. Tomlinson (Ed.), *Developing materials for language teaching* (2nd ed., pp. 63–87). London: Bloomsbury.

Stoller, F., L., & Robinson, M., S. (2014). An interdisciplinary textbook project: Charting the paths taken. In N. Harwood (Ed.), *English language teaching textbooks—content, consumption, production* (pp. 262–298). Basingstoke: Palgrave Macmillan.

Timmis, I. (2014). Writing materials for publication: Questions raised and lessons learned. In N. Harwood (Ed.), *English language teaching textbooks: Content, consumption, production* (pp. 241–261). Basingstoke: Palgrave Macmillan.

Tomlinson, B. (Ed.). (1981). *Talking to learn*. Port Vila: Government of Vanuatu.

Tomlinson, B. (1995). Work in progress: Textbook projects. *Folio, 2*(2), 26–31.

Tomlinson, B. (2003). Developing principled frameworks for materials development. In B. Tomlinson (Ed.), *Developing materials for language teaching* (1st ed., pp. 107–129). London: Continuum.

Tomlinson, B. (2010). What do teachers think about EFL coursebooks? *Modern English Teacher, 19*(4), 5–9.

Tomlinson, B. (2013a). Developing principled frameworks for materials development. In B. Tomlinson (Ed.), *Developing materials for language teaching* (2nd ed., pp. 95–118). London: Bloomsbury.

Tomlinson, B. (Ed.). (2013b). *Applied linguistics and materials development*. London: Bloomsbury.

Tomlinson, B. (2015). Key issues in EFL coursebooks. *ELIA, 15*, 171–180.

Tomlinson, B. (Ed.). (2016). *SLA research and materials development for language learning*. New York: Routledge.

Tomlinson, B. (in press). Making typical coursebook activities more beneficial for the learner. In D. Bao (Ed.), *Creative concerns in ELT materials development: Looking beyond the current design*. Bristol: Multilingual Matters.

Tomlinson, B., Bao, D., Masuhara, H., & Rubdy, R. (2001). Review of adult EFL courses. *ELT Journal, 55*(1), 80–101.

Tomlinson, B., & Masuhara, H. (2013). Adult coursebooks. *ELT Journal, 67*(2), 233–249.

Van den Branden, K., Bygate, M., & Norris, J. M. (2009). *Task-based language teaching: A reader*. Amsterdam: John Benjamins.

Viney, P. (2007). Featured writer questions: Peter Viney. *Folio, 11*(2), 32–33.

Zacharias, N. T. (2005). Teachers' beliefs about internationally-published materials: A survey of tertiary English teachers in Indonesia. *RELC Journal, 36*(1), 23–37.

Zemach, D. (2006). Working with an editor. *Folio, 10*(2), 37–39.

Zemach, D., & Viney, P. (2007). Author test. *Folio, 11*(2), 25–27.

7

Developing Digital Materials

Introduction

In this chapter, we will explore the development of digital materials. What do we mean by "digital materials"? We define them simply as "materials delivered digitally." In other words, the definitive feature of digital materials is their mode of delivery. Be they paper materials in the 1970s or digital materials today, the most distinctive difference is how the content and methodology are communicated. As McLuhan (1964, p. 8) rightly points out, "Each medium, independent of the content it mediates, has its own intrinsic effects which are its unique message" and the delivery mode is likely to influence our perceptions.

What really matters for teachers and learners, however, remains the effect of the particular materials on learners and on the quality of their learning. The validity of the content and methodology needs to be carefully evaluated regardless of the mode of delivery. The medium of delivery, software and applications (e.g. apps) change day by day (e.g. web 2.0 to 3.0 or beyond; smart phones, tablets, smart watches; phablets, i.e. phones with a larger screen that are hybrids of the phone and the tablet) but the main question remains whether digital materials provide improvement in the quality of learning that cannot otherwise be achieved.

In this chapter we are going to focus on samples of accessible digital materials and to predict the effects of the use of digital materials for language learning by using the second language acquisition (SLA) principles summarized in Tomlinson (2013b, 2016). We will also discuss how user friendly (e.g. versatile, navigable and resource friendly) digital materials are for the teachers and learners who use them.

If you are specifically interested in evaluating mobile language learning resources, Reinders and Pegrum (2016) provide a very concise, comprehensive but user-friendly evaluation framework. Their framework involves five categories; for example, the "Educational Affordances Exploited in Learning Design" category looks at how well the tools' affordances have been exploited (e.g. does the material make good use of such strengths of the smart phone as portability, connectivity and social interactivity). Their framework also includes "General Pedagogical Design" (e.g. constructivist; collaborative learning), "SLA Design" (e.g. comprehensible input; comprehensible output; meaning negotiation; feedback) and "Affective Design" (e.g. engagement; affective filter). This framework could be adapted for use in the evaluation of any type of digital material.

The Complete Guide to the Theory and Practice of Materials Development for Language Learning,
First Edition. Brian Tomlinson and Hitomi Masuhara.
© 2018 John Wiley & Sons, Inc. Published 2018 by John Wiley & Sons, Inc.

What Does Research Say about the Effectiveness of ICT in Language Education?

There is now a massive literature on the use of digital media for language learning, for example recent publications by Chapelle (2010); Grgurović, Chapelle, and Shelley (2013); Hockly (2013); Kiddle (2013); Motteram (2013); Thomas, Reinders, and Warschauer (2013); Mishan and Timmis (2015); Reinders and Pegrum (2016). In addition, articles related to ICT assisted learning feature regularly in major journals in applied linguistics (e.g. *Applied Linguistics*; *ELT Journal*; *Studies in Second Language Acquisition*; *TESOL Quarterly*) as well as in specialized journals on technology (e.g. *CALICO Journal*; *CALL Journal*; *ReCALL*; *Technology and Language Learning*).

We searched for research that reports or predicts the effects of the use of digital materials for language learning and found that most of the literature tends to focus on the identification of resources and affordances (i.e. capabilities of apps, software or equipment for potential user performance) and discusses ways of exploiting ICT resources for language learning. Some attempts are being made to ascertain the effectiveness of the use of ICT in learning. Grgurović et al. (2013), for example, examined 37 effectiveness studies that satisfy their stringent criteria (e.g. pre-and postlanguage test design) between 1970 and 2006 and apply a meta-analysis method to enable comparison across different studies (see also Felix, 2008). They find that overall results favor "small but statistically significant effect size" for technology-supported pedagogy (Grgurović et al., 2013, p. 165). They notice possible other factors that could influence the results, such as language proficiency, difference of language (e.g. most of the studies are in in EFL/ESL and Spanish). Their "analyses of instructional conditions, characteristics of participants, and conditions of the research design did not provide reliable results." They conclude their article by stating, "Perhaps more important for educational decision-making today, the overall results did not indicate that CALL was inferior to classroom conditions" (Grgurović et al., p. 192).

From the perspective of materials development, we would need more specific details of the materials, of the medium, and of the likely factors influencing the effect on language learning. The kinds of research we would welcome include:

- content analysis and evaluation of materials (e.g. linguistic and task authenticity; modality combinations such as text, visual and sound, and their effects on learners);
- measures of the processes (e.g. materials and user interaction such as frequency of access to the materials; complexity and richness of learner interactions induced by digital modes and procedural design; affective elements such as interest, motivation and intensity of attention);
- outcomes evaluation (e.g. development of targeted language proficiency; improvement in presentation of spoken and / or written data; motivation for autonomy).

Diverse Levels of Digital Adoption in Education

Dedeney and Hockly (2012) provides a very accessible account of how technology has been introduced and developed in language education. How much technology has been normalized in our environment may depend on personal and teaching contexts. Peacock (2013) provides an interesting anecdote in the foreword of Motteram (2013):

> I remember as a fledgling teacher in the British Council teaching centre in Hong Kong listening to the Director of Studies giving a welcome speech to teachers at the start of the new academic year. The centre had begun investing heavily in computers and had just opened its "Classroom of the Future"—a classroom with specially adapted furniture which gave students relatively painless access to computers built into desks. The Director of Studies was talking about the role of technology in the future of language learning and rather dramatically made his point by closing with the following epithet: "The British Council needs teachers who are confident with technology. You are either into technology or you are in the way and had better start looking for a new job."
>
> Strong words indeed—and at the time quite a wake-up call for a number of teachers in the room who looked nervously around at their colleagues and no doubt made mental notes to get to grips with this new-fangled email malarkey.
>
> Times have changed, teachers have evolved, and we now have a new breed of learning technologists. As in Hong Kong, the first changes began in the classroom itself—new technologies such as overhead projectors, interactive whiteboards, laptop computers and wireless internet have opened up the classroom to the outside world. Teachers who spent their lives managing with a textbook, a tape recorder and a blackboard are now adept at using PowerPoint to present grammar, playing podcasts to practise listening skills, pulling texts off the world wide web to introduce reading skills and perhaps most ground-breaking of all—empowering students by giving them access to a wide range of web-based tools that allow them to publish work and engage with live audiences in real contexts.
>
> (Peacock, 2013, p. 2)

Motteram (2013) provides various case studies from primary schools to adult education in various countries, including Taiwan, Turkey, and South Africa. What the book shows is how teachers are creatively making use of available and accessible Internet resources and of digital programs and apps to try out new approaches to teaching.

In our own cases, Brian works for two universities: one in the United Kingdom and the other in the United States. He delivers an EdD course module for the university in the United States. as part of an online course. He teaches through live webinars (i.e. seminars on the web) and participates in forum discussion online while the students are spread around the globe in different time zones. Virtual language environments (VLEs) provide a stable platform for all the necessary educational transactions (e.g. announcements, course specifications, resources for each session, assignment submission) between teachers and students. Unlike the real university, VLE is available anytime and anywhere. Hitomi worked at the National University of Singapore from 1997 to 2000 and the university expected all the lecturers to build a web site for each module on the VLE environment. Hitomi now works for the University of Liverpool, which uses Blackboard (a paid VLE provider). In her previous university, the open source Moodle (http://moodle.org) was used as a VLE platform. There is a slightly different feel in each VLE platform but once you get the knack you can move from one to another easily. When we teach sessions we incorporate YouTube videos as well as images that were collated by doing Google searches on to the Powerpoint Presentation software that comes as part of a package by Microsoft. We also surf the Internet and find a lot of information. Our students may use Wikipedia (i.e. an online encyclopedia written and revised by the users). They write their assignments using computers and submit via VLE. We sometimes use Google Docs to share the same documents. Of course emails are the main tools of communication. We use Skype (i.e. a free communication tool owned by Microsoft since 2011) for video-conferencing or meetings (https://www.skype.com/en/). Behind all this exists the global Internet environment of Web 2.0 (the second generation of the World Wide Web), which allows users to communicate, share and collaborate. We carry very portable tablets that allow us to get information whenever we need to and to check emails. Information and communication technology (ICT) is part of our normal personal and professional lives.

From our experience, and from the latest reports, we know that such a situation is NOT the norm in schools in the vast majority of countries. Motteram (2013) explains that:

> In most classrooms the drivers of activity are the examination and a centralised curriculum. And as a result textbooks and teaching often reflect this. In many parts of the world, for example, spoken language is not examined and so, although it might appear in the curriculum, it does not get taught.
>
> (Motteram, 2013, pp. 303–304)

Such an observation is confirmed by the results in the British Council's survey (2015) conducted in South Asia, specifically, Afghanistan, Bangladesh, India, Nepal, Pakistan and Sri Lanka. The research team investigated access to technology and the need for continuing professional development of 892 carefully selected representative teachers from each country. The quantitative and qualitative analyses of multiple data reveal that:

- The majority of the teachers are positive about using technology for their own language development and professional development.
- They welcome opportunities to interact with other educators that will facilitate community development and collaboration.
- The technological devices that are available are TV, radio, computer and mobile phones.
- Computers and mobile phones are the most preferred channels.
- Low levels of digital literacy and ICT skills were noted among the group surveyed.
- Many of the teachers reported problems of maintenance or of getting permission to use computer labs.
- In some schools mobile phones are banned, meaning that teachers are unable to use them in their classrooms.

A similar picture emerges from the papers from the British Council India English Language Teaching Research Partnerships (ELTReP) Awards scheme which Brian is currently editing for publication in 2017. Hardly any access to, and very little use of, digital materials is reported in 21 research studies of what happens in primary, secondary, and tertiary classrooms in various regions of India.

The discussion of diversity often leads to the topic of the digital divide (Hilbert, 2011, 2016) between urban and rural areas and of global inequality. But the situation in education seems a lot more complex. For example, Vrasidas (2010) reports a national survey conducted by CARDET (a Center for the Advancement of Research and Development in Educational Technology which is based in Cyprus but conducts research projects with partners globally) on teachers use of ICT and the challenges they face. The results revealed that ICT is available in most schools and classrooms but teachers use it mainly for preparing educational material and lesson plans. The teachers are aware of the benefits of ICT in their classrooms but the majority of these teachers did not integrate ICT in their teaching. The reasons given were (50.5% return rate—531 responses out of 1,051 samples):

- extent of the curriculum that needs to be covered during the year (81.4%);
- time constraints (71.7%);
- time required for preparing ICT-based activities (60.4%);
- availability of infrastructure (53.5%);
- amount of quality content (50.7%);
- lack of in-classroom teacher support (50.2%);
- lack of participation of teachers in decision making (43.4%);
- need for professional development (37%).

Thomas (2015) explains similar challenges in Japan to attempts to genuinely incorporate technology-mediated task-based learning (or any innovation for that matter). He points out (p. 241) that "… this kind of learning requires not just a digital shift, but also a fundamental shift in policy and approach…" Thomas (2015) questions the optimistic views of technology by ICT proponents (e.g. Chapelle, 2014) by saying:

> While language learning technologies have made significant strides over the last decade as broadband has improved around the world, it is nevertheless clear from the current volume [Thomas and Reinders, 2015] that neither TBLT nor digital technologies currently occupy anything approaching what might be called a hegemonic or normalized position in language education. This is true of the West but is especially relevant in the Asian context …
>
> (Thomas, 2015, pp. 229–230)

It is promising that surveys (e.g. Vrasidas, 2010; The British Council, 2015) confirm that teachers see the potential benefits of digital materials and that they are positive about using them for preparation and, some, for teaching. However, for the use of digital materials to become a routine part of classroom practice the whole curriculum will have to be reappraised and digital elements situated in it. Policy changes and teacher development, as we know very well from the past, require a very strong political will as well as planning and investment at national, regional and institutional levels. We have, for example, seen language laboratories gathering dust in Nigerian institutions in the 1960s and language laboratories being used for air conditioned meetings with visitors to schools in Indonesia in the 1980s. The Nigerian institutions lacked reliable sources of electricity and the Indonesian schools lacked appropriate software and alternative air-conditioned rooms.

However we do believe that accessible, well-structured and principled digital materials could help the majority of teachers worldwide to grasp how technology could provide resources that are likely to engage, empower, and facilitate language learning.

Are Digital Materials Better at Facilitating Second-Language Acquisition?

Second Language Acquisition Principles

Tomlinson (2011, 2013b, 2016, see also Chapter 8 in this book) reviews SLA literature and proposes principles that could be used in evaluating materials. Tomlinson (2013b) explains that it is generally agreed that SLA is facilitated by:

1. A rich and meaningful exposure to language in use.
2. Affective and cognitive engagement.
3. Making use of those mental resources typically used in communication in the L1 (e.g. visual imaging and the inner voice).
4. Noticing how the L2 is used.
5. Being given opportunities for contextualized and purposeful communication in the L2.
6. Being encouraged to interact.
7. Being allowed to focus on meaning.

Samples of Digital Materials

Based on our arguments that "accessible and well-structured principled digital materials" that are readily available could help teachers realize "how technology could provide resources that are likely to engage, empower and facilitate language learning" we searched the web for such materials. As we predicted, our initial search revealed thousands of sites by non-profit-making organizations as well as commercial enterprises. In order to make our search feasible, we set up a scenario in which moderately IT competent teachers with access to the Internet and to a computer try to find digital materials more or less ready to be used in their classes. They are pressed with time and do not wish to spend a long time searching or carefully evaluating the materials. Those teachers would appreciate digital materials which:

- can be accessed free;
- are appropriate for their learners (e.g. age, language proficiency, appeal);
- are easy to navigate;
- are approved by some authority in the English language teaching field;
- seem to offer quality in learning experience;
- seem to offer approaches in line with current thinking.

Using these criteria, we continued our search and selected three globally well-known sites:

- the British Council *LearnEnglish*;
- *Onestopenglish* by Macmillan;
- *Lessonstream* by Jamie Keddie.

Match Between the SLA Principles and Selected Digital Materials

Our aim was to find how SLA principles are being realized in selected digital materials. Our investigation was NOT meant as a systematic selection and evaluation of digital materials as you may find in a regular *ELT Journal* survey. We would welcome such an evaluation, though, as we have found many potentially useful materials which we do not get to discuss in detail in this chapter. The approach we took was to experience some of the materials by following the activity instructions as language learners and then reflect on the processes we went through in relation to the SLA principles listed above and also on our reactions as users of the digital materials.

No SLA researcher would disagree that exposure to comprehensible input (i.e. input that can be sufficiently understood) is a prerequisite for language acquisition. The World Wide Web provides a massive amount of multimodal and textual resources. More, however, is not necessarily better. In an ICT-rich context, we can, for example, experience a cognitive overload of unreliable, misleading and outdated information. What is crucial is the quality and potential effect of the comprehensible input that is likely to facilitate authentic experience of language in use. Users of digital materials in this sense are likely to welcome a digital environment that offers carefully selected materials. Such platforms can be created at institutional level and teachers can share materials and communication.

LearnEnglish (http://learnenglish.britishcouncil.org/en)

The British Council *LearnEnglish* provides a systematic and well-structured web site for users with different attributes, learning styles, needs and wants. *LearnEnglish* gives choices in the menu bar at the top in relation to:

- learner attributes (i.e. young learners, teenagers and teachers; proficiency level);
- learning objectives (e.g. skills, grammar and vocabulary, exams, literature, contemporary British studies);
- multimodal presentations (e.g. video, audio, texts);
- genre and types (e.g. magazine, documentary, animations, games).

We tried the teenage materials and found that, apart from some language learning videos and exercises, the materials seem to provide authentic experience of the viewing of interesting contents, for example a 5 minute video report by a teenage reporter talking to the actress Kate Winslet about her experience of being involved in making the recent film *Steve Job* (http://learnenglishteens.britishcouncil.org/uk-now/film-uk/kate-winslet-strong-women-and-learning-lines). This video was in fact developed by Into Film (http://www.intofilm.org/), an organization that uses film and media production to develop skills in young people in the United Kingdom.

In terms of SLA principles, the authentic videos in the "UK Now" section in *LearnEnglish* are often cognitively and affectively engaging (i.e. Principle 2) and they seem to entice repeated viewing (repetition is one way of increasing "exposure" in Principle 1).

How comprehensible are the authentic videos? *LearnEnglish* provides a rough level of proficiency in terms of the Common European Framework of Reference (CEFR). It is useful even though comprehensibility may also depend on various factors in addition to level of language proficiency (e.g. interest, background knowledge, topic familiarity, motivation).

We felt somewhat put off, however, by the product-based pre- (e.g. pre-teaching of vocabulary) and post-activities (e.g. Multiple choice, True or False) that seem to feature in every video (e.g. http://learnenglishteens.britishcouncil.org/grammar-vocabulary/grammar-videos/future-forms). The downloadable pdfs of the activities may be meant to be used as class materials but the activities without the eye-catching colorful graphics and the interactivity become mere tests of declarative knowledge. The underlying assumption seems to be that explicit teaching of vocabulary and grammar can lead to language acquisition and that this can be evidenced by scores on the accompanying comprehension questions. We find it such a pity that engaging authentic videos get this treatment. The content of the videos is not exploited for communication for real-life purposes (i.e. Principles 5 and 6) or for Principle 4: "Noticing how the L2 is used."

The grammar and vocabulary section does use animation videos, presumably, in an attempt to contextualize grammar or lexis. But the contrived audio script is read aloud and we saw no difference between the digital materials and the much criticized inauthentic DVDs provided with many coursebooks. No opportunity is given for the users to notice significant language features within meaning focused interaction (i.e. Principle 4). The explicit prescriptive explanation of grammar takes away the point of providing contexts and the teaching method is far from matching contemporary learner-centered learning theories. We can only imagine that conventional practice / testing exercises are what the writers assumed that teachers and learners want.

In the Games section in the Study Break, we found a mixture of quality in the materials. Some games exploit the interactivity of digital media well but some could be played with only visual clues without understanding any language. "Magic Gopher," the most popular game (9201 likes and 414 feedbacks when accessed on 28 August, 2016), involves an interactive magic trick (http://learnenglishteens.britishcouncil.org/study-break/games/magic-gopher). Users are instructed to choose a number and, after being asked to do a few additions and subtractions, Magic Gopher guesses what number (expressed in a symbol) the viewers had in mind (Principle 2: Affective and cognitive engagement).

The language interaction comes in the form of reading Gopher's instructions and following them in stages (Principle 6: Being encouraged to interact; Principle 7: Being allowed to focus on meaning). If learners do not understand they can click the help sign held by the icon of an assistant gopher and all the instructions are displayed. (Repetition and recycling that leads to Principle 1: A rich and meaningful exposure to language in use.) We tried it a few times and The Magic Gopher guessed the answers correctly. Comments on message boards sometimes share similar experiences but the asynchronous nature of the message board often leads to incoherent threads of viewers' one-way comments. The viewers of the Magic Gopher however seem to have shared the same goal of wanting to find out the trick behind the Gopher's "magic," thus helping the thread of messages to cohere and interact and providing purposeful reading for all of us users (Principle 1: A rich and meaningful exposure to language in use).

Onestopenglish (http://www.onestopenglish.com/)

Onestopenglish, with a £42 annual charge, uses a similar web site to that of *LearnEnglish* by the British Council (N.B. other major publishers provide similar community web sites). The main menu bar at the top gives various choices such as Business, ESP, and CLIL. Each category has a drop-down menu and a list of all the materials available. There are a lot of lesson plans by established coursebook writers and aspiring writers as well as teachers' award-winning lesson plans. For comparison with *LearnEnglish* videos, we typed "videos for teenagers" in the search box. We got a lot of results but the top 30 were lesson plans. Many of them were for helping learners to make videos. On the right hand column, "Search by ..." appeared. The categories included Language Focus, Age Group, Level, Content area, and so on, but not media such as "video" as a search tag. We then chose the Teenagers section from the top menu. In the main section there are boxes of categories such as Spot on News for teenagers, Time to Travel, etc. We felt that the web site could have been structured in a little more user-friendly way. We felt as if we had gone into a shop filled with goods in rough categories but you had to open each box to find what was in it.

After trying out some materials, we decided to focus on a unit of CLIL material called: "Webquest: Water" at Intermediate to Upper-Intermediate level, as it did make use of various media as part of the material (http://www.onestopenglish.com/teenagers/topic-based-materials/webquests/webquest-water/554199.article). There was no attribution regarding the writer. There are seven activities that lead up to a project involving a questionnaire survey and a presentation. The first three activities are mainly reading and comprehension activities like the following:

- Activity 1. Water facts—take the quiz. Users are instructed to answer 11 multiple questions and then find out answers by linking to www.explainthatstuff.com/water.html. There is a very interesting information site about water with photos but it is very extensive.
- Activity 2. Storing and Treating Water: Users are instructed to go to www.scottishwater.co.uk/clearer-fresher-learning/all-about-water/all-about-water/water-treatment and to fill in a chart, to sequence the steps for water treatment and to fill in gaps This is potentially interesting but it features another very long text.
- Activity 4 involves the learners brainstorming ways of saving water. Then they watch videos for more ideas.
- Activity 5 involves reading an existing webpage on irrigation.
- Activity 6 involves reading about water aids in Tanzania.
- Activity 7 is a project involving a questionnaire and a presentation.

In terms of SLA principles, there is a lot of "rich and meaningful exposure to language in use" (Principle 1). The texts are written for L1 adults so we wonder how "comprehensible" L2 intermediate to upper intermediate learners might find them (especially if they cannot connect the topic to their lives) and how long reading the texts online might take. What would the class dynamics and atmosphere be like? The topic and content is intellectually interesting but again we are not so sure if L2 teenagers would be "Affectively and cognitively engaged." If the class is made up of L2 learners from different countries, water could be an excellent topic for exploring the situations in their own countries. It seems to be an opportunity missed.

There are no instructions about what happens after the learners do the comprehension, gap filling, and true or false activities. We do not see any obvious activities for "Noticing how the L2 is used" (Principle 4). The project in Activity 7 may provide "Opportunities for contextualized and purposeful communication in the L2" (Principle 5) and "Being encouraged to interact" (Principle 6).

All in all, this is a very worthy CLIL activity. In relation to Principle 2 "Affective and cognitive engagement," according to Ortega (2009, p. 189), "Motivation is usually understood to refer to the desire to initiate L2 learning and the effort employed to sustain it" (see also Ushioda & Dörnyei, 2012). Based on new neurobiological evidence regarding the fundamental role of emotion in cognition, Immordino-Yang and Damasio (2007, p. 9) argue that "it is simply not enough for students to master knowledge and logical reasoning skills in the traditional academic sense" and that "When we educators fail to appreciate the importance of students' emotions, we fail to appreciate a critical force in students' learning. One could argue, in fact, that we fail to appreciate the very reason that students learn at all." They also point out that unmemorable knowledge does inherently not transfer well to the real-world situation. For details of a 10-hour blended learning unit also focusing on saving water (but including responding to poems about water and inventing a water-saving device) see Tomlinson and Avila (2011, pp. 150–151).

Onestopenglish provides a potentially useful community for teachers. The teachers would probably appreciate it even more though if:

- navigation was more user friendly;
- reassurance was given about how the quality of the materials has been assured;
- materials were included after being trialed with target learners.

Lessonstream by Jamie Keddie (http://lessonstream.org/materials/video-lesson-plans/)

Lessonstream is an online resource of visual activities for teachers created by Jamie Keddie supported by crowdfunding (https://www.indiegogo.com/projects/videotelling-storytelling-for-screenagers-youtube-video"/). It won a British Council ELTon award in 2009. *Lessonstream* consists of YouTube videos in which Jamie Keddie talks to the viewers and discusses issues and then the main YouTube video follows. There are downloadable materials for each lesson stream. The menu at the top shows: Browse the Lessons, Language levels, Learner type, Time, Main activity, Language aim, Topic and Materials. Browse the Lessons provides boxes containing necessary information in a reader-friendly way. All the lessons have been tried out and thus the author can indicate approximate times taken by activities and suitable levels. We found the site to be easy to navigate. We sampled some stream videos and enjoyed them because they were personal, quirky and entertaining. They also made us think. For example, one video is called Owning English (http://lessonstream.org/2016/03/15/owning-english/). It starts with a video with the author and his friends talking about Camden and debating about whether the word "touristic" is acceptable or not while walking in a park in London. The author then decides to talk to various people in Camden and solicits their opinions about various issues. Two other short videos show the author talking about the difference in use of English between two generations and discussing acceptable use of language with his mother. Through these videos the author explores various aspects of accents and use of language in a very informal and engaging manner. The stream as a whole contains "A rich and meaningful exposure to language in use" (Principle 1) and the material is potentially "Affectively and cognitively engaging" (Principle 2). It also "makes use of those mental resources typically used in communication in the L1" and helps the learners "Notice how the L2 is used." The relaxed but interesting discussions are thought provoking. Watching the video "allows the learners to focus on meaning." This particular lesson stream does not have a lesson plan as most of the other videos do. But the videos have illustrated a lot of issues, therefore it is not difficult to develop activities such as small projects for discovering differences of the use of English by different generations or finding out how language evolves. For each stream there is a message board. For each comment, the author responds. Therefore, there is a feel of genuine interaction even though the interaction is asynchronous. So *Lessonstream* does provide "opportunities for con-textualized and purposeful communication in the L2" (Principle 6) and the users are "being encouraged to interact" (Principle 7). There is a sense of an ongoing relationship between the viewers and the author as the video is uploaded periodically. As we are writing this in the summer of 2016 the most popular lesson stream has been downloaded 26,014 times. What we appreciate is the fact that it exploits the media effectively and it is well-designed both for learners and for teachers.

Very similar principles to those we have used to evaluate the three web sites above are also used by Tomlinson and Avila (2011) to drive suggested webquest, weblog and wiki based activities with the goal of humanizing foreign language teaching.

What Are the Strengths and Weaknesses of Digital Materials?

Basic Requirements

Digital materials require:

- financial resources;
- hardware (e.g. computers, mobile phones, tablets);
- robust network connectivity;
- applications (i.e. software);
- digital literacy such as computing skills, ability to use the Internet, ability of teachers, students and learners to use the technology;
- technical support;
- a digital community to interact with.

Some learners have all of the above. Some may have none. Some might not even be able to afford coursebooks. Publishers nowadays produce various components for their courses, some printed, and some digitalized. This pushes up the cost of global course-book production and is reflected in the price. It is promising, however, that the sale of mobile phones has overtaken computers and other devices in so-called deprived areas of the world, making *Lessonstream*, for example, cheaply and easily available.

Durability

Technology progresses and devices need upgrading. It is in the manufacturers' inter-est that consumers feel the need to replace their computers every 4–6 years, and smart phones in a couple of years, if not every year. Compatibility of applications then becomes an issue as digital devices are upgraded. Newer applications can read the digital mate-rials developed with previous versions but older applications may no longer be able to cope with the materials produced with the latest versions. This urges the consumers to purchase new devices.

Likewise, web sites are updated and sometimes sites move. Some web sites become obsolete. When digital materials are published, some links may no longer work. Multimodal materials require a huge amount of memory and fast and reliable Internet connectivity. Digital materials could frustrate teachers and learners if they do not have the appropriate devices and networks. The imagination and creativity of teachers and students, on the other hand, are always up-to-date and are therefore more durable and reliable.

Choice

Each individual has preferences such as topics, learning styles (e.g. visual, auditory) and proficiency level. Digital materials enable individual learners to choose the content and modes of learning (e.g. *LearnEnglish*, *OnestopEnglish*). *LearnEnglish* and *Onestopenglish* offer a lot of choice in a hierarchical menu. The options are given in the main menu bar at the top with subcategories in pull-down menus. Quick links next to the main section highlight information that could be useful for the user choice (e.g. most popular sites). Having choice facilitates personalization: for example, frequent visits made by a particular user could affect how the same site is organized next time the user logs in.

Choices could mean, however, distraction and loss of focus. Our working memory is known to have limited capacity and multitasking is only possible by shifting our main attention to one task at a time, with the other tasks idling in the remaining working memory slots (e.g. Shell et al., 2010; Wen, 2016). When distracted by a stronger stimulus, a previous weaker task gives way to a new one. In face-to-face instruction, teachers tend to have fuller influence on learners' focus in classroom but in a purely autonomous online environment, learners are left on their own to manage their learning. How teachers or materials designers plan their interventions requires even more careful thought in digital materials. Visual processing-wise, just as a cluttered and overbusy layout of a printed coursebook can confuse learners, being greeted by too many digital choices may baffle the novice and result in wasted hours before any learning can take place. One solution to this problem would be blended learning courses, which combine the advantages of both face to face interaction and of digital delivery (see Mishan, 2013 for discussion of the value of blended learning and Tomlinson and Whittaker, 2013 for case studies of blended learning courses in design and use).

Linking

Web 2.0, the second generation of the Internet, allows interaction and collaboration between users. Linking (e.g. one webpage links with another) is one way of achieving such connection. In writing a book, we refer to other people's articles and books. In digital materials we are able to link one medium (e.g. a weblog) with many different media (e.g. photos, videos, digital newspaper articles).

Interactivity

Second language acquisition researchers emphasize the fundamental role of interaction as a source of language acquisition. In a face-to-face classrooms various interactions take place (e.g. spontaneous small talk; teacher talking with students; students talking in pairs or groups; students talking to the whole class in, for example, a presentation). Compared to the direct face-to-face classroom situation, digital communication tends to be indirect and different. For example, the Magic Gopher in *LearnEnglish* involves some virtual synchronous interaction between the Gopher and the user and asynchronous interactions between the writers of comments. Synchronous interaction can also be achieved by video conferencing, Webinars (i.e. Web Seminars), Skype (i.e. software that enables video/audio conversation) and synchronous texting. These digital means can be used regardless of the distance between the participants. If a task requires group work, students could share a document online (e.g. Google Docs, Drop Box) and negotiate by texting and Skyping.

Digital materials offer fewer, if any, opportunities for spontaneous synchronous interactive feedback. Ultimately, just as babies need direct interaction with all the senses to achieve L1 acquisition, L2 learners could be said to acquire language best through live face-to-face interactions with peers and the teacher with instant verbal and nonverbal feedback (e.g. meaning negotiation, recasts, clarification, encouragement with nonverbal affirmation).

Mobility

Mobility can be achieved by coursebooks, mobile devices (e.g. phones, networked tablets, phablets) and portable devices (e.g. laptops). However, Apple started a massive storage system called iCloud in 2011 with some shared storage with Microsoft and Amazon. Once you save your data in iCloud, you are able to access it from anywhere anytime as long as there is an internet connection. So digital materials, in theory, can be used anytime, anywhere with all their multifunctionality and interconnectivity.

Multifunctionality

Digital materials are capable of achieving various different functions (e.g. switching from text to video; gathering information through the internet during a task; using a corpus—see Cobb, 2009; conducting communication at a distance, to name a few).

A publication that emphasizes many of the above potential strengths of digital materials and exemplifies them with reference to the resources now available to teachers and learners is (Wilkinson, 2016). This chapter links CALL to input and interactionist theories, to cognitive theories and to constructivist theories, proposes principles for selecting and evaluating ICT resources and gives detailed examples of two related forms of multimodal literacy, digital storytelling and documentary journalism, which bring many of the advantages of digital materials together in an "Integrated Constructivist ICT-Infused Project" (p. 269). It also contains a useful list of resources available on the web, which could help teachers to "begin exploring ICT in the L2 classroom" (p. 273).

A Summary of the Potential Benefits and Problems of Using Digital Materials

Potential Benefits

- Class hours are limited; technology enables individual autonomy and collaborative interaction (e.g. Skype, SMS texting, Microsoft messenger software, Google Talk) anytime, anywhere.
- Collaborative and interactive writing at a distance (e.g. Google Docs, wikis i.e. a collaborative writing tool such as Wikipedia for which entries are written and revised by willing individuals with knowledge).

- Collaboration beyond the classroom (e.g. between difference classes, different schools, or different countries—Motteram, 2013).

Problems

- Digitalization of education needs political will, careful interactive planning between the government and / or institutions and the grassroots teachers, huge funding, teacher development and IT support.
- There are costly requirements such as technological devices and network connections before digital materials can be used.
- Technology changes so fast and often bemuses teachers. It is "constantly evolving" and it is nearly impossible for educational systems, teaching, learning and assessment to keep up with these changes.
- Technology is only a support.
- There "is no necessary relationship between the surface attraction of electronic communication and the quality and quantity of learning which result" (Maley, 2011, p. 388). This could be particularly true in relation to the current enthusiasm for microlearning, a way of delivering learning in short, very focused bursts through attractive videos with high production values (e.g. "Why Microlearning is HUGE and how to be part of it"—https://elearningindustry.com/why-microlearning-is-huge). This is an approach, originating in business learning, which is now being applied to language learning. Focusing on one learning point for a short time (usually no more than four minutes) through an engaging video is very appealing to learners but contradicts what we know about frequency and variety of input, prolonged engagement, opportunities for contextualized use and the delayed effect of instruction.

Our Recommendations for Using and Developing Digital Materials

We recommend that:

- Digital materials should always be designed and evaluated according to criteria developed to maximize the likelihood of language acquisition.
- Ministries of education and institutions should not impose the use of digital materials just so as to appear to be modern and up to date. Before introducing or further developing the use of digital materials they should consider both their likely learning effectiveness and their cost effectiveness, as well as their relevance to the curriculum and to examination preparation, the training and attitudes of their teachers and the inclinations of their learners.
- Teachers should be helped to increase their awareness of the potential value of digital materials and of the digital materials available for their use.
- In contexts where digital materials are affordable and sustainable consideration should be given to the development of blended learning materials so that the considerable benefits of face-to-face interaction and of teacher feedback and support can be retained whilst gaining the additional benefits offered by digital materials of flexibility, of convenience and of massively increased opportunities for exposure to and use of the target language.
- Teachers should not lose confidence in the validity of their teaching regardless of whether it is with or without technology and ultimately they should be responsible

for decisions regarding which digital materials to use and how to exploit them for the benefit of their learners.
- We should all remember that technology is only a tool and what matters is not how marvelous the technology is but how it is used by teachers and learners to facilitate learning.
- Student should always be at the center of their learning, not technology.

Conclusion

We fully endorse the developments that are taking place in the design and delivery of digital materials for language learning. However, at the same time we agree with the voices advising caution, especially with those insisting on principled development, on quality control and on recognition that the majority of language learners in the world do not have access to digital learning materials. These learners would, at least for the time being, be better served by small investments in cheap and available quality paper materials than in expensive digital materials which their institutions might not have the expertise, software, spare parts or even electricity to take advantage of. After all, it is arguable that one relatively cheap "big book" might be more valuable and durable for learners in a classroom than one expensive computer which needs feeding with software, updates, and expertise.

Although many digital materials are designed for self-access use by autonomous learners we would argue for the importance of teacher mediation, support and encouragement and of the provision of opportunities for learner interaction with teachers and with other learners. A good example of this is that in the Self-Access Learning Centre at Kanda University in Japan learners working with digital materials can go and talk to a teacher and can work with other learners around the same device if they wish. Brian once conducted a research project for a learning company in Singapore and found that primary school students benefitted more from CALL materials when working two at a computer than when working alone (especially in relation to the development of creative skills).

It is noticeable that we have made very little reference to research into the effectiveness of digital materials. There is some such research demonstrating small gains for learners whose materials are delivered electronically (e.g. Chapelle 2010, 2014; Chapelle & Lui, 2007; Grgurović et al., 2013) but if we were in a low resourced context we would need a lot more and a lot more convincing research to persuade us to risk investment in costly digital delivery of materials which might not be any more effective in facilitating language acquisition than the paper materials already in use.

What Do You Think?

1. Think of a particular language-teaching context and then decide what the advantages and disadvantages would be of using digital materials in that context.
2. Do you think it would be worth trying to introduce blended learning materials (i.e. combining digital and face-to-face delivery) in the context you thought of in 1 above? Why?
3. In the context in 1 above, do you think it would be possible to use a flexi materials approach in which all the learners in a class were doing the same generic

tasks but with texts they have found for themselves individually or in groups from the web? Do you think this would be a useful approach for the learners in your context?

4. What do you think are the potential advantages of each the following? Which do you think has the greatest potential for use in facilitating language acquisition:
   - Weblogs?
   - Webquests?
   - Skype?
   - Downloadable practice exercises?
   - Mobile phones?
   - Web libraries of extensive readers?

5. What advice about the use of digital materials would you give to:
   - Ministries of Education?
   - Examination bodies?
   - Publishers?
   - Materials developers?
   - Parents?
   - Teachers?
   - Language learners?

Tasks

1. Find any example of digital materials available to you and then evaluate their potential effectiveness by answering the following questions about them:
   - Which features (if any) are likely to facilitate language acquisition?
   - Which features (if any) could inhibit language acquisition?
   - Are the materials more flexible than their paper equivalent would be?
   - Are the materials more convenient to use than their paper equivalent would be?
   - Are the materials cheaper than their paper equivalent would be?
   - Do you prefer the materials to their paper equivalent? Why?

2. Specify a group of language learners (i.e. age, level, gender, location, objectives) and then design a unit of blended learning (see Further Reading 3 below) for these learners, which would afford them many of the advantages of both digital and paper materials and of online and face-to-face interaction.

Further Reading

For those who would like to learn more about apps-driven materials, Kiddle provides an excellent commentary: Kiddle, T. (2013). Developing digital language learning materials. In B. Tomlinson (Ed.), *Developing materials for language teaching* (2nd ed., pp. 189–206). London: Bloomsbury.

For those who are interested in mobile learning: see Reinders, H., and Pegrum, M. (2016). Supporting language learning on the move. In B. Tomlinson (Ed.), *SLA research and materials development for language learning* (pp. 219–231). NewYork: Routledge.

For those who are interested in blended learning: see Tomlinson, B., and Whittaker, C. (Eds.). (2013). *Blended learning in English language teaching: Course design and implementation*. London: The British Council and Mishan, F. (2013). Demystifying blended learning. In B. Tomlinson (Ed.), *Developing materials for language teaching* (2nd ed., pp. 207–224). London: Bloomsbury.

References

British Council. (2015). *Technology for professional development: Access, interest and opportunity for teachers of English in South Asia*. New Delhi: British Council.

Chapelle, C. A. (2010). The spread of computer-assisted language learning. *Language Teaching, 43*(1), 66–74.

Chapelle, C. A. (2014). Afterword—technology mediated TBLT and the evolving role of innovator. In M. González-Lloret, & L. Ortega (Eds.), *Technology-mediated TBLT. Researching technology and tasks* (pp. 323–334). Amsterdam: John Benjamins.

Chapelle, C. A., & Lui, H. M. (2007). Theory and research: Investigation of "authentic" CALL tasks. In J. Egbert & E. Hanson-Smith (Eds.), *CALL environments* (2nd ed., pp. 111–130). Alexandri a, VA: TESOL Publications.

Cobb, T. (2009). Necessary or nice? Computers in second language reading. In Z. Han & N. Anderson J. (Eds.), *Second language reading research and instruction—crossing the boundaries* (pp. 144–172). Ann Arbor: Michigan University Press.

Damasio, A., & Carvalho, G. B. (2013). The nature of feelings: Evolutionary and neurobiological origins. *Nature Reviews Neuroscience, 14*(2), 143–152.

Dedeney, G., & Hockly, N. (2012). ICT in ELT: How did we get here and where are we going? *ELT Journal, 66*(4), 533–542.

Felix, U. (2008). The unreasonable effectiveness of CALL: What have we learned in two decades of research? *ReCALL, 20*(2), 141–161.

Grgurović, M., Chapelle, C. A., & Shelley, M. C. (2013). A meta-analysis of effectiveness studies on computer technology-supported language learning. *Recall, 25*(2), 165–198.

Hilbert, M. (2011). The end justifies the definition: The manifold outlooks on the digital divide and their practical usefulness for policy-making. *Telecommunications Policy, 35*, 715–736.

Hilbert, M. (2016). The bad news is that the digital access divide is here to stay: Domestically installed bandwidths among 172 countries for 1986–2014. *Telecommunications Policy, 40*(6), 567–581.

Hockly, N. (2013). Designer learning: The teacher as designer of mobile-based classroom learning experiences. *The International Research Foundation for English Language Education*,

Immordino-Yang, M. H., & Damasio, A. (2007). We feel, therefore we learn: The relevance of affective and social neuroscience to education. *Mind, Brain, and Education, 1*(8), 3–10.

Kiddle, T. (2013). Developing digital language learning materials. In B. Tomlinson (Ed.), *Developing materials for language teaching* (2nd ed., pp. 189–206). London: Bloomsbury.

Maley, A. (2011). Squaring the circle—Reconciling materials as constraint with materials as empowerment. In B. Tomlinson (Ed.), *Materials development in language teaching* (2nd ed., pp. 379–402). Cambridge: Cambridge University Press.

McLuhan, M. (1964). *Understanding media: The extensions of man*. New York: McGraw Hill.

Mishan, F. (2013). Demystifying blended learning. In B. Tomlinson (Ed.), *Developing materials for language teaching* (2nd ed., pp. 207–224). London: Bloomsbury.

Mishan, F. & Timmis, I. (2015). *Materials development for TESOL*. Edinburgh: Edinburgh University Press.

Motteram, G. (2013). Developing language-learning materials with technology. In B. Tomlinson (Ed.), *Materials development in language teaching* (2nd ed., pp. 303–327). Cambridge: Cambridge University Press.

Ortega, L. (2009). *Understanding second language acquisition*. London: Hodder Education.

Peacock, M. (2013). Foreword. In G. Motteram (Ed.), *Innovations in learning technologies for English language teaching* (pp. 2–3). London: British Council.

Reinders, H., & Pegrum, M. (2016). Supporting language learning on the move. In B. Tomlinson (Ed.), *SLA research and materials development for language learning* (pp. 219–231). New York: Routledge.

Shell, D. F., Brooks, D. W., Trainin, G., Wilson, K. M., Kauffman, D. F., & Herr, L. M. (2010). *The unified learning model—how motivational, cognitive, and neurobiological sciences inform best teaching practices*. London: Springer.

Thomas, M. (2015). A digital shift is not enough: Cultural, pedagogical and institutional challenges to technology-mediated task-based learning in japan. In M. Thomas & H. Reinders (Eds.), *Contemporary task-based language teaching in Asia* (pp. 228–243). London: Bloomsbury.

Thomas, M., & Reinders, H. (2015). *Contemporary task-based language teaching in Asia*. London; New York: Bloomsbury Academic.

Thomas, M., Reinders, H., & Warschauer, M. (2013). *Contemporary computer-assisted language learning*. [Electronic book]. London: Bloomsbury Academic.

Tomlinson, B. (2011). Introduction: Principles and procedures of materials development. In B. Tomlinson (Ed.), *Materials development in language teaching.* (2nd ed., pp. 1–34). Cambridge: Cambridge University Press.

Tomlinson, B. (Ed.). (2013a). *Developing materials for language teaching* (2nd ed.). London: Bloomsbury.

Tomlinson, B. (2013b). Second language acquisition and materials development. In B. Tomlinson (Ed.), *Applied linguistics and materials development* (pp. 11–29). London: Bloomsbury.

Tomlinson, B. (2016). Achieving a match between SLA theory and materials development. In B. Tomlinson (Ed.), *SLA research and materials development for language learning* (pp. 3–22). New York: Routledge.

Tomlinson, B., & Avila, J. (2011). Web 2.0: A vehicle for humanizing FLL. *Anglistik: International Journal of English Studies*, *22*(1), 137–151.

Tomlinson, B., & Whittaker, C. (2013). *Blended learning in English language teaching: Course design and implementation*. London: British Council.

Ushioda, E., & Dörnyei, Z. (2012). Motivation. In S. Gass & A. Mackey (Eds.), *The Routledge handbook of second language acquisition* (pp. 396–409). New York: Routledge.

Vrasidas, C. (2010). Why don't teachers adopt technology? A survey of teachers' use of ICT in the Republic of Cyprus. *Elearning Magazine*. Retrieved from http://www.elearnmag.org/subpage.cfm?section=case_studies&article=46-1

Wen, Z. (2016). *Working memory and second language learning: Towards an integrated approach* (1st ed.). Bristol: Channel View Publications.

Wilkinson, M. (2016). Language learning with ICT. In W. A. Renandya & H. P. Widodo (Eds.), *English language teaching today: Linking theory and practice* (pp. 257–276). New York: Springer International.

8

Developing Materials for the Acquisition of Language

Introduction

We have used the term "acquisition" deliberately in the title of this chapter as we believe that language is acquired gradually and developmentally over a long period as a result of multiple and varied experiences of language, some rich, experiential and subconscious, others focused, analytical and conscious. Languages cannot just be taught and learned. Language learners can be taught explicit declarative knowledge about language and this can be learned. However, this is not enough. Learners need to acquire the ability to use the grammar, the lexis and the pragmatic exponents of a language and not just know about them. Yet in our experience, many materials still focus on learning about and practicing language with the result that many of the learners who use them might be able to pass target examinations but not achieve effective communication in their L2. Of course, they also need to develop the skills of reading, writing, listening, and speaking and this development will be focused on in Chapter 9.

The Acquisition of Grammatical Competence

Coursebooks

Apart from a few years in the 1970s and early 1980s when functions (and very briefly notions) were central, grammar has dominated the syllabus (or at least the map of contents) of most materials. As Benevides (2016, p. 6) says, "Language learning courses have long been organized according to a generalized grammar syllabus; that is, to a sequence of language forms meant to be taught one after the next, regardless of the learners' specific needs or their learning context." What is worrying about that to those of us who believe that grammar is overemphasized in most language courses to the detriment of engagement, motivation, and communicative achievement is that, as Richards (2014, p. 19) says, "Coursebooks often determine the goals and content of teaching, as well as the methods teachers use." We have just looked at the map of contents for the preintermediate or intermediate level of four global coursebooks in current use taken at random from our shelves, *Pre-Intermediate Outcomes* (Dellar & Walkley, 2010), *Speakout intermediate* (Clare & Wilson, 2012), *Global intermediate* (Clandfield & Robb Benne, 2011) and *The big picture intermediate* (Goldstein, 2011). Despite making claims on their blurbs about authenticity, natural, real-life English and English as it is used, they

The Complete Guide to the Theory and Practice of Materials Development for Language Learning, First Edition. Brian Tomlinson and Hitomi Masuhara.
© 2018 John Wiley & Sons, Inc. Published 2018 by John Wiley & Sons, Inc.

all place "Grammar" most prominently in the first column of their list of "Contents" for each unit. *Outcomes* does also have an introductory "in this unit you learn how to" column and *Speakout* actually heads the first column "Grammar / Functions," although in each unit two sections focus on grammatical structures and one section focuses on a function (e.g. Unit 4.1 focuses on "must, have to, should," 4.2 on "used to and would" and 4.3 on "reaching agreement"). The pedagogical approach of the three books seems to be PPP (Presentation, Practice, Production), with the emphasis very much on controlled practice, the presentation being through rules and contrived texts and the production through short, simple writing or speaking activities with models to follow when writing or speaking. For example, in *Outcomes,* Unit 13 on p. 95, advice is given on how to use the present perfect continuous, two controlled practice activities follow and then learners ask questions about each other following a model that contains a present perfect continuous. In *Speakout* Unit 4, on p. 45, there is a modal verb matching activity, a making sentence from prompts exercise using "the positive or negative form" of the modal in brackets and a making sentences exercise with a model to follow. In *Global* there seems to be more emphasis on presentation with advice on how to use a structure (e.g. the present perfect continuous on p. 59) and rule-completion exercises (e.g. for using phrasal verbs on p. 61). *The big picture* also features information and advice on using structures plus a lot of controlled practice exercises involving identification, matching and gap filling and some sentence writing activities with help. To be fair, though, in the actual units grammar seems to be less prominent than in the list of contents.

The four books analyzed above, although published between 2010 and 2012, are still in frequent use in language schools in the United Kingdom and in many institutions overseas, as recent visits have confirmed. Just to make sure that recently published coursebooks are suddenly not grammar centric we checked the web. *New Headway Intermediate* 4th Edition (Soars & Soars, 2012) is definitely dominated by "Grammar," with 28 grammar sections in the nine units and just as much controlled practice as in the books analyzed above, with a claim to have a "strong grammar focus" in the Oxford University Press advert for the book on the web and with "Grammar" heading the first column in the Contents of the book. *Outcomes intermediate,* 2nd edition (2016), does have a list for each unit of what the learners will "learn how to" but still the first column of the Table of Contents is headed "Grammar." *Topnotch 2,* 3rd edition (Saslow & Ascher, 2015), does seem to have a greater focus on doing things in English but also has new "Extra Grammar Activities" in every section and new "Grammar Coach Videos," which "explain each grammar point and provide further examples." *Face2face intermediate,* 2nd ed. (Redston & Cunningham, 2013), stands out as being rather different in that "Vocabulary" heads the first column of the Contents and "Grammar" the second column, there do seem to be more vocabulary activities than grammar activities and some of the grammar activities do take a consciousness-raising approach. What worries us though is that so many of the activities focus on grammar at sentence level when in fact in actual communication grammar operates at textual and contextual levels and choice of appropriate and effective grammatical form is influenced by so many factors in addition to accuracy. We would certainly agree with Richards and Reppen (2014, p. 23) that, "A pedagogy for the teaching of grammar seeks to develop learners' awareness of the nature of texts and the functions of grammar within them, and to expand the grammatical resources learners make use of when they engage in the production of spoken and written texts."

See Tomlinson, Dat, Masuhara, and Rubdy (2001), Masuhara, Haan, Yi, and Tomlinson (2008), and Tomlinson and Masuhara (2008, 2013) for detailed evaluations of global coursebooks which provide similar evidence of the predominence of grammar and of PPP pedagogy in global coursebooks.

The pedagogical pattern described above is not necessarily true of institutional and locally published materials, probably because there is less of an imperative to sell the materials to administrators and teachers convinced of the centrality of grammar in the language learning process. In *English Empowers 2* (Poh-Knight & Kepler, 2011), for example, communication skills predominate but there is a section at the end of the book that focuses on Language in Action (Grammar and Vocabulary) in which learners are asked to reflect on language used in texts encountered previously in the book and to analyze new (and rather contrived) texts so as to notice how specific language features are used. This is fairly typical of the approach of coursebooks for Singapore secondary schools these days, an approach which is influenced by the genre approaches popular in Australia and which is exemplified also in *Life Accents 3* (Davis, Tup, and Aziz, 2003), a coursebook which only puts grammar in the seventh column of its "Contents" and which uses a presentation, discovery, delayed production approach to gaining grammar. *English for Life 1* (Tomlinson, Hill, & Masuhara, 2000) is another coursebook for Singapore secondary schools, which puts grammar in the seventh column. This book follows a discovery, practice, production approach, a compromise between the writers' beliefs and the editor's expectations. *Use your English* (Tomlinson & Masuhara, 1994) is a coursebook that caters for first-year university students in Japan. It does so by following a rather radical approach (approved by the publishers) of not drawing attention to grammar at all, of focusing on "using English rather than learning about it" and of aiming to help its users to develop high-level communication skills. The book followed a principled text-driven approach in which the students experience potentially engaging texts before being challenged to produce similar texts of their own. The book was popular with its users but, needless to say, it did not sell very well. Other coursebooks we know of, which are principled, take a radically different approach to grammar and are popular with their users are:

- *On target* (1995), a text-driven coursebook for Namibian secondary school students which was written by a team of thirty teachers and followed a discovery approach to grammar.
- *Search 10* (Fenner & Nordal-Pedersen, 1999), a very rich and engaging coursebook for Norwegian secondary school students which follows a text-driven approach and deliberately pays very little explicit attention to grammar (though it does in its revised form as *Searching 10* (Fenner & Nordal-Pedersen, 2006)).
- *Improve your English* (Tomlinson, 2004) is a coursebook written by a team of writers from Leeds Metropolitan University and the University College of St Mark and St John, Plymouth to help primary teachers in Ethiopia to improve their communication skills. This book also uses a text-driven framework and follows a discovery approach to grammar.

The books above are just a few examples of how some locally published coursebooks have deviated from the predominant model of PPP followed by almost all global coursebooks and also by most local publishers in their assumption that they are adhering to an established and validated norm. Most of the innovative institutional and locally published books above specify or assume that responsive teaching will take place whilst students are engaged in production tasks—in other words that the teacher will respond to students requests for help in deciding on a grammatical structure or on a lexical item.

Ironically it is possible that more and more useful grammar teaching takes place when using such books than when using coursebooks which give conspicuous prominence to grammar and that, because learners learn best what they need and want when they need and want it, there is more learning of grammar too.

Pedagogical Approaches

Presentation Practice Production (PPP)

As we mentioned earlier, PPP is the dominant pedagogical approach in commercial coursebooks. PPP in our view it is an approach that can only achieve shallow and ephemeral learning because of its narrow focus, its lack of contextualization, its lack of affective and cognitive engagement, its inadequate provision of exposure to language in use, its inadequate provision of opportunities to use the language for authentic communication, its lack of spaced and varied recycling and its impossible attempt to help learners to achieve instant acquisition. (As Mishan, 2005, p. 38, says, PPP constrains "the learners to immediate production of a particular grammatical form.") It "reflects neither the nature of language nor the nature of learning" (Lewis 1993:190). However, it does create an illusion of systematicity, success and coverage, and is therefore popular with teachers and students. Timmis (2005, 2013) reports how McCarthy explains that the authors of the corpus-based coursebook, *Touchstone* (McCarthy, McCarten, & Sandford, 2005/2006), used a situational PPP approach as this would be familiar and undemanding for the teachers. PPP is not popular with most researchers, though, and Scrivener (1994), Willis (1994), Woodward (1993), Skehan (1998), Mishan (2005), Tomlinson (2011) and many others have criticized its lack of correspondence with the research findings and theories of second language acquisition (SLA) and its ineffectiveness in promoting communicative competence. Masuhara (2016) says, "it may be a convenient teaching procedure but it ignores what we know about when, why and how the brain learns" (p. 29). Because of the predominance of PPP in coursebooks and its apparent face validity with teachers and students Tomlinson (2011) suggests modifying it so that the Production phase is seen as an opportunity for feedback and reinforcement, or it is postponed until a later unit when more exposure, instruction and practice have been given. Better still, in our view now, would be to start with a Production task to see what learners can do and then to follow this with Presentation and Practice relating to what learners found problematic in the Production phase. The conventional PPP approach does however have some advocates. If you google PPP you will find many blogs from teacher trainers explaining PPP and praising it as a simple, common sense approach. You will also find reference to some academic articles defending it. For example, Criado (2016) first of all asserts the relevance for foreign language learners of skill acquisition theory (SAT), with its emphasis on "explicit instruction, meaningful practice and feedback" (p. 122) in order to help the learner to progress from conscious declarative knowledge to automatized procedural knowledge (i.e. from explicit knowledge about language to implicit knowledge about how to use it). She then claims that PPP (with its sequence of explicit teaching, followed by conscious and focused practice and then by attempts to produce the target structure) matches SAT theory and is therefore the ideal way to teach language to foreign language learners. Unfortunately neither Criado (2016) nor any of the other advocates of PPP we have read provide any evidence in support of their claims. But then, to be fair, we have never seen any empirical evidence that PPP does not foster communicative competence either.

Discovery Approaches

Our preference for discovery approaches to grammar learning developed from a conviction that what students find out for themselves is more likely to be learned and retained than what they are told by a teacher or book (a conviction shared by Ellis, 2010), provided that it is relevant and useful to them and that they have multiple subsequent encounters with similar manifestations of language use to those that triggered the discovery. In our case our instincts were confirmed and reinforced by Kolb's theory of experiential learning (Kolb, 1984, 2015; Kolb & Kolb, 2009) in which experience stimulates apprehension, which can eventually be converted into comprehension through reflection, analysis and discovery. It was further reinforced by Schmidt's (1992) theory of noticing, which claims that exposure to comprehensible input is necessary but not sufficient as we need to notice how a feature is used so we will be aware of it again in subsequent input and eventually be able to acquire it. Some recent coursebooks (e.g. *Speakout*—Clare & Wilson, 2012) have started to include consciousness-raising activities in which the students are guided towards discovering a predetermined answer to a grammatical question, for example completing the rules for the present perfect and past simple on p. 21 of *Speakout* (Clare & Wilson, 2012). Often the evidence provided to the learners is at sentence or short paragraph level (e.g. Ellis, 2010, p. 50) and it is often contrived to make the discovery point as obvious as possible. Ellis (2010) provides a rationale for consciousness raising (CR) activities, lists the various options open to the task designer and mentions some limitations of CR tasks (e.g. that they are less suitable for young learners who prefer "doing" to "studying" and for older learners who are not intellectually inclined). Mishan (2005, 2013) is an advocate of consciousness-raising approaches but she, quite rightly in our view, insists that it is only "the first step towards learning" and that learners need to be exposed to "as rich a variety as possible of (authentic) language input" (Mishan, 2005, p. 37). Mishan (2013) refers to coursebooks that have introduced CR approaches but she is critical of how controlled the activities are, of how they have right answers, and of how they are often followed by practice activities (as demonstrated also by Nitta & Gardner, 2005).

We prefer an open-ended language awareness approach (Tomlinson, 1994a, 2007, in press) in which the learners first of all experience an extended and authentic spoken or written text whose meaning they respond to personally. They then, in pairs or small groups, focus on a particular language feature of the text in order to make discoveries about how it is formed and used. They share their discoveries with other pairs or groups and then, for homework, look for other instances of the focused feature in use. Later they pool their out-of-class discoveries and then try to formulate generalizations about the particular feature (in our case in a loose-leaf file or a computer document titled "A Grammar of English by X" to which they return many times to update their instances and revise their generalizations). Other discovery approaches include research approaches in which the learners make use of multiple authentic resources inside and outside the classroom to solve a grammar problem (e.g. What's the difference between some and any?) and translation approaches in which the learners are given words and phrases in the L2 which they do not know and are then asked to translate sentences from the L1 through trial and error in order to provide data for learner discovery. Another approach gets learners to analyze concordance lists extracted from corpora (e.g. the British National Corpus—http://www.natcorp.ox.ac.uk/corpus/) in order to discover features of the form and functions of the highlighted language feature (e.g. 20 instances of the use of the subordinator "although"). When using this approach we find it is sometimes better to get the learners to assemble their own concordance lists from sources that they understand and are interested in so as to avoid the lexical and contextual problems which can arise when using a published corpus. For ideas for making discoveries from published corpora see Reppen (2011) and for suggestions for teacher and student assembly and exploitation of their own concordance lists see Willis (2011). Other authors who have written about discovery approaches to grammar include Tomlinson (1994a, 2007, in press), McCarthy and Carter (1995), Harmer (1998), Bolitho (2003), Bolitho et al. (2003), Cullen and Kuo (2007), Jones (2007), Mishan (2005), Timmis (2005, 2013), and Thornbury (2006). Textbooks that contain discovery activities include Hall and Shepheard (1991), Carter, Hughes, and McCarthy (2000) and Bolitho and Tomlinson (2005). Some of these authors add practice to discovery in order to facilitate acquisition (Cullen & Kuo, 2007) or to check the validity of discovered generalizations (Jones, 2007; Timmis, 2013). Other authors add production, for example Harmer (1998) proposes an Engage, Study, Activate model and Thornbury (2006) advocates moving from awareness raising to proceduralization to autonomy. We believe that production is the best way of checking generalizations and we often set learners a production task likely to involve use of the focused feature (e.g. a story involving a conversation between two characters when investigating the differences in function between direct and indirect speech). Sometimes we get learners to produce a text before they explore the core text. After subsequently making discoveries from the core text they then do another similar production task. In our view it is important to realize that such activities are an investment in the future and are not intended to promote instant acquisition.

Sokol (2005) describes and exemplifies a novel approach to using grammar discovery activities. He uses a "Thinking Approach" (p. 28) in which the teacher sets the students a grammatical problem related to what Lewis (1986) calls grammar-as-choice (as opposed to grammar-as-fact). The teacher then conducts a whole-class discussion to help the students to come up with solutions to the problem and in doing so adheres to the following principles:

- "Explicit grammar teaching … is avoided …"
- "Learners are always presented with a situation where the solution is not known to them …"
- "Learners compose their own models of grammar by applying tools offered by the teacher."
- "The teacher does not evaluate the quality of the proposed models …"
- "Students reconsider their models by collecting and analysing samples of language where the model doesn't work" (p. 29).

Another type of grammar discovery approach is the III (illustration-interaction-induction) approach first advocated in Carter and McCarthy (1995), exemplified in the coursebook *Exploring grammar in context* (Carter, Hughes, & McCarthy, 2000), and illustrated and commented on in Carter, Hughes and McCarthy (2011). This is an approach that makes use of language awareness activities in the induction stage and which helps learners to make contextually effective choices of manifestations of spoken grammar through observation and interaction with the data provided (corpus informed data that is sometimes modified to suit learner level and need).

Focus on Form (FoF)

Long (1991) made a distinction between focus on form (FoF) and focus on forms (FoFs). The former refers to the drawing of learners' attention to language forms "as they arise incidentally in lessons whose overriding focus is on meaning or communication" (Long, 1991, p. 46). The latter refers to the traditional approach (still followed in most coursebooks today) of pre-selecting discrete language teaching points and then focusing on them one by one, unit by unit. As Fotos and Nassaji (2007) point out about focus on form, this "construct has been interpreted and used differently by different researchers" (p. 12). In addition to its original concept as a reactive response to communication problems it is now also conceived as a proactive approach focusing on a particular structure which has been found to be problematic.

See Fotos and Nassaji (2007) for information about all the variations of these two approaches to FoF, none of which, as far as we know, have been applied to coursebook development, apart from input enhancement through highlighting and through flooding ("an artificially increased incidence of the form in focus," Williams & Evans, 1998, p. 141). Fotos and Nassaji (2007) refer to studies claiming that FoF can lead to awareness of the target structure that favorably affects acquisition but they do not say how acquisition was measured or how authentic it was.

Task-Based Approaches

In our view one of the most promising ways of getting learners to focus on form is to engage them in a task-based lesson in which the main emphasis is on meaning and communication but attention is paid to the form of structures both during the production of language and after it in a reflection or discovery task. As Tomlinson (2015, p. 328) points out there is a rich literature on the principles and procedures of task-based language teaching (TBLT), there is some literature reporting research findings, there is some literature reporting TBLT projects "but there is hardly any literature focusing on materials and curriculum design for TBLT." Van den Branden (2006) does contain some chapters describing how TBLT materials were developed in Belgium and Thomas and Reinders (2015) includes chapters on materials and curriculum design for TBLT in Asia. The strong version of TBLT insists that the structures paid attention to should not be predetermined but should arise incidentally during the task performance. The weak version encourages "pre-teaching of language which could be useful when doing the tasks and in doing so risks changing the task into a practice activity" (Tomlinson, 2015, p. 329). The only use of strong TBLT tasks in course materials that we know of are in materials which we have been involved in developing (e.g. Tomlinson, 1981, 1994b; Tomlinson & Masuhara, 1994; Tomlinson, Hill & Masuhara, 2000) and in *Widgets* (Benevides & Valvona, 2008), a book that, as Mishan (2013, p. 273) says, is effectively an extended "role play, putting the students into the position of employees in an international company." There are numerous examples of weak TBLT tasks in Thomas and Reinders (2015), many of them deliberately weakened by their designers and often further weakened by teachers in order to satisfy the need for accuracy promoted by examinations and the belief still prevalent in Asia (and elsewhere) that students need to learn the language required by a task before they can be asked to do it. There are also examples of weak TBLT approaches in global coursebooks. Mishan (2013) says that "tasks" now appear in the free language production stage of PPP dominated coursebooks such as *Headway advanced* (Soars & Soars, 2003), *Touchstone full contact* (McCarthy, McCarten, & Sandiford, 2008) and *English in mind 2* (Puchta & Stranks, 2010). Mishan (2013, p. 273) says the only coursebook she knows (apart from *Widgets*) which attempts a TBLT format is *Cutting edge* (Cunningham & Moor, 2008) but she is critical of it for undermining the most essential principle of TBLT by presenting 'the language focus as the precursor to the task rather than as the outcome of it.'

Benevides (2016) advocates using a themed task-based approach which begins "with meaning and then" progresses "through to forms" by following a "themed syllabus" that "restricts learner attention to a specific topic, subject, or genre over an entire course, allowing language to emerge and be recycled naturally" (e.g. "Love and Dating, in which the class might read a graded reader version of Romeo and Juliet, watch a film such as Bridget Jones' Diary, discuss blog articles on celebrity relationships, write fictional love letters, and prepare presentations on topics such as How to meet your ideal partner" (p. 7). Tomlinson (2016a) proposes a text-driven task-based approach in which a menu of potentially engaging written and spoken texts drive communication tasks that eventually serve as sources of linguistic investigation as well as driving follow-up tasks. This is a deliberate riposte to Long (2015, p. 305) who urges task designers and teachers to "Use task not text, as the unit of analysis." We find that many of the textless tasks in the literature are trivial and unengaging (e.g. many of the spot the difference and picture story tasks) and we prefer to engage learners affectively and cognitively in spoken, written or video texts before involving them in production tasks. Our texts are not models to emulate but stimuli to production, and they can also serve later as a source of grammatical, lexical and pragmatic discovery.

Ellis (2016) states that "Acquiring an L2 primarily involves the development of implicit knowledge" but acknowledges that "Explicit knowledge can play a role in both L2 use and acquisition" (p. 204), especially when participating in careful writing, which allows time to draw on explicit knowledge for formulation and for monitoring and also as a result of noticing the use of features during communication. Ellis is critical of coursebooks for focusing on text-manipulation activities which typically treat language "as an *object* to be studied or practised" with 'the primary focus on specific linguistic forms' and with "no communicative purpose" (p. 207). His preference (and ours) is for text-creation activities in which "language is treated as a tool for achieving some kind of communicative outcome" (p. 208). He also prefers to guide learners to "an understanding of how specific grammatical features function' to 'simply telling them how they work" (p. 211) and refers to research that indicates that consciousness-raising "tasks do help learners build their explicit knowledge and that learners find them more motivating than knowledge-telling" (p. 211). Like us, Ellis is in favor of "text-rich input" (p. 213) and of teachers helping students in need during text-creation activities.

Other Approaches in the Literature

Interestingly, although grammar seems to be predominant in coursebooks and features prominently in web blogs for teachers and in series of how-to-teach handbooks (e.g. Harmer, 1987; Thornbury, 2000; *Teaching grammar*, 2016) it does not play a dominant role in publications about materials development. For example, the ELT-Teacher2Writer series of handbooks on Training Teachers to be Writers (http://www.eltteacher2writer.co.uk/) has 18 handbooks but none of them are on materials for the teaching of grammar. *SLA research and materials development for language learning* (Tomlinson, 2016b) has numerous chapters on vocabulary, pragmatics, and interaction but only one on grammar. This is a chapter that reviews theoretical approaches to the teaching of grammar, analyzes the grammar activities in a number of workbooks and reveals that the highest percentage of activities in all three series analyzed are grammar activities, of which the most frequent type in all the books is accuracy-centered reproduction (Baleghizadeh, Goldouz, & Yousefpoori-Naeim, 2016). *English language teaching materials: Theory and practice* (Harwood, 2010) is another book that focuses on materials aiming at the development of skills but has one chapter with a focus on materials for grammar teaching, a chapter by Ellis (2010), which, as well as focusing on consciousness-raising tasks (see Discovery approaches above), justifies and exemplifies "interpretation activities" that "aim to teach grammar by inducing learners to process the target structure through input rather than by eliciting production of the structure" (p. 44). *Materials evaluation and design for language teaching* (McGrath, 2002), *Methodology and materials design in language teaching* (Renandya, 2003), *Teaching materials and the roles of EFL/ESL teachers* (McGrath, 2013), *Materials and methods in ELT: A teacher's guide* (McDonough, Shaw, & Masuhara, 2013) and *Issues in materials development* (Azarnoosh, Zeraatpishe, Faravani, & Kargozari, 2016) make no explicit reference to the development of materials for teaching grammar at all.

One publication that does focus on developing materials for the teaching of grammar is Arshad (2003). This starts by considering the validity, relevance and practicality of such language learning theories and grammar teaching models as comprehensible input theory, universal grammar, interactionist theories, input enhancement, skills approaches, grammar consciousness raising, processing instruction, interpretation tasks and reconstruction tasks. Some theories are dismissed as being too vague and lacking in specification of techniques and interaction theories, whilst being appreciated, are considered to be impractical in "many Asian classrooms where students tend to remain quiet, passive and dependent on the teacher" (p. 120). Unlike Bao (2007, 2013) who considers ways of effecting change in Vietnamese classrooms, Arshad accepts this apparent status quo and insists that a language-learning theory should be interventionist and should "support teacher intervention and indicate how the teacher can affect the language learning process" (Arshad, 2003, p. 119). Arshad favors an eclectic approach making use of the comprehension approaches suggested in Ellis (1995) in which teachers "must try to focus learners' attention on noticing and understanding specific grammatical features in the input rather than … student production of the target language through tasks such as drills" (p. 122). In focusing on comprehension of input Arshad stresses the value of enhanced input in which targeted structures are highlighted through, for example using bold letters, 'brief explanations or exemplary sentences on the sidebar' and adding the targeted structures on the screen "whenever they are used in a sentence in the conversation" (p. 123). He also emphasizes the importance of the input being meaningful and contextualized and of requiring student processing of target structure (through, for example grammatical problem solving) and reflection. We would agree with Arshad on everything but artificial input enhancement (which we have found interrupts the learners' focus on meaning) and on the central role that Arshad assigns to the teacher in grammar activities. The use of a comprehension approach to grammar acquisition is also endorsed by Barnard (2007) in her study of a large-scale comparison of comprehension versus production approaches for beginners learning Bahasa Indonesia in Singapore.

Mishan (2005) reviews the literature on instructed language teaching with particular reference to formal grammar instruction and decides that order of acquisition and accuracy of acquisition are not positively affected by explicit grammar instruction but that rate of acquisition can be affected by classroom instruction (provided that the learners are also exposed to sufficient comprehensible input). She calls for research (which is so far insufficient) on ultimate proficiency and durability of learning, concludes that "the traditional presentation and practice of grammar rules has no overwhelming empirical justification in terms of enhanced language acquisition" (p. 35) and recommends discovery approaches, task-based approaches and learner autonomy as approaches more likely to positively impact on acquisition. As teacher trainers who have had to suffer observing the boredom of learners all over the world being subjected to the tedious presentation and practice of grammar rules we would appeal to publishers to take note and to make use of more engaging and more educationally valuable approaches to fostering language acquisition, which have greater potential for durable effectiveness too. On our teacher development courses we always stress that learners of an L2 in an educational institution need to benefit educationally from their courses as well to acquire communicative competence in the L2. If they gain no educational benefit in terms of, for example, furthering their development of higher level skills but gain some acquisition, the course has failed them. If they gain neither educational development nor language acquisition the course has been a disaster.

Of course, there are studies that demonstrate increases in accuracy resulting from a focus on forms but in our experience the tests are of explicit declarative knowledge rather than of communicative production. For example, Morris & Tremblay (2002) demonstrated an increase in morphological accuracy resulting from closed dictation activities but did so by reporting the experimental students improvement in gap filling.

Richards (2007) writes about a form-focused instruction (FFI) perspective to materials development and in doing so argues that the materials writer needs to gain an understanding of such theoretical issues as interactionist views of language learning, noticing and language awareness and should then develop a syllabus (e.g. "a functional syllabus, a text-based syllabus, or a process syllabus" (p. 152) and a set of instructional principles. He then provides the following set of instructional principles which "integrate FFI within a communicative framework" (p. 155):

1. L2 learning is facilitated when learners are engaged in interaction and meaningful communication.
2. Effective classroom learning tasks and exercises provide opportunities for students to negotiate meaning, expand their language resources, notice how target forms are used, and take part in meaningful interpersonal exchange.
3. Meaningful communication results from students processing content that is relevant, purposeful, interesting and engaging.
4. Communication is a holistic process that often calls upon the use of several language skills or modalities.
5. Language learning is facilitated both by activities that involve inductive or discovery learning of underlying rules of language use and organization, as well as by those involving language analysis and reflection.
6. Language learning is a gradual process that involves creative use of language and trial and error.
7. Learners develop their own routes to language learning, progress at different rates, and have different needs and motivations for language learning.
8. Successful language learning involves the use of effective learning and communication strategies.
9. The role of the teacher in the classroom is that of facilitator, who creates a classroom climate conducive to language learning and provides opportunities for students

to use and practice the language and to reflect on language use and language learning

10. The classroom is a community where learners learn through collaboration and sharing.

Richards (2007, pp 155–156)

We would completely endorse these learner-centered principles, though we wonder how many published coursebooks, if any, can claim to have completely applied these principles (including those written by Jack Richards and those written by ourselves). Certainly something to aspire to though.

Stranks (2013) is critical of the continued domination of grammar in coursebooks and of how "concern with grammatical form continues to take precedence over meaning considerations" (p. 337) and he attributes this to the "inherent conservatism of ministries of education and the major publishing houses" (p. 338) as well as to the buyers of materials settling for "the comfortingly familiar" (p. 338). He analyzes and criticizes current grammar materials and argues that grammar materials "should see" grammar "as part of language, not as a separate feature to be learned for its own sake" (p. 349), that practice activities should "develop a theme" (p. 341) so that they provide language practice and not just grammar practice and that we should adopt a receptive approach to grammar which, like the approaches suggested by Lewis (1986) and Ellis (1995), focuses on identifying and understanding the meaning(s) of a structure in a text rather than on practicing and producing that structure. Mishan and Timmis (2015) have a six-page section on Materials for Teaching Grammar in which they review approaches to grammar teaching and advocate an eclectic approach which takes into account the learners' age, level, expectations and abilities, as well as the nature of the language point, in deciding whether to use a proactive or reactive approach, an explicit teaching or a gradual awareness from input approach or a receptive, practice or productive approach.

Our Recommendations

We very much prefer a discovery approach that aims to develop gradually increasing language awareness through exploration of language features initially in texts already experienced and then subsequently in other texts searched for. Here is a flexible procedure which we would recommend:

1. Find a potentially engaging listening, reading or viewing text.
2. Devise a readiness activity connecting the learners to the theme / topic / location of the text (e.g. "Have you ever been with somebody to an event which you didn't really want to go to? Did you try to get away from it as soon as possible? How?").
3. Write instructions to get the learners to experience the text (e.g. "Read this story about a teenager taking his girlfriend to a football match. As you read it try to see the faces of the boy and the girl and think about why the girl went to the game").
4. Devise an intake response activity inviting the learners to think about and articulate their personal responses to the text (e.g. 1 "Do you have any sympathy for the boy? Why / why not?" 2 "Do you have any sympathy for the girl? Why / why not?").
5. Devise a production task inviting the learners to write a similar text to the one they have read (e.g. "A few weeks after the match the girl decides to forgive the boy and invites him to go with her to a ballet performance. The boy is happy to be reunited with his girlfriend but he has no interest in ballet. Write the scene in the interval at

the theatre in which the boy is trying to persuade the girl to leave the theatre with him").

6. Devise a discovery task in which the learners are asked to go back to the core text and to try to make discoveries about a specified feature (e.g. "Go back to the story at the football match and in groups work out how the boy tried to persuade the girl to stay and how the girl tried to persuade the boy to leave the game with her").

7. Devise a research task to give to the learners for homework (e.g. "Try to find as many examples as you can of modal verbs being used to persuade people to do something").

8. Devise a generalization task (e.g. "In your group look at all the examples you've found of modals used for persuasion—including those from the story at the football match. Try to write generalizations about modals used for persuasion and then copy them with examples into your Grammar of English file. When you come across other examples add them to your Modal section and revise your generalizations if you want to").

9. Devise a further production task similar to the one in 5 above (e.g. "It's the girls' birthday. The boy has bought tickets for a classical music concert. The boy is bored by the music and keeps falling asleep. At the interval he tries to persuade the girl to leave the concert hall with him. Write this scene").

N.B.—If you want to avoid being accused of sexual stereotyping, the roles in the tasks above could be reversed with the girl taking her boy friend to a football match. No students have ever complained though when doing the tasks outlined above.

The procedure outlined above is only of value in relation to effective and durable acquisition if the learners meet the discovered feature many times again when engaged in authentic listening, reading and interaction in the L2. So our approach involves stimulating learners to experience a potentially engaging text, getting them to produce a text with connections to the core text, getting them to explore the core text to make discoveries about a specified feature, getting them to look for texts likely to include the focused feature, getting them to articulate generalizations about the use of the focused feature, getting them to produce a similar text to their first one and making sure they have multiple opportunities for extensive reading, listening, and viewing and for authentic interaction both inside and outside the classroom (Tomlinson, 2014; Pinnard, 2016). For an outline of a similar procedure designed to facilitate learner noticing when used with a video of a chef getting celebrities to do things for him see Tomlinson (2010).

We have just noticed that a procedure not mentioned at all in our review of the literature on developing materials for grammar above is recycling. Yet this is so important for the acquisition of grammatical competence. Multiple and varied encounters with a structure (both with and without deliberate noticing) are necessary for the eventual acquisition of that structure and yet it does not seem to be a major concern for materials developers. This seems to be true of ourselves too, though we have earlier in this chapter stressed the need for further encounters with a language feature in use subsequent to paying attention to it in a language awareness task and we do point out the potential value of teacher recasting of learner utterances in meaning focused tasks on the accuracy and appropriacy of immediate and delayed communicative production (see Avila, 2007; Tomlinson, 2007). Also, in teacher training sessions we have asked participants to check the amount of structural recycling in coursebooks and usually they have found hardly any. We have just done this with the second conditional in *Speakout intermediate* (Clare & Wilson, 2012). The second conditional is focused on in 6.2 of Unit 6. The learners read a short review of a TV program, which has been flooded with underlined utterances using the second conditional. They then use these utterances to complete rules, they look for other examples in a longer text on the previous page, they listen and complete conversations, they complete sentences with the correct form of verbs in a box, and they complete sentences about their classmates. They are now primed ready to notice second conditionals in subsequent input and there are a number of them in the speaking and writing activities that immediately follow and at the end of the unit there is a "Lookback" practice activity on the second conditional. However, the only subsequent encounters with the second conditional we can find are two "If you had to …" questions in Unit 9, one "If I were you …" completion in Unit 10, and some further practice activities in the Language Bank at the back of the book. We can only find one small encounter with the second conditional in any of the reading or listening texts before Unit 6 ("It'd be great if we could meet" on p. 10) and only one in the units after it (in a short text on p. 162 of the Communication Bank). The learners' only chance of eventually acquiring the second conditional is if they have many meaningful (and sometimes attentive) encounters with it in their extensive reading, listening, and viewing and in their out-of-class interactions. We know that coursebook writers are usually constrained by a shortage of space and an excessive syllabus but it would be good to see attempts to expose learners to a structure both before and after they pay attention to it in a unit. But then maybe most learners do not need to acquire such structures as the second conditional at all.

The Acquisition of Lexical Competence

Vocabulary has now gained center stage in the literature on language teaching and is becoming far more prominent in language learning materials, too. As Maley (2013) says, both Willis (1990) and Lewis (1993) "advocate making lexis the central feature of language courses" and "this has influenced the way lexis is dealt with in many language coursebooks" (p. 103). For example, it is placed in the second column of the contents of the coursebooks we looked at for the "Acquistion of Grammatical Competence" section above, and there are more vocabulary activities than grammar activities in these books (e.g. in Unit 5 of *Speakout intermediate* (Clare & Wilson, 2012) there are 17 vocabulary activities and only five grammar activities). In the blurb for *How to write grammar presentations and practice* (Kerr, n.d.) it says "Vocabulary has gained its rightful place at the centre of modern language learning syllabuses, but how does a writer select which items to present and practise?" This reinforces the point we make above but also illustrates the assumption made by many coursebook writers and most teachers that vocabulary needs to be presented and practiced.

Coursebooks

There are numerous vocabulary activities in each unit of *Global intermediate* (Clandfield & Robb Benne, 2011) but they all seem to be identification exercises (e.g. "Underline the words which refer to inexact numbers or times" (p. 79)), text-manipulation exercises that make use of existing explicit knowledge of lexical items (e.g. "Use the words in the box to make expressions with take …" (p. 66)) or practice exercises making use of provided words (e.g. "Work in pairs. Choose three questions and ask and answer them … use the expressions in exercise 1" (p. 79)). None of the activities seems to be input rich nor to involve interpretation of lexical items in contextual use, discovery of meaning from context, text creation, or using lexical items for communication. Most other coursebooks seem to feature a similar range of restricted vocabulary exercises with *Speakout intermediate* (Clare & Wilson, 2012), for example, featuring sentence completion, matching phrases to meanings, using phrases in a sentence, explaining the meaning of words in bold, and asking and answering questions in pairs with a model to emulate. Both books do, though, make an attempt to relate the activities to the students' lives and have some questions that do not predetermine answers.

Pedagogical Approaches

Although vocabulary is now central in the literature on language teaching we can find only a few publications on materials development for vocabulary learning.

A long time ago Ellis and Tomlinson (1980) wrote a long chapter on the teaching of vocabulary, which summed up what was known about how lexical items achieve contextual meaning and recommended such criteria for the selection and grading of lexical items on a course as frequency, availability (i.e. frequency in a particular type of context), teachability (i.e. how easy an item is to teach) and coverage (i.e. the capacity of an item to take the place of other items). In doing so they stressed the need to focus on lexical items and not dictionary words and on the fact that "items capable of obvious ostensive definition (e.g. 'handbag') are easier to teach than items whose referents are abstract (e.g. 'sincerity')" (p. 76). In relation to presentation they recommend intensive reading plus subsequent focus on salient lexical items, presenting new items together with known items in situations in which the items are frequently associated, recycling and communicative use. They stress that the presentation of a lexical item should include, for example:

1. Exemplification of the referent of the item through some form of ostensive definition (when this is possible).
2. Exemplification of the implied meanings of the item (if any).
3. Exemplification of the registers in which the item can appropriately be used.
4. Exemplification of the item in actual use. (Ellis & Tomlinson, 1980, p. 84)

At the beginning of the report of his evaluation of vocabulary in Malaysian secondary school textbooks Mukundan (2010) stresses two vital points about the learning of vocabulary. He insists (quite rightly in our view) that "the more a word is repeated and recycled, the more the chances are of it being remembered" (p. 292) and he reports Thornbury (2002) as claiming that "students remember words which are repeated at least seven times over a spaced interval (providing the words are meaningful and salient)" (Mukundan, 2010, p. 292). Mukundan also quite rightly emphasizes the point that "learners cannot hope to remember very many new words that are all introduced at the same time and within a short duration" (p. 292), a point endorsed by Nation (2013) when saying that if twelve new words are introduced in a unit only five or six are likely to be learned. Mukundan is critical of Malaysian textbooks for not adhering to these principles and, for example, for introducing far too many new words at lower levels, for not introducing some of the 2,000 most frequently used words and for insufficient spaced repetition.

Paul Nation is recognized as one of the leading experts on the teaching and learning of vocabulary. He has also written on the development of materials for vocabulary acquisition in, for example, Nation & Macalister (2010) Nation & Webb (2011), and Nation (2013). In Nation (2013) he advocates focusing on the 3,000 most frequently used word families, as they cover 90% of most texts. He then puts forward a pedagogical approach that is informed by the following conditions for vocabulary learning:

1. Noticing. According to Nation "we learn what we focus on" (see Barcroft's, 2006, research) "and typographical enhancements" (e.g. putting the word in italics or bold, defining the word orally, or in the text, or in a glossary) tend to bring about small improvements in knowledge of word form (p. 353).

2. Retrieving. Nation (2013) states that retrieving can strengthen and establish the learning that remains once a word has been noticed. Retrieving can be receptive or productive and involves recalling the meaning or part of the meaning of a form when hearing or reading it or when wanting to express a meaning through speech or writing. It can be encouraged through meaning focused skills activities and "through activities like re-telling, role play or problem solving where input … is the basis of the production of the output" (pp. 353–354).

3. Elaborating. Nation does not define elaboration but he gives such examples as "meeting a known word … where it is used in a way that stretches its meaning for the learner … using a known word in contexts that the learner has not used it in before … having rich instruction on the word which involves giving attention to several aspects of what is involved in knowing a word" (Nation, 2013, p. 354). He refers to Laufer and Hulstijn (2001) when stressing that the "further one moves from noticing to retrieval, to varied use and to elaboration, the better learning is likely to be" (Nation, 2013, p. 353). We would prefer the first stage to be experience of the word in contextual use and the second stage to be response to the contextual meaning of the word. Then we would happily follow Nation's stages—but would replace typographical enhancement with a noticing activity involving some cognitive challenge (e.g. What attitude towards "typographical enhancement" does the word "replace" indicate?). We would also only use typographical enhancement in a second version of a text as we have found that we cannot pay attention to the global meaning of a text if it has been manipulated to draw our attention to certain lexical items. And we are (we think) proficient readers.

We would strongly agree with Nation's championing of extensive reading, his emphasis on opportunities afforded by graded readers for "spaced receptive retrieval of appropriate vocabulary" (Nation, 2013, p. 354), his appreciation of the value of intensive listening and reading in vocabulary acquisition and his recommendation to ask postlistening / reading questions that require the learner to use target vocabulary when answering them. We are less enthusiastic though about his support for the teacher identifying and defining new words prior to student reading / listening, for the use of glossaries and for the learner skimming through the text to "select five or six words to focus on" while reading the text. Such interventions might increase the students' knowledge of words but they risk student memorization of definitions rather than student deduction of meaning from context, they encourage intolerance of ambiguity and they encourage teachers to pre-teach the language in texts rather than stimulate learners to enjoy and make use of holistic experience of the texts for themselves. We have seen lessons in which the teacher has spent so long pre-teaching the vocabulary of a text that the students never have time to read it. First of all help the learners to experience and respond to the meaning of a text and then go back and focus on problematic vocabulary in the text has always been our advice. We have similar problems with Nation's recommendations for speaking and writing activities. He gives examples of potentially valuable communication activities but in our view overemphasizes the value of pre-teaching, glossaries and dictionaries in these activities too. As you might have appreciated by now we prefer task-based approaches in which learners initially use their existing linguistic resources for a spoken or written communication task and then make use of their performance and other input to extend their lexical awareness. We have no objection though to learners seeking help from the teacher and from each other during preparation or even performance as learners learn best what they need at the time they need it. We have no objections either to Nation's suggestions for vocabulary fluency development which put into practice his three conditions of "easy demands, meaning focus and opportunity to perform at a higher than normal level" (p, 362), for example teacher reading (and rereading) of stories from blown up books which the students sit around, the teacher reading a chapter a day of a graded reader, a listening corner with recorded stories to choose from, "continuous writing where the focus is on writing a lot on familiar topics" (p. 363). See Nation (2001) and Nation (2007) for further elaboration and examples of these ideas.

Maley (2013) stresses that learners need to meet a word in context many times (15–20 times according to Waring, 2006) before it starts to become part of their vocabulary and that learners need repeated encounters with words in contextualized texts (as also stressed by Nation and Macalister, 2010) in order to understand their dynamic nature in use and to appreciate how their contextual meaning is informed by negotiation between users, contextual factors, the attitudes of the users, the creativity of the users, and the unpredictability of the interaction. Maley also lists the components of knowing a word (e.g. being able to recognize it, pronounce it, spell it, use it grammatically, understand its core meaning, be aware of its common collocations, interpret it in different contexts, etc.) and again stresses the need for multiple encounters in context in order to gain this knowledge. However, he does agree with Nation (2008) that at least 25% of teaching time should be devoted to explicit teaching of vocabulary and that the focus should be on high frequency words as they are the ones with the highest payback' (p. 104). Maley recommends three types of in-class activities:

1. Explicit instruction of, for example, word formation, prefixes / suffixes, roots, new words and collocations (See McDonough, Shaw and Masuhara (2013) for similar points for explicit instruction plus connotation and superordination).
2. Student use of words in, for example, games, dictations, retelling of stories, translation activities, and dictionary activities.
3. Student experience of words through, for example, extensive reading, teacher reading aloud, performance of poems, sketches, and plays and creative writing of short poems, minisagas or stories.

Maley (2013) also recommends such out-of-class activities as extensive reading, creative writing and self-study activities such as using reference tools, revision, using notebooks and word cards to record words they encounter and noticing how words are used in street signs, advertisements, headlines, etc.

Nakata and Webb (2016) aim "to gauge the relative efficacy of' learning vocabulary 'from flashcards, cloze exercises and crossword puzzles" (p. 123), three exercise types commonly featured in language learning materials. To do so they follow Nation's (2013b) guidelines for vocabulary activities and make use of Nation and Webb's (2011) Technique Feature Analysis (TFA) to "determine which components of the activities contribute to learning" (p. 123). Nation's guidelines are that vocabulary activities should facilitate vocabulary learning, should not involve a lot of work on the part of the teachers, should provide a balance of meaning-focused input, meaning-focused output, language-focused learning and fluency development, should be efficient and should be able to be used many times. Nakata and Webb (2016) use an adapted version of the TFA that asks questions about the likely achievement of the five criteria of motivation, noticing, retrieval, generation, and retention (e.g. "Does the activity involve multiple retrieval opportunities for each target word?" (p. 125). They conclude, for example, that "although flashcard learning may be very effective in terms of retrieval, its ability to promote generation may be limited," that "although crossword puzzles may be motivating, they may not be very effective in terms of generation and retention" and that "Flashcard learning may have additional value because it requires less work from teachers and time on task" (p. 135). Their recommendation is to "combine different activities so that they can compensate each other's weaknesses." Our worry is that none of these three common types of vocabulary activities is typically input-rich and none of them typically involves interpretation in context or text creation for communication (although cloze activities do have greater potential if the learners are completing an extended and engaging text rather than isolated sentences).

Boers and Strong (2016) support the many corpus linguists and psycholinguists whose research has revealed the abundance and significance of lexical phrases (p. 139). In particular they stress the frequency of lexical phrases in natural discourse and their importance in achieving both receptive and productive fluency. They differentiate between fixed idioms (e.g. sit on the fence) and collocations ("i.e. collocations of words whose co-occurrence is so common that substituting one of the words by a near synonym sounds wrong" (p. 139) (e.g. "make an effort" versus "do an effort") and then they review the research on the effectiveness of collocation exercises in textbooks. Their conclusions are that "unless the collocations are already known by the learner, the task of deciding which words form partnerships—while potentially serving a useful awareness-raising purpose—often fails to establish the desired partnerships in the learner's mental lexicon" and that "decontextualized, discrete-point exercises … may never be a substitute for more genuine communicative practice, where learners incorporate (and evaluate the appropriateness of) learned phrases in their own discourse to express their own messages" (p. 149).

An interesting new book, which combines theory and practice, is Dellar and Walkley (2016b). It advocates an approach that the authors call teaching lexically, in which grammar and lexis are taught in combination, contextualization is essential, and richness and utility of input are stressed. Part A discusses the theories and principles behind the approach, Part B provides sample activities for teachers to use and Part C discusses the issues involved in using a lexical approach in the classroom.

We recently conducted research into the learning of vocabulary for the English Profile Project (Cambridge University Press and the University of Cambridge). We devised and supervised the research with classes of B1 level learners in Universiti Putra Malaysia, the ELS language school in Kuala Lumpur and a senior high school in Seville. In each institution one class was a control class and received no treatment, one class received an extensive reading treatment and one class received a text-based, discovery + practice treatment. In all three institutions, all three classes took an identical pre-test and post-test to assess their knowledge of 15 lexical items from the English Profile B1 level list. In all three institutions the control class increased its knowledge of the items very slightly but the treatment classes made considerable improvements. In Universiti Putra Malaysia the extensive reading group made the most progress but in the ELS and in the

Seville high school the text-based discovery + practice group improved the most. This difference was attributed by teachers to the Universiti Putra Malaysia students being Malay and having a liking for stories and experiential approaches whereas the ELS students were Chinese and preferred analytical approaches. The Seville students were about to take important examinations, which would test their explicit knowledge of vocabulary. We came to the following conclusions:

- Students might acquire frequently used lexical items without instruction (especially if they are immersed in an English-rich environment) but they are unlikely to acquire infrequently used lexical items without pedagogic intervention.
- Extensive reading can help students to acquire lexical items providing the items are salient and recycled.
- Text-based vocabulary teaching can help students to acquire lexical items providing the items are salient and recycled.
- The most effective means of facilitating vocabulary acquisition depends to some extent on the social and educational culture of the learners.

(Tomlinson and Masuhara, 2012)

Our Recommendations

Our strong preference is for giving vocabulary building the main emphasis in materials for language learning (especially at lower levels) as "understand utterance no grammar not understand utterance no vocabulary." If not being asked to compromise by a publisher, sponsor or ministry we would develop materials which rely mainly on incidental and incremental learning through meaningful experience but which also contain activities that teach what is teachable (e.g. spelling rules) and activities that allow learners to develop lexical awareness by noticing what is noticeable and discovering what is discoverable. In other words, our materials would aim to "help learners to make use of their explicit knowledge in the process of developing their implicit knowledge" (Ellis, 2016). They would do so through:

1. A rich and varied menu of texts for extensive reading, extensive listening and extensive viewing from which learners would make selections according to their potential for engagement and to which they would be encouraged (but not obliged) to discuss with themselves using their inner voices and with other learners through "book club"-like forums held through social media and face to face.
2. A text-driven, task-based approach (see Tomlinson, 2013, Chapter 5 in this book and "Materials for Grammatical Competence" above) in which learners would experience a potentially engaging written, spoken or visual text, respond to its meaning, perform a task in which they produce a similar text, explore the core text to make discoveries about the use of particular lexical items in that text, produce a revised version of their own text and then for homework look out for and note further uses of the lexical items investigated in class.
3. Vocabulary strategy activities in which learners practice with teacher guidance such learning strategies as tolerance of ambiguity, deduction of meaning from context and effective use of the dictionary, as well as such communication strategies as circumlocution, coining, and seeking clarification. We have found such explicitly focused activities to be very useful in, for example, getting students to lose their fear

of unknown words and their dependence on their dictionary and helping them to interact successfully when they do not understand a word used by an interactant or when they do not know or recall a word they need to use. And of course communication strategies can also be learning strategies, as was the case with the student who eventually elicited the word "gloves" by saying he wanted to buy "socks for hands" and the student who eventually elicited "customs officer" by saying his father worked as a "customer" at the airport.

4. Getting students to keep notebooks (in either hard or soft copy) in which they keep a record of lexical items they have investigated in class activities and items they have noticed whilst looking out for the L2 outside the classroom. These notes would not just contain definitions and translations but comments on noticed connotations, collocations, register, and so forth, as well as on their own and other people's effective and ineffective use of the items.

"That's all very well but what do you do with beginners?" would be a very reasonable question at this point. Our answer would be to start with TPR Plus (Tomlinson, 1994c), dramatic reading of stories by the teacher and word games—as was done on the PKG (By the Teacher for the Teacher) program in Indonesia, mentioned in numerous chapters in this book (Tomlinson, 1990). When the learners were ready to read and to attempt oral communication we would then make use of our suggestions 1 and 2 above and allow discussions to take place in the L1 if one was shared by the learners.

The Acquisition of Pragmatic Competence

In the late 1970s and early 1980s some coursebooks focused on functions such as agreeing, apologizing, arranging, deciding, declining, inviting, and requesting. They did so in the main by using a PPP approach in which exponents of the function were introduced in sentences or dialogues, practiced in drills and then "used" by the students in role plays. We can vividly remember observing rather painful lessons such as the one in which a teacher used a coursebook to teach such exponents of requesting as "Would you mind …", "I'd be grateful if," and "Could you please …" The students did drills in which they chanted out the exponents in sentences from the coursebook and then in pairs they performed a role play in which one student was asking another to turn down a radio. The exponents to use were written on the board and most students mechanically worked thorough them one by one without any consideration of which would be most appropriate and effective in achieving the intended effect in the situation. Moving from grammar practice to function practice was blamed by many authorities and teachers for a perceived increase in grammatical inaccuracy and soon coursebooks (and much applied linguistic research) returned to the centrality of grammar. For example, Wang (2006) surveyed four prestigious Chinese applied linguistics journals and found that, in 2003, the largest percentage of articles on teaching Chinese as a foreign language focused on grammar (e.g. 36 out of 92 articles in *Zhongguo Yuwen* (Chinese language)), that three of the journals published no articles on pragmatics at all, and that the 10 articles on pragmatics research in one journal were all of a pragmalinguistic nature. One reason for the comparative neglect of pragmatics could be the rise in significance of corpus linguistics. It is much easier to identify and then explore the use of lexical items and of manifestations of structures than it is pragmatic features and competencies. However, in the last decade many researchers have stressed the importance of pragmatic competence whilst not necessarily connecting their research and recommendations to language learning. Recently though some researchers have begun again to stress the importance of learners of a language developing pragmatic competence (i.e. being able to achieve and perceive intended effect), some have connected this to materials development and some course-books have started to feature functions again. This is probably because of the perceived need to conform to the very influential *Common European Framework of Reference for Languages: learning, teaching, assessment,* http://www.coe.int/t/dg4/linguistic/source/framework_en.pdf, which stresses the need for learners to perform competencies (e.g. at B2 level "Can outline a case for compensation, using persuasive language to demand satisfaction and state clearly the limits to any concession he / she is prepared to make" (p. 80)). Interestingly the emphasis in the document is on competencies but the emphasis in most teaching materials is, as we will see below, mainly on gaining explicit pragmatic knowledge.

The Coursebooks

The *Big picture upper intermediate* (Brewster & Lane, 2012) has a one-page section on functional language in each unit (compared to three substantial sections on grammar and two on vocabulary). The functional language sections tend to focus on teaching exponents of a featured function (e.g. checking understanding in Unit 5) and do so through a basically PPP approach (with the production activity usually recommending using certain phrases—e.g. "Then act out the situation using suitable phrases from 4" (p. 100)). There is, though, also an attempt to include consciousness raising. Some of the questions do invite discovery from evidence (e.g. "Which word in each sentence is long and drawn out? How does this affect the meaning?" (p. 100)) but most of them test what the learners already know (e.g. "Which expressions in 4 … concede a point in an argument" (p. 100)—the expressions in 4 are in isolated sentences without any context. None of the functional language sections are text rich and none of them invite text creation for communication. *Speakout intermediate* (Clare & Wilson, 2012) and *Global intermediate* (Clandfield & Robb Benne, 2012) are similar to *Big picture upper intermediate* in that they devote one page per 10–11-page unit to a function and that they teach its common exponents using a primarily PPP approach. *Speakout intermediate* does sometimes start with extended input (though the listening text in Unit 4 for example is very conspicuously flooded with target exponents) and it does come closest to text creation in the production stage with a fairly free role play. However, none of these books (nor any of the other coursebooks that we have looked at) actually provides learners with opportunities to achieve intended effects in actual communication, which is, after all, the main aim of most language learners. And none of them pays any attention to the pragmatic strategies involved in achieving intended effects (e.g. implying potential benefits for the interactant when trying to persuade them to do something that would benefit you). Yet the ability to use and to counteract such strategies is vital for communicative success.

The Literature

Tomlinson (1994a) focuses on helping learners to develop pragmatic awareness which "can help learners when participating in planned discourse," can "contribute to the learner readiness required for language acquisition," and can "help learners to develop cognitive skills and to gain more independence as language learners" (p. 119). The article discusses the theories underlying pragmatic awareness activities (e.g. noticing, learner readiness, learner autonomy), recommends an approach that exposes "learners to language use in such a way that they are guided to make discoveries for themselves," which will then help them to note the gap between "their use of the target language and that of proficient users" (p. 119) and then gives and discusses a detailed example of a unit of pragmatic awareness material. This unit for upper intermediate learners is based on an extract from *The graduate* by Charles Webb and in it the learners are invited to make their own discoveries about how the interrogative is used to persuade and the imperative is used to resist persuasion and "about how interaction between context and language form is used to achieve illocutionary force" (p. 119).

McCarten and McCarthy (2010) focus on conversation strategies and do so by first of all suggesting useful ways of making use of corpora data on conversation strategies, providing suggestions for adapting corpus texts, and giving examples of corpus-informed coursebook materials for helping learners to develop conversational competence (McCarthy, McCarten, & Sandford, 2005/2005/2006). Whilst being more "authentic" than most coursebook materials and yet being welcomingly familiar to materials writers, teachers, and students with their following of a PPP approach we found the materials to be disappointingly conventional. Most of the activities are typical decontextualized controlled and guided practice exercises (e.g. fill in the gap) and the texts follow the advice of, "Keep speakers 'polite' … and not confrontational or face-threatening" (McCarten & McCarthy, 2010), thus perpetuating the image of the bland, safe, harmonious EFL world.

Cohen and Ishihara (2013) review what we know about pragmatic ability (i.e. "how meaning is conveyed and interpreted in communication" (p. 113), what we think we know about it, and what we need to know about it, with a particular emphasis on speech acts ("namely the specific functions that people carry out in speaking and writing, such as apologizing, complaining, making requests, refusing things / invitations, complimenting or thanking" (p. 114)). They also review the research on teaching pragmatic ability in coursebooks, make suggestions for adapting coursebooks, and make suggestions for materials development. The research they refer to (e.g. Uso-Juan, 2008; Nguyen, 2011) is generally critical of coursebooks, as we are, for teaching speech acts out of context "without steps to draw students' attention to this variable and its effect on the speech produced" (p. 116). They recommend teachers to supplement their coursebooks by, for example, drawing attention to:

- "the appropriate situations in which to use certain forms" (p. 116);
- "the semantic formulas (i.e. speech-act-specific strategies) … (e.g. for apologies, "acknowledgement of responsibility," and "offer or repair" (p. 117);
- "research-based materials of a cross-cultural nature that pertained to the given speech act" (p. 117).

They also recommend getting 'students to go out into the community and collect data of their own on a given speech act as well as the development of materials which help learners to both notice (i.e. 'simply register a surface language structure') and understand (i.e. 'understand the principles behind how the language form interact with the context')" (p. 121). In addition they give examples from coursebooks that do exceptionally help learners to develop awareness from analysis of naturally occurring conversations of interactions between speech act manifestations and contexts (i.e. Riddiford & Newton,

2010; Wong, 2011) and they suggest supplementing the somewhat stilted dialogues typically found in beginners' textbooks with dialogues at differing levels of formality from naturally occurring data featuring the same speech act (e.g. greeting exchanges).

Ishihara and Paller (2016) repeat the criticisms of other researchers of pragmatics that many coursebooks "offer students few opportunities to develop their pragmatic competence" (p. 87), are inauthentic and stilted and rarely "facilitate the analysis of contextualized language use by learners" (p. 87). They refer to recent research highlighting the shortcomings of pragmatic materials in coursebooks and they make the very important point that we need more "research informed pragmatic material" because "pragmatic failure could have greater repercussions than grammatical failure" (p. 88). However they also direct attention to "a few recently published materials that have been developed in better alignment with current SLA theories and research-based information in the realm of pragmatics" (p. 87). They refer in particular to *Workplace talk in action* (Riddiford & Newton, 2010), a text-based coursebook which makes use of conversations "from a corpus of 1,500 natural conversations collected in 20 workplaces in New Zealand" (p. 95), which organizes its seven units by pragmatic principles and which makes use of a framework of "(A) observation of workplace action; (B) workplace conversations analysis of additional workplace conversations; (C) analysis of workplace e-mails; (D) categorization of useful phrases relating to the pragmatic feature (e.g. agreeing and disagreeing); (E) practice using these phrases" (p. 95). The learners are given opportunities to practice the pragmatic feature in simulated settings but Ishihara and Paller (2016), whilst praising the book for being "a prime example of research-informed materials for pragmatic development" (p. 96) wonder, as we do, "about the extent to which learners are given opportunities to produce language in authentic interactive contexts" (p. 96). Ishihara and Paller (2016) also praise *Touchstone* (McCarthy, McCarten, & Sandiford, 2005/14) for being corpus informed and for teaching conversation strategies (e.g. using "I mean" to repeat ideas) but again doubt whether enough interactive output practice is provided. "Another potentially successful book" (p. 97) is *Conversation Strategies* (Kehe & Kehe, 2011) which is designed to "enhance the learners' spoken communicative ability" (p. 97). Ishihara and Paller (2016) wonder though how affectively and cognitively engaging the many controlled activities are likely to be and feel that the teacher would need to add "meta-pragmatic information regarding when certain expressions are appropriate and why" (p. 98) as well as opportunities for pragmatic noticing.

Ishihara and Paller (2016) conclude their chapter by recommending other research-informed textbooks as well as practically oriented publications that "can serve as resources for research-based instruction in pragmatics" (p. 99). They also make the following statement, which we would endorse not just for pragmatics but for all areas of applied linguistics and language instruction:

> Through reflective and exploratory practice … based on the use of … research-informed materials, the instruction can be further refined to reflect the real-world issues teachers and learners encounter in authentic everyday classrooms, which in turn could contribute to the development of research in instructed SLA.
> (Ishihara & Paller, 2016, p. 99)

The "use of spoken corpora for the development of materials for the teaching of pragmatic routines" (p. 250) is the focus of Bardovi-Harlig and Mossman (2016). They refer to research that indicates the value of "interaction with conversation in the target language with both native speakers and other learners" (p. 250) for the development of pragmatic competence. However, they stress that research has also shown that instruction can facilitate the acquisition of pragmatic routines (i.e. expressions such as "You're right" and "That's true") but only if decontextualized presentation and practice (as is typical of many coursebooks) is avoided and pragmatic authenticity is achieved. They recommend developing materials "that provide (1) input (as a necessity, as a model, and as meaningful and motivating exposure to language); (2) fidelity of input to the target language; and (3) input and activities consistent with L2 acquisition processes" (p. 251). They then demonstrate how corpora can be used in the development of pragmatic materials by (1) "selecting the corpus, (2) identifying expressions, (3) extracting examples, (4) preparing corpus excerpts for teaching, (5) preparing noticing activities, (6) developing production activities" (p. 252). The chapter provides many very useful references to suitable corpora and exemplifies principled and potentially effective materials, for example, an open-ended noticing activity, which gets students to really think about why an interactant in an authentic interaction used particular pragmatic routines when ordering her food; a production activity in which "students get to play 'TV star' and act out scenes from the television shows used in the corpus" (p. 263). They also make the following strong statements with which we completely agree:

- "Turns that contain the target expression should *not* be modified, but rather they should appear in the teaching materials exactly as they do in the corpus" (p. 258).
- "It is not sufficient for learners to have a list of expressions. They must be contextualised" (p. 260).
- "Among other benefits production allows learners to notice the gap between what they want to say and what they can say," thus, in our view, creating a need that can be responded to by the teacher.
- "Corpora provide two important resources for materials developers, namely frequency information and authentic language use that serves as input" (p. 265), providing, we would add, that this authentic language use is contextualized.

However, we would not agree with the suggestion that 'to enhance the salience of the corpus examples, delete non-sequential turns … reduce repetition, repair, overlap, false starts, and unfinished sentences" (p. 258). In our view this would reduce the fidelity of the input and provide an inauthentic experience of target language interaction.

Our Recommendations

We believe that pragmatic competence is not teachable through the explicit provision of declarative knowledge. This might be of some value for monitoring and noticing but "teaching" pragmatic competence is much more a question of providing a rich and authentic experience of language being used in contexts to achieve specific effects, of getting learners to notice how language users (including themselves) achieve and fail to achieve their intended effects and of providing the learners with multiple opportunities to achieve intended effects in actual communication. A text-driven, task-based approach is in our view the most effective way of doing this using a flexible framework similar to the following:

1. Readiness activity (activating learners' minds in readiness for experiencing the core text).

2. Text experience (getting learners to read, listen to or view an authentic text in which language is used to achieve intended effects and encouraging them to visualize and use their inner voices whilst doing so).
3. Intake response activity (encouraging learners to deepen and articulate their personal responses to the text).
4. Development task 1 (getting learners to try to achieve similar intended effects to those in the core text in a communication task).
5. Input response task (getting to learners to focus on a pragmatic aspect of the core text and to make discoveries about how an intended effect was or was not achieved).
6. Development task 2 (getting learners to try once more to achieve similar intended effects to those in the core text in a communication task).

Ideally we would provide learners with access to further input outside the classroom in which they might notice the target pragmatic feature in use, we would encourage them to look out for such input themselves and we would postpone development task 2 to allow for the delayed effect of the learning experience.

Tasks

1. What is your opinion of the following statements:
   a) Controlled practice is of very little value in developing grammatical competence.
   b) Learner noticing of grammar in use is much more valuable than teachers giving the learners notes about grammatical features.
   c) An institution, coursebook or teacher syllabus of grammatical teaching points is counterproductive as learners only learn what they want and need and only learn it when they want and need it.
   d) Simplified generalizations about grammar (e.g. "some" is used in affirmative statements; "any" is used in negative statements and questions) are of no value to learners. It is more valuable for them discover typical use for themselves.
   e) Learners will only acquire grammatical competence if they are exposed to a rich and varied input of the language in use, they are helped to notice features of language use for themselves and they are eventually given many opportunities to use the language for communication.
2. Look at a unit from any L2 coursebook and answer the following questions about it.
   a) What pedagogical approach does it take to the learning of grammar?
   b) Do you think this approach is likely to facilitate the acquisition of grammatical competence?
   c) What adaptations (if any) would you make to the grammar activities when using this book?
   d) What revisions (if any) would you make to the grammar activities if you were tasked with developing a revised version of this book?
   e) What pedagogical approach does the book take to the learning of vocabulary?
   f) Do you think this approach is likely to facilitate the acquisition of lexical competence?
   g) What adaptations (if any) would you make to the vocabulary activities when using this book?
   h) What revisions (if any) would you make to the vocabulary activities if you were tasked with developing a revised version of this book?

i) Does the book give any attention to the development of pragmatic competence? If it does:
- What pedagogical approach does it take to developing awareness of pragmatic functions?
- Do you think this approach is likely to facilitate the acquisition of pragmatic competence?
- What adaptations (if any) would you make to the pragmatic awareness activities when using this book?
- What revisions (if any) would you make to the pragmatic awareness activities if you were tasked with developing a revised version of this book?

Further Reading

Tomlinson, B. (Ed.). (2013). *Applied linguistics and materials development.* London: Bloomsbury.
Tomlinson, B. (Ed.). (2016). *SLA research and materials development for language learning.* New York: Routledge.

References

Arshad, A. S. (2003). Developing materials for the teaching of grammar. In J. Mukundan (Ed.), *Readings on ELT material* (pp. 118–127). Selangor Darul Ehsan: Universiti Putra Malaysia Press.
Avila, J. (2007). The value of recasts during meaning focused communication 2. In B. Tomlinson (Ed.), *Language acquisition and development: Studies of learners of first and other languages* (pp. 162–170). London: Continuum.
Azarnoosh, M., Zeraatpishe, M., Faravani, A., & Kargozari, H. R. (Eds.). (2016). *Issues in materials development.* Rotterdam: Sense.
Baleghizadeh, S., Goldouz, E., & Yousefpoori-Naeim, M. (2016). What grammar activities do ELT workbooks focus on? In B. Tomlinson (Ed.), *SLA research and materials development for language learning* (pp. 153–165). New York: Routledge.
Bao, D. (2007). Enhancing the language learning process for reticent learners of Vietnamese and of English in Vietnam. In B. Tomlinson (Ed.), *Language acquisition and development: Studies of learners of first and other languages* (pp. 205–224). London: Continuum.
Bao, D. (2013). Voices of the reticent: Getting inside views of Vietnamese secondary students on learning. In M. Cortazzi & L. Jin (Eds.), *Researching cultures of learning: International perspectives on language learning and education* (pp. 136–154). Basingstoke: Palgrave Macmillan.
Barcroft, J. (2006). Can writing a word detract from learning it? More negative effects of forced output during vocabulary learning. *Second Language Research, 22*(4), 487–497.
Barnard, E. S. (2007). The value of comprehension in the early stages of the acquisition and development of Bahasa Indonesia by non-native speakers. In B. Tomlinson (Ed.), *Language acquisition and development: Studies of learners of first and other languages* (pp. 187–204). London: Continuum.

Bardovi-Harlig, K., & Mossman, S. (2016). Corpus-based materials development for teaching and learning pragmatic routines. In B. Tomlinson (Ed.), *SLA research and materials development for language learning* (pp. 250–267). New York: Routledge.

Benevides, M. (2016). Text and context: Innovating the coursebook. *Between the Keys, 24*(1), 6–8.

Benevides, M., & Valvona, C. (2008). *Widgets*. Hong Kong: Longman.

Boers, F., & Strong, B. (2016). *An evaluation of textbook exercises on collocations*. In B. Tomlinson (Ed.), *SLA research and materials development for language learning* (pp. 139–152). New York: Routledge.

Bolitho, R. (2003). Materials for language awareness. In B. Tomlinson (Ed.), *Developing materials for language teaching* (pp. 422–425). London: Continuum.

Bolitho, R., Carter, R., Hughes, R., Ivanic, R., Masuhara, H., & Tomlinson, B. (2003). Ten questions about language awareness. *ELT Journal, 57*(2), 251–259.

Bolitho, R., & Tomlinson, B. (2005). *Discover English* (3rd ed.). Oxford: Macmillan.

Brewster, S., & Lane, A. (2012). *The big picture upper intermediate*. Oxford: Richmond.

Carter, R., Hughes, R., & McCarthy, M. (2000). *Exploring grammar in context*. Cambridge: Cambridge University Press.

Carter, R., Hughes, R., & McCarthy, M. (2011). Telling tails: Grammar, the spoken language and materials development. In B. Tomlinson (Ed.), *Materials development in language teaching* (2nd ed., pp. 78–100). Cambridge: Cambridge University Press.

Carter, R., & McCarthy, M. (1995). Grammar and the spoken language. *Applied Linguistics, 16*(2), 141–158.

Clandfield, L., & Robb Benne, R. (2011). *Global intermediate*. Oxford: Macmillan.

Clare, A., & Wilson, J. J. (2012). *Speakout intermediate*. Harlow: Pearson.

Cohen, A. D., & Ishihara, N. (2013). Pragmatics. In B. Tomlinson (Ed.), *Applied linguistics and materials development for language learning* (pp. 113–126). London: Bloomsbury.

Criado, R. (2016). Insights from skill acquisition theory for grammar activity sequencing and design in foreign language teaching. *Innovation in language learning and teaching* [Guest editor B. Tomlinson], *10*(2), 121–132.

Cullen, R., & Kuo, V. (2007). Spoken grammar and ELT materials. *TESOL Quarterly, 41*(2), 361–386.

Cunningham, S., & Moor, P. (2008). *Cutting edge intermediate*. Harlow: Longman.

Davis, C., Tup, F., & Aziz, D. (2003). *Life accents*. Singapore: Times Media.

Dellar, H., & Walkley, A. (2010). *Pre-Intermediate outcomes*. Andover: Cengage Learning.

Dellar, H., & Walkley, A. (2016a). *Intermediate outcomes* (2nd ed.). Andover: Cengage Learning.

Dellar, H., & Walkley, A. (2016b). *Teaching lexically: Principles and practice*. Peaslake: Delta.

Ellis, R. (1995). Interpretation tasks for grammar teaching. *TESOL Quarterly, 29*, 87–105.

Ellis, R. (2010). Second language acquisition research and language teaching. In Harwood, N. (Ed.), *English language teaching materials: Theory and practice* (pp. 33–57). Cambridge: Cambridge University Press.

Ellis, R. (2016). Language teaching materials as work plans: An SLA perspective. In B. Tomlinson (Ed.), *SLA Research and materials development for language learning* (pp. 203–218). New York: Routledge.

Ellis, R., & Tomlinson, B. (1980). The teaching of vocabulary. In R. Ellis & B. Tomlinson. *Teaching secondary English: A guide to the teaching of English as a second language* (pp. 60–95). London: Longman.

Fenner, A. N., & Nordal-Pedersen, G. (1999). *Search 10*. Oslo: Gyldendal.

Fenner, A. & Nordal-Pedersen, G. (2006). *Searching 10*. Oslo: Gyldendal.

Fotos, S., & Nassaji, H. (Eds.). (2007). *Form-focused instruction and teacher education: Studies in honour of Rod Ellis*. Oxford: Oxford University Press.

Goldstein, B. (2011). *The big picture intermediate*. Oxford: Richmond.

Hall, N., & Shepheard, J. (1991). *The anti-grammar grammar book*. Harlow: Longman.

Harmer, J. (1987). *Teaching and learning grammar*. Harlow: Longman.

Harmer, J. (1998). *How to teach English*. New York: Longman.

Harwood, N. (Ed.). (2010). *English language teaching materials: theory and practice*. Cambridge: Cambridge University Press.

Ishihara, N., & Paller, D. L. (2016). Research-informed materials for teaching pragmatics: The case of agreement and disagreement in English. In B. Tomlinson (Ed.), *SLA Research and materials development for language learning* (pp. 87–102). New York: Routledge.

Jones, C. (2007). Spoken grammar—is "noticing" the best option? *Modern English Teacher, 16*(4), 155–160.

Kehe, D., & Kehe, P. D. (2011). *Conversation strategies*. Brattlebaro, VT: Pro Lingua Associates.

Kerr, P. (n.d.) *How to write vocabulary presentations and practice*. ELT Teacher2Writer. Retrieved from http://www.eltteacher2writer.co.uk/how-write-vocabulary-presentations-and-practice

Kolb, A. Y., & Kolb, D. A. (2009). The learning way: meta-cognitive aspects of experiential learning. *Simulation and Gaming: An Interdisciplinary Journal of Theory, Practice and Research, 40*(3), 297–327.

Kolb, D. A. (1984). *Experiential learning: Experience as the source of learning and development*. Englewood Cliffs, NJ: Prentice Hall.

Kolb, D. A. (2015). *Experiential learning: Experience as the source of learning and development* (2nd ed.). Upper Saddle River, NJ: Pearson.

Laufer, B. & Hulstijn, J. (2001). Incidental vocabulary acquisition in a second language: the construct of task-induced involvement. *Applied Linguistics, 22*(1), 1–26.

Lewis, M. (1986). *The English verb: An exploration of structure and meaning*. Hove: Language Teaching Publications.

Lewis, M. (Ed.). (1993). *The lexical approach: The state of ELT and the way forward*. Hove: Language Teaching Publications.

Long, M. (1991). Focus on form: a design feature in language teaching methodology. In K. de Bot, R. Ginsberg & C. Kramsch (Eds.), *Foreign language research in cross-cultural perspective*. Amsterdam: John Benjamins.

Long, M. (2015). *Second language acquisition and task-based language teaching*. Malden, MA: Wiley Blackwell.

Maley, A. (2013). Vocabulary. In B. Tomlinson (Ed.), *Applied linguistics and materials development* (pp. 95–111). London: Bloomsbury.

Masuhara, H. (2016). Brain studies and materials for language learning. In B. Tomlinson (Ed.), *SLA research and materials development for language learning* (pp. 23–32). New York: Routledge.

Masuhara, H., Haan, M., Yi, Y., & Tomlinson, B. (2008). Adult EFL courses. *ELT Journal, 62*(3), 294–312.

McCarten, J., & McCarthy, M. (2010). Bridging the gap between corpus and coursebook: The case of conversation strategies. In Mishan, F. & Chambers, A. (Eds.) *Perspectives on language learning materials development* (pp. 11–32). Bern: Peter Lang.

McCarthy, M., & Carter, R. (1995). Spoken grammar. What is it and how should we teach it? *ELT Journal, 49*(3), 207–217.

McCarthy, M., McCarten, J. & Sandford, H. (2005/2006). *Touchstone.* Cambridge: Cambridge University Press.

McCarthy, M., McCarten, J., & Sandford, H. (2008). *Touchstone full contact.* Cambridge: Cambridge University Press.

McDonough, J., Shaw, C., & Masuhara, H. (2013). *Materials and methods in ELT: A teacher's guide* (3rd ed.). Chichester: Wiley-Blackwell.

McGrath, I. (2002). *Materials evaluation and design for language teaching.* Edinburgh: Edinburgh University Press.

McGrath, I. (2013). *Teaching materials and the roles of EFL/ESL teachers: Practice and theory.* London: Bloomsbury.

Mishan, F. (2005). *Designing authenticity into language learning materials.* Bristol: Intellect.

Mishan, F. (2013). Studies of pedagogy. In B. Tomlinson (Ed.), *Applied linguistics and materials development.* (pp. 269–286). London: Bloomsbury.

Mishan, F., & Timmis, I. (2015). Materials development for TESOL. Edinburgh: Edinburgh University Press.

Morris, L. & Tremblay, M. (2002). The impact of attending to unstressed words on the acquisition of written grammatical morphological by French speaking ESL students. *Canadian Modern Language Review, 58*(3), 364–385.

Mukundan, J. (2010). Words as they appear in Malaysian secondary school English language textbooks: Some implications for pedagogy. In B. Tomlinson & H. Masuhara (Eds.), *Research for materials development in language learning: Evidence for best practice* (pp. 291–304). London: Continuum.

Nakata, T., & Webb, S. (2016). Vocabulary learning exercises: Evaluating a selection of exercises commonly featured in language learning materials, In B. Tomlinson (Ed.), *SLA research and materials development for language learning* (pp. 123–138). New York: Routledge.

Nation, I. S. P. (2001). *Learning vocabulary in another language.* Cambridge: Cambridge University Press.

Nation, I. S. P. (2007). The four strands. *Innovation in Language Learning and Teaching, 1*(1), 1–12.

Nation, I. S. P. (2008). *Teaching vocabulary: strategies and techniques.* Boston: Heinle Cengage Learning.

Nation, I. S. P. (2013). *Materials for teaching vocabulary.* In B. Tomlinson (Ed.), *Developing materials for language teaching* (2nd ed., pp. 351–364). London: Bloomsbury.

Nation, I. S. P., & Macalister, J. (2010). *Language curriculum design.* New York: Routledge.

Nation, I. S. P., & Webb, S. (2011). *Researching and analysing vocabulary.* Boston: Heinle Cengage Learning.

Nitta, R., & Gardner, S. (2005). Consciousness raising and practice in ELT coursebooks. *ELT Journal, 59*(1), 3–13.

Nguyen, M. T. T. (2011). Learning to communicate in a globalized world: To what extent do school textbooks facilitate the development of intercultural pragmatic competence? *RELC Journal, 42*(1), 17–30.

On target. (1995). Grade 10 English Second Language Learner's Book. Windhoek: Gamsburg *Macmillan.*

Pinnard, L. (2016). Looking outwards: using learning materials to help learners harness out-of-class learning opportunities. *Innovation in language learning and teaching* [Guest editor B. Tomlinson], *10*(2), 133–143.

Poh-Knight, L., & Keppler, G. M. (2011). *English empowers 2*. Singapore: Marshall Cavendish.

Puchta, H., & Stranks, J. (2010). *English in mind* (2nd ed.). Cambridge: Cambridge University Press.

Redston, C., & Cunningham, G. (2013). *Face2face intermediate* (2nd ed.). Cambridge: Cambridge University Press.

Renandya, W. A. (Ed.). (2003). *Methodology and materials design in language teaching*. Singapore: RELC.

Reppen, R. (2011). Using corpora in the language classroom. In B. Tomlinson (Ed.), *Materials development for language teaching* (2nd ed., pp. 35–50). Cambridge: Cambridge University Press.

Richards, J. (2007). Materials development and research: towards a form-focused perspective. In Fotos, S. & Nassaji, H. (Eds.), *Form-focused instruction and teacher education: Studies in honour of Rod Ellis* (pp. 147–160). Oxford: Oxford University Press.

Richards, J. C. (2014). The ELT textbook. In S. Garton & K. Graves (Eds.), *International perspectives on materials in ELT* (pp. 19–36). Oxford: Palgrave Macmillan.

Richards, J., & Reppen, R. (2014). Towards a pedagogy of grammar instruction. *RELC Journal, 45*(1), 1–25.

Riddiford, N., & Newton, J. (2010). *Workplace talk in action: An ESOL resource*. Wellington: Victoria University of Wellington.

Saslow, J., & Ascher, A. (2015). *Topnotch 2* (3rd ed.) Harlow: Pearson.

Schmidt, R. (1992). Psychological mechanisms underlying second language fluency. *Studies in Second Language Acquisition, 14*, 357–385.

Scrivener, J. (1994). *Learning teaching*. Oxford: Heinemann.

Skehan, P. (1998). *A cognitive approach to language learning*. Oxford: Oxford University Press.

Soars, L., & Soars, J. (2003). *Headway advanced*. Oxford: Oxford University Press.

Soars, L., & Soars, J. (2012). *New headway advanced* (4th ed.). Oxford: Oxford University Press.

Sokol, A. (2005). Creatively proGRAMMARed. *Folio, 9*(2), 27–32.

Teaching grammar. (2016). Cambridge English Teacher. Cambridge: Cambridge University Press. Retrieved from https://www.cambridgeenglishteacher.org/courses/details/18599.

Stranks, J. (2013). Materials for the teaching of grammar. In B. Tomlinson (Ed.), *Developing materials for language teaching* (2nd ed., pp, 337–350). London: Bloomsbury.

Thomas, M., & Reinders, H. (Eds.). (2015). *Contemporary task-based teaching in Asia*. London: Bloomsbury.

Thornbury, S. (2000). *How to teach grammar*. Harlow: Pearson.

Thornbury, S. (2002). *How to teach vocabulary*. Harlow: Pearson.

Thornbury, S. (2006). *An A–Z of ELT: A dictionary of terms and concepts used in English language teaching*. Oxford: Macmillan.

Timmis, I. (2005). Towards a framework for teaching spoken grammar. *ELT Journal, 59*(2), 117–125.

Timmis, I. (2013). Spoken language research: the applied linguistic challenge. In B. Tomlinson (Ed.), *Applied linguistics and materials development* (pp. 79–94). London: Bloomsbury.

Tomlinson, B. (Ed.). (1981). *Talking to learn*. Port Vila: Vanuatu Ministry of Education.

Tomlinson, B. (1990). Managing change in Indonesian high schools. *ELT Journal, 44*(1), 25–37.

Tomlinson, B. (1994a). Pragmatic awareness activities. *Language Awareness, 3*(3/4), 119–129.

Tomlinson, B. (1994b). *Openings*. London: Penguin.

Tomlinson, B. (1994c). Materials for TPR. *Folio, 1*(2), 8–10.

Tomlinson, B. (Ed.) (2004). *Improve your English*. Addis Ababa: Ministry of Education.

Tomlinson, B. (2007). The value of recasts during meaning focused communication 1. In B. Tomlinson (Ed.), *Language acquisition and development: Studies of learners of first and other languages* (pp. 141–161). London: Continuum.

Tomlinson, B. (2010). Helping learners to fill the gaps in their learning. In F. Mishan & A. Chambers (Eds.), *Perspectives on language learning materials development* (pp. 87–108). Berlin: Peter Lang.

Tomlinson, B. (2011). Introduction: principles and procedures of materials development. In B. Tomlinson (Ed.), *Materials development in language teaching* (2nd ed., pp. 1–34). Cambridge: Cambridge University Press.

Tomlinson, B. (2013). Developing principled frameworks for materials development. In B. Tomlinson (Ed.), *Developing materials for language teaching* (pp. 98–118). London: Bloomsbury.

Tomlinson, B. (2014). Looking out for English. *Folio, 16*(1), 5–8.

Tomlinson, B. (2015). TBLT materials and curricula: from theory to practice. In M. Thomas & H. Reinders (Eds.), *Contemporary task-based teaching in Asia* (pp. 328–339). London: Bloomsbury.

Tomlinson, B. (2016a, April). *Text-driven task-based approaches*. Presentation at the IATEFL Conference, Birmingham.

Tomlinson, B. (Ed.). (2016b). *SLA theory and materials development for language learning*. New York: Routledge.

Tomlinson, B. (in press). *Discovery-based instruction*. In J. I. Liontas (Ed.) TESOL encyclopedia. Hoboken, NJ.: Wiley.

Tomlinson, B., Dat, B., Masuhara, H., & Rubdy, R. (2001). EFL courses for adults. *ELT Journal, 55*(1), 80–101.

Tomlinson, B., Hill, D. A., & Masuhara, H. (2000). *English for life 1*. Singapore: Marshall Cavendish.

Tomlinson, B., & Masuhara, H. (1994). *Use your English*. Tokyo: Asahi Press.

Tomlinson, B., & Masuhara, H. (2008). Materials used in the UK. In B. Tomlinson (Ed.), *English language learning materials: A critical review* (pp. 159–178). London: Continuum.

Tomlinson, B., & Masuhara, H. (2012). *The English Profile Vocabulary Project*. Unpublished report.

Tomlinson, B., & Masuhara, H. (2013). Review of adult ELT textbooks. *ELT Journal, 67*(2), 233–249.

Uso-Juan, E. (2008). The presentation and practice of the communicative act of requesting in textbooks: focusing on modifiers. In E. S. Alcon & M. P. Safont (Eds.), *Intercultural language use and language learning* (pp. 223–243). Netherlands: Springer.

Van den Branden, K. (2006). *Task–based language education: From theory to practice*. Cambridge: Cambridge University Press.

Wang, H. (2006). Pragmatics in foreign language teaching and learning: Reflections on the teaching of Chinese in China. In M. W. Chan, K. N. Chin, & T. Suthiwan (Eds.), *Foreign language teaching in Asia and beyond* (pp. 93–108). Singapore: National University of Singapore.

Waring, R. (2006). Why extensive reading should be an indispensable part of all language programmes. *The Language Teacher, 30*(7), 44–47.

Williams, J., & Evans, J. (1998). What kind of focus and on which forms? In C. Doughty & J. Williams (Eds.), *Focus on form in classroom second language acquisition* (p. 139). Cambridge: Cambridge University Press.

Willis, D. (1990). *The lexical syllabus.* London: Collins Cobuild.

Willis, J. (1994). Task-based language learning as an alternative to PPP. *The Teacher Trainer, 8*(1), 17–20.

Willis, J. (2011). Concordances in the classroom without a computer: assembling and exploiting concordances of common words. In B. Tomlinson (Ed.), *Materials development for language teaching* (2nd ed., pp. 51–77). Cambridge: Cambridge University Press.

Wong, J. (2011). Pragmatic competency in telephone closings. In N. Houck & D. Tatsuki (Eds.), *Pragmatics: Teaching natural conversation* (pp. 135–152) Alexandria, VA: Teachers of English to Speakers of Another Language.

Woodward, T. (1993). Changing the basis of pre-service TEFL training in the UK. *IATEFL TT. SIG Newsletter, 13*, 3–5.

9

Developing Materials for the Development of Skills

Introduction

In this chapter, we will focus on developing materials for the "four modes of communication" (i.e. listening, speaking, reading and writing), which are typically referred to as "the four skills". We will firstly review the literature that tries to distinguish the concepts of "skill" and of "strategy", as the terms are still widely used despite the fact that no agreement has been reached on what exactly they refer to. Skill and strategy teaching attracted a lot of attention in the latter half of the twentieth century, so we will briefly provide a retrospective account of materials for teaching skills and strategies and the rationale behind them. There have been a lot of changes in our understanding of the processes involved in listening, speaking, reading and writing, reflecting developments within applied linguistics, second language acquisition and beyond; for example, insights from other disciplines such as cognitive psychology and neuroscience. The current thinking seems to be that learners may acquire communicative competence best in an holistic environment in which the learners are provided with meaningful and motivated exposure as well as opportunities to use the target language in various communicative modes and to pay selective conscious attention to language use and strategies (e.g. Han & D'Angelo, 2009; Gass & Mackey, 2012; Richards and Rodgers, 2014; Long, 2015; Ellis, 2016a; Tomlinson, 2016).

Rather than discussing each skill separately, we will take an integrated approach in our attempt to capture interconnected and fundamental elements that underlie all four skills and to discuss how materials could best help learners to listen, speak, read and write.

Skills and Strategies

The Notion of Skills

Around the 1970s when the communicative approach challenged the existing views of language, learning and teaching, the contrast was made between "linguistic competence" and "communicative competence" (Hymes, 1972; Canale & Swain, 1980; see Richards & Rodgers, 2014 for an historical account). In traditional grammar-based approaches around that time (e.g. the grammar translation method), learning a

The Complete Guide to the Theory and Practice of Materials Development for Language Learning,
First Edition. Brian Tomlinson and Hitomi Masuhara.
© 2018 John Wiley & Sons, Inc. Published 2018 by John Wiley & Sons, Inc.

language usually meant learning "language knowledge" by consciously studying words and grammar in the target language (Richards and Rodgers, 2014). In the communicative approach, on the other hand, the focus is more on learners becoming able to use the target language for communication. Common sense tells us that just because *we have accumulated knowledge about tennis* it does not mean *we can play tennis*. We also need to *acquire some kind of sensor, motor, cognitive, and strategic abilities to be able to play tennis*. Likewise, in order to become able to listen, speak, read and write in a target language, we also need to acquire the sensor, motor, cognitive, and strategic abilities necessary for using a language too.

The notion of "skills" for language use, however, turned out to be rather elusive and difficult to define. Identifying what exactly a skill consists of was even more challenging. Alderson (2000, p. 110), in discussing assessment of reading skills, pointed out that "The notion of skills and subskills … is enormously pervasive and influential, despite the lack of clear empirical justification."

The notion of skill has long been discussed and researched in education, information processing and psychology but the use of the term, when examined closely, is varied and vague (e.g. see Afflerbach, Pearson, and Paris, 2008 for a survey of how the term is used in the United States). For example, Richards and Schmidt (2010, p. 532), in the *Longman dictionary of language teaching and applied linguistics*, define skill as, "an acquired *ability* to perform an activity well, usually one that is made up of a number of co-ordinated processes." The equation of skills and abilities has been observed in official curriculum documents since the 1920s (Afflerbach et al., 2008, p. 367). Richards and Rodgers (2014, p. 26), however, define skills as, "integrated sets of *behaviors* that are learned through practice. They are made up of individual components that may be learned separately and that come together as a whole to constitute skilled performance." Defining skills as "actions" or "behaviors" derives from behavioral learning theories in the 1960s when psychologists were investigating motor skills, routine habits, and activities that were automatic and needed less conscious effort (Afflerbach et al., 2008).

Is "skill" then "ability" that we possess internally (e.g. Richards and Schmidt, 2010)? Or is it "behavior" or "action" that is externally observable (Afflerbach et al., 2008; Richards and Rodgers, 2014)? If we choose the former, we are dealing with a mental "construct" (i.e. a theoretical and hypothetical idea or substance containing various conceptual elements) that is difficult to observe or measure. These days we hear about "problem-solving skills" and "critical thinking skills" or "life skills." What are they and what do they consist of? As mental constructs are not amenable to direct inspection, researchers have conducted their investigations using different probes (e.g. verbal protocols; statistical factor analysis of behavioral tests) to get some indication that their hypotheses are likely to be verified. As a result, we are left with an unsettling number and variety of lists of skills and subskills (N.B. also called macro and micro skills). In fact, after reviewing the literature on reading skills, Williams and Moran (1989) noted inconsistencies among the proposed list of skills. They pointed out (p. 224) that "Although no two lists of reading skills are identical, casual inspection suggests that the skills might be grouped roughly into 'language-related' skills (e.g. guessing the meaning of unknown words) and 'reason-related' skills (e.g. identifying the main idea)."

If we accept the latter definition of observable "behaviors," it excludes so-called mental "skills" such as "inferencing" and "identifying the main idea" that we often see in educational literature and curricula. These mental skills are supposed to be part of the "higher order skills" (e.g. Anderson & Krathwohl, 2001) that are considered vital in education.

The Notion of Strategy

Cohen (2011, p. 682) provides a generally accepted definition of strategies: "Language learning strategies can be defined as thoughts and actions, consciously selected by learners, to assist them in learning and using language in general, and in the completion of specific language tasks" (see also Oxford, 2011a; Oxford, 2011b). As Cohen implies, there are learning strategies to facilitate language learning and communication strategies to facilitate communication.

Oxford (2011a) provides a very useful research timeline on strategies from various perspectives. For example, she traces back the three broad influences on strategy concepts—for example, general strategy concepts such as strategies in war from the Greek period; the self-regulation concept (e.g. Van der Veer & Valsiner, 1991); autonomy concepts mainly from the seventeenth century. She then examines key publications in eight different categories including effectiveness, theories and models, instruction and language area strategies—including those for "the four skills." The studies of good language learners showing more awareness and control in strategy use in the 1970s stimulated further strategy research (see Griffiths, 2008 for a review). Oxford (1990) published a strategy-assessment questionnaire, the Strategy Inventory for Language Learning (SILL) (see Oxford & Burry-Stock, 1995 for an ESL and EFL version). Note that strategy studies became widely studied in L1 educational contexts and then applied in L2 situations.

Differentiating Skills and Strategies—Are We Any Clearer?

Terminological inconsistency was noted by Williams and Moran (1989) regarding skills and strategies. Each term was often not used consistently and sometimes they were used interchangeably. Almost 20 years later Afflerbach et al. (2008) discuss similar confusions among the users of these terms. In order to clarify the confusions regarding various definitions of reading skills and strategies, they conducted a thorough analysis of the publications by various authoritative organizations and historically influential literature in psychology, information processing, and education in the United States. They provide the history of how the terms "skills" and "strategies" have been defined and developed in various disciplines Based on their investigation, they describe the defining differences between skills and strategies in relation to reading:

> Reading skills are automatic actions that result in decoding and comprehension with speed, efficiency, and fluency and usually occur without awareness of the components or control involved. The reader's deliberate control, goal-directedness, and awareness define a strategic action.
>
> (Afflerbach et al., 2008, p. 368)

They then continue to explain:

> A concrete example may clarify the distinction. Suppose a student determines he or she has only a vague understanding of a paragraph as he or she reaches the end of it. The student wants to do something to clarify his or her comprehension so the student slows down and asks, "Does that make sense?" after every sentence. This is a reading strategy—a deliberate, conscious, metacognitive act. The

strategy is prompted by the student's vague feeling of poor comprehension, and it is characterized by a slower rate of reading and a deliberate act of self-questioning that serves the student's goal of monitoring and building better comprehension. Now imagine that the strategy works and the student continues to use it through-out the school year. With months of practice, the strategy requires less deliber-ate attention, and the student uses it more quickly and more efficiently. When it becomes effortless and automatic (i.e., the student is in the habit of asking "Does that make sense?" automatically), the reading strategy has become a reading skill. In this developmental example, skill and strategy differ in their intentionality and their automatic and non-automatic status.

(Afflerbach et al., 2008, p. 368)

If we follow their argument, skimming (i.e. a behavior of reading a text quickly to get an overall idea) can be called a skill if the person does it automatically without any effort. Those who are not used to the idea may use a skimming strategy consciously in a purposeful way. Skimming is an action; therefore it counts as a skill if you follow the definition by Richards and Rodgers (2014). Note here that if we subscribe to the other definition of skills as acquired mental abilities (Richards & Schmidt, 2010), the behav-ioral nature of skimming may be categorized as a strategy and not a skill. No wonder confusion between skills and strategies persists.

Teaching Skills and Strategies—a Matter of Faith?

How can skills be taught? If we choose to define a skill as "an acquired ability" (Richards & Schmidt, 2010), a question follows: can "ability" such as the listening skill be "taught" in the first place? Even if we concede that a new ability can be taught, should an abil-ity be separated into subskills that are then taught separately? Or is skill a unitary phenomenon? If we choose to define skills as "behaviors or actions with finesse" (e.g. Richards & Rodgers, 2014), what kinds of "controlled practice" will help beginners to develop the ability to manage actions or behaviors like expert users of the target lan-guage?

Despite the fact that there were no clear agreements in relation to the definitions and the value of teaching discrete language skills and strategies, skill-based books were pub-lished and were popular in the 1970s onwards (e.g. the Oxford Skills Series). Nuttall (1985, p. 199) commented, in her review of materials for teaching reading, "That it is possible to promote reading skills and strategies … is still largely a matter of faith, but the number of materials produced show that it is a faith widely held."

The typical procedures for teaching skills and strategies seemed to involve a phase in which explicit teaching of a specific skill or strategy takes place followed by practice (e.g. Greenall & Swan, 1986; the Oxford Skills series—e.g. Tomlinson & Ellis, 1987). The implicit assumption regarding the learning process seems to be that conscious practice will eventually transfer to become subconscious skill.

What is the rationale behind such skills and strategy based approaches? Littlewood (1984) proposed a skills-learning model, which he claims to be compatible with the com-municative language approaches, which had both a cognitive and a behavioral aspect:

The cognitive aspect involves the internalisation of plans for creating appropri-ate behaviour. For language use, these plans derive mainly from the language systems—they include grammatical rules, procedures for selecting vocabulary, and social conventions governing speech. The behavioral aspect involves the automation of these plans so that they can be converted into fluent performance in real time. This occurs mainly through practice in converting plans into performance.

(Littlewood, 1984, p. 74)

Following Littlewood, if a "plan" happens to involve a particular grammatical rule, learners need to practice it until they can use it automatically. Learning then becomes a process of habit formation of the grammatical rule. In audiolingualism, an oral model was presented and the learners practiced it to form a habit. In Littlewood's version of skills learning, the grammar rules seem to be demonstrated or explained in some way and then communication practice follows in order to form a habit. It seems to us that Littlewood's suggestion seems to resemble the procedures of P-P-P (Presentation, Practice, Production). According to Littlewood (1984), the "plan" may be "procedures for selecting vocabulary" or "social conventions governing speech." If the plan happens to be "procedures for selecting vocabulary" we hit the dilemma we discussed above of trying to identify skills and subskills.

Johnson (1996) searched for inspiration from skills acquisition theory in cognitive psychology, specifically Anderson's Adaptive Control of Thought (ACT) (Anderson, 1982). Skills acquisition theory distinguishes three types of knowledge: declarative; procedural and automatized. Johnson and Jackson (2006, p. 534) explain that "declarative knowledge" is "knowledge about," for example, grammar, tennis techniques. They contrast "Procedural knowledge" as "knowledge how to." Note here that procedural knowledge could include sensory or nonverbal elements. According to Johnson and Jackson (2006, p. 534), "it is both important and difficult to convert declarative into procedural knowledge—by the process known as proceduralisation ..." According to DeKeyser (1998, p. 61), currently one of the major proponents of Skills Acquisition Theory (Dekeyser, 2007; Dekeyser, 2015), "proceduralization is achieved by engaging in the target behavior—or procedure—while temporarily on declarative crutches."

Johnson and Jackson (2006) investigate how teaching may facilitate proceduralization in performance in other subjects such as music, sport and flight simulation. They identify some similar sequences between ELT and performance-based teaching such as the "deep-end strategy"; for example, let learners swim in the sea and the instructor identifies the learner needs → trains them in a pool → lets learners swim in the sea again. They also recognized a pretask → task → posttask sequence in which performance related feedback is included.

Strategy instruction, on the other hand, evolved independently of skills teaching and became more prominent in the 1980s to 1990s (e.g. for examples of learner strategy training see Ellis and Sinclair, 1989; Littlejohn and Hicks, 1998; Hicks and Littlejohn, 2003). Rather than focusing solely on "the four skills," strategy proponents emphasize how strategic training enhances self-regulation, learner autonomy, and successful performance by teaching what good learners do.

Oxford (2011a), in her research timeline that traces major publications on strategies, argues for the validity of strategy instruction and the efficacy of it:

Cohen & Macaro [2007] produced a landmark volume three decades after the birth of the field of L2 learning strategies. This book presented many challenges to the field (such as terminology problems, research issues, and conflicting typologies), but showed that progress had been achieved, particularly in research on strategies related to certain L2 areas, such as reading, writing, speaking, and listening.

Relationships were shown to exist between strategy use and proficiency in multiple L2 areas. (Oxford, 2011a, p. 179)

What researchers seem to agree is that:

- good language learners tend to be aware of and be able to use a variety of strategies effectively;
- guided practice is likely to help learners become strategic and improve their proficiency and autonomy;
- there is a considerable number of possible categories of strategies and substrategies.

What should the syllabus and methodological approaches be? Should the syllabus for strategy teaching involve selection from an available list of strategies, as much of the efficacy research in strategy studies has done (see part 2 of Cohen and Macaro, 2007)? Should teachers then spend time demonstrating and explaining the selected strategies and then the learners practice them until the strategies become automatized? As was the case with skills, the actual methodology seems to resemble PPP. Will one-fits-all pre-selected strategies, even specifically designed for the target learners, cater for the individual level of strategy awareness and control? There is also an inherent paradox in teacher-controlled strategy training that claims to enhance learner autonomy. McDonough in Archibald (2006) and Littlejohn (2008), in fact, point out the danger of learner training restricting the time spent on language learning. When do learners listen, speak, read and write extensively in the target language? In many EFL contexts, the classroom is the only place for learners to be exposed to English. And if you analyze coursebooks you will find that the students spend very little time actually reading, writing, speaking or listening. For example, in *Outcomes Pre-Intermediate* (Dellar & Walkley, 2010) in Unit 11 there are 31 sections either giving information on or providing practice of language points or testing the learners' knowledge or comprehension and only 13 sections in which they read (1), write (0), listen (3) or speak (9) in order to communicate. At the back of the book there are two-page "writing lessons" for each unit. However, most of the activities in these lessons consist of grammar and vocabulary practice and there is only one writing activity, in which the learners are instructed to "Use as much language from these pages as you can" (e.g. p. 143). Interestingly there are no examples of skills or strategy training in the writing lessons or elsewhere.

Taking the example of teaching reading skills, Masuhara (2013) questions the feasibility and value of teaching skills and strategies:

Reading is a complex operation, which could involve many potential skills / strategies. Each skill or strategy may involve a number of subskills and sub-strategies. Take an example of the commonly recognized strategy of "guessing the meaning of an unknown word" … possible strategic options include: identifying parts of speech of the word, analyzing morphological components of the word, making use of any related phrases or relative clauses in the nearby context, analyzing the relationships between the surrounding clauses and sentences, etc. The list is far from complete and those listed are strategies related only to vocabulary. In addition, learners might need grammar-related strategies, discourse-related strategies, strategies solving ambiguity by inferencing, etc. The difficulty a learner might face in reading could be any combinations of various skills / strategies. Materials writers have to predict and choose the major ones but there is no guarantee that their selections are the ones each individual needs.

(Masuhara, 2013, p. 375)

Many EFL curricula all around the world are still based on grammar-based language syllabuses. However, with the emphasis on communication across different cultures, pragmatic competence for communicative interaction is sometimes added in line with the competency-based Common European Framework. Adding a skills and strategy inventory would be likely to make the already massive syllabus even larger.

There may also be language level prerequisites to strategy instruction. Based on their 8-week strategy training in reading with 89 Japanese university female preintermediate / intermediate students, Masuhara, Kimura, Fukada, and Takeuchi (1996) speculate that the apparent positive results in L1 strategy teaching may be due to the fact that successful L1 readers are able to shift their attention to efficient reading strategies because bottom-up processing is automatized. High scorers on the pretest in the Masuhara et al. (1996) studies with Japanese EFL learners tended to welcome the strategy training whereas the low and middle scorers found the extra metacognitive attention taxing to their language processing load during the reading process. Masuhara et al. suspect that strategy training may cause cognitive overload and interfere with the reading process in the case of L2 learners who still require conscious attention for bottom-up processing. They observe that the majority of L2 learners are tackling two things at a time: processing language and constructing meaning of the content. Strategy training imposes a third cognitive load: monitoring the use and control of strategies. The verbal protocol data of L2 learners revealed that they were paying more attention to metacognitive processing than to the meaning construction that is the whole point of reading. The struggles experienced by low to middle scorers may be due to the limited capacity of working memory (Shell et al., 2010; Wen, 2016).

Masuhara (2013) argues that:

> The efficacy of the Skills / Strategies Approaches solely depends on the premise that the conscious training will eventually transfer to become subconscious skills. If a person learns consciously how to play tennis well, will (s)he become a good tennis player? Perhaps, if only (s)he has enough experience of playing tennis. The majority of procedural skills are learned subconsciously just as the majority of cognitive skills are.

(Masuhara, 2013, p. 375)

The literature on skills and strategies we have surveyed does not seem to include extensive discussion of how skills and strategies should be incorporated into curricula or of a suitable methodology for skills / strategy instruction that is in line with current understanding of language learning theories. If skills / strategy instruction means that an inventory of pre-selected skills / strategies is taught and discussed one by one followed by practice, then the methodology seems to remain as P(resentation), P(ractice) and additional communicative P(roduction), which seems to have very little support these days from SLA researchers. After a certain period of training of skills / strategies, learners may be able to demonstrate automatized communication of the skills / strategies that were taught and practiced. What happens if the situation requires unpractised sets of skills / strategies, which is more the case in real communication?

There is another vital aspect of learning, which is often missing in strategy research—the learners' affect and motivation, which, Masuhara (2016) argues strongly, lies at the very core of learning based on findings in brain studies. The aforementioned Masuhara et al. (1996) used the pretest→ 8-week treatment → posttest design to compare the effects of strategy training and extensive reading. Both groups' respective improvement was statistically significant in terms of the mean scores of differences between pre-tests and post-tests. Therefore both interventions (i.e. strategy and extensive reading treatments) seem to be beneficial. Interestingly, the extensive reading group's mean scores increased much more than the strategy group. The difference of mean scores between the two groups was not statistically significant but the remarkable differences were in the qualitative data. All the high, middle, and low scorers in the extensive reading group reported that they enjoyed the 90-minute once-per-week free voluntary reading. A lot of them reported that they were pleasantly surprised that they could actually manage to read extensively without the teacher's guidance and that they felt more confident in their capabilities. The positive association between reading and pleasure seemed to provide an incentive for future autonomous reading according to the feedback data submitted at the end. A follow-up study could have provided additional verification of their findings. Krashen (1991, p. 409; 2004) argues that reading is another source of comprehensible input, which stimulates language acquisition. He argues against scholars who assume that skills must first be taught directly and are made "automatic" by reading. He claims that genuine reading for meaning is far more valuable than workbook exercises and that "it is the source of 'skills.'"

Though we have doubts about the value of skills and of strategy training (despite including such training in some of our coursebooks) we do acknowledge that "teaching" easily applied communication strategies such as coining, circumlocution and asking for help whilst communicating can be useful. Only last night we heard the Liverpool FC manager, Jurgen Klopp, say in a television interview, "wet heat … what's it called?" "Humidity?", offered the interviewer. "Yes, humidity," responded a grateful Klopp. And we have taught communication strategies to students who have then managed to buy socks by asking for "gloves for hands" and communicate their father's occupation by saying "He's a customer at the airport." In both cases, like Jurgen Klopp, they also managed to elicit the word they were searching for from their interlocutors. There is research evidence of the value of teaching communication strategies, something that very few coursebooks do. For example, Moazen, Kafipour, and Soori (2016) report the beneficial effects of teaching an experimental group communication strategies in addition to teaching them coursebook based lessons that were identical to those taught to the control group at a university in Iran—though we should note that the main benefit reported was an increased student perception of the value of communication strategies rather than necessarily an increased use of them.

Language Teaching Must Go On?

Though influential, "the communicative approach" and the exploration of skills and strategies did not seem to have dramatically affected grammar-based curricula globally. The literature we have looked at questions if skills and strategy training can directly contribute to language teaching. In fact, "learning about learning" in strategy training could take away the time in the curriculum in which the learners actually spend time listening, speaking, reading, and writing. Traditions and the face validity of the structure-based syllabus go hand in hand with assessment and examinations. The awareness of the importance of lexis has attracted a lot of attention due to findings in corpus studies (e.g. Sinclair, 2004; McCarthy, O'Keeffe, & Walsh, 2010) since the 2000s. Skills teaching of the four modes of communication still continues to feature though alongside grammar and lexis in syllabuses (see for example the content map of any coursebook and an analysis of content maps of currently used global coursebooks in Chapter 8 of this book). Note that, due to logistical reasons, listening and speaking tend not to be tested in many country-level high-stake examinations. This has caused a negative washback effect on local coursebooks and on classrooms in such countries, especially in EFL situations. The heading of this section mentions "language teaching." Our main concern is how learners can LEARN best to become able to listen, speak, read and write in a target language and how materials can facilitate such learning processes.

Towards Unification of Current Thinking in Different Strands of Disciplines for Developing Materials for the Four Skills

While discussions and debates were taking place in relation to the efficacy of skills / strategy training in the latter half of the twentieth century, we are now witnessing relevant theoretical developments in different fields (e.g. discourse analysis, corpus linguistics, second language acquisition, English as an international language / global English, psychology, neuroscience).

We would like to explore how current thinking from different strands can be fed into developing optimal materials for the four modes of communication (i.e. listening, speaking, reading, writing) that are both theoretically valid and practically useful. First, we would like to discuss convergent factors that influence our planning for developing materials for all four skills. Before our discussion, we would like to provide a classroom scenario of L2 listening to make our discussion more concrete.

Does This Sound Familiar?

"Teacher, the tape is too fast and I can't catch the words" (a quote by Jing Erl—a pseudonym—provided by Renandya and Farrell, 2011, p. 52). Based on our experience of observing numerous classes on consultancies and whilst working with teachers and postgraduate students from all around the globe, we think that Renandya and Farrell (2011) capture a familiar reality of EFL listening classes in Asia and elsewhere.

We suspect that Jing Erl is learning English in a context in which most, if not all, the learners have very few or no opportunities to listen or interact meaningfully face to face with speakers of the target language inside or outside the classroom. The teachers, parents and students seem to still, consciously or subconsciously, buy into the "perfect native-like English" myth as an ultimate target. Consequently, teachers feel that their pronunciation is not good enough so they rely on the native-speaker tape (or the affordable equivalent CD, DVD or web link). The use of tapes in class means that learners act as overhearers of whoever is talking on the audio materials (one of the most difficult subskills of all). In such a situation, learners do not know the context of the talk or have a purpose for listening. They do not have control of the flow of the conversation except for asking the teacher to pause or let them listen to the tape again as Jing Erl did. What is worse is that the learners know that what follows after listening will be Q & A, gap filling, or true or false questions that will test their understanding of discrete sections of the recorded text and they are thus unwilling to tolerate any ambiguity. The teacher is also likely to nominate students to report their answers, a potential face-losing occasion for students who are not confident. Stress and anxiety mount and effective understanding is almost impossible for many students (including us when we were trying to learn a number of foreign languages).

Convergent Factor 1: Beliefs and Myths about the Native Speaker Model and their Consequences

The "native-speaker myth" still seems to persist among teachers, learners, parents and other stakeholders (e.g. government officials, syllabus designers, inspectors, decision makers in schools, materials developers, publishers). The assumptions are that:

- "Native speaker performance provided in the materials" is the ideal and that the learners should become able to comprehend, simulate and perform likewise.
- Listening to or reading non-native speakers' English, including that produced by teachers and learners, could have detrimental effects on learning (e.g. bad pronunciation, grammatical mistakes, bad style). For example, we have just received an e-mail from a researcher in Iran reporting concerns that the absence of native-speaker teachers of English is leading to the development of a variety of Iranian pidgin English.

Not widely known is the fact that "The native speaker performance on the tape" is likely to be the result of actors reading out in a recording studio the scripts of written dialogues or monologues. Analyses of spoken English reveal distinctive differences between written English and spoken English (e.g. Carter & McCarthy, 2006; O'Keeffe, McCarthy, & Carter, 2007). Materials writers and publishers attempt to incorporate some of the typical features of authentic real-life spoken interactions but comparison of coursebook interactions and authentic conversations has revealed marked differences (e.g. Angouri, 2010).

The bias toward "certain varieties of native-speaker English" also seems rife (see Kirkpatrick, 2010 for the varieties and nature of use in World Englishes). International high-stake examinations may contribute in re-enforcing such a bias. Governments and employers may still favor certain types of "native or native-like" teachers.

What is significant is that, as a result, teachers feel that their English is not good enough and tend to rely heavily on the use of tapes or affordable equivalents (e.g. CD, DVD, YouTube). Teachers are also aware of the expectations of learners, parents and other stakeholders. Barker (2011) reports how he initially faced strong resistance from Japanese university students when he tried to persuade them to speak in English with their peers in and out of class as members of an English club. They confided to him that they did not want to listen to their peers because they feared that they would pick up "bad English" and that they felt strange speaking English when they could converse better in Japanese. Criticisms against pair or group work as part of communicative approaches or task-based approaches include similar arguments. It seems to us that the argument that "non-native speaker's English" contaminates learning cannot explain the fact that the emphasis on native speaker English since the audiolingual method era in the 1960s has not prevented learners from having accents or making grammatical mistakes.

Meanwhile, SLA researchers emphasize that language acquisition requires motivated exposure to rich, relevant, and meaningful input as well as abundant opportunities for meaning negotiation in order for language acquisition to take place (e.g. Ellis, 2016a; Gass & Mackey, 2012; Long, 2015; see also Tomlinson, 2011b; Tomlinson, 2013b; Tomlinson, 2016 for discussion connecting SLA with materials development). The "native-speaker" myth seems to hush the teachers and learners in relation to "the four skills" even though the teachers and learners *are* the unrecognized best resources for such interactions vital for language acquisition. The Japanese university students who did regularly use English in and out of class in Barker (2011) made marked progress not only in relation to confidence and in motivation to speak but also in producing longer and richer utterances and in holding turns in English.

Convergent Factor 2: Process and Product-Based Approaches

The distinction between process and product-based instruction is often made, especially in relation to so-called receptive skills (i.e. listening and reading). Most of the processes in listening and reading happen as mental operations that are not amenable to observation. Therefore, researchers have to measure the success of comprehension (i.e. the product) indirectly by looking at the scores of comprehension tests (e.g. comprehension questions, gap filling, true or false). Researchers also use verbal protocols (e.g. introspection, think aloud) as probes to uncover some of the invisible mental processes. Verbal protocols are known to be vulnerable and to result in fragmented and contradictory findings. Thinking aloud during the process is supposed to capture some parts of the ephemeral internal processes but, as Littlejohn (2008, p. 73) comments, "As one wit recently commented, it may be akin to trying to understand the processes of digestion by asking people to talk while eating."

Materials for teaching receptive skills tend to rely on "testlike activities" (see evaluations of listening materials in Ableeva and Stranks, 2013; Hill and Tomlinson, 2013; Mishan and Timmis, 2015; Santos, 2015; of reading materials in Maley and Prowse, 2013; Masuhara, 2013; Timmis and Mishan, 2015; of writing materials in Hyland, 2013; Timmis and Mishan, 2015; and of speaking materials in Bao, 2013; Norton, 2015; Timmis and Mishan, 2015). Consult the references above also for examples of and suggestions for principled good practice as well as Al-Busaidi and Tindle (2010) for a critique of an innovative in-house textbook for developing writing skills, Mackey, Ziegler, and Bryfonski (2016) for a research-based advocacy of task-based approaches to stimulate production skills, and Tomlinson (2011b) for suggestions for helping learners develop visualization skills for reading.

Materials tend to use activities that are likely to involve the target skills (e.g. putting pictures in a correct sequence to see if learners can follow instructions; asking the learners to summarize the speaker's / writer's opinion to see if they are able to infer what is not obvious in a listening / reading text). These common activities are focused on the *product* of listening or reading (thus they are sometimes called product-based approaches). If the answers are correct then we assume listening or reading was successful. The fact that product-based tests can be created easily may explain why they dominate the majority of skills activities. There is an inherent mechanism of product-based listening and reading activities becoming tests for "perfect comprehension." Going back to the listening class scenario and Jing Erl, her worry that she is not catching the words seems to testify to this consequence.

The problem with product-based approaches is that learners do not normally receive any feedback on what caused misunderstandings nor support for how they can be helped in their future attempts. The product-based approaches also tend to overlook the very fact that, in real life listening or reading, we do not listen or read intensively to get "correct answers." Instead, we have intended goals for listening or reading, and we achieve a sufficient interpretation based on our own personality and past experience necessary for the goals to be achieved. For example, we would read a magazine article differently from how we read a medical diagnosis sent by a specialist.

Process-based approaches, on the other hand, pay attention to the processes that listeners / readers go through and try to support them prior to, while and after listening or reading. There are many suggestions how such help could be offered. Goh (2010) and Vandergrift and Goh (2012) advocate encouraging learners' autonomy in becoming strategic listeners / readers. Goh (2010), for example, offer sequences in listening involving self-appraisal and self-regulation all through listening. Field (2008, 2012) suggests how conventional product-approaches can be modified to include stages of reflection and discussion and repeated listening. He also makes a strong case in relation to the difficulties of decoding in listening and suggests that diagnostic instruction should help learners with the bottom-up decoding process. McDonough, Shaw, and Masuhara (2013) survey the major publications on the four skills and provide lists of pre-, while- and post-activities that are likely to help the learners.

Convergent Factor 3: The L1 Acquisition Order of the Four Skills—Listening is the Most Fundamental of all the Skills!

Most of the literature on methodology and materials for skills instruction treats the four skills separately (e.g. Harwood, 2010; Burns and Richards, 2012; Tomlinson, 2013a, b; Mishan and Timmis, 2015) and few add an integrated skills chapter (e.g. McDonough et al., 2013). The sequence in which the four skills are presented seems to be either following the categorization of "receptive skills versus productive skills" or "spoken versus written."

We would like to present a new angle and strongly argue that the listening skill deserves much more attention as the fundamental skill that supports the other skills. Let us explain by looking at what we understand about the listening process, at a comparison of how the development of listening skills takes place in the L1 and the L2, and at the nature of real-life listening texts.

The Listening Process

Vandergrift (2007), in his overview of listening research and pedagogy, comments that:

> L2 listening remains the least researched of all four language skills. This may be due to its implicit nature, the ephemeral nature of the acoustic input, and the difficulty in accessing the processes. In order to teach L2 listening more effectively, teachers need a richer understanding of the listening process. A narrow focus on the right answer to comprehension questions (product) does little to help students understand and control the processes leading to comprehension. Listening

is often perceived by language learners as the most difficult language skill to learn … and, consequently, can become a source of anxiety for L2 learners …

(Vandergrift, 2007, p. 191)

Such views are shared by various researchers on listening (Rost, 2005; Field, 2008; Goh, 2010; Field, 2012; Vandergrift & Goh, 2012; Goh & Aryadoust, 2016). Field (2008 and also earlier publications) argues for the significance of the decoding process (often called bottom-up processing) which has been overlooked in the fields of researching and teaching listening.

From a neuroscientific point of view, there seems to be consensus in that listening is the very foundation of all the other skills in the L1. Thousands of years of evolution have genetically programmed the human brain to acquire spoken languages. "Written language must stand on the shoulder of oral language …" explains Tallal (2003) based on neuroscientific evidence. Tallal (2003) calls the brain an "experience-dependent learning machine." She describes how the brain is programmed to process the sensory world, turn that into phonological representations, and turn those into syllables, words and phrases, and ultimately allow us to develop a written code, which is the orthography or letters that go with those sounds. Babies are known to recognize some significant speech sounds even before birth and children tune in to spoken language in their environment (see Masuhara, 2007 for a comparison of L1 and L2 acquisition).

Comparison of Learning Skills in L1 and L2

Masuhara (2007), in her investigation of reading skills, finds a stark contrast in her comparison between L1 acquisition and L2 simultaneous learning of all four skills.

L1 children are genetically programed to acquire aural / oral abilities but this does require a lot of nurturing. In fact they spend 4 to 5 years, establishing the necessary neural networks through an incredible amount of gradual exposure, time, and resources involving both *bottom-up processing* (i.e. perceptive processing from phoneme to syntactic and semantic chunks) and *top-down processing* (i.e. meaning construction combining existing knowledge in the brain with incoming information). N.B. The processing is considered to be interactive and parallel and not linear, reflecting the parallel processing of neural networks in the brain (Gazzaniga, Ivery, & Mangun, 2013).

Healthy, normal child development is encouraged by affective and cognitive stimulus and a sense of security and pleasure. L1 learners have control over the interaction and negotiation of meaning that takes place.

By the time L1 children begin formal education in which reading and writing starts, they have established the neural connections to:

- process rapidly successive acoustic changes in incoming speech and recognize the phonological constituents such as phonemes, phonological chunks (e.g. syllables, words, lexical bundles) and prosodic features of utterances (e.g. rhythm, pitch, tone, stress);
- connect sound-meaning relationships with pragmatic coloring (e.g. automatized recognition of words, lexical bundles and formulaic expressions; understanding implied messages);
- recognize 4,000–5,000 aural / oral words (Nation & Waring, 1997);

- make use of intuitive knowledge of communicative syntax (see Cullen, 2012 for discussion of the difference between traditional sentence based grammar and communicative grammar);
- make conscious use of strategies only when they find difficulty in automatic processing.

They acquire such abilities in an environment in which they have plenty of proficient users around to help them negotiate meaning in real-life communications that are vital for life sustenance and development. What is most significant is the fact that, in L1, there is a fundamental language acquisition period through aural / oral modes! On the basis of more or less automatized aural / oral abilities that do not tax the limited capacity of working memory in learning, orthography (e.g. graphemes) and reading and writing conventions are gradually learned after children start formal education in primary schools.

In Japanese secondary schools for 13–15 year olds, on the other hand, Masuhara (2007) reports:

> In the L2 formal learning context, many non-native EFL teachers prefer to lecture in Japanese to a large class about vocabulary or grammar knowledge of English. In the worst cases, audiotapes are probably the only source of authentic one-way input. Also frequent testing features heavily in L2 instruction, which could nurture negative association when learning L2 language and reading.
>
> (Masuhara, 2007, p. 24)

N.B. English became a compulsory subject in the fifth and sixth grades for 10–12 year old children in Japanese primary schools in 2011.

When and how do L2 learners receive instruction in "the four skills"? Do they receive the time, resources, support or affective reassurance to establish the necessary neural networks for a new language that L1 toddlers get prior to reading and writing being introduced? Judging from Jing Erl's request in Renandya and Farrell (2011), she is not likely to have acquired the automatic phonological segmentation prerequisite for meaning-focused fluent listening, speaking, reading and writing.

Masuhara (2007) reports that L2 learners often resort to compensatory measures by employing conscious cognitive strategies and relying on top-down processing (see Field, 2004; Farrell and Mallard, 2006 in relation to French learners' invariable use of strategies across the different proficiency groups). She speculates that L2 learners may be making use of available mental resources in the brain that they have developed in the L1 to compensate for the lack of L2 automatized language processing ability.

Convergent Factor 4: Explicit Learning and Implicit Learning

We notice that teachers receive conflicting advice from experts. On the one hand, extensive reading or free voluntary reading is highly recommended as it is said to enhance the likelihood of language acquisition and the development of skills (e.g. Krashen, 2004; Maley, 2008; Maley & Prowse, 2013). Experts argue for holistic learning approaches involving affective engagement for the development of reading skills. "Learning by doing" is advocated by experiential learning proponents (e.g. Kolb, 1984), and constructivists (e.g. Liu & Matthews, 2005) encourage inductive approaches.

On the other hand, teachers hear about how important it is to consciously practice skills until they are automatized (e.g. DeKeyser, 2015; Johnson, & Jackson, 2006) and how strategy training instruction (Oxford, 2011b; Vandergrift & Goh, 2012) will help learners become autonomous and strategic. The skill and strategy proponents may also recommend diagnostic evaluation, coaching of useful metacognitive awareness strategies and practicing control.

Beneath the surface differences lie fundamentally different views about learning. Han and Finneran (2014) explain the differences:

> Ever since Krashen (1977, 1981, 1982) explicitly hypothesized that adult second language (L2) learners have two independent paths for developing ability in an L2, namely, subconscious acquisition and conscious learning, a spirited debate has ensued among researchers over whether or not L2 learners develop one or two knowledge systems, explicit and / or implicit, and what role consciousness partakes in that process. Following Paradis (2009), explicit knowledge is synonymous with metalinguistic knowledge, neurolinguistically subserved by declarative memory, which contrasts with implicit knowledge, neurolinguistically subserved by procedural memory.
>
> The two types of knowledge also differ putatively in (a) that explicit knowledge is open to introspection, but implicit knowledge is not, and (b) that use of explicit knowledge is deliberate and intentional, but use of implicit knowledge is effortless and non-intentional.
>
> (Hulstijn, 2005)

> To date, SLA researchers have remained divided in their views on the relationship between explicit and implicit knowledge, with three vying positions persisting: the non-interface, the strong-interface, and the weak interface. By "interface," it is often meant that there is a connection or overlap between the two types of knowledge.
>
> (Han & Finneran, 2014, pp. 370–371)

In Krashen's view (1982), language learning is too complex to be explained or learned explicitly. For example, can we explain prosodic features (e.g. intonation, stress) that are highly context dependent? Even if the learners understood some elements, will they be using such explicit declarative knowledge naturally in their performance? Second language acquisition researchers agree that the majority of learning takes place in an implicit manner (Ellis, 2005; Ellis, 2016a, b). Note that explicit teaching of discrete items or in the form of error correction is very different from the explicit learning that SLA researchers talk about (see Ellis, 2016b) in which various approaches are used to raise the awareness of learners in terms of improving effective language use or strategies in learner performance. In this sense, current thinking seems to discourage blind insistence of teaching discrete knowledge of vocabulary (see O'Keeffe, 2012 for recommendations), grammar (see Cullen, 2012) or strategies in product-based instruction.

There are promising studies on how exactly explicit learning interacts with implicit learning and the role of consciousness and working memory (e.g. Yang & Li, 2012; Wen, 2016). There are also interdisciplinary efforts as Shell et al. (2010) put it:

In education, the words theory and model imply conjecture. In science, these same words imply something that is a testable explanation of phenomena able to predict outcomes of experiments. This book presents a model of learning that the authors offer in the sense of scientists rather than educators. Conjecture implies that information is incomplete, and so it surely is with human learning. On the other hand, we assert that more than enough is known to sustain a "scientific" model of learning. This book is not a review of the literature. Instead, it is a synthesis. Scholars and many teachers likely have heard much if not most or even all of the information we use to develop the unified learning model. What you have not read before is a model putting the information together …

(Shell et al., 2010, p. v)

What the Literature Says About Materials for Skills Development

There is a massive literature on skills development but not much on materials for facilitating it. However, some recent books on materials development do include chapters on materials for L2 skills development. For example, in Harwood (2010) there are chapters on innovative approaches to developing materials for reading, for writing, for listening and for speaking, most of them favoring process- rather than product-based approaches. Tomlinson (2013a) includes a section in which chapters focus on materials development for one of the four skills, critique typical materials, and make suggestions for principled good practice. In Harwood (2014), Freeman (2014) provides a detailed critique of the use of different types of reading comprehension questions in current coursebooks but does not question the tendency of coursebooks to test the product of the students' reading of a text rather than to provide a rich experience of reading or suggest ways in which the learners could learn from and improve their process of reading. Also in Harwood (2014), Dixon et al. (2014) research textbooks for training teachers to teach reading and seem to favor an explicit strategy training approach. Mishan & Timmis (2015) gives more attention to materials development for "the four skills" than most books do and includes a chapter on materials to develop reading and listening skills and a chapter on materials to develop speaking and writing skills. Although they have separated the skills for focused attention they stress that they would advocate an approach to "teaching language skills, operating within prevailing pedagogies (communicative, task-based) all tending towards integrated and multi-skilled instructional models" (p. 99). This is an approach that is advocated and discussed in detail in McDonough et al. (2013).

A recent publication that contains separate chapters on the different skills is Renandya and Widodo (2016). What is distinctive about this book is a research-supported emphasis on learners using the skills in order to further develop their ability to use them rather than being advised how to develop them, a preference for learners using different skills at the same time (e.g. simultaneous reading and listening in Renandya and Jacobs, 2016, and in Chang, 2016), a focus on the value of extensive experience of using the skills, and a much greater emphasis on extensive listening and extensive viewing than in most other publications.

It is noticeable that nearly all the contributions to the literature referred to above focus on particular skills in isolation. This probably reflects the approach, which still prevails in coursebooks, of including in every unit a section in which the exercises and activities focus on a particular skill. We have just looked at six global coursebooks currently used around the world to teach intermediate level young adults. They are all dominated by grammar and vocabulary practice activities, they all separate the skills, though *Global intermediate* (Clandfield & Robb Benne, 2011), for example, does have some sections labelled "Reading and Listening" (e.g. p. 68), and they all make use of skills activities to provide further experience and practice of target language points (*Face2Face intermediate* (Redston & Cunningham, 2007) even has sections labeled "Reading and Vocabulary" and "Reading and Grammar"). All the books seem to use a product approach in which students are tested on their comprehension of texts or their immediate use of the vocabulary or structure introduced in the unit. None of them gives advice on skills development or invites students to reflect on their performance. In contrast some locally published coursebooks focus on skills development rather than language learning. For example, *English access 2* (Singh, 2011)—like many other books published for Singapore schools—has four substantial sections in each unit on skills development and only one on "Language in Action" (i.e. grammar and vocabulary). It devotes a lot of space to teaching strategies, for example, predicting events in a narrative, skimming for main ideas, scanning for details, reading a short story, and categorizing details in Theme 3.

Our Recommendations on Developing Materials for the Four Modes of Communication

1. For beginners, provide rich, recycled, meaningful and comprehensible input through extensive listening as the foundation for speaking, reading and writing. Tomlinson (2001) offers an extensive discussion and suggests ways of making a smooth transition from an aural / oral phase to skillful reading. Hill and Tomlinson (2013) provide lots of examples of effective and feasible activities. Total Physical Response and Total Physical Response Plus (Tomlinson, 1994) provide ample opportunity for aural learning. L1 reading acquisition literature recommends the use of rhymes, songs, and games. Similar approaches for L2 learners could be fun, provided that the content is made suitable for L2 learners' cognitive levels. Listening to stories and participating in drama would be another effective avenue to explore (Park, 2010).

2. Create situations in which learners need and want to listen to (and use) the target language more outside the classroom. Just as L1 babies and toddlers need more than 4 years of willing exposure in order for them to become able to segment the speech stream and make meaning, L2 learners need a massive amount of motivated listening. Class hours are hardly enough. Discuss with learners how to find ways of increasing meaningful, enjoyable and sustainable extensive listening and reading. Our recommendations include an extensive listening library with cassettes, CDs, DVDs, and English social clubs in which learners only speak in English (e.g. Barker, 2011).

3. Provide engaging opportunities for exposure to authentic and meaningful language in use. Rather than passively listening to strangers' dialogues or monologues about their hobbies, ambitions or anecdotes on a CD Rom or DVD, live interactions would provide much more engaging opportunities for exposure to authentic and meaningful language in use. Task-based approaches or projects that require clear real-life outcomes (not language practice!) would provide a clear target and focus for learner interaction. If a video of a surprising invention is available, teachers could let the

learners watch it. The learners could then be asked to plan a commercial presentation of the invention to perform. The preparation would involve learners' repeated viewing and listening of the video, interaction within the group, watching and analyzing successful commercials, writing scripts, rehearsals with a clear real-life purpose and audience, working on content and then focusing on accuracy with the help of peers and teachers. The actual commercial would be a group performance. Masuhara (2015) provides a sequence of task activities that involve the four skills plus their rationales (see Chapter 11 for a summary). Van den Branden (2006) reports actual cases of task-based language teaching from primary to tertiary, as well as of task-based assessment and teacher development.

4. Make use of pedagogic approaches in which "the four skills" are integrated. A number of approaches that are increasingly used involve integration rather than separation of skills. For example, text-driven approaches (Tomlinson, 2013c) involve the learners engaging in thinking and discussion activities prior to experiencing listening to or reading a potentially engaging text, which they respond to by articulating their personal reactions and then by producing texts of their own. Other approaches in which "the four skills" are integrated include scenario approaches, in which learners prepare for and then perform in contextualized interactions in which they do not know what their interactant is going to say (e.g. di Pietro, 1987); task-based approaches in which a written, spoken or audio-visual text drives communication tasks (e.g. Tomlinson, 2017); CLIL approaches in which other subjects are taught in the target L2 (e.g. Coyle, Hood, & Marsh, 2010), and comprehension-based approaches in which the learners start by listening and gradually move onto reading, writing and speaking when they are ready (e.g. Barnard, 2007). Unfortunately very few global coursebooks follow any of these approaches and most achieve face validity by having a separate section in every unit on each of the four skills. Each skills section is typically brief, training or even advice is rarely given, and the main objective usually seems to provide extra practice of the main grammar and / or vocabulary teaching points of the unit. The listening and reading texts usually feature examples of target structures and vocabulary and the learners are usually told to use target structures, words or expressions in the speaking and writing activities (e.g. when doing a writing activity in Unit 6 of *The big picture intermediate* (Goldstein, 2012) the learners are told to "Use expressions from 5a where possible)."

5. Make sure that students have resources available to enable them to do as much listening, reading, speaking and writing as possible in relation to topics, themes, genres and text types that interest and relate to them. Ultimately, the ability to read confidently, fluently, and effectively develops gradually from engaged experience of reading. Experience is a prerequisite for listening, speaking and writing too and so the main aim of materials and of teachers should be to provide ample experience of reading, writing, listening and speaking (ideally in situations where the "skills" are integrated). Typically the coursebook does not (and cannot) provide enough experience and so supplementary experiential materials need to be provided by publishers, teachers need to develop resources and provide opportunities and students need to be encouraged to look for opportunities themselves to listen to, speak, read, and write the target language outside the classroom. See, for example, Renandya and Farrell (2011) for extensive listening resources and Tomlinson (2013b) and Pinnard (2016) for suggestions for helping learners to experience the target language in use outside the classroom.

6. Do not use materials to teach language and skills at the same time. Most course-books make use of their skills sections to introduce, reinforce or provide practice in the structures and / or lexis taught in the unit. For example, in Unit 9.1 of *Speakout intermediate* (Clare & Wilson, 2011), the grammar teaching point, the third conditional, dominates all the skills sections. It is a salient structure in the reading passages, the students are prompted to use it in the speaking activity, it is the dominant structure in the model text for the writing section, and it is expected to be used in the essay-writing activity. So, the whole sub-unit, and not just the grammar section, is driven by a Presentation, Practice, Production approach to the teaching of a grammatical point. This seems to be the pattern throughout this and other current global coursebooks (maybe that is what sells coursebooks), though in *Speakout intermediate* a few sub-units (e.g. 9.3) are driven by a function rather than a grammar point. In our experience this continued focus on grammar or vocabulary might aid the learning of the language teaching point but it is unlikely to contribute to the development of the skills as learners tend to prioritize the teaching (and therefore testing) points. If, for example, a reading text is flooded with highlighted exemplars of a target structure, the learners are likely to focus their processing energy on those exemplars rather than to read the text for a global understanding of its meaning (especially if the comprehension questions focus on that structure too).

7. Help students to make use of the skills of sensory imaging and of the use of the inner voice that they have already developed in the use of their L1. When using one or more of "the four skills" in the L1 we typically visualize, smell, listen, touch, and taste in our minds and we make use of our inner voice to repeat and to "discuss" what we listen to and read as well as to prepare what we are going to say and write. For example, if we are going to describe a market we visited in Nigeria we will see mental pictures of the market, we will feel the humidity, we will smell the odors we remember and we will mentally recreate our affective responses to the visit. We will also use our inner voice to prepare what we want to write or say and to monitor what we produce. When reading a story set in a school we are likely to visualize both our own experiences of school and those described in the story, as well as using our inner voice to repeat in our minds what we read on the page and to talk to ourselves, to the writer and to the protagonists about what is happening in the story. Yet in an L2 we do not seem to do this until we are advanced enough to not worry about decoding every word when reading or listening or to not worry too much about always achieving accuracy in our speech and writing. In Japan and Oman we have trained lower intermediate level students to make use of sensory imaging and their inner voice with noticeable increases in confidence, motivation and communicative effectiveness. For discussion of the theories underlying such training and their practical application in imaging and inner voice tasks see Tomlinson & Avila (2007a, b) and Tomlinson (2011b).

8. Make sure that the learners are affectively and cognitively engaged when participating in "skills" activities. Unless the learners are stimulated to feel and to think, the activities are likely to have little impact, to be unmemorable, and to result in shallow processing. See Tomlinson (2013b, 2016) and Chapter 8 in this book for theoretical justifications of this statement.

N.B. Perhaps the most effective type of communication to help learners develop their language skills involves a proficient user of the language talking or writing to an engaged novice, as the proficient user will have to modify their discourse to make it comprehensible. This can be easily achieved by the teacher talking and writing to the learners in the L2 on topics that interest them rather than always instructing them about the L2.

What Do You Think?

1. Do you think skills can be taught or are they best developed through experience? Why?
2. Do you think skills should be focused on separately or in an integrated way? Why?
3. Do you think that teaching strategies to learners helps them to read, listen, write, and speak or does it overload the learners and impede their performance? Why?
4. Do you think that it is beneficial to make use of skills materials to reinforce and practice grammar and lexis? Why?
5. Think back to your experience of learning to use "the four skills" in an L2 you are now proficient in and ask yourself what the main contributors were to the development of your proficiency as a reader, writer, listener, and speaker of that language.
6. Think back to your experience of learning to use "the four skills" in an L2 you have not achieved proficiency in and ask yourself what the main contributors were to your inability to achieve proficiency as a reader, writer, listener, and speaker of that language.
7. What advice would you give to a coursebook writer about helping users of the book to achieve proficiency as a reader, writer, listener, and speaker of the target language.

Tasks

1. Take any coursebook that deals with the "four skills" in separate sections and come up with ideas for revising a unit from the book so that the skills are integrated rather than separated.
2. List learning strategies (if any) which you think are worth "teaching" and then, for each one, think of the best way to "teach" it.
3. List communication strategies (if any) which you think are worth "teaching" and then for each one think of the best way to "teach" it.
4. List ways in which you could encourage learners to read, write, listen to, and speak the target language outside the classroom.

Further Reading

We would recommend the following for developing materials for skills development:

McDonough, J., Shaw, C., & Masuhara, H. (2013). *Materials and methods in ELT* (3rd ed.). Chichester: Wiley.

Mishan, F., & Timmis, I. (2015). *Materials development for TESOL*. Edinburgh: Edinburgh University Press.

Tomlinson, B. (Ed.). (2013). *Developing materials for language teaching* (2nd ed.). London: Bloomsbury.

References

Ableeva, R., & Stranks, J. (2013). Listening in another language—research and materials. In B. Tomlinson (Ed.), *Applied linguistics and materials development* (pp. 199–211). London: Bloomsbury.

Afflerbach, P., Pearson, P. D., & Paris, S. G. (2008). Clarifying differences between reading skills and reading strategies. *The Reading Teacher, 61*(5), 364–373.

Al-Busaidi, S. & Tindle, K. (2010). Evaluating the effect of in-house materials on language learning. In B. Tomlinson & H. Masuhara (Eds.), *Research for materials development in language learning: Evidence for best practice* (pp. 137–149). London: Continuum.

Alderson, J. C. (2000). *Assessing reading*. Cambridge: Cambridge University Press.

Anderson, J. R. (1982). Acquisition of cognitive skill. *Psychological Review, 89*(4), 369–406.

Anderson, L. W., & Krathwohl, D. R. (Eds.). (2001). *A taxonomy for learning, teaching, and assessing: A revision of Bloom's taxonomy of educational objectives*. Boston, MA: Allyn & Bacon.

Angouri, J. (2010). Using textbook and real-life data to teach turn taking in business meetings. In N. Harwood (Ed.), *English language teaching materials—theory and practice* (pp. 373–394). Cambridge: Cambridge University Press.

Archibald, A. (2006). Learner strategies: An interview with Steven McDonough. *ELT Journal, 60*(1), 63–70. doi:10.1093/elt/cci083

Bao, D. (2013). Developing materials for speaking skills. In Tomlinson, B. (Ed.), *Developing materials for language teaching* (2nd ed., pp. 407–428). London: Bloomsbury.

Barker, D. (2011). The role of unstructured learner interaction in the study of a foreign language. In S. Menon, & J. Lourdunathan (Eds.), *Readings on ELT materials IV* (pp. 50–71). Petaling Jaya: Pearson Malaysia.

Barnard, E. S. (2007). The value of comprehension in the early stages of the acquisition and development of Bahasa Indonesia by non-native speakers. In B. Tomlinson (Ed.), *Language acquisition and development: studies of first and other language learners* (pp. 187–204). London: Continuum.

Burns, A., & Richards, J. C. (Eds.). (2012). *The Cambridge guide to pedagogy and practice in second language teaching*. Cambridge: Cambridge University Press.

Canale, M., & Swain, M. (1980). Theoretical bases of the communicative approach to second language teaching and testing. *Applied Linguistics, 1*(1), 1–47.

Carter, R., & McCarthy, M. J. (2006). *Cambridge grammar of English: A comprehensive guide to spoken and written English grammar and usage*. Cambridge University Press: Cambridge.

Chang, A. C. S. (2016). L2 listening: In and outside the classroom. In W. A. Renandya & H. P. Widodo (Eds.), *English language teaching today: Linking theory and practice* (pp. 111–126). New York: Springer International.

Clandfield, L., & Robb Benne, R. (2011). *Global intermediate*. Oxford: Macmillan.

Clare, A., & Wilson, J. J. (2011). *Speakout intermediate*. Harlow: Pearson.

Cohen, A. D. (2011). Second language learner strategies. In E. Hinkel (Ed.), *Handbook of research in second language teaching and learning II* (pp. 681–698). New York: Routledge.

Cohen, A. D., & Macaro, E. (Eds.). (2007). *Language learner strategies: Thirty years of research and practice*. Oxford: Oxford University Press.

Coyle, D., Hood, P., & Marsh, D. (2010). *Content and language integrated learning*. Cambridge: Cambridge University Press.

Cullen, R. (2012). Grammar instruction. In A. Burns & J. C. Richards (Eds.), *The Cambridge guide to pedagogy and practice in second language teaching* (pp. 258–266). Cambridge: Cambridge University Press.

DeKeyser, R. M. (1998). Beyond focus on form: Cognitive perspectives on learning and practicing second language grammar. In C. Doughty & J. Williams (Eds.), *Focus on form in classroom second language acquisition* (pp. 42–63). Cambridge: Cambridge University Press.

DeKeyser, R. M. (Ed.). (2007). *Practice in a second language: Perspectives from applied linguistics and cognitive psychology*. New York: Cambridge University Press.

DeKeyser, R. M. (2015). Skill acquisition theory. In B. Van Patten & J. Williams (Eds.), *Theories in second language acquisition. an introduction.* (pp. 94–112). London: Routledge.

Dellar, H. & Walkley, A. (2010). *Outcomes Pre-Intermediate*. Andover, Cengage.

Di Pietro, R. J. (1987). *Strategic interaction: Learning languages through scenarios*. Cambridge: Cambridge University Press.

Dixon, L. Q., Wu, S., Burgess-Brigham, R., Joshi, R. M., Blinks-Cantrell, E., & Washburn, E. (2014). Teaching English reading: What's included in the textbooks of pre-service general education teachers. In N. Harwood (Ed.), (2014). *English language teaching textbooks: Content, consumption, production* (pp. 111–144). Basingstoke: Palgrave Macmillan.

Ellis, G., & Sinclair, B. (1989). *Learning to learn English*. Cambridge: Cambridge University Press.

Ellis, N. C. (2005). *At the interface: Dynamic interactions of explicit and implicit language knowledge. Studies in Second Language Acquisition, 27*(2), 305–352.

Ellis, R. (2016a). Focus on form: A critical review. *Language Teaching Research, 20*(3), 405–428. doi:10.1177/1362168816628627

Ellis, R. (2016b). Language teaching materials as work plans: An SLA perspective. In B. Tomlinson (Ed.), *SLA research and materials development for language learning* (pp. 203–218). Oxon: Routledge.

Farrell, T. S. C., & Mallard, C. (2006). The use of reception strategies by learners of French as a foreign language. *The Modern Language Journal, 90*(3), 338–352.

Field, J. (2004). An insight into listeners' problems: Too much bottom-up or too much top-down? *System, 32*, 363–377.

Field, J. (2008). *Listening in the language classroom*. Cambridge: Cambridge University Press.

Field, J. (2012). Listening instruction. In A. Burns, & J. C. Richards (Eds.), *The Cambridge guide to pedagogy and practice in second language teaching* (pp. 207–217). Cambridge: Cambridge University Press.

Freeman, D. (2014) Reading comprehension questions: The distribution of different types in global EFL textbooks. In N. Harwood (Ed.). (2014). *English language teaching textbooks: Content, consumption, production* (pp. 72–110). Basingstoke: Palgrave Macmillan.

Gass, S. M., & Mackey, A. (Eds.). (2012). *The Routledge handbook of second language acquisition*. Oxford: Routledge.

Gazzaniga, M. S., Ivry, R. B., & Mangun, G. R. (2013). *Cognitive neuroscience—the biology of the mind* (4th ed.). New York: W. W. Norton.

Goh, C. C. M. (2010). Listening as process: Learning activities for self-appraisal and self-regulation. In N. Harwood (Ed.), *English language teaching materials—theory and practice* (pp. 179–206). Cambridge: Cambridge University Press.

Goh, C. C. M., & Aryadoust, V. (2016). Learner listening: New insights and directions from empirical studies. *International Journal of Listening, 30*(1), 1–7. doi:10.1080/10904018.2016.1138689

Goldstein, B. (2012). *The big picture intermediate.* Oxford: Richmond.

Greenall, S., & Swan, M. (1986). *Effective reading.* Cambridge: Cambridge University Press.

Griffiths, C. (2008). *Lessons from good language learners.* Cambridge: Cambridge University Press.

Han, Z., & Finneran, R. (2014). Re-engaging the interface debate: Strong, weak, none, or all? *International Journal of Applied Linguistics, 24*(3), 370–389. doi:10.1111/ijal.12034

Harwood, N. (Ed.). (2010). *English language teaching materials: Theory and practice.* Cambridge: Cambridge University Press.

Harwood, N. (Ed.). (2014). *English language teaching textbooks: Content, consumption, production.* Basingstoke: Palgrave Macmillan.

Hicks, D., & Littlejohn, A. (2003). *Primary colours activity book.* Cambridge: Cambridge University Press.

Hill, D. A. & Tomlinson, B. (2013). Coursebook listening activities. In B. Tomlinson (Ed.), *Developing materials for language learning* (pp. 429–442). London: Bloomsbury.

Hulstijn, J. (2005). Theoretical and empirical issues in the study of implicit and explicit second language learning: Introduction. *Studies in Second Language Acquisition, 27*(2), 129–140.

Hyland, K. (2013). Materials for developing writing skills. In Tomlinson, B. (Ed.), *Developing materials for language teaching* (2nd ed., pp. 391–406). London: Bloomsbury.

Hymes, D. (1972). On communicative competence. In J. B. Pride & J. Holmes (Eds.), *Sopciolinguistics* (pp. 269–293). Harmondsworth: Penguin.

Johnson, K. (1996). *Language teaching and skill learning.* Oxford: Blackwell.

Johnson, K., & Jackson, S. (2006). Comparing language teaching and other-skill teaching: Has the language teacher anything to learn? *System, 34*(4), 532–546. Retrieved from doi:http://dx.doi.org.liverpool.idm.oclc.org/10.1016/j.system.2006.08.002

Kirkpatrick, A. (2010). *The Routledge handbook of world Englishes.* New York: Routledge.

Kolb, D. A. (1984). *Experiential learning: Experience as the source of learning and development.* Englewood Cliffs, NJ: Prentice Hall.

Krashen, S. (1977). Some issues relating to the Monitor Model. In H. D. Brown, C. Yorio & R. Crymes (Eds.), *On TESOL '77: Teaching and learning English as a second language: Trends in research and practice* (pp. 144–158). Washington: TESOL.

Krashen, S. (1981). *Second language acquisition and second language learning.* New York: Pergamon Press.

Krashen, S. (1982). *Principles and practice in second language acquisition.* Oxford: Pergamon Press.

Krashen, S. (1991). The input hypothesis: An update. In J. E. Alatis (Ed.), *Georgetown University round table on languages and linguistics 1991.* Washington DC: Georgetown University Press.

Krashen, S. (2004). *The power of reading* (2nd ed.). Portsmouth, NH: Heinemann.

Littlejohn, A. (2008). Digging deeper: Learners' disposition and strategy use. In G. Cane (Ed.), *Strategies in language learning and teaching* (pp. 68–81). Singapore: RELC.

Littlejohn, A., & Hicks, D. (1998). *Cambridge English for schools.* Cambridge: Cambridge University Press.

Littlewood, W. (1984). *Foreign and second language learning.* Cambridge: Cambridge University Press.

Liu, C. H., & Matthews, R. (2005). Vygotsky's philosophy: Constructivism and its criticisms examined. *International Education Journal, 6*(3), 386–399.

Long, M. H. (2015). *Second language acquisition and task-based language teaching.* Hoboken, NJ: Wiley-Blackwell.

Mackey, A., Ziegler, N., & Bryfonski, L. (2016). In B. Tomlinson (Ed.), *SLA research and materials development for language learning* (pp. 103–118). New York: Routledge.

Maley, A. (2008). Extensive reading: Maid in waiting. In B. Tomlinson (Ed.), *English language learning materials—A critical view* (pp. 133–156). London: Continuum International Publishing Group.

Maley, A., & Prowse, P. (2013). Reading. In B. Tomlinson (Ed.), *Applied linguistics and materials development* (pp. 165–182). London: Bloomsbury.

Masuhara, H. (2007). The role of proto-reading activities in the acquisition and development of effective reading skills. In B. Tomlinson (Ed.), *Language acquisition and development: Studies of learners of first and other languages* (pp. 15–45). London: Continuum.

Masuhara, H. (2013). Materials for developing reading skills. In B. Tomlinson (Ed.), *Developing materials for language teaching* (pp. 365–391). London: Bloomsbury.

Masuhara, H. (2015). "Anything goes" in task-based language teaching materials?—the need for principled materials evaluation, adaptation and development. *The European Journal of Applied Linguistics and TEFL, 2*, 113–127.

Masuhara, H. (2016). Brain studies and materials for language learning. In B. Tomlinson (Ed.), *Second language research and materials development for language learning* (pp. 23–32). New York: Routledge.

Masuhara, H., Kimura, T., Fukada, A., & Takeuchi, M. (1996). Strategy training or / and extensive reading? In T. Hickey & J. Williams (Eds.), *Language, education and society in a changing world* (pp. 263–274). Clevedon: Multilingual Matters.

McCarthy, M., O'Keeffe, A., & Walsh, S. (2010). *Vocabulary matrix—understanding, learning, teaching.* Andover: Heinle Cengage Learning.

McDonough, S. (2012). Review of teaching and researching language learning strategies. *ELT Journal, 66*(2), 253–255.

McDonough, J., Shaw, C., & Masuhara, H. (2013). *Materials and methods in ELT* (3rd ed.). Chichester: John Wiley & Sons, Ltd.

Mishan, F., & Timmis, I. (2015). *Materials development for TESOL.* Edinburgh: Edinburgh University Press.

Moazen, M., Kafipour, R., & Soori, A. (2016). Iranian EFL learners' perception of the use of communication strategies and gender effect. *Pertanika Journal of Social Sciences and Humanities, 24*(3), 1193–1204.

Nation, I. S. P., & Waring, R. (1997). Vocabulary size, text coverage and word lists. In N. Schmitt & M. McCarthy (Eds.), *Vocabulary: Description, acquisition and pedagogy* (pp. 6–19). New York: Cambridge University Press.

Norton, J. (2015). Developing speaking skills: How are current theoretical and methodological approaches represented in coursebooks? *The European Journal of Applied Linguistics and TEFL, 4*(2), 53–72.

Nuttall, C. (1985). Recent materials for the teaching of reading. *ELT Journal, 39*(3), 198–206.

O'Keeffe, A. (2012). Vocabulary instruction. In A. Burns & J. C. Richards (Eds.), *The Cambridge guide to pedagogy and practice in second language teaching* (pp. 236–245). Cambridge: Cambridge University Press.

O'Keeffe, A., McCarthy, M., & Carter, R. (2007). *From corpus to classroom: Language use and language teaching.* Cambridge University Press: Cambridge.

Oxford, R. (2011a). Strategies for learning a second or foreign language. *Language Teaching, 44*(2), 167–180.

Oxford, R. (2011b). *Teaching and researching language learning strategies.* Harlow: Pearson Longman.

Oxford, R. (1990). *Language learning strategies: What every teacher should know.* Boston, MA: Heinle & Heinle, 1990.

Oxford, R., & Burry-Stock, J. A. (1995). Assessing the use of language learning strategies worldwide with the ESL/EFL version of the strategy inventory for language learning (SILL). *System, 23*(1), 1–23. Retrieved from doi:http://dx.doi.org.liverpool.idm.oclc.org/10.1016/0346-251X(94)00047-A

Paradis, M. (2009). *Declarative and procedural determinants of second languages.* Amsterdam: John Benjamins.

Park, H. (2010). Process drama in the Korean EFL secondary classroom: A case study of Korean middle school classrooms. In B. Tomlinson (Ed.), *Research for materials development in language learning* (pp. 155–171). London: Continuum.

Pinnard, L. (2016). Looking outwards: using learning materials to help learners harness out-of-class learning opportunities. *Innovations in language learning and teaching 10*(2), 133–143.

Redston, C., & Cunningham, G. (2007). *Face2Face intermediate.* Cambridge: Cambridge University Press.

Renandya, W. A. & Farrell, T. S. C. (2011). "Teacher the tape is too fast!" Extensive listening in ELT. *ELT Journal, 65*(1), 52–59.

Renandya, W. A., & Jacobs, G. M. (Eds.). (2016). Extensive reading and listening in the L2 classroom. In W. A. Renandya & H. P. Widodo (Eds.), *English language teaching today: Linking theory and practice* (pp. 97–110). New York: Springer International.

Renandya, W. A. & Widodo, H. P. (Eds.). (2016). *English language teaching today: Linking theory and practice.* New York: Springer International.

Richards, J. C., & Rodgers, T. S. (2014). *Approaches and methods in language teaching* (3rd ed.). Cambridge: Cambridge University Press.

Richards, J. C., & Schmidt, R. W. (2010). *Longman dictionary of language teaching and applied linguistics* (4th ed.). Harlow: Longman.

Rost, M. (2005). L2 listening. In E. Hinkel (Ed.), *Handbook of research in second language teaching and learning* (pp. 503–528). Mahwah, NJ: Lawrence Erlbaum Associates.

Santos, D. (2015). Revising listening materials: What remains, what is changed and why. *The European Journal of Applied Linguistics and TEFL, 4*(2), 19–36.

Shell, D. F., Brooks, D. W., Trainin, G., Wilson, K. M., Kauffman, D. F., & Herr, L. M. (2010). *The unified learning model—how motivational, cognitive, and neurobiological sciences inform best teaching practices.* London: Springer.

Sinclair, J. McH. (Ed.). (2004). *Trust the text—Language, corpus and discourse.* New York: Routledge.

Singh, B. (2011). *English access 2.* Singapore: Marshall Cavendish.

Tallal, P. (2003). *Neuroscience, phonology and reading: The oral to written language continuum* [Televised interview conducted by Children of the Code]. Retrieved from http://www.childrenofthecode.org/interviews/tallal.htm

Tomlinson, B. (2000). Beginning to read forever. *Reading in a Foreign Language, 13*(1), 523.

Tomlinson, B. (2001). Materials for TPR. *Folio, 1*(2), 8–10.

Tomlinson, B. (1994). Materials for TPR. *Folio, 1*(2), 8–10.

Tomlinson, B. (Ed.). (2011a). *Materials development in language teaching* (2nd ed.). Cambridge: Cambridge University Press.

Tomlinson, B. (2011b). Seeing what they mean: helping L2 readers to visualize. In B. Tomlinson (Ed.), *Materials development in language teaching* (2nd ed., pp. 357–378). Cambridge: Cambridge University Press.

Tomlinson, B. (Ed.). (2013a). *Developing materials for language teaching* (2nd ed.). London: Bloomsbury.

Tomlinson, B. (2013b). Second language acquisition and materials development. In B. Tomlinson (Ed.), *Applied linguistics and materials development* (pp. 11–29). London: Bloomsbury.

Tomlinson, B. (2013c). Developing principled frameworks for materials development. In B. Tomlinson (Ed.), *Developing materials for language teaching* (pp. 98–118). London: Bloomsbury.

Tomlinson, B. (2016). Achieving a match between SLA theory and materials development. In B. Tomlinson (Ed.), *SLA research and materials development for language learning* (pp. 3–22). New York: Routledge.

Tomlinson, B. (2017). Text-driven approaches to task-based language teaching. *Proceedings of the NILE Conference on Transforming Teaching*, August 2016.

Tomlinson, B., & Avila, J. (2007a). Applications of the research into the roles of audio-visual mental aids for language teaching pedagogy. In B. Tomlinson (Ed.), *Language acquisition and development: studies of first and other language learners* (pp. 82–89). London: Continuum.

Tomlinson, B., & Avila, J. (2007b). Seeing and saying for yourself: the roles of audio-visual mental aids in language learning and use. In B. Tomlinson (Ed.), *Language acquisition and development: studies of first and other language learners* (pp. 61–81). London: Continuum.

Tomlinson, B., & Ellis, R. (1987). *Reading upper intermediate*. Oxford: Oxford University Press.

Van den Branden, K. (Ed.). (2006). *Task-based language education*. Cambridge: Cambridge University Press.

Vandergrift, L. (2007). Recent developments in second and foreign language listening comprehension research. *Language Teaching, 40*, 191–210.

Vandergrift, L., & Goh, C. (2012). *Teaching and learning second language listening: Metacognition in action*. New York: Routledge.

Van der Veer, R., & Valsiner, J. (1991). *Understanding Vygotsky. A quest for synthesis*. Oxford: Blackwell.

Wen, Z. (2016). *Working memory and second language learning: Towards an integrated approach* (1st ed.). Bristol: Channel View Publications.

Williams, E., & Moran, C. (1989). State of the art: Reading in a foreign language. *Language Teaching, 22*(4), 217–228.

Yang, J., & Li, P. (2012). Brain networks of explicit and implicit learning. *Plos One, 7*(8). Retrieved from http://journals.plos.org/plosone/article?id=10.1371/journal.pone.0042993

10

Developing Materials for Young Learners

Introduction

Different researchers have different views as to how old young learners are. In this chapter we are going to follow Bland (2015a) in categorizing young learners as those between the ages of 3 and 12, because 3 year olds are now being taught English as a foreign language (in, for example, China and South Korea) and "there is no sudden cut-off at age ten or eleven with regard to a need for child-centred pedagogy, rich in oral input and child-centred learning" (Bland, 2015a, p. 1).

The development of materials for the teaching of foreign languages to young learners is a distinctive field in a number of ways. It is distinctive in that in the last 20 years there has been a massive increase both in the amount of research dedicated to finding out what does and what does not facilitate the acquisition of a foreign language by young learners and in the number of courses published for young learners. This has been fueled mainly by the increase in the number of countries (mainly in Europe, South Asia and the Far East) that now require primary school pupils to learn a foreign language (usually English) but also by a growing dissatisfaction with the ways in which many young learners are typically taught to learn a language that is of no immediate relevance, value, or interest to them. It is also distinctive in that most of the researchers are focused on what happens in the classroom rather than on the outcomes of "laboratory" experiments designed to confirm the hypotheses of the researchers. Many of the researchers have been primary school teachers themselves and most of them are involved in training primary school teachers either in teacher training colleges, development projects, or universities. They are what we would call researcher / practitioners as opposed to the researcher / academics who dominate many other areas of applied linguistics.

Perhaps the most distinctive feature though is the disparity between what published materials typically ask young learners to do and what researcher / practitioners recommend they should be doing. There are notable exceptions but what published materials typically ask young learners to do is to learn grammar and vocabulary from explicit instructions and drills whereas researcher / practitioners typically do not view such learning as feasible or desirable (see, for example, de Keyser, in press) and recommend that the focus should be on more age realistic and educational goals such as:

- Implicit learning through language experience both inside and outside the classroom (e.g. Enever, 2011; Lefever, 2012; de Keyser, in press).
- Learning holistically.

The Complete Guide to the Theory and Practice of Materials Development for Language Learning, First Edition. Brian Tomlinson and Hitomi Masuhara.
© 2018 John Wiley & Sons, Inc. Published 2018 by John Wiley & Sons, Inc.

- The development of positive attitudes towards the target language and its acquisition.
- Learning both what and how to learn (e.g. see Ellis & Ibrahim, 2016, for 10 pedagogical principles for teaching young learners to learn and Ellis and Ibrahim, 2015, for a detailed discussion of principles and procedures for teaching young learners to learn.

The research-based literature on teaching young learners is elegantly summed up by Read (2015, p. xi) who talks about the importance of "rich exposure to language" and of "Opportunities for natural interaction and meaningful repetition in engaging contexts leading to creative outcomes." She sees "the advantages of such an approach not narrowly in terms of measurable linguistic outcomes but rather in terms of the whole learner and the more elusive social, psychological, cognitive, metacognitive, affective and emotional benefits that underpin children's motivation and learning success." She also makes the significant claim that "Early foreign-language learning is also integrally linked to the development of intercultural understanding, empathy, self-awareness and respect for others, and to broadening children's view of the world." Read is not specifically talking about materials development but for many years we have been recommending the application of this holistic, experiential, humanistic approach to the development and use of materials for young learners. Occasionally our advice has been taken but often it has been opposed by experts and publishers who consider it lacks the face validity required by parents and teachers used to the paradigm of discrete, incremental, and explicit learning. In Vanuatu it was followed on a project in which a set of communicative activities developed by primary school teachers and teacher trainers at a workshop was published by the Ministry of Education (Tomlinson, 1981). The activities were intended as examples for teachers to use and as models for developing their own locally specific activities. "In these activities the pupils are not told what to say and they do not practise particular structures or items of vocabulary. Instead they are put into situations which require them to use spoken English to achieve a particular purpose" (Tomlinson, 1981, p. i). This book helped to transform the classroom from somewhere where meaningless drills were endured to somewhere were meaningful discussions were enjoyed. For example, on approaching a primary school on a small island the loud noise of "We are standing up. We are sitting down. We are standing up" could be heard half a mile away. A few months later this had been replaced by the sound of excited chat, including, in one classroom, 8 year olds making up in pairs a story about The Old Man and the Boy on a small island and in another 10 year olds talking in elementary English about the famous photo of a young girl suffering napalm burns in Vietnam. In Indonesia 12 year olds on the nationwide PKG (By the Teacher for the Teacher) program (Tomlinson, 1990) gained motivation, enjoyment of English, and higher marks on the end-of-year examination by using materials developed by teachers following such experiential approaches as TPR Plus (Tomlinson, 1994a), extensive reading, and language discovery. However, in China we were dropped from one materials development project because our task-based materials did not contain any explicit teaching or grammar drills and we were compromised on a number of others by the insistence that the grammar and vocabulary items specified by the curriculum had to be taught in the sequence they were prescribed.

The Literature

One of many young learner researcher / practitioners we respect for being firmly based in the classroom is Irma-Kaarina Ghosn, who works at the Lebanese

American University in Byblos and conducts her research in the primary schools and refugee camps of Lebanon. We are going to refer to her work extensively because we feel that it serves as an excellent example of good practice in terms of research-based, principled development of materials. There are many other equally principled researcher / practitioners but most of them focus on methodology rather than on materials development (see, for example, many of the chapters in Bland, 2015a).

In Ghosn (2003) she acknowledges that the coursebook "is often the only exposure to English, aside from the teacher, that students receive" (p. 291) and she investigates what teachers and students actually do with their coursebooks in the classroom. She does so by reporting "a non-experimental exploratory study in six primary school classrooms in Lebanon" (p. 292) in which she found both qualitatively and statistically relevant differences between groups following a coursebook-based course (n 78) and groups following a "literature-based course" (n 85) (p. 293). Ghosn provides transcribed examples of the typical interactions from the two different types of groups and concludes from the evidence of her transcriptions of 12 hours of videotaped interactions that:

1. Interactions driven by the coursebook tended to:
    - be focused on accuracy of form (e.g. when students used their own words instead of repeating those in the book teachers tended to correct them);
    - be at word, phrase and sentence level;
    - sound like drills;
    - focus on content that learners will have already shared in their L1 (e.g. "family members, hobbies etc." (p. 296)) or which is of no relevance to the lives of the students (e.g. coin collecting, caring for pets, gardening, the four seasons).
2. Interactions stimulated by reading stories tended to:
    - be "interactive and often carried over several turns" (p, 298);
    - include elaboration and clarification of responses;
    - include student initiated language and content;
    - include negotiation of meaning;
    - show signs of "high motivation level" with students "eagerly waving their hands, bidding for turns" (p. 301).

In her conclusion Ghosn puts forward a proposal that accords with what we typically do—that is, instead of moving from accuracy practice to reading comprehension, start with the reading of a story "to generate discussion and link the content to learners' experiences" (p. 302) and then use "dialogues, literary journals, letters to the characters and so on" (p. 302) for accuracy practice, preferably with the activities selected by the students.

Ghosn has continued her research on the effects of coursebooks in primary classrooms in Lebanon as well as her search for more effective alternatives. For example, in Ghosn (2007) she focuses on the value of using children's literature instead of coursebooks in a 15-week classroom-based experiment with young Arabic speaking children (*n* 140) of ages 9.5–12. The experimental classes received story-based instruction (SBI) once per week whilst the control classes continued with their regular coursebook-based instruction. Ghosn found SBI had a positive influence on the L2 writing of the students in the experimental classes "resulting in longer and more expressive writing with clearer organisation and supporting detail" (Ghosn, 2007, p. 171). The students in the experimental classes also showed in the post-test that they had acquired a broader vocabulary base than those in the experimental classes and that they were capable of using more creative expressions. In Bacha, Ghosn, and McBeath (2008), Ghosn participates in an evaluation of materials used in primary schools in the Middle East and a survey of the research on how they are typically used. The evaluation concluded that while much of the content of global and local coursebooks was potentially interesting, the global coursebooks presented language in unfamiliar contexts and both types of coursebooks featured activities that did "not challenge the learners to negotiate meaning or engage them affectively or cognitively" (Bacha, Ghosn, and McBeath, 2008, p. 286). The survey of coursebook use suggested that the coursebook controlled the classroom, that pre-teaching was dominant, that very often promisingly communicative activities were subverted into meaningless drills and that texts were typically read aloud round the class by the children. In Ghosn (2010) she continued to assert that instruction based on children's literature was more valuable for young learners than that based on coursebooks. She reports the results of a 5-year experiment in four schools in Lebanon in which she eventually compared the vocabulary, grammar, and reading comprehension of 10–11 year old children in classes that had been using literature-based reading anthologies for 5 years with those in classes that had been using global coursebooks. Ghosn thinks the findings that the children in the literature-based classes reached higher levels of vocabulary, grammar, and reading comprehension can be attributed to the fact that they read more texts and longer texts and therefore encountered more concepts and vocabulary and that they encountered language frequently and naturally recycled in by now familiar contexts and were better able to make inferences. She thinks that their gains in vocabulary and background knowledge helped them quickly to become better readers, that this helped them to gain even more vocabulary and background knowledge, and that they were more able to relate to the concepts in the stories than their counterparts were to many of the concepts (for example, pocket money) in the practice exercises in the global coursebooks. Ghosn compares her findings with very similar findings in other reading studies with young learners and, for example, quotes Bernhardt's (2000) conclusion that "extended reading experiences over time with authentic, not grammatically sequenced or altered, texts promoted greatest gains in comprehension over time" (p. 800). Interestingly, Ghosn (2010) concludes by saying that the literature-based approach is probably most effective in monolingual classes in which a teacher who speaks their shared L1 can encourage the children to use their L1 when they are stuck in discussions and can then recast their utterances into the target L2.

In Ghosn (2013a) she reports how it was decided in 2010 that the Lebanese national coursebooks were not suitable for the lower primary-grade Palestinian refugee children they were being used with in refugee camps in Lebanon and that they should be replaced by more relevant materials. It seems that less than half of the grade four children in the camps passed the annual English examinations and an evaluation of the coursebooks considered them to be "intended for children who were fairly advanced in their oral language and literacy skills in English" (Ghosn, 2013a, p. 253), as most of the equivalent Lebanese children were because of their attendance at pre-schools. The evaluation also concluded that the coursebooks were too text heavy for the Palestinian children, that the vocabulary levels were too high for them, and that the "topics and concepts" had "little or no relevance to young Palestinian children living in a refugee camp" (p. 254). Ghosn was made responsible for writing a new three-level series for the Palestinian children, which was pointedly called *Enjoy English* (Ghosn, 2011 / 12). This series applied such research- and observation-based young learner principles as relevance to target learners' lives, cultural appropriacy, meaningful connection to the learners' interests, enthusiasms, views attitudes and feelings, focus on meaningful communication rather than on language itself, recycling of concepts and language, and gradual increase in difficulty. It also took into account the "holistic development of the young learner, who is still developing not only linguistically but also cognitively and psycho-socially" (Ghosn, 2013a, 252). It aimed to increase learner attention, motivation, and confidence to facilitate the achievement of the main goal of increased language and academic literacy. At the time of writing, Book One had been in use for a year. No formal evaluation had been undertaken but Ministry of Education officials reported their pleasure in observing active engagement in classroom activities (especially those involving the use of "big books") and in hearing children use English rather than just recite it. In Ghosn (2017) she returns to her investigation of the differences between how teachers use coursebooks and how they use storybooks in class. Again, she found that the coursebook was in control and often acted as a syllabus to be followed and that the teacher determined and dominated the discussions engendered by coursebook activities. In contrast she found there was more interaction in class discussion stimulated by storybooks and that the teacher focused much more on meaning in her contributions.

Ghosn (2013b) takes a broader approach by considering what we know facilitates language acquisition and development for young learners and then evaluating four young learner coursebooks to discover the degree of match between their content and approaches and the recommendations of researchers in the field. She begins by agreeing with other researchers that the optimal ages for second language acquisition are between 6 and 15, providing that "instructional materials … take into account children's developmental characteristics" (p. 61). Ghosn highlights the following facilitators of young learner L2 acquisition:

- teacher and coursebook tolerance of developmental errors;
- conversational teacher recasting of learner utterances;
- utilizing procedural memory through exposing learners repeatedly to target structures being used in context;
- exposure to "stimulating, enriched environment" (Ghosn, 2013b, p. 64) which is "novel, emotionally relevant or personally significant" (p. 64);
- affective and cognitive engagement;
- compelling narrative;
- social interaction;
- relevance of content and of activities;
- avoidance of explicit instruction and correction;
- rich exposure rather than restriction to specific teaching points.

We would agree that all the above factors are potential facilitators of young learner L2 acquisition and we have tried to make use of them when contributing to materials development for young learners. We would add the following facilitators (most of which Ghosn does highlight in other publications):

- catering for the young learner tendency to prefer learning by doing;
- bizarreness of texts and tasks;
- outcome feedback (i.e. feedback on the effectiveness of the communicative use of language rather than just on the accuracy of the output);
- learner choice;
- use of the L1 or mixed codes in preparation for L2 "performance."

Ghosn's (2013b) evaluation of four young learner coursebooks reveals many positive matches with the literature on child L2 acquisition (e.g. potentially motivating use of "stickers, cut outs, songs, chants and craft projects" (p. 68) but she also found that not much of the content was "novel, curious or surprising" (p. 68), there was very little use of stories, there was very little evidence of recycling, and the books progressed rapidly in difficulty with the same pace demanded from all the learners. In her recommendations to materials developers Ghosn stresses the importance of remembering that young learners "learn best through play and active exploration and experimentation and acquire language within the context of meaningful human interaction rather than through formal book-based lessons" (p. 60). She advocates the use of storybooks rather than traditional-type coursebooks and recommends, in particular, the use of big books displayed by the teacher on an easel and used to stimulate, for example, retelling, dramatization, oral summaries, story writing, rewriting and games. Having observed big books used in this way in, for example, the South Pacific we would definitely endorse this recommendation.

In Ghosn (2016) she also argues against the use of formal coursebook-based instruction as this actually disadvantages very young learners who have not yet developed the cognitive ability needed to analyze bits and pieces of language. She recommends (as we do) that the learning environment be set up to encourage acquisition rather than instruction and argues in particular for a constructivist whole language approach in which children "learn about language, both oral and written, when they are presented with natural—'whole'—language rather than simplified chunks of language typical in lower primary school language teaching coursebooks," in which they "engage in authentic activities rather than decontextualized drills" and in which "vocabulary and skills are acquired within the context of these activities." Once again, she advocates the use of big books and elaborates on how they can be used in a shared reading approach in which students interact with each other and with their teacher whilst reading the same story from the same book at the same time.

Many other practitioner / researchers have reported similar findings and / or have made similar recommendations to those made by Ghosn. For example, Arnold and Rixon (2008) report the results of a survey of teacher attitudes towards young learner coursebooks. Seventy-six teachers from 28 countries responded. They mentioned 78 different courses or series and were in general favorable about their provision of fun and enjoyment, their emphasis on listening and speaking, their promotion of interaction, and their topic- or task-based approaches. They were less favorable, though, about some of them being heavily grammar based, not stretching the learners, being boring and repetitive, not recycling vocabulary, lacking connections and making "sudden jumps of level and difficulty" (p. 47). Some books were praised for being holistic and whole-language based but some teachers said that they had difficulties using them because of the more traditional expectations of parents and authorities (perhaps the biggest problem we have found in our attempts to be innovative in materials development for young learners, especially in East and Southeast Asia). As one teacher said, "I like the programme but we failed to implement it … It's holistic and whole language based and Korean parents want translating, vocabulary study … lots of fill in the blanks etc." (p. 47). The authors also did their own evaluation of 16 published young-learners' courses. They were positive about the cognitive levels of most of the courses but were very critical of the lack of help given by most (but not all) the courses to target learners whose L1 does not use the Roman alphabet. They were also critical of the unrealistic language content of the courses, the way learners were expected to "make productive use of all the language items they encountered" (Arnold & Rixon, 2008, p. 49), the focus on accuracy (even in supposedly task-based courses) and the emphasis on assessment. An interesting question is whether parents', teachers' and authorities' expectations stem from coursebook norms or whether they determine them. When we tried to break away from the four norms mentioned above in a primary course we were contributing to in China we were criticized for not matching expectations. We went ahead though and included incidental vocabulary in our dialogues and stories only to find that teachers were testing students on every lexical item in each unit. We were told that the students liked the richer texts but that their parents definitely did not like their reduced test scores.

Ghosn is a strong supporter of story-based materials for young learners. Many other practioners / researchers also put strong arguments forward (as we do) for young learner materials based on story listening, story reading, storytelling and story writing, and are critical of many published courses for neglecting the potential power of stories. For example, Arnold (2010) reports the positive effects of an extensive reading program in Hong Kong primary schools in which the students were treated as real readers who chose which books they wanted to read and which follow up activities they wanted to do. In advocating oral storytelling in the L2 primary classroom Bland (2015b) puts forward a very persuasive argument for oral narrative being central to human experience and being of great educational value in the classroom in addition to "providing rich high-quality input," which plays to the strengths of young children—"particularly their aural perception and their ability to learn implicitly" (p. 184).

Other recommendations that have been made by practitioner / researchers in relation to materials development for young learners include:

- Immersing young learners in the target language by teaching at least 50% of their curriculum in the L2 and preferably using holistic, experiential approaches in which the L2 is used for communication (Kersten & Rohde, 2015). This approach has been implemented in many countries, the earliest we have experienced being in Cameroon as long ago as the mid-1960s and the most famous being in Canada (Cummins, 2009), where English-speaking children are given most or all of their instruction for an initial period in French. Such immersion usually seems to facilitate the development of communicative competence but can lead to fossilization of errors (a problem that is being addressed through language-awareness lessons in the Canadian immersion programs).
- Helping young learners to acquire grammar through engaged and extended repetition in their input and their output. Bland (2015d) recommends taking advantage of young learners' tolerance of ambiguity, their love of rhythm, and their joy in performance to learn grammar incidentally from experiencing poetry in the L2. Tomlinson (2015) also stresses the importance of "repeated and meaningful exposure" (p. 283) and recommends using poetry, as well as jokes, cartoons, songs and stories. Kolb (2012) reports a variety of kinesthetic and multisensory activities designed to provide meaningful repetition in a primary English classroom in Germany.
- Using picture books in which the interdependence of pictures and words not only facilitates comprehension but can also provide a richer, more engaging and more memorable experience than words alone. Mourao (2015) provides powerful arguments in support of picture books with young learners and advocates in particular the use of multilayered picturebooks, which create gaps for the learners to fill and

that "provide multiple opportunities for interpretation, promoting discussion and language use" (p. 200). Bland (2013) also advocates the use of such picturebooks and we do too. We believe that what matters is that the interaction between pictures and words opens gaps for the learners to fill through visualizing, through the use of their inner voice and through discussion, and we agree with Mourao (2015) that picturebooks in which there is a one-to-one correspondence between pictures and words can "encourage passivity, for little effort is needed to understand the picturebook" (p. 200). For an interesting account of how a picture-book story course for young learners in Japan proved to be a positive language learning experience both for the young learners who enjoyed the course and for the university students who designed it see Brown (2016).

- Using technology to provide opportunities to experience language being used for communication, both through exposure to other people's interaction and through interacting themselves. This can be achieved, for example, through the use of mobile phones, through videoconferencing and through Skyping, providing that the teacher provides support as an organizer, mentor, and encourager and does not act as an instructor or corrector. For a description and analysis of a videoconferencing project involving primary schools in France and in Germany see Schmid and Whyte (2015).
- Catering for the shorter attention span of young learners by breaking lessons into short phases and providing "a mix of stirring and settling activities as well as different participatory structures" (Kolb, 2012, p. 34).
- Starting both the reception and later the production phases with unanalyzed chunks of language (e.g. "What's in your lunch box?"—Kolb (2012, p. 34), a practice recommended and justified by many experts (e.g. "Young children learn L2 languages without analyzing the input by simply absorbing what they hear. They remember new language in 'chunks'" (Pinter, 2012, p. 106). See Kersten (2015) for a survey of the literature on the acquisition of formulaic language and recommendations for how to utilize young learners' ability to learn and use it.
- Using a topic-based approach in which "the topics are taken from the children's real life and surrounding environment" (Kolb, 2012, p. 34).

Most experts on helping young learners to acquire an L2 would agree with the recommendations above. One area that does attract disagreement, though, is the teaching of L2 reading to young learners whose first language has a different writing system. Some advocate an experiential approach reliant on frequent and repeated exposure while others recommend a more systematic approach with the learners being taught the orthographical and phonemic systems of the L2. For an analysis of how L2 coursebooks teach young learners to read, a discussion of the issues involved and recommendations for materials development see Rixon (2013). See also Gersten and Geva (2003) for a discussion of the issues in teaching young learners to read in an L2, Hughes (2013) for recommendations for developing a "literacy environment" (p. 190), and Nunan (2013) for a report of a successful innovation in South Korea in which young learners were "taught" to enjoy extensive reading through a blended learning course involving a "brain-based phonemic awareness-phonics-fluency-vocabulary programme" (p. 243). See especially Noronho (in press), which reports the success of the Mobile Outreach Program (MOP) in Goa. MOP is an open access program that provides a library experience to primary school children after school within the community space. "The guiding theoretical principle … resides in the understanding that language is acquired as a whole and not in bits and pieces. The program therefore keeps language whole and involves participants in using it functionally and purposefully to meet their own needs" (Noronho, in press). The MOP is informed in particular by the whole-language approach of Goodman (1986) and follows Goodman's advice that what makes language easy to learn is when it is real, natural, whole, sensible, interesting, and relevant, when it belongs to the learner, when it is part of a real event, when it has social utility, when it has purpose for the learner, when the learner chooses to learn it, when it is accessible to the learner, and when the learner has power to use it. And perhaps most significantly on MOP "The most powerful of learning aids is used to teach language. That of the story." (Noronho, in press)

Our Recommendations for Developing and Using Materials for Young Learners

Make Maximum Use of Stories

Anybody who has had young children (or can remember being a young child) will know that what attracts children most is stories. Anybody who knows something about young learner L2 acquisition will appreciate that stories have the greatest potential for achieving the attention, the curiosity, the focus on meaning, the recycling of concepts and language, the rich and comprehensible input, the novelty, the impact, the affective and cognitive engagement and the motivation that can facilitate the gaining of positive attitudes, the achievement of L2 communicative competence and the cognitive development of a child. We would like to stress that stories have great potential but that potential is only realized if the emphasis is on experiencing and enjoying well-told stories and not on studying or learning from texts. One way of achieving this we have found is for the teacher to give a dramatic reading of a story and to occasionally pause and invite the learners to shout out the next word or phrase in either the L2 or the L1 (thus, for example, getting the learners to predict that Norman the bear disguises himself as a bee in order to enroll at Bee School and gain easy access to honey in the story *The Bumblebear* (Shireen, 2016)). Another effective way is for the teacher to use glove puppets to dramatize a story she is telling to her class. Yet another way is to use visuals, props and sound effects to enhance the appeal and increase the accessibility of a story.

In order to fully realize the potential of stories we would recommend materials developers to start every unit with a story, preferably told live by a teacher rather than by a recording. It should be made clear to students that this story is for them to enjoy and that there will be no questions on it afterwards. At the end of the lesson the teacher should provide access to a written version of the story for those students who would like to read it. Doing this in every unit would massively increase and enrich the students' exposure to the target language in use. We would also strongly recommend dramatic reading or telling of stories by the teacher. This could (as we have said above) involve the teacher making use of props, of visuals, and of sound effects to reinforce the language of the story. For example, one story that we have told in this way is about an old man who gets out of a taxi, walks slowly along a street, looks at the numbers of houses, and then stops outside number 10. The teacher telling the story reinforces the words by making the sound of a taxi screeching to a halt and miming an old man in a hat getting out of the taxi, walking slowly with a stick, looking at the numbers of houses drawn on the board and then stopping outside number 10. The story continues with the old man knocking on the door, an old lady in a scarf opening it, both people smiling at each other, the old man going into the house and then a very loud laugh coming from inside the house. The teacher reads (or preferably tells) the story line by line and reinforces each line with actions, props and sound effects. The teacher then tells the whole story again so that the students can create visual and auditory images of it, leaves the students in silence for a minute and then asks the questions "Who laughed? Why did they laugh?" The students answer the questions in groups (using their L1 if they want to) and then they act out or mime what happened after the old man went inside, first in rehearsal and then in performance to another group, whose task is to improvise a narrative for the scene they are watching.

Of course, storytelling by the students can also be very useful both for the teller and the listeners, providing that the tellers choose, find or ideally make up their own stories, that the tellers have had time to practice telling their stories (preferably with feedback from a peer), and that the tellers are encouraged to dramatize their stories rather than just read them out or recite them. One way we have used to stimulate student story-telling is to provide in the materials a visualization prompt. For example, we have told students:

- See in your mind a picture of your village.
- See the people in your village.
- See what the people are doing.
- See pictures of an interesting person in your village.
- See what he or she is doing.
- Tell yourself a story in your mind about this person.
- Tell your story to yourself aloud.
- Tell your story to a partner.

Another way we have used is the circle story. The students are given a prompt, which could be, for example, the beginning of a story, a short video scene without sound or a bizarre picture, and then they are asked to sit in groups in a circle to make up a story based on the prompt. Each student is given a number and then number one is asked to tell the first sentence of the story, then number two, then three, and so forth, and then round and round the circle until their story comes to an end. The students are told not to think for a long time before speaking and are encouraged to focus on telling an interesting story and to not worry about making mistakes. When they have concluded their story they tell it again as quickly as possible, making any changes they want. Then they tell it a third time but this time they pause and suggest improvements if needed to the language and content of each sentence, with the teacher making herself available to help if invited. Then they tell their story to another group and maybe eventually to the whole class.

We would also recommend story reading (once the young learners have enough vocabulary to read extensively without worrying about the meaning of every word), either done as shared reading with big books in class, as individual task-free reading in or out of class, or as part of a text-driven unit of materials (Tomlinson, 2013). Here is an example of a text-driven lesson for young learners in which the students do eventually read a story aloud to others but only after they have heard a similar story read aloud by the teacher and have had time to practice reading their story privately:

1. Do you ever make your parents annoyed? (Teacher mimes being annoyed.) See a picture of yourself annoying your parents. What are you doing? What are they doing? What are you saying? What are they saying?
2. I'm going to read you a story about a boy called Bernard. As I read it I want you to see pictures of what happens in the story. (Teacher reads McKee, D. (2005). *Not now, Bernard*. Sydney: Andersen Press.)
3. I'm going to read the story again. This time I want you to act the story as you listen to it. You're going to play all the parts. (Teacher reads the story while students act it out).
4. Who was to blame for Bernard's death? Who's fault was it? What do you think? Share your answer with other students.
5. What does, "Not now" mean in the story? Talk about it with other students.
6. Form a group of four. Write a similar story about a girl in your country. In your story there is a girl, her mother, her father, and a monster.
7. Practice reading your story aloud with each student playing one of the characters in the story.
8. Read your story to another group and listen to their story.

If the teacher / materials writer is going to select stories for a text-driven unit of material we would recommend looking for stories with the potential to engage the target learners rather than selecting stories whose language matches teaching points on a syllabus. If the teacher / materials writer is going to write stories we would definitely recommend writing authentic stories with the potential to be comprehensible, meaningful and engaging for the target students rather than contriving stories to illustrate lexical or structural teaching points.

Student story writing can be valuable, if the students are writing the stories for their own and other people's enjoyment rather than as a test of the accuracy of their written English. In our materials we have tried to stimulate young learners to write stories:

- after a similar visualization activity to the one about the village above;
- as a continuation of a story listened to or read (as with the *Not now, Bernard* story above);
- as an account of a personal experience;
- as a circle story with each member of a circle writing one sentence on a piece of paper and then passing it on to the next student in the circle (or with students moving from computer to computer or e-mailing their sentences on);
- as a development stage in a text-driven approach (i.e. after reading or listening to a story and doing an intake response activity designed to activate and deepen the students' personal responses to it).

We would usually follow a process approach with young learners in which they are encouraged to "write" a first draft in their minds, write a second draft quickly on paper or on a computer, write a third draft more carefully paying attention to accuracy as well as fluency, seek feedback from peers or a teacher and then write their final version. We would usually let students decide if they wanted to write individually, in a pair or in a group but sometimes we would encourage group writing of the first part of a story in class and continuation of the story individually at home.

Most of the stories we would use would be fiction but we would also make use of narrative accounts of processes and procedures. Most children seem to enjoy finding out how things are made or done and then, if possible, making or doing them themselves. For example, listening to the story of how chocolate is made and then simulating the process themselves or listening to the story of how a local ceremony is performed and then performing it themselves. We would also make use of dialogues that tell an interesting story and have them performed by the teacher (or preferably by two teachers whose classes have been combined) before being performed impromptu by the students. Here is an example of such a "dialogue" to be used with a Young Learners' class in Turkey:

> Darici is a young boy who supports Galatasary. Tonight is the big game v Fenerbahçe and Darici wants to stay up to watch it on tv. Tomorrow he's taking an important exam and his father wants him to go to bed early. His father doesn't like football at all. His mother is a Beşiktaş supporter.

> FATHER: Time for bed.
> DARICI: But the game is just coming on.
> FATHER: Yes, but your exam is more important.
> DARICI: It's a really big game. And I'm ready for the exam anyway.
> FATHER: You need the sleep. There'll be another game.
> DARICI: Just the first half?
> MOTHER: I'll be watching the Barcelona v Real Madrid game anyway.
> DARICI AND FATHER: What?
> MOTHER: I want to watch Messi and Suarez.
> DARICI: Only because your team's no good.
> FATHER AND MOTHER: Go to bed now.

TPR Plus

The young learners on the PKG program in Indonesia (and learners in many other countries) seemed to be at their happiest when they were involved in a TPR Plus story activity (Tomlinson, 1990, 1994a). This involved the teacher telling a dramatic, bizarre, or humorous story, which the students acted out as the story was told, or the teacher telling the students how to cook a tasty meal and the students cooking it (with ingredients they had been asked to bring from home), or the teacher hiding sweets all over the school grounds and the students listening to clues and then going off in groups to look for the sweets, or even the teacher "dictating" a mural and the students painting it on the classroom wall. Sometimes there were follow-up activities that involved recalling the teachers' words and then making use of them for follow up activities. We were always amazed at the content accuracy of the students' recall and attributed it to the fact that the original words had stimulated both visualization and enactment, ideal activities for promoting intake from input. For example, having acted out "They Came from the Sea Part 1"(a story about four strange creatures who suddenly appeared offshore standing on a circular ship and then took a man and a woman from the beach as prisoners back to their ship), young learners in Indonesia were able to retell the story very accurately by shouting out completions of sentences started by the teacher. They were also able to develop creatively silly continuations of the narrative as circle stories.

Games

It is not surprising that most young learners in our experience enjoy and benefit from playing games that involve exposure to and use of the target language (Tomlinson & Masuhara, 2009). Most children in most cultures enjoy playing games. Some enjoy board games, some enjoy quizzes, some enjoy games involving physical activity. Some enjoy individual games, some enjoy group games, and some enjoy team games. Some enjoy competitive games and some enjoy collaborative games. A very good example of this was a group of young learners in a primary school in Vanuatu who were being introduced to dominoes. When a boy put down the winning domino the whole group cheered as though they had all won—a dramatic demonstration of the Melanesian tendency to prefer collaboration over competition. The important point is that young learners should be exposed to different types of games and then given plenty of opportunities to play the types they enjoy. If they are enjoying a game and that game requires them to understand the L2 in use and / or to use it in order to play the game, there is a very good chance they will achieve sufficient cognitive and affective engagement for the experience to contribute to their acquisition of the L2, especially if the game recycles or helps them to recycle language items and structures, as most children's games do. Here is an example of such a game:

> You're going to play Newspaper Hockey. I'm going to give you instructions to help you to play the game. Here they are.

> - The students on this side of the room move your desks to the nearest wall.
> - Put your chairs in a line facing the opposite wall.
> - Now the students on this side of the room move your desks to the nearest wall.
> - Put your chairs in a line facing the opposite wall so that you face the other students.
> - This is Team A and this is Team B.
> - Move your chairs so that you are directly opposite a player from the other team.
> - Team A put a chair at this end of the room in between the two teams. This is the goal you are defending.
> - Team B put a chair at this end of the room in between the two teams. This is the goal you are defending.
> - Team A you are defending this goal and attacking that goal.
> - Team B you are defending this goal and attacking that goal.
> - I'm going to give each team some newspapers. Now each team make three balls. Make them as hard as you can.
> - I'm going to give each team some more newspapers. Now each team make three hockey sticks. Make them as strong as you can.
> - Each team put your strongest hockey stick on your team's chair, that's the one you are defending.
> - Team A put your strongest ball in the middle of the room in between the two teams and in between the two goals.
> - I'm going to give each player a number. Listen carefully to your number. (The teacher gives a number to each player in each team with number 1 being the player nearest their team's goal.)

- Remember, when I call your number jump up, grab the hockey stick from your goal and try to hit the ball into your opponent's goal. Keep playing until a goal is scored or I stop you. Remember also, you can only hit the ball with your stick. If you touch the ball with your hand or foot it's a penalty to the other team.

The teacher reads the above instructions instruction by instruction and makes sure the students understand and follow them. The learners play the game until one team scores seven goals. The teacher acts as the referee and also reminds the players of the rules if they are confused. Then learners play a more complicated version of the game in which they have to work out mentally the answer to a mathematical problem. The answer is the number of the player who should jump up and try to score (e.g. "The number of sides in a triangle plus the number of musicians in a trio divided by the number of wheels on a tricycle.") Team members can help each other and can shout out encouragement in the target language (and possibly be penalized if they use their L1), The learners could then be asked in groups to make up another game involving the use of newspapers and to write instructions for their game. They could then be given written instructions for the game they have played and told to make use of them to revise the instructions for their own game. Then they could give their instructions to another group and help them to play their game.

Computer games obviously have great potential for engagement and language learning (see Chapter 7) but it is important that the games can only be played if the students have to understand instructions and advice in the target language and ideally if the players have both to think and to interact in the target language. We once saw a French lesson in which young English-speaking learners played computer games whose format was obviously familiar to them. The students seemed to enjoy playing the games but they seemed to be able to do so automatically without reading or listening to the instructions and any interaction between them was in English. We thought it highly unlikely that the games were facilitating language acquisition.

A recent project in which games do seem to have been successful in facilitating language acquisition is Peace through Traditional Toys and Games, an Erasmus + KA2 Strategic Partnership Project led by Pakmaya Primary School in İzmir, Turkey, in collaboration with three schools from Portugal, Romania, and Greece. The project was fully funded by the European Union and lasted for 2 years (2014–2016). It aimed to show that traditional toys and games could be used as effective teaching materials in school education, and especially in language teaching, in order to promote communication, integration and peace, and as an incentive for children to go back to street games and to learn and communicate the games culture of their area. As we write, an article on the project by the Project Leader, Mehmet Ates, is likely to appear in the MATSDA journal *Folio* in early 2017.

Drama

Acting out dialogues, short plays, cartoons, short films and improvisations can offer many opportunities for fun, for exposure to language in use, and for using the target language for communication. We have found that the sillier the drama is the more fun and language experience the learners gain, that it is very important that learners are not compelled to perform in front of the whole class if they do not want to, and that no correction of language is made by the teacher whilst the learners are acting. Most of our drama activities with Young Learners have involved groups rehearsing until they are ready to "perform" to another group. An example of a very popular silly drama is to ask learners to act out is *Mine's bigger than yours* (Willis & Reynolds, 2008), either as a whole class with teacher narration or in small groups with student narration. This is the story of a Little Hairy Monster and a Scary Monster and involves Scary Monster trying to take Little Hairy Monster's lollipop by chasing her and threatening her with such boasts as "My roar's bigger than yours … Give me your lollipop or I'll deafen you." The drama that the students act out is full of action and noise, as well as exposure to one of the functions of the comparative, to lots of demonstrable vocabulary and to a surprise ending.

Songs and Chants

Most Young Learner coursebooks do include songs and chanting but often the songs and chants have been contrived to illustrate a language point and language work follows quickly on after the singing or chanting. We believe that the songs and chants should be selected or devised for their potential to achieve impact and engagement and that the focus should be on their performance rather than any analysis of them. Ideally, the songs and chants should be contextualized and meaningful, though again impact is often most easily achieved if they are bizarre. One way of achieving impact through novel repetition is to make use of jazz chants as developed and popularized by Caroline Graham ("Jazz Chants are exercises when students repeat rhythmically words and short phrases to music" (Wikipedia: https://en.wikipedia.org/wiki/Jazz_Chants).

Drawings

Most young learners in most (but not all) countries love to draw, provided that they are not assessed on their artistic ability and are free to express themselves creatively. If they are drawing their interpretations of stories they have heard or read in the L2, if they are drawing to instructions given in the L2, or if they are participating in collaborative drawing in which they either talk with each other in the L2 when deciding what to draw or give a presentation in the L2 on their drawing, then they are gaining valuable experience of the L2 whilst participating in a potentially engaging activity. Again, this is especially true if the drawing they produce is intriguingly bizarre. For example, we have made up bizarre stories using apparently unconnected sentences from drills in the coursebook and then asked students to draw the stories.

Making Things

Most young learners in most (but not all) countries love to make things, provided that they are not assessed on their artistic ability and are free to express themselves creatively. We have seen, for example, young learners very happily make masks to wear when acting, make puppets in character for performing their made up stories and make "mock" shoes, scarves, and caps from materials brought from home. In a Vanuatu primary school one very resourceful teacher got her students to make string puppets, which were hung from the classroom wall and then frequently used to perform bizarre stories made up to illustrate language points from their rather boring coursebook. In an

Ethiopian primary school there was a large stock room full of artefacts made to instructions by students and available for anybody to make use of in English lessons.

All the activities described so far involve physical activity and cater for young learners' tendency to prefer kinesthetic, experiential ways of learning. In our experience these activities are most effective when they follow our DEEPA approach:

- **D**aft
- **E**njoyable
- **E**xperience of language and
- **P**hysical
- **A**ctivities

This is an approach based on the principles that young learners:

- need daft activities so that the bizarreness of the experience will be salient and memorable;
- need to enjoy their experience of learning and gain self-esteem and confidence from it;
- need meaningful experience of the language in use in order to acquire it;
- learn more through physical activity than from studying books;
- benefit from the deep processing that comes from willing investment in meaningful experience of language in use;
- do not gain much from the shallow processing that comes from instructed participation in meaningless drills;
- need to achieve affective and cognitive engagement in order to learn.

Scenarios

A scenario is a type of role play in which two students play roles and try to influence each other's views or actions. Each student knows what role the other is playing but does not know what he is going to try to get him to think or do. This means that they are not playing out a script but are genuinely interacting. We have developed a version of scenarios that is based on Di Pietro (1987). In Indonesia, for example, young learners took part in locally relevant scenarios in which the task was to use English to achieve an intention (e.g. persuading your mother to let you stay up to watch a badminton tournament on television; trying to make sure you get the birthday present you want). In each scenario there were usually two roles. Half the class in groups prepared to act out one role and half prepared to act out the other. The students knew who the other role was but not what they were going to say and do. After the preparation of strategies, a representative from each half played out the scenario and tried to achieve their intention. At any time a "time out" could be called and advice could be given to the representative or a substitution could be made. After the interaction was finished, the teacher led a postmortem in which the strategies and language used were reviewed by the teacher and suggestions were made by the students for what might have been more effective. Here is an example of a scenario for three characters developed for young learners in Istanbul and based on the dialogue we presented earlier in this chapter:

DARICI   You are a young boy who supports Galatasary. Tonight is the big game v Fenerbahçe and you want to stay up to watch it on tv, even though you have an important exam tomorrow. Try to persuade your parents to let you stay up to watch the game. Your father doesn't like football at all and your mother is a Beşiktaş supporter.

FATHER   Your son is a young boy who supports Galatasary. Tonight is the big game v Fenerbahçe and he wants to stay up to watch it on tv, even though he has an important exam tomorrow. You don't like football and you don't intend to watch the game. You also think your son should go to bed early to make sure he is fresh for his exam. Your wife is a Beşiktaş supporter and is unlikely to want to watch the game.

MOTHER   Your son is a young boy who supports Galatasary. Tonight is the big game v Fenerbahçe and he wants to stay up to watch it on tv, even though he has an important exam tomorrow. You like football but you are a Beşiktaş supporter and you don't intend to watch the game. You want to watch the Barcelona v Real Madrid game instead because you are a great fan of Lionel Messi. You also think your son should go to bed early to make sure he is fresh for his exam.

Content and Language Integrated (CLIL) Activities

In CLIL approaches students gain new knowledge and new skills through instruction in the L2 and at the same time they acquire communicative competence in the L2. Content and language integrated materials are designed with both goals in mind.

Content and language integrated activities in the L2 in which students gain knowledge and / or develop skills related to other primary school subjects can be engaging, if they are driven by potentially engaging texts (e.g. a story about dinosaurs) and / or they involve kinesthetic activity (e.g. acting out the cultivation of a crop from the sowing of seeds to the harvesting of the crop). We have found, though, that they can be even more engaging if they introduce young learners to interesting aspects of an unfamiliar pursuit (e.g. teaching young German learners in English how to play cricket), teach them a new skill (e.g. how to play a musical instrument), or provide new information about something they are really interested in (e.g. the Premier League in England or the making of a cartoon feature film). For information about the theory and practice of CLIL see Coyle, Hood, and Marsh (2010) and for detailed accounts of young learner CLIL projects in Europe (and examples of materials used on them) see Bentley (2015).

Tasks

Meaning-focused tasks in which young learners work together to achieve an intended outcome can provide valuable experience of the L2 provided they receive input in the L2 (ideally from an engaging written or spoken text), they need to use the L2 to achieve the desired outcome and they are not inhibited by teacher correction. An example of such a task would be for groups of students to be given three weekly comics in the L2 to look through before deciding which one they want to be subscribed to for the class library and then giving a short presentation to support their recommendation.

See Tomlinson (1981) for a book of tasks developed by teachers for use in primary schools in Vanuatu; see Van Gorp and Bogaert (2006) for advice on developing tasks for primary and secondary learners of an L2 and see Pinter (2015) for a detailed discussion of research tasks and pedagogic tasks for young learners.

Discovery Activities

Discovery activities involve the learners in making discoveries about how the L2 is used from exploring spoken or written texts that they have recently enjoyed. For example, the learners make discoveries about the functions of "Not now X" having enjoyed and responded to the story *Not now Bernard* (McKee, 2005), they make discoveries about the differing functions of the simple past and the past continuous after acting out and then reading the story *They came from the sea Part 1*, they make discoveries about how the comparative is used after acting out *Mine's bigger than yours* (Willis & Reynolds, 2008) and they work out how to give instructions in Japanese after acting out instructions in the context of a Japanese song. All these activities involve groups of learners first identifying the target item or structure in the text, then discussing how it is used and finally attempting to formulate a generalization about its functions (s). They might share their generalizations, discuss them in a plenary session with the teacher, revise them and then record them together with examples in the "book" they are writing about the target language (e.g. *English grammar* by Willy Widodo). At lower levels we would recommend that this is done in the L1 to make sure that understanding is achieved (though any intervention by the teachers should be in the L2 to maximize the learners' exposure to language in use). Many experts consider such activities to be too cognitively demanding but we have seen that young learners get very excited when they have independently made discoveries. For example, in Indonesia a teacher was obliged by the syllabus to focus on regular and irregular adverbs with her class of 11 year olds. Instead of teaching them she told them a story about a party and they acted it out as she narrated it. In their acting of the story the students did things in many different ways (e.g. slowly, more slowly, quickly, more quickly, well, better, badly, worse). The teacher did not focus on the adverbs but on stimulating enjoyable activity. Afterwards the teacher gave the students the story to read. Then she told them to look for words that described how things were done and to underline them. She told them to find two different types of these words. Suddenly a boy jumped up excitedly and rushed to the board. He wrote a list of regular adverbs from the story and a list of irregular adverbs and shouted "Two types." The teacher congratulated him and then labeled one list Regular Adverbs and the other one Irregular Adverbs before challenging the class to find other examples from the story. See also Ellis and Ibrahim (2015) for claims that young learners are more capable of gaining from cognitively demanding challenges than most people think.

We would recommend the use of discovery activities with young learners instead of drills, language practice, and language teaching. The aim is not immediate mastery of an item or structure but rather the beginning of a noticing process that can eventually (given sufficient exposure) facilitate the acquisition of an item or structure. It is also to develop curiosity about the target language and a capacity for autonomous learning.

For discussion and examples of discovery activities see Bolitho et al. (2003) and Tomlinson (1994b, 2007).

Multi-dimensional Representation Approaches

A multi-dimensional representation approach is one that enables the learners to make full use of the resources of their minds (Tomlinson, 2000; Masuhara, 2005) and which to do so follows the principles of personalization, affective engagement, cognitive engagement, use of mental imagery, use of the inner voice and raising of esteem. Bonilla and

Vargas (2015) did a 5 months' internship at a private language school for 10–12 year olds in Bogota. During this time they observed lessons, analyzed and evaluated materials, interviewed teachers and students, and did a needs analysis. They found that the coursebook in use was very unpopular with the teachers because it was too easy and with the students because it was boring and remote. They then wrote their own materials using a developmental framework proposed by Jolly and Bolitho (1998) and the principles in Tomlinson's (2000) article on the multi-dimensional approach. Their coursebook was "narrated" by an endearing but complex monkey who, for example, confessed to bullying a newcomer in his class at school and helped to find the owner of a lost banana. The activities consisted mainly of personalization activities (e.g. "What would you do?") and mini creative tasks. The materials have not been evaluated yet but we were certainly engaged by them.

Conclusion

We would like to end by stressing a number of vital points about materials for young learners.
Young learners:

- gain languages through motivated experience of them rather than from being instructed about them (see Enever, J. (2011) and Lefever (2012) for studies demonstrating young learners' ability to acquire language incidentally from exposure to, for example, the Internet and subtitled television programs and films—a reason given recently for young children in Finland being already able to communicate in English when they first go to primary school.);
- should not be pushed into premature production in the target language (and the inevitable experience of making multiple errors) but should be allowed to acquire sufficient vocabulary through engaged listening first;
- do not in most cases have any immediate need to use the target language and therefore it does not matter which lexical items and structures they acquire as long as they develop a positive attitude to learning the language and some ability to communicate in it;
- are typically kinesthetic rather than studial learners and benefit most from learning through doing;
- learn most from enjoyable engagement with the target language.

See Arnold and Rixon (2008) for an evaluation of young learner coursebooks in relation to many of the principles and procedures we have advocated above.

What do You Think?

1. We agree with some of the following statements and very much disagree with others. Which of the statements do you agree with? For each statement, say why you agree or disagree.
   a) If young learners have no immediate need to use the target language it doesn't matter what language they do or do not learn. What matters is that they develop a positive attitude towards learning the language and are keen to learn more.

b) If you don't correct young learners' errors the errors will fossilize and the learners will never achieve accuracy.

c) Teachers of young learners don't need a syllabus and a coursebook to follow. What they need is an easily accessible library of potentially engaging texts, tasks, games and songs.

d) Young learners shouldn't be pushed into premature production. They should first enjoy a comprehension approach in which they are exposed to the language in comprehensible use and only be asked to produce language when they are ready to do so.

e) Young learners need to be tested frequently on their knowledge of grammar as well as their use of the four skills. Otherwise their teachers will not know what to teach them next.

f) It is often said that there is no gain without pain. But if young learners find learning an L2 painful they are unlikely to be successful in learning it.

2. What are your answers to the following questions? Give reasons for your answers.

a) What age do you think is best for young learners to start learning an L2?

b) Do you think readers for young learners should be graded according to language level or just written intuitively for them to understand and enjoy?

c) Do you think the teacher of classes of young learners should use the L1 or the L2 when talking to the learners?

d) Do you think instructions in young learners' coursebooks should be in the L1 or the L2?

e) Do you think it is useful for young learners to be taught the grammar of the target language?

Tasks

1. Take a young learners' coursebook and analyze a unit from the book to find out the percentage of activities that involve the learners:

a) experiencing the target language in use;

b) using the target language for communication;

c) being taught about the target language;

d) practicing the target language;

e) making discoveries about the use of the target language;

f) being tested.

2. Evaluate the unit you analyzed in 1 above using the following criteria:

a) To what extent are the texts likely to engage the learners affectively?

b) To what extent are the texts likely to engage the learners cognitively?

c) To what extent are the activities likely to engage the learners affectively?

d) To what extent are the activities likely to engage the learners cognitively?

e) To what extent are the texts likely to seem relevant to the learners?

f) To what extent are the activities likely to seem relevant to the learners?

g) To what extent are the learners likely to enjoy using this unit?

For each criterion give a score out of 5 and justify your score.

3. Try to improve the unit so that it gets higher scores on the evaluation criteria and it contains a higher percentage of the types of texts and activities you think it should provide.

Further Reading

Bland, J. (Ed.). (2015). *Teaching English to young learners: Critical issues in language teaching with 3–12 year olds.* London: Bloomsbury.

Ellis, G. & Ibrahim, N. (2015). *Teaching children how to learn.* Peaslake: Delta Publishing.

References

Arnold, W. (2010). A longitudinal study of the effects of a graded reader scheme for young learners in Hong Kong. In B. Tomlinson & H. Masuhara (Eds.), *Research for materials development in language learning: Evidence for best practice* (pp. 37–49). London: Continuum.

Arnold, W., & Rixon, S. (2008). Materials for teaching English to young learners. In B. Tomlinson (Ed.), *English language learning materials: A critical review* (pp. 38–59). London: Continuum.

Bacha, N., Ghosn, I.-K., & McBeath, N. (2008). The textbook, the teacher and the learner: A Middle-Eastern perspective. In B. Tomlinson (Ed.), *English language learning materials: A critical review* (pp. 281–299). London: Continuum.

Bentley, K. (2015). CLIL scenarios with young learners. In J. Bland (Ed.), *Teaching English to Young Learners: Critical issues in language teaching with 3–12 year olds* (pp. 91–112). London: Bloomsbury.

Bernhardt, E. (2000). Second-language reading as a case study of reading scholarship in the twentieth century. In M. L. Kamil, P. B. Mosenthal, P. D. Pearson & R. Barr (Eds.), *Handbook of reading research* (vol. 3, pp. 791–812). Mahwah, NJ: Lawrence Erlbaum.

Bland, J. (2013). *Children's literature and learner empowerment.* London: Bloomsbury.

Bland, J. Ed. (2015a). *Teaching English to young learners: Critical issues in language teaching with 3–12 year olds.* London: Bloomsbury.

Bland, J. (2015b). Oral storytelling in the primary English classroom. In J. Bland (Ed.), *Teaching English to young learners: Critical issues in language teaching with 3–12 year olds* (pp. 183–198). London: Bloomsbury.

Bland, J. (2015c). Drama with young learners. In J. Bland (Ed.), *Teaching English to young learners: Critical issues in language teaching with 3–12 year olds* (pp. 219–238). London: Bloomsbury.

Bland, J. (2015d). Grammar templates for the future with poetry for children. In J. Bland (Ed.), *Teaching English to young learners: Critical issues in language teaching with 3–12 year olds* (pp. 147–166). London: Bloomsbury.

Bolitho, R., Carter, R., Hughes, R., Ivanic, R., Masuhara, H., & Tomlinson, B. (2003). Ten questions about language awareness. *ELT Journal, 57*(2), 251–259.

Bonilla, P. B., & Vargas, J. D. G. (2015). *"Living up the world": The materials development process of a module for fifth graders following a multi-dimensional approach* (Unpublished PhD dissertation). Pontificia Universidad Javeriana, Bogota.

Brown, D. N. (2016). Implementing English picture book story time to build confidence in ELL. In T. Pattison (Ed.), *IATEFL 2015 Manchester conference selections* (pp. 116–117). Faversham: IATEFL.

Coyle, D., Hood, P., & Marsh, D. (2010). *CLIL: Content and language integrated learning.* Cambridge: Cambridge University Press.

Cummins, J. (2009). Bilingual and immersion programmes. In M. Long & C. Doughty (Eds.), *The handbook of language teaching* (pp. 159–181). Oxford: Wiley-Blackwell.

de Keyser, R. M. (in press). Age in learning and teaching grammar. In J. I. Liontas (Ed.), *TESOL encyclopedia*. Hoboken, NJ: Wiley.

Di Pietro, R. (1987). *Strategic interaction: Learning languages through scenarios.* Cambridge: Cambridge University Press.

Ellis, G., & Ibrahim, N. (2015). *Teaching children how to learn.* Peaslake: Delta Publishing.

Ellis, G., & Ibrahim, N. (2016). Teaching children how to learn. In T. Pattison (Ed.), *IATEFL 2015 Manchester conference selections* (pp. 103–105). Faversham: IATEFL.

Enever, J. (Ed.). (2011). *ELLiE: Early language learning in Europe.* London: British Council.

Gerston, R., & Geva, R. (2003). Teaching reading to early language learners. *Educational Leadership, 60*(7), 44–49.

Ghosn, I.-K. (2003). Talking like texts and talking about texts: How some primary school coursebooks are realised in the classroom. In B. Tomlinson (Ed.), *Developing materials for language teaching* (pp. 291–305). London: Bloomsbury.

Ghosn, I.-K. (2007). Output like input: Influence of children's literature on young L2 learners' written expression. In B. Tomlinson (Ed.), *Language acquisition and development: Studies of learners of first and other languages* (pp. 171–186). London: Continuum.

Ghosn, I.-K. (2010). Five-year outcomes from children's literature-based programmes vs programmes using a skills-based ESL course—The Matthew and Peter effects at work? In B. Tomlinson & H. Masuhara (Eds.), *Research for materials development in language learning: evidence for best practice* (pp. 21–36). London: Continuum.

Ghosn, I.-K. (2011 / 12). *Enjoy English Grade One.* Beirut: UNRWA Education Programme.

Ghosn, I.-K. (2013a). Developing motivating materials for refugee children: From theory to practice. In B. Tomlinson (Ed.), *Developing materials for language teaching* (2nd ed., pp. 247–268). London: Bloomsbury.

Ghosn, I.-K. (2013b). Language learning for young learners. In B. Tomlinson (Ed.), *Applied linguistics and materials development* (pp. 61–74). London: Bloomsbury.

Ghosn, I-K. (2016). No place for coursebooks in the very young learner classroom. In B. Tomlinson (Ed.), *SLA research and materials development for language learning* (pp. 50–66). New York: Routledge.

Ghosn, I.-K. (2017). They do talk—when there's something worth talking about: The curious case of language class discourse. In H. Masuhara, F. Mishan, & B. Tomlinson (Eds.), *Practice and theory in materials development for L2 learning* (pp. 211–229). Newcastle upon Tyne: Cambridge Scholars.

Goodman, K.S. (1986). *What's whole in whole language.* Richmond Hill, Ontario: Scholastic.

Hughes, A. (2013). The teaching of reading in English for young learners: Some considerations and next steps. In B. Tomlinson (Ed.), *Applied linguistics and materials development* (pp. 183–198). London: Bloomsbury.

Jolly, D., & Bolitho, R. (1998). A framework for materials writing. In B. Tomlinson (Ed.), *Materials development in language teaching.* Cambridge: Cambridge University Press.

Kersten, S. (2015). Language development in young learners: The development of formulaic language. In J. Bland (Ed.), *Teaching English to young learners: Critical issues in language teaching with 3–12 year olds* (pp. 129–146). London: Bloomsbury.

Kersten, K., & Rohde, A. (2015). Immersion teaching in English with young learners. In J. Bland (Ed.), *Teaching English to young learners: Critical issues in language teaching with 3–12 year olds* (pp. 72–89). London: Bloomsbury.

Kolb, A. (2012). Teaching English in primary school. In Eisenmann, M. & Summer, T. (Eds.), *Basic issues in EFL teaching and learning.* Heidleberg: Winter.

Lefever, S. (2012). Incidental foreign language learning in young children. In A. Hasselgreen, I. Drew & B. Sorheim (Eds.), *The young language learner: Research-based insights into teaching and learning.* Bergen: Fagbokforlager.

Masuhara, H. (2005). Helping learners to achieve multi-dimensional mental representation in L2 reading. *Folio, 9*(2), 6–9.

McKee, D. (2005). *Not now Bernard.* Sydney: Andersen Press.

Mourao, S. (2015). The potential of picturebooks with young learners. In J. Bland (Ed.), *Teaching English to young learners: Critical issues in language teaching with 3–12 year olds* (pp. 199–218). London: Bloomsbury.

Noronho, S. (in press). Supporting language learning through a library program. The ELTRePA Project. Kolkata: British Council.

Nunan, D. (2013). Innovation in the young learner classroom. In K. Hyland & L. L. C. Wong (Eds.), *Innovation and change in English language education* (pp. 233–247). Abingdon: Routledge.

Pinter, A. (2012). Teaching young learners. In A. Burns & J. C. Richards (Eds.), *The Cambridge guide to pedagogy and practice in second language teaching* (pp. 103–111). Cambridge: Cambridge University Press.

Pinter, A. (2015). Task-based learning with children. In J. Bland (Ed.), *Teaching English to young learners: Critical issues in language teaching with 3–12 year olds* (pp. 114–127). London: Bloomsbury.

Read, C. (2015). Foreword. In J. Bland (Ed.), *Teaching English to young learners: Critical issues in language teaching with 3–12 year olds* (pp. xi–xiii). London: Bloomsbury.

Rixon, S. (2013). Authors' knowledge, rationales, and principles—Steady flow-through or stuck in the publishing pipeline? The case of early reading with young learners. In B. Tomlinson (Ed.), *Developing materials for language teaching* (pp. 229–246). London: Bloomsbury.

Schmid, E. C., & Whyte, S. (2015). Teaching young learners with technology. In J. Bland (Ed.), *Teaching English to young learners: Critical issues in language teaching with 3–12 year olds* (pp. 239–260). London: Bloomsbury.

Shireen, N. (2016). *The Bumblebear.* London: Random House.

Tomlinson, B. Ed. (1981). *Talking to learn.* Port Vila: Government of Vanuatu.

Tomlinson, B. (1990). Managing change in Indonesian high schools. *ELT Journal, 44*(1), 25–37.

Tomlinson, B. (1994a). Materials for TPR. *Folio, 1*(2), 8–10.

Tomlinson, B. (1994b). Pragmatic awareness activities. *Language Awareness, 3*(3 and 4), 119–129.

Tomlinson, B. (2000). A multi-dimensional approach. *The Language Teacher, 24*(7), 1–6.

Tomlinson, B. (2007). Teachers' responses to form-focused discovery approaches. In S. Fotos & H. Nassaji (Eds.), *Form focused instruction and teacher education: Studies in honour of Rod Ellis* (pp. 179–194). Oxford: Oxford University Press.

Tomlinson, B. (2013). Developing principled frameworks for materials development. In B. Tomlinson (Ed.), *Developing materials for language teaching* (2nd ed., pp. 95–118). London: Bloomsbury.

Tomlinson, B. (2015). Developing principled materials for young learners of English as a foreign language. In J. Bland (Ed.), *Teaching English to Young Learners: Critical issues in language teaching with 3–12 year olds* (pp. 279–293). London: Bloomsbury.

Tomlinson, B., & Masuhara, H. (2009). Playing to learn: A review of physical games in second language acquisition. *Simulation and Gaming, 40*, 645–668.

Van Gorp, K., & Bogaert, N. (2006). Developing language tasks for primary and secondary education. In K. Van den Branden (Ed.), *Task-based language education: From theory to practice* (pp. 76–105). Cambridge: Cambridge University Press.

Willis, J., & Reynolds, A. (2008). *Mine's bigger than yours*. London: Andersen Press.

11

Developing Materials for Teenagers and Adults

Introduction

In English language teaching, who are most likely to enroll in courses such as general English, EAP (English for academic purposes) and ESP (English for specific purposes)? Could this be the same for all modern languages? Of all the published language-teaching materials, who may be the most targeted users? What is their age range?

The blurbs of global coursebooks normally claim that they are intended for "adult" and sometimes also "young adult" learners. Judging from the fact that global coursebooks cater for the largest possible markets, the answers to the questions above are likely to be young adults and adults.

Who do we mean by "young adults" and "adults"? When coursebooks claim to cater for "young adults and adults," to which specific age groups are they referring? Can and should young adults and adults be bundled together for commercial reasons (see Chapter 6, "Developing Coursebooks"): do late teens, adults in their thirties, or retirees have similar needs and wants?

We also wonder about individuality: as we grow older, we tend to cultivate individual identities. For example, Sen (2006), an economist and philosopher, contemplates on the identity of an adult:

> In our normal lives, we see ourselves as members of a variety of groups—we belong to all of them. The same person can be, without any contradiction, an American citizen, of Caribbean origin, with African ancestry, a Christian, a liberal, a woman, a vegetarian, a long-distance runner, a historian, a schoolteacher, a novelist, a feminist, a heterosexual, a believer in gay and lesbian rights, a theater lover, an environmental activist, a tennis fan, a jazz musician, and someone who is deeply committed to the view that there are intelligent beings in outer space with whom it is extremely urgent to talk (preferably in English). Each of these collectivities, to all of which this person simultaneously belongs, gives her a particular identity. None of them can be taken to be the person's only identity or singular membership category. Given our inescapably plural identities, we have to decide on the relative importance of our different associations and affiliations in any particular context (Sen, 2006, xii–xiii)

Imagine this person has decided to learn an additional language, say, Spanish. Once she is classified as a "student" or "learner," somehow her multiple identities seem to be

The Complete Guide to the Theory and Practice of Materials Development for Language Learning,
First Edition. Brian Tomlinson and Hitomi Masuhara.
© 2018 John Wiley & Sons, Inc. Published 2018 by John Wiley & Sons, Inc.

swallowed by the language-teaching labels (see Cook, 2013, for an insightful discussion), for example, of proficiency level (e.g. A1 Beginner) or of learning purposes (e.g. business Spanish). Teachers' concerns tend to center around which Spanish sounds, vocabulary, grammar and expressions this person should learn or if her proficiency is progressing. In typical language learning situations, this person's personality with all her capabilities, skills, strategies, strengths and achievements rarely matters. Instead, she is encouraged to strive for the impossible target of attaining "native-like" perfection, which often results in learners feeling inadequate all along from beginner to advanced.

Considering the majority of users of coursebooks are young adults and adults, what we find perplexing is the seeming scarcity of literature that investigates and makes recommendations for suitable teaching approaches and for developing materials for teenage, young adult and adult learners. They are often the course participants and target learners but the literature rarely seems to focus on their age-specific characteristics or the ways they learn. There is abundant literature on needs analysis for language learning (e.g. Long, 2005; Huhta, Vogt, Johnson, & Tulkki, 2013) but it tends to focus on academic or occupational needs and research methodology. There are some age-group-specific psychological studies: of youth (e.g. Goldner & Berenshtein-Dagan, 2016; Yu, Li, & Zhang, 2015) and university and adult education (e.g. O'Toole & Essex, 2012; Suwanarak, 2015). But they do not discuss materials development for learning languages for these age ranges. Surprisingly, age-specific focus does not seem to feature as a category in the list of contents in major publications in materials development (McGrath, 2002, 2013, 2016; Gray, 2010, 2013; Harwood, 2010, 2014; Tomlinson & Masuhara, 2010; McDonough, Shaw, & Masuhara, 2013; Tomlinson, 2013a, 2016; Garton & Graves, 2014; Mishan & Timmis, 2015; Masuhara et al., 2017).

Two exceptions we have found are Mishan and Chambers (2010) and Tomlinson (2013b). Mishan and Chambers (2010) has a section called "Tailoring materials for learner groups" and includes chapters on preuniversity EAP students in Venezuela (St. Louis, Trias, & Periera, 2010), on Tunisian university students on an English Culture course (Mason, 2010), and on adult ESOL in the United Kingdom (Hann, Timmis, & Masuhara, 2010) but the focus tend to be more on the designing of materials for courses. Tomlinson (2013b) contains a section called "Developing materials for target groups" and it provides two chapters, which do discuss developing adult materials: "Adult Spanish beginners" (Cives-Enriquez, 2010) and "Adult beginners in English and modern languages" (Cook, 2013).

In the fields of psychology and second language acquisition, "age factors" have attracted a lot of attention in relation to the unresolved controversy of the so-called "critical" or "sensitive period" in language learning. Note that these studies often compare success rates of language attainment between pre-puberty and post-puberty immigrants in terms of nativelike proficiency in various aspects such as pronunciation, lexis, and collocation (Ortega, 2009; Granena & Long, 2013; DeKeyser, 2016). The significance of such "nativeness" (which "natives"?), however, may be a context dependent issue in our era when global English is sought after by the majority of English users (Pennycook, 2010). In business negotiations between Chinese and Saudi Arabians, for example, what matters is establishing mutually intelligible and effective means of communication.

The invariable target of native-speaker-like proficiency seems to be assumed in ELT courses and coursebooks. If the Chinese and Saudi Arabians referred to above enrolled on Business English courses, for example, they might find the repeated emphasis on accurate use of English based on British English or American English norms to be somewhat demotivating. In addition, for adult learners outside the EU who have already gone through an institutional education, a coursebook syllabus based on exam specifications or the Common European Framework (see Chapter 6, "The Process of Publishing Coursebooks") may seem irrelevant.

In this chapter, therefore, we intend to:

- define what teenagers, young adult and adult learners may mean;
- try to identify age-group-specific characteristics;
- consider principled approaches that may be appropriate for teenagers, young adults and adults;
- explore future directions for the materials that cater for teenager, young adult and adult learners.

Teenagers

Descriptions of Teenagers

The definitions of teenagers in various dictionaries seem very similar. A teenager, or teen, means a person whose age falls within the range between 13 and 19. This is due to the fact the terms between those ages in English all end with "teen."

Note here that, according to the World Health Organization, "Adolescent development," 10–19 years old, is called "adolescent," i.e. a period of transition from child to adult. The key developmental experience includes:

> The process of adolescence is a period of preparation for adulthood during which time several key developmental experiences occur. Besides physical and sexual maturation, these experiences include movement toward social and economic independence, and development of identity, the acquisition of skills needed to carry out adult relationships and roles, and the capacity for abstract reasoning. While adolescence is a time of tremendous growth and potential, it is also a time of considerable risk during which social contexts exert powerful influences. (http://www.who.int/maternal_child_adolescent/topics/adolescence/dev/en/)

So the teenage years (i.e. 13–19) are part of the adolescence which is described by WHO (2016) as "one of the critical transitions in the life span and is characterized by a tremendous pace in growth and change that is second only to that of infancy." WHO also points out that "The biological determinants of adolescence are fairly universal; however, the duration and defining characteristics of this period may vary across time, cultures, and socioeconomic situations."

The Royal College of Psychiatrists in the United Kingdom divides adolescence into pre-teens (10–12) and teens (13–19) (http://www.rcpsych.ac.uk/healthadvice/parentsandyouthinfo/parentscarers/adolescence.aspx). Puberty, according to the report in the United States, starts during the pre-teens and completes during the teens, around the age of 17 (Palo Alto Medical Foundation, 2015).

The adolescent years coincide with the basic institutional education period. Educational systems vary from one country to another but 5–11 year olds tend to go to primary schools; 12–18 year olds are likely to be receiving education in secondary schools (e.g. middle school, junior, and senior high schools); 19 year olds may be continuing on to higher education in a college or university. Despite the lack of agreement on the "critical / sensitive period" for acquiring a language, some governments have started teaching foreign languages in primary schools or even earlier. The introduction of English at primary (or even pre-primary) level means that students enter secondary school after they have gone through different kinds and levels of English learning experience. The successful ones are at quite high levels whereas the unsuccessful ones may already have become false beginners, possibly, with low motivation and negative attitudes. The timing and sequence of the introduction of L2 literacy has a significant influence on the achievement levels of the four skills among teenagers (Masuhara, 2007). So teaching teenagers means teaching multilevel learners with varied motivation and confidence sitting in the same classroom. Each of them is trying to manage biological, social and personal growth that is unfamiliar and difficult to control. Furthermore, teenagers study English for general purposes as a school subject (i.e. for no particular purpose). There is no urgent or specific goal. Unless English learning is fascinating or has a strong personal significance, teenage students may not be too focused on their language learning. This is the ultimate challenge for teachers and for materials developers. Some teachers therefore may resort to stimulating students' instrumental motivation by mentioning quizzes and exams. Teenagers, however, might discover lifelong passions and become aware of issues in life and society through their learning. Teenagers in fact may be giving teachers and materials developers a lesson or two by being discerning and by paying selective attention only when the teaching and materials are "OK."

Characteristics of Teenagers

Though all of us have gone through the teenage period it may be useful to refresh our understanding about the psychological and cognitive characteristics of teenagers. Cultural contexts and individual differences should be carefully investigated to avoid stereotyping. However, some universally convergent characteristics seem to be evident in authoritative medical and psychological literature. For example, the following general tendencies of teenagers are observed in the United States and in the United Kingdom:

- Peers of their own age matter more than family. Long phone calls, texting, Internet chatting and going out with friends are ways of establishing identities and independence from family. Experimentation with clothes, appearance, music, hobbies, and certain behaviors may be their ways of expressing solidarity with like-minded peers. They gain social skills through sharing experience with peers.
- Questioning and challenging conventions in family and school lives. They judge things as good or bad, right or wrong as part of forming their own views. The rejections of conventions and consequent conflicts against family members or adults are likely to be their expressions of asserting their own identities rather than intending to attack others. They may recklessly try new things and take on challenges only to find that they lack expertise or experience, thus affecting their level of self-esteem and confidence. They want to be independent and left alone but, at the same time, they may be seeking for sympathetic and guiding support. By late teens onwards they may gradually start to see other possible interpretations, consequences of their actions and effects of what they say.
- Moodiness. Rapid biological, social, intellectual, and psychological changes may result in emotional ups and downs. They become very self-conscious—an appearance

of a pimple could be felt as the end of the world. "Being upset, feeling ill or lacking confidence can make them feel vulnerable. They may show this with sulky behaviour rather than obvious distress" (http://www.rcpsych.ac.uk/healthadvice/parentsandyouthinfo/parentscarers/adolescence.aspx).

- Being curious and seeking excitement. Teenagers are interested in trying out new things that are "exciting," which could include some antisocial behavior. From our personal experience, the majority of youths seem to somehow manage to find engaging activities that do not infringe laws, such as sports, music, art, and many other activities that simulate them intellectually and emotionally.

Teenage learners may sometimes be stereotyped. Teenagers in the United Kingdom, for instance, may be described as those who:

- are hard to please;
- often do not like the materials that books provide;
- enjoy rebelling against a prescriptive approach;
- get bored quickly;
- crave independence;
- often have stronger opinions about life than many adults (http://www.onestopenglish.com/teenagers/topic-based-materials/).

You may find some of these descriptions familiar. Hitomi taught for 10 years in a co-educational Japanese secondary school. Despite being culturally stereotyped as polite, Japanese teenagers, both male and female, can be rebellious and challenging, in some cases due to deep-rooted personal and social problems. All in all, however, as the author of the blog in *Onestopenglish* above points out in another bullet point, despite their stereotypical behaviors, "Left to their own devices teenagers are often more responsible, cooperative and sensible than we give them credit for." In Hitomi's case, she found that her students (i.e. 15–18 years old) were carefully assessing if teachers were genuinely and sensitively making efforts to reach the students' true selves (Goldner & Berenshtein-Dagan, 2016). If the students liked a particular teacher in spite of her / his own shortcomings and felt that they could trust her / him, then they were more likely to open up and be willing to share thoughts and feelings (but only when they were prepared to do so).

Some Recommended Principles and Approaches that are Likely to be Suitable for Teenagers

Principles of Materials for Teenagers

We believe that the following principles may be appreciated universally by teenagers based on our own teaching experience of teaching and observing numerous classes and trials of our materials in various projects, as well as our reading of relevant literature on teaching methodology and learning theories (e.g. second language acquisition, psychology, education and neuroscience). Teenagers seem to appreciate materials that are:

- relevant (e.g. related to their lives in some ways);
- affectively engaging (e.g. funny, surprising, scary, helping to raise self-esteem and confidence);

- cognitively challenging (e.g. makes them think; entices them to work out the under-lying mechanisms);
- meaningful (e.g. means something to their true selves);
- useful (e.g. in raising their scores in exams).

We think that teenagers tend to be more motivated if materials:

- lead to learning new useful skills (e.g. building a model; doing magic tricks);
- involve working with peers;
- provide achievable challenges;
- satisfy cognitive levels in a linguistically accessible way;
- provide opportunities for competitions that they can potentially win (and which do not cause serious problems if they lose);
- connect to learning outside the classroom (e.g. connection with the community, making use of media, engaging with adults with expertise);
- provide potential social rewards (e.g. getting acknowledgement from their peers, family and community for the value of their work);
- help them feel self-fulfilled (e.g. satisfy inner needs and wants);
- learn about adults whom they can respect and relate to;
- provide opportunities to contribute to society (e.g. connection with real people, institutions);
- satisfy different learning styles and preferences;
- make use of multimodality in production (e.g. miming to stories, drawing crucial scenes and explaining them) as well as reception (e.g. video, visuals and audio input);
- allow weaker learners to hide and observe others without being threatened or being dragged under the spotlight;
- offer individual support when they need it.

In sum, teenagers seem to need materials that help them to acquire and develop "communicative competence", "linguistic competence" and "personal competence" (Stevick, 1982).

Approaches

Mishan (2013) describes the changes in pedagogical approaches from the 1950s to the present and provides a useful account and examples of current approaches:

> The recognition of the crucial role that learners play in their own learning is reflected in the evolution of language pedagogy over the latter half of the last century. Thus we see the movement from the controlled and controlling language learning methods of the 1950s and 1960s, such as the audiolingual method, the direct method and grammar translation, to the Communicative Approach in the 1970s and thence to approaches and pedagogies which explicitly foster autonomy, such as task-based learning in the 1980s (Willis and Willis, 2007), learner autonomy in the 1980s and 1990s (Benson, 2001), and latterly, Content and Language Integrated Learning (CLIL) [Coyle, Hood, & Marsh, 2010] and Problem-based Learning (PBL) [Barrett, Mac Labhainn, & Fallon, 2005].
>
> (Mishan, 2013, p. 269)

What seems to emerge is a shift of focus from teaching to learning. We know that what we teach does not automatically lead to what learners learn. Instead, by exploring how learners learn, teaching can be tailored to maximize the effectiveness of learning. Studies in learning and in second-language acquisition inform us how such a learning process can be facilitated. Mishan (2013) points out that current approaches have been influenced by early twentieth-century educational philosophies. For example, various versions of constructivist philosophy (e.g. Bruner, 1973; Piaget & Cook, 1953; Stevick, 1982; Vygotsky, 1978) emphasize learners' active engagement in learning through discovery, problem solving, and communicative and social interactions. Some attempts have been made to incorporate such fundamental philosophies and approaches into education and empirical research has been undertaken (e.g. De Witte & Rogge, 2016 for an up-to-date review of problem-based approaches in secondary schools and universities).

Based on the characteristics and strengths of teenage learners and approaches we have discussed so far, we believe that teenagers would welcome experiential approaches (Kolb, 1984) in which they can try and learn new skills and collaborate with peers (e.g. communicative language teaching; task-based approaches; text-driven approaches; project work; learner training). Content and Language Integrated Learning offers the potential for satisfying learners with different interests in relation to subject matter (e.g. technology, science, history, home economics, music, art). They are likely to enjoy challenges such as problem solving (e.g. Mishan, 2010), and experience an extra buzz of competition as a form of creative play (Maley, Masuhara, Pugilese, & Tomlinson, 2014). If a motivating task or project is presented in a way in which their intellectual curiosity is stimulated then they might autonomously surf the Internet to try to achieve their target well (e.g. discovery approaches, extensive reading, listening for purposes, use of multimedia). If the Internet is not available then they can read relevant publications or talk to people in the community. The presentation or publication of their products will give them a boost of confidence. If target success requires accuracy, teenagers are likely to make conscious efforts to revise for accuracy (e.g. language awareness; consciousness raising). They can be ambitious and then they might welcome sensitive support as they navigate their ways into discovery (Tomlinson, 2016). Teenagers may also enjoy extensive listening (e.g. Renandya and Farrell, 2011) or video viewing (Keddie, 2014). Research testifies to the effectiveness of extensive reading (see Maley, 2008, for a review; latest information in http://erfoundation.org/wordpress/) but it may not be an obvious choice for teenagers. Text-driven approaches (Tomlinson, 2013c) make use of engaging texts containing universal topics and activities that could bridge the classroom to independent reading. Fenton-Smith (2010) explores extensive reading with post-reading classroom activities which may help teenagers develop the reading habit.

Example of Task-Based Materials for Teenagers

We have so far explored principles and various procedures for materials development we think are suited for teenagers. Seemingly different strands of approaches such as the task-based, the text-driven, discovery and problem-based approaches can be combined as series of coherent tasks.

Let us use an example of adapted materials in Masuhara (2015). She uses a task introduced in a chapter by Van Gorp and Bogaert (2006, pp. 92–93) in Van Den Branden (2006). Note that Van den Branden (2006) makes a unique and valuable contribution to the literature on task-based language learning as it bridges theory and practice. It not only discusses theories but also provides reports of actual task-based teaching practices in Belgium from very young learners to tertiary levels, including for assessment and teacher development.

The chapter by Van Gorp and Bogaert (2006, pp. 92–93) presents an interesting text on an Indian magician's trick titled "A Gruesome Performance," from a textbook based on a task-based syllabus for a Flemish secondary school.

The original material in the secondary school textbook divides the text "A Gruesome Performance" into two sections: the magic and an explanation of the tricks with the teacher reading the first part of the text. Masuhara (2015) provides a summary of the text:

> The first section of the text explains how an Indian magician scares and fascinates his audience at the same time through his magic performance. His magic involves: an ordinary rope standing up in the air; his assistant climbing up the rope; the magician following the disobedient assistant up the rope then dismembering his assistant in the air with a knife; the magician coming down and helping the assistant emerge from a basket, intact and smiling in front of the stunned audience.
>
> (Masuhara, 2015, p. 120)

The textbook asks the learners to individually think of how the trick is done. Then three possible answers are given. After students have made a choice, they are asked to find out if other students nearby have made different choices. The students are then instructed to go on and read about how the trick was done in the latter part of the text.

Masuhara (2015) finds the text to be potentially engaging for teenagers but does not think that the "discussion tasks" in the textbook qualify as genuine tasks as they lack a "nonlinguistic real life outcome," which can be seen as the distinguishing feature between a task and a communicative activity. Furthermore, the question of guessing the mechanism of the magic trick is weakened by the following task of selecting one possible answer from the three choices. The next instruction just asks the students to find out if others have made the same choice. The resulting conversation does not require the kinds and quantity of meaning negotiation that SLA researchers recommend. If the students have access to the second part, teenagers are likely to quickly skim through and find the answers before they are instructed to read on.

Masuhara (2015) proposes adapted materials that involve three subtasks (one subtask intended for one lesson), leading up to the main task, using the text "A Gruesome Performance."

Subtask 1: A Bit of Magic (Listening and Speaking)

1. The teacher announces the main theme: "magic" (*typical starting point of The Task-Based Approach*). She asks the students if they know of any magic tricks (*emphasis on relevance*). She shows a short video of Tommy Cooper's Vase Trick (https://www.youtube.com/watch?v=Y4c4zkMl8Ro). In the video, the British Comedian uses his knowledge and skills (or his tactfully exaggerated lack of) for magic in his act (*use of multimodal input; achieving impact, laughter, preparation for the teacher performance*).

2. She then tells the students that she will demonstrate a magic trick. After her performance, she asks the students to form groups and discuss how the magic trick works (*problem-based approach; interactions; collaboration*).

3. She then shows a YouTube video of a teenager performing the same magic trick and then explaining how the trick works (https://www.youtube.com/watch?v= 9HfVwzBuckQ) (*use of multimodal input; extensive listening for a purpose*).

4. She sets a group task for the following week: group performance of magic tricks (*task-based approach; experiential approach; autonomous learning; learning of new skills; creativity; multimodal output*). The students are given criteria: being entertaining, achieving clarity and impact (*task-based approach in terms of goal setting*). She shows how they can find magic tricks revealed on YouTube. She makes herself available if the students need help and guidance (*responsive teaching*).

Subtask 2: Group Performance of their Magic Trick (Reading and Writing during Preparation; Speaking during the Performance)

5. The teacher invites the volunteering groups to perform (*part of task-based approach; experiential approach; peer appreciation*), while the rest of the class gives feedback rating according to the criteria (entertaining, clear, impactful). The students are encouraged to add some comments if they want to (*use of group-to-group peer feedback*). The feedback is given to the group who performed the trick. She suggests if they want to they can upload their videos onto YouTube (*connection to real life; opportunities for language awareness / consciousness raising; nonlinguistic real-life outcome of a task; potential outside class interactions*). She makes herself available if the students need help and guidance (*responsive teaching*).

Subtask 3: Compiling a Booklet of Party Tricks to Sell at School Events (Writing of Instructions)

6. The teacher instructs the groups to write up their performance so that they can produce a class booklet of magic to sell at the School Exhibition Day (*connection to real life; opportunities for language awareness / consciousness raising*).

7. The teacher instructs the groups to swop their draft with another group and to request feedback for content and sequence (*use of group-to-group peer feedback; communicative focus*).

8. The groups revise according to the feedback. The teacher instructs the students to swop their second draft and ask for feedback on language use (*linguistic focus; language awareness / consciousness raising*).

9. The teacher instructs the groups to submit their final draft by a set date.

10. Prior to the following session she picks out major linguistic areas that many students seem to have problems with (*responsive teaching*).

11. The teacher shows some examples of typical mistakes and elicits suggestions for improvement from the students (*linguistic focus; language awareness / consciousness raising*). If necessary, form-focused teaching could take place in a meaningful context (responsive teaching).

12. (Optional.) The teacher suggests the students promote their booklet at the school exhibition day. If there should be any profits, the class decides how to use them (*connection to real life; nonlinguistic real-life outcomes as a result of tasks*).

Subtask 4. Writing the Second Part of the Text on Indian Magic Revealed (Integrated Skills and Expository Writing)

13. The teacher reads the first part of "A gruesome performance", instructing the students to visualize (*extensive listening for a purpose*).

14. She reads it a second time but instructs students to mime as she reads along (*catering for different learning styles and mixed abilities; experiential approach*).

15. She instructs the students to read the text individually and work out how the magic works (*problem-based approach*).

16. She tells the students to form groups and agree on how the tricks are designed (*collaborative learning; interaction; meaning negotiation through communication*).

17. She invites groups to report what they think. She takes notes on the board (*collaborative learning; interaction; communication; reporting*).

18. She instructs the groups to write a draft of the next section of the text Indian Miracle Revealed (*task-based approach; creative writing; collaborative learning; interaction; communication*).

19. She lets the students read the next section of the text to see the similarities and differences in terms of content (*language awareness / consciousness raising; building up linguistic competence*).

20. She instructs the students to individually compare their group draft with the text in terms of expressions and structures (*language awareness / consciousness raising; building up linguistic competence*).

21. She tells the groups to list major differences and similarities between the group draft and the text in terms of language (*language awareness / consciousness raising; building up linguistic competence*).

22. She conducts a whole class discussion regarding linguistically salient aspects of the texts (*language awareness / consciousness raising; building up linguistic competence*). If necessary, form-focused teaching could take place (*responsive teaching*).

23. She sets a homework task of individually revising the group draft based on the language discoveries (*task-based approach with a real-life outcome of a narrative account of a magic trick*). She announces a deadline for submission of the revised version to her. The students' narrative accounts can be published in some form (e.g. submission to an external internet site) (*task-based approach with a real-life outcome*).

This adaptation did not take up a lot of time or effort: searching for videos, making use of text-driven and task-driven approaches (Tomlinson, 2013c provides an easy to follow framework) and making some use of constructivist approaches such as problem-based, experiential, and discovery approaches.

To evaluate if the adapted task-based materials in Masuhara (2015) incorporated teenage learners' characteristic needs and wants, we have created a table (see Table 11.1) "Comparing teenager characteristics with learning principles and learning approaches." To provide an example we have compared the adapted task-based materials "a gruesome performance" with the teenage characteristics in the first column and we think they have achieved an effective match. You could try to compare a unit of a coursebook for teenagers (or a unit of the materials which you use to teach teenagers) with the teenage characteristics in the first column. You could also use the list of characteristics to help you to develop or adapt a unit of materials for teenagers and then compare your unit with the list of characteristics.

Other Published Examples for Teenage Learners

There are some coursebooks specifically designed for teenagers such as Campbell, Metcalf, and Robb Benne (2015) and Puchta, Stranks, and Lewis-Jones (2016). Though this is

Table 11.1 Comparing teenager characteristics with learning principles and learning happroaches

Teenagers' characteristics and needs	Learning principles	An example ("Magic") of task-based learning material	Materials that you are using	Your own material
Search for independence	Active roles of learners; Opportunity for self-expression; Goal-orientated learning	x		
Search for identity	Autonomous learning; Peer and social interaction; Feeling of self-fulfilment	x		
Importance of peers	Peer and social interaction and collaboration	x		
Curiosity for something new and exciting	Discovery approach; Play competition with a fair prospect for winning	x		
Connection beyond classroom	Contributing to the community and societies; Use of Internet; Opportunities for global communication	x		
Psychological vulnerability	Affective and cognitive engagement; Different learning styles; Learning and receiving support from adults and peers	x		
Need for communicative competence	Opportunity for using language for communication	x		
Need for lingusitic competence	Language aware-ness / Consciousness raising; Error feedback	x		
Need for personal competence	Opportunity for self-expression; Experiential approach; Problem-solving skills; Autonomous learning; Goal-orientated learning	x		
Need for guidance	Scaffolding by the more experienced e.g. teacher, expert	x		

not stated explicitly, the supplementary materials seem to reveal that the target users are adolescent learners in European Union countries. Both books make use of texts specially chosen for teenagers and involve discussions of personal and social issues. For example, the web site for Think by Puchta et al. (2016) provides author interview videos in which Puchta explains the teenager characteristics and rationale for designing the course. The downloadable samples demonstrate that they include some problem-based activities designed to encourage critical thinking and guided writing activity (80–120 words) for a purpose—e.g. "school magazine." The supplements seem to include videos that can be viewed with digital devices such as tablets and mobiles. We welcome such efforts by authors and publishers. Most of the activities, however, seem to be conventional gap filling of lexical bundles, questions and answers and matching of linguistic items. There seem to be no follow ups after discussions. Role plays seem to be part of the production phase of a PPP approach. The online materials and workbooks seem to provide mainly language practice. It would make an interesting research task to analyze the proportion of these language exercises in both courses compared with genuinely communicative activities. Another focus of research could be if the teenage learners confirm what the course claims to provide. As discussed in Chapter 6, "Developing Coursebooks," perhaps the buyers (administrators and teachers) may be mindful of examinations. Whether doing these practice exercises leads to higher scores in examinations would be another interesting research focus.

As for other resources for teenage materials, The British Council's "Learn-English," has a teens section (British Council LearnEnglish Teens, http://learnenglis hteens.britishcouncil.org/). It also hosts a site in collaboration with the BBC (British Broadcasting Corporation) World Service called "TeachingEnglish" for teachers and it has a "Teaching teens site" in which various resources and articles are freely made available (http://www.teachingenglish.org.uk/). Publishers also seem to be actively using blogs to create a teacher community. Once we subscribe to it, we can access online materials and discussion forums and enjoy teacher development opportunities (e.g. participating in webinars with renowned authors and researchers). Some publishers offer competitions with prizes and the winners' materials and blogs are shared on their community sites: a win-win way of marketing and promoting the courses. The active members may be invited to become reviewers or be considered for participation in a writing project—opportunities for the publishers to spot talent. Macmillan Publishers, for example, offer Onestopenglish in which various kinds of materials for different topics (e.g. business, skills) are made available as resources. One of the tabs includes resources for teenagers (http://www.onestopenglish.com/teenagers/topic-based-materials/). It offers links to other blogs such as project work, webquests and interactive games. The users can give a rating with Facebook likes. This can offer incentives for writers, user-rating information for potential users and talent spotting opportunities for publishers.

Regarding the interactive online communities that provide resources, we wish there were authors' names and information about authors' credentials. We would also welcome a clear explanation by the web / blog organizers about the date of updates, who is responsible for quality control of these materials, and how such evaluation takes place. We also hope that ease of navigation in these sites in general will be improved so that users will not drown in the sea of accumulated materials.

Materials for Young Adults and Adults

The term "pedagogy" derives from Greek via old French and it originally meant education for children. The term "andragogy" (i.e. literally means leader of man), on the other hand, was originally coined by German high school teacher in 1983 and was popularized by Knowles' (1984) influential work, *The adult learner: A neglected species.*

Knowles argued that adults have different learning needs and wants and prefer different approaches compared to children. His views of adults being self-directed, focused and motivated may reflect some elements of adult learning styles but current understanding is that adults are more likely to have different styles coming from their backgrounds and previous learning experience. They choose what and how they learn according to their needs, purposes and contexts at a particular time. In addition to lifelong learning (i.e. learning from birth to senior years), the concept of "lifewide" learning has been acknowledged (see the paragraph headed "Lifewide education community interest company" at http://www.lifewideeducation.uk/about.html). Lifewide learning embraces all the kinds of learning we do. It may mean synchronous or combined engagement in any kind of learning activities including formal education in universities or colleges, work-based professional development, community adult education, like-minded communities of people sharing voluntary learning, self-directed learning.

Descriptions of Young Adults and Adults

The definition of adult, compared to teens, seems rather nebulous. Biologically, adult seems to mean postpuberty and in some cultures people are considered to be adults if they are capable of reproduction. Legally, though variable according to social contexts, adult often means aged 18 or over and considered to be able to take on social and economic responsibility (e.g. voting, driving, marrying). Psychologically, Levinson (1986) divides adulthood into young adult (17–45 years old), middle adult (40–65), and late adult (60 onwards). The overlapped years are considered to be transitions. The publishing world seems to have different conventions in that young adult fiction seems to be marketed to readers of around 15–20-something.

We will refer to "young adults" to mean someone who is around 18 to mid-20s. Adults may be subdivided into "adults" (mid-20s to 65) and "senior adults" (65 onwards). Young adults (i.e. 18 to mid-20s) may still be in a formal educational system. In relation to English-language education, they may enroll in English for academic purposes (EAP) courses or general courses in language schools, combining study with living in English-speaking countries.

Adults who are mid-20s to 65 are likely to be engaged in some way in work or employment. Therefore they may be interested in ESP (English for specific purposes—e.g. business, medicine, law). They may decide to do an online distance modern language course or a course in a blended mode in which various face-to-face and distance modes of learning are combined (see Chapter 7). In England, the term ESOL (i.e. English for Speakers of Other Languages) is used to refer to teaching adult refugees and immigrants. Such learning could take place in a community college or in a workplace.

People aged 65 onwards are likely to be retired and they may take up learning languages for various reasons. They may enjoy lifelong learning and take foreign language courses in community adult education centers.

The difficulty in defining young adults and adults in itself testifies to the fact that the one-fits-all concept does not work for adults in materials development. When global coursebooks claim that their target learners are adults (and young adults), who do they mean? Where are they learning? In Chapter 6, "Developing Coursebooks," publishers explained that their syllabus is based on tried and tested examination-defined-syllabuses and on the Common European Framework. Do young adults and adults still need a grammar syllabus that prepares them for an examination? Which examination?

Characteristics of Young Adults and Adults

O'Toole and Essex (2012), based on their considerable experience of adult education in Australia, point out that adult learners tend to:

- have clear objectives;
- have specific personal, social and professional needs;
- be motivated to learn;
- expect high-quality, relevant, and meaningful content;
- expect skillful and qualified teachers;
- expect their needs to be met;
- have other multiple commitments;
- tend to be pressed with time;
- bring in various lifelong and lifewide learning experiences;
- have conscious and unconscious learning preferences and learning styles;
- "have strong values and need to unlearn and have these values challenged".

(O'Toole and Essex, 2012, p. 190)

Interestingly, O'Toole and Essex (2012, p. 187) report that "Attention spans between adults and children are not as wide as one might think" and they emphasize the importance of adults being engaged, just as children, through changes of dynamics by making use of a variety of activities, "mixing talk with participation and action." And we have found that adults enjoy stories just as much as young learners (even, in our experience, stories intended for L1 children).

Classroom learning is just one of many learning modes. Adult learners may welcome other modes such as e-learning, workplace-based learning, distance learning, individualized guidance and collaborative learning. Note here, though, that the learners might need clear guidance and support to keep the focus and motivation going in these individualized modes.

Principles of Materials for Young Adults and Adults

Castaño Muñoz, Redecker, Vuorikari, and Punie (2013) and Redecker (2014) describe "Open Education 2030" for adult education, a key element of the European agenda. They have identified four major scenarios for adult learning choice involving the two axis (x = learning contexts and y= learning goals). One scenario is self-guided discovery: usually involving an autonomous lifelong learner who is happy and confident in setting her own learning goals and manages to make use of available open resources through self-regulation and self-evaluation without external guidance. The opposite scenario is a guided journey: usually involving a person who prefers institutions or teachers to set the goals and help her learn for certification. Another scenario is guided discovery: usually involving someone who sets learning goals himself but prefer to be guided (e.g. by a community of experts). The last scenario is a self-guided journey: usually involving someone whose learning goals are set by others (e.g. a certified course online) but regulates and takes responsibility for his own learning. What the European Commission is investigating is how to establish a system in which each of the scenarios is possible and does not disadvantage anyone. Depending on the choice, the materials, teaching mode and approaches will be different. The current print coursebook used in language schools is an example of a guided journey experience. Distance online courses may be suited to those who prefer guided discovery to save having to sift through masses of unevaluated digital resources. Resource materials carefully constructed or selected by experts based on needs analyses may suit Guided Discovery learners. Self-guided autonomous learners would be discerning users of online and print materials. They might also welcome specific need-based resource materials.

Our Recommendations for Developing and Using Materials for Young Adults and Adults

Young adults and adults are aware that being proficient in languages, especially in global English, is vital. Long (2015, p. 11) questions the point of offering everything in a textbook "without identifying the learner goals and an analysis of their present or future communicative needs to achieve those goals":

> Language learning requires a huge investment of time, effort and money on the part of students and, in many cases, their parents or employers. With the need for new languages so crucial for so many, more and more learners, especially college students and young adults, are reluctant to accept courses that were clearly not designed to meet their needs. "General-purpose" (nebulous or no purpose) courses may teach too much, e.g., all four skills, when learners may only need, say, listening, listening and speaking, or reading abilities, and / or too little, e.g., nothing comparable to the content and complexity of the tasks and materials with which learners will have to deal or the discourse domain in which they will have to operate.
>
> (Long, 2015, p. 11)

Cook (2013) analyzes modern language textbooks as well as English teaching materials and points out shortcomings in themes, methods and language. Furthermore, he argues that materials should reflect the situations, roles and language of adult L2 users needs in the target language.

Based on our exploration of definitions, characteristics and research of goals and contexts of learning for young adults and adults, our recommendations include the following:

1. Find the goals, specific needs and wants of the learners. The materials should be:
   - relevant;
   - immediately useful;
   - rewarding;
   - self-discovering and self-fulfilling;
   - time saving;
   - facilitative in achieving learner goals;
   - helpful in terms of learner training.
2. Make use of learners' own experience. It is vital to establish rapport with adult learners. Engaging stories, poems, jokes, case studies and personal anecdotes could help make connections. In return, they are likely to open up and be willing to share their experiences, which could spark off opportunities for genuine negotiation of meaning for communication. It is also important to involve adult learners in planning what

and how they would like to learn. Ottley (2016) describes how he set up a focus group when he started teaching in Iraqi Kurdistan with a totally unfamiliar group of students with multiple ethnic, racial, and religious backgrounds. He used the course map from the global coursebook so he could satisfy requirements but adapted the materials in the light of students' interests and requests. In our experience, adult learners will welcome opportunities to reflect on and discuss learning strategies, their progress, and the adjustment of their learning experience.

3. Engage adults with affectively and cognitively engaging materials. Malu (2013) describes how children's picture stories can be so engaging for adults. Cives-Enriquez (2013) reminds us of the importance of fun in sessions with company executives. We have found that although adults object to being asked to do childish things, they can be persuaded to be childlike and to play with the language in ways that can be conducive to language acquisition (Cook, 2000). We have also found that problem-based approaches in which adult learners need to collaborate to solve problems (Mishan, 2010) can result in usefully heated discussion in the L1 and detailed reading and research. Such deep engagement can then often lead to sustained motivation and to durable learning.

4. Use adult learners' strengths. Adult learners are conscious learners who are likely to welcome cognitively challenging discovery approaches and the sort of cognitively engaging activities, projects, and tasks which, for example, Skeldon (2008) reports and advocates for the teaching of English for science and technology (EST).

Conclusion

We believe that consideration of age-specific factors has been overlooked and we would like to see more research conducted and more discussion in this area. As for suitable approaches for teenagers, young adults and adults, we have made recommendations based on the literature available (e.g. descriptions of characteristics; educational theories). Identifying appropriate approaches and implementing them through materials in different contexts would require careful consideration of many more factors in addition to age-specific factors by the respective stakeholders (Joy & Kolb, 2009; Bowden, Abhayawansa, & Manzin, 2015). What we argue is that numerous research findings supporting current methodological thinking seem to testify to the fact that the traditional teacher-centered knowledge-transmission approach for teenagers and young adults may not be the most appropriate or effective in terms of language acquisition. Such an approach does not provide opportunities for the motivated communicative interaction that is vital for language acquisition and development or for developing creativity or fostering life skills. Communicative proficiency in English seems to be considered to be a prerequisite for political, economic and social survival in the global world (Graddol, 2006; Euromonitor International, 2012; Loh & Renandya, 2015). Recent reforms by governments all around the world may be based on their awareness that good language education holds the key. The content and the systems of examinations seem to be major constraints for the development of materials for teenagers. As most adults no longer demand exam preparation, there is no reason why global coursebooks need to be so dictated by a grammatical syllabus. Instead, the development of adult materials has great potential for innovation.

What do You Think?

1. In this chapter, we described teenager characteristics based on the information provided by the World Health Organization and on data based on teenagers in the United Kingdom and United States. Do you think your learners are different? If so, how? Why do you think that they are different? Should the materials differ accordingly?
2. Look at Table 11.1 "Comparing teenager characteristics with learning principles and learning approaches." What would be the differences between teenager characteristics and adult characteristics? Do you think we should use different approaches for adults from the ones we use with teenagers? If so, what differences do you suggest?

Tasks

1. Download a set of publishers' sample materials for teenagers. Evaluate a unit using the following criteria:
   - To what extent are the texts likely to engage the learners affectively?
   - To what extent are the texts likely to engage the learners cognitively?
   - To what extent are the activities likely to engage the learners affectively?
   - To what extent are the activities likely to engage the learners cognitively?
   - To what extent are the texts likely to seem relevant to the learners?
   - To what extent are the activities likely to seem relevant to the learners?
   - To what extent are the learners likely to enjoy using this unit?

   For each criterion give a score out of 5 and justify your score. Try to improve the unit so that it gets higher scores on the evaluation criteria and it contains a higher percentage of the types of texts and activities you think it should provide.

2. Develop a set of typical characteristics of adult learners in a learning environment you are familiar with (see Table 11.1 for a set of teenage characteristics). Analyze a unit from a young adult coursebook to measure the match between the coursebook and your set of characteristics. Suggest ways of adapting the unit so that it achieves a greater match with your set of characteristics.

Further Reading

Cook, V. (2013). Materials for adult beginners. In B. Tomlinson (Ed.), *Developing materials for language teaching* (2nd ed., pp. 289–308). London: Bloomsbury.
Redecker, C. (2014). The future of learning is lifelong, lifewide and open. *Lifewide Magazine*, 9, 12–17. Retrieved from http://www.lifewideeducation.uk/magazine.html

References

Barrett, T., Mac Labhainn, I., & Fallon, H. (Eds.). *Handbook of enquiry and problem-based learning: Irish case studies and international perspectives.* Galway, Ireland: CELT, National University of Ireland Galway and All Ireland Society for Higher Education.
Benson, P. (2001). *Teaching and researching autonomy in language learning.* London: Longman.

Bowden, M. P., Abhayawansa, S., & Manzin, G. (2015). A multiple cross-cultural comparison of approaches to learning. *A Journal of Comparative and International Education, 45*(2), 272–294.

Bruner, J. S. (1973). *The relevance of education.* New York: Norton.

Campbell, R., Metcalf, R., & Robb Benne, R. (2015). *Beyond B1 plus.* Oxford: Macmillan Education.

Castaño Muñoz, J., Redecker, C., Vuorikari, R., & Punie, Y. (2013). Open education 2030: Planning the future of adult learning in Europe. *Open Learning, 28*(3), 171–186.

Cives-Enriquez, R. (2010). Materials for adults: "I am no good at languages!"—inspiring and motivating L2 adult learners of beginner's Spanish. In B. Tomlinson (Ed.), *Developing materials for language teaching* (2nd ed., pp. 270–287). London: Bloomsbury.

Cook, G. (2000). *Language play: Language learning.* Oxford: Oxford University Press.

Cook, V. (2013). Materials for adult beginners. In B. Tomlinson (Ed.), *Developing materials for language teaching* (2nd ed., pp. 289–308). London: Bloomsbury.

Coyle, D., Hood, P., & Marsh, D. (2010). *Content and language integrated learning.* Cambridge, Cambridge University Press.

DeKeyser, D. (2016). Age in learning and teaching grammar. In J. Liontas (Ed.), *TESOL encyclopedia.* Hoboken, NJ: Wiley.

De Witte, K., & Rogge, N. (2016). Problem-based learning in secondary education: Evaluation by an experiment. *Education Economics, 24*(1), 58–82.

Euromonitor International. (2012). *The benefits of the English language for individuals and societies: Quantitative indicators from Algeria, Egypt, Iraq, Jordan, Lebanon, Morocco, Tunisia and Yemen.* London: Euromonitor International Ltd.

Fenton-Smith, B. (2010). A debate on the desired effects of output activities for extensive reading. In B. Tomlinson & H. Masuhara (Eds.), *Research for materials development in language learning* (pp. 50–61). London: Continuum.

Garton, S., & Graves, K. (2014). *International perspectives on materials in ELT.* Basingstoke: Palgrave Macmillan.

Goldner, L., & Berenshtein-Dagan, T. (2016). Adolescents' true-self behavior and adjustment: The role of family security and satisfaction of basic psychological needs. *Merrill-Palmer Quarterly, 1*, 48.

Graddol, D. (2006). *English next—why global English may mean the end of "English as a foreign language."* London: The British Council.

Granena, G., & Long, M. (2013). *Sensitive periods, language aptitude, and ultimate L2 attainment.* Amsterdam: John Benjamins Publishing Company.

Gray, J. (2010). *The construction of English: Culture, consumerism and promotion in the ELT global coursebook.* Basingstoke: Palgrave Macmillan.

Gray, J. (Ed.). (2013). *Critical perspectives on language teaching materials* [Electronic book]. Basingstoke: Palgrave Macmillan.

Hann, N., Timmis, I., & Masuhara, H. (2010). ESOL materials: Practice and principles. In F. Mishan & A. Chambers (Eds.), *Perspectives on language learning materials* (pp. 202–223). Bern: Peter Lang.

Harwood, N. (Ed.). (2010). *English language teaching materials—theory and practice.* Cambridge: Cambridge University Press.

Harwood, N. (Ed.). (2014). *English language teaching textbooks—content, consumption, production.* Basingstoke: Palgrave Macmillan.

Huhta, M., Vogt, K., Johnson, E., & Tulkki, H. (Eds.). (2013). *Needs analysis for language course design: A holistic approach to ESP.* Cambridge: Cambridge University Press.

Joy, S., & Kolb, D. A. (2009). Are there cultural differences in learning style? *International Journal of Intercultural Relations, 33*(1), 69–85.

Keddie, J. (2014). *Bringing online video into the classroom.* Oxford: Oxford University Press.

Knowles, M. (1984). *The adult learner: A neglected species* (3rd ed.). Houston: Gulf Publishing.

Kolb, D. A. (1984). *Experiential learning: Experience as the source of learning and development.* Englewood Cliffs, NJ: Prentice Hall.

Levinson, D.J. (1986). A conception of adult development. *American Psychologist, 41,* 3–13.

Loh, J., & Renandya, W. A. (2015). Exploring adaptations of materials and methods: A case from Singapore. *The European Journal of Applied Linguistics and TEFL, 4*(2), 93–111.

Long, M. H. (Ed.). (2005). *Second language needs analysis.* Cambridge: Cambridge University Press.

Long, M. H. (2015). *Second language acquisition and task-based language teaching.* Hoboken, NJ: Wiley-Blackwell.

Maley, A. (2008). Extensive reading: Maid in waiting. In B. Tomlinson (Ed.), *English language learning materials—A critical view* (pp. 133–156). London: Continuum.

Maley, A., Masuhara, H., Pugliese, C., & Tomlinson, B. (2014). C is for creativity. *English Teaching Professional, 95,* 14–17.

Malu, K. F. (2013). Exploring children's picture storybooks with adult and adolescent EFL learners. *English Teaching Forum, 51*(3), 10–18.

Mason, J. (2010). The effects of different types of materials on the intercultural competence of Tunisian university students. In B. Tomlinson & H. Masuhara (Eds.), *Research for materials development in language learning: Evidence for best practice* (pp. 67–82). London: Continuum.

Masuhara, H. (2007). The role of proto-reading activities in the acquisition and development of effective reading skills. In B. Tomlinson (Ed.), *Language acquisition and development: Studies of learners of first and other languages* (pp. 15–45). London: Continuum.

Masuhara, H. (2015). "Anything goes" in task-based language teaching materials?—the need for principled materials evaluation, adaptation and development. *The European Journal of Applied Linguistics and TEFL, 4*(2), 113–127.

Masuhara, H., Mishan, F., & Tomlinson, B. (Eds.). (2017). *Practice and theory for materials development in L2 learning.* Newcastle upon Tyne: Cambridge Scholars.

McDonough, J., Shaw, C., & Masuhara, H. (2013). *Materials and methods in ELT: A teacher's guide* (3rd ed.). Oxford: Wiley-Blackwell.

McGrath, I. (2002). *Materials evaluation and design for language teaching.* Edinburgh: Edinburgh University Press.

McGrath, I. (2013). *Teaching materials and the roles of EFL/ESL teachers.* London: Bloomsbury.

McGrath, I. (2016). *Materials evaluation and design for language teaching* (2nd ed.). Edinburgh: Edinburgh University Press.

Mishan, F. (2010). Withstanding washback: Thinking outside the box in materials development. In B. Tomlinson & H. Masuhara (Eds.), *Research for materials development in language learning—evidence for best practice* (pp. 353–368). London: Continuum.

Mishan, F. (2013). Studies of pedagogy. In B. Tomlinson (Ed.), *Applied linguistics and materials development* (pp. 269–286). London: Bloomsbury.

Mishan, F., & Chambers, A. (Eds.). (2010). *Perspectives on language learning materials development*. Bern: Peter Lang.

Mishan, F., & Timmis, I. (2015). *Materials development for TESOL*. Edinburgh: Edinburgh University Press.

Ortega, L. (2009). *Understanding second language acquisition*. London: Hodder Education.

O'Toole, S., & Essex, B. (2012). The adult learner may really be a neglected species. *Australian Journal of Adult Learning, 52*(1), 183–191.

Ottley, K. (2016). Why one-size-fits-all is not fit for purpose. In B. Tomlinson (Ed.), *SLA research and materials development for language learning* (pp. 268–279). New York: Routledge.

Palo Alto Medical Foundation. (2015). Parents and teachers: Teen growth and development, years 11 to 14. Retrieved from http://www.pamf.org/parenting-teens/health/growth-development/pre-growth.html

Piaget, J., & Cook, M. T. (1953). *The origins of intelligence in children*. Oxon: Routledge.

Pennycook, A. (2010). The future of Englishes—one, many or none? In A. Kirkpatrick (Ed.), *The Routledge handbook of world Englishes* (pp. 673–687). Oxon: Routledge.

Puchta, H., Stranks, J., & Lewis-Jones, P. (2015). *Think*. Cambridge: Cambridge University Press.

Redecker, C. (2014). The future of learning is lifelong, lifewide and open. *Lifewide Magazine*, (9), 12–17.

Renandya, W. A., & Farrell, T. S. (2011). "Teacher, the tape is too fast!" Extensive listening in ELT. *ELT Journal, 65*(1), 52–59.

Sen, A. (2006). *Identity and violence: The illusion of destiny*. London: Allen Lane.

Skeldon, P. (2008). Materials for English for science and technology. In B. Tomlinson (Ed.), *English language learning materials—A critical review* (pp. 59–73). London: Continuum.

Stevick, E., W. (1982). *Teaching and learning languages*. Cambridge University Press: Cambridge.

St. Louis, R., Trias, M., & Periera, S. (2010). Designing materials for a twelve-week remedial course for pre-university students: A case study. In F. Mishan & A. Chambers (Eds.), *Perspectives on language learning materials development* (pp. 249–270). Bern: Peter Lang.

Suwanarak, K. (2015). Learning English as Thai adult learners: An insight into experience in using learning strategies. *English Language Teaching, 8*(12), 144–157.

Tomlinson, B. (Ed.). (2011). *Materials development in language teaching* (2nd ed.). Cambridge: Cambridge University Press.

Tomlinson, B. (Ed.). (2013a). *Applied linguistics and materials development*. London: Bloomsbury.

Tomlinson, B. (Ed.). (2013b). *Developing materials for language teaching* (2nd ed.). London: Bloomsbury.

Tomlinson, B. (2013c). Developing principled frameworks for materials development. In B. Tomlinson (Ed.), *Developing materials for language teaching* (2nd ed., pp. 95–118). London: Bloomsbury.

Tomlinson, B. (2016). Discovery-based instruction. In J. Liontas I. (Ed.), *TESOL encyclopedia*. Hoboken, NJ: Wiley.

Tomlinson, B., & Masuhara, H. (2010). *Research for materials development in language learning: Evidence for best practice*. London: Continuum.

Van den Branden, K. (Ed.). (2006). *Task-based language education*. Cambridge: Cambridge University Press.

Van Gorp, K., & Bogaert, N. (2006). Developing language tasks for primary and secondary education. In K. Van den Branden (Ed.), *Task-based language education* (pp. 76–105). Cambridge: Cambridge University Press.

Vygotsky, L. S. (1978). *Mind in society: The development of higher psychological processes.* Cambridge, MA: Harvard University Press.

Willis, D. & Willis, J. (2007). *Doing task-based teaching.* Oxford: Oxford University Press.

Yu, C., Li, X., & Zhang, W. (2015). Predicting adolescent problematic online game use from teacher autonomy support, basic psychological needs satisfaction, and school engagement: A 2-year longitudinal study. *Cyberpsychology, Behavior, and Social Networking, 18*(4), 228–233.

12

Developing Materials for Different Levels, Users, and Purposes

Introduction

In our view there is no one best methodology for teaching an L2; it depends on the context, the learners, their targets in learning the language, and their teachers. For the same reasons, there is no template for the best course of materials. In this chapter, we will look at how the purposes for learning an L2, the language levels of the learners, and the attitudes, experience, and preferences of the learners and the teachers are determiners of the optimal course materials for facilitating the achievement of learner goals.

There is a large literature on the teaching of English for different purposes but very little on materials development for learners of an L2 for different purposes. There is not much literature on the teaching of L2s for different levels and users and even less on materials development for different levels and users. In fact, there are many major books on the learning and teaching of second or foreign languages that make no reference to different levels, users, or purposes at all. For example, a recent comprehensive guide to teaching English for speakers of other languages (TESOL) (Liu and Berger, 2015) makes no reference in the list of contents to the teaching of ESOL for different, levels, users, and purposes and this is largely true also of such books as Larsen-Freeman (2000), Mishan (2005), Eisenmann and Summer (2012), McDonough, Shaw, and Masuhara (2013), McGrath (2013) and Richards and Rodgers (2014). This probably reflects the views of the authors that what they have to say about teaching and learning languages as L2s applies universally regardless of the learning context (e.g. "This list of abilities is applicable not just to ESP but to all forms of English language teaching," McGrath, 2013, p. 24). A notable exception is Hinkel (2005), which has a 174-page opening section with separate chapters on ESL in elementary education, in secondary schools, in adult education, for academic purposes, for specific purposes, in the workplace and in different contexts of learning (e.g. Tomlinson, 2005a). Most of these chapters make very little reference, though, to materials development for the type of learners or purposes they are focusing on. This is also true of Byram and Hu (2013), which has sections on, for example, beginner language learners, English for specific purposes, gender in language learning and large classes but makes little reference to materials development. This apparent neglect of the role of materials development is evident, too, in the literature focused on the learning and teaching of an L2 for learners of different ages and in the abundant literature on individual differences in L2 learning. For example, Ioup (2005) details the effects of different learner ages on the outcomes of learning but makes no reference to how this

The Complete Guide to the Theory and Practice of Materials Development for Language Learning, First Edition. Brian Tomlinson and Hitomi Masuhara.
© 2018 John Wiley & Sons, Inc. Published 2018 by John Wiley & Sons, Inc.

affects or should affect materials development (but see Chapters 10 and 11 in this volume for considerations of materials for young learners and for teenagers and adults respectively), and Ellis (2008), whilst rightly elaborating the effects of differences of affective states, age, aptitude, attitude, beliefs, learning styles, motivation and personality on the outcomes of language learning, makes no reference to how these differences are affected by materials nor to how materials could cater for these differences. Ortega (2009) also draws attention to the outcomes of these individual differences whilst making no reference to the potential impact of materials. Nation and Macalister (2010) has a chapter on the impact of environment analysis on curriculum development and focuses in particular on such situational factors as purposes for learning, preferred ways of learning, the training, confidence, and time available of the teachers, the suitability of classrooms, the time available for the course, and the availability of resources. The potential impact of such constraints on course delivery is discussed but not the implications for materials development. Granema and Long (2013) focuses in particular on differences of age and on differences of aptitude. Its main concern is with research findings in both classroom and naturalistic settings but it does contain a concluding section on implications for educational policy and language teaching, a section that makes no reference at all to implications for materials development. Liu and Nelson (in press) focuses on diversity in the classroom and discusses how each learner in a classroom is differentiated from all the others in relation to such factors as linguistic, cultural and social backgrounds, preferred learning styles, personality and motivation. Pedagogic implications are considered and individualized teaching is recommended but no reference is made to differentiation in materials or in their use.

We feel that what is needed is a publication that discusses and exemplifies the implications for materials development of the findings and theories on individual differences reported in such publications as those above. After all, if each individual in a class is different, how can a coursebook, for example, cater for the needs of each learner in that class? In our view the answer is to develop multilevel / purpose / user materials and / or generalizable sets of activities to be matched by teachers or students to an appropriate selection of texts from an extensive menu, an answer we will elaborate on below.

There are many books on materials development that also make little or no reference to developing materials for different levels, users and purposes, for example, McGrath (2002, 2013) and Mishan and Timmis (2015). There are some books on materials development, however, which do make reference to the development of different materials for different levels, users, and purposes; for example, Mishan and Chambers (2010) devotes a complete section to Tailoring Materials for Learner Groups (pp. 175–270), and these will be referred to in the sections below.

It is interesting to speculate on why materials development seems to be neglected in publications about the learning and teaching of L2s and why many publications on materials development neglect to consider how differences in levels, users, and purposes does and should affect materials development. We think that some of the reasons could be that:

- Materials development has only recently gained respectability as an academic field of study.
- It is considered impractical to vary materials according to so many differences.
- Many pedagogical procedures, such as presentation, production, and practice (PPP), task-based language teaching (TBLT), content-based learning, and communicative

language teaching, seem to be considered to be generalizable to all levels and types of learners.

- The allocated number of pages in many books seem to have been taken up by what are considered more fundamental issues.
- There has been very little research on catering for difference through materials development (probably because of the difficulty of measuring effects and of isolating materials as the sole variable).

Materials for Different Levels

The Literature

Despite the fact that all publishers produce coursebooks for beginner, for elementary, for intermediate, and for advanced-level learners we can find very little literature that actually focuses on the differentiation of materials for different levels of learners. There are many publications that focus on the performance and / or teaching of students at different levels of proficiency but most of them make little reference to materials. For example, Bernhardt (2011) provides a detailed analysis of the research literature on advanced second-language reading but includes only one-and-a-half pages on materials, in which she welcomes recent moves towards the provision of authentic texts but is critical of reading exercises (e.g. fill in the blank) that do not "require the reader to use any of the knowledge sources required for comprehension" (p. 64) and of the emphasis on "procedures to be practised, outside of texts, that are then supposed to transfer to texts"(p. 65). These are both valid criticisms that we would like to see developed into practical suggestions for material development.

One publication that does focus on materials for a specific level of learner is Cook (2013), which evaluates six coursebooks for L2 adult beginners, two for teaching French, two for teaching Italian, and two for teaching English. Although focusing on the teaching of beginners, Cook is also concerned with the importance of catering for the adult, thus emphasizing the need to consider all the characteristics of the learner profile when developing materials and not just the most obvious one(s). Cook is critical of these coursebooks for their blandness and triviality and for being insufficiently "adult in theme, teaching method and language" (p. 293). Cives-Enriquez (2013) is also concerned with materials for the teaching of adult beginners. She focuses on ways of humanizing materials for teaching Spanish to adult beginners and in particular on ways of promoting emotional engagement, self-confidence, autonomy, and the taking of risks. Unlike Cook (2013), though, she does not insist on everything being adult and encourages adults to be childlike in their willingness to play games and to play with the language they are learning.

We can find hardly any literature on materials for teaching at intermediate or advanced levels, Maley (2009) being one of the few exceptions by being a book that offers a wealth of ideas for developing supplementary materials to stimulate, challenge, and extend advanced learners. There are many tips on the web, though, for ideas and lesson plans for intermediate and advanced learners, as you will find if, for example, you google "teaching English to advanced learners." Nearly all these publications focus on adding "real-life" activities and none of them seems to offer any help in developing materials for different levels. For example, Maley (2016) offers 17 ideas for use with advanced learners but interestingly, although they are published on a publisher's web site, they are all ideas for supplementary activities (e.g. keeping journals, writing real letters, writing film scripts, writing subtitles for films, teaching lower level classes) and none of them involves using developed materials. We have always advocated and practiced the use of authentic literature in English with advanced learners so we were pleased to see a recent article reporting very positive empirical results for a study of the use of literature with an advanced adult group of learners (Kim, 2016). One of the findings of this study was that using literature with advanced learners led to "a more purposeful, contextually-situated, and pragmatic understanding of language" (p. 18).

Published Materials

We have just picked a current coursebook series at random from our bookshelves and have investigated it to find out what the differences are between its coursebooks at different proficiency levels.

The series is *Speakout* (Clare & Wilson, 2011; Eales & Oakes, 2011), which won the NSU "Best course this year" award. What we found is presented in Table 12.1.

It seems that the main differences between each coursebook and the one below it in level are a slight increase in the length of texts, slightly less emphasis on grammar and vocabulary practice, slightly less control of content and expression in "production" activities and slightly more intelligent content. The pedagogical approach is basically the same throughout the course but with a gradual move from closed to more open activities. Students at the lower levels of proficiency seem to be treated as though they have less experience of the world and less capacity for thought than their more "advanced" counterparts. What is true for *Speakout* seems fairly typical of the way most published coursebooks, in our experience and on our shelves, approach progression through their different levels of proficiency. What we find amazing is that advanced learners are still taught and asked to practice language items and are not asked to interact with reading texts longer than 600 words, yet they probably have a higher level of communicative competence than the average native speaker.

Recently we visited the Liverpool School of English to see what their approach is to teaching learners with different levels of proficiency. They told us that their students prefer consistency and continuity and so they tend to use the same coursebook series at all levels of proficiency. They also told us that their students (many of whom are preparing for the IELTS examination) have expressed a preference for coursebooks with explicit teaching of grammar and that, for this reason, their coursebook of choice is *New English file* (Oxenden, Latham-Koenig, & Seligson, 2012), a choice endorsed by most of the teachers. For two of the four terms in the year the teaching in the morning classes is driven by an institutional syllabus and by *New English file*. Other courses are used in the other two terms but *New English file* remains the favorite, though *Outcomes* (Dellar & Walkley, 2010) is also popular with some teachers because of its interesting texts. The director and assistant director of studies expressed their own personal pedagogic preferences for different proficiency levels and accepted that their policy of selecting the same course for all levels is unlikely to allow them to follow up these preferences. However, they considered that from a management point of view it was more important to achieve consistency and standardization (especially in view of their commercially necessary continuous enrolment policy) than to follow their pedagogic inclinations. Their personal preferences were for an emphasis on core vocabulary at the lower levels,

Table 12.1 Analysis of *Speakout*.

Level	Content	Texts	Activities	Approach
Starter	General topics (e.g. people, places, things, life, routines, shopping) Safe topics with little risk of controversy	Reading: 100–250 words. Listening: Conversations of between 5–15 short turns. Monologues of between 50–100 words.	Mainly controlled practice activities such as sentence completion, blank filling, underlining, matching, correction, sentence writing, surface questions and true / false	Mainly a grammar-based PPP approach with the emphasis on presentation and controlled practice (and with most of the production activities being really guided practice activities)
Elementary	General topics (e.g. people, places, food, transport, holidays) Safe topics with little risk of controversy	Reading: 100–250 words. Listening: Conversations of between 6–28 short turns plus interviews with turns of up to 100 words. A few monologues of up to 300 words.	Mainly controlled practice activities such as sentence completion, blank filling, underlining, matching, correction, sentence writing, surface questions and true / false. A few simple think questions per unit	Mainly a grammar-based PPP approach with the emphasis on presentation and controlled practice (and with most of the procuction activities being really guided practice activities)
Preintermediate	General topics (e.g. life, work, travel, money, technology) Safe topics with little risk of controversy	Reading: 100–400 words. Listening: Conversations of between 6–28 short turns plus interviews with turns of up to 100 words. A few monologues of up to 300 words.	Mainly controlled practice activities such as sentence completion, blank filling, underlining, matching, correction, sentence writing, surface questions and true / false. A few simple think questions per unit and some pair / group guided discussion activities	Mainly a grammar-based PPP approach with the emphasis on presentation and controlled practice (and with most of the production activities being really guided practice activities).

(continued)

Table 12.1 *(Continued)*

Level	Content	Texts	Activities	Approach
Intermediate	Some general topics (e.g. jobs, history, world communities) Mainly safe topics with little risk of controversy plus some more open-ended topics with the potential for personalization and disagreement (e.g. identity, solutions, emotion, success)	Reading: 100–450 words. Listening: Conversations of between 6–28 short turns plus interviews and discussions with turns of up to 100 words. Some monologues of up to 400 words.	Mainly controlled practice activities such as sentence completion, blank filling, underlining, matching, correction, sentence writing, surface questions and true / false. Some think questions, some pair / group guided discussion activities and some "What do you think questions?"	Mainly a grammar based PPP approach with the emphasis mainly on presentation and controlled practice (and with most of the production activities being really guided practice activities)
Upper intermediate	Mainly safe topics with little risk of controversy but a lot more open-ended topics with the potential for personalization and disagreement (e.g. issues, ideas, age, trouble)	Reading: 100–500 words. Listening: Conversations of between 6–28 short turns plus a number of interviews and discussions with turns of up to 100 words. Some monologues of up to 500 words.	Mainly controlled practice activities such as sentence completion, blank filling, underlining, matching, correction, sentence writing, surface questions and true / false. Some think questions, some pair / group guided discussion activities and some "What do you think questions?"	Mainly a grammar based PPP approach with most of the production activities being really guided practice activities.
Advanced	Mainly safe topics with little risk of controversy (e.g. places, trends, time) but a lot more open-ended topics with the potential for personalization and disagreement (e.g. opinion, freedom, justice, inspiration).	Reading: 100–600 words. Listening: Dialogues with turns averaging about 15 words plus a number of interviews and discussions with turns of up to 100 words. Some monologues of up to 600 words.	Many controlled practice activities such as sentence completion, blank filling, underlining, matching, correction, sentence writing, surface questions and true / false. More think questions, pair / group discussion activities and many "What do you think questions?"	Still mainly a grammar based PPP approach but with more production activities offering freedom of content and expression

moving towards a more task-based approach with greater freedom of expression at the upper levels. They accepted though that it was inevitable that publishers would base their courses on satisfying intermediate level learners first (their main market) and that coursebooks below and above this level would basically then follow the established format to allow the continuity that institutions need and students seem to welcome.

This visit to the Liverpool School of English reminded us of the realities of language school teaching and the inevitable tension between management priorities and pedagogic principles, with the priority ultimately being to choose a course that helps to achieve standardization as well as satisfying expressed customer preference and with the course being chosen initially because it satisfies requirements at the intermediate level (the entry level of the majority of students). Of course, publishers are well aware of these institutional constraints and tailor their courses accordingly.

Our Recommendations

We believe, like Klein (1986), that L2 acquisition is functionally driven and we advocate a gradual syntactization approach (see Ellis, 1994, pp. 369–373 for a summary) for materials development, in which an emphasis on meaning, communication and confidence at the lower linguistic levels is added to with increasing concern with form, accuracy and effectiveness as the levels progress through intermediate to advanced. The point is that, in natural language acquisition, learners only start to really pay attention to syntax when they have acquired enough vocabulary and confidence to achieve some success in communication in the L2 and we are saying that materials for beginners and elementary L2 learners should reflect this natural process and focus on the acquisition of vocabulary and confidence rather than the study and practice of grammatical accuracy. No learner, whether acquiring an L2 naturally or in a classroom, has ever started by communicating effectively and accurately so why do we persist in expecting our learners to achieve the impossible, and in so doing, push premature and erroneous production that can induce negative feelings of failure and erode confidence?

Our recommended approach would be as follows.

Beginner / Elementary

A comprehension approach (Winitz, 1981; Barnard, 2007) in which the emphasis is initially on listening for meaning and in which production is postponed until the learners have acquired enough vocabulary and confidence to achieve readiness. Our approach to materials would be to develop a set of flexible scripts for the teachers to make use of to drive TPR Plus activities (Tomlinson, 1994a) in which the learners act out stories as they are narrated or songs as they are sung, make models, meals, and murals as they are instructed, play games and, for example, dance or exercise to directions. The scripts would be meaning and function driven but language items would be recycled when natural from one script to another. Gradually more and more of the scripts would be given to the learners to read as well and eventually the learners would be asked to respond to scripts kinesthetically without having listened to them first. The learners would also eventually be asked to analyze scripts that they have performed to make discoveries about pragmatic, discourse and linguistic points, to attempt to articulate their discoveries (in the L1 in a monolingual class) and to look out for similar utterances outside the classroom (Tomlinson, 2014b).The amount and depth of discovery work would depend on the age and maturity of the learners but even young learners would do some of these activities. At the elementary stage the learners would also start extensive reading and would read what they wanted to read without being asked to do any exercises or summaries.

Lower Intermediate / Intermediate

We would follow a text-driven approach (Tomlinson, 2013d and Chapter 5 in this volume) in which potentially engaging spoken and written texts drive speaking and writing tasks. These materials would be supplemented by extensive reading, listening and viewing and by pragmatic awareness tasks (Tomlinson, 1994b), encouraging learners to make discoveries about how the L2 is used to achieve communicative effect from the texts they have already experienced and from those they find for themselves.

Upper Intermediate / Advanced

We would continue to follow a text-driven approach but would also encourage even more reading, listening to, and viewing of the L2 in authentic use and even more analysis of how the L2 is typically used, making use of data from corpora of L1 and of proficient L2 use and of learner research projects in which the learners investigate the use of the L2 outside the classroom.

One of the realities of language teaching is that learners are placed together through placement testing in language schools and according to age in primary and secondary schools, and then every learner in a class is usually allocated the same coursebook. They are treated as though they are learning in a homogeneous group and often they all use the same coursebook, on the same page at the same time, and yet within that group there are great differences in background, aptitude, motivation, personality, and even language level. There are publications that discuss ways of catering for mixed levels in the same classroom. For example, Bell (2012) provides useful suggestions for assessment, classroom organization and curriculum development for such classes and advocates a theme-based approach. Prabhu (2001) (as cited in Maley, 2011) proposes an approach to materials development in which a menu of semi-materials and meta-metamaterials are provided for the teacher to select from and to decide when and how to use, semi-materials being either single type activities (e.g. a reading skills exercise) or "raw" input consisting of texts without activities and meta-materials being pedagogical procedures without texts (e.g. role play; dictation). Maley (2011) puts forward and exemplifies the idea of flexi-materials, which "combine the notion of semi-materials with that of meta-materials" (p. 386). Teachers "are provided with a set of 'raw' texts and 'a set of generalisable procedures … which may be applied to any or all of the texts in any combination'" (p. 386). Prabhu (2001), and Maley's (2011) ideas allow teachers to make their own choices of content, sequence and pace and therefore to cater more effectively for a mixed group than when just following the coursebook. Tomlinson (1994c) is a textbook that provides the teacher (and the learners) with a set of potentially engaging "raw" texts from contemporary world literature in English and separately with a set of tasks for the teacher to select from for each text. Tomlinson (2013d) goes a step further by describing and demonstrating an approach in which the learners are provided with (and / or are encouraged to build up) a library of texts which they then select a text from to use with a set of generalizable procedures. "Or the materials can be based on units of text genres (e.g. advertisements, reports, jokes, announcements stories etc.) and the learners can be asked to find an appropriate and engaging text from the internet" (p. 111) as in the example Tomlinson provides for a set of activities to be used with any newspaper report (pp. 111–114). Nuangpolmak (2014) describes a project in Thailand in which supplementary multilevel materials were designed for use at the same time with different levels of learners in the same class. We did something similar to this when we were involved in a British Council project developing materials for future "leaders" in sub-Saharan African countries. The target classes were similar to each other in being composed of future "leaders" in politics, sport, entertainment, business, etc., but in each class the learners differed considerably from each other in level of language proficiency and of communicative confidence and competence. We catered for these differences by offering choice of different versions of the same text, of task, and of amount within each unit of material and trialed the materials in Senegal. The teachers were skeptical about the value of the materials as they assumed that the learners would opt for the shortest and easiest texts and tasks. In reality this was not the case, with many learners opting to be challenged by going for the most difficult version of a text or by going for an easier version first and then reading one of the more difficult versions of it.

Materials for Different Users

The Literature

One of the first publications to draw attention to the importance of materials being suitable for the age, social background, cultural background, and learning context of their target learners was Cunningsworth (1984), a book that includes among its recommended criteria for evaluating and selecting materials considerations of the potential interest, appeal and relevance of the materials to the learning context of the students, as well as their match with the capabilities of the teacher and the resources available. More recently, Tomlinson and Masuhara (2004) focused on the importance of considering such situational factors in evaluations when differentiating between universal criteria (i.e. those which "apply to any language learning materials anywhere for any learners" (p. 6)) and local criteria (i.e. those that "relate to the actual or potential environment of use" and measure "the value of the materials for particular learners in particular circumstances" (p. 7). This distinction between universal and local criteria is also focused on in Tomlinson (2003, 2013a), publications that stress the importance of using the same criteria for both the development and the evaluation of a set of materials. Typical features of the environment that should inform the development of materials are given as:

- the type(s) of institutions;
- the resources of the institution(s);
- class size;
- the background, needs and wants of the learners;
- the background, needs and wants of the teachers;
- the language policies in operation;

- the syllabus;
- the objectives of the courses;
- the intensity and extent of the teaching time available;
- the target examinations;
- the amount of exposure to the target language outside the classroom.

(Tomlinson, 2013a, p. 42)

Examples of local criteria are given as:

- To what extent are the stories likely to interest 15-year-old boys in Turkey?
- To what extent are the reading activities likely to prepare the students for the reading questions in the Primary School Leaving Examination in Singapore?
- To what extent are the topics likely to be acceptable to parents of students in Iran? (Tomlinson, 2013a, p. 42)

One obvious implication of using such environmental features to inform criteria is that global coursebooks are unlikely to satisfy local criteria because in trying to cater for learners everywhere they can rarely "engage learners anywhere" (Tomlinson, 2012, p. 272). In Tomlinson (2008a) the same 10 universal criteria were used to evaluate both the local and the global coursebooks used in different regions of the world. The 10 criteria asked questions about exposure to authentic use, meaningful exposure, interesting texts, achievable challenges, affective engagement, cognitive engagement, discovering English in use, meaningful activities, feedback opportunities, and positive impact. Although the criteria were universal, their application inevitably involved connecting many of them to local environments (e.g. "To what extent is the exposure to English in use likely to be meaningful to the target learners?" "To what extent are the texts likely to interest the learners?") (p. 77). These criteria were used in evaluations of coursebooks in Africa (Lumala & Trabelsi, 2008), Argentina (Barrios, de Debat, & Tavella, 2008), Australasia (Mol & Tin, 2008), Central and Eastern Europe (Bolitho, 2008), Japan (Smiley & Masuim, 2008), Malaysia (Mukundan, 2008), the Middle East (Bacha, Ghosn, & McBeath, 2008), Southeast Asia (Bao, 2008), the United Kingdom (Tomlinson & Masuhara, 2008), the United States (Frazier & Juza, 2008) and Western Europe (Prodromou & Mishan, 2008). It was found, for example, that many locally published materials "do provide comprehensible connections to the culture of the learners" (p. 321) but that many of the global coursebooks were "Anglo-centric or Euro-centric in their topics and themes and in their assumptions about the best ways to learn" and portrayed "non-European cultures superficially and insensitively" (p. 320). Gray (2010) addresses this issue of inappropriate and / or irrelevant cultural content in global coursebooks. He reports a study of 20 teachers in a Barcelona language school who objected to the stereotypical representation s of Britain and "the inclusion of irrelevant or incomprehensible cultural information about Britain" (p. 18) and he is critical of the "culturist" approach of many EFL coursebooks, which reduce the student to "a set of cultural stereotypes and all behaviour is then explained in terms of cultural stereotypes" (p. 36). Gray evaluates four best selling global coursebooks, interviews teachers and interviews publishers. He concludes that there is a pervasive Anglo-centric ideology in most global coursebooks and that the solution is more regionally based publishing projects involving local teachers, a solution that we have found could be successful on publishing projects we were involved with in Bulgaria, Morocco, Namibia, Turkey and Vanuatu.

There are a number of publications questioning the validity of "imposing" so-called Western culture and / or methodology on learners in non-Western cultures (especially through the medium of global coursebooks) and Holliday (1994) has argued in particular for the use of context appropriate methodology. Other publications arguing against the dominance of Western culture and / or methodology in materials being used in non-Western cultures include Kramsch and Sullivan (1996), Cortazzi and Jin (1999), Gray (2002), McKay (2003), Holliday (2005), Pham (2007), and Byram and Masuhara (2013), who argue for collaboration with local teachers, publishers, and experts in order to develop materials for specific target contexts. There are also publications that demonstrate the inappropriate stereotyping of cultures in global coursebooks and a tendency to portray Western cultures more positively than non-Western cultures (see, for example, Bao, 2016).

One publication that discusses in some detail the issues involved in using materials and methodology for teaching English as an L2 in different cultural contexts around the world is Tomlinson (2005b). Consideration is given to the issues of:

- The applicability of generally agreed learning principles (e.g. establishing a relaxed atmosphere, affective engagement, encouragement of learner autonomy) in non-Western cultures of learning.
- The need to "pay attention to local conditions rather than taking a set of ideas" around the world (Stubbs, 2000, p. 16).
- The universality of the school culture, with its aim to maintain the status quo and its insistence on conformity and control.
- Learner expectations and attitudes, and how they can easily change as a result of teacher justification and enjoyably useful experience.
- Teacher expectations and attitudes, and how they can eventually change as a result of reflection on the effectiveness of current practice, official encouragement, incentives to change and improved learner performance.
- The dangers of overgeneralizing about the teaching and learning styles of particular cultures.
- The universality in ways in which foreign languages are naturally acquired regardless of the cultures they are acquired in.
- The universality of the characteristics of the good language learner and the good language teacher regardless of cultural norms.
- The universality of what interests and engages learners regardless of culture (e.g. narrative, humor and incongruity).
- The potential value of breaking the norm and stretching the culture.

Our extensive experience of developing and using materials in many different cultures has led us to question cultural stereotyping (for example, the most teacher-centered language teaching we have observed has been in Western Europe and the most innovative use of materials in such non-Western cultures as Iran, Indonesia, and Vanuatu) and to believe that, in any materials development, universal principles of language acquisition should drive procedures that can become locally acceptable. We have always tried to be sensitive to the needs, wants, and expectations of the target users of our materials but have never seen the point of only using procedures that conform to local norms and expectations but have not been very successful in helping learners to achieve communicative effectiveness. Instead, we have used procedures that aim to engage learners affectively and cognitively and to provide a challenging but enjoyable experience of language learning (an approach that we have found to have a universal appeal to learners of all ages). These procedures have sometimes worried local academics and teachers but have rarely been resisted by local learners. Accommodation has sometimes been necessary to appease and win over teachers who would otherwise feel threatened by an apparently alien approach (as it is very important that the teacher believes in the materials they are using) but often teachers eventually became enthusiastic about new approaches once they had time to trial and understand them and to make them their own. Bao (2002, p. 272) quotes a teacher in one of his communicative experiments in Vietnam as saying, "Some strategies don't work because I am simply not familiar with employing them. These will have to take time to develop into my own techniques." Ultimately we believe that the basic principles of SLA are universal and that procedures for applying them are "more flexible and amenable to modification than is generally acknowledged," that "most teachers and learners are willing to experiment with change providing that the change is non-threatening and potentially beneficial," and that teachers "should teach in ways which suit their beliefs and personality while being sensitive to the needs and wants of their learners and to the prevailing norms of the cultures in which they are teaching" (Tomlinson, 2005a, p. 150). In the *Guardian* on Saturday July 2, 2016, Philip Oltermann quoted Margret Rasfeld as saying "In education you can only create change from the bottom—if the orders come from the top, schools will resist." Rasfeld is the head teacher of the Evangelical School Berlin Centre, a school that does not grade or timetable its students, which offers such courses as "responsibility" and "challenge," yet achieves impressive examination results. Rasfeld also says "Ministries are like giant oil tankers: it takes a long time to turn them around. What we need is lots of little speedboats to show you can do things differently" (p. 23). We agree with Rasfeld but we would add that a dynamic tension between top and bottom in education is ideally a good thing, with a conservative top ensuring stability and a more innovative bottom achieving beneficial change.

The type of class, classroom, and institution in which learners are learning an L2 can be a factor in determining the use of materials. Some fairly obvious points are that:

- Materials designed for use in well-resourced schools with reliable access to the Internet are of little value in schools with unreliable access to the Internet (especially if the electricity supply is unreliable too). We once contributed to a self-access project in Ethiopia in which it was assumed that the participants would be able to communicate with each other at a distance only to find that very few of them would have reliable access to the Internet or to electricity.
- Materials designed for teenagers or young adults with a liberal education will need to be adapted before being used in cultures where many topics are taboo (and even when being used with culturally mixed classes).
- Materials written for mixed-gender classes might need adaptation when used with single-gender classes.
- Materials designed for use with small, self-enrolled, motivated classes in language schools (as many global coursebooks seem to be) will need adapting before being used with very large classes of learners in state institutions who are being compelled to learn an L2.

There are publications focusing on how teachers can adjust their teaching to cater for students in large classes. Shamin (2012) reviews the literature on teaching an L2 in large classes, defined as "50 or more students" (p. 96). She concludes that most teachers consider teaching large classes to be "both problematic and burdensome" and reports such problems as "low levels of student involvement, issues in classroom management, assessment and feedback, limited resources and physical discomfort" (p. 96). She looks at some of the solutions that have been proposed (e.g. small-class approaches, communicative approaches, small-group work, task-based approaches, peer assessment) but concludes that teachers often abandon innovative strategies and revert to "survival strategies" such as "dictating essays or writing essays on the board for students to copy and learn by rote" (p. 96). However Shamin considers that "Large classes do not always lead to ineffective teaching" (p. 96) and can stimulate innovation. She reports a successful learner autonomy approach in Pakistan (Sarwar, 2001), a successful task-based approach in Indonesia (Coleman, 1987), and a successful small-group approach in Spain (Burgess, 1989). However, she does not explicitly deal with the vital issue of developing and / or adapting materials for large groups. We have enjoyed teaching large groups of up to 90 students in, for example, Japan, Singapore, and Oman, and we have found that the energy generated by the teacher at the beginning of a lesson can become "contagious" and self-sustaining in a large class, as the resistance of a few individuals has little impact. We also have used learner autonomy, task-based and small group approaches with large classes but what we have found most successful has been adapting and developing materials so that whole-class approaches in which all the students participate in activities together can become engaging, enjoyable and communicative. See Chapter 4 in this volume and Tomlinson (2016a) for suggestions and examples of how to do this (for example, by specifying a previous relationship between the shop assistant and the customer in a textbook dialogue and then getting half the class to imagine and then act out together the "performance" of one of the characters and the other half to do the same for the other character).

One type of learner who features in the literature on language learning is the self-access learner—that is, the learner who is learning an L2 outside the classroom without a teacher, either at home alone or in a self-access center in the company of other learners. Cooker (2008) focuses mainly on self-access centers and says that in her experience the materials available in them can be published materials in a paper-based format, online or in non-web, computer-based formats, or in some cases they are designed by learners themselves (Malcolm, 2004) or by teaching staff (Lin & Brown, 1994). Cooker says that there are very few materials published specifically for self-access learners and lists the typical types of materials available in a self-access center as:

- authentic materials such as magazines, television programs, films and music;
- graded readers;
- language-learning software / web-based resources;
- drama-based language learning materials;
- coursebooks;
- texts for specific skills;
- examination preparation texts.

After describing each of these types of materials in some detail, Cooker provides an evaluation of a sample or representative of each type and concludes by calling for more attempts from publishers of self-access materials to engage learners affectively and cognitively, to stimulate learner creativity, to help learners to achieve self-diagnosis, and to provide models of successful L2 users for learners to compare themselves with.

Tomlinson (2011) claims that most publications on self-access (e.g. Gardner & Miller, 1999; Benson, 2006) have little to say about the development of self-access materials. He also claims that most self-access materials "still consist of controlled or guided practice activities which use cloze, multiple choice, gap filling, matching and transformation activities to facilitate self-marking and focused feedback" (p. 414) and which restrict learners to "closed activities requiring a narrow left brain focus and little utilisation of prior personal experience, of the brain's potential learning capacity or of individual attributes or inclinations" (pp. 414–415). Tomlinson (2011) praises Littlejohn (1992), Gardner and Miller (1999), McGrath (2002), McDonough and Shaw (2003), Mishan (2005), and Cooker (2008) for their reaction against the restriction of self-access materials to narrowly focused practice activities and for their advocacy of authentic materials, creativity, exploration, and enjoyment. He also advocates and exemplifies "access-self activities" (p. 416) that offer choice of activities and pace, are open-ended, involve the learners as individual human beings, stimulate left- and right-brain activity at the same time, provide a rich, varied, and comprehensible input, and provide opportunities to make linguistic and pragmatic discoveries. This humanistic approach is procedural-ized through using a text-driven approach (Tomlinson, 2013d), through the provision of commentaries rather than answer keys and through follow up suggestions. McDonough et al. (2013) and Tomlinson (2010, 2013e) also advocate and exemplify more individual-ized and open-ended approaches to materials for self-access and more encouragement for learners to look out for English outside the classroom.

Published Materials

Apart from materials published for self-access there are very few materials published specifically to cater for user difference. Many British and American publishers now do publish local versions of some of their global coursebooks but, inevitably, they tend to treat all learners in a specific target area as being undifferentiated. This is also true of most locally published coursebooks that target a particular region or country. Such courses do tend to offer more relevant and potentially engaging materials to their target learners than most global coursebooks but they are no more likely to cater for differences in motivation, preferred learning styles, social background, needs and wants. The only such differentiation we know of is in China, where we were told by a publisher we were writing materials for that we needed to provide more language drills for learners from rural areas, and in Singapore where publishers normally produce three different versions of each level of their secondary school courses. For example, *Life Accents 3A—An English Language Course for Upper Secondary* (Davies, Tup, & Aziz, 2003) has a special / express version for those proficient in English (often those from homes where English is often spoken and there is exposure to English through television, books, newspapers, and music), a normal (academic) version for those with some competence in English (often those from homes where there is some access to English through television, books, newspapers and music), and a normal (technical) version for those with little competence in English who are considered the weakest academically and are following a vocational pathway (often those with very little access to English through television, books, newspapers and music). *English for Life 1* (Tomlinson, Hill, & Masuhara, 2000) though, for example, caters for special express and normal (academic) in one version.

Our Recommendations

Our view is that, while it is impractical to provide different courses for learners in the same classroom who are different, it is possible to provide a lot more choice within a course of approaches, routes, texts, tasks, and follow ups to cater for differences in, for example, social background, cultural background, prior experience, preferred learning style, personality, attributes, language proficiency, gender, and motivation. For example, one of our MA students devised an audio course in which the students sampled different instructor voices, different pedagogical approaches and different activity types before deciding on a route through the materials. And we have used an approach in which learners have responded personally to listening to and then reading a potentially engaging text (e.g. a poem beginning, "I'm an old, old lady") and have then walked round the classroom reading task cards on the wall. The tasks differ in level of language proficiency (e.g. "Learn to recite the poem in the voice of the old lady" versus "You are the old lady. Write a letter to your son in Australia"), in medium of expression (e.g. "Paint a picture of the poem" versus "You are related to the old lady. Form a family group with other 'relatives' and discuss how to help the old lady"), and in type of task and expression (e.g. "Every day in summer the old lady sits on a bench in the park. Today there is an old man sitting there. Write the conversation between the old woman and the old man" versus "Answer the following comprehension questions about the poem"). Each student chooses a task, sits down near its card and then decides whether to work individually, in a pair or in a group. The students can change tasks at any time and can do another one if they finish early. Later any student who wants to can "perform" their task to the class (e.g. show their painting and answer questions on it).

Materials for Different Purposes

The Literature

For many years materials could be divided into those for general purposes (see Masuhara & Tomlinson, 2008) and those for specific purposes. Recently, however, materials for a whole series of subspecific purposes have been developed along with accompanying academic disciplines. At first the division was between general academic purposes and professional purposes, then there were further splits into, for example, English for science and English for business, and now there are very specific disciplines, such as English for accountants, English for architects, English for computer studies and English for medicine. There is now also a big demand in the United Kingdom for materials for learners of ESOL (English for speakers of other languages), most of whom are adult immigrants seeking job opportunities or looking for advancement in the jobs they already have. The big question, though, is "Are these disciplines so significantly different as to warrant separate academic disciplines, courses and coursebooks?" There is now a significant literature attached to these subdisciplines and many case studies of the development of materials for them, most of which assume that each sub-purpose requires a separate needs analysis and a separate inventory of language items and skills. At the MATSDA / University of Liverpool Conference in June, 2016, on authenticity in materials development for language learning, 18 of the 52 presentations were case studies of an L2 for a specific purpose and each purpose was different and very specific, including

A course book for EFL cosmetology students, a coursebook for signing in EFL in which all the texts were social media postings (Park & Park, 2016), and a coursebook especially for visitors and newcomers to Bogota wanting to learn Spanish (*Bogota: Vivela en Español*, 2016). There is also an assumption that any student wanting to learn an L2 for academic or professional purposes has already developed a basic communicative competence in the language. This has certainly not been the case, in our experience, for many students doing EAP (English for academic purposes) courses prior to commencing subject studies in English at such highly respected English-medium universities as Bilkent University in Ankara, King Saud University in Riyadh, and Sultan Qaboos University in Muscat. And it was certainly not the case with all students on such courses as English for Saudi Arabian policemen, English for French businessmen, and English for Omani nurses at a language school in England. On one course at Bell College, Saffron Walden, post-PhD students from China became very accurate and fluent in the technical language of their scientific specializations but had great problems in communicating socially with the fellow scientists they ultimately worked with in laboratories at Cambridge University. This was reported to be a significant problem as the scientists said that they rarely used technical language in discussions about their work as most of them took place over a coffee or a drink in a pub and there they used vague and informal language.

Materials for English for Specific Purposes (ESP) and English for Academic Purposes (EAP)

Dudley-Evans (2001) claimed that "English for specific purposes (ESP) has for about 30 years been a separate branch of English Language Teaching" with "its own approaches, materials and methodology" and with a focus on "classroom-based activity," and "materials production and text analysis rather than with the development of a theory of ESP" (p. 131). He goes on to discuss the importance of needs analysis, target situation analysis, text analysis and genre analysis but, like most publications on ESP in our experience, does not actually explain what is so distinctive about ESP approaches, materials or methodology. He claims that ESP is "materials driven" but does not provide any examples of ESP materials or say what their defining characteristics are. Paltridge (2012, p. 179) characterizes an ESP class as usually being adult, homogeneous, "typically an upper intermediate level or above," having limited time and following a course focusing on "the language skills and genres appropriate to the specific activities the learners need to carry out in English." Paltridge traces the history of ESP back to the 1960s and describes how it focused initially on sentence-level language (e.g. the passive in research reports), then in the 1970s on such rhetorical functions as cause and effect, then in the 1980s on strategies identified from needs analysis, and now on "the abilities, knowledge and skills that learners need in order to perform particular spoken and written genres" (p. 180). Paltridge draws attention to how corpus studies have informed current genre approaches, a point made forcibly by O'Keeffe, McCarthy, and Carter (2007) in their detailed account and exemplification of how corpus studies have informed the materials and the pedagogy for the teaching of academic and business English. The focus of Paltridge's chapter is on course design, teaching and assessment but, in a paragraph on evaluating ESP materials, Paltridge makes the important points that the materials selected for an ESP course (usually a mixture of coursebooks and in-house material) need to be "usable in the particular situation, able to be adapted to suit the learners' needs and flexible enough so that this can take place" (p. 182). We certainly agree with

Paltridge and would always stress the need for all teachers of an L2 (and especially teachers of an L2 for specific purposes) to be trained to adapt the materials they are using to the specific needs of the actual class they are currently teaching (see Chapter 4 in this volume for recommended procedures for principled adaptation). One early publication that does demonstrate a concern with appropriateness and usability is Hidalgo, Hall, and Jacobs (1995). This book contains five chapters describing the development of materials for learners of ESP and focuses on such issues as collaborating with subject specialists, authenticity of text and task, needs analysis, the importance of encouraging teachers to develop locally relevant materials, team writing and planning. Whilst there is some reference to stipulations of methodology the main concerns of the chapters are with the process of developing materials and with ensuring the relevance of the topic and language content to the needs of the learners. There is very little reference to principles of language acquisition.

Much of the literature on English for academic purposes (EAP) focuses on needs analysis and curriculum development. However, Hamp-Lyons (2001) does make and exemplify the point that most EAP textbooks have started as in-house materials "based on needs analysis of the immediate situation" and have then been "polished into textbooks" (p. 129). Interestingly, this is what used to happen with nearly all coursebooks. Teachers "developed materials for their classes, found they were popular, and then submitted them to a publisher" (Tomlinson, 2013b, p. 209). However, global general English coursebooks have for a long time been commissioned by publishers to fill a gap in the market. It seems to us that this has now also happened with EAP materials as certain tertiary courses become increasingly popular with overseas students in the United Kingdom, United States, Australia and New Zealand, as well as in English-medium universities in such countries as Malaysia, Oman, Thailand, Turkey, and the United Arab Emirates (e.g. architecture, business studies, computer studies, engineering and medical studies).

According to Brick (2012), the emphasis in EAP was originally on academic study skills but has now moved on to a focus on "the discourse of academia and of the specific disciplines in which" the students "are enrolled" (p. 171), with a split between those experts favoring an English-for-general-purposes (EGAP) approach and those favoring an English-for-specific-purposes (ESAP) approach. At the heart of both approaches, according to Brick, is the concept of genre and the need for students to become familiar with the text structures of relevant genres (e.g. lectures, literature reviews and research reports if you follow Swales, 1990; narrative, explanation and discussion if you follow Martin, 1993). Both approaches, whether following Swales or Martin, are text based and their materials use authentic texts as models for students to analyze and make use of, ideally, according to Brick, with "several different examples of a genre, as writers can and do vary in the ways they use generic structure and language" (p. 177). We have found that using a text-based approach to EAP material development (i.e. one that encourages students to mine the text for features to emulate) can result in rather mechanical copying of genre characteristics. We prefer a text-driven approach (Tomlinson, 2013d) in which a potentially engaging text drives a unit of material with students initially responding to the meaning of the text before developing a draft of a related text of their own without analysis of the original (e.g. a report of their carrying out an experiment suggested in a scientific report of another experiment). After developing their own text the students go back to make a linguistic, discourse or pragmatic discovery from the core and other connected texts, which they then use in revising their own text.

Many of the materials developed for ESP and EAP courses can be criticized for focusing more on relevant content and less on appropriate pedagogy, a focus probably reinforced by sponsors of courses who are specialists in the content but not in pedagogy and by the short time often available for such courses (according to Basturkmen, 2006, the aim of EAP "is to speed learners through to a known destination"). Often, in our experience, this can lead to a transmission of knowledge approach in which a lot of relevant language content is learned but not applied and is then quickly forgotten. Mol and Tin (2008), for example, are critical of EAP materials used in Australasia which do "not integrate current research on language teaching methodology" and "focus on *what* to teach rather than *how* to teach" (p. 88). Skeldon (2008) is critical of many of the 1970s and 1980s materials for English for science and technology (EST) because of their inability to "negotiate the tricky line between the boringly familiar and the bafflingly new"(p. 60), because of the apparent assumption that "because the students had limited English, their knowledge of science was also limited, or even their intelligence" (p. 61), because "the level of the language in the materials was way beyond the students"(p. 61), because there was a neglect of reading, because texts were constructed just to illustrate language points, because examples and drills contained sentences which "no one would ever dream of saying" (p. 62) and because many of the activities (usually typical textbook exercises like True / False, matching, and multiple choice) were trivial and unchallenging. Skeldon contrasts these "first generation of EST materials" (p. 62) with current project-based materials and advocates making use of (or compiling from web sources) more engaging scientific articles to drive more challenging activities, developing a series of science based extensive readers and developing communication activities based on science and technology. We would be interested to know Skeldon's views on the materials developed by the University of Sheffield for a recent project aimed at providing both language support and subject knowledge for non-native speaking primary school students learning both English and science. We suspect that he would approve of the autonomous learning opportunities and the use of parental resources built into the take-home materials in Afitska (2016). We hope he would also approve of the way that de Kocha (2016) makes use of learner research, board games, video, songs, and team writing on an adult EAP course as well as of the way that senior staff at the Liverpool School of English (see report of our visit above) recommend a greater use of case studies, of tasks and of problem solving activities in EAP / ESP materials.

We have had personal experience of designing EAP materials and of giving presentations on materials development at EAP conferences (e.g. the BALEAP conference in the United Kingdom) when we have been told that our humanistic approaches are too "soft" for EAP and that EAP students need a "hard" approach in which relevant language and skills are taught to the students as quickly as possible. However, there were many positive responses to Tomlinson (2008b)—an article that sympathized with EAP teachers for often having to attempt so much with so little time, was critical of many EAP coursebooks for assuming that what the teacher teaches the students will learn, and advocated the humanizing of EAP. It also described how an EAP coursebook was humanized when used at Sultan Qaboos University in Oman by subverting, personalizing, and localizing the texts and activities and by adding challenges, enjoyment and potentially engaging texts and tasks. Recently the article stimulated the construction of the following set of criteria for evaluating how humanistic a set of EAP materials are:

1. To what extent do the materials:
    a) Respect the learners as individual human beings?
    b) Encourage the learners to take responsibility for their own learning?
    c) Challenge the learners to use high-level skills?
    d) Help the learners to connect what is in the materials to what is in their minds?
    e) Encourage the learners to visualize?
    f) Encourage the learners to make use of their inner voices?
    g) Encourage the learners to personalize the materials?
    h) Help the learners to connect the materials to their own lives?
    i) Encourage the learners to be creative?
    j) Encourage the learners to be constructively critical?
    k) Encourage the learners to make discoveries for themselves?
    l) Encourage the learners to look out for English outside the classroom?
    m) Offer choice of texts to the learners?
    n) Offer choice of tasks to the learners?
    o) Provide a rich exposure to relevant language in use?
    p) Offer opportunities to use the language for relevant communication?
2. To what extent are the materials likely to:
    a) Engage the learners affectively?
    b) Engage the learners cognitively?
    c) Be enjoyable for the learners?
    d) Have a positive impact on the learners' motivation?
    e) Help the learners to achieve deep processing of language input?
    f) Relate to the learners' linguistic needs?
    g) Relate to the learners' academic needs?
    h) Relate to the learners' personal wants? (Rasti & Tomlinson, 2016)

McGrath (2002) attributes the problems with early ESP materials to the fact that the teachers had "to design much of their own material" (p. 144) and that this led eventually to the use of standard exercises, which saved the teachers a lot of time because they could be used with any text. A good example of a framework developed to help such teachers is Rafik-Galea and Cortazzi (2003), a very thorough and helpful developmental framework but one that stresses the satisfaction of discovered needs and the selection of relevant content rather than the use of appropriate methodology. However, there are now many notable exceptions to this neglect of principled pedagogy. For example, Heah and Yun (2003) report the development of communication skills materials for engineers on courses at Nanyang Technical University in Singapore. The materials were developed in collaboration between communications skills staff and engineering staff and were driven by five main pedagogic principles, including the encouragement of creativity and variety of responses and, in particular, the cognitive engagement of the learners. As problem solving is "the dominant mode of thinking in civil engineers," it became the dominant task type in the materials and the tasks were designed to promote cognitive engagement, creativity, and variety of response. Prior to embarking on a task, the students received input in their materials provided both from language specialists and from technical specialists, and were given opportunities to analyze and then synthesize relevant language content. A similarly principled approach was used in developing an oral communication-skills course for teachers in ASEAN countries. As one of the authors of the course recounts in Poedjosoedarmo (2003), the activities consisted of participants exploring the features of spoken English relevant to a particular teaching activity, evaluating sample teaching activities and then devising teaching activities. Research reports on a number of pedagogically principled ESP / EAP materials development projects are reported in Tomlinson and Masuhara (2010). For example, Mason (2010) discusses the findings from his study of the effects of different types of materials on the intercultural competence of EAP students at a Tunisian university, Trabelsi (2010) evaluates the effects of the authentic materials he developed for business English students at a Tunisian university, St. Louis (2010) presents a case study of the effects of a reading course for science and technology students at a university in Venezuela, Al-Busaidi and Tindle (2010) report on the development and effects of an in-house writing course for EAP students at a university in Oman, McCullagh (2010) provides an evaluation of the effects of a course for medical English, and very unusually, Cullen (2010) reports the development and effects of materials he developed in Japan for L2 songwriters. What is distinctive about these chapters is that they all focus on appropriate pedagogy and are not restricted to the usual concerns with needs analysis, content and curriculum development of most publications on EAP / ESP materials development. Mason developed materials to "meet learners' wants, achieve connections with learners' own lives, stimulate emotional engagement and promote visualization" (p. 73, quoted from Tomlinson, 2003, p. 20) and he found them to be far more effective than the conventional knowledge transmission materials they replaced. Trabelsi was successful in replacing conventional knowledge transmission based materials with a set of materials that were authentic in the sense that they "were tailored to the learners' profile and … suitable to the stakeholders' (teachers and employers) expectations and demands" (p. 116). St. Louis's project introduced well-received activities to promote affective engagement, discovery, criticality and autonomy, and Al-Busaidi and Tindle were also successful in introducing locally focused activities to stimulate affective and cognitive engagement, to promote discovery and to develop criticality. Cullen combined a language-centered approach, a skills-centered approach and a learner-centered approach in developing materials that helped L2 songwriters to improve their ability to write effective songs in an L2, and McCullagh focused on the development of authentic inputs and processes that would help medical students to improve their ability to communicate with patients and with professionals. Interestingly McCullagh (and the coauthor of her coursebook Ros Wright) aimed at pedagogical outcomes, educational outcomes and "psychosocial outcomes relating to individual development" (p. 385), outcomes not typically aimed at by most EAP / ESP courses.

A number of principled approaches to developing EAP / ESP materials are also reported in Harwood (2010a). Jones and Schmitt (2010) recount the development and initial evaluation of academic-discipline-specific materials on a CD-ROM that made use of a "Needs-Driven Spoken Corpus" (p. 225) and a number of language-awareness activities to help students acquire the discipline specific lexis they need in order to interact "with native speakers in formal and less formal academic settings" (p. 242). Feak and Swales (2010) also report on a corpus-driven course of materials, in their case developed for postdoctoral fellows in perinatology, which made use of consciousness-raising and genre-analysis activities. Hewings (2010) describes materials he uses at the University of Birmingham to help international students improve their ability to write essays in English. What is particularly interesting to us is that the materials for each key feature of essays start with the reading and then writing of a nonacademic text and then include a lot of whole-class brainstorming and pair discussion prior to the writing of academic texts. Harwood (2010b) reports a research-driven materials development project in which "a critical pragmatic approach" (p. 301) was used that encouraged students to evaluate the appropriateness of models of citation in relation to their own citation requirements, and Curry and Lillis (2010) describe their research-driven project to develop materials that provided data of academic text production to students and invited them to relate and then apply the data to their own text production. Harwood (2010a) also contains three chapters on the development of ESP materials. Bosher (2010) refers to the materials developed to help students on a nursing course to develop such skills as "critical thinking," "writing progress reports," and "understanding culturally sensitive topics" (p. 346). Angouri (2010) reports his findings, which show "a discrepancy between the textbook language taught and the actual language" used in business meetings (p. 373), and he shows "how real-life data can be used in the language classroom to complement the Business English textbook" (p. 373). Jakubiak and Harklau (2010) also examine "approaches to materials design in adult English as a Second Language programs in immigrant receiving nations" (p. 395). Interestingly, all the EAP / ESP materials development projects reported in Harwood (2010a) are driven by pedagogical principles as well as by researched subject content; they are all in-house projects; they all include elements of learner discovery and criticality; they all seem to have been instigated because of discovered deficiencies in published textbooks but none of the projects seem to have resulted in commercial publication. Harwood continues to promote such chapters in Harwood (2014). For example, Feak and Swales (2014) recount how they revised two EAP textbooks they had written and stress, in particular, the need for compromise between satisfying the "immediate audience (editors and external reviewers …) and the more remote audience (the end users, namely students and instructors)" (p. 316). McGrath (2002) refers to a much earlier report of the revision of EAP materials (Lynch, 1996). Like Feak and Swales (2014), Lynch makes many interesting and valid points about materials revision but says little about what is distinctively different about developing EAP materials. Stoller and Robinson (2014) also narrate the development of a textbook for chemistry students which was developed at Northern Arizona University as an interdisciplinary, collaborative project which used a genre and discovery approach and was committed to "authenticity of purpose, task and texts" (p. 275). Interestingly, unlike Feak and Swales (2014), the authors do not report any need to compromise with their publisher, Oxford University Press, as, even more unusually these days, the publisher had accepted the book as a proposal on the strength of very positive reviews rather than soliciting it to fill a discovered gap in the market.

A recent publication that focuses on the need for principled ESP and EVP (English for vocational purposes) materials is Widodo (2016), a chapter that advocates the use of text- and task-based materials, which puts forward seven "elements" as being essential ingredients of ESP / EVP materials and which stresses that "ESP materials should arouse students' prior knowledge or experience" (p. 283). Another publication that focuses on materials for facilitating workplace communicative competence is Jaidev and Blackstone (2016). This chapter advocates a project-based, problem-solving approach, and illustrates this with a report of a multimodal project for students at the National University of Singapore, which "required students to be actively engaged in identifying a problem, follow through by investigating and analysing it from different perspectives and then proposing a viable solution" (p. 293).

An author who is critical of (but understanding of the commercial need for) the "one-size-fits-all" approach of many EAP courses is Ottley (2016). Writing from recent experience of teaching EAP in Iraqi Kurdistan he points out the lack of relevance and appeal to his students of the EAP coursebook that he is using and suggests ways in which the students can be used to evaluate materials and to source more relevant and engaging materials, as well as creative and challenging ways of exploiting locally available authentic materials.

Materials for English for Speakers of Other Languages (ESOL)

Most learners of ESOL are immigrants to English speaking countries who are seeking job opportunities, looking for advancement in the jobs they already have or are preparing to take examinations in ESOL which are important for their continued stay in their new country. If you google ESOL, there are many references to institutional and online courses but very few to publications about ESOL and especially about the development of materials for it. One researcher who has specialized in writing about developing materials for ESOL is Naeema Haan. In Haan (2013) she reports case studies in the United Kingdom of ESOL for preparing learners for employment and of ESOL for helping workers in their workplace. She reviews the very few courses of materials that are available for such learners and criticizes their emphasis on assessment, she reports what ESOL students said helped them to improve their English (e.g. watching television with subtitles and reading children's books) and she recommends that materials for employability should, for example, "have templates which can be personalized for local purposes" (p. 185), "be rich enough to be 'mined' for multiple purposes" (p. 185) "encourage learner autonomy" (p. 186), "help the learner develop skills for learning" (p. 186) and "build confidence in the learner." Haan, Timmis, and Masuhara (2010) stressed the diversity of ESOL learners (and exemplified this by describing each individual in a class of ESOL learners at a Job Centre in Yorkshire), criticizes publishers for attempting to map existing EFL coursebooks to the adult ESOL core curriculum and establishes principles for ESOL materials design (e.g. "ESOL materials should provide cognitive and affective engagement as well as catering for learners' real and immediate needs" (p. 240). Haan (2013) focuses on ways of helping ESOL learners to develop learning strategies that they can use outside the classroom. She reports the results of a longitudinal study in Yorkshire of "factors supporting progress of ESOL learners" (p. 315) and, whilst congratulating the learners in her study for their resourcefulness, she suggests principles for the development of ESOL materials for strategy training that would help learners make better use of their environment outside the classroom. Tomlinson and Masuhara (2008) report how they googled "ESOL materials" and in 10 pages could not find a single reference to an ESOL coursebook. They reviewed the downloadable materials available and found them exam orientated and language focused. They also sampled the views of ESOL teachers on the materials available to them and found that, although they valued the wide choice, they resented the time required for finding, selecting and adapting materials and they were critical of the materials because they were insufficiently relevant to the "learner's previous and current lives" (p. 163).

English as an International Language (EIL) and English as a Lingua Franca (ELF)

A fairly recent development in the differentiation of purposes for learning an L2 has been the growth of publications calling for English to be taught as an international language (EIL) or as a lingua franca (ELF) to learners whose need is primarily to communicate in English with other non-native speakers of English. This is a recognition of the reality that the majority of interactions in English are not between or with native speakers but between L2 speakers who do not share an L1. There is by now a considerable literature on the needs of such learners and on the advocacy of differentiated curricula and courses for them, for example, Jenkins (2000, 2007, 2012), Kirkpatrick (2006), Wright (2009) and Seidlhofer (2010), who argues that English is already the "de facto lingua franca of Europe" (p. 357) and that it is very different from the language that features in the corpora of native speaker English. There is also a literature putting forward alternative positions—see, for example, Canagarajah (2007), who argues for a focus on lingua Franca English (LFE), which is a social process rather than a product, and Timmis (2002) for evidence of learners preferring to aim for native speaker norms rather than those of ELF. However, we know of very few publications other than Tomlinson (2006, 2016b) that actually make proposals for developing materials to meet the needs of learners of EIL and / or ELF. McKay (2006) discusses issues related to EIL curriculum development but focuses on models of language use without any reference to materials. Tomlinson (2006) includes a short section on materials in which he advocates, for example, developing materials that "teach … those features of the EIL core which are relevant, teachable and useful," provide "opportunities to interact with other EIL users … to achieve intended outcomes," "expose learners … to a rich variety of language use in a variety of genres and text types" and "help learners to accommodate their English … when interacting" (p. 144). Tomlinson (2016b) advocates exposing learners to authentic written, spoken and multimedium texts being used for lingua franca communication and involving learners in authentic tasks that require the use of the skills, strategies and pragmatic competence needed in typical lingua franca contexts, such as interaction on an international flight, at an international sports event, or during contract negotiations. He also recommends pragmatic awareness activities that involve learner investigation of pragmatic features of both successful and unsuccessful non-native speaker interaction, the reading of literature, newspapers, blogs, and so forth, written by non-native speakers of English and the teaching of those capabilities that are very important in lingua franca interaction (e.g. accommodation, seeking clarification, communication repair).

Materials for Examination Preparation

We recently walked into the resources room of the Norwich Institute for Language Education (NILE), an institution that specializes in teacher development courses, and were amazed how many shelves were filled with commercially published examination-preparation books. The same thing was true on a recent visit to the Liverpool School of English and to a number of well-resourced institutions overseas. There are high-stake examinations available at every stage these days, and publishers have grabbed the opportunity to help teachers to prepare students for taking them. As Bailey and Masuhara (2013, p. 305), say, students "can access a dizzying array of test preparation materials." Most teachers are grateful for this help as they and their institutions are judged by their students' examination results. Not all of them agree, though, with the typical approach that these books take, an approach that provides information on the syllabus of the examination being prepared for, teaches / revises language items and skills likely to be assessed, offers advice on how to tackle typical assessment tasks and provides a lot of practice in doing such tasks. What is often missing, though, is the affective and cognitive engagement vital for durable learning as well as learner opportunities for discovery. Alderson and Hamp-Lyons (1996), for example, investigated TOEFL preparation courses in the United States and found them to be serious, teacher-centered courses with little laughter and with less student talk, and with more teacher talk and use of metalanguage than in other courses. An alternative approach is to focus the course on stimulating affective and cognitive engagement and on providing a rich and varied exposure to relevant language use, opportunities to use the language for communication, and opportunities to make discoveries about language use. Then, a few weeks before the examination, the students are introduced to the format of the examination, are given advice, and are given opportunities to practice with past papers. This is an approach that was used on the By the Teacher for the Teacher (PKG) Project in Indonesia (Tomlinson, 1990) and the students in the experimental classes did better in the end-of-year examination than their equivalents in the control classes who had been taught to pass the examination.

As well as questioning the value of the advice and practice approach in examination preparation books, some of us are also concerned that such an approach is denying students new learning opportunities during the lengthy preparation period (Tomlinson, 2005b) and that it is having negative washback effects on classroom teaching, informal testing, and global coursebooks. See Bailey and Masuhara (2013) for a detailed discussion of these washback effects and an analysis of their impact on some recent global coursebooks. The almost exclusive focus on preparation for the target examination also means that students are likely to need another course once they have passed the examination, as emerged during our discussion at the Liverpool School of English (see above) where the view was expressed that IELTS preparation books did not typically prepare the students for the study skills they would need on their academic courses once they had passed the IELTS examination.

Materials Development for Teacher Training

We are both strong believers in the value of teachers developing materials as a major part of their initial and their in-service training as language teachers. We have found by running hundreds of such courses around the world (including a dedicated MA in materials development for language teaching which we ran at the University of Luton and at Leeds Metropolitan University) that developing materials is one of the best ways of helping teachers to:

- understand and question theories of language acquisition;
- apply theory to practice and practice to theory;
- develop the vital teacher skills of evaluation, adaptation and materials design;
- gain confidence, self-esteem and awareness;
- develop criticality and originality.

For publications supporting and exemplifying this view see Canniveng and Martinez (2003), Popovici and Bolitho (2003), Masuhara (2006), Masuhara (2011), Emery (2013), Tomlinson (2013c), Tomlinson and Masuhara (2013), and Edwards and Burns (2016). Some of these publications report on the development of materials by teachers in training, some on the development of materials for teachers in training, some on the development of actual materials for real students, and some on the development of materials as a part of a larger simulation. All of them report positive effects of such developments and the appreciation of the teachers involved, as does Tomlinson (2014a) in its report of a survey of teachers around the world who have taken part in materials development courses and projects. Tomlinson (2014a) found, for example, that the respondents to his questionnaire reported major increases in confidence, self-esteem, criticality and awareness of the principles of language acquisition, as well as improvements in the ability to make principled decisions and to evaluate, adapt and design materials.

Our Recommendations

We believe that the same principles apply to materials development regardless of the target learners' purposes for learning the L2. Whether learners have 6 years at school to acquire a language or 6 weeks on a course to develop specific capabilities, they need materials that will provide them with a rich, varied, and comprehensible input, offer them opportunities to use the language for communication, help them to make discoveries for themselves about how the language is used, provide them with an achievable challenge and, above all else, stimulate them to achieve affective and cognitive engagement. In our view all this is necessary to enable any learner to acquire communicative confidence and competence and it is better to reduce the inventory of language items and capabilities to be taught than to risk shallow learning. After all, many of the specialized lexical items and very specific capabilities can be quickly picked up on the job or the course provided the learners enter it with confidence and motivation gained from their language course.

Conclusion

We believe that it is very important to realize that ESP, EAP, ESOL, EIL and ELF, for example, are not distinct varieties of English with totally differing lexicons and syntax to be taught and learned, although, obviously, within each of these purposes there are subpurposes that do differ lexically and syntactically. Burns and Richards (2012), say "each learning context requires the mastery of specific genres of discourse with their own linguistic characteristics" (p. 9). It is true that there are differing purposes for acquiring an L2 and differing contexts in which to acquire it, and that each has some lexical items specific to it and some distinctive uses of syntax. However, what is important for materials designed to help learners of a specific purpose or from a specific context is that they help their target learners to develop the specific strategies, skills, and competences that they need and want. It is our view that materials for these differing purposes and contexts should not differ significantly in pedagogical approach but should differ in topic and linguistic content so as to be relevant, meaningful, and potentially useful to their specific target learners. We also believe that all materials for acquiring an L2 should share the same principles of language acquisition and should cater for their learners as human beings and not just as students of the L2 for a particular purpose. Where they should differ is in relation to what their target learners will eventually need to do in the L2. What they should share is a concern with helping their target students to do what they want to do in the L2 both whilst learning it and after their courses.

What Do You Think?

1. Do you think that materials for EAP and for ESP should use different pedagogical approaches from those for EGP (English for general purposes)? Why?
2. Do you agree that the same pedagogic principles should apply to the development of materials for any learners regardless of their ages, genders, levels, purposes and cultural backgrounds? Why?
3. Do you think that materials should be designed so that they can be easily adapted to suit learners of different levels, backgrounds and purposes? How do you think this could be achieved?
4. Do you think that materials should be developed to cater specifically for L2 learners who need to develop communicative competence in the target language so they can interact effectively with other L2 users of that language? Why? How would such materials differ from conventional materials?
5. What do you think should be the main distinguishing features between materials for beginners and materials for advanced learners?

Tasks

1. Specify a learner profile for a cohort of learners who are learning an L2 for specific purposes. Then take a unit at random from a coursebook or set of web materials and adapt it to suit your specified cohort of target learners.
2. Design a framework for developing materials so that they can be used effectively by learners of differing levels, backgrounds, purposes and aspirations in the same classroom.

References

Afitska, O. (2016). Scaffolding learning: developing materials to support the learning of science and language by non-native English-speaking students. *Innovation in Language Learning and Teaching* [B. Tomlinson guest editor], *10*(2), 75–89.

Al-Busaidi, S., & Tindle, K. (2010). Evaluating the impact of in-house materials on language learning. In B. Tomlinson & H. Masuhara (Eds.), *Research for materials development in language learning; evidence for best practice* (pp. 137–149). London: Continuum.

Alderson, J. C., & Hamp-Lyons, L. (1996). TOEFL preparation courses: A study of washback. *Language Testing, 13*(3), 280–297.

Angouri, J. (2010). Using text-book and real life data to teach turn taking in business meetings. In N. Harwood (Ed.), *English language teaching materials: Theory and practice* (pp. 373–394). Cambridge: Cambridge University Press.

Bacha, N., Ghosn, I-K, & McBeath, N. (2008). The textbook, the teacher and the learner: a Middle-East Perspective. In B. Tomlinson (Ed.), *English language learning materials: A critical review* (pp. 281–300). London: Continuum.

Bailey, K. M., & Masuhara, H. (2013). Language testing washback: The role of materials. In B. Tomlinson (Ed.), *Applied linguistics and materials development* (pp. 303–318). London: Bloomsbury.

Bao, D. (2002). *Understanding reticence: An action research project aiming at increasing verbal participation in the EFL classroom in Vietnam* (Unpublished PhD thesis). Leeds Metropolitan University, Leeds.

Bao, D. (2008). ELT materials used in Southeast Asia. In B. Tomlinson (Ed.), *English language learning materials: a critical review* (pp. 263–280). London: Continuum.

Bao, D. (2016). Cultural pigeon holes in English language teaching materials. *ELT World Online.com, 8*. Retrieved from https://blog.nus.edu.sg/eltwo/files/2016/07/0804-DAT-BAO-Cultural-pigeonholes-in-English-language-teaching-materials-2i27c6i.pdf

Barnard, E. S. (2007). The value of comprehension in the early stages of the acquisition and development of Bahasa Indonesian by non-native speakers. In B. Tomlinson (Ed.), *Language acquisition and development: studies of first and other languages* (pp. 186–204). London: Continuum.

Barrios, M. L., de Tabat, E. V., & Tavella, G. (2008). In B. Tomlinson (Ed.), *English language learning materials: a critical review* (pp. 300–316). London: Continuum.

Basturkmen, H. (2006). *Ideas and options in English for Specific Purposes*. Mahwah, NJ: Lawrence Erlbaum.

Bell, J. (2012). Teaching mixed level classes. In A. Burns & J. Richards (2012). *The Cambridge guide to pedagogy and practice in second language teaching* (pp. 86–94). Cambridge: Cambridge University Press.

Benson, P. (2006). Autonomy in language teaching and learning. *Language Teaching, 40*, 21–40.

Bernhardt, E. B. (2011). *Understanding advanced second-language reading*. New York: Routledge.

Bogota: Vivela en Español. (2016). Bogota: Pontificia Universidad Javeriana.

Bolitho, R. (2008). Materials used in Central and Eastern Europe and the former Soviet Union. In B. Tomlinson (Ed.), *English language learning materials: A critical review* (pp. 213–222). London: Continuum.

Bosher, S. (2010). English for nursing: developing discipline specific materials. In N. Harwood (Ed.), *English language teaching materials: Theory and practice* (pp. 346–372). Cambridge: Cambridge University Press.

Brick, J. (2012). Teaching English for academic purposes. In A. Burns & J. Richards (2012). *The Cambridge guide to pedagogy and practice in second language teaching* (pp. 170–178). Cambridge: Cambridge University Press.

Burgess, S. (1989). *Good news from the crowded classroom: Reflections on large classes as a stimulus to curriculum development*. Unpublished paper.

Burns, A., & Richards, J. (2012). *The Cambridge guide to pedagogy and practice in second language teaching*. Cambridge: Cambridge University Press.

Byram, M., & Hu, A. (Eds.). (2013). *Routledge encyclopedia of language teaching and learning* (2nd ed.). New York: Routledge.

Byram, M., & Masuhara, H. (2013). Intercultural competence. In B. Tomlinson (Ed.), *Applied linguistics and materials development* (pp. 143–159). London: Bloomsbury.

Canagarajah, S. (2007). The ecology of global English. *International Multilingual Research Journal, 1*(2), 89–100.

Canniveng, C., & Martinez, M. (2003). Materials development and teacher training. In B. Tomlinson (Ed.), *Developing materials for language teaching* (pp. 479–489). London: Continuum.

Cives-Enriquez, R. (2013). Materials for adults: "I am no good at languages!"—Inspiring and motivating L2 adult learners of beginner's Spanish. In B. Tomlinson (Ed.), *Developing materials for language teaching* (2nd ed., pp. 269–287). London: Bloomsbury.

Clare, A., & Wilson, J. J. (2011) *Speakout* [Pre-intermediate, intermediate and advanced levels]. Harlow: Pearson.

Coleman, H. (1987). Teaching spectacles and learning festivals. *ELT Journal, 41*(2), 97–103.

Cook, V. (2013). Materials for adult beginners from an L2 user perspective. In B. Tomlinson (Ed.), *Developing materials for language teaching* (2nd ed., pp. 289–308). London: Bloomsbury.

Cooker, L. (2008). Self-access materials. In B. Tomlinson (Ed.), *English language learning materials: A critical review* (pp. 110–132). London: Continuum.

Cortazzi, M., & Jin, L. (1999). Cultural mirrors / materials and methods in the EFL classroom. In E. Hinkel (Ed.), *Culture in second language teaching and learning* (pp. 196–219). Cambridge: Cambridge University Press.

Cullen, B. (2010). Learning materials for L2 songwriters. In B. Tomlinson & H. Masuhara (Eds.), *Research for materials development in language learning; evidence for best practice* (pp. 189–206). London: Continuum.

Cunningsworth, A. (1984). *Evaluating and selecting EFL teaching materials.* London: Heinemann.

Curry, M. J., & Lillis, T. (2010). Making professional academic writing practices visible: Designing research based heuristics to support English-medium text production. In N. Harwood (Ed.), *English language teaching materials: Theory and practice* (pp. 322–345). Cambridge: Cambridge University Press.

Davies, C., Tup, F, & Aziz, D. (2003). *Life accents 3—An English language course for upper secondary.* Singapore: Times Media.

De Kocha, K. (2016). Hands on EAP. *IATEFL Issues* [50th Anniversary issue], *1*, 6–7.

Dellar, H., & Walkley, A. (2010). *Outcomes: Real English for the real world.* Andover: Heinle.

Dudley-Evans T. (2001). English for specific purposes. In R. Carter & D. Nunan (Eds.), *The Cambridge guide to teaching English to speakers of other languages* (pp. 131–136). Cambridge: Cambridge University Press.

Eales, F., & Oakes, S. (2011) *Speakout* [Starter, elementary and upper intermediate levels]. Harlow: Pearson.

Edwards, E., & Burns, A. (2016). Action research to support teachers' classroom materials development. *Innovation in Language Learning and Teaching* [Special issue, B. Tomlinson guest editor], *10*(2), 106–120.

Eisenmann, M., & Summer, T. (2012). *Basic issues in EFL teaching and learning.* Heidelberg: Winter.

Ellis, R. (1994). *The study of second language acquisition.* Oxford: Oxford University Press.

Ellis, R. (2008). *The study of second language acquisition* (2nd ed.). Oxford: Oxford University Press.

Emery, H. (2013). Working with student-teachers to design materials for language support within the school curriculum. In B. Tomlinson (Ed.), *Developing materials for language teaching* (2nd ed., pp. 521–536). London: Bloomsbury.

Feak, C. B., & Swales, J. (2010). Writing for publication: Corpus-informed materials for postdoctoral fellows in perinatology. In N. Harwood (Ed.), *English language teaching materials* (pp. 279–300). Cambridge: Cambridge University Press.

Frazier, J., & Juza, P. (2008). Materials in the USA. In B. Tomlinson (Ed.), *English language learning materials: A critical review* (pp. 179–192). London: Continuum.

Gardner, G., & Miller, L. (1999). *Establishing self-access: From theory to practice.* Cambridge: Cambridge University Press.

Granema, G., & Long, M. (2013). *Sensitive periods, language aptitude, and ultimate L2 attainment.* Amsterdam: John Benjamins.

Gray, J. (2002). The global coursebook in English language teaching. In D. Block & D. Cameron (Eds.), *Globalization and language teaching* (pp. 151–167). London: Routledge.

Gray, J. (2010). *The construction of English: Culture, consumerism and promotion in the ELT global coursebook.* Basingstoke: Palgrave Macmillan.

Haan, N. (2013). Mining the L2 environment: ESOL learners and strategies outside the classroom. In B. Tomlinson (Ed.), *Developing materials for language teaching* (2nd ed., pp. 309–332). London: Bloomsbury.

Haan, N., Timmis, I., & Masuhara, H. (2010). ESOL materials: Practice and principles. In F. Mishan & A. Chambers (Eds.), *Perspectives on language learning materials development* (pp. 223–248). Berlin: Peter Lang.

Hamp-Lyons, L. (2001). English for academic purposes. In R. Carter & D. Nunan (Eds.), *The Cambridge guide to teaching English to speakers of other languages* (pp. 126–130). Cambridge: Cambridge University Press.

Harwood, N. (Ed.). (2010a). *English language teaching materials: Theory and practice.* Cambridge: Cambridge University Press.

Harwood, N. (2010b). Research-based materials to demystify academic citation for postgraduates. In N. Harwood (Ed.), *English language teaching materials: Theory and practice* (pp. 301–321). Cambridge: Cambridge University Press.

Harwood, N. (Ed.). (2014). *English language teaching textbooks: Content, consumption, production.* Basingstoke: Palgrave Macmillan.

Heah, C., & Yun, L. S. (2003). Collaborative materials design for communication skills training in an engineering context. In W. A. Renanyanda (Ed.), *Methodology and materials design in language teaching: Current perceptions and practices and their implication* (pp. 208–222). Singapore: RELC.

Hewings, M. (2010). Materials for university essay writing. In N. Harwood (Ed.), *English language teaching materials* (pp. 251–278). Cambridge: Cambridge University Press.

Hidalgo, A. C., Hall, D., & Jacobs, G. M. (Eds.). (1995). *Getting started: Materials writers on materials writing.* Singapore: RELC.

Hinkel, E. (Ed.) (2005). *Handbook of research in second language teaching and learning.* Mahwah, NJ: Lawrence Erlbaum.

Holliday, A. (1994). *Appropriate methodology and social context.* Cambridge: Cambridge University Press.

Holliday, A. (2005). *The struggle to teach international English.* Oxford: Oxford University Press.

Hutchinson, T., & Waters, A. (1987). *English for specific purposes.* Cambridge: Cambridge University Press.

Ioup, G. (2005). Age in second language development. In E. Hinkel (Ed.), *Handbook of research in second language teaching and learning* (pp. 419–436). Mahwah, NJ: Lawrence Erlbaum.

Jaidev, R., & Blackstone, B. (2016). Facilitating workplace communicative competence. In W. A. Renandya & H. P. Widodo (Eds.), *English language teaching today: Linking theory and practice* (pp. 293–307). New York: Springer International.

Jakubiak, C., & Harklau, L. (2010). Designing materials for community-based adult ESL programs. In N. Harwood (Ed.), *English language teaching materials: Theory and practice* (pp. 395–418). Cambridge: Cambridge University Press.

Jenkins, J. (2000). *The phonology of English as an international language. New models, new norms, new goals.* Oxford: Oxford University Press.

Jenkins, J. (2007). *English as a lingua franca: Attitude and identity.* Oxford: Oxford University Press.

Jenkins, J. (2012). English as a lingua franca from the classroom to the classroom. *ELT Journal, 66*, 486–494.

Jones, M., & Schmitt, N. (2010). Developing materials for discipline-specific vocabulary and phrases in academic seminars. In N. Harwood (Ed.), *English language teaching materials.* (pp. 225–250). Cambridge: Cambridge University Press.

Kim, W. (2016). Fostering L2 voices with literature: Pedagogical insights. *ELTWorldOnline.com, 8.* Retrieved from https://blog.nus.edu.sg/eltwo/files/2016/05/0803-WON-KIM-Fostering-L2-Voices-with-Literature-2ks0d3k.pdf

Kirkpatrick, A. (2006). Which model of English? Native speaker, nativized or lingua franca? In A. Kirkpatrick (Ed.), *English in the world* (pp. 71–83). London: Continuum.

Klein, W. (1986). *Second language acquisition.* Cambridge: Cambridge University Press.

Kramsch, C., & Sullivan, P. (1996). Appropriate pedagogy. *ELT Journal, 50*(3), 199–212.

Larsen-Freeman, D. (2000). *Techniques and principles in language teaching.* Oxford: Oxford University Press.

Lin, L. Y., & Brown, R. (1994). Guidelines for the production of in-house self-access materials. *ELT Journal, 48*, 150–156.

Littlejohn, A. P. (1992). *Why are ELT materials the way they are?* (Unpublished PhD thesis). University of Lancaster, Lancaster.

Liu, D., & Nelson, R. (in press). Diversity in the classroom. In J. I. Liontas (Ed.), *TESOL encyclopedia.* Hoboken, NJ.: Wiley.

Liu, J., & Berger, C. (2015). *TESOL: A guide.* London: Bloomsbury Academic.

Lumala, M., & Trabelsi, S. (2008). Materials used in Africa. In B. Tomlinson (Ed.), *English language learning materials: A critical review* (pp. 223–244). London: Continuum.

Lynch, T. (1996). Influences on course revision: An EAP case study. In M. Hewings & T. Dudley-Evans (Eds.), *Course evaluation and design in EAP, Review of ELT 6.1* (pp. 26–35). Hemel Hempstead: Prentice Hall Macmillan.

Malcolm, D. (2004). Why should learners contribute to the self-access centre? *ELT Journal, 58*, 346–354.

Maley, A. (2009). *Advanced learners.* Resource Books for Teachers. Oxford: Oxford University Press.

Maley, A. (2011). Squaring the circle—Reconciling materials as constraint with materials as empowerment. In B. Tomlinson (Ed.), *Materials development in language teaching* (2nd ed., pp. 379–402). Cambridge: Cambridge University Press.

Maley, A. (2016). Methodology: teaching at advanced levels. *OnestopEnglish.* Retrieved from http://www.onestopenglish.com/methodology/ask-the-experts/methodology-questions/methodology-teaching-at-advanced-levels/146378.article

Martin, J. (1993). Literacy in science: Learning to handle text as technology. In M. Halliday & J. Martin. *Writing science: Literacy and discursive power.* London: Falmer Press.

Mason, J. (2010). The effects of different types of materials on the intercultural competence of Tunisian university students. In B. Tomlinson & H. Masuhara (Eds.), *Research for materials development in language learning; evidence for best practice* (pp. 67–82). London: Continuum.

Masuhara, H. (2006). Materials as a teacher development tool. In J. Mukundan (Ed.), *Readings on materials development II* (pp. 34–46). Petaling Jaya: Pearson Malaysia.

Masuhara, H. (2011). What do teachers really want from coursebooks? In B. Tomlinson (Ed.), *Materials development in language teaching* (pp. 236–266). Cambridge: Cambridge University Press.

Masuhara, H., & Tomlinson, B. (2008). Materials for General English. In B. Tomlinson (Ed.), *English language learning materials: A critical review* (pp. 17–37). London: Continuum.

McCullagh, M. (2010). An initial evaluation of the effectiveness of a set of published materials for medical English. In B. Tomlinson & H. Masuhara (Eds.), *Research for materials development in language learning; evidence for best practice* (pp. 381–393). London: Continuum.

McDonough, J., & Shaw, C. (2003). *Materials and methods in ELT: A teacher's guide* (2nd ed.). Chichester: Wiley-Blackwell.

McDonough, J., Shaw, C., & Masuhara, H. (2013). *Materials and methods in ELT: A teacher's guide* (3rd ed.). Chichester: Wiley-Blackwell.

McGrath, I. (2002). *Materials evaluation and design for language teaching.* Edinburgh: Edinburgh University Press.

McGrath, I. (2013). *Teaching materials and the roles of EFL/ESL teachers: Practice and theory.* London: Bloomsbury.

McKay, S. (1992). *Teaching English overseas.* Oxford: Oxford University Press.

McKay, S. (2003). Towards an appropriate EIL pedagogy: re-examining common ELT assumptions. *International Journal of Applied Linguistic, 13*(1), 1–22.

McKay, S. (2006). EIL curriculum development. In A. Kirkpatrick (Ed.), *English in the world* (pp. 114–129). London: Continuum.

Mishan, F. (2005). *Designing authenticity into language learning materials.* Bristol: Intellect.

Mishan, F., & Chambers, A. (2010). *Perspectives on language learning materials development.* Bern: Peter Lang.

Mishan, F., & Timmis, I. (2015). *Materials development for TESOL.* Edinburgh: Edinburgh University Press.

Mol, H., & Tin, T. B. (2008). EAP materials in Australia and New Zealand. In B. Tomlinson (Ed.), *English language learning materials: a critical review* (pp. 59–73). London: Continuum.

Mukundan, J. (2008). Multi-media materials in developing countries: the Malaysian experience. In B. Tomlinson (Ed.), *English language learning materials: A critical review* (pp. 100–109). London: Continuum.

Nation, I. S. P., & Macalister, J. (2010). *Language curriculum design.* New York: Routledge.

Nuangpolmak, A. (2014). Multilevel materials for multilevel learners. In S. Garton & K. Graves (Eds.), *International perspectives on materials in ELT* (pp. 121–140). Hemel Hempstead: Palgrave Macmillan.

O'Keeffe, A., McCarthy M., & Carter, R. (2007). *From corpus to classroom: Language use and language teaching.* Cambridge: Cambridge University Press.

Ortega, L. (2009). *Understanding second language acquisition.* London: Hodder Education.

Ottley, K. (2014). Please read the text on page seven: It has nothing to do with you. *Folio, 16*(1), 12–14.

Ottley, K. (2016). Why one-size-fits-all is not fit for purpose: The problem with mass-produced teaching materials, and how one might creatively and sensitively confront this problem. In B. Tomlinson (Ed.), *Second language research and materials development for language learning* (pp. 268–279). New York: Routledge.

Oxenden, C., Latham-Koenig, C., & Seligson, P. (2012). *New English file* (3rd ed.). Oxford: Oxford University Press.

Paltridge, B. (2012). Teaching English for specific purposes. In A. Burns & J. Richards (Eds.), *The Cambridge guide to pedagogy and practice in second language teaching* (pp. 179–185). Cambridge: Cambridge University Press.

Park, S., & Park, H. (2016). *English for SNS*. Seoul: M J Books.

Pham, H. H. (2007). Communicative language teaching: unity within diversity. *ELT Journal, 61*(3), 193–201.

Poedjosoedarmo, G. (2003). Developing an oral communication skills training package: Process and product; problems and solutions. In W. A. Renanyanda (Ed.), *Methodology and materials design in language teaching: Current perceptions and practices and their implication* (pp. 192–207). RELC: Singapore.

Popovici, R., & Bolitho, R. (2003). Personal and professional development through writing: The Romanian textbook project. In B. Tomlinson (Ed.), *Developing materials for language teaching* (pp. 505–517). London: Continuum.

Prabhu, N. S. (2001). *A sense of plausibility*. Unpublished manuscript.

Prodromou, L., & Mishan, F. (2008), Materials used in Western Europe. In B. Tomlinson (Ed.), *English language learning materials: A critical review* (pp. 193–212). London: Continuum.

Rafik-Galea, S., & Cortazzi, M. (2003). Learning by experience: Effectuating changes in EAP materials development. In J. Mukundan (Ed.), *Readings on ELT material* (pp. 1–20). Selangor Darul Ehsan: Universiti Putra Malaysia Press.

Rasti, R., & Tomlinson, B. (2016). *How humanistic are the materials?* Unpublished manuscript.

Richards, J. C., & Rodgers, T. S. (2014). *Approaches and methods in language teaching*. Cambridge: Cambridge University Press.

Sarwar, Z. (2001). Adapting individualization techniques for large classes. In D. Hall & A. Hewings (Eds.), *Innovation in English language teaching: A reader* (pp.127–136). London: Routledge.

Seidlhofer, B. (2010) Lingua franca English: the European context. In A. Kirkpatrick (Ed.), *The Routledge Encyclopedia of World Englishes* (pp. 355–371). Abingdon: Routledge.

Shamin, F. (2012). Teaching large classes. In A. Burns & J. Richards (2012). *The Cambridge guide to pedagogy and practice in second language teaching* (pp. 95–102). Cambridge: Cambridge University Press.

Skeldon, P. (2008). Materials for English for science and technology (EST). In B. Tomlinson (Ed.), *English language learning materials: a critical review* (pp. 59–73). London: Continuum.

Smiley, J., & Masui, M. (2008). Materials in Japan: Co-existing traditions. In B. Tomlinson (Ed.), *English language learning materials: A critical review* (pp. 245–262). London: Continuum.

St. Louis, R. (2010). Can a 48 hour refresher course help first year English for science and technology reading students? A case study of English CIU at Universidad Simon Bolivar, Venezuela. In B. Tomlinson & H. Masuhara (Eds.), *Research for materials development in language learning; evidence for best practice* (pp. 121–136). London: Continuum.

Stoller, F. L., & Robinson, M. S. (2014). An interdisciplinary textbook project: charting the paths taken. In N. Harwood, N. (Ed.), *English language teaching textbooks: Content, consumption, production* (pp. 262–298). Basingstoke: Palgrave Macmillan.

Stubbs, M. (2000). Society, education and language; the last 2,000 (and the next 20?) years of language teaching. In H. Trappes-Lomax (Ed.), *Change and continuity in applied linguistics* (pp. 15–37). Clevedon: Multilingual Matters.

Swales, J. (1990). *Genre analysis: English in academic and research settings*. Cambridge: Cambridge University Press.

Timmis, I. (2002). Native speaker norms and international English: A classroom view. *ELT Journal, 56*, 240–249.

Tomlinson, B. (1990). Managing change in Indonesian high schools. *ELT Journal, 44*(1), 25–37.

Tomlinson, B. (1994a). Materials for TPR. *Folio, 1*(2), 8–10.

Tomlinson, B. (1994b). Pragmatic awareness activities. *Language Awareness, 3*(2 and 4), 119–129.

Tomlinson, B. (1994c). *Openings. Language through literature: An activities book* (New Edition). London: Penguin.

Tomlinson, B. (2003). Materials evaluation. In B. Tomlinson (Ed.), *Developing materials for language teaching* (pp. 15–36). London: Continuum.

Tomlinson, B. (2005a). English as a foreign language: Matching procedures to the context of learning. In E. Hinkel (Ed.), *Handbook of research in second language teaching and learning* (pp. 137–154). Mahwah, NJ: Lawrence Erlbaum.

Tomlinson, B. (2005b). Testing to learn. *ELT Journal, 59*(1), 39–46.

Tomlinson, B. (2006). A multi-dimensional approach to teaching English for the world. In A. Kirkpatrick (Ed.), *English in the world* (pp. 130–150). London: Continuum.

Tomlinson, B. (Ed.). (2008a). *English language learning materials: A critical review*. London: Continuum.

Tomlinson, B. (2008b). Humanizing an EAP coursebook. *Humanizing Language Teaching, 10*(2). Retrieved from http://www.hltmag.co.uk/apr08/sart01.htm

Tomlinson, B. (2010). Principles and procedures for self-access materials. *Studies in Self-Access Learning, 1*(2), 72–86.

Tomlinson, B. (2011). Access-self materials. In B. Tomlinson (Ed.), *Materials development in language teaching* (2nd ed., pp. 413–432). Cambridge: Cambridge University Press.

Tomlinson, B. (2012). Materials development. In A. Burns & J. Richards (2012). *The Cambridge guide to pedagogy and practice in second language teaching* (pp. 269–278). Cambridge: Cambridge University Press.

Tomlinson, B. (2013a). Materials evaluation. In B. Tomlinson (Ed.), *Developing materials for language teaching* (2nd ed., pp. 21–48). London: Bloomsbury.

Tomlinson, B. (2013b). Innovation in materials development. In K. Hyland & L. L. C. Wong (Eds.), *Innovation and change in English language education* (pp. 203–217). New York: Routledge.

Tomlinson, B. (2013c). Materials development courses. In B. Tomlinson (Ed.), *Developing materials for language teaching* (2nd ed., pp. 481–500). London: Bloomsbury.

Tomlinson, B. (2013d). Developing principled frameworks for materials development. In B. Tomlinson (Ed.), *Developing materials for language teaching* (2nd ed., pp. 95–118). London: Bloomsbury.

Tomlinson, B. (2013e) Looking out for English. *Studies in Self-Access Learning, 4*(4), 253–261.

Tomlinson, B. (2014a). Teacher growth through materials development. *The European Journal of Applied Linguistics and TEFL* [Special issue], *3*(2), 89–106.

Tomlinson, B. (2014b). Looking out for English. *Folio, 16*(1), 5–8.

Tomlinson, B. (2016a). Applying SLA principles to whole-class approaches. In B. Tomlinson (Ed.), *Second language research and materials development for language learning* (pp. 33–49). New York: Routledge.

Tomlinson, B. (2016b). Current issues in the development of materials for learners of English as an International Language (EIL). In W. A. Renandya & H. P. Widodo (Eds.), *English language teaching today: Linking theory and practice* (pp. 53–66). New York: Springer International.

Tomlinson, B., Hill, D. A., & Masuhara, H. (2000). *English for life 1*. Singapore: Times Media.

Tomlinson, B., & Masuhara, H. (2004). *Developing language course materials*. RELC: Singapore.

Tomlinson, B., & Masuhara, H. (2008). Materials used in the UK. In B. Tomlinson (Ed.), *English language learning materials: A critical review* (pp. 159–178). London: Continuum.

Tomlinson, B., & Masuhara, H. (2013). Simulations in materials development. In B. Tomlinson (Ed.), *Developing materials for language teaching* (2nd ed., pp. 501–520). London: Bloomsbury.

Trabelsi, S. (2010). Developing and trialling authentic materials for business English students at a Tunisian university. In B. Tomlinson & H. Masuhara (Eds.), *Research for materials development in language learning; evidence for best practice* (pp. 103–120). London: Continuum.

Widodo, H. P. (2016). Teaching English for specific purposes (ESP): English for vocational purposes (EVP). In W. A. Renandya & H. P. Widodo (Eds.), *English language teaching today: Linking theory and practice* (pp. 277–292). New York: Springer.

Winitz, H. (Ed.). (1981). *The comprehension approach to foreign language instruction*. Rowley, MA: Newbury House.

Wright, S. (2009). The elephant in the room. *European Journal of Language Policy, 1*(2), 93–120.

13

Visuals, Layout, and Design

Introduction

In this chapter we will explore visuals, layout, and design in published language-learning materials. We decided to do so because, despite increases in the sales of digital materials (and especially of e-materials), published materials in print form are still used in most language classrooms around the globe (see Chapter 2 and Tomlinson, 2015), because we felt that visuals, layout and design seem to be overlooked in our survey of the contents and indexes of the literature on materials development, and because we have already discussed visuals in digital materials in Chapter 9. In our literature search we could only find a few references that discuss visual elements in language learning materials (e.g. Prowse, 1998, 2011; Tomlinson, 1998, 2011; Hill, 2003, 2013; Masuhara, 2005) and only a few paragraphs on layout and design, mainly in MA assignments or guidelines on selecting material (e.g. *Evaluation and selection of learning resources: A guide*, 2008). We did, however, find a number of useful resource books and web sites that provide practical ideas for using visuals (e.g. Wright, 2008; Keddie, 2009).

Prowse (2011) provides insights into the process of materials development based on testimonials from various established writers and states that "it is axiomatic in publishing that design and illustration can make or break a book" (p. 162). The glossy and colorful magazine-like global coursebooks look so professional and dazzling. Who are these colorful visuals for? How do they help teachers conduct effective teaching? Are learners able to learn the target language more effectively with materials with such appealing visuals?

Some readers may think that visuals, layout and design are specialized areas that should be best left to professional materials developers or publishers. Others may think that visuals matter mainly in teaching young learners. Just reflecting upon what we read in our daily lives (e.g. books, newspapers, magazines, e-mails, texts on internet sites and social media messages) we realize how much we are surrounded and influenced by visuals as well as language. Visuals such as illustrations can convey a lot of meaning with or without language, for example in a simple line drawing in a satirical cartoon. Structural elements such as size, prominence, and placing of different sections in layout influence when and how we pay attention to visuals and texts. The use or nonuse of color, one aspect of design, can create a different atmosphere, mood, and tone in the background, which can influence our subconscious affective responses. Research in social semiotics provides ample evidence that our comprehension and reaction to linguistic text is influenced by visuals, layout and design at all ages (e.g. see Kress, 1997; Kress and Van Leeuwen, 2006 for extensive discussion). In this sense, we argue that visuals, layout and design are indispensable parts of meaning making and of language acquisition and development at all ages.

How and why we use visuals, layout and design, however, would be different depending on our roles in materials development and use. For example, if we were a publisher, one of our imperatives would be to increase the possibility of sales by using colorful and impactful visuals in strategic positions (e.g. the top right hand corner of pages in textbooks) so that potential buyers will be attracted to our products during their quick inspection. From a teachers' point of view, what matters would be how the visuals, layout, and design help us teach with maximum effect. Teachers may use visuals to spark curiosity, discussion, and creativity among learners with different learning styles and individual interests. Learners might be attracted by glossy presentation but they might also want to be able to find activities and references easily and they might prefer white space to cluttered presentation. We believe that raising awareness about visuals, layout and design will help all those involved in materials development to critically evaluate our current practice and explore future directions in a collaborative manner.

Visuals

Kinds of Visuals

By visuals, we mean graphic elements such as drawings, photos and animation as opposed to linguistic texts. In the materials development courses we run, we firstly brainstorm for kinds of visuals, followed by a treasure hunt activity, spotting kinds of visuals in published materials to add to our list. We then categorize them to see if we can find something different and innovative from the expanded list for later analyses.

The following list is not exhaustive but contains the major kinds of visuals we often find in published materials:

- photos;
- drawings;
- simplified figures (e.g. match stick figures, cutout figures, silhouettes);
- paintings;
- collages (i.e. an artistic technique of putting together various different materials such as photographs and pieces of paper or fabric in a single frame);
- cartoons;
- mock documents that simulate real life documents (e.g. letters, book covers, diary pages, newspapers, adverts, road signs);
- conceptual drawings (i.e. making abstract notions more concrete e.g. an arrow to represent a life cycle);
- graphs, charts, maps, diagrams;
- functional illustrations (e.g. graphically designed headings, word art, icons, arrows, speech or thought bubbles).

Materials for children might include interactive visuals that allow children to play actively with the visuals. Such materials enable children to, for example, open the door of a refrigerator in a book and find ice cream, cakes, and soft drinks that can be taken out and put back in. "The Very Hungry Caterpillar," the most widely used children's story according to a survey by Mourão (2015), provides opportunities for such tactile play as putting food through holes in an illustrated caterpillar.

Multimedia or Internet materials can expand the concept of visuals: for example, video, animation, three-dimensional pictures, or illustrations with sound effects (see Chapter 7, "Developing Digital Materials").

Objectives of Visuals

What really matters in terms of language acquisition and development, however, is what visuals are used for—i.e. the objectives of using visuals. Hill (2003) analyzed four intermediate-level student global young adult / adult coursebooks published by major international publishers and found that each page of materials had, on average, two illustrations per page. His closer evaluation of two coursebooks revealed that 55% of their visuals were purely decorative and did not serve any language learning or educational functions. Hill (2013) updated his analysis with three more current global coursebooks and found that:

> over half of the images (40.8% +12.6%) across the three books are still used purely for decoration, for example, if a conversation takes place in a restaurant, there is a photo or drawing of a restaurant beside the dialogue, but students are not asked to refer to the picture. (Hill, 2013, p. 160)

At the MATSDA / University of Liverpool Conference on Authenticity in Materials Development in June, 2016, Haedong Kim gave a presentation on learners' and pre-service teachers' opinions about illustrations in EFL textbooks in South Korea (Kim, 2016), in which he reported his survey of teachers' and students' attitudes towards different types of pedagogic and decorative illustrations in government authorized English textbooks in South Korea. His results showed that the use of illustrations to enhance authenticity was received positively and that the students considered pedagogic illustrations to be more interesting and more useful than decorative illustrations. Kim concluded his presentation by proposing that teachers should choose textbooks that use more pedagogic visual materials and textbook developers should make an attempt to exclude unnecessary decorative illustrations from their materials. This reminds us of *The mind's eye* (Maley, Duff, & Grellet, 1981), a book that uses ambiguously intriguing photos to drive language use activities and which we consider to be the ultimate example of the functional and educational use of engaging visuals.

We think it is very important that we try to identify the objectives behind visuals so that we can use them for valid and effective teaching. What are the objectives of using visuals? Looking at actual materials and identifying the objectives of each visual would make a useful teacher and materials development activity.

Visuals may be used to:

1. Provide a visual explanation / description for something that may be unfamiliar to the learners.
2. Provide context (e.g. introducing characters in a detective story, setting the mood and tone).
3. Show procedures (e.g. how to play a new game).

4. Induce affective responses (e.g. curiosity, interest, laughter).
5. Provoke thoughts and reactions (e.g. finding plausible reasons for a mystery; for and against an issue).
6. Provide a visual summary.
7. Achieve consistency and mark changes.
8. Provide an aesthetic experience.

The first three objectives above serve educational functions. An example of Objective 1 (i.e. visual explanation) can be seen in an extensive reader called *The Galapagos Islands* (Maclachlan, 2015), submitted for the 2016 Language Learner Literature Award (LLL Award) annually organized by the Extensive Reading Foundation (http://erfoundation.org/wordpress/). It would be difficult for the readers to imagine exotic animals or the geological structures of the islands without the photos, map, and illustrations. Note here that Hill (2013) differentiates visuals that are provided for low-level language practice of vocabulary (e.g. matching a word with a picture) and those that offer possibilities for creative use and for stimulating learner interactions. His analysis revealed that most visuals were of the former kind.

Objective 2 (i.e. providing context) is behind, for example, illustrations that provide historical background, as in stories from Shakespeare. As Byron and Baldridge (2007) point out, emoticon or emoji (e.g. smiley icons) are often used to provide contextual clues for the receivers of texts or e-mails. When the topic is sensitive, for example, the sender of the message may add emoticon to reduce the possibility of misunderstanding, which linguistic media such as texts and e-mails could potentially cause.

Objective 3 (i.e. showing procedures) may be familiar in instructions for assembling or using home appliances. Such visuals can be very useful as replacement or support for instructions in language learning materials, too. For example, one of our consultancies involved collaboration with the Educational Bureau in Guangzhou to develop primary-level coursebooks. In our materials, we often used quite complicated physical games and tasks. The problem was that the instructions in English were too difficult for the primary-school learners but we did not want to use Chinese instructions as we had stressed the importance of the teacher using instructions in English to provide meaningful and repeated exposure to English in use (see Chapter 14). The collaborating Chinese materials development team came up with an idea to use a series of photos of Chinese primary children playing the games or doing the tasks. In this way, the photos provided the procedural clues for the learners to work out what they have to do and the teachers supplemented this with English instructions given in the Teachers' Book.

Objective 4 (i.e. inducing affective responses) and Objective 5 (i.e. provoking thoughts and reactions) are vital in education and language acquisition (see Tomlinson, 2013; Ellis, 2016; Masuhara, 2016). Impactful visuals can spark off curiosity, motivation and personal responses that can facilitate meaningful discussions or provide reasons for reading or writing. "Battle for Big Tree Country" (Strong, 2015), one of the finalists of 2016 LLL Award, uses black-and-white illustrations that look like those in graphic novels or comics (Saraceni, 2003). The dramatic illustrations achieve impact that teachers could exploit in many ways (e.g. predicting events, working out how individuals may be feeling and why, guessing what happens next). Some of the illustrations also provide visual summaries (i.e. Objective 6) toward the end of the story.

Objective 7 (i.e. achieving consistency and marking changes) can be an important part of design by providing consistency but a change of illustrative style or kind of photo (e.g.

artistic paintings, historical documents, color, level of abstractness) can also provide a sense of variety and a fresh feel to different units within a course.

Objective 8 (i.e. providing aesthetic experience) is somewhat controversial. Hill (2013) quotes Harmer (2001, p. 135), who takes a positive view of aesthetic visuals without any obvious pedagogic value on the ground that they may interest or motivate some learners, especially those with visual orientation. Others would dismiss them as purely decorative.

Hill (2013) argues, on the basis of his analysis of visuals in three well-known global coursebooks, that:

> It seems to me that having over 50% of the pictures in a given coursebook used for purely decorative purposes is a great waste of effort on the part of the publisher and a great waste of opportunity for the language learner and teacher. (Hill, 2013, p. 163)

Hill (2013) does acknowledge the fact that the learners nowadays may prefer colorful visuals as reflecting their normal experience. Some learners may even be deeply affected by the artistic and aesthetic impact. Hill (2013, p. 161), however, questions if such reactions have a long-term and "direct effect on students attitudes to English or to language learning, or indeed help the learner to learn English better." Of course, the ideal would be visuals that both provide an aesthetic experience and facilitate an activity likely to promote language acquisition, as in, for example, *Search 10* (Fenner & Nordal-Pedersen, 1999), a Norwegian EFL coursebook, which makes use of famous paintings and unusual photographs to stimulate and facilitate language use.

We would strongly argue that we need to be very clear what the objectives of visuals are. Is there not a potential conflict between marketing objectives and language learning objectives? A colorful magazine-like appearance is costly. If we prioritized language learning as well as financial objectives, could we not make collaborative efforts so that the decorative 50% of the total space is used for engaging texts, activities and well-connected, aesthetic visuals that are more likely to lead to effective and durable learning?

Characteristics of Visuals

Visuals are a kind of tool. Just like a pair of scissors or glue, each has characteristics that may be appropriate for different uses. In materials development, once we are clear about our objectives, we need to be able to choose or develop the best possible visuals for whatever objective we set.

Based on his investigation, Hill (2003) points out that photos and drawings are the two major kinds of visuals most widely used in coursebooks. Photos are often used to illustrate people (portraits), objects and places in published materials. They are useful for teachers and materials writers if they wish to give impressions of reality and authenticity in terms of people, objects, and events and their historical and social significance. To achieve such effects, teachers could, for example, present to the learners a story with characters taken from their own photo resource library consisting of newspaper and magazine clippings. Possible weaknesses of photos may be that they could inhibit learners' imagination and date very quickly, and they are not very flexible if teachers want to focus on, emphasize, or highlight particular features within a photo.

Drawings, on the other hand, are often used in published materials to illustrate actions and interactions among people. This may reflect the strengths of the drawings in that they are much more flexible and can be made to order in terms of specificity, focus, emphasis, and details. For example, an exaggerated caricature of a person may highlight the personality much better than a photo can. Drawings can vary from simple and generic icons to realistic and detailed paintings. What is more useful to teachers is that drawing can create not only spatial but also temporary accounts of people, places and events; for example, teachers can draw simple stick figures on a board and tell a story by gradually adding details. The possible weaknesses of drawings may be a lack of assumed authority and the danger of particular artistic styles inducing positive or undesirable negative reactions.

In comparison with his analysis in Hill (2003), Hill (2013) noticed a much greater use of photos (75%, i.e. 392 cases out of 520 photos and drawings) than drawings (about 25%, i.e. 137 cases out of 520). He speculates that a possible reason may be "a greater and simpler access to different types of photographic images parallel to the increased use of electronic technology in publishing" (Hill, 2013, p. 159).

Knowing the strengths and weaknesses of different kinds of visuals enables teachers and materials developers to choose the right kinds of illustrations appropriate for their objectives, particular learners and teaching contexts.

For a quick but useful professional development, we recommend looking at the visuals in a unit of materials and investigating what kinds of visuals there are, what objectives they serve and how the visuals are used. What do you think you will find?

If you would like to try a criterion-based evaluation (see Chapter 3), we could develop pre-use or post-use criteria for visuals based on our discussion so far. Some examples of pre-use criteria are as follows:

To what extent are the visuals:

- Varied?
- Attractive?
- Likely to achieve impact in attracting learners' attention?
- Likely to be useful for language acquisition?
- Likely to help learners to make connections with the real world?
- Likely to help the learners to make connections to the world they know?
- Likely to help the learners understand new experiences they are being introduced to?
- Likely to facilitate learner creation of mental representation rather than imposing complete visual images? (see the second item in the Issues section below)

As you can see, we have turned some of the objectives of visuals into criteria so that we can evaluate whether the materials are likely to achieve their objectives or not. These criteria serve as reminders of what we want visuals to do in materials. We would also stress that visuals should:

- be selected or developed to achieve specific objectives;
- be comprehensible for the target learners;
- be suitable for the target learners (e.g. not seeming childish to adult learners; not being culturally alien);
- not replace or inhibit learner visualization;
- not impose interpretations of texts they are illustrating.

We think that teachers should be helped to appreciate the potential value of illustrations in materials and to gain awareness of how to maximize the potential of illustrations they develop and / or use (e.g. Wright, 2008). We also think that they should be helped to benefit from the publications available on easy ways of creating illustrations (e.g. Wright, 1985).

Layout

The Effects of Layouts

Layout means structural arrangement of parts (e.g. text and visuals). When we see a poster or advert in the media that is amusing, shocking or thought provoking, we realize the power of layout. For example, try searching for "unhcr poster" in your Internet browser. "UNHCR" stands for United Nations High Commissioner for Refugees. Find a poster that affects you. Then consider why the poster may have had such an effect on you. What attracted your attention first? How did your eyes move? Why in that sequence? What kind of emotional and cognitive responses have you experienced?

We are often not aware of structural placement but good layout can play a significant role, often at subliminal level, in:

- attracting attention;
- providing focus;
- sequencing smoothly;
- separating different sections;
- attracting aesthetic responses;
- giving consistent structure;
- providing impact by dramatically departing from the normal layout.

Factors that contribute to the effects of the layout may include:

- positioning;
- size;
- sequence (i.e. our eyes naturally seem to move from top to bottom. In the case of English, our eyes also seem to move from left to right);
- use of space;
- overall balance of visuals and text;
- separation;
- repetition of certain elements.

Good layout in materials supports teachers in managing teaching procedures smoothly with structural clarity. In analyzing layout we could use questions including:

- Are the activities clearly separated?
- Are connections between visuals and activities clearly signaled?
- Is it clear which activities instructions refer to?
- Is there enough white space to achieve clarity for the learners?
- Are sections of units clearly labeled?
- Are headings prominent?

Design

Design is the overall plan of appearance and functions of a set of materials. It could mean the design of the whole book such as the size, weight, covers, and binding or it could mean the design of the pages. Such design elements are likely to be finalized by the editor and designer at an earlier stage of materials production planning before the writing begins or finishes. Note that this could cause a mismatch between the materials writers' intentions, often based on pedagogy, and the visuals, layout, and design of the book (e.g. when a visual is given such clarity and prominence that it prevents learner whilst-reading prediction or imposes an interpretation of its accompanying text).

Materials with good design are likely to be:

- appealing;
- aesthetic;
- impactful;
- functionally clear;
- easy to use;
- cost effective.

Thus, good design can help teachers and materials writers to:

- achieve teaching objectives;
- stimulate affinity between users;
- give credibility to the materials;
- provide a reassuring consistency;
- achieve intended impact where necessary;
- control tones and moods.

Design has two major aspects: appearance and functions. Therefore evaluation criteria could be developed for each aspect. Note here that, unlike layout, design features can be evaluated in degrees.

Appearance

To what extent:

- Is the cover interesting?
- Is the cover appealing?
- Is the appearance potentially attractive to learners from all backgrounds and cultures?
- Does the book retain visual interest throughout?
- Does the book retain visual appeal throughout?
- Does the book give the appearance of being up to date?

Functionality

To what extent:

- Does the design provide consistency?
- Does the design offer variety?
- Is there consistency in the use of design features (e.g. icons, headings, labels, fonts)?
- Is the book portable?

Analyzing Visuals, Layout and Design—An Example

Let us now put into practice what we have discussed so far in relation to how visuals, layout and design work for or against smooth and effective teaching and learning. Major international publishers provide web sites for their global coursebooks and many of them offer free downloads (e.g. a sample unit of student books at different levels, accompanying audio files). In this chapter, we will use a two-page extract (pp. 20–21) from Unit 2 Lives and Legends in *Global intermediate*, published by Macmillan Education (Clandfield & Robb-Benne, 2010) and which is part of the freely downloadable sample unit (http://www.macmillanglobal.com/try-global). It would help if you had these two pages at hand but we will try to provide enough detail in any case to make our explanation self-standing. The choice of this sample has no significance other than it offers a slightly different layout compared to the current trend of a two columns per page layout in many of the widely available international coursebooks.

The main author of *Global* is Lindsay Clandfield and his blog (http://www.macmillanglobal.com/blog/author-blog/a-free-unit-and-some-more-free-resources) gives an overview of the section: "Lives 2: Read an extract from Booker award winner Zadie Smith's *White Teeth*. Students discuss family-related issues and debate sayings and proverbs about family life." Teaching points listed at the beginning of the unit are: vocabulary for relationships; grammar: past perfect and past simple; pronunciation: weak forms.

When we look at pages 20–21, our overall impression of the visuals, layout and design is positive. The design features such as use of round frames with coordinated color create an aesthetic and warm atmosphere. The placing of a black-and-white photo of, seemingly, an old English family on the left edge and a novelist's colored photo on the right edge create almost horizontal symmetry.

Page 20 consists of three columns. The first column gives the content list and indicates what the foci of the section are in terms of vocabulary, reading and grammar. Below the content list in the first column is a photo of an English family consisting of different generations. Note that the photo does not indicate who this family is.

The second column is used for vocabulary. The photo of the big family in the first column is adjacent to vocabulary section activity 2 (i.e. putting the two separate parts of a sentence together as an exercise for lexical bundles such as "… have a lot in common with …"). Based on our teaching experience, we suspect that some learners may be somewhat distracted by the photo in the first column in doing the activities in column 2. We wonder why this particular photo has to be placed next to activity 2—possibly because activity 1 in the second column is vocabulary for family members (e.g. the learners are asked for the differences between grandfather and great grandfather)? But the photo does not particularly help in answering the questions. At the bottom of the second column we see a two-color illustration of an old couple on a motor cycle with younger generations looking at them from a window. We could not work out how this drawing has anything to do with the vocabulary activities.

The third column is for reading-related activities 1–4. At the bottom of the third column, there is a two-color drawing of a man with a woman (who has a prominent wedding ring) holding onto the man's arm. In the background is another woman who looks at the couple with a sad expression on her face. The man's jacket and this third lady's dress share the same color. It looks as if she may have been the ex-girlfriend of the man.

We feel puzzled about the placing of the two drawings at the bottom of the second and third columns from a pedagogic point of view. The drawings in themselves are fine and could spark off interesting stories but the problem is that they have nothing to do with the activities or the novel. These visuals seem to us to be what Hill (2003, 2013) calls "decoration" as they do not make any apparent pedagogical contributions. In this case, these decorative visuals possibly disrupt the smooth flow of learning.

There is an issue about the layout in the third reading column. The instruction for activity 2 says, "Read and listen to the summary and extract from White Teeth. Summarize what the extract is about in one sentence. Compare your sentences with other students." The summary and extract are placed on the next page. The flow of activities so far has been to go down the column so our eyes went down only to realize that the sequence in reading activity 1 is supposed to go sideways to the next page. On page 21, we see no labels indicating "summary" or "extract." The proportion of the size of the frame for the summary in a black circle and of the extract in a rose-colored circular frame is not as prominent as the rest of the text. The space for the summary and extract is a little more than 1 / 7 of the whole two-page spread; 6 / 7 of the whole space is devoted to activities. The circular frames may achieve a unique appearance as a design but they restrict the size of the font. More significantly, the summary of the book is presented in the top left-hand corner (i.e. the priority position where the eye goes first) in the black round box on the left hand side of the extract on p. 21. This means that learners will read the summary first, "*White Teeth* is a story about two wartime friends—the Bangladeshi Samad Iqbal and the Englishman Archie Jones, and their families in London." This is where some learners could wrongly connect the old photo of a British family in Column 1 with Archie Jones' family in London. It is not helped by the fact that the photo and the two illustrations are all about English-looking people. The photo, illustrations, book cover, and summary black circle come before the novel extract and might make strong first impressions on learners. The actual extract from the novel is placed on the right-hand side of the summary. This means that learners will read the extract after reading the summary. The extract is all about the tensions between Bangladeshi Samad and Alsana, his wife.

So, all in all, the visuals, layout, and design do not seem to highlight the text that describes a family relationship, which seems to be the main focus intended by the coursebook writer (see Clandfield's blog, which we introduced earlier). This is unfortunate as we think that the actual extract is very affectively and cognitively engaging and that activity 4 is thought provoking. If those two strong elements were given fuller support, then this unit could offer many more opportunities for genuine communicative interaction, as recommended by second-language acquisition researchers. It could stimulate creativity (e.g. a creative role play between Samad and Alsana; predicting what happens to their relationship followed by the reading of a further section as an option). The language focus could include a language awareness activity encouraging discovery of how Alsana avoids giving direct responses plus research into such language use outside the classroom as an extension of reading activity 4 A. Furthermore, a cultural awareness activity could lead to interesting reflection on the learners' own cultures.

See Bao (2016) and Gray (2010) for further examples of culturally inappropriate visuals conflicting with the intentions of materials developers or the essence of a text or activity.

Some Issues in Using Visuals, Layout, and Design

1. Who ensures the valid and effective use of visuals, layout and design for effective language acquisition and development?

The repeated theme that emerges in this chapter is that teachers, materials writers and designers may have different concerns and targets. Ultimately teachers would look for pedagogic effectiveness, designers would aim for aesthetic appeal. In addition, materials writers and publishers may have to consider additional non-educational reasons such as copyright, budget, market research results, artists' fees and time constraints at every production stage. One of the materials writers testifies in Prowse (2011, pp. 161) that collaboration and agreements are vital among materials writers, designers and editors of publishers. Are such collaborations happening?

When we were writing a coursebook in Singapore, Hitomi used a poem in one of her units. The poem was "Miss, Sue is Kissing," by Michael Richards (Richards, 2004). The poem is about a girl who keeps on kissing tadpoles (i.e. baby frogs), whispering "Prince, prince …" When a boy asks why she is kissing tadpoles, she says she is trying to catch him young. After reading the poem, the learners are asked in groups to draw Sue. To do this task, learners need to visualize what Sue is doing and think hard why she is doing so. They also need to remember and connect the poem with the fairy tale "The Frog Prince," best known from the Brothers Grimm's written version which inspired Disney's film of "The Princess and the Frog" in 2009. The crucial part of this activity is for the learners to connect what they read with their own real lives and think why Sue thought she needed to catch the prince when he was young. Through drawing in groups, learners would have to reread the poems many times and negotiate with their group members what to draw as a group. From the very early stage we had requested meetings with artists and designers. Knowing how vital visuals, layout, and design are, we wanted to make sure the illustrator got it right. Such a meeting did not happen. So, Hitomi added an art brief that strongly requested that the illustration should come on a different page and the learners should not be able to see the illustration when they do the drawing activity. She also added an illustration of what Sue should look like to make doubly sure. We did not hear from the artists or the editors until the book was published. We were shocked to see right next to the poem the illustration of a beautiful princess who is around 18 to 20 years old with a tiara on her head in a gorgeous dress, with a think bubble in which a handsome prince is holding a white horse. This dazzling illustration totally destroyed the poem and the activity. Prowse (2011, pp. 61–162) provides reports from three coursebook writers who have had similar experiences.

Illustrators typically make use of visual redundancy to ensure clarity in their illustrations. To do so they often use conventions that are culture bound. For example, we once asked an illustrator on a materials-development course to draw, for a coursebook, a man standing on a station platform. He included five features of redundancy to make it clear that the man was on a station but unfortunately all the features would only be recognizable to somebody living in the United Kingdom (e.g. the then British Rail logo, a platform raised above the tracks, a serrated wooden overhang). A drawing in a coursebook being used by Brian in Nigeria depicted a man sitting in an obviously very hot office thinking of going for a swim after work. Unfortunately none of the Nigerian students were aware of the think bubble convention and many thought that offices in England had swimming pools in them.

Hill (2013), after providing a table comparing the ratio of functional and decorative visuals, comments:

> … these figures highlight what I see as one of the major problems in the production of coursebooks: the authors, unless they specifically provide a brief for a particular picture for use with an activity, leave the rest of the production process up to the editors and designers, and it is at that stage that the decorative images are usually added. And what goes onto a page is dependent upon a number of non-educational factors, such as space left once the necessary exercises and illustrations have been included, what illustrated straplines are included at the top of pages or start of chapters and how many pictures they can afford from picture agencies without going over budget. (Hill, 2013, pp. 160)

Hill (2013, pp. 160–161) fully acknowledges and praises the professional skills that go into producing attractive coursebooks and we agree with him. Our analyses of the visuals in the previous section, however, seem to reveal that the vital link between design and pedagogy seems to be often missing.

Prowse (2011) reports changing practices in publishing coursebooks:

> The digital revolution may mean that in the future the "print" coursebook as we know it vanishes, and the electronic materials which replace it are multi-authored packages assembled to meet the requirements of a particular group of students. Coursebook writers may increasingly be paid fees for sets of materials rather than sharing the risk of creating a whole book or series with the publisher by getting royalties. (Prowse, 2011, p. 172)

If we look at a global course at all the levels and see the names of the different authors, we can actually see examples of what Prowse describes about multi-component packages of materials created by multi-authors. More efforts for closer collaboration between authors, editors, and designers might create more cost-effective materials that also facilitate language acquisition and development. Meanwhile, teachers' critical evaluation of visual, layout and design becomes even more crucial.

2. Visuals in print and visualization in our minds

So far we have looked at visuals in the input. There is another fundamental issue, which is even more neglected: we should differentiate between the visuals in the materials in print (i.e. input) and the multi-dimensional representations we create from linguistic text in our minds (i.e. intake).

Imagine that you have read a book. You have created a mental representation of the main characters in the novel. Suppose you decided to watch a movie based on the novel. Guess what happens next. You may be disappointed that the choice of actors or actresses and that how the story was depicted was totally "wrong." You may prefer your own version, which you had subconsciously created in your mind. This mental representation (i.e. intake) is formed through our integration of the processed aural or written linguistic input with memories in our minds. So, if we hear about a cat or dog, we add our own personal interpretations based on our multitudes of experience stored in our various memory systems and we create our own mental representations of these animals. Such mental representation often involves affective and cognitive coloring. For example, those who love cats are more likely to have positive representations whereas those who have had bad experiences with them are more likely to create negative representations. Those whose dogs happen to be suffering from allergic reactions may create their own cognitive mental representation of incoming information about a dog.

We strongly believe, supported by our research and by the literature, that the ultimate objective of comprehension activities is to help the learners become able to create their own vivid mental representation of linguistic content in their minds, an achievement that can enhance understanding, retention, and recall (Masuhara, 2005; Tomlinson, 2011). Visuals do carry significant communicative values and visuals are abundant in what we encounter every day but the main medium for input still remains linguistic texts.

So the kinds of activities that encourage creating multi-dimensional mental representations might involve, for example, creating mental images, drawing interpretations, adding illustrations to stories, completing partial illustrations, creating pictorial summaries. We gave an example earlier in issue 1 about the group drawing activity of Sue in the poem "Miss! Sue is Kissing …". As our anecdote shows, the careless use of visuals can actually prevent such mental processes, as can visuals that are so detailed that they make the text redundant.

3. Outward appearance or inward significance?

Teachers seem to feel that their home-produced materials are inferior to professionally produced materials (see discussion of teachers' reluctance toward adaptation in Chapter 4, "Adaptation"). Students may feel that glossy global coursebooks are more likely to help them become better in language learning. But do such coursebooks actually contribute to durable motivation and actual learning of language? Is it not inward significance of materials that helps learning and inspires durable motivation? We would welcome research on the effect of coursebook appearance on durable attitudes and on learning effect. Meanwhile, teachers could take back educational control of visuals, layout, and design in their own adaptation (see Chapter 4) and development of materials (Chapter 5).

The Principles and Procedures of Visuals, Layout and Design that we Recommend

When Writing Materials for Materials Writers and Publishers

As we have explained and exemplified in this chapter, we would welcome greater efforts in putting pedagogical objectives as the main driver of visuals, layout, and design. We strongly believe that taking time for collaboration between writers, editors, designers and illustrators throughout a project would be more effective in terms of cost, validity, effects, and reputation. In our experience, the most successful cases have been when teachers became writers with the full support of sponsors and publishers and in collaboration with editors and designers, as in the development of the Namibian coursebook *On target* (1995) (see Chapter 5 for details) or in the Norwegian coursebook *Search 10* referred to earlier (Fenner & Nordal-Pedersen, 1999). We also find initiatives such as http://www.eltteacher2writer.co.uk/about-elt-teacher-2-writer—a series of e-books training teachers to be writers—to be potentially promising as a way of bringing back innovation, flexibility and coherence in materials development.

For Teachers

Depending on personality, experience and confidence, some teachers may feel that developing materials is beyond their abilities. However, we have seen all over the world teachers make successful adaptations of prescribed materials out of necessity. What they are doing is finding ways of motivating their students by tapping into learner creativity and into their own. They often do so by localizing and personalizing existing materials. Our recommendation is to find a very engaging text as the main driver (see Chapter 5) and then related visuals that could spark inspiration. We would like to recommend the following as enjoyable and efficient ways of using visuals in materials:

1. **Collect impactful visuals** that have succeeded in making you feel surprised, impressed and / or curious and in provoking thought and amusing you. Locally relevant visuals are obviously valuable as they tackle the problem of cultural appropriacy often raised by the critics and users of global coursebooks. Make sure you note down the sources where you get the visuals from in case they are protected by copyright and you need to get permission to use them. See the Appendix: Resources Useful for Materials Developers at the end of this book for sources of freely available images. See https://creativecommons.org/licenses/by/2.0/uk for information about how Creative Commons licenses make some texts and images available for educational use and see https://www.jisc.ac.uk/guides/open-educational-resources for learning materials that are available online.
2. **Invite colleagues, students and friends to share visuals**. Visuals brought to class by your students reflect what they are interested in and visuals contributed by friends and by colleagues can help you to build a library of authentic visual texts, which can be selected from to stimulate communication. Also by sharing visuals with colleagues you can collaborate in materials development, and gain useful feedback from their students as well as your own.
3. **Learn from effective use of visuals available** around you such as in media, books, posters, adverts and on the internet. Why did they achieve impact? How are visuals and texts positioned (i.e. layout)? They are authentic materials created by professionals for communicative purposes (e.g. to appeal, surprise, persuade, entertain) and they can teach us a lot about how to achieve our intended effects.
4. **Incorporate engaging and educationally useful visuals into your materials** and make drafts of your materials for trialing.
5. **Consider the objectives of activities in terms of language acquisition and development**. Engagement is a vital ingredient of language acquisition but is the engagement created by visuals also facilitating engaged interaction using the target language? This is where evaluation and analysis criteria become useful (see some examples of evaluation criteria and analysis questions in previous sections in this chapter; see also our recommendations for evaluation procedures in Chapter 3 and adaptation procedures in Chapter 4).
6. **When and how to use visuals** is vitally important. We explained the damage caused by misplacing the visuals to the poem "Miss! Sue is kissing…" If you can, **trialing your materials with your colleagues** (they can try theirs on you too) is highly encouraged.

They may point out the problems with layout or prominence of your visuals. This is in fact grassroots professional development that can easily be incorporated into busy teachers' lives.

7. **Use your materials** in your class. Students are the best source of feedback about how engaging your materials are.

We recommend Chapter 3, "Evaluation" for "Suggestions for how to Evaluate Your Materials," and you may also find Chapter 4, "Adaptation" and Chapter 5, "Developing Materials" useful in relations to making use of visuals in your materials. Also of help would be web resources for teachers on using visuals which are available for free download e.g.:

- http://lessonstream.org/materials/image-lesson-plans/
- https://atiyepestel.wordpress.com/2013/05/16/1000-pictures-for-teachers-to-copy-andrew-wright/

and we recommend accessing resource books for using visuals in language teaching (we found, for example, Wright, 1991 and Keddie, 2009 by searching on the web for "visuals in language teaching").

Our final recommendation is to look at any purely decorative but potentially engaging visual in materials you are using or developing and to either think of activities you could add to make immediate use of the visual for language activities or to make a note of the visual for future use in a different unit or set of materials.

Tasks

1. Select a unit of materials from any coursebook and then:
   - evaluate the visuals in relation to their potential effectiveness in facilitating language acquisition;
   - evaluate the lay out in relation to its potential value for (a) the students, and (b) the teachers;
   - evaluate the design in relation to its potential value for (a) the publishers, (b) the teachers, and (c) the students.
   For each of the subtasks above it would be useful to draw up a list of criteria, making selective use of our criteria above and of criteria added by yourself.
2. Redesign the unit of materials you have evaluated in 1 above so that it is of greater potential value for its target learners.

References

Bao, D. (2016). Cultural pigeon holes in English language teaching materials. *ELT WorldOnline.com, 8*. Retrieved from https://blog.nus.edu.sg/eltwo/files/2016/07/0804-DAT-BAO-Cultural-pigeonholes-in-English-language-teaching-materials-2i27c6i.pdf

Byron, K., & Baldridge, D. C. (2007). E-mail recipients' impressions of senders' likability: The interactive effect of nonverbal cues and recipients' personality. *Journal of Business Communication, 44*(2), 137–160.

Clandfield, L., & Robb-Benn, R. (2010). *Global intermediate*. Oxford: Macmillan Education.

Ellis, R. (2016). Language teaching materials as work plans: An SLA perspective. In B. Tomlinson (Ed.), *SLA research and materials development for language learning* (pp. 203–218). New York: Routledge.

Evaluation and selection of learning materials: A guide. (2008). Charlottetown, Prince Edward Island: Department of Education.

Fenner, A. N., & Nordal-Pedersen, G. (1999). *Search 10*. Oslo: Gyldendal.

Gray, J. (2010). The branding of English and the culture of the new capitalism: Representations of the world of work in English language textbooks. *Applied Linguistics, 31*(5), 714–733.

Harmer, J. (2001). *The practice of English language teaching* (3rd ed.). Harlow: Pearson Longman.

Hill, D. A. (2003). The visual element in EFL coursebooks. In B. Tomlinson (Ed.), *Developing materials for language teaching* (1st ed.) (pp. 174–182). London: Continuum.

Hill, D., A. (2013). The visual elements in EFL coursebooks. In B. Tomlinson (Ed.), *Developing materials for language teaching* (2nd ed.) (pp. 157–166). London: Bloomsbury.

Keddie, J. (2009). *Images*. Oxford: Oxford University Press.

Kim, H. (2016, June). *Learners' and pre-service teachers' opinions about illustrations in EFL textbooks in South Korea*. Presentation at the MATSDA/University of Liverpool Conference on Authenticity in Materials Development, Liverpool.

Kress, G. R. (1997). *Before writing: Rethinking the paths to literacy*. London: Routledge.

Kress, G. R., & Van Leeuwen, T. (2006). *Reading images: The grammar of visual design* (2nd ed.). London: Routledge.

Maclachlan, A. (2015). *The amazing Galapagos Islands*. Brentford: Compass Publishing.

Maley, A., Duff, A., & Grellet, F. (1981). *The mind's eye: Using pictures creatively in language learning*. Cambridge: Cambridge University Press.

Masuhara, H. (2005). Helping learners to achieve multi-dimensional mental representation in L2 reading. *Folio, 9*(2), 6–9.

Masuhara, H. (2016). Brain studies and materials for language learning. In B. Tomlinson (Ed.), *Second language research and materials development for language learning* (pp. 23–32). New York: Routledge.

Mourão, S. (2015). The potential of picturebooks with young learners. In J. Bland (Ed.), *Teaching English to young learners—critical issues in language teaching with 3–12 year olds* (pp. 199–217). London: Bloomsbury.

Prowse, P. (1998). How writers write: Testimony from authors. In B. Tomlinson (Ed.), *Materials development in language teaching* (pp. 130–145). Cambridge: Cambridge University Press.

Prowse, P. (2011). How writers write: Testimony from authors. In B. Tomlinson (Ed.), *Materials development in language teaching* (2nd ed.) (pp. 151–173). Cambridge: Cambridge University Press.

Richards, M. (2004). Miss! Sue is kissing… In M. Harrison & C. Stuart-Clark (Eds.), *A poem for everyone* (pp. 135–135). Oxford: Oxford University Press.

Saraceni, M. (2003). *The language of comics*. London: Routledge.

Strong, G. (2015). *Battle for big tree country*. Boston: National Geographic Learning.

Tomlinson, B. (1998). Seeing what they mean: Helping L2 readers to visualise. In B. Tomlinson (Ed.), *Materials development in language teaching* (pp. 265–278). Cambridge: Cambridge University Press.

Tomlinson, B. (2011). Seeing what they mean: Helping L2 readers to visualise. In B. Tomlinson (Ed.), *Materials development in language teaching* (2nd ed.) (pp. 357–378). Cambridge: Cambridge University Press.

Tomlinson, B. (2013). Second language acquisition and materials development. In B. Tomlinson (Ed.), *Applied linguistics and materials development* (pp. 11–29). London: Bloomsbury.

Tomlinson, B. (2015). Key issues in EFL coursebooks. *ELIA Journal*, *15*, 171–180.

Wright, A. (1985). *1000 pictures for teachers to copy*. Reading, MA: Addison-Wesley.

Wright, A. (2008). *Pictures for language learning*. Cambridge: Cambridge University Press.

Wright, A. (1991). *Visuals for the language classroom*. Harlow: Longman Pearson.

14

Writing Instructions for Language-Learning Activities

Introduction

In our view it is very important that both the teacher and the students are able to clearly understand all instructions in the materials that they use and that the students are able to make easy use of them. A number of materials writers have told us that their written instructions are not that important as the teacher will clarify them orally when setting activities for their students, and we were even told by materials developers at a workshop in Mauritius that their instructions in English did not really matter because the teacher would explain what to do to the students in French. However, we have often found when observing lessons in many different countries that the teacher has misunderstood instructions because they were insufficiently precise and clear, that many students forget or do not listen to their teacher's instructions and have to rely on their inadequate understanding of what it says in the textbook, and that often the teacher tells students to do an activity from the textbook in class or for homework without any reinforcement or clarification of the instructions. If students are not sure what to do, we have found that some of them assume that it is their fault rather than that of the materials writers, they approach the activity negatively and they are less likely to benefit from the activity than if they had started it with a clear understanding and in a positive frame of mind. Or some students end up doing the wrong thing and being rebuked by their teacher or different students do the activity differently and then the teacher has problems giving feedback. For these reasons we think it is vital that instructions for activities are absolutely clear and that materials developers and teachers are trained to achieve consistent precision and clarity when writing or giving instructions. We must admit, though, that we have observed lessons in which both the teacher and the students misunderstood the instructions for a coursebook activity and unintentionally turned it into a more open-ended and communicative activity (as happened once in Indonesia in one of the best lessons we have ever observed).

Given the importance of effective instructions we find it amazing that there is so little written on it in the literature on materials development for language learning. We searched through the major books on materials development for language learning and found nothing on instructions. Then we read again a section on writing effective instructions in a book we wrote for inexperienced teachers in South East Asia (Tomlinson & Masuhara, 2004). Finally we googled "writing instructions for language learning materials" and came across two interesting articles. McColl (2002, pp. 2–3), in writing about

The Complete Guide to the Theory and Practice of Materials Development for Language Learning,
First Edition. Brian Tomlinson and Hitomi Masuhara.
© 2018 John Wiley & Sons, Inc. Published 2018 by John Wiley & Sons, Inc.

the teaching of modern languages in Scotland, gives some very useful practical advice for teachers when they are writing or giving instructions, including:

- give no more than one or two instructions at a time;
- as well as giving the instructions orally, write them up on the board so that students who forget can quickly see what they have to do next;
- use a handheld electronic device to record the instructions as you give them to the class, then give the recording to whoever may need it to serve as a reminder;
- include commonly used instructions along with wall displays of classroom language, preferably associated with a drawing or icon to serve as a reminder;
- when setting out written instructions, whether on the board or on a worksheet, make the process clear by making each step into a separate sentence and setting them out in a numbered list;
- teach those students who have particular difficulty keeping on track to tick each stage as they complete it.

Corke Pelton (n.d.) turned out to be an article on teaching students to write instructions. Initially this did not seem to be relevant but then an obvious thought occurred to us. One potentially very useful way to help students to understand instructions better is to train them to write instructions themselves. This is something we have actually done many times without realizing it. For example, if the students have been doing a task that involves following written instructions (e.g. playing a game, following a recipe, solving a puzzle), one of the post-task activities we often do is to get the students to devise their own game, recipe, puzzle, and so on, then to investigate the instructions they followed in doing the task given to them, and then to revise the instructions they have written in the light of what they have discovered about writing clear instructions. Hopefully, this not only helped students to improve their writing of instructions but helped them to understand instructions more easily too. Something else we have done to help students to understand instructions is to give them unclear instructions to make something (e.g. a paper airplane), let them make a mess of it, teach them how to seek clarification, and then give them similar instructions on how to make something else (e.g. a paper boat).

Issues in Writing and Giving Instructions

Which Language should be Used for Writing and Giving Instructions?

In some countries (e.g. China, South Korea) instructions are sometimes written in the L1 in textbooks to make sure that the learners understand them. In many countries (e.g. Brazil, China, Indonesia, Japan, Portugal, Spain, and South Korea) we have seen or been told about teachers typically translating instructions from the target language to the L1 to ensure understanding and facilitate acquisition. For example, in Indonesia we have seen teachers reading the instructions in English and then translating them into Bahasa Indonesia. On the surface, using the L1 in giving instructions seems to make sense as it is more likely to achieve the main goal of clear understanding. However, what we have found is that doing so denies the learners exposure to the L2 in use in contexts with optimum potential for facilitating acquisition from need, from relevant and frequent recycling and from immediate situational feedback. On the PKG (By the Teacher for the Teacher) program in Indonesia (Tomlinson, 1990), for example, teachers were encouraged to use only English when giving instructions orally or in writing to beginners and to standardize the terms they used (e.g. "Tick the correct answer." Rather than "Select / choose underline the right / best answer"). The result was not only quick and easy understanding by the students but increased confidence and fluency in English from the teachers, who were initially reluctant but eventually enthusiastic.

Should Instructions be Exemplified?

It seems self-evident that providing examples of what to do helps learners to follow instructions. Doing so adds useful redundancy, which can reinforce and clarify the students' understanding of the instructions. The example is also often more memorable than the instruction as it is often more easily visualized and retained. However we have found that materials developers and teachers need to be very careful when illustrating instructions. If they provide linguistic examples, there is a danger of restricting the activity to varied repetition of the example or practice of a particular structure. Here are two examples of problematic exemplification:

1. "Talk to your partner about their likes and dislikes. For example, you can ask, 'Do you like basketball?'"
2. "Move around the room inviting classmates to your party. You could use 'Would you like to come…' or 'I'd like you to come…'"

In response to 1 we have heard students laboring through such "conversations" as the following:

A: Do you like basketball?
B: No.
A: Do you like football?
B: No.
A: Do you like dancing?
B: Yes.

In response to 2 we have heard conversations like the following:

A: Would you like to come to my party?
B: Yes. Thank you very much.
A: I'd like you to come to my party.
C: Thank you.
A: Would you like to come to my party?
D: Yes. Thank you very much.

In both cases the examples have become dominant and have so severely restricted the interactions that they have become meaningless drills rather than meaningful conversations.

Visual exemplifications can also be problematic. They can replace the linguistic instructions they are supposed to be illustrating and result in the students making no effort to understand the English to which they are being exposed. Worse still, they can cause misunderstanding of the instruction. For example, imagine the following instruction is illustrated by a drawing of somebody giving a photo of a girl to the person on his left. "Give your photo to the person on your left."

A male student might think he has to give a photo of a girl rather than of himself and that he has to give it to someone on his right (because the person in the drawing is on his right as he looks at the drawing).

Visual illustrations of instructions can be useful but it is very important that they reinforce and / or clarify an instruction and that they do not replace it or make it confusing.

Do Instructions Have to Be Linguistic?

As we have said above, we believe that giving instructions in the target language can facilitate the acquisition of that language because instructions can satisfy the optimum conditions for effective input. That is they can be relevant, meaningful, significant, comprehensible, and recycled, and following them can provide useful outcome feedback (i.e. learners will often know immediately if they have misunderstood the instructions). However, there is obviously a problem at lower linguistic and cognitive levels when attempting to communicate lengthy and complex instructions in the target language for a game or task.

When working on a course for Chinese primary school learners we wanted to include some fun games and tasks but had problems ensuring that the instructions were comprehensible. What we did was to get Chinese children of the target age to play the games and perform the tasks and to photograph the children doing so. In the published teachers' book there was a "script" in English for teacher instructions but in the student book there were only photos of children playing the games and doing the tasks. This was even more effective than we expected as the students identified with the children in the photos, who resembled them and were obviously enjoying the activities. We would now recommend replacing instructions with photos in the initial units of the students' book of a young learners' beginners' course, then writing captions to accompany photos in the middle units, and then adding instructions before photos in the later units.

How Can Instructions be Evaluated?

The best way to find out if instructions are effective is to give them to learners of an equivalent age and level and then observe them trying to carry out the instructions. If they have any problems you can try to find out why, both by observation and by discussion with the learners. Obviously, this is not always possible so we believe it is very important to establish criteria both to drive the instructions and later to make use of when evaluating the instructions. As you know what you intend, your instructions often seem sufficiently clear to you. It is therefore important that you ask colleagues to make use of your criteria to evaluate your instructions for you.

We have listed and explained our main criteria below.

Criteria for Writing and Giving Instructions

1. Salience

We have found that it really helps learners if the instructions for an activity are salient; that is, if they stand out from any adjacent text, description, comment, advice, and so forth. Otherwise there is a danger that some students might be confused by what seems to be a very long instruction or might have problems finding the instruction again when they want to check they are doing an activity in the way intended. Ways of making it clear which words are instructions and which are not include "putting the instructions in bold, in a distinctive font, in a different color or in a box" (Tomlinson & Masuhara, 2004, p. 29).

Good example	It's important that your drawings are easy to understand. In order to help your group members: **Write a caption underneath each drawing.**
Bad example	It's important that your drawings are easy to understand. Write a caption underneath each drawing in order to help your group members if they are confused.

2. Separation

Notice in the good example above the instruction not only stands out but it is separated from non-instructions too. Ideally instructions should be separated from each other to make it clear how many different things the learners need to do.

Good example	1. **Number the drawings.** 2. **Write a caption to go with each drawing.** 3. **Give a letter to each caption.** 4. **Give the drawings and the captions to your team members.** 5. **Get your team members to put the right caption under each drawing.**
Bad example	Number the drawings, write a caption to go with each drawing, give a letter to each caption, give the drawings and the captions to your team members and get them to put the right caption under each drawing.

3. Sequencing

We have found that it is very important that each instruction is presented in the same sequence as the action it is intended to effect. If the sequence of instructions is different from the sequence of target actions then students get confused and often prioritize the sequence in which the instructions are given. For example, when carrying out the following instruction some students are likely to ignore the key word "Before" and write the letters after folding the paper. This seems incredible but we must always remember that some students are so tense when following instructions in English that they do not have the confidence to question the instructions.

"You are going to fold the paper in half. Before this write A in the top left hand corner and B in the top right hand corner."

Good example	You are going to operate the machine in picture 1. **Write down what you need to know in order to operate the machine.** **Listen to instructions on how to operate the machine.** **Answer questions 1–6 in the box.**
Bad example	Listen to an account of how to operate the machine in the picture and answer the questions about it. Before you listen write down what you need to know about operating the machine.

4. Staging

Instructions should be given in stages so that the students do not have to remember a lot of instructions before starting to follow them. If there are a lot of instructions, the students should receive an instruction for the first activity, do the action, receive an instruction for the second activity, do the action, and so on.

Good example	8. **Listen to my next instructions. The first time just listen and visualize what you are going to do. The second time carry out the instructions.**
	9. **Put your balls in the circles so that:**
	   • **you have twice as many balls in A as in C**
	   • **you have twice as many balls in A as in B**
	   • **you have twice as many balls in B and C as you have in D**
	   • **you have one ball in between A, B, C and D**
	10. **Compare your answer with that of another pair nearby.**
	11. **Move two balls so that you have an equal number of balls in each circle.**
	12. **Join together with another pair.**
	13. **Make up another task involving balls and circles.**
	14. **Write instructions for your task.**

Bad example	8. Listen to my next instructions. The first time just listen and visualize what you are going to do. The second time carry out the instructions. Put your balls in the circles so that you have twice as many balls in A as in C, you have twice as many balls in A as in B, you have twice as many balls in B and C as you have in D and you have one ball in between A, B, C and D 9. Compare your answer with that of another pair nearby. Then move two balls so that you have an equal number of balls in each circle. 10. Join together with another pair, make up another task involving balls and circles and write instructions for your task.

5. Sufficiency

Sometimes materials writers in trying to keep their instructions as short and simple as possible do not give sufficient information to the learners. It is important that instructions are simple and succinct but it is equally important that they contain all the information that students need to carry them out as they are intended.

Good example	**Write a note for the company that is delivering your furniture to your new home.** **Tell the company:** **which room to put each item of furniture in;** **where to put each item of furniture in each room.**
Bad example	Write a note for the furniture delivery company telling them where to put your furniture in your new house.

6. Succinctness

Sometimes materials writers, in trying to help students, provide too much information in their instructions. This can cause confusion, annoyance, a negative attitude towards the activity, and delay in starting to do it. Ideally, instructions should contain all but only all the information needed to do an activity and they should be presented in the briefest and most concise way possible.

Good example	A friend has gone to live in Barcelona. You used to live in Barcelona so: **Write an e-mail to your friend.** **Recommend places, restaurants and things to do in Barcelona.**
Bad example	A friend you have known for many years has got a new job in Barcelona and went to live there last week. You used to live in Barcelona before you got married so you have decided to help your friend by writing an e-mail in which you recommend interesting places to visit, things to do and good restaurants to go to in Barcelona.

7. Simplicity

It seems fairly obvious that instructions should be as simple as possible. We argue that the language of instructions should be at a lower level than that of the texts in a set of materials; 100% comprehension is essential when following instructions. Engagement is vital when reading or listening to texts; 100% comprehension is not.

Ways of ensuring simplicity are:

- Only specifying one action in each instruction. (For example, X "Write your name in the middle of the piece of paper, draw a circle around it, draw another circle of the same size next to it and write the name of another group member in that circle.")
- Using common and familiar vocabulary. (For example, "Choose someone to write down your points" versus "Nominate a group secretary.")
- Using only imperatives, simple forms of verb tenses and the active voice. (For example, X "If you have been nominated you should draw two columns on a sheet of paper.")
- Not using subordinate clauses (For example, X "Give your drawing to a person who is not in your group and who has not read the story which you have depicted.")

● Not using coordinators (For example, X "Listen to the story and answer the questions below it.")

Good example	**See pictures in your mind of yourself on holiday in another country.** **Then tell a partner about:** **the places you visited,** **the people you met,** **the food you ate.**
Bad example	Imagine you have been taken to an exotic country for your holiday and tell a partner about the places that you visited, the people you met and the food that you ate when you were enjoying your vacation in that country.

8. Specificity

Many coursebook instructions tell students what to do but they do not tell them how to do it. For example:

● "Match the underlined words in sentences 1–10 with the pictures A to J." (What are the students supposed to do? How do they match the words to the pictures?)
● "Before reading the article about New York make up two questions about New York which you want to know the answer to. As you read the article ask yourself your questions. When you have finished reading answer your questions." (Do they write down the questions? Do they ask their questions aloud or in their heads? Do they write answers to their questions?)
● "There is a chemist, a florist, a newsagents and a convenience store on Haig St. Here is a list of items that you want to buy. Put each item in the right shop." (How do they do this? Write the name of the item next to the name of the shop? Draw the shops and draw the items in it? Mime carrying each item?)

We believe that instructions need to be specific about what to do and specific about how to do it too. Otherwise some students will not even start to do the activity and other students will do the activity in different ways. This can lead to student loss of esteem, confusion and even guilt, as well as making it very difficult for the teacher to lead a feedback session.

Good example	1. **Look at pictures 1–6.** 2. **Read questions a)–f).** 3. **Match each question to a picture by writing in pencil the letter of the question next to the picture.** 4. **Look at picture 1 again.** 5. **Try to answer the question about picture 1 in your mind.** 6. **Use your dictionary to find any words you need to answer the question.** 7. **Write an answer to the question in your exercise book.** 8. **Do 4–7 above for pictures 2–6.**
Bad example	Match each question to a picture and then answer the questions by looking at the pictures and making use of your dictionary.

9. Unambiguity

It is obviously important that nothing in an instruction is capable of two or more interpretations. We have found that, for example, pronouns, adverbials of position, co-ordinators and synonyms can be ambiguous and therefore we always avoid them when writing or giving instructions. Here are some examples of potentially ambiguous instructions:

- "You are a waiter in a restaurant. Your partner is one of the customers. You will find the menu *below* the drawing of a restaurant. Read *it* to *them*."
- "Pretend you are passengers sitting on a bus. Arrange your chairs as though they are on the bus and then sit on *them*. Your teacher is an old man who has just got on *it*. He is paying the conductor for *his* ticket. Offer your *seat* to *him*."
- "Look at the photo *above* of people at a football match. What is the man *on the left* wearing on his head, what is the *person* in front of him wearing and what is the *one* behind *him wearing*."
- "Listen to the story and tell your partner about it." (Whilst listening or afterwards?)

We recommend participants in our workshops to:

- use nouns or noun phrases instead of pronouns;
- indicate what is being referred to (e.g. instead of using adverbials of position (e.g. above, below, under, behind, in front of, next to, near, on the left) use numbers, letters, boxes, colors, etc.);
- use the same word or phrase again instead of using a synonym to refer to it.

Good example	1. **Write a caption in a box for each drawing.** 2. **Number the drawings.** 3. **Give a letter to each caption.** 4. **Give the drawings and the captions to your team members.** 5. **Get your team members to put each caption on the drawing which it describes.**
Bad example	After writing a caption under each drawing number them, give each one a letter and give them to your team members. Get them to match the drawings and the boxes.

10. Standardization

We are usually advised to avoid repetition when writing and to use synonyms when referring to a lexical item we have already used. This might be good advice when writing a story but we have found when writing instructions that it is safer to use the same lexical item to refer to a particular referent each time it is mentioned. We think the first instruction below is potentially confusing whereas the second is much clearer.

1. X "Look at p. 3 of the instruction booklet. Try to memorize the directions and then to repeat them without looking at the manual. Then check to see if your recollection of the instructions is the same as in the book."
2. **"Look at p. 3 of the manual.**
   Memorize the instructions.

> **Say the instructions aloud without looking at the manual.**
> **Check to see if your instructions are the same as those on p. 3 of the manual."**

The repetition of "instructions" and "manual" in 2 might not be stylistically aesthetic but it is much more likely to ensure clarity than the use of the synonyms in 1.

Good example	**Look at the picture of cows in a field.** **Tell yourself a story in your mind about what the cows are doing.** **Tell a partner your story about the cows.** **Listen to your partner's story about the cows in their picture.**
Bad example	Look at the drawing of cows in a meadow. Tell yourself a story about what the animals in the field are doing. Then tell your partner your narrative about the calves in the picture. When you have finished your tale listen to your friend's story about the cows in their photo.

11. Self-Evidence

It is vital that an instruction is self-evident and that it can be followed without clarification from a teacher or peer and without needing to refer to anyone or anything else.

Good example	**Look at the photo of the sun on p. 72 of your Student Book.** **Answer questions 1–10 on p. 72 of your Student Book.**
Bad example	Look at the photo of the sun setting on Pantai Cenang Beach on p. 72 of your Student Book. Then go to p. 10 of the Activities Book on the web and answer the questions there.

Have you noticed that most of our criteria begin with the letter S? We have had fun with this in workshops by challenging the participants to beat the "world record" for criteria for effective instructions beginning with S. The criteria must be valid and the participants must be able to justify them. The record is currently held by a group of primary teachers in Botswana who came up with 30 criteria beginning with S.

What Do You Think?

1. Do you agree with the materials developers who think we are being pedantic by insisting that instructions should be perfectly clear and easy to follow without clarification by a teacher? Or do you agree with us that without complete clarity and precision instructions can cause damaging confusion and negativity? What are the reasons for your answer?
2. Do you think the instructions in a coursebook should be standardized so that the same words are used over and over again? Why?
3. Do you think that the instructions for a set of materials should be drafted, evaluated, trialed and revised by the same writer(s)? Or do you think that having a

different writer evaluate, trial and revise the instructions would ensure greater clarity? Why?

Tasks

1. Write improved versions of the following instructions:
   a) Match the sentences in the story with the adjectives which describe it.
   b) What is your idea about the people who are described in the newspaper article?
   c) Listen to the song and fill in the blanks in the lyrics.
   d) Do you agree with the arguments that were put forward in the article for clearing the forest and then replacing it with a shopping center that would cater for the needs of the workers who will be working in the factory when it is built?
   e) Describe your picture to your partner using the verbs you have just learned in their right tenses.
2. a) Select five criteria from the evaluation criteria 1–11 above. Then use them to evaluate the following instructions:

> 1. Get into pairs please and decide who is A and who is B.
> 2. Take a piece of paper and make ten tiny balls.
> 3. Listen to what your teacher tells you to do. Just listen and visualize what you are going to do. The second time carry out the instructions.
> 4. On your other piece of paper draw four circles of equal diameters with two circles next to each other above the other two circles and each circle touching the circle next to it and the circle below it. Write A in your top left hand circle, B in your top right hand circle, C in your bottom left hand circle and D in your bottom right hand circle. Ask your teach questions if you're not sure of something or if you can't remember what she said.
> 5. If you have finished compare your circles with those of another pair nearby.
> 6. Listen to your teacher telling you what to next. Just listen and visualize what you are going to do. The second time carry out the instructions.
> 7. Put your balls in the circles so that you have twice as many balls in A as in C, twice as many balls in A as in B, twice as many balls in B and C as in D and one ball in between A, B, C and D. Compare your answer with that of another pair nearby.
> 8. Move two balls so that you have an equal number of balls in each circle.

Use Table 14.1 to help you in your evaluation of the instructions.

Table 14.1

Criterion	Grade out of 5	Suggested improvements
e.g.		

   b) Write an improved version of the eight instructions in (a) above.
   c) Use the other six criteria from the evaluation criteria 1–11 above to evaluate the following instructions:

> 1. Listen to the concluding comments from four meetings and match them with one of these meeting types: a monthly productivity meeting, a weekly departmental meeting, a problem-solving meeting, an informal discussion.
> 2. Listen again and choose the correct words in italics.
>   a. Let's finish *then/here.*
>   b. Thank you *for all your ideas/for every idea.*
>   c. Right, is that *all there is/everything*?
>   d. Is there *something/anything else* we need to discuss?
>   e. OK. Time *for tea/to conclude.*
> 3. You have been appointed meeting secretary. Write the minutes of one of the meetings.

Use Table 14.2 to help you in your evaluation of the instructions.

Table 14.2

Criterion	Grade out of 5	Suggested improvements
e.g.		

d) Write an improved version of the instructions in (c) above.
3. a) Go to a page at random in a textbook you know. Evaluate the instructions on that page using all of the criteria 1–11.
   Use Table 14.3 below to help you in your evaluation.

Table 14.3

Criterion	Grade out of 5	Suggested improvements

b) Write improved versions of the instructions of which you were critical.
4. a) Make up a game in which pairs of students compete against each other by moving small stones or pieces of paper from one circle to another.
   b) Read criteria 1–11 again and then write the instructions for your game that will appear in a student book of tasks.
   c) Use Table 3 in 3 (a) above to help you to evaluate your instructions.
   d) Revise your instructions.
   e) Give your instructions and criteria 1–11 to a colleague and get them to evaluate your revised instructions.
   f) Revise your instructions again.
   g) (If possible, give your revised instructions from (f) to two pairs of students and ask them to play the game. Observe them whilst they are playing and note any problems they have in following the instructions.)
   h) (Make final revisions to your instructions.)

References

Corke Pelton, B. (n.d.). *Writing "how to" instructions.* Retrieved from http://www.learnnc. org/lp/editions/invent-convent/6707

McColl, H. (2002). Modern languages for all, or for the few? *Scottish Languages Review*, 5. Retrieved from http://www.languageswithoutlimits.co.uk/commonbarriers.html

Tomlinson, B. (1990). Managing change in Indonesian high schools. *ELT Journal*, *44*(1), 25–37.

Tomlinson, B., & Masuhara, H. (2004). *Developing language course materials.* Singapore: RELC.

15

Materials Development Research

Introduction

When we began to focus on materials development with the founding of MATSDA (the Materials Development Association) in 1993, materials development was still viewed primarily as a practical undertaking but was beginning to become an academic field of study too. Most of the presentations at our first few MATSDA conferences and most of the articles in early issues of our journal *Folio* consisted of suggestions for approaches to materials development plus demonstrations of materials based on them. Many of the presentations and articles connected their suggestions and claims to applied linguistics theories but very few reported research. However, as materials development gradually became more academically "respectable," more postgraduate students, more university academics, and more teachers began to conduct research on various aspects of materials development and some of this research was reported at MATSDA conferences and in *Folio*. Nevertheless in 2005 Richards pointed out that materials development was still insufficiently supported by research. In a colloquium paper Richards (2005) stated that all materials reflect the writers' theories of language, of language use, and of language acquisition but that they normally do so implicitly and often without being aware of it (a point made by Maley, 1995, p. 220 when he described materials development as "a form of operationalised tacit knowledge" and said that his materials were informed by his "fundamental beliefs about the nature of language, the nature of learning and indeed about human nature itself" (p. 221)). Richards (2005) goes on to say that very few materials producers are also academic theorists and researchers and that there has been very little research into the development, use, and effects of materials. He then suggests useful ways of connecting research and materials development. He could have also mentioned that a number of well-known applied linguistics researchers were also quite prolific coursebook writers (e.g. Rod Ellis, Jeremy Harmer, David Nunan, and himself) but that, at that time, their research and theorizing was not directly connected to materials development. A few years later, in a plenary paper, Chapelle (2008) pointed out how remarkably little research had been published on materials evaluation. At that time the same point could still have been made about research on the development and use of materials. If you looked at the main literature on materials development you would find scholarship and theory but very little empirical investigation (e.g. in Cunningsworth,

The Complete Guide to the Theory and Practice of Materials Development for Language Learning, First Edition. Brian Tomlinson and Hitomi Masuhara. © 2018 John Wiley & Sons, Inc. Published 2018 by John Wiley & Sons, Inc.

1995; Hall, 1995; Tomlinson, 1998a, 2003, 2008; McGrath, 2002). If you looked at books on language acquisition and on classroom research (e.g. Hinkel, 2005; Ellis, 2008) you would find a lot of empirical investigation of the factors that facilitate language acquisition but very little reference to the role that materials play in the process of language acquisition. Tomlinson (2012) pointed out some of the reasons for the paucity of published research on materials development. He said that

> Empirical investigation of the effects of materials on language acquisition requires longitudinal research involving considerable investments of time and money. It also requires a careful control of variables which would be quite easy in controlled experiments investigating such immediate phenomenon as repair but very difficult to achieve in classroom research investigating enduring effects on language acquisition and development. How, for example, can you claim that it was a particular textbook which was responsible for a measured long term outcome and not the quality of the teaching, the rapport between teacher and class or the exposure to the target language gained by the students away from the textbook? Such research is possible but very demanding and could best be achieved by long term collaboration between publishers and universities. Publishers do, of course, conduct research into the effects of their materials on their users but, for good reasons, such research is usually confidential and rarely published. (Tomlinson, 2012, p. 168)

Tomlinson (2012) could have added that materials development was often still considered to be insufficiently academic by university departments and by academic journals (a problem we have both suffered from in applications for promotion). Instead, Tomlinson went on to point out that in spite of the problems he mentioned there was some published research, for example on the effects of materials on their users. He drew attention to the considerable research on the effects of extensive reading materials on learners of English, and referred to Elley (1991), Day and Bamford (1998), and Krashen (2004), reporting research findings that "demonstrate the positive power of free, voluntary reading in facilitating language acquisition" (Tomlinson, 2012, p. 168); to Maley (2008) providing a review of published research on extensive reading and listing web sites that reported current research projects on extensive reading; and to Fenton-Smith (2010) reviewing the research on "the desirability or otherwise of designing output activities to follow the extensive reading of a book" (Tomlinson, 2012, p. 168). Tomlinson (2012) also referred to the literature on the effects of CALL materials on their users (e.g. Chapelle 1998, 2001; Chapelle & Lui 2007) and to a number of then recent books on materials development that did include reference to research (e.g. Mishan, 2005, which reviews the research literature relevant to the issue of authenticity in materials development; Harwood, 2010a, which contains numerous chapters relating research-driven theory to materials development; and Mukundan, 2003, 2006a, 2006b, 2008, which include papers from MICELT materials development conferences in Malaysia that report research). Examples of research papers from MICELT conferences were given by Tomlinson (2012) as Chandran and Abdullah's (2003) report of a study of gender bias in Malaysian English-language textbooks, Mukundan and Hussin's (2006) report on the use of Wordsmith 3.0 to evaluate materials, Le and Ha's (2009) report on a study of foreignness in EFL global textbooks, and Menon's (2009) report on a corpus analysis of textbooks. Tomlinson (2012, pp. 168–169) also refers to Renandya (2003), which "includes research papers on textbook evaluation in Indonesia (Jazadi 2003), on the use of textbooks in Malaysia (Chandran 2003) and on localising ELT materials in Vietnam (Dat 2003)" and, whilst conceding that Tomlinson (1998a, 2003, 2008a, 2011a) focus mainly on suggestions for innovation in materials development, he points out that these books do also include reference to research.

> For example, Tomlinson (1998b, 2011b) reports on major research findings in second language acquisition and proposes ways of connecting them to materials development and (2011c) on research into L1 and L2 visual imaging, suggesting ways of applying the findings to developing activities for L2 learning. Donovan (1998) writes one of the few published accounts of a publisher's trialing of coursebooks, and discusses the lessons to be learned, Ellis (1998) reports the literature on research studies which evaluate language learning materials, and applies the findings to suggestions for conducting materials evaluations, Ellis (2011) reports research experiments on the effects of task-based materials in action and discusses their implications, and Masuhara (2011) reports and evaluates what little literature there is on research into what teachers want from coursebooks (this is another topic of enquiry that is investigated by publishers and reported confidentially). In one such report Tomlinson found that teachers in twelve countries around the world specified their main want as interesting texts and their main need as not having to spend a lot of time preparing lessons. In Tomlinson (2003) there are reports on research into the use of electronic materials (Derewianka 2003), hyperfiction (Ferradas Moi 2003), materials for beginners (Cook 2003), the realization of primary school coursebook tasks in the classroom (Ghosn 2003) and the development of textbooks (Lyons 2003, Popovici & Bolitho 2003, Singapore Wala 2003). In Tomlinson (2008a) there is a chapter on language acquisition and language learning materials (Tomlinson 2008a) and numerous chapters reporting systematic evaluations of materials in different regions of the world. (Tomlinson, 2012, p. 169)

Tomlinson (2012) also draws attention to Van den Branden's (2006) book on task-based learning, which contains papers reporting research on the effects of task-based language learning materials on their users in Belgium, and to Tomlinson (2007a), a book focused primarily on language acquisition and development. The latter book contains reports on research relating materials development "to the neuro-linguistic processes involved in early reading" (Masuhara 2007), to the inner voice and visual imaging (Tomlinson & Avila 2007), to influences on learners' written expression (Ghosn 2007) and to the value of comprehension approaches in the early stages of language acquisition (Barnard 2007)" (Tomlinson, 2012, p. 169).

So, despite what Richards (2005) and Chapelle (2008) said, there was already quite an extensive literature on research in materials development but, we have to admit, very little of it provided empirical evidence. However at that time we were supervising, advising on, and examining a number of PhD students who were conducting empirical investigations of the effects of materials, as were other practitioner / academics in universities around the world. Some reports of these studies have been published in books and journals (e.g. Barnard, 2007, on the effects of comprehension based materials for beginners of Bahasa Indonesia, Tomlinson and Dat, 2008, on the effects of materials designed to remedy oral reticence by students in Vietnam, and Gilmore, 2007, on the effects of the use of authentic materials). In Tomlinson and Masuhara (2010a) we put together reports on 22 materials development research projects in 14 countries around the world, many conducted by our PhD students, our visiting scholars, and our colleagues, and some conducted by teachers doing action research projects in their institutions. These reports focus, for example, on research on the value of extensive reading, on the effects of in-house materials designed for university students, on the effects of locally developed materials for language learners, and on the effects of different types of materials. As Tomlinson (2012, p, 170) says, "Interestingly, none of the projects reported was conducting research on the effects of global coursebooks, though many were reporting on projects to find replacements for them."

Chapelle (2008) argued the need to move materials evaluation forward into a more research-oriented framework so that claims could be made about the effects of materials on the basis of evidence from research. We completely agreed with Chapelle in 2008 and we still agree with her argument now—though, as you will see below, there has been considerable progress made in materials development research since 2008. We do, however, think there is a danger of overestimating the importance of empirical research and of underestimating the importance of informed, principled, and well-thought-out advocacy of approaches based on wide reading, deep thinking and considerable experience in the classroom. Garton and Graves (2014a, p. 654) say, "the field is generally undertheorised. Many of the books published are 'how to' books, with advice for teachers (see, for example, McDonough et al., 2013; McGrath, 2002; Tomlinson, 2003, 2011c)." We would say that these books are definitely not "how to" books and that what they are doing is connecting theory to practice and practice to theory in ways that are accessible to teachers and materials developers. We would say that they have stimulated more reflection on current practice and more innovation than many of the statistics dominated reports of empirical studies, which seem more concerned with gaining academic acclaim than influencing the development and use of materials (see Maley, 2016 for a critique of the often negative influence of research and academia in applied linguistics). What we need is both empirical investigation and application of theory, research and experience.

Recent Research

Tomlinson (2012) concludes by hoping that research would soon be reported on the actual effect of different types of L2 materials on the language acquisition and development of their users, a hope also expressed in Harwood (2014) and Tomlinson (2013b, 2015b). Tomlinson (2012) also expresses the hope that there would soon be reports of research on ways of encouraging teachers and learners to try new types of materials, on ways in which "commercial publishers can achieve face validity whilst introducing principled innovative approaches" (p. 170) and on ways in which learners can be helped to develop their own learning materials. Since then a number of publications have reported innovative research on materials development but none has really addressed the hopes articulated in Tomlinson (2012).

In Harwood (2014), Hadley (2014) reports a 6-year study of the effects of a global textbook on nearly 700 students in a university in Japan. Unfortunately he does not investigate which features of the textbook are responsible for the reported effects—although he does claim that the presentation-practice-production (PPP) approach of the textbook is the approach his students "most craved" (p. 221). Neither does he compare the use of the textbook with any other treatment nor investigate the effect of using the textbook on the language acquisition and development of the students. Instead he compares the scores of the students on the textbook placement test at the beginning of their first semester in April with the scores they achieved on the same test "in the second week of January the following year" (p. 223), and concludes that the textbook "appears to have played a major role in the students' improvement" (p. 230). The test on which Hadley relies for this conclusion is designed to match "learners to appropriate textbook levels" (p. 222). It "lasts for 50 minutes and consists of 70 multiple-choice items divided into three sections that assess listening … reading … and grammatical knowledge" (p. 232). This can hardly provide the empirical evidence that Hadley claims demonstrates the effectiveness of the textbook. The students might have become better at doing the sort of exercise practiced in the textbook (though in fact some of them did not) but there is no evidence that they improved (or did not improve) their ability to use English for communication. Nor is there any evidence that it was the textbook that was responsible for the observed effects, as there seems to have been no attempt to record the students' out-of-classroom experience of English or to investigate the teachers' actual use of the textbook. We are not saying that Hadley's research is not useful or informative. What we are saying is that it is very difficult to control the variables in post-use evaluation of the effectiveness of materials on their users, that it is very important to specify exactly what effects are being measured, and that it is dangerous to make strong claims about the effects of textbooks (as Hadley does) on the unconvincing "evidence" of the apparent effects of one textbook.

Also in Harwood (2014) there are reports of research on the "writing out of the working class" from ELT textbooks (Gray & Block, 2014, p. 45–46), the distribution of different types of reading comprehension questions in global EFL textbooks (Freeman, 2014), the content of "39 English reading textbooks for preservice general education teachers" in four countries (Dixon et al., 2014, p. 111), seven teachers' use of an ESP coursebook at a Saudi Arabian University (Menkabu & Harwood, 2014), and an experienced teacher's use of an EAP textbook in a UK university (Grammatosi & Harwood, 2014). In addition there are studies of textbook production by Timmis (2014) on a materials development project for a country in South East Asia, by Stoller and Robinson (2014) on the writing of an EAP textbook for students of chemistry, by Feak and Swales (2014) on their revisions of two EAP textbooks, and by Hadfield (2014) on her own writing process when co-authoring a resource book for teachers. All of these chapters make new and interesting contributions to the field but none of them is informative about the effects of materials on their users or about any of the other research topics we included on our wish list above. This is true also of the research reported in McGrath (2013). For example, McGrath reports studies by Gray (2000) on the use of textbooks by L2 teachers in Barcelona, by Yan (2007) on the use of textbooks by 30 trainees at a university in central China, by Tsobanoglou (2008) on the use of textbooks in schools in Greece, and by Sampson (2009) on the use of textbooks by experienced and by inexperienced teachers in Hong Kong. These studies in Harwood (2014) and in McGrath (2013) are helping to fill a gap that was commented on in Tomlinson (2012, p. 156): 'There seems to be very little published on what teachers and learners actually do with materials in the classroom.' This gap has also been partially filled by Wette (2011), Guerrettaz and Johnston (2013), Forman (2014), Loh and Renandya (2015), and Swe (2015), who all report on what teachers did in the classroom when using materials (e.g. Forman, 2014, reports how teachers in Thailand were faithful to the global coursebook they were using despite it being culturally distant). The paucity of research on what teachers actually do with materials is something focused on in Garton and Graves (2014a), which reviews the literature, focuses on the three areas of interaction with materials which were identified by Guerrettaz and Johnston (2013) (i.e. "curriculum, classroom discourse and language acquisition") and points "to future directions for research" (p. 654). How materials are actually used is also a feature of Garton and Graves (2014b), a book that focuses on local concerns in materials development and use. Interestingly though we can still find very little literature on what students actually do with materials. What do they do in their minds when they are using materials in the classroom? We know a little about this thanks to a few studies of what L2 learners do in their minds in relation to visualization and inner speech when reading, listening to, or writing texts (e.g. de Guerro 2004, 2005; Tomlinson & Avilla 2007; Tomlinson 2011c; Yi 2012). What decisions do students make when using self-study materials or when following a computer based course which facilitates independent use? We do not seem to know.

Unfortunately none of the above publications is telling us anything about the effects of different types of materials on their users. This is something focused on in Tomlinson (2013a) when the contributors were asked to concentrate on what was known about their field, what was thought to be known about the match between their field and materials development, and what needed to be found out about the match between their field and materials development. For example, Ghosn (2013b), in her section on what we know about young learners and language learning, focuses on such developmental features as "the emergence of linguistic features following a fairly predictable pattern" (p. 62), the creative use of second language syntax, the making of universal intralingual errors and the utilization of procedural memory. In her section on what we think we know about young learners and materials, she draws attention to the research-based belief that fun and enjoyment should be essential features of materials and to the apparent underestimation of the curiosity of young learners and their resultant restriction to "simple language and simple topics" (p. 66). She concludes by suggesting that research on young learners' materials should ask questions about their developmental appropriateness, their match with SLA theory, their relevance and their achievement of learner success and confidence. She also evaluates four young learner coursebooks in relation to these questions and suggests a principled storybook approach with the potential for positive evaluation in relation to her questions. Similar approaches are adopted, for example, by Hughes (2013) in relation to teaching reading to young learners, by Timmis (2013), and by Burns and Hill (2013) in relation to speaking skills, by Maley (2013) in relation to vocabulary teaching, by Cohen and Ishihara (2013) in relation to pragmatics, by Byram and Masuhara (2013) in relation to intercultural competence, by Maley and Prowse (2013) in relation to reading, by Ableeva and Stranks (2013) in relation to listening, and by Mishan (2013) in relation to pedagogy. They are all fairly critical of the published materials they evaluate and they all point out that we need to know a lot more about what effect materials actually have on their users. In the concluding comments, Tomlinson (2013c) makes a plea for research that focuses on "practical ways of applying attested theory to the development of coursebooks in ways which help them to retain face validity" (pp. 321–322) and makes suggestions for ways of doing this. Tomlinson (2013c) also expresses a hope for "innovative research experimenting with novel ways of applying theory to materials development" and makes suggestions for types of innovative materials that could be developed and researched (pp. 321–322).

To some extent these pleas for more research on the effects of different types of materials on their users and on the development of acceptable ways of matching SLA theory to practice in materials design have been answered but these answers are not yet, or are only just, in print. They have been responded to in presentations at a MATSDA Conference on SLA Research and Materials Development for Language Learning at the University of Liverpool in 2014 (for example, on research projects investigating students attitudes towards materials teaching grammar through PPP compared to materials using a noticing approach and on the effect of project-based learning on the motivation of students in China), at a MATSDA conference on motivation and materials development at the University of Limerick in 2015, and at a MATSDA conference on authenticity and materials development at the University of Liverpool in 2016, as well as in chapters for Masuhara, Mishan, and Tomlinson (2017), for Tomlinson (2016a), and for Maley and Tomlinson (in press), and in articles for Tomlinson (2015b, 2016c). In Masuhara et al. (2017) there are chapters, for example, on the comparative effects of teaching grammar using inductive and communicative materials, on the effect of task repetition on primary students' oral fluency, and on the effects of providing learners with something worth talking about. In Tomlinson (2016a), for example, there are chapters on the effects of task repetition and of task planning and on the effects of typical coursebook exercise types on language acquisition, and Tomlinson (2016b) specifically focuses on the likely effects of a number of coursebooks on the language acquisition of their users. There are also new comprehensive books on materials development by Mishan and Timmis (2015) and by Maley and Tomlinson (in press), which include reports on research investigating the effects of different types of materials on their users.

Most of the contributions to the recent publications mentioned above report the effect of materials on learners' attitudes, motivation or examination scores or on such easily measurable attainments as increased explicit lexical or pragmatic knowledge. There is still little in press or in prospect reporting the effects of different types of materials on the learners' ability to use English effectively for communication. One obvious reason for this is the difficulty of controlling such variables as teacher awareness, teacher enthusiasm, teacher rapport, learner motivation, and learner contact with English outside the course. Another is the apparent unreliability of tests of communicative competence. Another is the expense in time and money such an investigation would require given the delayed effect of instruction.

Areas of Research Referred to in this Volume

In almost every chapter of this book we have been referring to the materials development research relevant to that chapter. In this section of this chapter we are summarizing the materials development research we have referred to in other chapters for easy reference. In order to save space and to avoid controversy we are restricting "research" mainly to studies that collect and report data and are excluding publications that connect materials development to existing research, to theory or to personal experience (though personally we think that the latter are often more informative and stimulating than the former). It seems to us now when looking back at the research reported in this book that we could categorize it as follows:

Evaluating the Effects of Materials

There are numerous published research reports on studies aiming to find out what effects materials have on their users. Most of these make use of questionnaires, interviews and focus groups to find out what the attitudes and opinions are of the teachers and students who have used the materials. Some attempt to measure gains in knowledge of specific lexical items, grammatical structures or pragmatic exponents. Very few, though, attempt the demanding task of measuring gains in communicative competence. Here are the references to studies evaluating the effects of materials that we have mentioned in this book:

In Chapter 1 we refer to:

- Darici and Tomlinson (2016) reporting the effects of text-driven materials in a classroom in Turkey;
- Chapelle (1998, 2001), Chapelle and Lui (2007), and Chapelle and Jamieson (2008) evaluating the attitudinal and learning effects of CALL materials on learners;
- the case studies in Tomlinson and Whittaker (2013) of the effects of blended learning materials on learners;
- Elley and Mangubhai (1981), Davies (1995), Krashen (2004), and Fenton-Smith (2010) reporting the effects of extensive reading materials on learners;
- Swain and Lapkin (2005), and Barker (2010) reporting on the effects of learners being immersed in the target language;
- the numerous research studies reporting the effects of materials on learners in classrooms around the world in Tomlinson and Masuhara (2010a), Garton and Graves (2014b), Harwood (2014), Azarnoosh, Zeraatpishe, Faravani, and Kargozari (2016), Masuhara et al. (2017), Tomlinson (2016a, 2016b, 2016c), and Maley and Tomlinson (in press).

In Chapter 2 we refer to Al–Busiadi and Tindle (2010), Jones and Schmitt (2010), Hewings (2010), Mason (2010), Trabelsi (2010) and Troncoso (2010) reporting on the effectiveness of in-house materials developed for use with students at universities, and in Chapter 3 we refer to Ellis (2011) reporting four micro-evaluations of the effects of materials and to reports in Tomlinson and Masuhara (2010) and in McGrath (2013) of studies of materials development projects involving pre-use and post-use evaluation of newly developed materials (e.g. Law, 1995; Fredriksson and Olsen, 2006; Al-Busaidi and Tindall, 2010; Pryor, 2010; and Stillwell, Kidd et al., 2010; Stillwell, McMillan, Gillies and Waller, 2010). In Chapter 3 we also refer to evaluations of coursebook material in relation to SLA principles reported in Mukundan (2006b), Kennedy and Tomlinson (2013), Tomlinson (2010a, 2013d, 2013e), Harwood (2014), Boers and Strong (2016), Nakata and Webb (2016) and Tomlinson (2016). In Chapter 7 we refer to recent research on the effectiveness of materials delivered electronically which is conducted and / or reviewed by Chapelle and Lui (2007), Grgurović, Chapelle, & Shelley (2013), and Chapelle (2014). In Chapter 8 we refer to Tomlinson's (2007b), and Avila's (2007) accounts of successful use of meaning-focused teacher recasting, to Boers and Strong's (2016) and Nakata and Webb's (2016) research on the effectiveness of vocabulary materials and to research on the effectiveness of materials for teaching pragmatics by Uso-Juan (2008), Riddiford and Newton (2010), Wong (2011), Nguyen (2011), and Ishihara and Paller (2016). In Chapter 10 we refer to Read's (2015) account of the literature on the effectiveness of materials for young learners, to research on the effectiveness of materials for young learners in Lebanon by Ghosn (2003, 2007, 2010, 2013a, 2013b, 2016), to a survey of teacher views on materials for young learners by Arnold and Rixon (2008), to the Canadian immersion project (Cummins, 2009), to a report of a successful blended-learning extensive reading project (Nunan, 2013), to a report of a mobile learning project in Goa (Noronha, in press) and to studies demonstrating the ability of young learners to acquire language implicitly in Enever (2011) and in Lefever (2012). In Chapter 11 we refer to De Witte and Rogge's (2016) survey of problem-based approaches in secondary schools and universities and in Chapter 12 we refer to Bao's (2002) experiments with communicative materials in Vietnam and to research reports on EAP / ESP courses in Al-Busaidi and Tindle (2010), Cullen (2010), by Mason (2010), McCullagh (2010), Trabelsi (2010), St. Louis (2010), and Tomlinson and Masuhara (2010). In Chapter 12 we also refer to reports on studies of EAP courses in Harwood (2010a) by Angouri (2010), Bosher (2010), Curry and Lillis (2010), Feak and Swales (2010), Harwood (2010b), Jakubiak and Harklau (2010), Jones and Schmitt (2010), and to reports on studies of ESP courses by Lynch (1996), Feak and Swales (2014) and Stoller and Robinson (2014). Reports on ESOL studies by Haan, Timmis and Masuhara (2010) and Haan (2010, 2013) are also mentioned.

We should point out again that very few of the research studies mentioned above actually attempted to measure effects of materials on the communicative competence of learners (notable exceptions being Barnard, 2007, and Ghosn, 2010). Most of the studies focus on the opinions of users of materials and their perceptions of their effect on learner performance.

Evaluating the Effectiveness of Different Pedagogic Approaches

In Chapter 2 we refer to Al-Busaidi and Tindle (2010), McCullugh (2010), Troncoso (2010), Darici and Tomlinson (2016), and Heron (2013, 2016) reporting on the apparent effectiveness of their development and trialing of materials following a text-driven approach. In Chapter 9 we describe the research reported in Masuhara, Kimura, Fukada, and Takeuchi (1996) of their research into the comparative effects of strategy development and extensive reading approaches to reading skills development. There seems to be very little other research, though, which specifically focuses on the effects of the use of a particular pedagogy in materials for language learning.

Evaluating the Effects of Adaptations of Materials

In Chapter 4 we refer to adaptation studies in Garton and Graves (2014b) and Masuhara et al. (2017) and to detailed analyses of adaptation research studies reported in Shawer (2010a), Guerrettaz and Johnston (2013), Grammatosi and Harwood (2014), Bolster (2014 and 2015), Bosompem (2014), Loh and Renandya (2015), Abdel Latif (2017), and Tasseron (2017).

Analysis of Materials

In Chapter 3 we refer to Tomlinson (1999, 2013b) reporting an analysis of low-level coursebooks, in Chapter 4 we refer to analyses of the cultural content of coursebooks by Shin, Eslami, and Chen (2011), Tomlinson (2013f), Forman (2014), Messekher (2014),

Ottley (2014) and Tasseron (2017), and in Chapter 5 we refer to Douglas (2012) who analyzed six global coursebooks, and found very little evidence of publishers and materials writers making use of the information about the use of English provided in corpora. In Chapter 12 we refer to Gray's (2010) study of the attitudes to their coursebooks of 20 teachers in a Barcelona language school and to Bao's (2016) study of the inappropriate stereotyping of cultures in global coursebooks. In Chapter 13 we report Hill's (2003, 2013) and Kim's (2016) analyses of illustrations in coursebooks.

Discovering What Publishers Want from Materials

In Chapter 6 we summarize accounts of the publishing process by Donovan (1998), Singapore Wala (2003, 2013), Zemach (2006), Viney (2007), Amrani (2011, 2014), Aitchison (2013), Clandfield (2013), and McGrath (2013). We also refer to accounts of compromises made between authors and publishers in Bell and Gower (2011), Feak and Swales (2014), and Santos (2015).

Discovering What Publishers Do with Materials

In Chapter 3 we refer to Roxburgh (1997), Donovan (1998), Singapore Wala (2003), Amrani (2011), and Aitchinson (2013) reporting how publishers evaluate materials during and after development.

Discovering What Teachers Want from Materials

In Chapter 3 we refer to Masuhara (2011) discussing ways of eliciting from teachers what they want from materials and reporting what little literature there is on this topic.

Discovering What Teachers Do with Materials

In Chapter 1 we refer to Thomas and Reinders (2015) reporting on how teachers weaken task-based materials in Asia to achieve familiarity and to prepare students for their examinations and to the research reports in McGrath (2013) of what teachers do with materials in the classroom.

In Chapter 2 we refer to Ball and Fiman-Nermser (1988), Gray (2000), Be (2003), Tsui (2003), Chandran (2003), and Jazardi (2003) reporting on how novice teachers tend to follow their coursebooks as scripts, as well as to Tsui, (2003), and Gray (2000, 2010) reporting on how more experienced teachers tend to make use of their coursebooks as resources and to McGrath (2013) and Garton and Graves (2014a) reporting case studies of what teachers around the world do with their coursebooks in class. We also refer to Menkabu and Harwood (2014) reporting research by Cheng (1997), Pelly and Allison (2000), Lee and Bathmaker (2007), Shawer (2010a, 2010b), and Wette (2010), revealing what teachers actually do with their coursebooks and again to Thomas and Reinders (2015) revealing how teachers weakened task-based language materials in Asia.

In Chapter 4 we refer to Guerrettaz and Johnston (2013) reporting considerable use of the coursebook in lessons they observed but also to Bolster (2014, 2015) on teachers' flexible use of their coursebook.

Discovering How Writers Write Materials

In Chapter 1 we refer to Johnson (2003) reporting his research on the differences between how experts and how novices write materials. In Chapter 2 we refer to Prowse (2011) and Samuda (2005) reporting how teachers write materials in their research and in Chapter 5 we refer to accounts of how writers write in Flores (1995), Hidalgo, Hall, and Jacobs (1995), Pascasio (1995), Penaflorida (1995), Richards (1995), Sundara Rajan (1995), Prowse (1998), Johnson (2003), Samuda (2005), Bell and Gower (2011), Prowse (2011), and Hadfield (2014). We also refer to accounts of how they developed principled sets of in house materials by Evans, Hartshorn, and Anderson (2010), Harwood (2010b), Hewings (2010) and Jones and Schmitt (2010), as well as to accounts of principled development of materials in Harwood (2014).

Discovering what Learners Want from Materials

In Chapter 8 and 10 we report Noronha's (in press) and Modugala's (in press) research on what young learners in India want from materials (i.e. stories and activities) and in Chapter 8 we refer to Bao's (2013) research on what learners in Vietnam want.

The Authenticity of Materials

In Chapter 2 we refer to Cullen and Kuo (2007), Lam (2010), Timmis (2010), Tomlinson (2010), and Cohen and Ishihara (2013) reporting on the disparity between how language is used in coursebooks and the evidence of language use provided by data from corpora.

The Washback Effect of Assessment on Materials Development and Use

In Chapter 12 we refer to studies of washback by Alderson and Hamp-Lyons (1996) and by Bailey and Masuhara (2013).

The Impact of Materials Development on Teacher Development

In Chapter 1 we refer to Tomlinson (2010) reporting his research on the perceived impact of teachers who participated in materials development projects and courses. In Chapter 4 we refer to Canniveng and Martinez (2003), Tan (2006), Yan (2007), and to Bouckaert (2015) reporting studies in which teachers gained from participation in materials development and arguing for the value of including materials evaluation, adaptation and development as part of preservice training. In Chapter 5 we refer to Srinivas (2003) reporting on teacher involvement in textbook development in India and to Popovici and Bolitho's (2003) account of teacher development on a materials development project in Romania. In Chapter 12 we refer to studies of teacher materials development in Popovici and Bolitho (2003), Emery (2013) and Edwards and Burns (2016).

In looking back though our book we cannot find references to studies evaluating the effects of different modes of delivery or to studies evaluating what learners do with materials.

Proposed Areas of Research

We would like to end this chapter by proposing areas for research that we think would be very informative and which could stimulate improvements in materials development leading to more durable and effective acquisition of language and more successful development of communication skills.

The Effects of Different Types of Materials on the Learners' Ability to Use the Target Language Effectively

This is a very demanding research area, which, given the difficulty of controlling the variables and the time needed to allow for the delayed effect of instruction, ideally requires cooperation between an academic institution and a publisher. However, we do believe that it is possible for an independent researcher to produce data indicating (but not proving) such effects, especially if the researcher has the time and funding afforded by a PhD or EdD project, and if the researcher is able to influence teaching allocations in an academic institution. This is what happened in the case of Barnard (2007), who compared the effects of a comprehension-based approach to learning Bahasa Indonesia with those of a conventional PPP approach at the National University of Singapore where she was Head of Bahasa Indonesia. All the teachers in the department taught both the comprehension-based materials and the PPP materials. It is also what is going to happen in the case of Alper Darici, who plans to compare the effects of a text-driven approach with those of a PPP approach for students preparing for an international examination in Fatih schools in Istanbul, where he is Director of English. Our advice to Alper, and to all researchers of the effects of language learning materials, is to focus on a specific effect of a particular feature of the set of materials being used as the treatment in a research experiment. For example, to focus on the effect on self-monitoring of grammatical accuracy in written communication during the discovery activities in text-driven units of material or to focus on the value of teacher availability during the undertaking of a task in a unit of task-based materials. Such a focus makes the research more manageable and more informative and it is likely to make it more valid and reliable too. It also provides a focused way of evaluating an approach by conducting a separate experiment for each of its components. For many years we have been using and recommending a text-driven approach to materials development in which the starting point is the selection of a text with the potential for affective and cognitive engagement of the target learners (Tomlinson, 2013e). This text then drives all the activities in a unit of materials, for example in the following way:

1. A **readiness activity** to activate the learners' minds in relation to the location, topic or theme of the core text. (e.g. "Think back to your first day at school. Try to see pictures in your mind of you getting ready to go to school, of you on your way to school and of you in the classroom for the first time").
2. An **initial response activity** to help the learners to experience the text holistically rather than to follow their inclination to study the words in it (e.g. "Read the poem, 'First Day at School' and as you read it try to see pictures in your mind of what happens to the boy in the poem. Don't worry if you don't understand all the words").

3. An **intake response activity** to help the learners to express and deepen their understanding of the text (e.g. "Draw pictures of anything you can remember in the poem. Show your pictures to your group and tell them what you've drawn").

4. A **development task** in which the learners use the target language to produce a written or spoken text developed from or in response to the core text (e.g. "Write a poem about yourself called, 'First Day at University.' Read your poem to the other members of your group, listen to their poems and then discuss how your poems are similar and how they are different").

5. An **input response** activity in which the learners return to the core text to make discoveries about a salient language feature (e.g. "In the poem the boy seems to ask a lot of questions. In your group find these questions in the poem. Who is he talking to? Is he really asking questions? What is he using these 'questions' for?").

6. A **research task** in which the learners investigate other instances of the salient feature they focused on in 5 above (e.g. "In the readers in our class library find other examples of 'questions' which are not really asking questions. For each one decide what the 'question' is being used for").

7. Another **development task** in which the learners either produce another similar 'text' or revise their original text (e.g. "In your group choose one of your poems and then together write an improved version of it. You can insert some 'questions' if you like."). (Tomlinson, 2015a, 333–334)

A number of teachers have published reports of the effectiveness of such an approach (e.g. Troncoso, 2010; Heron, 2013; Vo, 2014; Tomlinson & Darici, 2016) but none has been able to specify which components of the approach are responsible for its apparent success. It would be very informative if each component was researched separately prior to an experiment in which the effect of combining all the components in a unit of materials was researched.

As a research task, select a specific feature of a type of language learning materials that you think is likely to help to achieve a specific learning effect. Try to measure the effectiveness of this feature when used with learners.

This way of evaluating the effects of an approach by evaluating each of its components separately first could be used to evaluate the effect of, for example, PPP approaches, task-based approaches, text-driven approaches, CLIL approaches, TPR approaches and discovery approaches. We would very much like to see it used to assess first of all each different component and then all the components of a text-driven approach because our reading, our research and our experience of the development of materials leads us to believe that this is a potentially valuable approach which is underused in coursebook development. Here is an example of a research task assessing the value of one component of the text-driven approach:

Get a teacher to use a coursebook with a control group for a semester. With an equivalent experimental group, get the same teacher to use the same coursebook but with the addition of a readiness activity at the beginning of each unit. Administer a pre-course communication test before using the coursebook and administer the same test again at the end of the semester.

For example:

1. Both the control group and the experimental group are given the same communication test at the same time. The test should involve purposeful reading and listening as well as communicating in writing and in speech to achieve intended effects and

should be marked by answering a number of "can do" questions about the students (e.g. To what extent can the student express personal views effectively?).

2. Both groups use a coursebook in the way intended but the experimental group does a readiness activity before starting each unit. For example, before starting Unit 05 RELAX in Dellar and Walkley (2010) the experimental group does the following activity:

   a) Think of your favorite ways of relaxing. See pictures of yourself relaxing in different ways and ask yourself, "Why do I find this relaxing?"

   b) If you want to, tell somebody else about how you relax and why you find it relaxing.

3. At the end of term both groups take the same communication test again and the improvement of the two groups is compared.

A similar approach can then be taken with each of the seven stages of the text-driven approach, as in the two examples below:

1. Get a different teacher to do the same research task as the one above but instead of giving the experimental group a readiness activity before starting each unit the teacher gives them an intake response activity immediately after they listen to or read a text. An example of adding intake response activities would be whilst doing Unit 05 RELAX in Dellar and Walkley (2010) the experimental group does the following activities:

   a) You've listened to somebody talking about the popularity of football. Tell a partner what you think about football.

   b) Which of the sports you've read about would you like to play? Which one would you like to watch? Tell somebody the reasons for your choices and see if they agree with you.

2. Get a different teacher to do the same research task as the one above but instead of giving the experimental group a readiness activity before starting each unit the teacher gives them a development activity to do. An example of adding development activities would be whilst doing Unit 05 RELAX in Dellar and Walkley (2010) the experimental group does the following activities:

   a) You've listened to somebody talking about the popularity of football. With a partner think of another sport that is popular and then write the script for a short radio talk about it.

   b) You've read about three unusual sports. With a partner invent a new sport and then write a paragraph describing it. Your paragraph should help anybody who wants to play your sport by making it clear what the players do.

In addition to getting different teachers to conduct research on the effectiveness of each component of the text-driven approach as in the examples above different teachers could research the effect of using all the components of a text-driven approach together. A teacher could use a coursebook with a control group for a semester. With an equivalent experimental group the same teacher could replace the coursebook with text-driven units that make use of the spoken and written texts in the coursebook but which replace the coursebook activities with the following text-driven activities:

- readiness activities;
- initial-response activities;
- intake-response activities;
- development activities;
- input response activities;

- research activities;
- development revision activities.

The teacher could administer a pre-course communication test before the materials are used and the same test again at the end of the semester. Another teacher could conduct a similar experiment but instead of using the texts from the coursebook used by the control group she could use potentially engaging texts of the same genres, text types, and topics as those in the coursebook.

A similar approach could be used to evaluate the effects of other approaches.

Researching the Effects of Typical Coursebook Activities

It would be usefully informative if the effects of conventional coursebook activities were evaluated. At the moment such activities as multiple-choice comprehension questions, filling in the blank exercises, cloze activities, sentence transformation activities and true / false questions are routinely used in most EFL coursebooks (Tomlinson & Masuhara, 2013; Tomlinson, 2016d) yet we know of no empirical evidence of their effectiveness. All the activities listed above are undeniably useful in testing (and in coursebooks) because of their ease of delivery and marking as well as their potential for reliability. However, how valid are they as sources of information about the communicative competence of learners and how valuable are they as facilitators of language acquisition and development? We need to find out in order to justify continuing their use in coursebooks or in order to replace them with more valuable activities. Here is an example of such research.

Select a typical coursebook activity and try to measure the effectiveness of the activity in achieving the intended learning effect.

For example:

Give a class of Intermediate students tests on the lexical items that feature in the matching exercises in Clandfield and Benne (2010) and then give them the matching exercises to do from the coursebook. Give an equivalent group the same tests and then give them study activities in which they are given definitions of the lexical items. Give another equivalent group the same tests and then give them reading texts in which the items are used in ways that make their meaning clear. Then give all three groups the same tests again and compare the improvement of the three groups.

For example:

Group 1 do the following matching exercise from Clandfield and Benne (2010, p. 23). Match adjectives 1–6 to definitions a–f

1. ancient	a very angry
2. filthy	b very bad
3. astonished	c very old
4. exhausted	d very surprised
5. furious	e very dirty
6. terrible	f very tired

Group 2 do the following. Study the following definitions:

1. ancient = very old
2. filthy = very dirty
3. astonished = very surprised
4. exhausted = very tired

5. furious = very angry
6. terrible = very bad

Group 3 do the following. Read the following story:

> What a trip! When I got to the car park I found the car I'd rented was so ancient that it made my 1998 Honda look new. It was also so filthy that I had to spend half an hour cleaning it before setting off for the coast. Everything went smoothly though for about an hour, but then in the middle of a forest on a very quiet road the car broke down. I was furious because I'd been promised a modern, reliable car. I was even angrier though when I found out my mobile didn't work and I had to set off walking to the nearest village five miles away. I managed to get a bus from there but then had to walk another three miles from the main road to my hotel. I was exhausted when I got there because I hadn't slept on the plane and I'd walked eight miles altogether with a heavy suitcase. I was astonished that I made it to the hotel because I hadn't walked so far for over twenty years. I was also astonished though that the hotel was beautiful. White, modern, by the beach, with a beautiful garden. I hadn't expected such an attractive hotel. For the first time in the day I was happy and looking forward to my holiday. Then I was shown to my room. It was terrible. Tiny, filthy, at the back of the hotel, overlooking the rubbish bins. I hadn't seen such a bad room since the days of my back packing round the world.
>
> And then I got a phone call to say that Mary was ill and wasn't going to join me. What a terrible holiday! I think I'll stay at home next year.

In the research experiments suggested above there would be obvious problems in controlling variables. The teacher's training, experience, beliefs, personality, credibility with the students, empathy with the students, ability to establish rapport with the students and even mood are important factors in determining the effects of the use of a set of materials, as obviously is the actual way in which the teacher uses the materials. It could be that a very effective teacher using a set of materials helps the learners to acquire language from those materials whereas an ineffective teacher prevents the learners from acquiring language from the same materials. We have found that when attempting to measure the effectiveness of a set of materials it is therefore important to try to control the teacher variables by doing at least one of the following:

- Ensure that the same teacher(s) teaches both the control group(s) and the experimental group(s).
- Teach both the control group(s) and the experimental group(s) yourself (although there is evidence, for example from Heron, 2013, that teaching your own materials can achieve greater effect than teaching somebody else's).
- Specify exactly how all the materials are to be used and then record the lessons to check adherence (though this, of course, contradicts the typical realities of flexibility and variability of use).
- Observe a number of a teacher's lessons and make notes on how the teacher uses the materials and on whether or not the teacher makes it apparent what his attitude(s) to the material are.
- Use many different teachers in the experiment, record their lessons and note differences in effect.

None of the above measures will completely nullify teacher effect and the only strong claim that could be made would be that a particular way of using a set of materials seemed to influence the learners' acquisition of language in a particular way. It could never be claimed that the set of materials per se was exclusively responsible for the observed effect on acquisition. It would also be very useful to make the teacher the focus of the research and to compare the effect of the same materials used by teachers with equivalent groups as well as comparing the effect of materials being used by the teacher who developed them with the effects of the same materials being used by teachers who did not contribute to their development.

Another variable that needs controlling is the learner variable. The effectiveness of a set of materials can be determined by the motivation, attitudes, previous experience of learning the language, learning preferences and capabilities of the learners. Their outside-class exposure to the target language is obviously another factor in determining acquisition. In order to ensure as much validity and reliability as possible we have found that it is important that:

- In any comparative study equivalence is established between the learners, not just of language level but of motivation, inclination and opportunity as well.
- In any case study typicality is established before generalization can be attempted.
- In longitudinal studies, records are kept of the learners' other experience of the language.
- Measures of effectiveness are made a number of times in order to take into account variability of performance.

In determining the effect of the use of materials it is also important to be specific in what is measured rather than to attempt generalized appraisal. For example, it is more informative and more reliable to measure the length of conversational utterances than to try to evaluate general improvement in conversational ability. It is also useful to try to isolate the specific feature of a set of materials that is responsible for a measured effect. For example, it is more informative and more reliable to try to measure the effect of adding affective impact to a text on recall of its content than it is to try to measure the effect of a text-driven approach (Tomlinson, 2013e) on reading comprehension. In our view, researchers often make the mistake of using ready-made tests to assess the effects of materials (e.g. Hadley, 2014, using a coursebook placement test to measure 'improvement'). It is obviously convenient to do so as such tests have already been assessed for reliability but often it is unclear what exactly the effect is that is being measured. What really matters in our view is not increase of declarative knowledge, not improvement in objective test scores, but acquisition of language and development of the ability to use it for communicative effect.

Researching the Implementation of Innovative Materials

Ways of Incorporating Principled Innovations in Conventional Coursebook Formats

One of the reasons that coursebooks published by commercial publishers remain so conservative is that publishing innovative coursebooks risks losing face validity and therefore sales. This has happened in the past with innovative courses such as *The sourcebook* (Shepherd, Cox, & Roberts, 1991), which invited teachers to select from resources rather than follow the usual sequential route through a coursebook. It also happened to *Openings* (Tomlinson, 1994), a book of language through literature activities in which Part

A consists only of texts for teachers and students to select from and Part B consists of a menu of suggestions for activities to be used with each text. It was popular with students on our language and teacher development courses in different parts of the world but certainly did not sell very well.

What we would like to see is research into how to incorporate innovative materials into conventional coursebook formats so as to maximize both their effect in facilitating language acquisition and their ability to attract teachers to use them. For example: develop four task-based units following a strong task-based approach in which there is no pre-teaching of language and no explicit teaching of forms (Tomlinson, 2015a). Print the materials in a booklet and include in it a brief introduction about the task-based approach. Then modify the draft materials so that they look like conventional coursebook materials (e.g. with specifications of grammar, vocabulary, pronunciation, function and skills learning points in a contents map, with topic headings, with learning point activity headings, with a grammar reference section). Publish these materials in a booklet too. Then:

1. Give the two booklets to a group of teachers together with a questionnaire asking them which booklet they would prefer to teach from and why.
2. Give the two booklets to a focus group of teachers and then ask them to talk about which booklet they would prefer to teach from and why.
3. Get teachers to use one of the booklets with a class and the other booklet with an equivalent class.
4. Interview the teachers about which booklet they preferred using.
5. Give the students a questionnaire asking them about their attitudes towards the materials in the booklet they used with regard to both interest and usefulness.
6. Analyze the data collected from 1 to 5 above to determine which booklet was preferred and why.

Ways of Persuading Users of the Value of Innovative Materials and of Helping Them to Benefit from the Innovations

Another problem with innovative material is that, even if a ministry of education, an institution or a publisher decides to introduce innovative materials, the users of the materials (i.e. administrators, teachers, and students) might resist the innovations, especially if they do not seem to provide explicit preparation for an important examination. We have found, for example, when observing lessons in schools that teachers often use innovative materials in the same way they used the materials they are replacing or (as Pelly and Allison, 2000, and Lee and Bathmaker, 2007, found) they only use those parts of the materials that are directly related to target examinations. What we would like to see is research on ways of persuading the users of innovative materials of the value of the innovations and on helping the users to benefit from the innovations.

For example, develop four task-based units following a strong task-based approach in which there is no pre-teaching of language and no explicit teaching of forms (Tomlinson, 2015a). Print the materials in a booklet. Then print the materials in another booklet with the addition of:

1. A brief introduction to the booklet specifying the principles and the benefits of a task-based approach.
2. A brief introduction to each unit specifying the learning objectives of the unit.

3. Reflection activities at the end of each unit inviting the students to reflect on what they have gained from each subtask in the unit.
4. A teachers' book explaining the principles and objectives of each subtask and giving practical advice for carrying out the tasks.

Then follow procedures 1 to 4 from the research task in "Researching the Implementation of Innovative Materials" above.

Since starting our careers as teachers of English a long, long time ago, we have appreciated the power of reading (Krashen, 2004, 2011) and, in particular, of the reading of stories with the potential to engage students both affectively and cognitively (Ghosn, 2013a). What we have found is that students can read stories that include unfamiliar structures and lexis, and, if they are engaged by the stories, they can gain sufficient access to enjoy them and be able to recall the stories. I have found in particular that most lower level students are not fazed by the appearance of a few unfamiliar present and past perfects in a story they are enjoying and, in fact, do not even notice they are there.

Researching the Effects of Unfamiliar Language on Students' Ability to Understand and Enjoy Stories

When Brian was working at Bell College in Saffron Walden in the 1980s an intermediate class was given a page from the novel *Vanity Fair* and the equivalent page from a graded reader version of the novel. Both pages described the atmosphere on the night before the Battle of Waterloo. Half the class was given the authentic version first and then the graded reader version and the other half of the class were given the graded reader version first. The students were then asked which version they enjoyed most and why. All the students preferred the authentic version and made comments like, "This one contained some difficult words but it was exciting. The other one was easy to understand but it was boring." Unfortunately, the data was never written up and the mini-experiment was never published. However, we have been trying to persuade commercial publishers that they are far too strict in their control of structure and lexis in their graded readers and that this control often leads to bland, unnatural texts. Without persuasive data they are never going to be convinced. What we would like to see is research investigating the effects of controlling and not controlling structures and lexis in potentially compelling stories. For example:

Either write or find a story at a slightly higher language level than a lower intermediate class (i.e. B1). Rewrite the story replacing structures likely to be unfamiliar with structures which you know will be familiar. Give the authentic story to one lower intermediate class and give the simplified version to an equivalent lower intermediate class. When the students have finished reading, collect in the stories and give the students a short questionnaire asking them how interesting and understandable they found the story and why. Then ask the students to write the story from memory.

Analyze the questionnaires, mark the stories using content points as criteria, and then determine if there is any difference between the enjoyment and understanding of the authentic version and the simplified version.

Another research task could be to do the same as in the one above only instead of replacing unfamiliar structures replace lexical items which you think would be unfamiliar to a lower intermediate class.

Alan Maley and Brian Tomlinson are so convinced from experience of the power of ungraded stories with the potential for affective and cognitive engagement that they intend to launch a series of extensive readers to be known as *It makes you think* for which authors will write stories with social issues intuitively for one of three broad levels. It would be very reassuring to have research evidence of the effectiveness of such an approach and it would make them rethink if the evidence was unexpectedly of the ineffectiveness of such an approach.

There are many other research studies we would be very interested in seeing undertaken. For example, studies of what students actually do both physically and mentally when using materials with a class or by themselves, studies of whether or not face validity and attractiveness of appearance are significant factors in the effectiveness of materials and studies of the value of giving learners choice of texts and tasks when using materials would usefully increase our knowledge of the interaction between materials and language acquisition and development. For further suggestions for materials development research studies see Tomlinson and Masuhara (2010b).

Conclusion

The length of this chapter and especially of its list of references is testimony to the fact that it can no longer be claimed that materials development is an atheoretical field or that there is no empirical research on materials development. Whilst we are personally pleased that materials development has become academically respectable, we would not like a situation to develop where materials development becomes obsessed with empirical research of what is measurable to the exclusion of the experience-based inspiration that has stimulated materials development to date. We have not included references to reviews of materials in this chapter because we do not want to be contentious in claiming that such evaluations constitute academic research. However, we do think that principled criterion-referenced evaluations make an extremely important contribution to the field and we have made extensive reference in Chapter 3 to those evaluations published in the literature (e.g. Tomlinson, Dat, Masuhara, & Rudby, 2001; Masuhara, Haan, Yi, and Tomlinson, 2008; Tribble, 2009; Wilson, 2010; Tomlinson & Masuhara, 2013).

We will never be able to claim conclusively that a particular type of language learning material is more effective in achieving a specified effect on learners than another type of material also intended to achieve that effect. As we have asserted frequently in this chapter it is not the materials per se that are responsible for learning effects but the ways in which they are used by teachers and by learners. However, this should not deter us from attempting to measure the effects of a specific feature of a set of materials in use on a specific aspect of learner performance in ways which will enable us to make the tentative claim that the use of a particular feature of materials design has the potential to achieve a specific effect on the performance of language learners. At the moment publishers know (or at least think they know) what types of language activities teachers want, theorists know what they think language learning materials should do but we do not know which types of language learning activities are actually most likely to be beneficial to language learners.

We need to find out.

What Do You Think?

1. What do you think has been indicated by the research on materials development that you have read? Has anything been proved by this research?

2. What research would you like to see undertaken in relation to materials development? Why? How would you undertake it?
3. Do you agree that informed reflection on the experience of developing and / or using materials can often be more informative than empirical research? Why?
4. What do you think are the main problems in applying SLA research to the development of materials for language learning? Can you think of ways of overcoming some of these problems?
5. Can you think of ways in which the development and use of materials can inform SLA research?

Tasks

1. Select one of the proposed research projects in "Proposed Areas of Research" above and then critique it for its validity and potential usefulness. If you discover problems with the project, suggest ways of revising it.
2. Add a proposed research project of your own that could provide new information relevant to materials development for language learning.

References

Abdel Latif, M. M. (2017). Teaching grammar using inductive and communicative materials: Exploring Egyptian EFL teachers' practice and beliefs. In H. Masuhara, F. Mishan, & B. Tomlinson (Eds.), *Practice and theory for materials development in L2 learning* (pp. 275–289). Newcastle upon Tyne: Cambridge Scholars.

Ableeva, R., & Stranks, J. (2013). Listening in another language—research and materials. In B. Tomlinson (ed.), (2013d), *Developing materials for language teaching* (2nd ed., pp. 199–212). London: Bloomsbury.

Aitchison, J. (2013). *How ELT publishing works* (Kindle ed.). Oxford: ELT Teacher 2 Writer.

Al-Busaidi, S., & Tindle, K. (2010). Evaluating the effect of in-house materials on language learning. In B. Tomlinson & H. Masuhara (Eds.), *Research for materials development in language learning: Evidence for best practice* (pp. 137–149). London: Continuum.

Alderson, J. C. & Hamp-Lyons, L. (1996). TOEFL preparation courses: A study of washback. *Language Testing, 13*(3), 280–297.

Amrani, F. (2011). The process of evaluation: A publisher's view. In B. Tomlinson (Ed.), Materials development in language teaching (2nd ed., pp. 267–295). Cambridge: Cambridge University Press.

Amrani, F. (2014). Ten things your editor never wants to hear you say. *IATEFL Materials Writing Special Interest Group Newsletter, 1.* Retrieved from http://free.yudu.com/item/details/1801448/Building-Materials-IATEFL-Materials-Writing-SIG-Newsletter-Issue-01

Angouri, J. (2010). Using text-book and real life data to teach turn taking in business meetings. In N. Harwood (Ed.), *English language teaching materials: Theory and practice* (pp. 373–394). Cambridge: Cambridge University Press.

Arnold, W., & Rixon, S. (2008). Materials for teaching English to young learners. In B. Tomlinson (Ed.), *English language learning materials: A critical review* (pp. 38–59). London: Continuum.

Avila, J. (2007). The value of recasts during meaning focused communication 2. In B. Tomlinson (Ed.), *Language acquisition and development: Studies of learners of first and other languages* (pp. 162–170). London: Continuum.

Azarnoosh, M., Zeraatpishe, M. Faravani, A., & Kargozari, H. R. (Eds.). (2016). *Issues in materials development*. Rotterdam: Sense.

Bailey, K. M., & Masuhara, H. (2013). Language testing washback: The role of materials. In B. Tomlinson (Ed.), *Applied linguistics and materials development* (pp. 303–318). London: Bloomsbury.

Ball, D. L., & Feiman-Nermser, S. (1988). Using textbooks and teachers' guides: A dilemma for beginning teachers and educators. *Curriculum Enquiry, 18*, 401–423.

Bao, D. (2002). *Understanding reticence: An action research project aiming at increasing verbal participation in the EFL classroom in Vietnam* (Unpublished PhD thesis). Leeds Metropolitan University, Leeds.

Bao, D. (2013). Voices of the reticent: Getting inside views of Vietnamese secondary students on learning. In M. Cortazzi & L. Jin (Eds.), *Researching cultures of learning: International perspectives on language learning and education* (pp. 136–154). Basingstoke: Palgrave Macmillan.

Bao, D. (2016). Cultural pigeon holes in English language teaching materials. *ELTWorldOnline.com, 8*. Retrieved from http://blog.nus.edu.sg/eltwo/

Barker, D. (2010). The role of unstructured learner interaction in the study of a foreign language. In S. Menon & J. Lourdunathan (Eds.), *Readings on ELT materials IV* (pp. 50–70). Petaling Jaya: Pearson Malaysia.

Barnard, E. S. (2007). The value of comprehension in the early stages of the acquisition and development of Bahasa Indonesia by non-native speakers. In B. Tomlinson (Ed.), *Language acquisition and development: studies of learners of first and other languages* (pp. 187–204). London: Continuum.

Be, N. (2003). *The design and use of English language teaching materials in Vietnamese secondary schools* (Unpublished PhD thesis). Victoria University, Wellington, New Zealand.

Bell, J., & Gower, R. (2011). Writing course materials for the world: A great compromise. In B. Tomlinson (Ed.), *Materials development in language teaching* (2nd ed., pp. 135–150). Cambridge: Cambridge University Press.

Boers, F., & Strong, B. (2016). An evaluation of textbook exercises on collocations. In B. Tomlinson (Ed.), *SLA research and materials development for language learning* (pp. 139–152). New York: Routledge.

Bolster, A. (2014). Materials adaptation of EAP materials by experienced teachers (Part I). *Folio, 16*(1), 16–22.

Bolster, A. (2015). Materials adaptation of EAP materials by experienced teachers (Part II). *Folio, 16*(2), 16–21.

Bosher, S. (2010). English for nursing: developing discipline specific materials. In N. Harwood (Ed.), *English language teaching materials: Theory and practice* (pp. 346–372). Cambridge: Cambridge University Press.

Bosompem, E. G. (2014). Materials adaptation in Ghana. In S. Garton & K. Graves (Eds.), *International perspectives on materials in ELT* (pp. 104–120). Basingstoke: Palgrave Macmillan.

Bouckaert, M. (2015). Perspectives on ELT materials development: Student teachers' voices. *Folio, 16*(2), 9–15.

Burns, A., & Hill, D. A. (2013). Teaching speaking in a second language. In B. Tomlinson (Ed.), *Applied linguistics and materials development* (pp. 231–248). London: Bloomsbury.

Byram, M., & Masuhara, H. (2013). Intercultural competence. In B. Tomlinson (Ed.), *Applied linguistics and materials development* (pp. 143–161). London: Bloomsbury.

Canniveng, C., & Martinez, M. (2003). Materials development and teacher training. In B. Tomlinson (Ed.), *Developing materials for language teaching* (pp. 479–489). London: Continuum.

Chandran, S. (2003). Where are the ELT textbooks? In W. A. Renandya (Ed.), *Methodology and materials design in language teaching* (pp. 161–169). Singapore: SEAMO.

Chandran, S. K., & Abdullah, M. H. (2003). Gender bias in Malaysian English textbooks. In J. Mukundan (Ed.), *Readings on ELT material* (pp. 91–101). Serdang: University Putra Malaysia Press.

Chapelle, C. (1998). Multimedia CALL: Lessons to be learned from research on instructed SLA. *Language Learning and Technology, 2*(1), 22–34.

Chapelle, C. A. (2001). *Computer applications in second language acquisition.* Cambridge: Cambridge University Press.

Chapelle, C. A. (2008, June). *The spread of computer-assisted language learning.* Plenary paper presented at the Association Canadienne de Linguistique Appliqué / Canadian Association of Applied Linguistics, Vancouver, British Columbia, 4–6.

Chapelle, C. A., & Jamieson, C. (2008). *Tips for teaching with CALL: Practical approaches to computer-assisted language learning.* Harlow: Pearson Longman.

Chapelle, C. A., & Lui, H. M. (2007). Theory and research: investigation of "authentic" CALL tasks. In J. Egbert & E. Hanson-Smith (Eds.), *CALL environments* (2nd ed., pp. 111–130). Alexandria, VA: TESOL Publications.

Chapelle, C. A. (2014). Afterword—technology mediated TBLT and the evolving role of innovator. In M. González-Lloret, & L. Ortega (Eds.), *Technology-mediated TBLT. Researching technology and tasks* (pp. 323–334). Amsterdam: John Benjamins.

Cheng, L. (1997). How does washback influence teaching? Implications for Hong Kong. *Language and Education, 11*, 38–54.

Clandfield, L. (2013). *How to plan a book* (Kindle ed.). Oxford: Teacher2Writer.

Clandfield, L., & Benne, R. R. (2010). *Global intermediate.* Oxford: Macmillan.

Cohen, A. D., & Ishihara, N. (2013). Pragmatics. In B. Tomlinson (Ed.), *Applied linguistics and materials development* (pp. 113–126). London: Bloomsbury.

Cook, V. (2003). Materials for adult beginners from an L2 user perspective. In B. Tomlinson (Ed.), *Developing materials for language teaching* (pp. 275–290). London: Continuum Press.

Cullen, B. (2010). Learning materials for L2 songwriters. In B. Tomlinson & H. Masuhara (Eds.), *Research for materials development in language learning; evidence for best practice* (pp. 189–206). London: Continuum.

Cullen, R., & Kuo, I. C. (2007). Spoken grammar and ELT course materials: a missing link? *TESOL Quarterly, 41*, 361–386.

Cummins, J. (2009). Bilingual and immersion programmes. In M. Long & C. Doughty (Eds.), *The handbook of language teaching* (pp. 159–181). Oxford: Wiley-Blackwell.

Cunningsworth, A. (1995). *Choosing your coursebook.* Oxford: Heinemann.

Curry, M. J., & Lillis, T. (2010). Making professional academic writing practices visible: Designing research based heuristics to support English-medium text production. In N.

Harwood (Ed.), *English language teaching materials: Theory and practice* (pp. 322–345). Cambridge: Cambridge University Press.

Darici, A. & Tomlinson, B. (2016). A case study of principled materials in action. In B. Tomlinson (Ed.), *Second language acquisition research and materials development for language learning.* New York: Routledge.

Dat, B. (2003). Localising ELT materials in Vietnam: A case study. In W. A. Renandya (Ed.), *Methodology and materials design in language teaching: current perceptions and practises and their implications* (pp. 170–191). Singapore: RELC.

Davies, C, (1995). Extensive reading: An expensive extravagance. *ELT Journal, 49*(4), 329–336.

Day, R., & Bamford, J. (1998). *Extensive reading in the second language classroom.* Cambridge: Cambridge University Press.

De Guerro, M. C. M. (2004). Early stages of L2 inner speech development: what verbal reports suggest. *International Journal of Applied Linguistics, 14*(1), 90–112.

De Guerro, M. C. M. (Ed.). (2005). *Inner speech—thinking words in a second language.* New York: Springer Verlag.

Dellar, H., & Walkley, A. (2010). *Pre-Intermediate outcomes.* Andover: Heinle.

Derewianka, B. (2003). Developing electronic materials for language teaching. In B. Tomlinson (Ed.), *Developing materials for language teaching* (pp. 199–220). London: Continuum Press.

De Witte, K., & Rogge, N. (2016). Problem-based learning in secondary education: Evaluation by an experiment. *Education Economics, 24*(1), 58–82.

Dixon, L. Q., Wu, S., Burgess-Brigham, R., Joshi, R. M., Blinks-Cantrill, E., & Washburn, E. (2014). Teaching English reading: What's included in the textbooks of pre-service general education teachers. In N. Harwood (Ed.), *English language teaching textbooks: Content, consumption, production* (pp. 111–144). Basingstoke: Palgrave Macmillan.

Donovan, P. (1998). Piloting—a publisher's view. In B. Tomlinson (Ed.), *Materials development in language teaching* (pp. 149–189). Cambridge: Cambridge University Press.

Douglas, J. (2012). *How are corpora of spoken English exploited for lexical items in materials development for general English coursebooks at upper intermediate level?* (Unpublished MA dissertation). Norwich Institute for Language Education / Leeds Metropolitan University, Norwich / Leeds.

Edwards, E., & Burns, A. (2016). Action research to support teachers' classroom materials development. *Innovation in Language Learning and Teaching* [Special issue: Innovation in Materials Development, Guest editor: Brian Tomlinson], *10*(2), 106–120.

Elley, W. (1991). Acquiring literacy in a second language: the effect of book-based programmes. *Language Learning, 41*(3), 375–411.

Elley, W. B., & Mangubhai, F. (1981) *The impact of a book flood in Fiji primary schools.* Wellington: NZCER.

Ellis, R. (1998). *The study of second language acquisition.* Oxford: Oxford University Press.

Ellis, R. (2008). *The study of second language acquisition.* (2nd ed.). Oxford: Oxford University Press.

Ellis, R. (2011). Macro- and micro-evaluations of task-based teaching. In B. Tomlinson (Ed.), *Materials development in language teaching* (pp. 21–35). Cambridge: Cambridge University Press.

Emery, H. (2013). Working with student-teachers to design materials for language support within the school curriculum. In B. Tomlinson (Ed.), *Developing materials for language teaching* (2nd ed., pp. 521–536). London: Bloomsbury.

Enever, J. (Ed.). (2011). *ELLiE: Early language learning in Europe*. London: British Council.

Evans, N. W., Hartshorn, K. J., & Anderson, N. J. (2010). A principled approach to content-based development for reading. In N. Harwood (Ed.), *Materials in ELT: theory and practice* (pp. 131–156). Cambridge: Cambridge University Press

Feak, C. B., & Swales, J. M. (2010). Writing for publication: Corpus-informed materials for postdoctoral fellows in perinatology. In N. Harwood (Ed.), *English language teaching materials: Theory and practice* (pp. 279–300). Cambridge: Cambridge University Press.

Feak, C. B., & Swales, J. M. (2014). Tensions between the old and the new in EAP textbook revision: A tale of two projects. In N. Harwood (Ed.), *English language teaching textbooks: Content, consumption, production* (pp. 299–319). Basingstoke: Palgrave Macmillan.

Fenton-Smith, B. (2010). A debate on the desired effects of output activities for extensive reading. In B. Tomlinson & H. Masuhara (Eds.), *Research for materials development in language learning: evidence for best practice* (pp. 50–61). London: Continuum.

Ferradas Moi, C. (2003). Hyperfiction: explorations in texture. In B. Tomlinson (Ed.), *Developing materials for language teaching* (pp. 221–233). London: Continuum Press.

Flores, M. M. (1995). Materials development: A creative process. In A. C. Hidalgo. D. Hall & G. M. Jacobs (Eds.), *Getting started: materials writers on materials writing* (pp. 57–66). Singapore: SEAMEO Language Centre.

Forman, R. (2014). How local teachers respond to the culture and language of a global English as a foreign language textbook. *Language, Culture and Curriculum, 27*(1), 72–88.

Fredriksson, C., & Olsen, R. (2006). *English textbook evaluation; An investigation into the criteria for selecting English textbooks*. Retrieved from https://dspace.mah.se/handle/2043/2842

Freeman, D. (2014). Reading comprehension questions: the distribution of different types in global EFL textbooks. In N. Harwood (Ed.), *English language teaching textbooks: Content, consumption, production* (pp. 72–110). Basingstoke: Palgrave Macmillan.

Garton, S., & Graves, K. (2014a). Identifying a research agenda for language teaching materials. *Modern Language Journal, 98*, 654–657.

Garton, S., & Graves, K. (Eds.). (2014b). *International perspectives on materials in ELT*. Basingstoke: Palgrave Macmillan.

Ghosn, I.-K. (2003). Talking like texts and talking about texts: How some primary school coursebooks are realised in the classroom. In B. Tomlinson (Ed.), *Developing materials for language teaching* (pp. 291–305). London: Bloomsbury.

Ghosn, I.-K. (2007). Output like input: Influence of children's literature on young L2 learners' written expression. In B. Tomlinson (Ed.), *Language acquisition and development: Studies of learners of first and other languages* (pp. 171–186). London: Continuum.

Ghosn, I.-K. (2010). Five-year outcomes from children's literature-based programmes vs programmes using a skills-based ESL course—The Matthew and Peter effects at work? In B. Tomlinson & H. Masuhara (Eds.), *Research for materials development in language learning: Evidence for best practice* (pp. 21–36). London: Continuum.

Ghosn, I.-K. (2013a). Developing motivating materials for refugee children: From theory to practice. In B. Tomlinson (Ed.), *Developing materials for language teaching* (2nd ed., pp. 247–268). London: Bloomsbury.

Ghosn, I.-K. (2013b). Language learning for young learners. In B. Tomlinson (Ed.), *Applied linguistics and materials development* (pp. 61–74). London: Bloomsbury.

Ghosn, I.-K. (2016). No place for coursebooks in the very young learner classroom. In B. Tomlinson (Ed.), *SLA research and materials development for language learning* (pp. 50–66). New York: Routledge.

Gilmore, A. (2007). Authentic materials and authenticity in foreign language learning. *Language Teaching, 40*, 97–118.

Grammatosi, F., & Harwood, N. (2014). An experienced teachers' use of the textbook on an academic English course: a case study. In N. Harwood (Ed.), *English language teaching textbooks: Content, consumption, production* (pp. 178–204). Basingstoke: Palgrave Macmillan.

Gray, J. (2000). The EFL coursebook as cultural artefact; how teachers censor and adapt. *ELT Journal, 54*(3), 274–283.

Gray, J. (2010). *The construction of English: culture, consumerism and promotion in the ELT coursebook.* Basingstoke: Palgrave Macmillan.

Gray, J., & Block, D. (2014). All middle class now? Evolving representations of the working class in the neoliberal era: The case of ELT textbooks. In N. Harwood (Ed.), *English language teaching textbooks: Content, consumption, production* (pp. 45–71). Basingstoke: Palgrave Macmillan.

Grgurović, M., Chapelle, C. A., & Shelley, M. C. (2013). A meta-analysis of effectiveness studies on computer technology-supported language learning. *Recall, 25*(2), 165–198.

Guerrettaz, A. M., & Johnston, B. (2013). Materials in the classroom ecology. *Modern Language Journal, 97*, 779–796.

Haan, N. (2010). ESOL for employability training materials in the United Kingdom: Contexts and effects. In B. Tomlinson & H. Masuhara (Eds.), (2010). *Research for materials development in language learning: Evidence for best practice* (pp. 172–188). London: Continuum.

Haan, N. (2013). Mining the L2 environment: ESOL learners and strategies outside the classroom. In B. Tomlinson (Ed.), *Developing materials for language teaching* (2nd ed., pp. 309–332). London: Bloomsbury.

Haan, N., Timmis, I., & Masuhara, H. (2010). ESOL materials: Practice and principles. In F. Mishan & A. Chambers (Eds.), *Perspectives on language learning materials development* (pp. 223–248). Berlin: Peter Lang.

Hadfield, J. (2014). Chaosmos: Spontaneity and order in the materials design process. In N. Harwood (Ed.), *English language teaching textbooks: Content, consumption, production* (pp. 320–359). Basingstoke: Palgrave Macmillan.

Hadley, G. (2014). Global coursebooks in local contexts: an empirical investigation of effectiveness. In N. Harwood (Ed.), *English language teaching textbooks: Content, consumption, production* (pp. 205–240). Basingstoke: Palgrave Macmillan.

Hall, D. (1995). Materials production: theory and practice. In A. C. Hidalgo. D. Hall & G. M. Jacobs (Eds.), *Getting started: Materials writers on materials writing* (pp. 8–24). Singapore: SEAMEO Regional Language Centre.

Harwood, N. (Ed.). (2010a). *Materials in ELT: theory and practice.* Cambridge: Cambridge University Press.

Harwood, N. (2010b). Research-based materials to demystify academic citation for post-graduate students. In N. Harwood (Ed.), *Materials in ELT: Theory and practice* (pp. 301–320). Cambridge: Cambridge University Press.

Harwood, N. (Ed.). (2014). *English language teaching textbooks: Content, consumption, production.* Basingstoke: Palgrave Macmillan.

Heron, M. (2013). *To what extent can using affectively engaging texts stimulate motivation in the learner centred classroom?* Unpublished MA dissertation. *Norwich Institute for Language Education* / Leeds Metropolitan University.

Heron, M. (2016). Using affectively engaging texts to stimulate motivation in the learner centred classroom. In M. Azarnoosh, M. Zeraatpishc, A. Faravani & H. R. Kargozari, (Eds.), (*Issues in materials development* (pp. 159–182). Rotterdam: Sense.

Hewings, M. (2010). Materials for university essay writing. In N. Harwood (Ed.), *English language teaching materials: theory and practice* (pp. 251–278). Cambridge: Cambridge University Press.

Hidalgo, A. C. D. Hall, J. G. M., & Jacobs, G. M. (Eds.) (1995). *Getting started: materials writers on materials writing.* Singapore: SEAMEO Language Centre.

Hill, D. A. (2003). The visual element in EFL coursebooks. In B. Tomlinson (Ed.), *Developing materials for language teaching* (1st ed., pp. 174–182). London: Continuum.

Hill, D. A. (2013). The visual elements in EFL coursebooks. In B. Tomlinson (Ed.), *Developing materials for language teaching* (2nd ed., pp. 157–166). London: Bloomsbury.

Hinkel. E. (Ed.). (2005). *Handbook of research in second language teaching and learning. Mahwah*, New Jersey: Lawrence Erlbaum.

Hughes, A. (2013). The teaching of reading in English for young learners: some considerations and next steps. In B. Tomlinson (Ed.), *Applied linguistics and materials development* (pp. 183–198). London: Bloomsbury.

Ishihara, N., & Paller, D. L. (2016). Research-informed materials for teaching pragmatics: The case of agreement and disagreement in English. In B. Tomlinson (Ed.), *SLA Research and materials development for language learning* (pp. 87–102). New York: Routledge.

Jakubiak, C., & Harklau, L. (2010). Designing materials for community-based adult ESL programs. In N. Harwood (Ed.), *English language teaching materials: Theory and practice* (pp. 395–418). Cambridge: Cambridge University Press.

Jazadi, I. (2003). Mandated English teaching materials and their implications for teaching and learning: The case of Indonesia. In W. A. Renandya (Ed.), *Methodology and materials design in language teaching* (pp. 142–160). Singapore: SEAMEO Regional Language Centre.

Johnson, K. (2003). *Designing language teaching tasks.* Basingstoke: Palgrave Macmillan.

Jones, M., & Schmitt, N. (2010). Developing materials for discipline-specific vocabulary and phrases in academic seminars. In N. Harwood (Ed.), *English language teaching materials: Theory and practice* (pp. 225–248). Cambridge: Cambridge University Press.

Kennedy, C., & Tomlinson, B. (2013). Implementing language policy and planning through materials development. In B. Tomlinson (Ed.), (2013). *Applied linguistics and materials development* (pp. 255–268). London: Bloomsbury.

Kim, H. (2016, June). *Learners' and pre-service teachers' opinions about illustrations in EFL textbooks in South Korea.* Presentation at the MATSDA / University of Liverpool Conference on Authenticity in Materials Development, Liverpool.

Krashen, S. (2004). *The power of reading. Portsmouth:* Heinemann. Westport: Libraries Unlimited.

Krashen, S. (2011). The compelling (not just interesting) input hypothesis. *The English Connection. A Publication of KOTESOL. 15*(3). Retrieved from http://www.koreatesol.org/sites/default/files/pdf_publications/TECv15n3-11Autumn.pdf

Lam, P. W. Y. (2010). Discourse particles in corpus data and textbooks: the case of well. *Applied Linguistics, 31*(2), 260–281.

Law, W. H. (1995). *Teachers' evaluation of English textbooks: An investigation of teachers' ideas and current practices and their implications for developing textbook evaluation criteria* (Unpublished M.Ed. dissertation). University of Hong Kong, Hong Kong.

Le, T. B. & Ha, P. L. (2009). Examining the foreignness of EFL global textbooks: issues and proposals from the Vietnamese classroom. In J. Mukundan (Ed.), *Readings on ELT materials III* (pp. 196–212). Petaling Jaya: Pearson Malaysia.

Lee, R., & Bathmaker, A. (2007). The use of English textbooks for teaching English to "vocational" students in Singapore secondary schools: a survey of teachers' beliefs. *RELC Journal, 38*(3), 350–374.

Lefever, S. (2012). Incidental foreign language learning in young children. In A. Hasselgreen, I. Drew & B. Sorheim (Eds.), *The young language learner: Research-based insights into teaching and learning*. Bergen: Fagbokforlager.

Loh, J., & Renandya, W. A. (2015). Exploring adaptations of materials and methods: A case from Singapore. *The European Journal of Applied Linguistics and TEFL, 4*(2), 93–111.

Lynch, T. (1996). Influences on course revision: an EAP case study. In M. Hewings & T. Dudley-Evans (Eds.), *Course evaluation and design in EAP, Review of ELT 6.1* (pp. 26–35). Hemel Hempstead: Prentice Hall Macmillan.

Lyons, P. (2003). A practical experience of institutional textbook writing: product / process implications for materials development. In B. Tomlinson (Ed.), *Developing materials for language teaching* (pp. 490–504). London: Continuum Press.

Maley, A. (1995). Materials development and tacit knowledge. In A. C. Hidalgo, D. Hall, & G. M. Jacobs (Eds.), *Getting started: Materials writers on materials writing* (pp. 220–239). Singapore: SEAMEO Regional Language Centre.

Maley, A. (2013). Vocabulary. In B. Tomlinson (Ed.), *Applied linguistics and materials development* (pp. 95–112). London: Bloomsbury.

Maley, A. (2016). "More research is needed"—A mantra too far? *Humanizing Language Teaching, 18*(3). Retrieved from http://hltmag.co.uk/jun16/mart01.htm

Maley, A., & Prowse, P. (2013). Reading. In B. Tomlinson (Ed.), *Applied linguistics and materials development* (pp. 165–182). London: Bloomsbury.

Maley, A., & Tomlinson, B. (in press). *Authenticity and materials development*. Newcastle upon Tyne: Cambridge Scholars.

Mason, J. (2010) The effects of different types of materials on the intercultural competence of Tunisian university students. In B. Tomlinson & H. Masuhara (Eds.), *Research for materials development in language learning* (pp. 67–82). London: Continuum.

Masuhara, H. (2011). What do teachers really want from coursebooks? In B. Tomlinson (Ed.), *Materials development in language teaching* (2nd ed., pp. 236–266). Cambridge: Cambridge University Press.

Masuhara, H., Haan, M., Yi, Y., & Tomlinson, B. (2008). Adult EFL courses. *ELT Journal, 62*(3), 294–312.

Masuhara, H., Kimura, T., Fukada, A., & Takeuchi, M. (1996). Strategy training or / and extensive reading? In T. Hickey, & J. Williams (Eds.), *Language, education and society in a changing world* (pp. 263–274). Clevedon: Multilingual Matters.

Masuhara, H., Mishan, F., & Tomlinson, B. (Eds.). (2017). *Practice and theory for materials development in L2 learning*. Newcastle upon Tyne: Cambridge Scholars.

McCullugh, M. (2010) An initial evaluation of a set of published materials for medical English. In B. Tomlinson & H. Masuhara (Eds.), *Research for materials development in language learning* (pp. 381–393). London: Continuum.

McDonough, J., Shaw, C., & Masuhara, H. (2013). *Materials and methods in ELT: A teacher's guide* (3rd ed.). Chichester: Wiley-Blackwell.

McGrath, I. (2002). *Materials evaluation and design for language teaching.* Edinburgh: Edinburgh University Press.

McGrath, I. (2013). *Teaching materials and the roles of EFL / ESL teachers.* London: Bloomsbury.

Menkabu, A., & Harwood, N. (2014). Teachers' conceptualization and use of the textbook on a medical English course. In N. Harwood (Ed.), *English language teaching textbooks: Content, consumption, production* (pp. 145–177). Basingstoke: Palgrave Macmillan.

Menon, S. (2009). Corpus analysis of prescribed Science and English language textbooks: potentials for language teaching and EST materials design. In J. Mukundan, (Ed.), *Readings on ELT materials III* (pp. 213–231). Petaling Jaya: Pearson Malaysia.

Messekher, H. (2014). Cultural representations in Algerian English textbooks. In S. Garton & K. Graves (Eds.), *International Perspectives on materials in ELT* (pp. 69–86). Basingstoke: Palgrave Macmillan.

Mishan, F. (2005). *Designing authenticity into language learning materials.* Bristol: Intellect.

Mishan, F. (2013). Studies of pedagogy. In B. Tomlinson (Ed.), (2013a), *Applied linguistics and materials development* (pp. 269–286). London: Bloomsbury.

Mishan, F., & Timmis, I. (2015). *Materials development for TESOL.* Edinburgh: Edinburgh University Press.

Modugala, M. (in press). Listening to children's perceptions and experiences of English language teaching material. In B. Tomlinson (Ed.), *The ELTRePA Project.* Kolkata: British Council.

Mukundan, J. (Ed.). (2003). *Readings on ELT material.* Sedang: Universiti Putra Malaysia Press.

Mukundan, J. (Ed.). (2006a). *Focus on ELT materials.* Petaling Jaya: Pearson Malaysia.

Mukundan, J. (Ed.). (2006b). *Readings on ELT materials II.* Petaling Jaya: Pearson Malaysia.

Mukundan, J. (Ed.). (2008). *Readings on ELT materials III.* Petaling Jaya: Pearson Malaysia.

Mukundan, J., & Hussin, A. A. (2006). Exploration of Wordsmith 3.0 as a textbook writer's guide and as an evaluation instrument. In J. Mukundan (Ed.), *Focus on ELT materials* (pp. 12–24). Petaling Jaya: Pearson Malaysia.

Nakata, T., & Webb, S. (2016). Vocabulary learning exercises: Evaluating a selection of exercises commonly featured in language learning materials. In B. Tomlinson (Ed.), *SLA research and materials development for language learning* (pp. 123–138). New York: Routledge.

Nguyen, M. T. T. (2011). Learning to communicate in a globalized world: To what extent do school textbooks facilitate the development of intercultural pragmatic competence? *RELC Journal, 42*(1), 17–30.

Noronha, S. (2017 forthcoming). Supporting language learning through a library program. In B. Tomlinson (Ed.), *The ELTRePA Project.* Kolkata: British Council.

Nunan, D. (2013). Innovation in the young learner classroom. In K. Hyland & L. L. C. Wong (Eds.), *Innovation and change in English language education* (pp. 233–247). Abingdon: Routledge.

Ottley, K. (2014). Please read the text on page seven: It has nothing to do with you. *Folio, 16*(1), 12–14.

Pascasio, E. M. (1995). Experiencing language: A response to the Philippine bilingual policy. In A. C. Hidalgo. D. Hall & G. M. Jacobs (Eds.), *Getting started: Materials writers on materials writing* (pp. 82–94). Singapore: SEAMEO Language Centre.

Pelly, C. P., & Allison, D. (2000). Investigating the views of teachers on assessment of English language learning in the Singapore education system. *Hong Kong Journal of Applied Linguistics, 5*, 81–106.

Penaflorida, A. H. (1995). The process of materials development: A personal experience. In A. C. Hidalgo. D. Hall & G. M. Jacobs (Eds.), *Getting started: materials writers on materials writing* (pp. 172–186). Singapore: SEAMEO Language Centre.

Popovici, R., & Bolitho, R. (2003). Personal and professional development through writing: The Romanian textbook project. In B. Tomlinson (Ed.), *Developing materials for language teaching* (pp. 505–517). London: Continuum.

Prowse, P. (2011). How writers write: Testimony from authors. In B. Tomlinson (Ed.), *Materials development in language teaching* (2nd ed., pp. 151–173). Cambridge: Cambridge University Press.

Pryor, S. (2010). The development and trialling of materials for second language instruction: A case study. In B. Tomlinson & H. Masuhara (Eds.), *Research for materials development in language learning: Evidence for best practice* (pp. 207–223). London: Continuum.

Read, C. (2015). Foreword. In J. Bland (Ed.), *Teaching English to young learners: Critical issues in language teaching with 3–12 year olds* (pp. xi–xiii). London: Bloomsbury.

Renandya, W. A. (Ed.). (2003). *Methodology and materials design in language teaching: Current perceptions and practices and their implications.* Singapore: RELC.

Richards, J. (1995). Easier said than done. In A. Hidalgo, D. Hall & G. Jacobs (Eds.), *Getting started: Materials writers on materials writing* (pp. 95–135). Singapore: RELC.

Richards, J. (2005, March). *Materials development and research—making the connection.* Paper presented at a colloquium on materials development and research. TESOL Convention, San Antonio.

Riddiford, N., & Newton, J. (2010). *Workplace talk in action: An ESOL resource.* Wellington School of Linguistics and Applied Language Studies, Victoria University of Wellington.

Roxburgh, J. (1997). Procedures for the evaluation of in-house EAP textbooks. *Folio, 4*(1), 15–18.

Sampson, N. (2009). *Teaching materials and the autonomous language teacher: a study of tertiary English teachers in Hong Kong* (Unpublished Ed.D. thesis). University of Hong Kong, Hong Kong.

Samuda, V. (2005). Expertise in pedagogic task design. In K. Johnson (Ed.), *Expertise in second language learning and teaching* (pp. 230–254). Basingstoke: Palgrave Macmillan.

Santos, D. (2015). Revising listening materials: What remains, what is changed and why. *The European Journal of Applied Linguistics and TEFL, 4*(2), 19–36.

Shawer, S. (2010a). Classroom level curriculum development: EFL teachers as curriculum-developers, curriculum-makers and curriculum-transmitters. *Teaching and Teacher Education, 26*, 173–184.

Shawer, S. (2010b). Classroom-level teacher professional development and satisfaction: Teachers learn in the context of classroom-level curriculum development. *Professional Development in Education, 36*, 597–620.

Shepherd, J., Cox, F., & Roberts, P. (1991). *The sourcebook—an alternative English course.* Harlow: Longman.

Shin, J., Eslami, Z. R., & Chen, W. (2011). Presentation of local and international culture in current international English-language teaching textbooks. *Language, Culture and Curriculum, 24*(3), 253–268.

Singapore Wala, D. A. (2003a). A coursebook is what it is because of what it has to do: Editor's perspective. In B. Tomlinson (Ed.), *Developing materials for language teaching* (pp. 58–71). London: Continuum.

Singapore Wala, D. A. (2013). Publishing a coursebook: The role of feedback. In B. Tomlinson (Ed.), *Developing materials for language teaching* (2nd ed., pp. 63–88). London: Bloomsbury.

Srinivas, R. (2003). Teacher involvement in textbook preparation in India. *Folio, 8*(1/2), 38–40.

Stillwell, C., Kidd, A., Alexander, K., McIlroy, T., Roloff, J., & Stone, P. (2010). Mutual benefits of feedback on materials through collaborative materials evaluation. In B. Tomlinson & H. Masuhara (Eds.), *Research for materials development in language learning: Evidence for best practice* (pp. 257–272). London: Continuum.

Stillwell, C., McMillan, B., Gillies, H., & Waller, T. (2010). Four teachers looking for a lesson: Developing materials with lesson study. In B. Tomlinson & H. Masuhara (Eds.), *Research for materials development in language learning: Evidence for best practice* (pp. 237– 250). London: Continuum.

St. Louis, R. (2010). Can a 48 hour refresher course help first year English for science and technology reading students? A case study of English CIU at Universidad Simon Bolivar, Venezuela. In B. Tomlinson (Ed.), *SLA and materials development* (pp. 3–22). New York: Routledge.

Stoller, F. L., & Robinson, M. S. (2014). An interdisciplinary textbook project; charting the paths taken. In N. Harwood (Ed.), *English language teaching textbooks: Content, consumption, production* (pp. 262–298). Basingstoke: Palgrave Macmillan.

Sundara Rajan, B. R. (1995). Developing instructional materials for adult workers. In A. C. Hidalgo. D. Hall & G. M. Jacobs (Eds.), *Getting started: materials writers on materials writing* (pp. 187–208). Singapore: SEAMEO Language Centre.

Swain, M., & Lapkin, S. (2005). The evolving sociopolitical context of immersion education in Canada: some implications for program development. *The International Journal of Applied Linguistics, 15*(2), 169–186.

Swe, S. T. (2015). *Evaluating the external materials used for cultural elements in ELT coursebooks through teacher perception and learning* (Unpublished PhD thesis). University of Essex, Colchester.

Tan, B. T. (2006). Student-teacher-made language teaching materials—A developmental approach to materials development. In J. Mukundan (Ed.), *Focus on ELT materials* (pp. 207–227). Petaling Jaya: Pearson Malaysia.

Tasseron, M. (2017). How teachers use the global ELT coursebook. In H. Masuhara, F. Mishan, & B. Tomlinson (Eds.), *Practice and theory of materials development in L2 learning* (pp. 290–311). Newcastle upon Tyne: Cambridge Scholars.

Thomas, M., & Reinders, H. (Eds.). (2015). *Contemporary task-based language teaching in Asia*. London: Bloomsbury.

Timmis, I. (2013). Spoken language research: the applied linguistic challenge. In B. Tomlinson (Ed.), *Applied linguistics and materials development* (pp. 79–94). London: Bloomsbury.

Timmis, I. (2014). Writing materials for publication: questions raised and lessons learned. In N. Harwood (ed.), *English language teaching textbooks: Content, consumption, production* (pp. 241–261). Basingstoke: Palgrave Macmillan.

Tomlinson, B. (1994). *Openings*. Harlow: Longman.

Tomlinson, B. (Ed.). (1998a). *Materials development in language teaching.* Cambridge: Cambridge University Press.

Tomlinson, B. (1998b). Introduction. In B. Tomlinson (Ed.), *Materials development in language teaching* (pp. 1–24). Cambridge: Cambridge University Press.

Tomlinson, B. (1999). Developing criteria for materials evaluation. *IATEFL Issues, 147,* 10–13.

Tomlinson, B. (Ed.). (2003). *Developing materials for language teaching.* London: Continuum Press.

Tomlinson, B. (Ed.) (2007a). *Language acquisition and development: studies of learners of first and other languages.* London: Continuum.

Tomlinson, B. (2007b). The value of recasts during meaning focused communication 1. In B. Tomlinson (Ed.), *Language acquisition and development: Studies of learners of first and other languages* (pp. 141–161). London: Continuum.

Tomlinson, B. (Ed.). (2008a). *English language teaching materials: A critical review.* London: Continuum.

Tomlinson, B. (2008b). Language acquisition and language learning materials. In B. Tomlinson (Ed.), *English language teaching materials: a critical review* (pp. 3–14). London: Continuum.

Tomlinson, B. (2010a). What do teachers think about EFL coursebooks? *Modern English Teacher, 19*(4), 5–9.

Tomlinson, B. (2010b). Helping learners to fill the gaps in their learning. In Mishan, F. & Chambers, A. (Eds.), *Perspectives on language learning materials development* (pp. 87–108). Berlin: Peter Lang.

Tomlinson, B. (Ed.) (2011a). *Materials development in language teaching* (2nd ed.). Cambridge: Cambridge University Press.

Tomlinson, B. (2011b). Principled procedures in materials development. In B. Tomlinson (Ed.), *Materials development in language teaching* (2nd ed., pp. 1–31). Cambridge: Cambridge University Press.

Tomlinson, B. (2011c). Seeing what they mean: helping L2 readers to visualise. In B. Tomlinson. (Ed.), *Materials development in language teaching* (2nd ed.). (pp. 357–378). Cambridge: Cambridge University Press.

Tomlinson, B. (2012). Materials development. *Language Teaching, 45*(2), 143–179.

Tomlinson, B. (Ed.). (2013a). *Applied linguistics and materials development.* London: Bloomsbury.

Tomlinson, B. (2013b). Second language acquisition and materials development. In B. Tomlinson (Ed.), *Applied linguistics and materials development* (pp. 11–30). London: Bloomsbury.

Tomlinson, B. (2013c). Concluding comments. In B. Tomlinson (Ed.), *Applied linguistics and materials development* (pp. 321–322). London: Bloomsbury.

Tomlinson, B. (Ed.). (2013d). *Developing materials for language teaching* (2nd ed.). London: Bloomsbury.

Tomlinson, B. (2013e). Developing principled frameworks for materials development. In B. Tomlinson (Ed.), *Developing materials for language teaching* (2nd ed., pp. 95–118). London: Bloomsbury.

Tomlinson, B. (2013f). Materials evaluation. In B. Tomlinson (Ed.), *Developing materials for language teaching* (2nd ed., pp. 21–48). London: Bloomsbury.

Tomlinson, B. (2014). Teacher growth through materials development. *The European Journal of Applied Linguistics and TEFL.* Special Issue. A. Maley (Ed.), *3*(2), 89–106.

Tomlinson, B. (2015a). TBLT materials and curricula—from theory to practice. In Thomas M. & Reinders, H. (Eds.), *Contemporary task-based language teaching in Asia* (pp. 328–340). London: Bloomsbury.

Tomlinson, B. (Ed.). (2015b). *The European Journal of Applied Linguistics and TEFL. Materials in the ELT classroom: Development, Use and Evaluation* [Special issue, guest editor B. Tomlinson], *4*(2).

Tomlinson, B. (Ed.). (2016a). *SLA and materials development.* New York: Routledge.

Tomlinson, B. (2016b). The match between SLA theory and materials development. In B. Tomlinson (Ed.), *SLA and materials development* (pp. 3–22). New York: Routledge.

Tomlinson, B. (Ed.). (2016c). Innovation in materials development. A special issue of *Innovation in Language Learning and Teaching* [Special issue, guest editor B. Tomlinson], *10*(2).

Tomlinson, B. (2016d). Making typical coursebook activities more beneficial for the learner. In B. Dat (Ed.), *ELT material development in Asia and beyond: Directions, issues, and challenges.* Newcastle upon Tyne: Cambridge Scholars.

Tomlinson, B., & Avila, J. (2007). Seeing and saying for yourself: The roles of audio-visual mental aids in language learning and use. In B. Tomlinson (Ed.), *Language acquisition and development: Studies of first and other language learners* (pp. 61–81). London: Continuum.

Tomlinson, B., & Darici, A. (2016). A case study of principled materials in action. In B. Tomlinson (Ed.), *SLA and materials development* (pp. 71–86). New York: Routledge.

Tomlinson, B, & Dat, B. (2004). The contributions of Vietnamese learners of English to ELT methodology. *Language Teaching Research 8*(2), 199–222.

Tomlinson, B., Dat, B., Masuhara, H., & Rubdy, R. (2001). EFL courses for Adults. *ELT Journal*, *55*(1), 80–101.

Tomlinson, B., & Masuhara, H. (Eds.). (2010a). *Research for materials development in language learning: Evidence for best practice.* London: Continuum.

Tomlinson, B., & Masuhara, H. (2010b). Applications of the research results for second language acquisition theory and research. In B. Tomlinson & H. Masuhara (Eds.), *Research for materials development in language learning: Evidence for best practice* (pp. 399–409). London: Continuum.

Tomlinson, B., & Masuhara, H. (2013). Review of adult ELT textbooks. *ELT Journal*, *67*(2), 233–249.

Tomlinson, B., & Whittaker, C. (2013). (Eds.). *Case studies of blended learning courses.* London: British Council.

Trabelsi, S. (2010). Developing and trialling authentic materials for business English students at a Tunisian university. In B. Tomlinson & H. Masuhara (Eds.), *Research for materials development in language learning: Evidence for best practice* (pp. 103–120). London: Continuum.

Tribble, C. (2009). Writing academic English—a survey review of current published resources. *ELT Journal 63*(4), 400–417.

Troncoso, C. R. (2010). The effects of language materials on the development of intercultural competence. In B. Tomlinson & H. Masuhara, (Eds.), *Research for materials development in language learning: Evidence for best practice* (pp. 83–102). London: Continuum.

Tsobanoglou, S. (2008). *What can we learn by researching the use of textbooks and other support materials by teachers and learners* (Unpublished MA dissertation). University of Nottingham, Nottingham.

Tsui, A. (2003). *Understanding expertise in teaching: Case studies of ESL teachers.* New York: Cambridge University Press.

Uso-Juan, E. (2008). The presentation and practice of the communicative act of requesting in textbooks: Focusing on modifiers. In E. S. Alcon & M. P. Safont (Eds.), *Intercultural language use and language learning* (pp. 223–243). Dordrecht: Springer.

Van den Branden, K. (2006). *Task-based language education: From theory to practice.* Cambridge: Cambridge University Press.

Viney, P. (2007). Featured writer: Peter Viney. *Folio, 11*(2), 32–33.

Vo, T. H. L. (2014). *A study into how materials design and teacher education can support the development of communicative competence in the Vietnamese workplace* (Unpublished PhD thesis). University of Portsmouth, Portsmouth.

Wang, H. (2006). Pragmatics in foreign language teaching and learning: Reflections on the teaching of Chinese in China. In M. W. Chan, K. N. Chin & T. Suthiwan (Eds.), *Foreign language teaching in Asia and beyond* (pp. 93–108). Singapore: National University of Singapore.

Wette, R. (2011). Meeting curriculum, learning and settlement needs: teachers' use of materials in courses for adult migrants. *TESOL in Context, 21*, 59–77.

Wilson, J. (2010). Recent IELTS materials. *ELT Journal, 64*(2), 219–232.

Wong, J. (2011). Pragmatic competency in telephone closings. In N. Houck & D. Tatsuki (Eds.), *Pragmatics: Teaching natural conversation* (pp. 135–152). Alexandria, VA: Teachers of English to Speakers of Another Language.

Wong, V., Kwok, P., & Choi, N. (1995). The use of authentic materials at tertiary level. *ELT Journal, 49*(4), 318–322.

Yan, C. (2007). Investigating English teachers' materials adaptation. *Humanising Language Teaching, 9*(4). Retrieved from http://www.hltmag.co.uk/jul07/mart01.htm

Yano Y., Long, M. H., & Ross, S. (1994). The effects of simplified and elaborated texts on foreign language comprehension. *Language Learning, 44*(2), 189–212.

Yi, Y. (2012). *The effects of visual image training on Chinese EFL learners' narrative writing* (Unpublished PhD thesis). Leeds Metropolitan University, Leeds.

Zemach, D. (2006). Working with an editor. *Folio, 10*(2), 37–39.

Conclusion

We hope that you have found our book informative and useful and that it will stimulate you to start, or continue, to take a principled and creative approach to developing, evaluating, adapting, using and researching materials for language learning. If it does we would really welcome your contribution to a MATSDA Conference and to the MATSDA journal *Folio*. For information about MATSDA please go to www.matsda.org

One recurrent theme throughout this book has been our reference to and our support for an appeal from researchers for a richer experience for language learners and a complaint about the impoverished experience often offered by coursebooks. Researchers have provided evidence in favor of supplying learners with much more experience of language in authentic use, many more opportunities to use the target language for communication, many more opportunities to make discoveries for themselves about language use, of offering much more choice to learners, of encouraging and facilitating learner autonomy, and of adopting humanistic, experiential approaches that have the potential to respect, engage, and stimulate learners. Researchers have also shown that commercially published coursebooks tend to focus on presentation and practice of language items, features and skills in decontextualized activities with little potential for engagement and little connection with the lives or aspirations of their target learners. We understand the commercial imperative that maintains the status quo and if we were publishers we would probably be very reluctant to risk making changes to our coursebooks that could threaten their face validity, fail to meet the expectations of potential customers, and risk financial disaster. We also understand that materials developers have to make compromises to get their coursebooks published (see Bell & Gower, 2011; Timmis, 2014) but we would hope they would put on more pressure to persuade their publishers to make some moves towards more principled publications. We also understand that there is little point in changing coursebooks if examinations do not change too. Even so, we remain optimistic that some progress will be made and that more research-informed, more engaging (but equally profitable) coursebooks will be published soon. After all, global coursebooks have made some positive changes and are, for example, more personalized, more politically correct, and more in touch with the contemporary world (both in themes and in their modes of delivery) than they were in the late 2000s. There are now many examples of locally published materials that are more relevant, more engaging and more principled than many of their global counterparts.

Our personal hope for the future is that practitioners and researchers will interact so that principled and coherent materials can be developed that are informed by both

The Complete Guide to the Theory and Practice of Materials Development for Language Learning,
First Edition. Brian Tomlinson and Hitomi Masuhara.
© 2018 John Wiley & Sons, Inc. Published 2018 by John Wiley & Sons, Inc.

the actualities of learning and of teaching an L2 and by research into second-language acquisition. If this happens, we hope that the affordances of digital delivery will stimulate blended learning courses that offer learners choices of delivery, of pedagogic approach, of texts, of tasks, of feedback and of assessment. We hope that these courses offer rich and varied exposure to the target language in use, opportunities to use the target language for monitored communication and opportunities to make discoveries about how the language is typically used for effective communication. If this happens, then L2 learners will have a much better chance of developing communicative competence in relation to their objectives for learning the language and of developing their awareness, skills, and personalities too.

As you will now know from reading our book, we hold strong views about materials development based on our considerable experience as writers, evaluators, adapters, users and researchers of materials for language learning. We hope that these views have not offended or disturbed anyone and that you will use them, not as something to accept or reject, but as a stimulus to thought and principled action. Most of our ideas have come from hearing about or seeing unfamiliar approaches in action, initially rejecting them because they are different from ours, reflecting on them, selecting from them, trying them out in our own way and then refining them as ours. We hope that you will do something similar with our views and approaches.

Enjoy developing!

Brian and Hitomi

Dr. Brian Tomlinson (University of Liverpool, Anaheim University, President of MATSDA) brianjohntomlinson@gmail.com

Dr. Hitomi Masuhara (University of Liverpool, Secretary of MATSDA) hitomi.masuhara@gmail.com

References

Bell, J. & Gower, R. (2011). Writing course materials for the world: A great compromise. In B. Tomlinson (Ed.), *Materials development in language teaching* (2nd ed., pp. 135–150). Cambridge: Cambridge University Press.

Timmis, I. (2014). Writing materials for publication: Questions raised and lessons learned. In N. Harwood (Ed.), *English language teaching textbooks: Content, consumption, production* (pp. 241–261). Basingstoke: Palgrave Macmillan.

Resources Useful for Materials Developers

These days developing materials is potentially easier than when we first started. The processing facility of the computer and easy access to the web have transformed the ways that materials are written. Libraries of texts and activities can be assembled and retrieved from without leaving the desk. Drafts of texts and activities can be inserted into materials in any order and then revised and sequenced later. They can also be easily sent to people for monitoring and easily abandoned or adapted. Materials can be developed by teams working at a distance from each other (though we personally still prefer the stimulus and collegiality that can be gained from face-to-face interaction). Student books and teachers' books can be developed at the same time. Materials can be designed and even illustrated as they are developed. Perhaps the greatest benefit, though, has become the easy access to resources on the web, which can inform, stimulate, and provide. Below we have listed some of these resources that we think can help teachers preparing materials for tomorrow's classes as well as materials developers preparing materials for eventual publication.

Associations with Materials Development Journals / Newsletters

The International Association of Teachers of English as a Foreign Language (IATEFL) is an international association based in the United Kingdom, which has a special interest group known as **MaWSIG (Materials Writers Special Interest Group)**. This group has a blog featuring guest posts by members on practical issues related to materials development and, having originally published *Building Materials*, a paper newsletter, in April, 2014, now publishes a web newsletter http://mawsig.iatefl.org/blog/newsletter/. For information about MaWSIG go to http://mawsig.iatefl.org/. Soon MaWSIG will start publishing a research-informed journal to be known as *ELT Materials Review*.

The **Japan Association of Language Teachers (JALT)** has a materials writers' special interest group **MWSIG**, which has a blog and which has been publishing a newsletter *Between the Keys* for many years. For information about MWSIG go to http://materialswriters.org/.

The **Materials Development Association (MATSDA)** is an international association based in the United Kingdom. MATSDA has been publishing a journal *Folio* for over 20 years, which is dedicated to connecting practice to theory and theory to practice and which welcomes contributions relating to materials for the learning of any language. For information about MATSDA go to htpp://www.matsda.org/.

The Complete Guide to the Theory and Practice of Materials Development for Language Learning, First Edition. Brian Tomlinson and Hitomi Masuhara.

Teachers of English to Speakers of Other Languages (TESOL) is an international association based in the United States with a materials writers' interest section (**MWIS**), which publishes a newsletter providing practical tips on materials writing. For information about MWIS go to http://www.tesol.org/connect/interest-sections/materials-writers/.

Corpora

There are now hundreds of corpora available on the web, some of them available free, some of them sampled free, and most of them available on payment of a fee. Here are some of what we think are the most useful corpora for teachers, materials writers, and researchers wanting to access information about how their target language is typically used.

- **The BASE Corpus (British Academic Spoken English)** (http://www2.warwick.ac.uk/fac/soc/al/research/collections/base/): 1,644,942 tokens taken from 160 lectures and 40 seminars recorded at the University of Warwick and the University of Reading.
- **The British National Corpus (BNC)** (http://www.natcorp.ox.ac.uk/): a 100 million-word data base of written and spoken British English.
- **Cambridge English Corpus** (http://www.cambridge.org/gb/cambridgeenglish/about-cambridge-english/cambridge-english-corpus): a multibillion-word data base of written and spoken texts taken from a variety of sources such as newspapers, web sites, books, magazines, the radio, educational institutions, the workplace, and conversations. It includes the **Cambridge Learner Corpus**—a 50 million-word collection of the scripts of students taking Cambridge exams worldwide.
- **CANCODE (Cambridge and Nottingham Corpus of Discourse in English)** (https://en.wikipedia.org/wiki/Cambridge_English_Corpus): a 5 million-word corpus of spoken English.
- **Collins Wordbanks Online English Corpus** (https://www.collins.co.uk/page/Wordbanks+Online): a 56 million-word corpus of British and American written and spoken English.
- **CORE (Corpus of Online Registers of English)** (http://corpus.byu.edu/core/): a 50-million word corpus of web texts, which is divided into many different registers to facilitate comparisons between registers. It also aids the creation of collections of texts of relevance to a specific area of interest.
- **The Corpus of American Soap Operas (SOAP)** (corpus.byu.edu/soap/): a 100 million-word corpus of data from 22,000 transcripts of American soap operas which offers a resource for exploring the use of informal spoken language.
- **The Corpus of Contemporary American English (COCA)** (http://corpus.byu.edu/coca/): a 520 million-word corpus of texts from spoken and written fiction, magazine, newspaper, and academic texts.
- **Global Web-based English (GloWbE)** (http://corpus.byu.edu/glowbe/): a 1.9 billion-word corpus of texts from 20 different countries from which full-text data can be downloaded.
- **ICE (The International Corpus of English)** (http://www.comp.leeds.ac.uk/ccalas/tagsets/ice.html): a huge collection of texts from 26 countries providing a corpus of national and regional varieties of English.

- **ICLE (The International Corpus of Learner English)** (http://www.uclouvain.be/en-cecl.html): a 2 million-word corpus of learner written English from 14 L1 backgrounds.
- **MICASE (The Michigan Corpus of Academic Spoken English)** (https://quod.lib.umich.edu/m/micase/): a 1.8 million-word collection of spoken academic English texts recorded at the University of Michigan.
- **The NOW Corpus (Newspapers on the Web)** (http://corpus.byu.edu/now/): a 3 billion-word corpus collected from contemporary web-based newspapers.
- **Webcorp** (http://www.webcorp.org.uk): an interface site that uses the Internet to run concordances.
- **The Wikipedia Corpus** (http://corpus.byu.edu/wiki/): the full text of Wikipedia containing 1.9 billion words in more than 4.4 million articles. It facilitates searches by word, phrase, part of speech, and synonyms and searches for collocates and re-sortable concordance lines for any word or phrase.
- **VOICE (the Vienna-Oxford International Corpus of English)** (http://www.univie.ac.at/voice/). A corpus of conversations in which English is used as a lingua franca (ELF).

For information about other corpora available online (including Business English corpora and non-English corpora) see O'Keefe, McCarthy & Carter (2007).

Journals with Relevance to Materials Development

Here are references to a few of the very many journals which, whilst not dedicated to materials development, do often contain articles on or related to the development of materials for language learning.

Research Journals

Applied Linguistics (https://applij.oxfordjournals.org/)
Annual Review of Applied Linguistics (www.journals.cambridge.org/jid_AP)
JALT Journal (www.jalt-publications.org/jj)
Language Learning Journal (www.tandfonline.com)
Language Teaching (www.journals.cambridge.org/LTA)
Language Teaching Research (ltr.sagepub.com/)
Modern Language Journal (www.onlinelibrary.wiley.com)
RELC Journal (rel.sagepub.com)
TESOL Quarterly (www.tesol.org/read-and-publish/journals/tesol-quarterly)

Professional Journals

English Teaching Professional (https://www.etprofessional.com)
English Language Teaching Journal (ELT Journal) (https://academic.oup.com/eltj)
Humanising Language Teaching (HLT) (www.hltmag.co.uk)
Language Teacher (www.jalt-publications.org/tlt)
Modern English Teacher (https://www.modernenglishteacher.com/)
Teacher Trainer (https://www.tttjournal.co.uk/)

Practical Guides to Materials Development

Baleghizadeh, S. (2012). *Materials development for English language teachers: A practical guide*. Tehran: SAMT Publishers.

Byrd, P. H. (1995). *Materials writers guide*. Rowley, MA: Newbury House.

Byrd, P. H. & Schuemann, C. M. (2012). Materials publication. *The Encyclopedia of Applied Linguistics*. Hoboken, NJ: Wiley-Blackwell.

ELT Teacher2Writer. Retrieved from http://www.eltteacher2writer.co.uk/. [A series of e-books training teachers to write materials.]

Núñez, A., Téllez, M. F., Castellanos, J. & Ramos, B. (2009). *A practical materials development guide for EFL pre-service, novice, and in-service teachers, Vol 1*. Bogota: Universidad Externado de Colombia, Facultad de Ciencias de la Educación.

Tomlinson, B. & Masuhara, H. (2004). *Developing language course materials*. Singapore: RELC Portfolio Series.

Recent Publications on Materials Development

Azarnoosh, M., Zeraatpishe, M. Faravani, A. & Kargozari, H. R. (Eds.). (2016). *Issues in materials development*. Rotterdam: Sense.

Garton, S. & Graves, K. (Eds.). (2014). *International perspectives on materials in ELT*. Basingstoke: Palgrave Macmillan.

Gray, J. (2010). *The construction of English: culture, consumerism and promotion in the ELT coursebook*. Basingstoke: Palgrave Macmillan.

Harwood, N. (Ed.). (2010). *Materials in ELT: theory and practice*. Cambridge: Cambridge University Press.

Harwood, N. (Ed.). (2014). *English language teaching textbooks: Content, consumption, production*. Basingstoke: Palgrave: Macmillan.

Maley, A. & Tomlinson, B. (Eds.). (in press). *Authenticity in materials development for language learning*. Newcastle upon Tyne: Cambridge Scholars.

Masuhara, H., M. Haan, Yi, Y. & Tomlinson, B. (2008). Adult EFL courses. *ELT Journal*, 62(3), 294–312.

Masuhara, H., Mishan, F., & Tomlinson, B. (Eds.). (2017). *Practice and theory for materials development in L2 learning*. Newcastle upon Tyne: Cambridge Scholars.

McDonough, J., Shaw, C. & Masuhara, H. (2013). *Materials and methods in ELT: A teacher's guide* (3rd ed.). London: Blackwell.

McGrath, I. (2013). *Teaching materials and the roles of EFL/ESL teachers: Practice and theory*. London: Bloomsbury.

McGrath, I. (2016). *Materials evaluation and design for language teaching* (2nd ed.). Edinburgh: Edinburgh University Press.

Mishan, F. & Timmis, I. (2015). *Materials development for TESOL*. Edinburgh: Edinburgh University Press.

Mukundan, J. (Ed.). (2006a). *Focus on ELT materials*. Petaling Jaya: Pearson Malaysia.

Mukundan, J. (Ed.). (2006b). *Readings on ELT materials II*. Petaling Jaya: Pearson Malaysia.

Mukundan, J. (Ed.). (2008a). *Readings on ELT materials III*. Petaling Jaya: Pearson Malaysia.

Tomlinson, B. (Ed.). (2008). *English language teaching materials: A critical review.* London: Continuum.

Tomlinson, B. (Ed.). (2011). *Materials development in language teaching* (2nd ed.). Cambridge: Cambridge University Press.

Tomlinson, B. (2012). Materials development for language learning and teaching. *Language Teaching: Surveys and Studies, 45*(2), 143–179.

Tomlinson, B. (Ed.). (2013a). *Developing Materials for Language Teaching* (2nd ed.). London: Continuum Press.

Tomlinson, B. (Ed.). (2013b). *Applied linguistics and materials development.* London: Continuum.

Tomlinson, B. (Ed.). (2016a). *SLA research and materials development for language learning.* New York: Routledge.

Tomlinson, B. (Guest Ed.). (2016b). *Innovation in Language Learning and Teaching (RILL)* [Special issue on materials development], *10*(2).

Tomlinson, B. (Guest Ed.). (2016c) *European Journal of Applied Linguistics and TESOL.* [Special issue on materials development], *3*(2).

Tomlinson, B. & Masuhara, H. (2007). *Developing language course materials.* Beijing: People's Educational Press.

Tomlinson, B. & Masuhara, H. (Eds.). (2010). *Research for materials development in language learning: evidence for best practice.* London: Continuum.

Tomlinson, B. & Masuhara, H. (2013). Adult coursebooks. *ELT Journal, 67*(2), 233–249.

Sources of Activities

The web is a very rich source of language teaching activities. It is very important, though, to evaluate activities available on the web against both universal and local criteria before using them; they are not all of the highest quality. Below is a small sample of the activities available. For access to many more just Google "Activities for language teaching."

Activities for ESL/EFL Students (a4esl.org/)

A Hive of Activities, *Tried and tested ELT ideas* (https://hiveofactivities. wordpress.com/)

British Council/BBC, *Teaching English* (https://www.teachingenglish.org.uk/teaching-teens/resources/activities)

British Council/BBC, *Vocabulary activities* (https://www.teachingenglish.org.uk/article/vocabulary-activities)

ELTgames.com (www.eltgames.com/)

English Club, *ESL Activities* (https://www.englishclub.com/esl-activities/)

ESL Kid Stuff, *ESL kids games and activities* (www.eslkidstuff.com/gamesmenu.htm)

ESL Library, *English conversation activities* (https://esllibrary.com/courses/76/lessons)

Internet TESL Journal, *Games and activities for the ESL/EFL classroom* (iteslj.org/games/)

Seven superb speaking activities that'll get your ESL students chatting . . . (www.fluentu.com/english/educator/blog/speaking-activities-for-esl-students/)

TEFL.net, *ESL activities* (http://www.tefl.net/esl-lesson-plans/)

Sources of Texts and Images

Newspapers

There are many web sites providing access to newspapers online. Here are a few of them:

Internet Public Library, *Newspapers and magazines* (www.ipl.org/div/news/).
Subject-categorized directory of authoritative web sites; links to online texts, newspapers, and magazines; and the Ask an ipl2 Librarian online reference service.

Online newspaper directory for the world (www.onlinenewspapers.com/). Listing of 10,000 newspapers from around the world, searchable by country and then by publication.

Refdesk.com, *Newspapers—USA and worldwide* (www.refdesk.com/paper.html). United States' newspapers online and worldwide newspapers in English.

World newspapers online (www.actualidad.com/).

Worldwide news in English (www.thebigproject.co.uk/news/).

Jokes

There are thousands of jokes available free on the web. You just need to google "Jokes on the web" and you will be given page after page of web sites. You have to be selective though. Many of the jokes could be offensive to students and/or teachers.

Poems

There are also thousands of poems freely available on the web. You have to be really selective, though, as many of them are by "amateur" poets seeking a readership. The best bet is to search for established poets who have web sites. Some of them post new poems that can be downloaded free. For example:

John Cooper Clarke, a very popular performance poet from Salford, makes his poems available on http://johncooperclarke.com/?p=33.
Carol Ann Duffy, the British Poet Laureate (www.carolannduffy.co.uk/) makes many of her poems available on www.sheerpoetry.co.uk, a web site that makes available poems, articles, workshops, interviews, and essays, question sessions and more, about and by Carol Ann Duffy, Gillian Clarke, Seamus Heaney, Simon Armitage, and others.
Roger McGough, perhaps England's most popular poet, makes some of his poems available on http://www.uktouring.org.uk/rogermcgough/.
Brian Patten, one of the famous Liverpool poets, has a web site http://www.brianpatten.co.uk/about.html, which gives you a poem of the month to download free and allows you to listen to Brian Patten reading some of his poems.
Michael Rosen, a well-known British poet and children's writer, makes many of his poems available on http://www.michaelrosen.co.uk/.
Benjamin Zephaniah, a popular British Jamaican poet makes all his poems available on http://www.poemhunter.com/benjamin-zephaniah/.

The web site http://www.poemhunter.com/ makes thousands of poems available, including the most popular 500 poems in English.

Stories

Most of the poets above are also story writers and make their stories available on their web sites. In addition you can search "Stories on the web" and find hundreds of sites that make children's and adult stories available, including:

Best stories on the web (short-story.me/).
Eastoftheweb short stories (eastoftheweb.com/short-stories/indexframe.html).
Fiction on the web (www.fictionontheweb.co.uk/).
Longreads (https://longreads.com/).
Stories from the web (www.storiesfromtheweb.org/).
Stories from the web—Internet safety (www.storiesfromtheweb.org/staysafe/internet 711activities.html).
Stories from the web—writing gallery (www.storiesfromtheweb.org/introwritinggallery. asp).
Ten websites where you can enjoy reading short stories and flash fiction (www.make useof.com/tag/10-websites-enjoy-reading-short-stories-flash-fiction/).
ViralNova (www.viralnova.com/).
Web of stories (www.webofstories.com/).

Adverts

Adverts are a potentially engaging source of language input. They are also short, contextualized, impactful, repetitive, and often funny and bizarre. The best free source of TV adverts on the web is probably http://www.tellyads.com/, which makes 21,000 adverts available to download.

Videos

Go to http://www.techsupportalert.com/5-Best-Free-Video-Streaming-Sites.htm for the pros and cons of the five most popular video streaming sites, with YouTube not surprisingly being the most recommended (https://plus.google.com/+YouTube or https://www.youtube.com/?gl=GB).

Another very popular source of potentially engaging videos is TED Talks (https://www.ted.com/talks) a huge collection of talks from expert speakers on education, business, science, technology, creativity and many other topics.

Images

Here are some of the web sites that make images freely available:

Author media (http://www.authormedia.com/where-to-find-free-legal-photos-online/). Eleven places to get a free and legal photo for your blog.

BootstrapBay (https://bootstrapbay.com/blog/free-stock-photos/). Twenty-one sites with breathtaking free stock photos.

Buffer (https://blog.bufferapp.com/free-image-sources-list). More than 53 free image sources for your blog and social media posts.

Google Images (https://images.google.co.uk/)

Pixabay (https://pixabay.com/). Free images.

Wikipedia (https://en.wikipedia.org/wiki/Wikipedia:Public_domain_image_resources). Public domain image resources.

When using any of the resources from web sites listed for the categories above please make sure that you are not infringing copyright. Two sites that enable you to make use of potentially engaging texts and images without infringing copyright are:

https://creativecommons.org/licenses/by/2.0/uk (Creative Commons licenses make some texts and images available for educational use);

https://www.jisc.ac.uk/guides/open-educational-resources (provides materials that are available free online for educational use).

All the resources in "Resources Useful for Materials Developers" are extremely useful. We would warn, though, about the danger of just using texts, activities, and images because they are easily available and save time and energy. We have worked, for example, with materials developers who have been happy to just use a time-saving tool which generates fill-in-the-gap activities without asking whether such activities would actually benefit the target learners. We would also urge teachers and materials developers not to neglect the live human resources readily available to them. Learners, colleagues and friends can be sources of spoken and written texts with great potential for engagement.

Reference

O'Keefe, A., McCarthy, M. & Carter, R. (2007). *From corpus to classroom: Language use and language teaching.* Cambridge: Cambridge University Press.

Index

The Complete Guide to the Theory and Practice of Materials Development for Language Learning,
First Edition. Brian Tomlinson and Hitomi Masuhara.
© 2018 John Wiley & Sons, Inc. Published 2018 by John Wiley & Sons, Inc.